The Available Man

Andrew Sinclair was born in Oxford, England, and studied at Eton and at Trinity College, Cambridge. His books include *Prohibition: The Era of Excess* and *The Better Half: The Emancipation of the American Woman*, as well as four novels. Mr. Sinclair has studied in America as a Commonwealth Fellow and under a fellowship from the American Council of Learned Societies.

THE
AVAILABLE MAN

The Life Behind the Masks of
Warren Gamaliel Harding

by

ANDREW SINCLAIR

Q

QUADRANGLE PAPERBACKS
Quadrangle Books / Chicago

CONTENTS

PREFACE

"Let me urge you again to write the Harding story," Brand Whitlock wrote to William Allen White, as one progressive Republican to another. "It has all the elements of an old Greek tragedy, with the angry and disgusted gods at the end wiping out all of the personages in a kind of Olympian Fury." [1] White did not write the Harding story. For the Kansas editor was as fervent a believer in the small-town myths of America as was his proposed subject. When the disgusted gods had wiped out Warren Gamaliel Harding and his friends, they had also begun to wipe out the myths that had made him President of the United States. Main Street was rarely to enter the White House so easily again.

Warren Harding became the most notorious President in American history because the myths that had formed him were not adequate to meet with the power and responsibility of the Presidency after the First World War. As Will Hays commented when he was a member of Harding's Cabinet, "The government is like a corner grocery which a few years ago could be run by one man, and now we try to use the same system in running Marshall Fields." [2] Harding could have run admirably a corner grocery, as he ran his small-town newspaper, the Marion (Ohio) *Star*. Unfortunately, social and political myths washed him into the Presidency and left him stranded there. He could not cope with the international and industrial complexity of postwar America with the beliefs of small-town Ohio. It was too late to muddle through.

As a man, Harding was uninteresting. He was not important

vi

in himself. But the reasons for his political success were all-important. As a representative of the power of folklore and past morality, he revealed how much politics was and is ruled by dead men. The concepts of the nineteenth century made him President in the twentieth. For his life and vocabulary nourished the Victorian and moral myths so dear to most American people that they could benefit from the machine without losing the values of the farm.

These myths, which formed Harding and in which he mostly believed, made him the Available Man in the Republican Party in 1920. There were the myths of the Country Boy, of the Self-made Man, of the Presidential State, of the Political Innocent, of the Guardian Senate, of America First, of the Reluctant Candidate, of the Dark Horse, of the Smoke-filled Room, of the Solemn Referendum, and of the Best Minds. With the help of these and other fictions, a most ordinary man reached the White House.

Harry Daugherty, the political manager of Harding, shrewdly pointed out how well Harding fitted the nostalgic folklore of American party politics when he pushed his candidate into the Presidential race in December, 1919. His eulogy of Harding was an admirable synthesis of the facts and fictions that made Harding both available and inadequate, the candidate who had not dared to be himself. Daugherty's statement was also something new in American politics. It was the first case of a manager selling his candidate as a winning image rather than as a great man:

Senator Harding has practically been forced into every contest for high honors he has ever received. He has been generous in supporting others. He is a thorough-going Republican partisan who always supports his own party but never offends those who belong to other parties. In many respects that make men great and attractive, no man was ever as much like McKinley as is Harding. He is patient, he does not rush in with a positive opinion until he has taken all the time necessary to consider a subject and receive all the good advice he can find or is offered. He is a charming man to meet and people like him immediately upon meeting him. The liking lasts. As a clear, convincing, pleasing orator he has no superior in the United States. When he takes a stand he stands there until he advances. He was born a poor boy and knows all the hardships that accompany a man who makes his own way in the world. He is kindly, considerate, sympathetic and good-natured. He is a great American and for everything that is American. There is no man so humble that he would not stop and stoop to do a favor and help lift up in the world. He is well posted and sound on all the great questions of interest to the welfare of our country. He is sound in his ideas about finances. He is of the McKinley type in his ideas on the protective tariff. He is a good judge of human nature. He has lived a pure life. He has the very appearance of a president of the United States. Harding is the one man sure to carry Ohio if the great Republican Party were to nominate him.[3]

Such was the image of the unknown politician who was nominated by his party and who reached the White House with the greatest majority of votes given to a President in a century. But once in the White House, Harding was faced with the reality of power. The myths faded or turned upon him. Main Street morality could not cope with Wall Street complexity. The "best minds" often disagreed. In an effort to prove yet another myth of democracy, that the office makes the man, Harding tried to free himself from the corruption and entanglements brought about by his small-town loyalties. He did too little too late, and he died too soon. After his death, this creature of myth became its victim, for the theories of conspiracy at the grass roots of democracy fed on new myths of the Poisoned President and the Ohio Gang. Harding, in his coming and his going, was the apotheosis of the American rural dream.

In this way, the Harding story is like "an old Greek tragedy." The old gods struck down a folk hero. For in his time Harding did seem to be hero enough. He seemed to represent the truth of many legends: that Presidents did come from the backwoods, that opportunities were equal, that small towns were the homes of goodness and democracy. On his death, he was mourned more than any President since Lincoln. But his example proved that Washington had become a world city and could no longer be ruled by the man from Marion. Harding was a small man in a great place, which was daily becoming greater.

Part One

THE NECESSARY MYTHS

"All great men must do a great many things for effect." WARREN HARDING

I

The Country Boy

"I believe that, if a wise God notes a sparrow's fall, no life can be so obscure and humble that it shall become of no consequence to America."   WARREN HARDING

To be born a white Protestant American in Ohio at the end of the Civil War was to be born a potential President. The accident of his birth in the hamlet of Blooming Grove on November 2, 1865, put Warren Harding on the road to the White House. In eleven of the eighteen national conventions of the Republican Party, between its founding in 1854 and 1924, sons of Ohio were nominated for the Presidency; and in four conventions, they were nominated for the Vice-Presidency.[1] And this was the period of the dominance of the Grand Old Party in national elections outside the South. As an Ohio-born Senator from the state of Washington observed shortly after Harding's death, "Every Republican President who has entered the White House by the votes of the people since the Civil War has come directly from Ohio or been born in Ohio. The only other two Presidents of the Republican Party who entered the White House have entered by way of the Vice-Presidency." [2]

Buckeye birth was only one of many political blessings showered on Harding's cradle. He was born a male Republican, the eldest of eight children, in a state dominated by the Republican Party.

Members of his family were among the original pioneers in Ohio and became dyed-in-the-wool Abolitionists. They claimed descent from Puritan and early Dutch ancestors.[3] Although his mother became a Seventh-Day Adventist, Warren Harding himself skirmished lazily with atheism and ended up as a Baptist.[4] As President Garfield before him, Harding always retained something of the ponderous sincerity of the preacher that his mother hoped he would become.

Yet most important for the Presidential childhood of Harding was his country background. He had the misfortune not to be born in a log cabin. "The log cabin stuff makes good copy, but unfortunately it is not true," he admitted to reporters.[5] But he had been born in the next most available place for Presidential timber —a frame farmhouse in a hamlet. His boyhood was passed in the little communities of Blooming Grove and Caledonia, where he learned to perform the chores of farm and village.

The Log Cabin and Country Boy myths were necessary for most Presidential candidates until recent times. Andrew Jackson had first made log cabins into the fit mangers of future Presidents. He had actually been reared in one somewhere in the backwoods of the Carolinas; his wife had been brought up in a similar hut. Ohio's first President, William Henry Harrison, had also claimed such a rude upbringing in the election campaign of 1840, against the urbane Van Buren. Harrison had actually been raised in a Virginia mansion; but the Log Cabin myth was already popular enough to make it wise for a politician to downgrade his origins.

Of course, the chief hewer of the Log Cabin myth was the hero of Harding's party, Abraham Lincoln. He had genuinely spent his early life in a log cabin in Kentucky. Although his birthplace was removed to the shelter of a mock-classical temple, this was only a formal recognition of the potency of myth. The log cabin was the shrine in which Republican candidates used to worship and accommodate their boyhood.[6]

Of the twenty-seven Presidents before Warren Harding, only two were associated with life in a large city, Arthur and Taft, and only one of these two was an Easterner. Neither was picked for the Presidency by an open convention. Arthur, from New York City, reached the White House because of the assassination of Garfield. He had been picked only to balance the ticket and he was not nominated again. Taft came more forgivably from the Midwestern city of Cincinnati, and he was the chosen candidate of the retiring Theodore Roosevelt, who delivered him the nomination on a plate. As the *New York Tribune* commented on Arthur's elevation to the White House in 1881, " 'the city man,' the metropolitan gentleman, the member of clubs . . . this is a novel species of President." [7]

As America was predominantly a rural nation until the census of 1920 and the election of Warren Harding, it was reasonable that most of the Presidents should have been reared on farms and in small towns. But the overwhelming preponderance of country-style Presidents argued a potent myth. Why was a rural background necessary for a President of the United States, when all the other leading nations of the world were habitually led by urban gentlemen?

The reason was that the New World felt itself new. The United States had been founded on the rejection of Europe, and that rejection was largely a denial of the governments and courts of the European city. From the time of Thomas Jefferson, democracy in America had been considered an agrarian democracy, founded on the town meeting and the vote of independent farmers. "The mobs of great cities," Jefferson wrote, "add just so much to the support of pure government, as sores do to the strength of the human body." [8] It was in obedience to this belief that state capitals were located in small villages such as Albany rather than in flourishing New York City. As early an American commentator as De Tocqueville repeated Jefferson's warning: "I look upon the size of certain American cities, and especially upon the nature of their population, as a real danger which threatens the future security of the democratic republics of the New World." [9]

If the Eastern cities were evil, because of their recent European immigrants and their European ways, the new states of the West were good, because Jefferson and every other American politician praised the farmers as the chosen people of God. Although early Ohio was called by a minister a land of "sinful liberty" because the frontiersmen had broken away from the restraints of life in the towns of New England, by the time of the Civil War Ohio represented a stable and settled farming society.

It was in the six decades after the Civil War that the fear of the European city in rural America became intolerable. That unholy institution seemed to have crossed the Atlantic with the immigrant ships. Although millions of Protestant Germans and Scandinavians arrived, they were outnumbered by the Irish, the Italians, the Poles, the Jews, and the Eastern Europeans. Country dwellers believed that these aliens had brought the slums and corrupt politics of the Old World into the New World and had made a Rome out of the Eastern seaboard. Between 1865 and 1900, the urban population increased fourfold, while the rural population only doubled. By 1906, Roman Catholics numbered two in three of the church members in the large cities, while Protestants numbered four in five of the church members in rural areas.

Up to that time, the population of the country still outnumbered that of the city. And thus, to attract the majority of Americans, a Presidential candidate had to be an old-stock Protestant American who was identified with the rural way of life. As the majority of the new immigrants themselves came from peasant backgrounds, they also found a welcome nostalgia in a rural candidate for office. People who had formerly lived on the farms of Europe and in the small towns of the United States filled the American city until the twentieth century. It is small wonder, then, that the political parties chose as Presidential candidates those men who, like the vast majority of the voters, had left the virtues of the country for the opportunities of the city.

The function of a democratic President, who represents many millions of people, is to make the citizens feel that they *share* in the government. This is the necessary fiction of a democracy. The American myth further adds that any American can rise from poverty to the White House if certain factors that allow the majority of Americans to identify with him make him available as a major-party candidate. Thus, when most Americans were poor and rural, the major parties liked to choose nominees who had been poor and rural. It is only now that most Americans are prosperous and urban that the major parties can afford to choose the sons of urban millionaires to carry the flag. When the fiction of the equality of opportunity was genuinely believed—as it was in America before the Great Depression—the poor country boy become President was the factual proof of the ideal. Nothing made a politician more available.

Warren Harding had the good fortune to be both a farmer and a small-town businessman. As a farmer, he was a failure. A boyhood friend refused to say that he "was a success at this sort of thing. He was not, with the accent on the Not." [10] Like other country boys, Harding would turn his hand to work when there was money in it. He painted barns, milked cows, planted wheat, and rode a cart to town, standing on a compost heap and drawn by one mule and one horse—a team that not even he could harmonize. Later in his journalistic and political career, he would always capitalize on his farm background, however much he preferred the life of town and office. His favorite story was one of riding hopefully toward Marion on a slow farm mule and being advised by a countryman, "If you are going to ride that mule, it is a farther distance than you will ever get." [11] He even went so far as to buy back the ancestral acres at Blooming Grove for his retirement from the Presidency. But, then, even such a sophisticated man as Franklin Delano Roosevelt, upon his arrival in the White House, wrote down his occupation as "Farmer."

His farm background was frankly to Warren Harding, as it was to generations of American youths, no more than a drudgery to escape and a memory to hallow—sometimes for political advantage. What was essential to him was the small towns of Ohio, in which he spent most of his adult life. Because he was a villager who had made good, he believed categorically that all villagers could make good:

> I grew up in a village of six hundred [he later stated of Caledonia, Ohio], and I know something of the democracy, of the simplicity, of the confidence in—aye, better yet, of the reverence for government, and the fidelity to law and its enforcement, as it exists in the small community. I do not believe that anywhere in the world there is so perfect a democracy as in the village. You know in the village

we know everybody else's business. I grew up in such a community, and I have often referred to it as a fine illustration of the opportunities of American life.

There is no social strata or society requirement in the village. About everybody starts equal. And in the village where I was born the blacksmith's son and the cobbler's son and the minister's son and the storekeeper's son all had just the same chance in the opportunities of this America of ours.

His speech went on to tell of his many village friends who had left home and made names for themselves in Ohio and the nation. But some had stayed in the village and had apparently failed. Myth demanded, however, that Harding should believe that these had chosen to follow the good rather than the successful path. The "pride of the school" had remained the janitor of his lodge and—naturally—"the happiest one of the lot." For by definition, "there is more happiness in the American village than any other place on the face of the earth."

This village creed allowed Harding to form his national philosophy. What was good for Blooming Grove and Caledonia was good for the United States. "So I like to preach," Harding continued, as an apparently logical deduction from the village state of opportunity and bliss, "the gospel of understanding in America, the utter abolition of class and every thought of it; the maintenance of American institutions, the things we have inherited, and above all continued freedom for the United States, without dictation or direction from anybody else in all the world." * [12]

The success of Harding and his philosophy of tradition and comfort is impossible to understand without an understanding of the importance of small-town life in America before the Great Depression. Mencken's attack on the "booboisie" of the backwoods, allied with the publicity given to the famous Jazz Age of the cities, has made many historians view the twenties as a predominantly *urban* period, when city standards overcame country values. In fact, as nearly every commentator of the time pointed out, the growing

---

* From *Our Common Country* by Warren G. Harding, copyright 1921, The Bobbs-Merrill Company. Renewed 1949, Carolyn H. Votaw, reprinted by permission of the publishers.

cities were filled with small-town or farm immigrants. The fact of urban life did not change the values of a country boyhood. Harding seemed an anomaly only to those whose eyes were dazzled by the booming cities, where over half the population of America had just begun to live. But to a vast majority of Americans, whose childhood had been spent close to the land, he was as natural as hayseed.

The continuing importance of the small town was demonstrated in two contrasting articles written while Harding was President. The first, by William Allen White, was written in *Collier's* as a counterattack on *Main Street* by Sinclair Lewis. The second was written by Louis Reid, and it appeared in the most famous attack on American values of its time, Harold Stearns's *Civilization in the United States.* The two articles put the case for and against the small town, while both continued to admit its importance. It was the most famous writer of all from Ohio, Sherwood Anderson, who in later life put the argument and the small town in proper perspective, although White had found Anderson's early collection of small-town stories, *Winesburg, Ohio,* "the picture of a maggoty mind; a snapshot from a wapperjawed camera." [13]

To White, the American small town in 1921 was "much like the Utopia of the mid-Victorian dream." Harding would have agreed with him. "Here great wealth is as unusual as bitter poverty. Water, light, communication, heat, books, grass plots, sanitation, clean streets, transportation are distributed equitably, almost equally. The telephone, the library, electric lights, running water in houses, schools, colleges, sewers, automobiles are either owned in common or used in common. . . . The Chamber of Commerce today in the American small town and in the American city is the leading exponent of altruism in the community."

Material improvement in small-town life had led to spiritual improvement through uplift. Collective neighborliness and kindliness marked the small town, suspicion and privacy the farmer and the city man. In these sentimental relations of men in the lodges and secret societies and churches, the New World was better than the Old. It was not the American blood or the Puritan spirit, or the melting pot, or "the voice that breathed o'er Eden," or manifest destiny that made small-town Americans tenderhearted. It was prosperity and economic surplus. The fear of poverty had been bred out of Americans in two or three generations of riches. "Anyone who has plenty and is not afraid of losing it likes to give." The small town was booming and better every year, and it was keeping pace with the city. [14]

So White spelled out the Harding creed: that all was good in the small town and that the progress of business there would bring riches and happiness to all. A huge mail of approval followed his article, thanking him for the truth of his observations. It was these people who saw in Harding one of their own and believed in the myths in which he believed. Although, in fact, the income of the small-town worker was declining rapidly compared with that of the city worker, he preferred not to think so. After all, even the progressive White, who had resolved to vote for Hoover throughout the Republican convention of 1920, had found himself cheering with the Kansas delegation for Harding's nomination.

The case against the small town by Louis Reid in 1922 represented the fact rather than the myth. He agreed with White that the small town was still a potent institution. The real culture of America in the 1920's lay in the secret societies of the small towns, the movies, the boosters' clubs, the evangelists, the church socials, and the pioneer picnics. Even though the young escaped into the cities, they took the small town with them. George Bernard Shaw had once remarked correctly that America was a nation of villages. America might think of itself as *rus in urbe*, "but between you and me and the chief copy-reader of the Marion [Ohio] *Star, in urbe* is a superfluous detail."

Yet if the civilization of the United States was still predominantly that of the small town, this had been a melancholy and funereal place, to be left for the city as soon as age and opportunity permitted. Although technical progress had made small-town life less isolated and more bearable, anything intellectual was given up for the social. The truthful man had been forced to flee from the small town by "the masks of respectability everywhere about him, the ridiculous display of caste." The businessman had been a refugee from lack of opportunity. Even the secret societies of the small town, the Elks and the Kiwanis and the Moose and the Masons, made their members class-conscious, not egalitarian. They enjoyed parading their superiority in front of the townsmen. "America can be divided into two classes, those who parade and those who watch the parade." Although most Americans remained sentimentally attached to the small town, it was doomed to stagnation unless intellect and prosperity and civic pride came to its rescue.[15]

Later in life, Sherwood Anderson, more mellow about his revolt from the small town of Ohio, explained its pervading force throughout American life. To him, the small town lay halfway between the cities, with their ideas, and the soil, from which men drew their strength. The townsmen could satisfy their hunger both for the land and for things of the mind. Factories had come to the small town, to rescue it from rural isolation. Since the advent of the bicycle and the Model-T Ford and the radio and the mail-order house and the chain store, the small town was open to urban influence. Technical progress had saved the small town from collapse and stagnation, although it had destroyed some of its atmosphere of intimacy and equality.[16]

It was as the representative of this later generation of small townsmen that Warren Harding was such a success. He was no pioneer hacking out a village from the wilderness or developing a town from nothing. His father, a homeopathic doctor, moved on from Caledonia to the county seat of Marion, in search of more patients, and Warren Harding and his brothers and sisters moved on with their father. Warren Harding himself put off the habits of the country boy for the habits of the small-town entrepreneur.

Marion in 1882 was a town of some four thousand people. As Harding later recollected in 1922, it had seemed to him at the age of seventeen the frontier of opportunity. "My first impression was that of very much a city, in which I feared I should be hopelessly lost. . . . I came from the farm and village, and the county seat of 4,000 loomed big in my vision, because I had seen nothing greater." During the next forty years, which Harding spent chiefly in Marion, the town grew to nearly thirty thousand people. Industry came to swell it from a mere center of farm and law-court trade. Harding's role was to help forward the community by "cheering and boosting" as a newspaper worker. And his pride, even as President of his country, remained in the hometown of his manhood. "There are communities in the world ten or twenty centuries old not half so important in world activities today; perhaps they have contributed to human progress infinitely less in all their time than Marion has in one century." [17]

Harding always remained the small-town booster, because he had seen Marion become a successful and industrial small town, "much like the Utopia of the mid-Victorian dream." In the ruthless competition of small towns for their very survival—two thousand nascent towns were abandoned in Iowa alone in less than a century—Marion had proved itself among the fittest of the small towns by surviving and prospering. Therefore, its inhabitants were among the fittest and the best, while the small town itself, by tradition, was both the reservoir and the hope of American democracy.

It was as the developer of the small town that Harding endeared himself to many of his countrymen. His career seemed to exemplify the myth dearest to the heart of America, the myth of the Self-made Man. As he himself wrote in a Presidential message to Iowa, celebrating the Diamond Jubilee of its statehood, in 1922, "It may fairly be said that there is no longer any frontier left; our national problem is not to subdue the wilds but to develop in the best possible fashion, with the most appropriate and helpful institutions, the great domain which we have now brought completely within the range of our activities." [18]

To Warren Harding, industry had come to develop the land of America and to confirm the equality of opportunity desired by the pioneers. As a self-made man, he could not or did not wish to see that the new institutions of industry that he supported were neither appropriate nor helpful to the dream of an equal chance for all.

2

The Self-made Man

"I do proclaim equality of opportunity, proved in America in making America the best land of hope in the world." WARREN HARDING

"Business shall be," Walt Whitman said, "nay is, the word of the modern hero." [1] When the young Warren Harding came to Marion at the age of seventeen, he came determined to become successful as a businessman. He was lucky that small-town life demanded little education or training in its young hopefuls. American business was not yet sophisticated enough to require the expert rather than the booster.

Harding's schooling was sketchy. As a local schoolboy, he had shone at nothing except the spelling of long words. He was graduated from an institution named Ohio Central College in Iberia, but the education there was inadequate. Harding left it with no more than a taste for making sonorous phrases in the Victorian style and an admiration for Napoleon and Alexander Hamilton, whose characters his did not resemble. Luckily for Harding, a higher education had never been a requirement for the White House. There is a basic suspicion of the intellectual and of the aristocrat in American democracy. University leaders, such as Woodrow Wilson, have rarely been successful in politics. Four of the Ohio Presidents before Harding—Hayes, Garfield, Benjamin Harrison, and McKinley—

had attended similarly backward academies or colleges. Harding himself, always putting the social values of the small town above the values of truth or of intellect, excused his lack of university training. "I am still persuaded that the smaller college, with the personal contact between the members of the faculty and student body, was the best educational institution of which we have ever been able to boast." [2]

Thus qualified, Harding was ready for nothing but the job of a country schoolteacher. He said later that he was ambitious to be a good schoolteacher; but, in fact, it was no profession to him, merely "a resort to youth's temporary earnings, to help prepare for something else." [3] After failing as an insurance salesman, Harding worked in a newspaper office in Marion as a reporter. Soon, with two associates, he bought up for $300 a mortgaged newspaper called the *Star* and was in business as a newspaper proprietor at the age of nineteen years.

It seems ludicrous now that a town of four thousand people could support three newspapers in 1884. The answer was that newspapers contained only a few pages and depended largely on political patronage. As Harding himself explained, "there was a bitterness and acerbity about political discussion which caused the factional newspaper to multiply if not to flourish. It was not difficult to start a newspaper in those days. A very small amount of cash and a little credit would procure a modest plant, and another journal would be 'established' to fight its owner's quarrels and divide the limited patronage of its limited field." [4]

Harding's opportunity lay in the fact that although Marion County was normally Democratic, Marion itself and the state as a whole were normally Republican. By making the daily *Star* "independent" and the weekly *Star* a partisan Republican newspaper— "for revenue only," as one of his competitors sneered—Harding could hope to keep solvent on political perquisites. His editorial policy, to avoid making enemies among political advertisers, was to praise the Republicans but not to damn the Democrats. Thus he won advertising away from the more partisan of the two rival newspapers of Marion, and eventually he put it out of business.

The success of Harding with the *Star* was certainly in the model of Horatio Alger. He started with nothing, and through working, stalling, bluffing, withholding payments, borrowing back wages, boosting, and manipulating, he turned a dying rag into a powerful small-town newspaper. Much of his success had to do with his good looks, affability, enthusiasm, and persistence. But he was also lucky. As Machiavelli once pointed out, cleverness will take a man far, but he cannot do without good fortune.

Harding was lucky in many ways. His greatest luck was that Marion grew. Once the Marion Steam Shovel Company had become a statewide success, the circulation of Harding's newspaper rose with the expansion of population in the town. By 1890, there were eight thousand people in Marion; by 1900, nearly twelve thousand; by 1910, eighteen thousand. Harding's consistent policy of supporting business and businessmen at all costs won him both advertisements from and stock in various companies. Harding was a speculator and a booster all his life, in the manner of every successful small-town businessman. Although a campaign biographer was to say that Marion "grew with the *Star*'s growth and strengthened with its strength," it would be more accurate to say that the *Star* grew with Marion's growth and strengthened with its strength.[5]

Nothing shows better Harding's speculative tendencies than his will. Although he was still poor enough in 1897, before his entry into major state politics, to have to buy a $50 bicycle on the installment plan, he left in 1923 an estate worth some $850,000.[6] Among these assets were many local stocks of no value, such as those in the Marion Base Ball Company, the Chautauqua Company, and various enterprises in engineering, oil, gas, and iron. His only major disaster was an investment in two thousand worthless $10 shares of the Metallic Mining S. and R. Company. As a friend noted, Harding was always boosting for new industries and was the first to take stock in them. Indeed, prosperous businessmen would advise against calling on Harding to sell stock, because of "his well-known penchant to subscribe for more stock than he could well afford."[7]

In this overeager way, Harding shared in the speculative fever that was to develop and loot the American landscape between the

Civil War and the Great Depression. In the age of the robber barons, Harding was an applauding shareholder. He never questioned the assumptions of what one critic of American conservatism has called the Great Train Robbery of American Intellectual History.[8] To him, the language of the Founding Fathers applied exactly to business conditions in the late Victorian age. Equality did not mean a moderately equal income for all men, but equality for all men to become as unequal with other men as they financially could. Liberty did not mean freedom for all men to live their lives as comfortably as one another, but liberty for the rich to become richer and the poor, if they were fortunate, to become rich. As Garfield had said, and Andrew Carnegie had quoted enthusiastically, "the richest heritage a young man can be born to is poverty." Harding robbed the vocabulary of the Constitution to justify the actions of the industrialists. For he himself, born a poor country boy, was to die nearly a millionaire.

In this worship of riches and the rich, Harding merely believed a popular opinion. The gospel of wealth stated that the rich were rich because they were the fittest and deserved to be so. As they were the best men in society, they would administer their riches wisely. Private charity or individual work would cure the ills of poor men, not federal action (legend had it that Warren Harding often went out from his newspaper office at Christmastime with pocketfuls of gold coins to give to the unfortunate). The poor were poor because they were shiftless and spendthrift. It was their own fault if they remained poor in the land of opportunity.

It is fair to Harding to say that the fictions of the equality of opportunity and the self-made man were widely believed in his youth. Emerson had clearly stated that each man was born to be rich and that poverty demoralized. In the rapidly expanding industrial economy of America after the Civil War, jobs and opportunities abounded for those with a talent for making money. An inquiry into the boyhood of eighty-eight prominent men in Springfield, Massachusetts, in 1880, revealed that only twelve had been brought up in a city, twelve in villages, while sixty-four were farmers' boys.[9] A rural background in Harding's youth seemed no obstacle to making a fortune, even if the means of doing so were increasingly shifting from speculation in land to speculation in industry.

This prevalent belief in the possibility of individual riches did much to explain the support Harding received throughout his life. He was both an example of and a believer in the self-made man. To him, however crafty the methods of business, they were virtuous if they provided jobs and wealth. He believed in advertisement rather than truth, in praise rather than criticism. And in an age when the very life of a small town depended on convincing people to settle there and to bring industry there, who can say that the exaggerations of the booster were anything more than the necessary words of a fighter for survival? If a continent was to be peopled and exploited in decades rather than in centuries, to the booster belonged the spoils.

In an interesting handwritten speech on "How We Advertise," delivered to friendly newspaper editors in Ohio in 1916, Warren Harding set out his lifelong faith as a speculator and a booster. It was an accurate reflection of the small-town mind, unedited for the benefit of posterity. He began by saying that honest advertising was necessary, for without it there could be no confidence. If confidence were hobbled, progress halted. If confidence were magnified, there was activity everywhere. But, Harding asked, moving into the sphere of categorical imperatives, what *ought* Americans to advertise? Did Americans put their best foot forward in their publicity, or did they need a few new ad writers on their staff?

Harding thought they did. Americans meant to advertise a new standard of liberty, but some of the ad writers distorted it to mean license, which hindered progress. Americans meant to proclaim equal rights and equal opportunity; but a lot of ad writers displayed big stuff to the contrary. Freedom to Harding did not mean freedom to do things that hindered the progress of American business, nor did it include freedom to criticize American institutions. In fact, censorship should be applied to knockers. Editors ought to crimp the publicity that opportunity was only for the favored few and advertise success as a thing to be desired, with happiness in its wake.

Harding continued to say that he was worried by the volunteer ad writers who, in the progressive age before 1916, called a state legislature a farmers' legislature or a businessmen's. This advertising claimed that government was not popular but class government. Perhaps the pretense exceeded the reality, but editors should insist on advertising the theory of legislation and administration without any discrimination, which was impartially representative of all the forces in American activity and was concerned with the general welfare and common weal. To Harding, there was no *truth* in political reporting. There was only propaganda. A reporter who pointed out that a state legislature was controlled by a business lobby was only an ad writer for the un-American idea of class. If all political writing *were* ad writing, as Harding claimed, then it *should be* written in terms of the American faith in equality and democracy. Unpleasant facts should be denied in order to keep up illusions in the traditional faith. To the booster, truth is treason where it conflicts with hope.

Harding continued with a message of nationalism. He wanted the creation of an American merchant marine in 1914 to take advantage of the Great War, and he wanted Americans to buy only American goods. Indeed, he advocated that American firms should boycott others that bought goods abroad, even in Canada. That was the American spirit that counted. That savored of the Germans' devotion to Made in Germany, which literally made Germany. Thus Harding, while already in the Senate of the United States, still displayed the narrow isolationism and suspicion of the small-town businessman who thought that all dollars earned in Marion should be spent there, even if the goods were better or cheaper in Columbus or Cleveland. Trade should be ingrown, or else money would be wasted; he believed in the "Middletown" dictum that "a dollar that is spent out of town never returns." This attitude was to remain with Harding throughout his life, and it led to a terrible blunder about the settlement of war debts.

Even the very values of the small town were a form of advertising to booster Harding. Americans advertised a welcome in village, city, state, or nation, to every agency of progress, and gladly acclaimed the establishment of public utilities; but it was not a sustained welcome. Once the thing was established, through some transformation *born* of the anvil, the majority of expressed opinion became hostile, and dividend-earning became a fancied menace to the public good. Harding had himself seen the railroad paid to come, but rarely was there a willingness to grant a compensation that enabled it to pay by staying.[10] To Harding, conscious that the coming of the railroad made or destroyed a hopeful small town, the railroad was only a blessing. Marion had been made by the Chicago and Atlantic Railroads, the Hocking Valley, and "the old Bee line, the first of railway lines to put us on a highway of commerce." [11] To Harding, a stockholder in all enterprises that promised to develop the industries of Marion and ensure its boom, dividends were the fair return of risk. If he did not consider that only a few of his fellow townsmen could afford to buy stock, it was because he had started poor himself. As a youth of fifteen, he had even worked one summer as a laborer during the laying of a railroad track. By his own sweat, Harding had become an owner of a little of a railroad, even if his youthful exertion had strained his heart. To Harding, the railroad and industry brought obvious benefits to all. They were owed a fair compensation.

Even Harding, however, did not unreservedly admire the rich. He was a small businessman, not a large one. Yes, Harding admitted, there had been "robber barons." But in the new era of things, of progressive days, businessmen should be treated as sinners were at revival meetings. They should now be forgiven for what they had had to do in the wicked days of quick development and should be allowed to walk on the straight and narrow path. It was Harding's conviction that a businessman shown where he had done wrong would not do wrong again. The system of competition and capitalism was right. And individuals were good—if sometimes mistaken.

Most indicative of Harding's traditional beliefs was his program for an improved civil service. He told the Ohio editors that he did not want a nonpartisan civil service. The way to good government was to put one party, preferably the Republican Party, in office for a generation. Then the spoils system would allow its appointees to become experienced in office, and good government would result. Until that happened, people should modify their advertising about civil-service reform. Harding remained true to the tradition of small-town politics that to the victor should belong the post office. His remedy for the inefficient government that was the result of the spoils system was not fewer partisan appointments to office, but more. The Republican Party was not to blame for rewarding its own. The voters were to blame for being fickle. It is a curiosity of American life that while the creed of business is efficiency, the creed of politics is loyalty. It is for this reason that businessmen have increasingly come into politics, in order to bring their efficiency with them.

Harding's speech continued with another contradictory belief, dear to the heart of the Midwestern town: that America was both the strongest and the most peaceful nation on earth. Preparedness for naval defense, Harding thought, was not preparation for invasion. American safety demanded a naval development commensurate with its growth and love of tranquillity. Peace through strength was Harding's creed, and it has remained the creed of the majority of his countrymen.

The hymn in praise of American technology and progress that followed was in the true style of the orators of the Kiwanis and the Elks and the Rotarians and the Masons and the Shriners—the businessmen's secret societies of which Harding was a member. Americans had drawn in the tropics for fruited sunshine in their winters and had made Oriental delights their Occidental necessities. They had mantled in silk from beggar to prince and had set the world motoring and had built roads in months that Europe was centuries developing. They spent millions on movies where once they spent pennies on books and pictures, and they lived in the ratio of dollars to what they once called cents. They now built palaces where they once reared huts, and the log cabin, fit for a Lincoln's birth, was no more than a fading tradition. American material progress was in the full pursuit of happiness for all, and Harding was joining in the halloo at its back.

As industry was making America richer and, by definition, happier, Harding ended his speech on a plea to the Ohio editors to be selective in what they advertised in the new progressive days of popular and direct government. It was essential to get right publicity in the conscientious press to make for stability and sure progress. To Harding, boosting *was* good American morality. The American ad writer ought to be a *patriot*, never a pretender; he ought to be a rational optimist, never a prattling pessimist; he ought to catch the measure of things accomplished and be able to foresee the things to come. And, in a final magnificent confusion of his boost of boosting and fact, Harding ended by saying that truth and conscience, honesty and honor, confidence and pride, appreciation and exaltation should be written in the publicity of growing Americanism so that all might go hopefully on.[12]

Such was the small-town creed of Harding, and such was his attraction to small-town businessmen of the usual breed. When the Lynds performed their seminal study of the average Midwestern town of "Middletown" (Muncie, Indiana), they found exactly the same beliefs prevalent there as had been mouthed by Harding. The growth of Muncie had paralleled that of Marion. While Marion had grown from eight thousand in 1890 to twenty-eight thousand in 1920, Muncie had grown from eleven thousand in 1890 to thirty-five thousand in 1924. It was mainly peopled, like Marion, by native-born American immigrants from neighboring farms, as Harding himself had been. The inhabitants of Muncie believed what Marion and Harding believed. Boosting was good, and knocking was bad; free competition was good, and government interference was bad; America should be strong and peaceful and stand alone; business would be good if business were left alone. This was Harding's "normalcy."

Muncie, like Marion, had seen the breakdown of the craft system before the imported factory and the collapse of the general store before the chain store. During this period, the caste system came to Muncie as the businessmen's clubs took over the social leadership of the town. "Middletown" mirrored exactly the social changes in the small town that Harding denied with his words.[13]

To Harding, America always remained the civilization of classless small towns that he had known personally, before the import of technology and communications had erected classes and urban standards in the small towns. He was fond of referring to the

Marion village blacksmith as the fountain of all wisdom. This black-smith had told him, after Harding had reached the White House, that things were so adjusted in modern times that it was not "very much trouble to be President anyhow." [14] Harding said that this was the only mistake the blacksmith had ever made.

Yet the revolution in communications that had made the President's job a hard one had destroyed the blacksmith's trade. He could not shoe a Model-T Ford. This fact Harding refused to recognize. While he boosted the railroads and automobiles and telephones that destroyed the classless American village, he spoke as if the village continued to be the home of equality and democracy. Like Henry Ford himself, who destroyed old America with his cheap cars and then tried to preserve it artificially by reconstructing a whole ancient village at Dearborn, Warren Harding profited from the present without shedding the fond notions of the past.

Harding's compromising nature, and the career that led him from farm through town to the capital of the United States, made him stress one important myth for a federal system—the myth of Unity. In Harding, the small town of the Midwest had harmonized the conflict between the frontier and the city, between the farmer and the industrialist, between the West and the East. Although he remained agrarian and American enough to think that the American experience was *different* and *apart* from that of Europe, he did seek to make Americans think of themselves as belonging to one nation. If strikers and discontented farmers refused to listen to his comforting words about a classless and open society, he did see himself as a born healer of the divisions among the groups and areas of his country.

Harding's success in politics seems, in many ways, to point out some of the great changes in society that recent sociologists have discerned about the beginning of the twentieth century. The fact that Harding was the first newspaper editor to be elected to the White House mirrored the increasing importance that the mass media were to play in political life. Rarely was a President more "inner-directed" than Woodrow Wilson or more "other-directed" than Harding.[15] Under Harding's regime, the rebellious middle classes of the progressive era seem to have begun the change to the docile white-collar workers of modern times.[16] The metamorphosis of the middle classes into white-collar and salaried positions went especially fast in the early 1920's.[17] Here Harding was something of an anachronism, an old-style entrepreneur; but his Cabinet system of devolved responsibility was in line with the increasing growth of decentralization of the great companies of the time; and he seemed to many Americans the first businessman President. If his tenure of office seemed to confirm the holding of political power in the hands of white rural old-American Protestants, his support of big business ensured that the technical changes that were revolutionizing American society would continue their upsetting path. He represented that mixture of the villager and the businessman that most Americans seemed to admire at the time.

For Harding was especially what a historian of the "image" in American life has called the celebrity—"the proved specimen of the average." [18] It so happened that the "average" changed officially on the year of his election to the Presidency from an average *rural* background to an average *urban* background. Yet his success is a necessary corrective to the view that urban ways immediately follow the census returns. It would take a generation before the children of the new city immigrants could find urban businessmen more "natural" representatives than were the rural self-made lawyers that their fathers had usually elected.

As a rural businessman, Harding represented both the past and the future. He was the last of the Ohio Presidents, although not the last of the Presidents from the small town. Yet because of his failure in office and because of the swift changes of society, no rural candidate after him and his fortunate successor, Calvin Coolidge, could run for the White House on the ticket of the small-town hero rather than that of the expert on American and foreign policy. One of Harding's mourning biographers wrote of him and Coolidge in 1923 that they had seen to "the re-establishment of the old order of elevation from rural obscurity to the highest office in the foremost nation of the world." The rapid growth of the great cities, the biographer continued, had "not yet closed that avenue to eminence and enduring fame." [19] It soon would, when the urban vote came to decide American Presidential elections.

In his final speech before becoming President, Warren Harding put forward the economic creed that had made him successful and had made him seem "the proved specimen of the average" to the mass of the country-born electorate, who were still used to the memory of a craft age and small industry, not to the age of huge corporations. "American business," Harding declared, "is everybody's business." Since six in ten factories were still small plants, "the big business of America [was] the little business of America." Work on the farm and in the home was business work. The American people were shareholders in their government, and it should be run like a good business. There was no conflict between capital and labor, because the "big inspiration in life" for all was "to get on." "We cannot get on all alike or be regarded precisely alike. God Almighty never intended it to be so, else He had made us all alike." The government should not try to run any business, for private enterprise was "the regular order of things."

Business, indeed, would save America from decay, as it had saved rural Marion. "The best social welfare worker in the world is the man or woman who does an honest day's work." The labor of each for himself would lead to the benefit of all. "American business is not a monster," Harding declared, true to the creed of "Middletown," "but an expression of God-given impulse to create, and the savior and the guardian of our happiness, of our homes and of equal opportunity for all in America. Whatever we do for honest, humane American business, we do in the name of social welfare." [20]

3

The Presidential State

"To all human appearance, this great valley is intended
by its great, good and wise Author, for a vast number
of people in which to live, move about, and act, and
eventually, to control forever, the destinies of the most
powerful nation on the globe."   CALEB ATWATER
A History of the State of Ohio, Natural and Civil (1838)

Between the Civil War and the 1920's, the White House was every
Ohio politician's retirement plan. It seemed the natural reward for
a lifetime of service to the Grand Old Party in the Buckeye State.
Before the age of Jackson, it had been the political myth that Presidents of the United States should come from Virginia; after the
Civil War, it was Ohio. The myth of the Presidential State is an
acute commentary on the taboos of availability in American
politics.

A Presidential candidate in a federal system must appeal to all
states and all groups. His support must be wide, if not deep. When
the main body of the United States was in a sprawl of states lying
along the Atlantic Coast, the chief division of attitudes was between North and South. In this situation, Virginia was, reasonably
enough, the mother of Presidents. It was agrarian enough to depend
mainly on tobacco and the plantation system. Thus it appealed to
the South. It was also mercantile enough to support a large trade
through Richmond to Europe and the West Indies, exporting

tobacco and importing slaves and manufactured goods. Thus it appealed to the North. Moreover, in the age of the Founding Fathers, when gentlemen were expected to rule, the Virginian aristocracy seemed born to command.

Yet the military hero of the American Revolution, George Washington, really made Virginia the Presidential state. He set the precedents for the office of Chief Executive. He had the nation's capital founded on Virginia's borders, where he owned a great deal of land. And he chose Virginians to help him in office. His very success in politics made the White House seem the natural stopping place of neighboring planters.

Except for the brief incursions of the Adams family from Massachusetts, Virginian planters sat in the White House for forty years, until Andrew Jackson's huge popular success changed the terms of availability for Presidential candidates. He brought the West into the area of choice and moved the birthplace of Presidents from the Atlantic Coast to the newly settled areas of America, which were demanding their share of political power. The sole Virginian to reach the White House again was John Tyler, and he did so from the Vice-Presidency, because of the death of the Western hero from Ohio, General William Henry Harrison. Jackson's success took the White House from Eastern aristocratic control and put it into the hands of politicians who boasted more democratic origins. Except for Zachary Taylor from Louisiana, the major parties nominated for the Presidency only lawyers and soldiers from the North and the West until the Civil War.

The Civil War again changed the terms of availability. Abraham Lincoln had come from Illinois, but his Secretary of War, the powerful Edwin Stanton, and his Secretary of the Treasury, Salmon Chase, had come from Ohio. This fact explained the enormous crop of Ohio men who reached high rank in the Union Army. *Appleton's Cyclopedia of American Biography* in 1900 mentioned only 406 Ohioans among 23,000 biographies; but, of these, 103 were military men, and 62 were political figures. From the days of fighting the Indians and the British to the Civil War, the chief way to fame for the sons of Ohio was war. Since, however, Washington had set the precedent for the White House as the reward of a successful general and since Jackson had enlarged the precedent to that of a successful Western general, Ohio's military men found, at the close of fighting, that the career of politics was naturally their peacetime occupation. Four of Ohio's Presidents were once Union generals, and one was a Union major.

Ulysses Grant, the victor of the Civil War, followed the precedent of Washington and Jackson and served two terms in the White House. He was supremely available, being nominated from Lincoln's state of Illinois and being born in Stanton's state of Ohio. Although his Administration in Washington was even more corrupt and inefficient than the later one of Warren Harding, his military glory and his memoirs saved his reputation for posterity, for he had enlarged the Jacksonian myth by his humility and average qualities. When Harding gave a speech in 1922 at Point Pleasant in Ohio, Grant's birthplace, he found in Grant "the supreme example of American opportunity." Harding brought the squalor of Grant's origins to the attention of those who thought "small-town vision to be pitifully circumscribed." To Grant, the small town gave "the inheritance of quality, and he dwelt and grew rugged in the freedom of democracy." [1]

Yet Grant did more practical things than confirm the myth of the Country Boy. He shifted the center of political power to the Midwest, particularly to Ohio. In an interesting analysis in 1923 of why the sons of Ohio had provided seven out of the twelve Presidents of the White House since 1869, Frank Kent dissected the myth of the Presidential state. [2] Ohio men were available because in Ohio the political currents of the country were thought to meet, mingle, and amalgamate. The electorate there was influenced by Eastern thought and Western feeling. It had even, to a certain extent, been settled by Southerners. It was "middle ground and battleground," and the drift of Ohio was apt to be the drift of the country.

This legend was moderately true. Ohio went solidly Republican from 1868 to 1908. In those years, only one Democrat, Grover Cleveland from New York, was elected to the Presidency. When Woodrow Wilson ran in 1912 and 1916, Ohio voted Democratic twice and then came back to the Republican fold in 1920 with

Harding. The truth of the matter was that Ohio was a normally Republican state at a time of normal Republican rule of the White House. The only two times that it voted Democratic before the coming of Franklin Roosevelt were when the Republican Party was split in 1912 and when Woodrow Wilson, four years later, won the German-American vote of the state with his promise of peace. Between the Civil War and the New Deal, Ohio was actually nearly as safe for the Republican Presidential nominees as the Solid South was for the Democrats.

Kent went on to claim that there was more genuine independent voting in Ohio than in any other state in the Union. In Columbus alone, he maintained, there were twenty-five thousand independent voters, and several hundred thousand throughout the state. This was, in fact, true in Ohio politics only after the turn of the century, when the rise of the Democrats there and of the progressives made a mayhem of the steady run of Republican candidates in state office. Until the opening of the twentieth century, however, Democrats in Ohio were often as rare as Tom Willard in Winesburg, who was a Democrat when it was a crime to be one and was "fairly hunted . . . with guns." [3] Harding's cry of "Back to Normalcy" meant to the Ohio Republicans a return to the good old days of Marcus Hanna, when the Republican boss picked the candidate and the people elected him.

Ohio's third reason for being a Presidential state, according to Kent, was the insecurity of political life there. To win, Ohio politicians had to be smarter and more unrestrained than those of other states. This explained to Kent the "frightful filth" of the Harding-Cox fight of 1920. Again, Kent's reasoning applied not so much to a fight *between* the two parties from the Civil War onward as to a fight *within* the dominant Republican Party to win political plums. Only in the progressive era did the Republicans really attend to the smears and innuendoes of interparty fighting.

The Governor of Ohio, in these fifty years, was an even more available Presidential candidate than the Governor of New York was and is. The curious thing about the Ohio myth was that the potency of the Ohio candidate scarcely depended on the strength of the state delegation in the national convention. It was rare that the delegation from Ohio was united behind one candidate. The reputation of the devious behavior of Ohio delegates at Republican conventions was made as early as 1860, when some of the Ohio delegates broke ranks behind Salmon Chase and gave the nomination to Abraham Lincoln. Murat Halstead's comment in the Cincinnati *Commercial* was, "I had imagined Ohio would be slippery enough for the crisis," while Lincoln found Chase himself like other Ohioans, "a little insane on the subject of the Presidency." [4]

The Presidential bee was so vindictive among Ohio Republicans that the Ohio delegation kept its slippery reputation until the nomination of Harding. In 1868 and 1872, the rebellious delegation prevented its favorite son from getting the Vice-Presidency, and it kept Senators Sherman and Foraker from ever gaining a Presidential nomination. It divided behind Taft in 1912 and Harding in 1920, although both won the Republican nomination. The most difficult part of getting to the White House for Buckeye Republicans was to keep the loyalty of their own party in their own state. The frontal assault at the convention was easy for such seasoned politicians to deal with, but they could never feel safe from a stab in the back.

The strategy of Ohio politicians at the Republican convention was often based on the theory of the deadlock. When neither of two leading contenders could gain the nomination, the convention always looked to the Buckeye State for its compromise candidate, for he, at least, could carry Ohio, the pivotal state of myth. Hayes and Garfield had both won the nomination by this tactic, as Harding also succeeded in doing. The potency of the Ohio myth always gave its favorite sons a huge advantage in a deadlocked convention, even when a favorite son was not a front-runner, such as Grant or McKinley or Taft.

Naturally, the continued choosing of Presidents from Ohio created a recurrent pattern. As Frank Kent observed, "the oftener Ohio nominates a Presidential candidate, the oftener she is likely to do so." Once an Ohio President was in office, he gave more federal jobs to Buckeye people than to those in any other state; for he had to keep the slippery state machine well greased to run smoothly behind him for his renomination. At least one Cabinet position, and sometimes two, went to Ohio men, and Cabinet positions made men available as future Presidents. In fact, the Ohio myth was so strong that Cleveland and Theodore Roosevelt and Wilson each gave a Cabinet position to an Ohio man, to keep the state sweet. Ohio not only provided more Presidents in fifty years than any other state, but it also provided more Cabinet members and federal jobholders.

The amount of power and loot available through pursuing a political career in the Republican Party gave the people of Ohio a particularly strong taste for politics. More Buckeye people engaged in politics, proportionately, because there was more to gain from politics. As Kent again observed, the more Ohio got, the more it was in a position to get. Ohio was the Presidential state for fifty years because it produced Presidential nominees in the Republican Party who won elections and who looked after their own. Ohio believed itself to be the mother of Presidents and thus persuaded others that it was. In politics, nothing succeeds like boosting.

To the young small-town booster Warren Harding, in search of fame and wealth, a mixture of business and Republican politics was the natural way to success. Like Brand Whitlock's hero Joshua Hardin, Warren Harding "poured the holy enthusiasm of his youth" into the Republican Party. "To him it was sacrosanct; he could not desert it." [5] In a political situation in which the faithful partisan could hope to work his way up to the White House after decades of service, Harding possessed a personal and tactical gift. This gift was good fellowship. Seeing that enemies within the party destroyed a Republican's chances of success, Harding sought to make friends even with his enemies. He sedulously fostered the myth of the Political Innocent, and his backers were glad to help him foster this myth, for it magnified their role in his success. Few Presidents have worked harder at politics or in office than Harding, and yet few Presidents have been thought so backward and lazy. He made his myth too well.

Nothing shows more clearly the continual power of Presidential Ohio than a letter sent out by the Harding for President Club before the Republican convention of 1920. It reveals once and for all how myth can make a President out of an undistinguished politician in America, if only he runs from the right place.

The fact still remains [wrote Harding's campaign secretary, Howard Mannington, after Harding had lost some of Ohio's convention delegates in the primary] that Ohio is a doubtful State in the election next November. There is not within the State any Republican who could be considered for the Presidential nomination stronger than Senator Harding. There is not a Republican outside the State who could be nominated for President stronger in Ohio than Senator Harding, who in his last election to the Senate carried Ohio by 107,000 majority; . . .

Never since the Republican Party came into existence, until 1912, has the electoral vote of the State gone to a Democratic candidate for President. It was the Roosevelt vote in 1912 that turned the vote of Ohio from Wm. H. Taft to President Wilson. In 1916 Ohio stood alone in the midst of the usually strong Republican states in its support of Wilson for re-election, giving him something like 90,000 majority, and with this vote the necessary electoral vote for his re-election.

The character of Ohio's citizenship has been changed during the past twenty-five years. The State is now a manufacturing community. The great steel, coal, rubber and various other manufacturing lines have brought into the State thousands of voters from adjoining States, particularly south of the Ohio River.

The urban population of the State greatly exceeds the rural population. In the cities of Cincinnati, Cleveland, Dayton, Columbus, Toledo, Akron, Youngstown, Canton, Hamilton, Springfield, Steubenville, not to mention other cities· of lesser importance, are contained three-fifths of the population of the State. In all these cities are large industrial enterprises. Ohio will be a doubtful state until the close of the polls in November, no matter what candidates are nominated. . . .

Senator Harding occupies the same strategic position now that he did before the Ohio primary. The geography of politics is still unchanged. Nationally he is as acceptable to both wings of the party. . . . If he should be nominated, there would be no danger of a bolt by the radical elements of the Party, such as may occur under some other circumstances. Senator Harding is acceptable to the East because of his known conservatism, and he is equally acceptable to the West because of his support of all reasonable so-called progressive measures.

He has deported himself in the canvass so as to avoid animosities, and his campaign has been characterized by the same scrupulous regard with a view to his nomination and the unification of the Party elements in his support in the coming election.[6]

The fact that the geography of politics had not changed for fifty years allowed Harding to succeed in 1920 in his chosen role of the political innocent, which he had been playing for thirty years.

4

The Political Innocent

"Some men have greatness thrust upon them, some are
born great, and some are born in Ohio."

CHAUNCEY M. DEPEW

When Warren Harding engaged in state politics in the last decade
of the nineteenth century, he saw the end of an age of boss politics.
The great Marcus Hanna, the power behind William McKinley,
still controlled with his industrial fortune a state that was predominantly rural. By the same alchemy that was to make Warren
Harding, the spokesman of big business, seem to be the representative of small business and the rural past, Hanna spoke up for the
old fictions of American capitalism. As his biographer, Herbert
Croly, noticed in 1912, as long as he lived, the American people,
partly because of his influence, remained true to the old system. He
carried with him the small traders and proprietors. "He added
nothing to the traditional system, except some improvements in
organization, and he took nothing away from it. He merely reflected it, and there is much to learn from the reflection." [1] Harding
merely reflected Hanna and the traditional system with his "Back
to Normalcy," and there is still much to learn from the reflection.

The small town's place in the history of American reform has
been curious and vital. As the fulcrum of American politics in the
nineteenth century, it went through a radical phase on its first

building. Some of the small towns of Ohio, such as Salem, in the 1850's, were hotbeds of antislavery and even feminist sentiment. These towns were essential in the founding of the Republican Party in its radical days. While the small towns of New England had already cooled into more conservative patterns, the new towns of the West could be fiery in their independence and dislike of Eastern control.

The frontier, however, moved rapidly westward. To the Far West, Ohio seemed to be an Eastern state. Conservative business and social groups took over the leadership of the small towns of Ohio. These grew increasingly traditional in their attitudes as a defense against the Southern poor whites and European immigrants that filled the slums of the new manufacturing cities of the state. Jesup Scott, the great city boomer of the early days of Ohio and one of the founders of Toledo, had predicted in 1852 just such an urban growth: "Who can doubt that railroads and telegraphs will make us one country in heart as in government; and that the great plain already preponderating in population will fix within her bosom, during the present century, the great seats of commerce and power of the nation?" [2]

Yet this growth of the cities of Ohio threatened Republican control of the state. Although the party of Lincoln could count on the Buckeye Negro vote, the Democratic Party, based in the cities, could count on the Southerners and many of the new immigrants from Europe. When Harding came onto the political scene, Ohio politics, which had always been personal and factional within the Republican Party, were becoming factional and personal both within and without the party.

For reformers had come to plague the assumptions of the comfortable politicians of the old era of the "robber barons." It is interesting that the first famous urban reformers of the progressive era appeared in Ohio—Samuel Jones and Brand Whitlock in Toledo and Tom Johnson and Newton Baker in Cleveland.[3] By their cleaning up of their respective cities, they provided the model for two decades of progressive urban reformers. From 1897, when Samuel Jones became Mayor of Toledo, until 1920 and the election of Warren Harding to the White House, traditional Republicans in Ohio could never feel free from the attacks of the progressives, who often ganged up with the Democrats to dispute control of the state.

Into such a disturbed Eden of Republican control, rapidly becoming a Sodom of interparty war, Warren Harding entered. He was all his life a believer in the old style of "normal" Republican politics, free from the worries of reformers and more democratic methods of election. He believed in party loyalty and the old faiths, just as Marion's business leaders believed in these things. Reformers were knockers. They rocked the boat. It was the duty of patriotic Americans to boost and steady the boat. For by definition, the American system of government was already the best in the world, and the best could hardly be improved.

As a Democratic newspaper wrote shrewdly of the unchanging Harding at home on his front porch at Marion in 1920, "Like the town, he is kindly of manner, good to look at—and conservative. There are no jangling notes of liberalism in the Harding philosophy, nor any traffic cops in Marion. Seeing Marion and knowing that Harding grew up there, and taking some stock in the theory that environment is the biggest factor in shaping character, one can understand a little better the standpatism of the Republican candidate. Harding is Marion." [4]

Harding was Marion in a political and Republican sense from his earliest days. At the age of twenty-two, he went as a Republican delegate from Marion to the state convention. He was present at these conventions as a delegate ever afterward. He was always available as a local party orator. He made the obligatory losing campaign in a race for county auditor, to prove his party loyalty. By 1899, he had earned his reward for a decade of service and narrowly won a nomination to the State Senate. His district comprised Democratic Marion County, but it also included three adjoining Republican districts. He was duly elected for two successive terms to the State Senate, although one term was the normal party reward to its faithful.

He was so successful that he became Floor Leader for the Republicans in the Senate and the acknowledged boss of Marion County in the political organization of the Grand Old Party. Thus he had become what the reforming Frederic Howe of Ohio called the "replica of Mark Hanna in every county. He took orders and desired to be known as a man who carried them out without question. He had things to protect; he wanted to rise; he hoped with the turn of the wheel to find himself at Columbus, at Washington, or postmaster at home." [5]

At this point, the myth of Harding as a Political Innocent began. It rested on three pillars: the claims of his wife, the claims of Harry Daugherty, and Harding's own claims. As it has been one of the most enduring myths in Harding's career, it bears detailed examination. For this myth has been a winner of votes and offices for many other politicians in American life.

At the age of twenty-six, Warren Harding married the divorced daughter of the richest man in Marion, Amos Kling. Local gossip had it that Florence Kling de Wolfe had married Warren Harding; for she was a driving, forceful personality, who rode horses "more like a man than a girl," while he had fostered his reputation as an affable figurehead. The facts of the case, however, prove gossip wrong. Florence Kling had nothing to gain socially from the match with a struggling newspaper editor, accused locally of Negro blood. All she had to gain was a handsome lover—a choice that she had made before when she had married her first, feckless drunkard of a husband. Harding, on the other hand, stood to gain both social acceptance and, perhaps, eventual control of a small-town fortune. Except sexually, Harding profited by his marriage—and, even so, by masculine small-town ethics, no good fellow was bound to remain faithful to his wife. If Harding miscalculated the length of Amos Kling's life and rage against him, he proved correct in the end. By 1907, he was voyaging to Europe with Kling and Kling's new wife, while Florence Kling Harding died a woman of some property.

Moreover, the business details of his life bored Harding. Politics and boosting were his passions. He thankfully turned over the role of making the *Star* a money-earner to his penny-pinching wife, as he was later to turn over the financing of his campaigns to Harry Daugherty. This behavior misled even such a famous newsboy of the *Star* as Norman Thomas, who wrote that "Mrs. Harding in those days ran the show. . . . Her husband was the front. He was, as you know, very affable; very much of a joiner and personally popular. He was a fine small-town or city booster." [6] What Thomas underrated was the fact that joining businessmen's societies and boosting is a full-time job for the would-be politician and successful owner of a newspaper. Harding never devolved business responsibility until he could, and he was always ready to spend all the time and money on public relations that he could spare. Few men have ever spent so much effort on appearing to spend so little.

Harding allowed the myth that he was run by his wife to continue, because it was useful to him. If he could not raise wages or meet expenses, he could blame it on the meanness of his wife. If he could not perform a favor demanded of him, it was because of the influence of his wife. It is often convenient to pose as a front in order to shrug off annoyances and details onto the so-called power behind the front. Yet Harding, to the end of his life, kept all major financial decisions about the *Star* and all major political decisions in his own hands. As Harry Daugherty, Harding's second and self-appointed *éminence grise*, wrote later, women were never allowed to influence any decision in Ohio politics.[7] Power and money were masculine preserves.

The myth that Harry Daugherty made Harding as a politician in Ohio and took him to the White House is as enduring as it is untrue. His relationship with Daugherty was, indeed, the most important relationship in Harding's life—not because it made him, but because it disgraced him. Without Daugherty, Harding would have been nationally known. Without Harding, Daugherty would have died an obscure lobbyist at Columbus.

Harry Daugherty was five years older than Harding. His background was similar, that of a poor boy who made good from a small town in Ohio. He had, however, picked up the usual first requisite of a politician, a law degree. He held office once as prosecuting attorney of Fayette County and twice as a Republican legislator in the House of Representatives at Columbus. But his career as a representative of the people was over before Harding's had begun.

Daugherty switched his legal knowledge and valuable contacts to the trade of lobbyist. The clients of his law firm included the

American Tobacco Company, Armour and Company, and the American Gas and Electric Company.[8] He remained a fringe politician in the Republican Party, always trying to put together the right combination of allies to win a slice of political patronage or a seat in the United States Senate. But he had no gift for keeping friends and no popular appeal. Thus he attached himself to the rising career of Warren Harding and later claimed that he had made him.

It was Harry Daugherty's trade to claim that he was more powerful and more important than his little eminence warranted. The lobbyist's pay depends on his ability to persuade his clients that he can fix people and things. Harry Daugherty did know how the Republican Party machine worked in Ohio, and he did have the ear of the machine politicians. While he could influence votes in the Upper and Lower House of the state legislature, he could not influence the votes of the people. He had to pretend that he was powerful all his life, but no one thought him so in Ohio politics until he suddenly struck it lucky with the nomination of Warren Harding at the Republican National Convention of 1920. It is only Daugherty's decades of bragging and the hindsight of historians that have given him something of the reputation of a Machiavelli in American politics. It should be remembered that Machiavelli himself was a political failure.

The relationship between Daugherty and Harding was casual in the extreme until Harding reached the State Senate. There he became very useful to lobbyist Daugherty, especially when he was elected to the position of Floor Leader in his second term. Daugherty cultivated him with minor presents and flattering appeals to party loyalty and straight sentimentalism. He found little resistance. Like Daugherty, Harding was a party regular and a believer in big business. Although Daugherty was to Harding at this time only one political contact among many at Columbus, Harding struck some chord in Daugherty. Perhaps, as Daugherty later related, he thought that Harding had the look of a President and could become one. More likely, Daugherty had lost most of the powerful political friends that he had had in Ohio and wanted to attach himself to the career of a rising politician.

In the surviving correspondence between Harding and Daugherty, it is noteworthy that it was always Daugherty who wooed Harding and not the other way around. Although Daugherty genuinely believed himself to be the chief political mentor of Harding, Harding believed that, in politics as well as in business, he was a self-made man. The shameful begging for affection shown in a letter of Daugherty to Harding in 1913 does not square with the legend of the weak Harding under Daugherty's hard thumb. In this letter, Daugherty reminded Harding that he had once introduced him during his losing campaign for Governor three years before. Daugherty's slogan had been: "He never dodged. He never scratched. He never sulked. He is a manly man."

> I am still a Republican [Daugherty continued in his letter to Harding]. Just old fashioned. Believing in the bridge which has carried us over the stream so many times. Willing to progress as fast as judgment, necessity and safety will permit. Hoping I will not make such a damn fool of myself as I know others have. Wanting to be natural and normal in all things. Knowing I do not know it all but knowing a man who thinks he does and is mistaken. Not downcast because I have not been more successful nor sour because many other men have been more successful than I have. Envy nobody anything. Hate nobody. Love my friends more and more every day and see more good than bad in every man who does not agree with me. Regret some things, among which is the fact that I don't see you oftener.
>
> With love
> Your friend
> H. M. Daugherty [9]

Such an unabashed and untrue appeal to the loyalty and sentimental streak in Warren Harding does not argue Daugherty's rule over his friend. Nor does the fact that Harding very nearly broke off contact with Daugherty altogether in the closing months of 1918, when he found out that Daugherty had been threatening to knife him in the back. The close contact between Harding and Daugherty in 1919 and 1920 was one of convenience for both men. Daugherty could take the fire for Harding's politicking, while Harding could continue in his role as the innocent.

After 1920, Daugherty's survival in Washington depended on how much he could exploit Harding's sense of gratitude. He fell from power with Harding's death and spent the rest of his life trying to prove how indispensable he had been to Harding's career. The truth was that he was never indispensable to Harding, who was ready at one time to dispense with him. It was only because Daugherty managed to convince so many people of his necessity that he has been considered the power behind Harding. Harding never thought so; he was merely more grateful than most politicians in Ohio, where, as Daugherty wrote, "rival leaders in the Republican Party have always fought each other with more ferocity than they fight Democrats." [10]

In his two terms in the State Senate, Warren Harding proved himself the perfect party regular. Although he had come up in the faction of Senator Foraker and Boss George B. Cox of Cincinnati, he was willing to do favors for all sections of the Republican Party in Ohio, the Hanna group in Cleveland, the Daugherty group at Columbus, and the statewide McKinley group, which was soon to disintegrate on McKinley's assassination and form again around Taft. He was energetic and ingratiating, and he soon became adept at getting things fixed. As the Governor of Ohio said, "There may be abler men in the Senate than Harding, but when I want things done I go to him." [11] Harding learned quickly how to deliver the goods for the machine.

Harding succeeded in state politics through personal charm. He accepted the rules of the game and was thus acceptable. "He was a regular he-man according to the sign-manual of the old days—a great poker player, and not at all averse to putting a foot on a brass rail." [12] All his life Harding knew how to play the hail-fellow-well-met to a political gang. The letters of his particular crony, F. E. Scobey, show a relationship of swappers of "parlor stories," more appropriate to wicked Paris than small-town America, and the casual favors expected between good fellows in politics.[13]

There is no question that Harding, like many businessmen and politicians of the time, accepted graft as a part of the wages of his jobs. His early correspondence is full of demands for free railway passes for his family in return for favorable publicity. In 1896, he had his sister appointed as a teacher in the State Kindergarten for the Blind, even though there were teachers better qualified.[14] His early correspondence with Senator Foraker was almost entirely about patronage, while Foraker in return asked him to bring "the right kind of delegation" from Marion County to the state convention.[15] Harding joined with other newspaper proprietors in price-fixing on bids for public printing and in dividing the profits of the successful "low" bidder.[16] But he made only a little through graft until he was elected to the State Senate, although he had to pay regular yearly assessments of $50 to the Republican machine. Upon his election, however, another State Senator wrote to him, "Now that the victory is ours we naturally think of the division of the spoils." [17]

It is impossible to calculate how much of the spoils went to Harding in his four years in the Senate. Records are not kept of graft. He was, however, useful to many business and political interests, for he believed "with the rectitude of a religious zealot" in party regularity.[18] One letter, however, from a newspaper friend in Bucyrus, Ohio, seems to show that Harding was not remiss in profiting himself and his intimates:

Dear Grandma—I mean Senator—I understand that there is a possibility of an appropriation bill being introduced in behalf of those three females who were appointed as a Parisian commission. I am told this idea originated in the depths of Hamilton country, the hotbed of all just and truly good legislative measures. On this account I have no hesitation in commending it to you as something worthy your best attention and indeed if it does come up I shall hope to see you on the band wagon next the driver so that you may take hold of the lines if necessary. I don't know the amount it is thought necessary to set aside for this female conception of maintaining the dignity and honor of the great Buckeye state in the Parisian capital but I trust you will see that it is sufficiently large that you and I may hope to get enough out of the Bucyrus end of the commission to thoroughly jag us on "cream" with a trifle left to invest in pepsin. Don't let the state of Ohio—and your friends—overwork you my dear boy. Look wise and "sox nix" and we'll run you for Governor after awhile. Don't forget I want to be the whole thing on the

Dairy (?) and food commission lay when you do get in. Mark that "taken" please.[19]

It is doubtful that Harding ever thought that there was anything dishonest in accepting the perquisites of position or office. Patronage and favors seemed the natural reward of party service in the days of Hanna. This was the lesson that the Republican Party taught Harding, and he saw no reason—since his ethics were those of a small-town businessman—to contradict his teacher. As Hanna wrote to him in 1899, "I am very glad to have this personal assurance of your intention to work with those of us who are interested in the success of pure politics and the principles of our party." [20] This letter was after a contact had assured Hanna that Harding would do nothing to which Hanna would take exception and that Harding wanted Hanna to express his views frankly on any public matters that might come up.

Harding's record in the State Senate showed his wooing of business and newspaper and political support. He stood pat except if a difficult situation made him wriggle. True to the dictates of enlightened self-interest, he introduced two bills lessening the law of defamation and the awarding of damages against the partisan press. Business leaders deafened his sympathetic ear with demands for laws to help state concerns against interlopers. Ohio First was Harding's policy, and it made him friends.

Only once did Harding oppose the political machine, and that was in response to a belief that was to haunt him all his life: that experts, or the best minds, had agreed on a solution that would solve all problems. Harding studied the findings of a committee of experts on municipal reform and pushed a bill through the State Senate for municipal reform. This naked attempt to gain the backing of the new progressive forces in the state, which were triumphant in Toledo and strong in Cleveland, brought down on Harding's head the wrath of the old-style corrupt city machines of George B. Cox and Foraker and Hanna. Harding was absent, conspicuously in Washington seeing Hanna, when the bill was reconsidered and killed. In another municipal bill, called the "Cox ripper," which confirmed the hold of the old machines on the cities, Harding voted against his conscience and for the bill as a party measure. His revolt had been short.

On the Prohibition issue, however, Harding had a bad time. No one could stand pat on the matter, which crossed party lines. In the urban areas of Ohio, wet votes organized by the saloons could put an end to any political career; in the rural areas of Ohio, dry votes organized by the Anti-Saloon League could do the same. Although Harding tried desperately to delay the consideration of a county option bill in the Senate, it was brought to the vote. By clever judgment, Harding, who relied mainly on rural votes, voted dry, while the majority of the Senators voted wet and thus placated the wet city machines that already thought well of Harding. In another debate on Prohibition, he admitted that he held stock in a Marion brewery and that he believed in fair treatment of the beer manufacturers. On the other hand, he was glad to be able to offer an amendment approved by the Anti-Saloon League, in the name of harmony.[21] Indeed, Harding could be so conciliating in the Senate that one admirer wrote to him, "Your speech sounded like a Democratic one, and I thought you were a Democrat, until you admitted that you were not." [22]

It was as a harmonizer of the irreconcilable that Harding made his name. To him, the world was something to adjust, not to change. Factions and differences existed. The thing to do was to arrange that everybody got something of what he wanted and was moderately satisfied. It was this philosophy that made Harding, with his comforting and sonorous phrases and zealous belief in the Grand Old Party, supremely available whenever the factions in the Republicans became embittered over a patronage quarrel and had to be reunited behind a candidate for an election. On one notable occasion in 1904, when four of the warring Ohio bosses had been named on the same slate as delegates-at-large to the Republican National Convention, Harding called them in the speech that presented them "harbingers of harmony."

It was this talent of choosing to ignore the rifts in social and party life that made Harding liked everywhere. He represented the drum of oil kept on ships to pour overboard in a storm. This policy of the harmonizer, however, did not prevent Harding from fighting hard for what he wanted. Both in his first nomination for State Senator and in his nomination for Lieutenant Governor of Ohio in 1902, he fought the bosses who opposed him. With the help of Foraker and George B. Cox, he beat the candidate of Hanna himself in 1902 and received Hanna's admiration for his shrewd politicking in his own interest.[23] Harding was never a political innocent when his own political career was in question. He fought it out with the craftiest politicians of his day. He played the political innocent only when his hope of success lay in becoming the compromise candidate of warring factions.

As Lieutenant Governor under Hanna's man, Myron Herrick, Harding had little to do, and he did it very well. He was, by law, presiding officer over the Senate and thus could increase his contacts and power there. Florence Kling Harding, however, was becoming critically ill, and Harding decided to make a strategic withdrawal from politics in 1905, in order to further his business interests with the help of all the new contacts he had won.

The time was ripe, moreover, for withdrawal. Although Hanna was dead, Herrick and Foraker and George B. Cox were quarreling more bitterly than ever. The Democrats were on the rise in the state. Their candidate defeated Herrick on his second try for the Governorship. Moreover, the position of Lieutenant Governor was relatively unimportant, and Harding wanted to wait until the wheel of fortune gave him enough allies to win a nomination for the Governorship of the state or for a seat in the United States Senate. Harding had come a long way on his own, and he wished to rise higher. He chose to wait at Marion, as his hero Napoleon had on Elba, until the time was ripe.

Only personal ambition can explain Harding's behavior in 1908. In his treatment of Senator Foraker, Harding showed neither personal loyalty to the man who had given him the entry into state politics nor political innocence. Foraker had been bitten by the Presidential bee for twenty-five years, and he was growing old. There had always been other candidates from Ohio at the Republican national conventions with prior claims to support from the state's delegation, such as John Sherman, William McKinley, and Marcus Hanna. But they were now dead, and Foraker could hope to be Ohio's favorite son in 1908, when President Theodore Roosevelt would step down and leave the field open, and perhaps deadlocked, for Foraker's advantage.

Theodore Roosevelt, however, had put another Ohioan in his Cabinet, William Howard Taft, and was threatening to designate Taft as his chosen successor to a packed convention. "They'll take Taft or they'll get me," he was quoted as saying.[24] Foraker was already under fire in Ohio from George B. Cox, who had swung to his enemy Herrick's support, and from the Daugherty faction and from the new power group in Cleveland centering around Congressman Theodore Burton, who wanted Foraker's seat in the Senate. Only the remnants of Hanna's Cleveland machine, led by the junior Senator from Ohio, Charles Dick, still supported Foraker —and, of course, Warren Harding.

Foraker had chosen, too, to pick a personal quarrel with Theodore Roosevelt. When Roosevelt had discharged with ignominy a battalion of Negro soldiers involved in a manufactured shooting incident in Brownsville, Texas, Foraker had protested in order to win the favor of the important Negro vote of Ohio. Roosevelt never forgave Foraker for this action.

Thus Foraker, in his attempt at the Presidency in 1908, had little support in Ohio and none in Washington. His chances to reach the White House were small; added to that, he had to seek the party's nomination again, in order to gain a third term in the United States Senate. His political future as a power in Ohio politics appeared doomed if Taft, as was likely, became President and gained control of federal patronage in Ohio. At this moment, Warren Harding, who had endorsed him for the Presidency at the meeting of the Ohio Republican League, changed sides. It was not, as Senator Ashurst was later to remark on the subject of one of his own changes of mind, because he saw the light but because he felt the heat. In the Marion *Star*, always at the service of the dominant group in the Republican Party, Harding declared for Taft. "This is not a bandwagon climb," he asserted; "it is the calm recording of the trend in Ohio politics." [25] Harding would swim with the tide the moment he saw its direction.

Foraker, in his memoirs, said that Harding's betrayal was for reasons that Harding found satisfactory, conscientious, and sincere. Yet Harding's defection was disastrous, "not so much because of his personal strength" as because he set the example. When Harding struck Foraker down, he led the renegades. And he was duly to receive his reward.

Harding's desertion of Foraker was well timed, as his refusal to run for Lieutenant Governor a second time had been. In September, the Hearst newspapers, which were muckraking against the influence of the Standard Oil Company in American politics, accused Foraker of being a paid lobbyist for Standard Oil in Ohio. He was further accused of accepting $50,000 in order to protest against an antitrust bill in the Senate of the United States. Foraker denied the charges, saying that he had been employed by Standard Oil only in his private capacity as an attorney and that he had never allowed Standard Oil to influence his judgment on legislation. Even though there was some truth in Foraker's defense of himself, he was known as a friend and supporter of big corporations. And Standard Oil was anathema in Ohio, where it was accused of ruining local oil companies.

Theodore Roosevelt took his revenge on Foraker for the Brownsville affair, denouncing him as a paid agent of the lobbyists and a traitor to his party. Although Harding, who had never seen any conflict of interest between private business deals and public politics, offered Foraker support in his campaign for renomination to the Senate, Foraker was doomed.[26] Taft's half brother, himself interested in the Senate seat, pressed the Hearst charge in his Cincinnati newspaper, the *Times-Star*. The seat finally went, however, to Congressman Theodore Burton of Cleveland, since Taft refused to back his half brother. Harding, who secretly hoped for the seat for himself on Foraker's failure, was never in the running. Even Daugherty backed Burton.

The sudden removal of Foraker from a position of power in Ohio left Harding to find a new backer. Here his policy of harmony and good fellowship paid off. If, like many politicians, he had allowed himself to back one man alone in Ohio, he might have ridden to the Governorship on his chosen hero's coattails, fighting his battles and sharing his rewards. But by refusing to fight for

Foraker all the time, Harding did not involve himself in Foraker's unexpected ruin. He had not taken his golden eggs all from one goose. When Foraker was eliminated, Harding had a record of helping other bosses in Ohio. He had been a popular vote-getter as Lieutenant Governor, and he had led the way in betraying Foraker for Taft in 1908. Thus, although he had lost strength with Foraker's fall, he had ingratiated himself enough with the new forces that controlled the Grand Old Party in Ohio.

Harding's reward was the Republican nomination for Governor in 1910. There was no question about his being a reluctant candidate for the office. Through much correspondence, he had kept up many contacts among newspaper owners and businessmen and local politicians, who were favorable to him because of his charm and readiness to make speeches. In July, 1909, he wrote to a friendly newspaper proprietor that a good many fellows were urging him to be a candidate. He thought that all the signs were favorable, and he was willing, but he did not wish to rush his friends into the thing until he could make what the medical men called a "favorable prognosis." He was, however, halting no booster, and he rejoiced to see the fellows promoting the thing. If they would only do enough of it to convince the big fellows to keep hands off or be for him, it would be easy.[27]

Harding's policy of trimming paid him handsomely. If President Taft intervened, Harding had no hope of the nomination. By pretending that he had not canvassed for support on his own behalf, Harding persuaded Taft to keep his hands off the fight for the nomination. He went to Washington to see the President and to gain his assurance that Harding's candidacy "would not be considered distasteful . . . or in any way inimical" to Taft's interests. Harding protested that he had always been a supporter of Taft's, both as an editor and as a public speaker. He had, indeed, deserted Foraker at the right time. This was not, Harding maintained to Taft, in order to gain his favor, but so that he could gain his neutrality. "I acquit you of any obligation to me," Harding wrote to the President, "except the right to be treated fairly; and that right you have accorded me always." [28]

Taft agreed to remain neutral; but his supporters in Ohio swung behind Harding, who was to get the same unsatisfactory reward as the first Judas. Walter Brown of Cleveland, a Roosevelt supporter, and the Taft machine backed Harding. Foraker opposed him, and George B. Cox played a watching game, officially opposed, but in fact using Harding to head off the powerful candidacy of the wealthy Nicholas Longworth, a Congressman from Ohio who had married a Roosevelt.

By the time Harding had won the nomination, however, he was reported to have said that he would have given a thousand dollars to have lost it.[29] Although he thanked Taft for playing fair before the convention, Taft had ruined his prospects of election by splitting with Roosevelt that summer, when Roosevelt tried to continue to play the President from the wings. While Foraker now swung toward Harding because he hated Roosevelt, Brown and Longworth swung away from Harding because of their new dislike of Taft. Although Roosevelt appeared in Ohio to give a few lukewarm speeches for Harding, many progressive Republicans obviously preferred the incumbent Democratic Governor, Judson Harmon, to the standpat Harding.

Even if Harding the harmonizer appealed desperately for the support of all Republicans, declaring that he would have "no monkey wrenches thrown into the machine," he could not oil the wheels in the party. Harmon cleverly made "boss control" the issue of the campaign, and he quoted Harding's many endorsements of Boss George B. Cox of Cincinnati to prove that Harding was, in Brand Whitlock's words, Cox's "creature." The liquor issue also hurt Harding. Although Harding had sometimes voted dry, Boss Cox was too notorious a wet not to drench his old supporter. The progressive Harmon beat Harding by 100,000 votes, the only important defeat of Harding's career. It is interesting to note that Harry Daugherty managed Harding for the first time on this losing campaign, although Harding did not hold it against him.

Before the election, Harding had written to his sister that "this time I shall attain the very distinguished honor or I shall henceforth and forever free myself from all public political participation—*and be much better off.*" [30] After the election, he was confirmed in his decision, and he wrote to the same newspaper friend who had boosted his candidacy in 1909 that he was serene and happy, if not quite so confident as he had been in the good faith of all people. He had had the germ eradicated from his system, and he could now go ahead and do other things, things that pleased him more than hunting men of "abiding honesty" to appoint to places or listening to the appeal for the pardon of the dishonest ones in the penitentiary. He would not in the future have to be either wet or dry or have to shape his course within the lines of any faction. While he still insisted the guilt was personal, he did not feel that defeat was personal, in its intention at least.[31]

Hope, however, springs eternal in the breasts of gamblers, fishermen, and politicians. The germ was not eradicated from Harding's system. When the forces of Taft and Roosevelt were gathering delegates for the momentous Republican National Convention of 1912, Taft thought of Harding as the man needed to bring harmony to the split Ohio delegation, in which Daugherty had managed to hold 14 votes for Taft against 34 for Roosevelt. "I may have been a little rough on the Colonel," Daugherty wrote later, "but it was no time for pleasantries." [32] Harding the harmonizer was chosen to put Taft's name in nomination at the convention in Chicago.

Harding was proud of this tribute to his oratory, which would bring him national attention for the first time. He could not foresee that this honor would make him give up his cherished policy of neutrality. It was normal for Republican Presidents to win a second nomination. No one could foresee the secession of Roosevelt. Taft seemed to be the winner, and Harding could not anticipate the hostility that his action would provoke among Roosevelt's supporters. Longworth's wife called him a crook to his face.[33] For once, Harding had to antagonize, while he sought only to harmonize.

Harding's nominating speech for Taft contained his usual slurring sentences that blunted the edges of all differences in a confusion of meaning. He refused to allow the difference between progressive and regular Republicans, for "progression" was the first essential of Republican fellowship. By confusing the word "progression" with "progressivism," Harding tried to make Taft seem the leader of the progressive forces that opposed him. "Progression is not proclamation nor palaver. It is not pretense nor play on prejudice. It is not of personal pronouns, nor perennial pronouncement. It is not the pertubation of a people passion-wrought, nor a promise proposed. Progression is everlastingly lifting the standards that marked the end of the world's march yesterday and planting them on new and advanced heights to-day. Tested by such a standard, President Taft is the greatest *progressive* of the age." [34]

Unfortunately for Harding, who was always a regular and a partisan, he could not keep his speech on this lofty plane of mellifluous nonsense. He accused the opposition to Taft's renomination of being without precedent or reason or excuse, "born of expediency and fostered in mendacity." The disloyalty in the Republican ranks was "inspired by pap rather than patriotism." At this point, disorder among Roosevelt's many supporters broke out in the hall, and Harding had to return to his pristine plan of pious platitudes and praise of the President. While Roosevelt and his supporters sat mute, Harding and the regular organization voted for the nomination of Taft. Roosevelt, who had won nearly all the delegates elected by the vote of the people in the primaries, called the convention "a steal." He succeeded with his supporters and became the candidate of the new Progressive Party.

The succeeding campaign was bitter and bloody. Daugherty earned the undying enmity of the Roosevelt supporters in Ohio by making them register on the ballots as Progressives, as distinct from Republicans. Harding attacked Roosevelt in the *Star* with all the partisan venom of his youth, before he had decided to play the role of the healer. Yes, the *Star* said, Theodore Roosevelt thought himself a progressive—"from one term to another." He was "the greatest fakir of all times." He resembled Aaron Burr in towering ambition and ruthlessness and bullying, in "egotism and greed for power and the same tendency generally." Although Harding later succeeded in making friends with Roosevelt, who was similar to Harding in forgiving those who could be useful to him, the *Star*'s attacks of 1912 continued to be waved in Harding's face throughout his career.

The years 1908 to 1912, when the progressive tide ran high in American politics, saw Harding's fortunes at the ebb. During this time of swiftly changing political situations, he had chosen to betray his backer, Foraker, to fight a losing campaign for Governor against a liberal Democrat, and to fall out with the powerful Roosevelt group in Ohio. Not only had Woodrow Wilson and the Democrats carried the White House and Congress, but Ohio had also voted for the Democratic Presidential candidate for the first time since the Civil War. Harding no longer appeared to be the harmonizer or the Political Innocent. He stood with the discredited and defeated forces of Taft, who, despite the backing of the regular Republican Party, had been beaten by Roosevelt in the election, so that the Grand Old Party stood in third place. Ohio itself was so infected with progressivism that a state constitutional convention had seen to the institution of municipal reform and of a statewide primary and civil-service system. Increased democracy, that anathema of the machine politician, was triumphant. And James M. Cox, a progressive Democrat and newspaper owner, had won the first of three terms as Governor.

At this nadir of Harding's political career, good fortune smiled. The ruin of Foraker had led to Theodore Burton's election to the former's seat in the Senate. Burton, however, plunged into a prolonged nervous depression in 1914. The split of the Republican Party between the regulars, such as himself, and the Progressives persuaded him that reelection would be difficult. Atlee Pomerene, a Democrat, had won the other Senate seat from Ohio in 1912. And now, by an amendment to the Constitution, the election of United States Senators had at last been made over to the popular vote, not to the vote of the state legislature. Burton, a regular machine politician, not only would have to fight a popular election, but also would have to defeat his Republican and Progressive rivals in the new popular primary enacted at the state constitutional convention.

The election of 1914 looked to be the bleakest year for regular Republicans in their history. Both the Democrats and the Progressives had been strong in 1912, and their popularity showed no signs of abating. The thin-skinned Burton, who found the prospect of two statewide campaigns "distasteful," decided to make a temporary and strategic withdrawal from politics, as Harding had done ten years before. By this means, he could avoid making enemies among either the regular or the progressive Republicans. Although Daugherty and Burton's Cleveland backers pleaded with him not to withdraw, he was adamant. As his statement of retirement said, "someone who has been less involved in the factional dissensions of the last two years would be more favorably regarded." [35] His private informants had told him that his chances of reelection against a Progressive were small.

This unusual withdrawal from high office created an unexpected vacuum. Foraker, who had always despised the vote of the people, decided that the people would reinstate him to the Senate, and he entered the primary. A lesser-known Republican, Ralph Cole, also entered. Daugherty himself might have entered, but Burton got hold of Harding and encouraged him to run.

Although legend later credited Daugherty with pushing Harding into the race, it was a legend spread by Daugherty. He asserted that he had found Harding "sunning himself like a turtle on a log" in Florida, and had "pushed him into the water." [36] In fact, Daugherty did not back Harding until he found out that Burton was backing Harding. Daugherty still hoped himself to go to the Senate, as his abortive campaign in the Senatorial primary of 1916 was to show. It was Burton himself who persuaded Harding to become a candidate.[37]

While the primary campaign gathered momentum, Burton changed his mind. He tried to win back the support of his Cleveland machine and of Daugherty, but they had already committed themselves and the regular Republican machine to Harding. Burton had decided to retire too early and to run too late. This wavering gave Harding his unexpected chance to reach Congress as the junior Senator from Ohio.

Throughout his life, Harding was to speak bitterly of the "democracy" of primary campaigns. To him, many of the ills of government could be cured if "party sponsorship" could "thoroughly supersede the expression of individual ambition." The convention system had its abuses, Harding admitted, but the primary system was worse.[38] Such a party zealot was Harding that he believed that the individual ambition of a man *within* a party was for the good of the party. It was only when a man sought office *outside* the party and relied wholly on the votes of the people that he expressed personal ambition.

For the myth of the Political Innocent depends on the struggle for power being hidden within secret party councils. Once the struggle for power is bared by the primary system, no man can pretend to be innocent. His ambition shows. Harding disliked the primary system because it made difficult for him the role of the reluctant candidate. No politician is innocent. Few are reluctant for office. None can be made to accept what he does not wish to accept, as General Sherman's famous refusal of the proposed Presidential nomination had showed. But the fictions of innocence and reluctance and party unity are important for candidates who choose to appeal to split parties and voters as modest flowers of the field. The more democratic the procedures of election, the more naked is the ambition of a seeker after office.

In the primary campaign of 1914, Warren Harding performed the distasteful actions of a vote-getting politician, sitting with Foraker and Cole in a row at the Republican outing "like so many big pumpkins at a county fair." [39] He was afraid that the seasoned Foraker might still have enough political influence to swing the primary against him. He feared treachery and, indeed, the machine in Foraker's old city of Cincinnati delivered an overwhelming majority for its home son. Harding tried to conduct his campaign so that he should have "nothing to repent" after the vote was cast. The contest, in his opinion, was "to be settled very largely on the question of expediency." [40] Thus Harding declared openly that his policy of compromise and conciliation was dictated not by his character but by the political situation. His friendliness to his rivals was meant to gain their later support.

Despite the backing of the party machine, Harding did badly in the primary. He won only 88,540 votes to the 76,817 votes of Foraker and the 52,237 of Cole. This minority approval seemed to augur ill for Harding's campaign against both a Progressive and a Democrat. Yet again luck was on his side.

The small towns of Ohio and the Protestant suburbs of the cities did not like Roman Catholics. Religious prejudice ran deep in the state. No Roman Catholic was to be elected to major office there until 1944, and this prejudice was to be a factor in President Kennedy's unexpected loss of the state to Nixon in 1960. In 1914, however, a progressive Roman Catholic, Timothy Hogan, won the Democratic nomination for the seat in the Senate. He had been Attorney General of Ohio and had relentlessly prosecuted those guilty of election frauds. He had thus made many enemies, both because of his principles and because of his religion. The Progressive candidate, A. L. Garfield, was a nonentity.

In his campaign against Hogan and Garfield, Harding was helped by the normal midterm swing against the party in power, by the loss of nerve of the Progressives, by his policy of conciliation, and by religious prejudice. The elections of 1914 saw Republican gains everywhere; both the Democrats and the Progressives lost ground, showing that the flood tide of the reform wave had been reached two years before and was now receding. As Foraker correctly observed to Harding, "the people are tired of the radical ideas that have prevailed . . . they are anxious to give business a rest." [41] The Progressives themselves had no patronage to distribute, and their machine was ramshackle and amateur. They had failed with Roosevelt—the most popular American of his time—and now they felt that they would fail again, as they did.

Many rebellious Progressives of 1912 were welcomed back into the Republican fold because of the policy of forgiveness adopted by Harding and others in the regular party. No deal was made with the Progressives, but as a friend of Harding wrote, "Our action is, to assure those who got off the reservation in 1912, and who intend to continue to be Republicans, not only for the good of the Republican party, but the good of their own country, that they are welcome to continue with the Old party." [42] Harding did indeed welcome them, and Garfield ran a poor third in the election, a threat to no one. But Harding was not fair enough to repudiate the campaign of hate against Hogan, part of which entailed the plastering of the walls and fences of Ohio with the slogan:

Read the *Menace* and get the dope,
Go to the polls and beat the Pope.[43]

This campaign marked the beginning of the flood of nativist
hatred that was to supersede progressivism and persecute aliens
during the First World War and rise to an apex of disgrace in the
Red Scare of 1919. The forces of nativism and nationalism always
helped Harding, who quickly learned how to gain their support.

Yet politics has always been something of a dirty business in
Ohio. Harding won against Hogan by some 100,000 votes, the
same number by which he had been defeated in the race for the
Governorship four years before. He had reached the pinnacle of
the ambition of a Buckeye politician, a seat in the Senate. Only the
White House could be a greater reward, and that seemed too distant a prospect. At the moment of Harding's success, his future
rival, Governor James M. Cox, suffered his only defeat in four
campaigns for the Governorship in eight successive years. The dry
vote, marshaled by the normally Republican Anti-Saloon League,
led to the victory of the colorless Republican regular, Frank B.
Willis.

Harding's rise to the Senate displayed a determined and politic
mind. Throughout his career, he made calculations and struck out
boldly for office when the omens looked favorable. He made fewer
mistakes and fewer enemies than his rivals in the Republican Party.
His good looks, cordial manner, memory for names and faces, and
comforting phrases conformed to the image of the successful politician that people treasured in their minds. He could inspire undying
loyalty, as in his dry contact in the Anti-Saloon League stronghold
of Westerville, Mary Lee. He was always available as a speaker and
as a compromiser of difficult situations. He never saw any reason
why the lion should not lie down with the lamb, as long as both
would vote for him.

Thus he received his reward. He was inferior mentally to most
of the Senators that came from Ohio, but he was conscientious and
hardworking and dignified. He looked a great man even if he was
not one. And the rewards of office are not for the intelligent, but

for those who can pick winners. As Taft said, when he endorsed Harding for the Senate race in 1914, he was "a man of marked ability, of sanity, of much legislative experience, and he is a regular Republican of principle, and not a 'trimmer.' " [44] Harding was praised for his experience and his long service, not for his brain and certainly not for his political innocence.

5

The Guardian Senate

"The traditions and courtesies of the Senators and Representatives stand in the way of the Executive, however,
as defined by the Constitution, and no man who is trained
in the congressional school fails to suffer by them in a
way that men of merely executive experience know nothing of."   RUTHERFORD B. HAYES

"I do not know much about books," declared Senator George
Hearst of California, who made a fortune in gold and had crowned
his career with a seat among the wise men of the nation. "I have
not read very much; but I have traveled a good deal and observed
men and things, and I have made up my mind after all my experience that the members of the Senate are the survival of the fittest."[1]

Given the fierce competition among businessmen and politicians for seats in the Senate, Senator Hearst was right. If the fittest
meant the richest and those most able to manipulate state legislatures, the Senate certainly represented the survivors. But until
1913 it did not represent the people, who elected Senators only
at secondhand, through their state representatives. In fact, until
the passage of the Seventeenth Amendment to the Constitution,
the Senate had been the pinnacle of power and pension scheme of
the leaders or backers of the dominant party in their home state.

Warren Harding was among the first group of Senators elected
directly by the votes of the people in 1914. He was also to be

the first Senator elected to the White House. There was no coincidence in this. The Seventeenth Amendment changed the rules of availability, because it proved that successful Senators could also be vote-getters. Until 1913, Senators of a state were not as good Presidential timber as Governors, because they had rarely proved their ability to gather in the votes of the people. Now they had to win votes to get to the Senate, and thus they became more available.

Although, in the early days of the Republic, many Presidents had been Senators during their public career, none had proceeded to the White House directly from the Senate. The failure of Henry Clay seemed to prove that Senators could not win a majority of the people's votes. Between the Civil War and the First World War, Benjamin Harrison was the only President, and James G. Blaine the only major-party nominee, who had served in the Senate. James A. Garfield of Ohio, however, stepped directly from the House of Representatives into the White House. If he had not won the Republican nomination in 1880, he would have entered the Senate. Yet in his brief time as President before his assassination, he did not allow his Congressional past to sway him. "It better be known at the outset," he declared, "whether the President is the head of the government, or the registering clerk of the Senate." [2]

This was the struggle which had been fought throughout American history and which was to put Harding in the White House. Until the Seventeenth Amendment, a strong President could claim that he had a more direct mandate from the people. Against this theory, which had been held by all the Presidents from Washington to Van Buren, the Senate could use the theory of Ohio's first President, William Henry Harrison, who had set forward his belief in a strong Congress in his inaugural speech. Harrison himself had been chosen by the Whig Party in 1836 and 1840 as a figurehead, and his theory had suited his Congressional backers. "It is preposterous," he had declared, "to suppose that a thought could for a moment have been entertained that the President, placed at the capital, in the center of the country, could better understand the wants and wishes of the people than their own immediate representatives, who spend a part of every year among them, living with them, often laboring with them, and bound to them by the triple tie of interest, duty, and affection." [3]

This Whig theory of the weak Chief Executive, buttressed by the Southern Democrats' theory of strong states rights, led to the tenure of nine weak Presidents in office before Harding. Four of these came from Ohio—William Henry Harrison, Grant, McKinley, and Taft. Thus, while the Senate had gradually established itself as the superior of the House of Representatives, it had also established itself as the rival of the President. Under a strong President who believed in the power of his office, the Senate obstructed him or bowed to him. Under a weak President who believed his power to be limited, the Senate ruled. Occasionally, as in the time of Andrew Johnson, the Senate tried to overthrow the President and even to impeach him. For the Presidency was an exceedingly *personal* office, made by the man itself. And the Senate was a jealous body, ready to profit from any weakness in the Chief Executive. .

When Harding arrived in the Senate in 1915, he found a situation that was intolerable to those Senators who believed in the theory of a strong Senate and a weak Chief Executive. Woodrow Wilson had dominated the Senate to an extent unparalleled. As he had declared in 1907 in his book *Constitutional Government in the United States*, "The President is at liberty, both in law and conscience, to be as big a man as he can. His capacity will set the limit." [4] By the good fortune of the election of 1912, Wilson had been given the chance to be a big man.

The Republican split had led to the election of a large Democratic majority of seventy-three in the House of Representatives. The progressive tide had changed the faces in the House; 114 of the 290 members had been elected for the first time. Wilson easily was master of this fledgling body, especially as the old-style Democratic leaders of the House realized that they had to support Wilson in order to keep him in the White House in 1916—he had won only 2 votes in 5 in the previous election. In the Senate the Democrats had long had a majority, because of the Southern bloc; in 1912, this majority was sixteen Senators. But an infusion of progressive Democrats had entered the Senate, and the President—by accident of birth a Virginian, although resident in New Jersey—could still play the Southern gentleman well enough to gain backing among the Southern Senators.

With this powerful conception of his office and a majority in both Houses, Wilson had railroaded a mass of progressive legislation through Congress. It was his successful "dictatorship" that had helped to discourage the traditionalist, Senator Theodore Burton, who declared "that the legislative branch of the Government is completely submerged by the Executive and that arguments and logic are of absolutely no avail in the framing of legislation." [5] The election of 1914, however, had lessened Wilson's power. The Democratic majority in the House was reduced to twenty-five, although the voting strength of Wilson's party in the Senate was unchanged. The progressive tide was ebbing. "We are saddened by many defeats," Louis Brandeis declared. Harding, helped into office by the trend of the times, reached the Senate as the only Republican Senator from Ohio, at a time when the Old Guard of the Senate was angered at the President and longed for a time when his power would be lessened. If the popular reaction against the progressives continued, its chance would come.

As Senator-elect, Harding was ready to assure his old friends of his continuing support. At an address to the Railway Business Association in 1914, he accused the progressives of hammering the trusts for political gain and of developing "the American inclination to be of scant appreciation . . . the greatest weakness of a people governed." But the progressives were losing, and Harding assured the railway businessmen that intelligent public thought was now demanding just treatment of the American railroads. Kansas, indeed, had only been "seething with the unrest of good fortune," brought to it by the Santa Fe Railroad. There had been bad financing and stock-watering in the construction of the railroad empires, but that period of plundering was over and had been necessary to unify the various companies.

Harding wanted to harmonize as usual. "There must be—there is—a righteous mean between plundering on the one hand and popular assault on the other, and the problem of the day is to find that righteous mean, and give to our railroads our boasted square deal." Harding was unalterably opposed to government ownership of the railroads, although that was "the logical drift. . . . We might as well adopt paralyzing socialism." [6]

Harding's economic conservatism was not changed at Washington; it was confirmed. For he took with him to the nation's capital his creed as a Marion man. He even took as a secretary the son of his Marion neighbor, George B. Christian, Jr. Of the men around Harding, Christian rapidly developed into the most influential. He made it his life's task to protect Harding from annoyance, and he made access to the Senator difficult, although not difficult enough. Thus Harding was allowed to play the friend of all in peace, without wasting too much of his time. Christian also took care of Harding's correspondence, fobbing off some inquirers with letters beginning, "I will show this to the Senator," or "The Senator is not gratified." McKinley, Harding's hero, had also had such a secretary, who had called himself McKinley's "Brutal Friend." Christian should have been more of a brutal friend, for he left too many of the unnecessary details to Harding.

Throughout Harding's career, Christian remained his shadow. He did not make Harding's policy so much as limit the decisions Harding had to make. And he was proud of himself. When Harding appeared to be a possibility for the White House, Christian was asked by a friend whether he felt he was up to playing the role of Woodrow Wilson's powerful secretary, Tumulty. Christian's answer was humorless. "Am I big enough for Tumulty's role? I know that I am big enough for his job. This is frankly admitted by myself and friends." [7] He increasingly felt his power in office, and his replies to people seeking to get at the President showed more and more asperity. Although Harding answered far too many of his letters personally when he first reached the White House, Christian increasingly replied for his tiring master, writing that "the most fertile mind in America, housed in the most industrious physique," could not answer all his Presidential letters.[8]

Harding entered the Senate in 1914, along with one other new Republican Senator, James Wadsworth, Jr., of New York. Wadsworth, as did most of the second-rate Senators, found Harding likable and, indeed, honest. "He disliked sham and was deeply concerned over the influence of demagogues in American public life." Of course, what Harding called sham and demagoguery, others called truth and progressivism. "By nature," Wadsworth continued on Harding, "he was a conservative, but he kept his mind open toward genuinely progressive movements." This meant that Harding voted against his standpat philosophy when a popular progressive measure was bound to pass and might tell against him in the future at the polls. "What he feared most of all," Wadsworth ended on the subject of Harding, "was the breakdown of representative government, especially through the block system in the Federal Congress." [9] Like Burton, Harding could not forgive the Democratic majority for supporting the President. To him, a Republican majority was normal, and it should have obstructed Wilson.

Harding's record in the Senate was undistinguished even in that undistinguished body. In six years, he introduced 134 bills, of which all but 12 were on local or pension matters. None of the twelve bills was of national importance. He failed to appear on more than two in five roll calls—a low average even for the Senate. He spoke rarely. His vote was in line with that of the Republican minority on all major matters. His absence was usually calculated to avoid a roll call on a delicate subject that might antagonize a voting minority. On subjects that affected the labor vote, for instance, he voted seven times in favor of labor, eleven times against, and did not vote another ten times. On subjects that affected big business, he was usually present and always favorable to private enterprise. In his most acute biographer's opinion, he was "an extreme reactionary," following the dictates of the conservative Senators.[10] As another Senator praised him ambiguously, "for better or for worse, he is just what he appears to be." [11]

Harding did vote his conscience on minor matters. He was notably liberal in backing exemption from military service for religious objectors and in opposing the censorship clause in the Espionage Bill, which he later supported. Yet such behavior did not affect his political standing. On two divisive matters, however, where a wrong choice would have made him unavailable in 1920, he showed the trimming side of his nature, which made him always vote in favor of public opinion rather than conscience. These matters were woman suffrage and prohibition.

The feminists and the drys bothered politicians in both parties. Women in the Western states and drys in all states had the vote. To antagonize them meant to risk losing an election. For the drys could certainly deliver a bloc vote, and the feminists claimed that they could do so. The tide of both prohibition and woman suffrage was slowly creeping in from the West to the Midwest and the East, and Harding watched it rise with his usual circumspection. He was not King Canute to order the waves not to wet his feet. He preferred to float on them.

In 1915, a delegation of women suffragists called on Harding in Columbus, and he was frank with them. He said that he had never been "permitted" to go into the suffrage question in detail and that he was "utterly indifferent" to the question, neither hostile nor friendly. But as a Senator, he supposed he would have to look at it from the national viewpoint. As a representative of Ohio, however, he would be justified in opposing a suffrage amendment to the Constitution, because the suffragists had been turned down by the people of Ohio when they had tried to amend the state constitution. Yet, Harding trimmed, he would look into the matter.

He then gracefully passed the buck and disclaimed responsibility: "Personally I am a believer in government through political parties. I am a very strong believer in sponsorship of the political party, and my own conviction is that suffrage will never become a fixed thing until some political party—not a pretended political party—assumes sponsorship for the suffrage cause. Believing as I do in political parties and government through political parties, I had much rather that the party to which I belong should, in its conferences, make a declaration, than to assume a leadership or take an individual position on the question." [12] Where the Old Guard of the Republicans led, Harding would follow. He would not choose alone and thus could not be blamed alone for the sins of his party.

It was Harding's good fortune that the people of Ohio increasingly voted for woman suffrage and that the Republicans in the Senate decided to support the Nineteenth Amendment once the Southern Democrats had proved their unalterable opposition.

When the important votes came, Harding was found to be on the side of woman suffrage. His appointed watcher, Mrs. Harriet Taylor Upton, a dry suffragist from Ohio, wrote that she had always been sure of his vote.[13] Like the rest of the Senators outside the South, he had changed sides because his constituents had changed sides.

On prohibition, however, Harding trod more delicate ground. The problem had plagued him all his life. He was a wet himself, but the Anti-Saloon League in Ohio had to be placated. In the Senate, Harding felt sufficiently removed from its influence to vote wet on every occasion that presented itself. Yet before the Eighteenth Amendment to prohibit the liquor trade came up to the vote, Harding was in contact with Wayne B. Wheeler of the Anti-Saloon League and proposed a time limit of six years for ratification of the amendment.[14] This time limit was a sop to those wet Senators such as Harding who wished to pass the responsibility of the prohibition amendment on to the state legislatures. They assumed that the amendment would never pass thirty-six of these legislatures, and in this way they could divert the dry pressure from Washington to the states.

Harding's final explanation of why he was changing his consistent wet vote in the Senate to support the Eighteenth Amendment was, perhaps, the frankest confession of his trimming that he ever made. As usual, he apologized for his rather rambling remarks, then proceeded to ramble on. "I am not a prohibitionist, Mr. President," he declared, "and never have pretended to be. I do claim to be a temperance man. I do not approach this question from a moral viewpoint, because I am unable to see it as a great moral question. I can remember very distinctly, when I was a boy, during the early days of a hardy rural citizenship in Ohio some of the most moral people the State boasted had a jug of whisky in the fence corner during the harvest time. I am not saying that I favor that. I only cite it as an instance that it is not always and invariably a moral question."

Yet, Harding continued in his tortuous straddle, there was an "ethical and economical" side to the prohibition question. Even so, it was "unwise, imprudent, and inconsiderate" to force the issue in time of war. This did not mean, Harding hastily added, that he questioned the high purpose of the prohibition forces, but it was a great misfortune to divide Americans into wet and dry camps when Congress should be "promoting the concord of citizenship" essential to winning the war.

Harding did not judge the Eighteenth Amendment by the yardstick of effective legislation—he did not think it would be effective. But he was fed up with being judged "by the wet and dry yardstick." It was time to settle the question once and for all by kicking it out of Congress and referring it "to the people who must make the ultimate decision." At this point, Harding did not ask himself why the state legislatures should be any more the representatives of the people than an elected Senator; he just wished to pass the buck and have peace. "This submission," he declared, "is a sort of a compromise between the contending forces, and I am willing to be counted *a compromising agent*." Yet even as a compromising agent, Harding finally declared that he had voted "from a strong sense of justice" and that if the Eighteenth Amendment were ratified, he would try to make it effective.

In the long history of a politic Congress, there has rarely been such a display of evasion, qualification, confusion, and contradiction. But it was Harding's vote that the Anti-Saloon League wanted, and this they received. They also received his vote on the second vital dry measure—the passage by Congress of the Volstead Act to enforce the dry law over the President's veto. On the matter of prohibition, Harding never showed to more disadvantage what one observer called "that vertebral weakness which is the one material infirmity in his character." [16]

For Harding desperately sought approval all his life. He hated to be forced to decide on matters that might antagonize people. At any given moment of his career, he was prepared to trim his sails in order to please. For instance, he made a curious confession, when he was already in the White House, that he had once even betrayed his most firm conviction, that of economic conservatism, to please his audience. As usual, Harding was being frank in front of a

Chamber of Commerce—this time, that of the whole United States. For it would understand the businessman's ethic that made him put public relations above integrity.

He told of making Chautauqua speeches a decade before in order to raise money. The manager had told him that the Chautauqua audiences were "very much concerned along certain reformative lines." Therefore, President Harding reminisced, "commercially inclined, I adjusted my subject to the suggestions of the management," although not too radically. Some six years later, however, he had reached the Senate, so that when the Chautauqua manager had suggested a second tour, he had replied, "I do not believe that I could subscribe to any radical program which you have in mind." The manager had then answered Harding's new display of firmness with the very reason for which Harding was standing firm: "My dear sir, we could not sell a reformer on the platform now at any price." [17]

Such a frank admission by a President of the United States, that he had ever been prepared to adjust his views to the suggestions of the management and public opinion, displayed the curious willingness of Harding to make a virtue of his weaknesses. He was always ready to hang out his dirty linen in public when that public had been brainwashed, like him, into thinking that dirty linen used for business purposes was bleached miraculously clean. Harding's vision of himself as "a compromising agent" in the disharmonies of life was even stronger than his vision of himself as William McKinley, risen again to stand foursquare on the creeds of nationalism and big business and a high tariff and the Republican Party.

Yet Harding's image of himself as McKinley was indeed powerful. In his first important speech in the Senate, Harding chose the subject of the government of the Philippine Islands. He broke his silence on this question because it was McKinley who had led in planting the American flag in the Philippines. Naturally, the Middle West did not support imperialism; but once the United States had accepted the government of the Philippines, they should use a strong hand. Some Senators wished to liberalize the United States government there and to give the Filipinos more independence. But, Harding said, the way to grant Philippine independence was to grant it. "We accepted the sponsorship; and if that is binding, we have no right to set them adrift. If it is not binding, the majority in this Chamber ought to vote unanimously to set them adrift at the earliest possible day." In fact, what had been done under McKinley had been well done. To reform it would be a Democratic and a partisan measure.

Harding's following eulogy of the Spanish-American War would have sounded exaggerated from anyone who was not on his knees before the image of McKinley: "We are the first nation on the face of the earth that ever unsheathed the sword on behalf of suffering humanity. We did that in Cuba in 1898. Perhaps someone will question the statement. I grant that Congress in making its declaration of war had more in mind an act of revenge for the destruction of the battleship *Maine*; but the great, kindly soul that was at the head of this Republic at that time put it on a higher plane. He disavowed any intention of the acquirement of territory, and literally went to war for humanity's sake. Then, out of the fortunes of that war, we acquired the Philippine Islands."

Harding immediately switched from his extremely charitable account of McKinley's motives—which he was not to apply to Woodrow Wilson's later statement about going into the First World War to make the world safe for democracy. He spoke in terms of *Realpolitik*, as a man of the world. "We have never heretofore been seriously concerned," he said, "about the 'consent of the governed.'" Had anyone worried over that with the Louisiana or the Gadsden Purchase, with the Mexican cession, or with the acquisition of Hawaii and Alaska and Puerto Rico? As an Infinite Hand was looking after the continuing expansion of America, its destiny must be to elevate other people to the standard of American citizens. The whole history of America was written "about the covenant of our nationality." America needed the Philippines to get into Eastern trade, and it could not show weakness in front of armed and warring Europe.

The Filipinos, indeed, were not ready for independence. It was America's mission to go "unfalteringly on, spreading our boasted American civilization throughout the world." Harding closed his speech with a declaration about empire and Christianity that would not have shamed H. Rider Haggard himself: "It seems to me, if it has been our privilege and our boast that we have established and developed the best popular Government on the face of the earth, that we ought to go on with the same thought that impelled Him who brought a plan of salvation to the earth. Rather than confine it to the limitations of the Holy Land alone, He gathered His disciples about Him and said, 'Go ye and preach the gospel to all the nations of the earth.' " [18]

Harding's maiden speech on the Philippines plays a strange counterpoint to his later attacks on Wilson over the League of Nations. It was Wilson who went out to preach the gospel of democracy to all the nations of the earth. It was Wilson who refused to acquire any territory after the First World War. It was Wilson who insisted that the war was for humanity's sake. Yet Harding, because the Old Guard Republicans in the Senate were at loggerheads with Wilson, contradicted nearly every position he had taken as a young Senator.

Again, as the keynoter and chairman of the Republican National Convention of 1916, Harding pushed the theme of internationalism. It had been McKinley who, after all, had first declared that "the period of exclusiveness" was past and who had extended American soil thousands of miles into the Pacific Ocean. The First World War had made Harding see that America could not stand alone. "Noting the elimination of distance," he declared to the assembled Republican delegates, "and the passing of our onetime isolation, we ought to have a navy that fears none in the world."

Among more conventional appeals to the flag and Republican principles, Harding made another strong appeal to internationalism. "We must assume the responsibilities of influence and example, and accept the burdens of enlarged participation. The cloistered life is not possible to the potential man or the potential nation. Moreover, the Monroe Doctrine, stronger for a century's maintenance, fixes an obligation of new-world sponsorship and old-world relationship. Our part must not be dictatorial, it must be trusted leadership in a fraternity of American republics. . . . My countrymen, Americanism begins at home and radiates abroad." [19]

Although Harding complained that the Old Guard Senators had

rewritten his speech until it was "a rag carpet," he did not complain that they had slanted it toward internationalism.[20] His speech on the Philippines of that year had made his mind run in that direction. He was angry, however, that he had spoiled his chance to become the orator of the party at the convention. Although many Republicans, gifted with the prophecy of hindsight, claimed that he had been a success as the chairman of the convention, the general opinion of the time was that he was a failure. One Michigan delegate wrote to a friend that the speech was wonderful and that he would not be surprised to see Harding as the nominee of the party, but he was almost alone in his opinion.[21] Daugherty's suggestion of Harding as keynoter at an earlier meeting of the Republican National Committee seemed to have misfired.

Harding, indeed, had been selected in his former role of harmonizer. He was intended to soothe the erstwhile Progressives at the convention and to persuade them to rejoin the Grand Old Party. This they did because the moderately progressive Charles Evans Hughes won the Republican nomination and because Theodore Roosevelt refused the nomination of the Progressive Party. They did not rejoin the Republican Party because of Harding's oratory, which nettled the Progressives and obscured the issues, as had his nominating speech for Taft in 1912. Again Harding declared that there was not a really reactionary Republican at the convention and that no party could endure that was not progressive; therefore, the Republican Party, by its endurance, was "genuinely progressive."

For his pains, he earned the hatred of Rooseveltians such as William Allen White, whose description of Harding was hardly that of a compromising agent: "He was a handsome dog, a little above medium height, with a swarthy skin, a scathing eye, and was meticulously clad in morning clothes with a red geranium as a boutonnière, and he had the harlot's voice of the old-time political orator. But he was bitter, scalding-bitter, to Theodore Roosevelt. I distrusted him, and into my distrust came something unpleasantly near to hate; for I thought he was deliberately, cruelly unfair. Of course, he represented the tip of the salient on the right."[22]

Over matters that might lose the votes of the people, Senator

Harding was ready to compromise. Over matters of party loyalty, however, he was unforgiving. Yet when Roosevelt contemptuously turned down the Progressive Party nomination, suggesting that the party nominate the reactionary Henry Cabot Lodge, Harding was ready to welcome the Colonel back into the regular fold. For Harding desperately needed the support of Roosevelt's friends in Ohio if he wanted a second term in the Senate in 1920, while Roosevelt needed the support of the regular Republican politicians if he wanted a third term in the White House. As Harding had betrayed Foraker for his own ambition, so Roosevelt betrayed the Progressives. It was time for all good men of politics to unite behind the banner of their old party and of their own interest.

It was Harding who first held out a hand to Roosevelt, although —true to his myth that to receive was better than to seek—he later claimed that Roosevelt had called him to a conference. Immediately after Roosevelt's betrayal of the Progressive Party, Harding wrote to him "with very great satisfaction," complimenting him on his action. This deed would "re-enlist the devotion of thousands of Republicans who have never been lacking in their personal esteem," but who were swayed against Roosevelt for a considerable period because of party differences. "I believe you will have your reward," Harding ended significantly, "in the high opinion of your fellow-countrymen." [23]

Roosevelt knew the significance of his action as well as Harding did. If Hughes were defeated in the election by Woodrow Wilson —as indeed he was—then Roosevelt would be the front-runner for the Republican Presidential nomination in 1920. By returning to the party fold and the high opinion of his Republican fellow countrymen, Roosevelt would be hard to beat in a race for the White House again. He had both destroyed and healed the Republican Party. Harding, calculating immediately and wisely, threw his support to the future winner. And Roosevelt, needing support from party regulars, accepted the offer, calling Harding to a conference about the state of the Republican Party.

From that time on, this alliance of expediency caused Harding to become the mouthpiece of Roosevelt's personal ambition in the

Senate. After Congress had declared war on Germany on April 6, 1917, with Harding's vote in full agreement, Roosevelt offered to raise and lead a volunteer division to France before the regular Army could arrive, in order to boost the morale of the Western Allies. To Roosevelt, the Flanders mud seemed much the same as the jolly charge up San Juan Hill with the Rough Riders in the Spanish-American War. Wilson refused Roosevelt's request contemptuously. He did not intend to allow the likely Republican candidate for the White House in 1920 to make such easy political capital through military action.

Roosevelt switched his request through his friends in the Senate into the form of an amendment to the Selective Draft Bill. Harding was chosen by Roosevelt's supporters to sponsor the amendment, since he was hardly known publicly as a Roosevelt man. Harding pleaded for the Roosevelt volunteer division on the floor of the Senate. The Allies needed "the earliest possible moral encouragement and soulful heartening," since they were fighting America's battles as well as their own. "The psychic moment awaits, and the special volunteer force for Europe will afford the ringing answer." Roosevelt's action would also help recruiting. "It will not hinder the universal-service plan; it will popularize the enactment." Americans should, anyway, get into the fight quickly, since the triumph of the Allies in Europe was the only guarantee America had against ultimate invasion.

God forbid, Harding continued, that Roosevelt's division should be stopped because of politics at home. Although he was an extreme partisan, Harding said, he had supported Wilson's war measures. "This is not a Democratic Party war. It is not an administration war. It is a war of the American Republic, or it will fail miserably." Harding denied that it was a war for democracy, as McKinley's war had been in 1898. Yet it was a war for all Americans. There was but one Theodore Roosevelt in the world, and to give him command over the 121,000 volunteers who had already offered him their services was "the natural thing and the heartening thing and the harmonizing thing to do." [24]

Wilson refused Roosevelt and did not call up a volunteer army. The bitterness of the Republicans against the President rose. "Nothing in the world except partisan bias," Harding complained to Roosevelt, "led to the refusal of a tender of a volunteer army, after Congress saw fit to make provision for such in the Army bill." [25] Senator Henry Cabot Lodge also complained to Roosevelt of Wilson's "mean soul" and his effort to make the war "a party war and shut out all persons of eminence who are Republicans from any share in it." [26] Roosevelt's links to the embittered Old Guard Republican Senators grew stronger, since they all felt personally wronged by the President.

Harding himself, at peace with Roosevelt and protesting his patriotism and support of the war, remained a vehement partisan. In the election of 1916, the Democrats had lost two seats in the Senate to the Republicans, and Wilson had only scraped back into the White House on the "peace" vote of Western women and the German-Americans—a vote that he soon alienated by declaring war. Harding and the other Republicans saw the popular tide running their way again and stepped up their attacks on the Administration, which was trying to hog all the credit for the war.

In a notable clash on the Senate floor, Harding came under fire for terming the Liberty Bond campaign "hysterical and unseemly" in Columbus on Memorial Day, for soothing the German vote in Ohio by claiming that he wished Americans loved their country as much as the Germans loved their Kaiser, and for appealing to the Progressives to support the Republicans and Roosevelt, kept out of France by Wilson's jealousy. Harding's defense was that the campaign for Liberty Bonds was hysterical and had to be, because no one wanted to buy bonds when the government was financing the war in such an unsound way. Had not Wilson himself called the drive for preparedness in 1914 hysterical? Harding repeated that he wished Americans to be as loyal to the Stars and Stripes as Germans were to their Kaiser, but there was not an ounce of pro-German sympathy in his body. He yielded to no man in the Senate "in a devotion and a willingness to serve these United States of America."

Parties had been preserved, however, for the days that were to come. Harding said that he had not forgiven the Democrats, who had campaigned against him in 1914, for saying that only a Democrat should be elected to "stand by the President . . . in trying times like these." It was the Democratic Party that had made the war partisan. And here Harding injected a dangerous smear. He claimed that the cooperation of the Republicans was shown by their refusal to call for "investigation, which would disturb the confidence of the American people of this day in the conduct of the war." He knew, from a secret session of the Senate, damaging facts against the Administration.

Senator Reed of Missouri immediately put Harding on the hook. A statement of that kind, Reed declared, was "much more damaging than any possible fact could be if laid bare in the Senate and to the country." Harding, who obviously had no facts, was forced to backwater. He refused to be led by heckling "to make a sensational statement inclined to disturb American tranquillity." He would continue to boost "popular confidence in this hour of need." He was no knocker. In fact, it was time to halt this "unseemly talk." His remark had been something of a joke. "In the good humor of the moment I have enjoyed the sallies on the question of partisanship."

But Harding was not to be let off his smear lightly. Senator Lewis of Illinois demanded that he clarify his smear, or else hundreds of thousands of Americans reading the newspapers the next day would believe that "some great impending slander" or scandal was imminent. Harding desperately denied that his smear held "any implication of scandal." But Reed would not let him go. He also demanded clarification. Harding then appealed for "a becoming understanding" of his statements. He admitted that there was not "anything dishonorable nor anything of a scandalous nature" in the unpreparedness of America. Yet, he still hinted darkly, he had too much regard for the state of the public mind to be drawn into a statement of specific details.

Reed had one of the sharpest tongues in the Senate, and he flayed Harding. He pointed out that Harding had reduced his smear to the statement that America was not as well prepared as it ought to be. In that case, Americans should buy *more* Liberty Bonds. As for his remarks on Germans loving their Kaiser more, surely this meant that Americans did not esteem their liberty so much as Germans loved their chains? And then Reed made his most interesting statement. He claimed that Harding was slandering the great country of America, over which "the Senator was ambitious to preside as Chief Executive." At least to Democratic Senators, Harding's Presidential ambitions were well known as early as 1917.

Harding did not attempt to reply to Reed's logic. He was defeated. He only rose to preserve his image as the political innocent from the Buckeye State. He said he had no ambition to be President. "I should like it said," he declared, "since this question has been raised, that *I think too well of my country to wish one of such incapacity in so exalted a position.*" The triumphant Reed then left Harding alone with a sneer: "Mr. President," he declared amidst mocking laughter, "the humility of the Senator doth most become him." [27]

Although Harding remained a rabid partisan, he was careful after this hammering to stick to his role as the harmonizer on the Senate floor. Once he became involved with the best minds among the Senate debaters, he was trounced. He preferred the great platitude or the folksy story, neither of which drew the fire of the best minds. His ambition and partisanship was obviously more clear to the Democrats than he allowed it to seem to himself; for Harding always clung to the kindly image of his own actions, however much he betrayed this image in his narrow support of his party.

As to working in the Senate committees in order to help win the war, Harding did little. As a junior member of the Senate, he was given few important assignments. But Henry Cabot Lodge, who needed a yes-man in his chosen field of power, did get Harding a place on the Foreign Relations Committee. With other positions on three committees—Commerce and Territories and Naval Affairs—Harding could later claim some knowledge of world politics, although his attendance at these committees was perfunctory. He also became a member of six other minor committees and was chairman of the Committee on the Philippine Islands—the subject that had first loosed his oratory on the Senate.

Off the Senate floor, Harding was assiduous in making friends who might help him later. He tried to do all things for all men in order to bind them to him through gratitude. He appeared suddenly in Herbert Hoover's office, asking for no present favor, just to be of help to Hoover in his relief work. He was always ready to help any Senator of either party. He was usually affable and smiling, the perfect image of the representative of the people. The current saying had it that no man could possibly be as much a Senator as Harding looked.

It is unquestionable that a man with a good image of himself will do *some* good. Harding enjoyed being of service to others because it flattered his opinion of himself. He liked to be kindly, except when duty to his party made him cruel. "He was one of the most charming persons in a social way," wrote the intelligent Democrat Cordell Hull, "one would ordinarily meet." [28] That was why his name always cropped up as a compromising agent when the best minds were deadlocked and could think of nothing better. Warren Harding was supremely available at being available.

Harding was politic, however, even as a partisan. He was prepared to support many of Wilson's war measures for fear of being considered unpatriotic by the voters of Ohio. Yet to one creed he remained devoted. His vote was always given on the side of big business.

When the bill for a revenue and excess-profits tax came up for debate in the Senate, Harding was moved to folksy eloquence. Although the Senate was nearly empty, Harding wished to make his "illuminating address" for the benefit of the gallery and the *Congressional Record.* He stood against $226,000,000 worth of "unfair, unjust, unreasonable, and uncalled-for class tax upon the great corporations of this land." He knew it was not popular to rise and speak in defense of corporations. Most Congressmen had made their careers "by going about swatting corporations." But, Harding pointed out, the swatters usually come from communities that had no corporations in them. "That is why they are communities instead of cities." He had seen Marion grow into a city because corporations had come there and had built it up.

The tax on the corporations that had developed the United States was a class tax, wrong in principle. Corporations were thought of as soulless things, but they were not. Harding knew, for his own *Star* was a little corporation, with its employees both unionized and sharing in the profits. Little corporations become great had made the villages of the pioneers into the cities of the middle classes. Those who founded corporations took risks. Nine in ten failed. It was envy that taxed the successful tenth one unjustly. The excess-profits tax was both a class and a sectional tax, against businessmen and against the industrial city. It was "encouraging the belief that those who have ought to be plundered," thus "dividing American citizenship along the most dangerous lines to be found in the development of this Republic." At a time when America should feel one, in harmony together, this tax would split it apart. "Those who do, those who accomplish, those who succeed, are to take up the burden of taxation and the support of the Government, and somehow or other the tendency of this legislation is to array Kansas and the Dakotas against Pennsylvania, Ohio, and New York."

Harding denied that he was a spokesman for Wall Street, about which he knew precious little. But the United States, in his opinion, depended on the cooperation of Wall Street with Main Street, not their antagonism. The less successful would always be in the majority, for God did not create men with equal enterprise. But it was wrong and demagogic to appeal to that envious majority and to emphasize class differences. Because a few munitions makers were profiteering, this was no reason to sandbag the whole of honest American industry. "Mr. President," Harding concluded, "I believe in success, and I despise the man who cries out against it. In my observations in life I have found that one man's success ought invariably to be made another man's inspiration to succeed; and I have had the experience to know that corporate and partnership success is not founded so much on capital as it is on talent, genius, industry, stick-to-itiveness, ability to do things." [29]

It was such consistent declarations by Harding that made him one of the darlings of the financial powers that backed the success of the Republican Party. Wall Street knew that it need not fear with a White House or a Senate full of Hardings. He believed so fervently in the right of the rich to become richer, and the right of the poor to try to imitate them, that he could not be more available to the standpat businessmen of America.

On one matter, however, Harding briefly contradicted his hatred of government intervention. When war was declared, he reverted to his early admiration of Hamilton and Napoleon. In a curious interview in 1917, he declared that wartime America needed a supreme dictator, with sole control and sole responsibility. The obstruction of Congress, in which Harding liked to join, was bad for winning the war. Wilson would have to override all opposition, as Lincoln and Washington had done.

Congress was admirably adapted for peace, Harding declared. But it was useless in war, with its "debate and delay." It was not that Congressmen were unpatriotic, but that the system was wrong. "Men are elected to legislative bodies for the purpose of discussing legislation. It is too much to expect that they will not, at least in a respectable minority, fulfill the strict letter of their function, even if 'Hannibal is knocking at the gates.'" Even those few Senators who had opposed the war altogether, in Harding's careful opinion, were sincere and courageous men. They were doing their duty. It was the system that made them seem unpatriotic.

Democracy, in fact, was useless in war. Autocracy must be fought with autocracy. Congress should not be abolished, but relegated to the position of a jury, "ready to impeach any dictator it might select." The only way to put out a large prairie fire was with a small one. Although a thousand letters to Harding complained about the virtual abdication of Congress to Wilson's power, Harding supported total abdication. Of course, Harding added in his private notes on the interview, Americans should preserve appearances, out of regard for their boasted democracy, and Congress should remain on guard; but it would go on delegating power, because human nature in a crisis turned to one commander.[30]

This strange declaration by Harding, so out of line with his usual partisan hatred of Wilson and fear of Presidential power, revealed a hidden side to his character. There was in him—the perfect machine politician—a basic contempt for the processes of democracy. He admired authority. He liked to follow a leader. Only the appearances of democracy were necessary in times of crisis, not the facts. Congress was an inefficient institution. A strong hand was needed in a threatening time, even if a weak hand would do in time of peace. Of course, Harding may have hoped to encourage Wilson to seize total power and thus hang himself. Strong war leaders suffer in the reaction of peace. Yet the authoritarian streak in Harding, based on the careers of his boyhood heroes, explains sufficiently the reasons for his strange admiration of a strong war President and a contempt for the processes of Congress.

This one major inconsistency in Harding's utterances gives a rounded picture of the man. He would have liked to be strong, but he had made a career of pleasing. He could be ruthless, but only when it was to his own advantage. He admired the great, but he wanted popularity more. He was a Hamilton only in his contempt for the vote of the people and in his admiration for the tycoon. Otherwise, he wore sheep's clothing. He dreamed, as average men dream, of being above the average; but when average men elected him to the position of his dreams, he found that he was little more than the average man he had always pretended to be.

As the war continued and as Wilson assumed more and more of the powers of the dictator that Harding had wished on him, Harding himself became more and more the obstructive Senator. On March 6, 1918, he warned the President that America had "gone war mad." In the name of war efficiency, the President was undermining the form of American government. The War Finance Corporation was an instrument to make the Treasury dominant over American business and to dictate the period of peace after the war.[31]

A month later, he repeated his warning over a bill to coordinate executive bureaus and agencies. He reneged on his previous support of a war dictatorship. "We accepted the challenge of the German war party," he declared, "that a republic is not so constituted that it can defend itself; and then, the moment that we are involved, we propose to entirely put aside our popular form of government and dwell in America under the most autocratic form of government on the face of the earth." While Harding said that he was ready to coordinate, concentrate, and consecrate all American power to the winning of the war, he was not willing as a Senator to surrender the functions and duties of his office. The trouble with the war legislation was that it would be continued into peace. The requisitioned railways, Harding prophesied incorrectly, would always remain nationalized. The war government had come to stay and had put an end to democracy in America.[32]

This change in Harding back to the disgruntled Senator was swift. It can be explained in terms of Harding's reversion to his usual beliefs, after a brief patriotic glow of cooperation at the beginning of the war. What had angered him, as it angered other Senators, was Wilson's increasingly high-handed treatment of Congress. One of Wilson's Assistant Secretaries of State had referred to Congress in Harding's presence as "the numskulls on Capitol Hill." And Harding was a vain man, exceedingly proud of his status. Wounded in his vanity, as Henry Cabot Lodge was to be when Wilson failed to take him to Versailles, Harding reverted to his partisan ways—although he continued to protest his patriotism. His smears of the Democrats continued. Unable as always to ferret out the dirty facts, he alleged broadly that there must be scandals in the conduct of the war, because there always were. "There are cormorants by land and sea that hover wherever there is a sanguinary conflict." In a prophecy of his own weakness as President, Harding accused Wilson of making the mistake of "putting into responsible positions men who are not fitted for them." [33]

Harding became more and more the defender of Congressional rights when he opposed a proposal to limit debate on the Senate floor on June 10, 1918. The man who had objected to the delays of debating a year before now objected to any surrender of the "privilege of full and free debate." He claimed that he still held his early opinion that the Senate "fiddled" away a great deal of time in "promiscuous talk." He hated the filibuster, but he hated more the stopping of debate. "The reformation of the Senate has long been a fad," he declared. Freedom of debate there was "one of the highest guaranties" of American liberty. Senators were not unpatriotic in refusing to follow Wilson in everything he wanted. The Senate was "not merely a collection of automatons, where, by playing on the keys, some greater intellect shall register his will and proclaim it through this medium and transmit it to the people of the Republic."

Harding then proceeded to advocate that return to the past which was to endear him to the old bosses in his party. After the war, he said, the great task would be to establish again "the inherited American Republic." He looked on Wilson's threats to appeal directly to the American people over the head of Congress as another proof of the dangerous demagoguery of the progressives. "Though he may be mightily sincere in his purposes, the man who advocates a pure democracy for the United States of America is as great an enemy to the Republic as the German who would undermine our institutions." [34] In his role of small-town businessman, Harding harbored an unholy fear of the mass of the people even after they had elected him to the White House by the largest majority given to a President in a century.

Harding's increased attacks on Wilson and the Democrats were also explained by the politics of an election year. The Republicans, while protesting their patriotism, could not support a Democratic President who openly asked the voters to send back only supporters of the President to Congress. For these out-and-out supporters were, demonstrably, Democrats. Even in wartime, no political party can be expected to plunge a bayonet in itself rather than in its rivals. To Wilson's statement that politics was adjourned, the Republicans had to reply that politics was flourishing. "The statement that politics is adjourned," Harding said to the Ohio Republican State Convention in the August before the election, "needs revision." Disloyalty and indifference were adjourned, but politics never. It could not be in a nation governed through popular political parties. "Abolish them and personal government becomes the substitute, and absolute, and violates every conception of representative popular government." Wilson had become what Harding had once seen as desirable in the inexorable logic of war, a dictator, and now Harding attacked him bitterly for this. In the time of reconstruction ahead, after the war was won, Harding urged a reaction from "granting excess power to the executive." Only the Republicans would restore the "inheritance of the founding fathers." The Democrats, through their leader, revealed "a tendency towards usurpation," which savored "more of autocracy than representative democracy."

Above all, Harding asserted, the war was *not* "the President's war." It was not "a party war," because the majority party in Congress was too divided to declare it and too divided to prosecute it. Democratic Party politics had not been adjourned for one hour by the government. If Americans wished to survive the appeal to mass against class and stick to proven policies against organized might, then they must turn back to the Republicans. "We are far adrift toward the socialized state." The railways had already been seized. Step would follow step. "No man can mark the halting place." War authority was almost limitless. While America's sons fought overseas, radicals at home were bringing in state socialism. In this saturnalia of extravagance and autocracy, the American people must send back Republicans to Congress to keep a check on the President.[35]

The American people responded to the appeal of the Republicans. War does regiment and does make the wartime leader appear an autocrat. There were controls. There was wishful thinking for the golden days before the war, which sometimes had existed and sometimes were imagined. And, above all, the German-American vote, concentrated in the Midwest, returned to the Republican Party, while some of the Irish-American vote, annoyed at the British alliance, also joined the Republicans. Anger that the new prosperity of the cities, made rich by the war, had not reached the farms brought out Insurgent and Farmer-Labor voters in the West. As Francis Bacon had once pointed out, wealth, like muck, should be well spread, and it was not.

The result was that the Republicans won a majority in the House of Representatives and in the Senate, forty-nine to forty-seven. There were twelve new Republican Senators, although progressives from the West such as La Follette and Borah and Norris could not be relied upon to support the standpat Republican vote. On the other hand, conservative Democratic Senators from the South would support the Republicans on some issues. Woodrow Wilson lost control of a majority in the Senate at the very time that he most needed its support to approve of the peace. No peace treaty could be ratified without a vote of two-thirds of the Senate, a vain body, which Wilson had treated roughly for six years.

It is less strange that Wilson lost the issue of the League of Nations than the fact that he nearly won it. He committed the partisan error of taking no Senators with him to Paris to help negotiate the Treaty of Versailles. He did this knowing that the Republicans held a majority in the Senate. He was sure enough of his own power over the American people to force the approval of the Senators through the pressure of their constituents. It was a proud gamble, and it failed.

Harding was one of the minor characters who assisted in its failure. As he more and more fell under the sway of Wilson's chosen enemy, Henry Cabot Lodge, he struck up a more and more jingoistic and nationalistic position. The dream of internationalism of his early days in the Senate disappeared. His time in Congress seemed to have broadened his horizon only from Ohio First to America First.

In the rioting and revolution that followed the armistice in Europe, Harding wanted to lock the doors to foreign influence. While Wilson was still in Paris, the great harmonizer threatened hostility to come. He warned Wilson from the Senate floor that he did not agree with the President's "notions of a new internationalism paralyzed by socialism." He did not agree with Wilson's sowing the seed "of a modified and magnified democracy throughout the world." In fact, the world, trembling under the menace of Bolshevism, owed "a very large part of that growing menace to the policies and utterances of the Chief Executive of the United

States." [36] The Senate, if Harding had anything to do with the matter, would stop the autocrat of the war from writing the peace and would return to the good old days of strong Congresses and weak Presidents who believed in America First.

6

America First

"America's present need is not heroics, but healing; not nostrums, but normalcy; not revolution, but restoration; not agitation, but adjustment; not surgery, but serenity; not the dramatic, but the dispassionate; not experiment, but equipoise; not submergence in internationality, but sustainment in triumphant nationality."

WARREN HARDING

Woodrow Wilson had hesitated to declare America's entry into the First World War for fear that this would loose the spirit of ruthless brutality in American life. In the history of American reform movements, nativism and violence had always played their role. The spirit of the Know-Nothings and the Ku Klux Klan was the dark side of the Grangers and the Populists; for all these movements were inspired by the fear of immigrant control of the Eastern cities, by the fear of rum and Rome and European capital. Even in the progressive movement, the rural progressives outside the cities were still inspired by nativist fears. And once the First World War began in Europe, the prejudices behind the progressive movement began to grow, until hate took the place of reform.

Once the battle lines had been drawn in the Old World, the sense of the New World as different and better had surged. This feeling had contributed to Harding's victory in the Senate race against a Roman Catholic and to the defeat of Progressives in that year. The nationalist wing of the Progressive Party, led by Theodore Roosevelt, had grown more and more strident in its demands for preparedness and loyalty. In this chorus, chauvinists such as Harding had joined enthusiastically. The best garb for a politician is the flag.

The result of this vocal campaign for armed loyalty was the encouragement of the attack on the alien and the foreign. The nativism of the rural progressives and of old-stock Americans came into the open. Bills to limit immigration into the United States were passed by both Houses of Congress with the support of progressives. Only Wilson's continuing vetoes kept the doors of America open, although Congress passed a literacy test for immigrants over the President's veto. Things German became things suspicious as America's financial commitments to England and France grew. The pacifist group among the Progressives, led by Senator La Follette of Wisconsin, had already been defeated in the Progressive Party convention of 1912, which had preferred the belligerent Roosevelt to La Follette. It lost any influence that it had once had over progressive thought with America's increasing involvement in the war.

By the time of the election of 1916, it was generally believed that the warmongering Roosevelt, now returned to the Republican fold, had committed Hughes and the Republican Party to entering the war. Thus the German-Americans and the pacifist wing of the Progressives had voted for Wilson. His later declaration of war bred an excessive patriotism among the American people and then an excessive revulsion. Harding, so often the reflection of the average, mirrored both excesses—and exploited them. As an old-stock American from Ohio, he was in the majority and on its side.

There were two complicating factors in Harding's fervent patriotism, one personal and one political. His wife was of German descent, and his father-in-law spoke German. There was also a large German-American vote in Ohio, particularly in Cincinnati. Only by stressing that America came first and that there could be no loyalties to any other country did Harding ignore the real problem of a division of loyalties. In the same way, he had tried to ignore the quarrel between the Progressives and the standpat Republicans. The myth of America First superseded in Harding's mind the myths of Marion First and Party First and Ohio First. The train of thought was, however, the same: that all differences would be magically resolved if a higher loyalty were invoked. To Harding, all parts fell into place in the rapt contemplation of the whole.

To a German-American constituent, O. A. von Lueblow, Harding set forth his creed before the declaration of war on Germany. This German-American had asked for a popular referendum before entering the war. Harding opposed such a plan, because it was contrary to the Constitution. Moreover, a war referendum would only reveal the divided state of the public mind, while the great essential was to prove an abiding nationality.[1]

Harding elaborated his thesis in a later letter to Von Lueblow; he remained cautious of the power of the German-American vote. He found no fault with anyone for sympathizing with the land from which he or his forefathers came. It was the most natural thing in all the world. Germany, however, was provoking America into declaring war by its submarine policy in the Atlantic. There evidently came a time when a person had to be for his country or for the enemy that proposed to abridge its rights. When that test came, Harding was for his country, first, last, and always. He believed, on sober reflection, that Von Lueblow was ready to be of the same mind, notwithstanding the sympathies that he had justly felt for the Central Powers.[2]

When the vote for war came up in the Senate, Harding was not one of the six Senators who voted against entering the war. Yet he was still being careful of the German-American vote in Ohio when he declared in the Senate his reasons for supporting the war. He did not want war "in response to the alleged hysteria of a subsidized or English-owned press." He did not want war "in response to the campaign of the munition makers, for there has been none." And he did not want war in the name of democracy. The sort of government other people chose to have was not

America's concern. "The German people evidently are pretty well satisfied with their Government." Harding, indeed, said that he wished Americans were as loyal to their government as Germans were to theirs.

"I want it known to the people of my State," Harding asserted, "and to the Nation that I am voting for war to-night for the maintenance of just American rights, which is the first essential to the preservation of the soul of this Republic." Somehow, the fires under "the American melting pot" had been damped, and it looked as if Americans were a divided people. But this war, declared in response to affronts, would at least put a soul into American life. "A war not for the cause of the allies of Europe; a war not for France, beautiful as the sentiment may be in reviving at least our gratitude to the French people; not precisely a war for civilization, worthy and inspiring as that would be; but a war that speaks for the majesty of a people popularly governed, who finally are brought to the crucial test where they are resolved to get together and wage a conflict for the maintenance of their rights."

This narrow war of nationalism defined by Harding had the appeal of discriminating against no one who felt loyal to any European fatherland, whether autocracy or democracy. It was a practical war for practical American ends. And its ideal—if there were an ideal—was an American one: the quickening Americanization of the immigrant in his loyalty toward the embattled United States. Harding quoted in disgust a letter from a constituent who had asked him, "Why seek to preserve American rights? There is no distinctly American nationality." Harding's answer came wrapped in Old Glory. "If there is no one who is distinctly American, then, in the name of the Republic, it is time that we find one." [3]

Although Harding's public speeches outdid even Roosevelt's in the fervor of his devotion to the flag, he remained wary of the power of the German-American vote. The frenzy against all things German passed mania and approached delirium, with German measles and dachshunds renamed "liberty" measles and "liberty" dogs, with outbreaks of violence against individual German-Americans in most of the villages and cities of America. Harding, however, did not join in this frenzy, and he was to reap his reward in 1920 for his forbearance. He even spoke up for the German-language press in the Senate. In the debate over a bill to prosecute seditious acts and utterances, Harding declared that he came from a state with a great many German-language newspapers. He hoped, indeed, that the day was near at hand "when the making of a really American Republic demands that we have a one-language Republic." Yet he knew of many German-language newspapers that carried "the finest utterances of American devotion and loyalty" that were printed in the land. Perhaps many a traitor was hiding behind the camouflage of these publications. Even so, Harding supported an amendment to the act that would allow religious publications in a foreign language to be carried in the mails of the United States.[4]

In this way, Harding tried still to get the best of both worlds, speaking up for the American patriot and yet refusing to victimize the powerful German-Americans. Playing both sides had been his successful strategy in his early days in Ohio politics, when he had supported Foraker and refused to criticize Hanna. He applied the lesson now, for the making of friends was a good and the making of enemies an evil. He defended safe things, such as American rights, and attacked safe things, such as traitors to America. For once, he acted more wisely than most Americans—indeed, most intellectual Americans—who plunged into a debauch of anti-Hun hysteria.

The excessive patriotism of many of the old Progressives is difficult to understand. Wilson loosed not only the spirit of ruthless brutality in American life, but also the spirit of dominant unreason. A country can keep its equilibrium when patriotism is the last refuge of a scoundrel, but not when it is the last refuge of an intellectual. The propaganda forces mobilized by George Creel came from the best universities in the land. The hatred they help to foment against the German and the alien gave a chance to the bigoted to take control in many areas of American life.

The nativism at the back of the rural progressive movement became naked. It was the reforming Senator Beveridge, the supporter of child-labor laws, who now praised Indianapolis businessmen for suppressing strikes by force. It was Theodore Roosevelt who endorsed for reelection such reactionaries as Senator Albert Fall, known as "Petroleum" Fall in the Senate, for his continual support of the large oil companies. To Roosevelt, Fall was an American after his own heart. And it was the progressive Democrat and Attorney General A. Mitchell Palmer who decided to run for the White House on the Red Scare.

With the success of the Bolshevik Revolution in Russia and with Communist uprisings in Hungary and Germany in 1919, a Red revolution seemed to be near. Although the Bolsheviks of America, the International Workers of the World, had been persecuted and broken up during the World War, enough of them still remained to cause worry to the comfortable. Even if Wilson himself was bitterly anti-Socialist—he refused to let Socialist leader Eugene Debs out of the jail to which he had been sent for opposing the war—the current joke in Ohio had it that IWW meant "I Woodrow Wilson." [5] Sporadic bomb attempts by the anarchists whipped a fear into a terror. These were followed by massive strikes against the soaring cost of living in 1919. Even the Boston police went on strike, giving over the city to looters, before Governor Calvin Coolidge cannily took the credit for restoring order.

With this widespread fear of revolution, Attorney General Palmer, whose own house had been bombed, decided to show the iron fist. He had been popular with labor and the foreign-born in his progressive days; but seeing the temper of the times, he decided to put all supposed revolutionaries in jail. Several thousand radicals were arrested, although few could be charged with any crime; 249 of them, including the anarchist Emma Goldman, were deported to Russia on an army transport ship. Palmer emerged as a popular hero, although the Wilsonian intellectuals were turning away in disgust from an administration that would allow such a wholesale assault on the liberties of Americans.

Harding, who feared a social revolution as much as any rich American, naturally joined in the attack on the radicals. He had been attacking them all his life. He took his stand on the safest ground in America—the Constitution. Every man, in Harding's opinion, who did not "subscribe heartily and loyally to the Constitution ought to go to Russia or some other land of tragic experiment." [6] The Constitution was the base of all Americanism, the ark of the covenant of American liberty, "the very temple of equal rights." The freedom of speech that it guaranteed had become more sacred than the document itself. There was no longer room in the United States for those who wanted to destroy the Constitution. "Any class or mass that opposes the Constitution is against the country and the flag."

Harding, so careful of the German-American vote in the World War, was not so careful of the foreign vote when social revolution threatened at home. "This republic has never feared an enemy from without," he told the Ohio Society of New York on January 10, 1920. "It no longer intends to be menaced by enemies from within. . . . One cannot be half American and half European or half something else. This is the day for the all-American." While the attitudes of many progressives had changed to the illiberal, the attitude of Harding had changed to the reactionary. With the social system at stake—and the vote of the agitator in Ohio worthless—Harding could damn his chosen enemy and fear nothing except a surfeit of praise.

It was in this season of fear of revolution that Harding coined his slogan of "Back to Normalcy" and referred to "a sane normalcy . . . to be reached in deliberation and understanding." Sane normalcy demanded the cooperation of capital and labor, the lessening of the power of government, the deportation of agitators, and the isolation of America from the Red plague of Europe. "Let Russia experiment in her fatuous folly, until the world is warned anew by her colossal tragedy. And let every clamorous advocate of the Red regime go to Russia and revel in its crimson reign. This is law-abiding America!"

By thrift and work and praise of honest success, by the old values of old America, normalcy could be regained. The new immigrants could also be saved by "complete and rejoicing Americanization." There was no selfishness in nationalism. A country should put its own house in order before it attempted to dictate to the world. "Let the internationalist dream and the Bolshevist destroy." As for Harding, he thought it an inspiration to patriotic devotion

To safeguard America first.
To stabilize America first.
To prosper America first.
To think of America first.
To exalt America first.
To live for and revere America first.[7]

Thus it was that the Red Scare confirmed Harding in the nationalism that he had always felt and had seemed to outgrow in his early days in the Senate. His horizons, bounded by hometown and home state and Grand Old Party and country, had once seemed about to include something of the world. But partisan feeling had begun his retreat from his brief internationalism. The Red Scare confirmed him as an isolationist. He was no better and no worse than the American people, who had backed reform and internationalism at one time, but now reverted to conservatism and nationalism for fear of revolution at home. The plague of the Old World led to the quarantine of the New.

It was against this background of the Red Scare that the drama of the League of Nations was played out. The failure of Wilson and the League cannot be understood unless the reawakening of America's traditional fear of Europe is understood. Harding, as he often did, mirrored the reaction of the average and the majority. Not until the autumn of 1919 could he stand firmly in his favorite position on the far right and be sure, as he had not been sure for more than a decade, that he would meet with popular approval.

The change had been swift. For when Wilson returned from Versailles early in 1919 with the peace treaty and the League of Nations wrapped in one bundle for the approval of Congress, the country was overwhelmingly on his side. Wilson, knowing of the opposition of the jealous Senate, hoped to capitalize on the popular desire for an immediate peace by inserting the League of Nations in the peace treaty. It was a package peace, the work—in the Secretary of State's opinion—of a "foxy ward politician." Only a few

Western Irreconcilables, such as William Borah of Idaho, seemed to be standing out wholly against the League of Nations.

The nationalist Harding was indeed so frightened at that time that he asked Borah to speak against the League in Ohio. He would arrange the dates if Borah would not tell anybody that he had arranged them. "I'd like to get in the fight against this League of Nations," he declared to Borah, "but the people of my State are all for it." [8] It was the later change of Buckeye sentiment that allowed Harding to declare himself the rabid nationalist who put America first.

As a member of the Senate Foreign Relations Committee, Harding had received a thorough grounding from Henry Cabot Lodge in the role of the Senate as a maker of foreign policy. In its long struggle with the Chief Executive, the Senate had used to the full its veto power over foreign treaties negotiated by the President. Being a conservative body, it had clung to the old American traditions first formulated by Washington and Jefferson and Monroe: involvement with Europe was bad, and the Americas were the sole concern of the United States. A military policy that involved more than the protection of the Americas was also dangerous. America First—and no more—was the traditional policy of the Senate.

In the two decades before the struggle over the League of Nations, the Senate had shown itself normally destructive. Determined to keep or expand its power, it had rejected in 1897 and 1911 general arbitration treaties with Great Britain. For if the principle of general arbitration were allowed, the Chief Executive could settle matters of foreign policy without consulting Congress. Even Theodore Roosevelt had been unable to win the Senate's acceptance of the principle of general arbitration or of any international peace-keeping agreement that would reduce the Senate's power in foreign affairs.

Against this consistent policy of Senatorial hostility, Wilson opposed the revolutionary concept of the League of Nations. The League went much further than the principle of general arbitration. The contentious Article Ten of the treaty, which Wilson called the heart of the covenant of the League of Nations, pro-

vided for the possibility of armed intervention by the United
States in the event of aggression against a member of the League.
Such an entanglement in world affairs broke every tradition of
American policy. On this sure ground, the personal and Republican
enemies of Wilson took their stand.

After the defeat of the Democrats in the election of 1918,
Theodore Roosevelt had warned the Allied leaders negotiating
with Wilson that the American people had repudiated their President. Before his death two months later, he had urged Lodge and
the influential Republican Elihu Root to devise a program of
amendments to hamstring the League, while professing public
loyalty to the idea. Wilson, on a brief return from Paris, was struck
enough by the anger of the Senate to accept certain modifications
in his plan for America's entry into the League. Yet Lodge and
his followers, by this time, were intent on the defeat and humiliation of Wilson. In the middle of March, 1919, thirty-nine Senators
signed a resolution opposing the League. This was more than the
one-third vote of the Senate needed to kill the League.[9]

From this time onward, the battle was joined between the White
House and the Irreconcilables, allied with the Reservationists, in
the Senate. Compromises were suggested, but more as camouflage
than in earnest. Lodge pretended to show a willingness to negotiate,
as did Wilson, but both were determined to fight to the finish. On
one attempt at reconciliation, Harding accompanied his mentor
Lodge to the White House with thirteen other Senators. Despite
an adroit performance by Wilson, who claimed that entry into
the League of Nations involved more of a moral than a legal commitment to the world by the United States, the Senators remained
unsatisfied.

Harding showed himself an able questioner in this meeting with
Wilson. First he asked the President why, if there was only a
moral commitment on the part of League members, Article Ten
was necessary. If every nation had only a moral commitment to
the League, was not the League useless? Wilson evaded the question by saying that a moral obligation was superior to a legal one,
but that it allowed an element of judgment in particular situations.

Harding, however, protesting his slow mind, was not prepared to let Wilson go. He asked whether, in case of a revenge war by the Balkans against Italy, the United States would be obliged to intervene. The President answered that the American government would decide on that case when it came up; it was not obliged to intervene. Yet Harding was still worried over the question of moral obligation—by folk belief, the morality of the New World was superior to that of the Old. The consciences of European countries, although not of America, might be warped by racial and geographical prejudices. Would not the moral obligation of America, then, be surrendered "to the prejudices or necessities of the nations of the Old World," dominant in the League? Should not America alone, unswayed by what the League thought moral, determine its own moral obligations? Harding was deeply worried that America, which had rejected Europe in order to rise above it, would now have to descend again to its level.

Wilson reminded Harding that if the moral judgment of Europe agreed on something *without a League* and if America dissented, then the New World would still receive the censure of the Old. In this case, Harding asked, what was the permanent value of the League? Here Wilson made himself clear. In his opinion, the United States would generally concur with the moral judgment of the world. Germany would never have dared to start the First World War if it had known that America generally stood with the moral judgment of the Allies. Harding shied away from this idea of international morality. It was America's own moral judgment that had made it enter the World War. Yes, the President replied, but it had agreed with the judgment of the world. Then why, Harding asked, was it necessary to have "a written compact" for America to fulfill its duties to civilization? It was not necessary, the President answered; but America would steady the whole world if it promised beforehand to stand by the right.[10]

In this exchange of remarks, Harding and Wilson displayed the hopelessness of reconciliation, for both were moved by different beliefs. Harding believed in a past tradition of isolation, backed by a personal suspicion of wicked and chaotic Europe. Wilson believed in a future of world involvement, backed by the personal acclaim of the European crowds. Like a snail, Harding had briefly stretched out nervous horns toward internationalism, but had quickly retreated inside his shell of nationalism. Wilson, seeing what Harding claimed to have seen in 1916, that technology and communications were making one world, tried to change the pattern of more than a century of American diplomacy. Harding's occasional sops to internationalism were the pious hopes of Rotary that men of goodwill of all countries should live in peace. Wilson's scheme of the League of Nations was the first practical step toward controlling the national state, which was becoming dangerous and obsolete in the new age of quick communications. If Wilson lost and Harding won, it was because the past rules the present more than the future does.

In the Senate debate on the League of September 11, 1919, Harding made his major speech in the Senate, obviously relishing his new role as a spokesman on foreign affairs. His correspondence now showed him that public opinion had swung against a League without reservations.[11] He could now speak his mind at last. Thus he openly backed Lodge's extreme position: the Senate would not accept the covenant of the League of Nations without crippling reservations, which would leave America as uncommitted as it had ever been. In Harding's opinion, the covenant of the League was one of peril to America. "To accept it unaltered would be a betrayal of America." This was the thought of an American who was "jealous of the Republic's nationality" and who feared "paralysis in that internationality which is the League's loftiest aim."

Harding declared that his love of peace was as great as the President's; there was no Wilsonian monopoly on loving peace. "It was the truth, last year, two years ago, three and four years ago, the people of this country were heedlessly and overwhelmingly for a league of nations, or a society of nations, or a world court, or some international association." Always in line with popular temper, Harding confessed that he had signed a resolution in favor of such an international association. But "nobody stopped to think of the involvements then. We are only learning them now."

Wilson should have counseled with the Republican Party after the election of 1918 had repudiated international involvement. He did not. He went in for "the excessive proclamation of democracy and humanity . . . mainly for home consumption." In fact, the war had been fought only to defend America's *national* rights. Harding did not even reproach Wilson for going to Paris to settle the peace and leaving all Senators behind. He did, however, reproach him for his dreams in settling that peace, for such a world as Wilson saw could not be realized "until that millennial day that marks the beginning of heaven on earth."

Wilson had been deceived in Paris, according to Harding, by the selfish and secret ambitions of the Allies. For the League, he had bartered away true American national interests. The Allies wanted the League only in order "to guarantee in perpetuity the selfishness of the Old World." Although a world court might be a good thing, the "supergovernment" of the League of Nations was a dangerous thing. And if the League were not a supergovernment, then it would prove "the colossal disappointment of the ages." In either case, the United States should keep out.

The League, indeed, would not solve the most important questions, such as disarmament or arbitration between nations. It would either involve America inextricably through Article Ten or be useless. No reservation on Article Ten written by the Senate could safeguard America's moral commitment to international action dictated by "the prejudices, ambitions, hatreds, and jealousies of the Old World."

Indeed, Harding continued, America now had an expanded influence and a world interest, but there was yet for the United States "a splendid isolation." In entering the war, Americans were not concerned with governing the universe, but in protecting their just rights. The President might be touring America, speaking in Ohio about the need for the people to support the League, but as a Senator from Ohio, Harding had an equal right to tell the people not to support the League without reservations. Europe was still asking for American troops to settle the question of Armenia, and Harding was not deaf to the wails of suffering humanity there. But he was "thinking of America first. Safety, as well as charity, begins at home. Selfishness? No. It is self-preservation." America was not strong enough to meddle in all the troubles of the world. Every time it meddled, moreover, it alienated a group of immigrants, and Americans were already too divided among themselves.

"In the travail of war," Harding declared, "the American soul was born, and we have preached and practiced Americanization ever since, and we mean to go on and make this Republic American in fact as well as in name. No republic can endure half loyal and half disloyal; no citizenship is of permanent value whose heart is not in America. I had thought the war worth all its cost, in spite of its unutterable expenditure in lives and treasure, to have found ourselves. It was an inspiration to find the adopted sons of the Republic consecrated to the common cause. Yet, sirs, the unhappy aftermath is resurrecting the old lines of divided citizenship. We are restoring hyphenism under internationalism."

In a frank reaction against anything new and anything European, Harding lumped together "the propagandists of the hour and the proponents of the league." The drives to nationalize industry, denationalize government, and internationalize the world were all linked. All were contrary to everything that had made America what it was. For "nationalism inspired, assured, upbuilded." If the Senate chose to defend nationalism, it was doing its sworn duty. "A Senator may be as jealous of his constitutional duty as the President is jealous of an international concoction, especially if we cling to the substance as well as the form of representative democracy. The dictatorship was for the war only, and does not abide in the aftermath." Those who dismissed the League were "splendidly patriotic."

Harding finally declared his support for strong reservations to the League, which Lodge and the Old Guard of the Republicans supported. "I could no more support 'mild reservations' than I could sanction mild Americanism. These reservations come of a purpose to protect America first." If such a course delayed reconstruction, reconstruction must wait. It was the President who had made the blunder, which the Senate had to correct.[12]

So Harding finally spoke out for nationalism, pure and unadorned. Thousands of copies of his speech were distributed in Ohio. He spoke out at the first moment that the tide of popular sentiment seemed to be swinging away from Wilson and the League. His stand was naked. America First seemed a safe cry, with Bolshevism breaking out in Europe and apparently imminent in America itself. The Senate agreed with him and voted down the peace treaty and the League of Nations.

Of course, America First was a myth. Wilson had never put America second. He had merely claimed correctly that the future security of the New World now depended, to some extent, on that of the Old. But he was gathering the hatred of most of the recent immigrants from the Old World, who were still involved with the lands of their fathers. The Irish-Americans swung away from the Democrats because Wilson had declared himself for the principle of self-determination and yet had not insisted that the British give independence to Ireland. The Italian-Americans were furious that Wilson had blocked Italian ambitions in the Adriatic. And the German-Americans, angry enough at the American entry into the war, were further angered by Wilson's agreement to the Allied revenge on Germany, which lost its empire and the Saar and had to pay immense reparations.

Wilson also seemed rapt in his intent to win the League and to do nothing for reconstruction. "Reconstruction," anyway, was an ugly word in American history because of the aftermath of the Civil War. The army took a long time to demobilize, and few could understand why their sons took a year to come home after the armistice. Wilson refused a progressive plan for nationalizing the railroads, and he restored them to modified private control. The War Industries Board, which had organized the nation's economy, dissolved when fighting stopped; its hundred business experts returned to private industry, although the problems of demobilization can be far greater than those of war.

The result was galloping inflation in 1919, with such a rise in prices that the gain in real wages of the prosperous war years was almost wiped out. The hatred of Huns now turned to hatred of Reds and even of Negroes; in Chicago, a bloody race riot showed that color could incite as much aimless prejudice as origin or creed. In this melting pot of social and economic discontent, those who preached a return to mythical stability were bound to be more popular than those who preached more new commitments. The Hardings came into their own against the Wilsons.

Even so, Wilson might have carried a version of the League through if he had not suffered a paralytic stroke, which probably affected his brain. At once, his chief asset—the remarkable personality that had awed even his enemies—was removed. He lay incapacitated in the White House from the fall of 1919 to the spring of 1920. The government was effectively in the hands of his individual Cabinet members, his physician, and his uneducated second wife. His secretary, Joseph Tumulty, desperately tried to make Wilson accept the League reservations of moderate Senators; but Mrs. Wilson kept Tumulty away, and the President remained unmoving in body and mind.

Eventually, when the Senate had finally killed the League, a letter that purported to come from the President refused to accept the action of the Senate as the decision of the nation. The treaty could not be rewritten. The next election should stand as a great and solemn referendum on the treaty. When the reactionary Senator Fall insisted on calling on Wilson to see whether he were mentally competent and fit to be President, Wilson made a show of speech and movement from his bed just good enough to send Fall away "reassured but . . . disappointed." [13]

In this virtual interregnum, those who opposed the League won the ear of the nation. With Wilson's collapse, the Senators who hated him, such as Harding, were openly triumphant. They had nothing to fear now. The newspapers openly declared that a madman or a dying man lay in the White House. Was not the League, then, the concoction of this crazed mind, driven insane by power? Harding, in his last speech in the Senate on the League, delivered on November 19, 1919, did not display his boasted generosity toward his stricken opponent.

"There was but one man in the United States of America," he claimed, "who did not know that this treaty could never be ratified without reservations." Thus Wilson had made "the colossal bunder of all time," and those who supported him participated in "a knowing betrayal of the Republic." Wilson had sought to press on, with his towering ambition, "in that disregard for the Senate which grew out of war conditions, in that little consideration for this body which followed a state of submergence." Therefore, by ignoring the Senate, Wilson had brought about his own humiliation in its rejection of the League. "That is not the fault of the Senate; that is the fault of him who negotiated . . . without recognizing that there is a Senate." It was a great misfortune that the Senate should repudiate its President, but the inheritance of the Republic was more important than the wounded feelings of the ambitious Wilson.[14]

So Harding spoke on the deathbed of the League and on the presumed deathbed of its author. These were the public words of a man who claimed to be modest, magnanimous, and generous to a fault when he sought to be Wilson's successor in the White House. For this was the necessary myth of the Reluctant Candidate.

7

The Reluctant Candidate

"I was quite reluctant to get into the presidential game but I came to find out that a man in public life cannot always map out his way according to his own preferences. Therefore, I decided to go in and do the best that I could, under more or less difficult circumstances."

WARREN HARDING

There are two ways to a Presidential nomination. One is by assault, and one by flirtation. The first demands a bold bid to seize the primaries. The second demands an insincere refusal of all high office. The front-runner may charge through to the nomination, but he risks alienating the support of those whom he needs to clinch his victory. The dark horse may break a deadlock, but he risks losing all to the determined candidate. The strong approach makes friends and enemies, who choose or reject. The weak approach makes acquaintances, who nod their second choice. The strategy of a candidate is determined by his personality, his backers, his home state, and his ability to attract popular support. By personality, management, geography, and popular appeal, Warren Harding was bound to play the role of the reluctant candidate.

By temperament, Harding liked to avoid a quarrel—except in the name of party. His known preference for appealing to all sides had made him available as a harmonizer on many occasions. He was one of the few politicians who could straddle wide and yet seem upright. He liked to protest his humility and incapacity even when he was doing a competent job of partisan hatchet work. In his own image of himself, Harding liked to think, incorrectly, that office had come to him without his seeking for office. In fact, he was an ambitious man.

This self-deception of Harding suited Harry Daugherty's image of himself as the man who made Harding run. Thus he spread far and wide the myth of Harding's reluctance for office. He did not mention that his plan to put Harding in the White House was Harding's own—a traditional one, based on an old strategy of politicians from Ohio. Nor did he mention that the role of the reluctant candidate was also forced on Harding because of his total lack of popular appeal outside his home state.

The date on which Harding decided to try to reach the White House is obscure. Certainly, such an ambition was the most distant of dreams until his election as Senator in 1914. But at that time, he immediately became available for the White House. His only serious rivals from Ohio, after Taft's political debacle, were ex-Senator Burton, ex-Governor Herrick, and the new Governor of Ohio, Frank Willis. But when, in 1916, Burton failed to get the Presidential nomination and Herrick failed to become the junior Senator from Ohio and Willis lost to Democratic ex-Governor James M. Cox, Harding became the only Republican in high office from Ohio, and thus its most available man. Therefore, from November, 1916, Harding may well have suffered premonitions of the Presidency. At least his Democratic opponents in the Senate accused him of this the following year, while he protested his incapacity.

One Ohio industrialist, Joseph Butler, Jr., claimed that Harding wanted the White House from the moment that he was elected to the Senate. At a meeting of the Youngstown Chamber of Commerce on November 23, 1914, Butler introduced Senator-elect Harding as a man who would be the future President of the United States. Harding was, Butler recollected later, "likely the only man hearing me make this prediction who then believed it would come true." In a letter to Butler from the White House, President

Harding later wrote that he thought Butler was entitled to a certificate for being actually "the original Harding man." [1]

Yet Harding's chance of reaching the White House was not great until he became the leading favorite son of Ohio after the election of 1916. His rivals were then effectively eliminated, and he became the titular head of the Buckeye Republicans. Before the election, he had been one partisan chieftain among many. He had knifed his rivals in a letter to his friend Malcolm Jennings, executive secretary of the Ohio Manufacturers' Association. Willis had made a mess as Governor, Harding wrote, and could not be reelected. Nobody enthused much about ex-Senator Burton for the White House; he did not seem to have the faculty for nailing anything down. Without being disloyal, Harding thought that Hughes would get the Republican Presidential nomination. As for ex-Governor Herrick, in Harding's opinion Harry Daugherty "would make five times as effective a senator." [2] In fact, Harding seemed to endorse Daugherty openly against Herrick, gaining praise for being such "a big man" to endorse such an obvious loser.[3] When Herrick won the Senatorial primary easily from Daugherty, Harding calmly wrote the latter off. Although he felt "a very sincere personal disappointment" on Daugherty's behalf, Daugherty's utter defeat meant "his complete retirement." [4]

In his correspondence with Jennings, Harding completely denied any ambition for the Presidency in 1916. If the progressive advance continued, he declared, he would even lose his Senate seat in 1920. He was already sickened "at the demonstration of the destructive tendencies on the part of radicals . . . well entrenched in the Senate." If their power grew, he would be content to leave the Upper House.[5] As for the White House, Jennings knew that Harding was unsuited:

> Honestly [Harding declared safely, since his chances for the Presidential nomination in 1916 were minimal], I would not have the place if I could reach out and grasp it, and I really do not want any of my friends to promote it in any way. On the contrary, I should prefer that every suggestion should be promptly punctured. I find it difficult to make a good many people believe that one can feel

this way, and I think Wilson was quite right when he said to the Gridiron Club that any man would be an audacious fool *to wish the Presidency on his own account.* Of course, I am human enough to enjoy having friends who think well enough of me to suggest me for that position, and I confess some pleasure in knowing that events have so broken thus far that I should attract some favorable mention, but when it comes down to serious consideration I am wholly truthful when I say that I had rather no mention were made whatever.[6]

Thus Harding's strategy of reluctance was developed *by himself.* When the situation was hopeless, he wanted no one to think him ambitious enough to seek the White House, for only an audacious fool would wish the Presidency on his own account. Harding was, however, flattered when friends wished the Presidency on him and when he had attracted favorable mention. But once serious consideration was brought to bear on his hopeless situation in 1916, opposed by progressives and not even Ohio's favorite son, it was best to make no mention of Harding for the White House. As with all his protestations against being a Presidential hopeful, Harding began with an avowal of incapacity and unwillingness; he continued with a conditional acceptance: his friends and the situation would have to wish it upon him. It was only when the odds were too great that he wanted silence on the subject.

One great figure stood between Harding and the White House after Hughes's defeat by Woodrow Wilson in 1916, when Herrick and Willis were also defeated by the Democrats in Ohio. Theodore Roosevelt, it was generally conceded, was the obvious Republican nominee for President in 1920. It was for this reason that Harding made his politic peace with Roosevelt as soon as he could. As long as Roosevelt was alive, Harding's own chances of getting to the White House were small. He needed Roosevelt's support in Ohio, where Walter Brown led the Colonel's friends, to succeed himself in the Senate.

Harding was running for reelection to the Senate every day that he was a Senator. His letters to and replies from Jennings show how closely he kept watch on the pulse of his home state, at least as it appeared to the secretary of the Ohio Manufacturers' Association. Jennings felt sure enough of Harding to criticize him openly and to advise him on how to write his speeches and on how to vote. Harding's answers were frequently almost humble, for fear of alienating the industrialists of Ohio. That he followed Jennings' advice is incontestable. He once read a speech of Jennings and declared that it might have been his own.

It was Jennings, for instance, who first advised Harding to speak out openly against pro-German feeling in Ohio. No man, according to Jennings, "in public life ever lost anything by boldly asserting the rights of his country and upholding its flag and its honor. It has been said that all the world loves a lover, which is not entirely true, but certainly all the world loves a fighter." [7] In response to this advice, Harding spoke out more firmly against traitors and for his country. He was also quick to furnish Jennings with five hundred copies of his speech on a revenue bill in favor of big business and against a profits tax, for distribution to Buckeye manufacturers, so that they should know that their Senator spoke up in their interests.

While Jennings kept Harding informed of the situation in Ohio, he also pointed out that Harding was becoming more and more mentioned as Presidential timber. Sometimes he succumbed to fears over the future and saw only the end of the Presidential system altogether. Harding agreed. "Many a moment," he declared on December 31, 1917, "I am convinced that we are doomed to the rule of something similar to the Bolsheviki on the one hand or a very strong military autocracy on the other." [8] In either case, of course, Harding saw no future for himself as either Senator or President.

As the election of 1918 approached, Harding waited on the result, to see whether a rival would come out of the field to take from him the leadership of the party in Ohio. Willis again won the nomination as Republican candidate for Governor, and Harding, who doubted Willis' ability to beat James M. Cox, saw no way to stop him without "creating menacing factions." It was a delicate matter to handle, Harding confessed, although he kept his hands off. Those people who said that his ambitions conflicted with those of Willis were fools. Harding repeated that he did not want Ohio to support him for the Presidency, even if Willis had that ambition. Walter Brown was, anyway, set on delivering the state to Roosevelt, and it might transpire that Roosevelt would be "the one best bet for the party to make." [9] In all, it was a pity that there should be "so much of so-called presidential politics" within the Republican Party two years before the next national convention.[10]

Harding, however, was not totally disinterested in these so-called Presidential politics. He kept up a detailed correspondence not only with Malcolm Jennings but also with Charles Hard, the assistant secretary of the Ohio Republican State Advisory Committee. Hard warned Harding of all the attempts of the pro-Willis forces and the pro-Roosevelt forces to take over the regular Republican organization in Ohio in order to be in a favorable position to nominate delegates to the national convention two years later.

In fact, the loss of Willis to Governor Cox for the second time, in 1918, while the Republicans won elsewhere on the discontented German-American and farm vote, largely eliminated him from consideration as Ohio's favorite son. That honor seemed to be reserved now for Harding if the Roosevelt faction did not seize control of the party. Willis was, however, now casting envious eyes at Harding's seat in the Senate. Suddenly, in November of 1918, Harding found himself in the familiar position of an Ohio politician—a desperate twist to avoid being struck down by many knives in the back. In the ensuing struggle for power, he showed considerable political skill and ambition. He was finally saved once again by extraordinary luck—the death of the great chieftain, Theodore Roosevelt.

Harding first noticed rumors of an attempt to deprive him of his political power in Ohio on November 14, in the wake of the election. Willis and Daugherty and the Roosevelt forces were maneuvering to organize the Republicans in the General Assembly in order to get the lion's share of the political spoils for their own supporters. It was in Harding's interest that no personal faction controlled the party organization and spoils in Ohio, for he was the obvious choice as Ohio's favorite son. He did not want the party

run "by either pin-heads or bull-heads in difficult times like these,"
even if he was an old enough hand at the game to know that factions liked to divide the spoils after a party victory in the elections.
Harding confessed to Hard that he would try to confer with
Daugherty and persuade him to take a "rational course." To protect himself, Harding wanted to continue as the head of the old
State Advisory Committee, a special inner group of Buckeye
politicians endorsed by the state convention and charged with fixing "Party plans for the ensuing two years." [11]

As November advanced, the situation for Harding worsened.
Party chieftains wanted to throw Harding off the State Advisory
Committee or leave it moribund. Daugherty wanted to fight it out
with the wet Roosevelt forces from Cincinnati for control of the
General Assembly, declaring that they were responsible for Willis'
loss of the election. He was also threatening to join the dry Willis
backers, who were opposed to Harding. The party seemed ready
to split apart in personal quarrels, and Harding wanted it as a
united group behind his back in 1920.[12]

Harding revealed his intention to fight if the forces against him
in the State Central Committee tried to end the State Advisory
Committee and Harding's influence over party policy. For then
power would go to the State Central Committee, in which Harding was powerless. "I prefer to dwell in harmony," he declared,
"and am always willing to yield to the limit to maintain that harmony, but if we are developing a situation in Ohio which demands
a fight, I think I can take my part therein and get a reasonable
degree of satisfaction out of it." [13]

It was at this moment that Harding became certain that Daugherty was working against him in order to increase his own personal
power. In a letter to Daugherty of November 29, Harding said
that he did not want Daugherty to push any quarrel that would
split the party in Ohio or the cordial relations between himself
and Daugherty: "We cannot have a successful Republican Party
in Ohio if we map our course with a view to making reprisals and
everlastingly baring to the public view the grievencies [sic] of
campaigns which have passed. I think the time has come for the
assumption of the broadest possible viewpoint and the endeavor to

unite the Party in Ohio for future triumph." If Daugherty would play Harding's game and drop his vendetta against the Cincinnati wets, Harding offered his support. "I do not know of anyone who wants to put you out of the Party in Ohio or seeks to discredit you and I know full well that I would take issue with anyone who sought to adopt such a course. On the other hand, I cannot join you in riding other people out of the Party because they are not in complete accord with you." Harding wanted to prevent any single man from becoming boss in Ohio, in order that he himself would remain Ohio's most important Republican. Thus he preached party unity and harmony under himself.[14]

Daugherty, however, was a born intriguer. On one hand, he was warning Harding of plots against him by the Cincinnati wets and Rooseveltians.[15] On the other hand, he was plotting with the drys and the Willis forces to take over control of the state legislature and party and perhaps to try to deliver Harding's seat in the Senate to Willis in 1920. To Harding, Daugherty kept the fair face of the seasoned campaigner instructing the political innocent on the wiles of men. "I have been in a position somewhat different from you," he declared to Harding, "and where I have been compelled to study the motives of men more than you have, and in the past I have rarely been mistaken." As an old and trusted friend, Daugherty advised Harding to back him in his bid for party control, otherwise Harding would fall a victim to his enemies.[16] In effect, he was telling the lamb in the Senate to lie down with the old Buckeye dog to stop himself from being eaten by the wolves.

Harding's reply to Daugherty's patronizing tone was frosty. At a personal meeting, he told Daugherty flatly that "some things he was committed to could not be." Harding also told him that some things that Harding wanted would be done, or else "responsibility for a lack of harmony program" would land on Daugherty. According to Harding, Daugherty left the interview promising to cooperate.[17] Yet Harding continued to resent Daugherty's air of superiority, writing curtly that he understood the situation in Ohio, despite Daugherty's "poor opinion" of his political intelligence.[18]

Harding's political intelligence was so good, indeed, that he knew almost at once that Daugherty was working against him. While Daugherty had assured Harding that he would back him and the State Advisory Committee, he assured others that the State Advisory Committee was doomed. Harding swallowed his "pride of opinion" and his "disappointments" and his "selfish ends" to appeal to Daugherty for his support over fixing a meeting of the Advisory Committee. Daugherty may have betrayed him once, but Harding was ready to forgive him.[19]

Daugherty's reaction was one of injured innocence. He said that Harding's letter was the most unfortunate letter that Harding had ever written. He protested his sincerity and the reality of the wet Rooseveltian plot against Harding, who knew him well enough to be sure that he could "never play any cards under the table in politics or anything else." He even said that he was not carrying on a vendetta against his party enemies, since he was "not in the fertilizer business" and did not "consider it profitable to pursue or puncture dead horses." He claimed that the sources of Harding's information in Ohio—chiefly Hard and Jennings—were unfriendly to him. In fact, Harding would be well advised to break with the Cincinnati wets and to give up all idea of a harmonious Advisory Committee, which might include those who were plotting against Harding.[20]

Harding replied with the same protestations of personal friendship for Daugherty. But he still claimed that Daugherty was wrong and was pursuing a vendetta against those who had defeated him in his bid for the Senate in 1916. Harding would not believe that there was a plot against himself personally. For if everyone, including Daugherty, were trying to "flim-flam" him, there would not be enough sincerity left in politics to make the game worthwhile. Harding had always forgiven his enemies, including Roosevelt. The thing was to look forward in politics, not backward. Perhaps, Harding said, he lacked "a real attribute of character" in submitting as he did, but he would find his enemies too numerous to punish if he tried to punish them. Forgiveness and harmony were the best *practical* policies.

It was at this point that Harding declared the superiority of his strategy of harmony and humility to Daugherty's policy of intrigue and vendetta. "The trouble with you, my dear Daugherty," Harding wrote loftily, "in your political relations with me, is that you appraise my political sense so far below par that you have no confidence in me or my judgement. Pray do not think because I can and do listen in politeness to much that is said to me, that I am always being 'strung.' I cannot and will not suspect everyone of wanting to use me. I must and will believe in professed political friendship until I find myself imposed upon. It is the only way that I know of to political happiness." [21] And by political happiness, Harding meant his own political success in gaining high office, compared with Daugherty's total failure. In fact, Harding was ready to break off relationships with Daugherty at this time. He felt quite capable of managing his own battles—against Daugherty, if need be. He had gone a long way by himself, and he could go further. Daugherty, with his many enemies, was indeed a liability in Harding's strategy of harmony.

Thus, when Charles Hard suggested a pact with Daugherty, Harding turned him down flat. He wrote, "I will make no arrangement of any kind in the future with Daugherty. I felt myself under very great obligations to him and have very highly valued his political friendship. He is a brilliant and resourceful man but his political hatreds have come to a point where they bias his judgement and I do not think him always a trustworthy adviser. More than that, he was not frank and open with me in discussing the situation, though I was perfectly sincere and open with him. . . . All this has destroyed my confidence and I would not consider a deal under any circumstances." [22]

Daugherty had even gone so far as to intimate "in a veiled way" that Harding was inviting an opposition candidate in 1920 for his place in the Senate unless he went along with Daugherty. Harding declared that he refused to give way under such a threat. Apart from Daugherty's determination to control the party organization, there was no conflict in Ohio. Harding refused to believe that Willis was in league with Daugherty, even though Hard had told him so. Harding, by his own strategy, wished to take Willis at face value, and Willis had assured him of support.[23] The beauty of Harding's strategy was that by refusing to treat double-dealers as enemies, he could pretend that friendship had always existed once he had scotched their plots.

Daugherty, seeing Harding's determination to fight and perhaps suspecting Harding's plan to break with him and outmaneuver him, tried to mend their relationship. He wrote on December 30, 1918, that Harding indeed had as much good political judgment as he did; but that, like himself, Harding could be mistaken and misled. He still claimed honesty and no connection with Willis against Harding. In fact, he said he was against Willis as a political candidate, because of Willis' defeats, although it might be "impossible" for him to oppose Willis. He repeated that he was not bitter in politics: "I do not cry over spilled milk in politics or business ventures; I follow the plan of looking out for a fresh cow in some convenient pasture," a remark hardly flattering to Harding. Daugherty declared that he had finally decided to back Harding in regard to the State Advisory Committee and even in regard to Harding's Presidential ambitions. He would stand with Harding if Harding would let him. If Harding wanted to be Ohio's favorite son, Daugherty would help. If Harding wanted to deliver Ohio to Roosevelt in 1920, Daugherty would acquiesce even in this triumph of his enemies.[24]

By this remarkable change of tone, Daugherty confessed that Harding had beaten him. He ate humble pie for fear of being pushed out of political power altogether. In the letter, he even talked of making a public announcement that he would "never again engage in any active political work." He saw clearly that Harding, who had made his peace with Roosevelt personally, might put together such an alliance of standpat and progressive Republicans in Ohio as would squeeze Daugherty out of the scene. Daugherty had tried with Willis to capture Harding and use him against the Roosevelt faction. If he had succeeded, Harding's reward might well have been a knife in the back in order to run Willis for the Senate. Harding had, however, shown strength and finesse by refusing to be scared and by appealing successfully to all people. Daugherty found himself stranded and alone. The trouble with the professional intriguer is that not even his friends can trust him.

Within the first week of January, 1919, Theodore Roosevelt unexpectedly died. This event changed the whole political situation. As Harding immediately wrote to Hard, ". . . the death of Col. Roosevelt will somewhat change the plans of some Republicans of Ohio, especially in their attitude toward state organization. I may be very over-confident about the situation, but I think we are going to be able to organize without any serious friction." [25] With the Roosevelt forces suddenly leaderless until a successor could be found, Harding stepped into the vacuum—and got what he wanted. Overnight, he became Ohio's favorite son and a definite possibility for the White House. "This makes a big change all over the country," Daugherty exulted to Harding. "I have some ideas about this thing now which I will talk over with you." [26]

Harding, of course, attended Roosevelt's funeral and later gave a moving oration to the Ohio legislature in late January. He used the Colonel's memory to boost his own policy. He recalled his own championship of Roosevelt, with his remark in the Senate, "If Theodore Roosevelt had been President . . . the *Lusitania* would not have been sunk!" He claimed that Roosevelt had said to him in private conference after the election of 1916, "Harding, we have all got to get together and restore the Republican Party to power in order to save this great country of ours." Roosevelt's most exalting quality was what Harding himself advocated, "Americanism . . . his appealing, vigorous, fearless, American manhood." Yes, Roosevelt had left the Republicans in 1912; but, Harding claimed, he had followed the Progressives only *after* they had left the Republicans. In fact, Roosevelt would rather have stayed faithful to the Republicans. "He was really," Harding the harmonizer correctly declared, "less the radical than he ofttimes appeared." [27]

So Harding, true to his policy of obscuring the differences between men, claimed the following of the deceased Roosevelt in the name of party harmony in Ohio. But they did not listen to his words. To Walter Brown and Roosevelt's other backers, Harding still stood pat on the far right. The political victory that Harding had won in Ohio on Roosevelt's death was to turn into something perilously close to defeat when Roosevelt's heir, General Leonard

Wood, came to claim his inheritance. It was then that Harding clung to all the support that he could find and became finally bound by gratitude to Harry Daugherty, the man whom he had declared that he could not trust.

Immediately after his defeat by Harding and after Roosevelt's death, Daugherty appointed himself manager for Harding's Presidential campaign. As in his campaign for the Governorship of Ohio ten years before, Harding never discouraged an early booster, although he would never admit to having encouraged one. He liked his supporters to go out and intrigue for him, while he disclaimed personal ambition and pretended to be reluctant for high office. Although Harding no longer trusted Daugherty, he found him increasingly useful. And Daugherty made it his business to be useful to the most powerful man in Ohio politics, a potential President. He tested the wind, used Harding's name to raise money, and built up again a relationship with his old friend.

As early as January 30, 1919, Daugherty was exploring the possibility of Harding's gaining delegates for 1920 in Nebraska, with or without Harding's approval. From Ohio, Harding continued to get news from Charles Hard about the situation there. On February 24, Hard warned Harding that two or three men of importance in Ohio politics were trying to swing the state to Taft in 1920, but that a Taft boom was not serious and would not affect Harding's chance to be favorite son. Hard even hinted that Daugherty might be involved in the matter, although he said that he thought not.[28] As Harding trusted Hard, he may still have been wary of Daugherty at this time.

Daugherty, however, blithely continued on his self-appointed mission as Harding's manager and adviser. He took it upon himself to report public opinion in Ohio to Harding, so that Harding could suit his speeches to his audiences. On April 2, he advised Harding that "the popular position" was to accept the peace treaty and get the boys home and be relieved from European obligations and enter a League of Nations that backed the Monroe doctrine.[29] Harding carefully ducked Daugherty's reading of the situation, saying that the public was not yet ready to hear a flat declaration against the League of Nations and that he would be silent until he knew the party line of the Senate Committee on Foreign Relations. He was hoping, however, to get into opposition to Wilson's dreaming.[30]

By July, however, Harding went a little further because he saw public sentiment changing. Charles Hard had warned him that the bankers and the church congregations were all for the League of Nations and that support for it was great since money was "the root of all evil and a tremendous amount of politics." [31] Harding, however, was testing the wind a little more correctly. His judgment to Daugherty was that the strong Reservationists would win, so that there would be no "excessive danger" in going into the League of Nations. "I am not sure," he continued, "that the growing sentiment of opposition will enable us to do even more than that. Personally, I should prefer to go further." [32]

Thus Harding ran deliberately and exactly in the middle ranks of public opinion, revealing his own mind only when he felt that his proposals would win majority support. Such a cautious approach to the public was certainly the strategy of a man who was running for election in 1920, either to the Senate or to the White House. Harding would make no definite commitment to any policy unless it was a moderate one that could be interpreted as sanely progressive or reasonably conservative. As he wrote to Daugherty about the passage of the Volstead Act, he supported the Anti-Saloon League leaders, who were deliberately seeking a moderate measure. "I think you know me well enough," he declared, "to believe I incline to a middle of the road course." [33]

Daugherty continued in his course of wooing the wife and friends of the reluctant candidate. To Florence Kling Harding, he wrote that he never complained because she saw things in a different light. He always insisted on telling her "just what I think about anything in the most inoffensive, conscientious, God-fearing and man-loving way I know of." [34] And he encouraged Harding along his path of more open resistance to the League. "If our red blood has run out, no league of nations will save us." [35] Wilson's speech on the League had been badly received at Columbus. "It seems to me Wilson is getting deeper and deeper into hot water and that you are going along now all right." [36] The "loyal and sensible people" were turning against the League.[37] Leaning more heavily now on Daugherty's advice, Harding declared himself more strongly against the League in the Senate.

It was to Daugherty that Harding wrote on October 4, telling of Woodrow Wilson's collapse: "He has an extreme case of nervous breakdown with hysterical symptoms and unmistakable flights of mental disturbance. . . . I understand that he has cursed the Republicans in the Senate in language that would do credit to you in one of your most irritated moments." [38] This collapse of Wilson had further cleared the field for Harding's ambition. For, until his collapse, Wilson might have demanded and received the Presidential nomination for the third time in order to carry on the fight over the League. And a two-time winner would be a formidable opponent in 1920 for any Republican Presidential nominee.

The situation in Ohio, however, increasingly demanded that Harding declare his intentions. Under the existing election laws of the state, it was doubtful that a man could run both for the Senate and for the Presidential nomination at the same time. Thus Charles Hard advised Harding to have the electoral law modified on his behalf, so that he could run for both.[39] Harding's reply, on August 26, was a model of that professed humility and real ambition with which he pursued the Presidency. "I do think we ought to have some modification," he declared, "without any selfish interest in the matter whatever. I always like to be frank and dependably truthful to you and I know you will believe me when I say I am not greatly concerned about the embarrassment involved in the conflict between a candidacy for the presidency and for a renomination for the Senate. I do not expect at any time to enter the presidential contest and really have no ambitions in that direction. If I knew of a perfectly consistent way to do so, I would say as much in a public way, but I am extremely reluctant to put myself in the ridiculous attitude of taking myself too seriously." [40]

Thus Harding tried to keep the door open, while protesting his total lack of ambition. Daugherty, with the true gambler's instinct of winner takes all, wanted Harding to declare himself frankly interested in the White House. If he ran for both, he might lose both. If he still wanted the Senate seat, no one would take his Presidential race seriously. Yet if he gave up ambition for the Presidency, he might effectively give up his power in Ohio politics. The only way to control the Ohio delegation at the national convention was to be its favorite son for the White House. Of course, Daugherty's advice may not have been disinterested; he may still have wanted Harding's seat in the Senate for another.

Yet it was not Daugherty who accused himself of being Harding's false friend; he merely accused everybody else in Ohio of that role. "They would trade you off for a yellow dog at any time," he warned Harding, "if they could go patronage rabbit hunting with the dog." The old friends of Roosevelt wanted to deliver the state to his heir, General Leonard Wood. But Daugherty claimed that he had never been "a gum-shoe, slippery-elm man in politics" and that he would never be one.[41] Harding did not seem to think that Daugherty protested too much. According to his usual role, he took this new avowal at its face value. "You are certainly a very devoted friend for anyone to have," he replied. "I should like you to know of my very genuine appreciation." [42] To Harding, anyone who claimed to be working wholly in his cause was working in a good cause.

Yet Harding's strategy won. He wanted to run for both the Senate and the White House at the same time. So Daugherty gave the fighting statement to the newspapers that Harding did not propose at that time "to be run out, smoked out or knocked out for either." [43] But he immediately went behind Harding's back to Harding's secretary in order to commit Harding still more deeply in the Presidential race. "Now I think we should without Harding knowing about it," he wrote to Christian on November 2, "canvass and keep in touch with the big field. He need say no more that he would not be a candidate for the Presidency. He will of course not say that he is. He don't have now to do much talking or know much. Presidents don't run in this country like Assessors you know." [44]

In these statements, Daugherty was falling into his usual error of underestimating Harding, who had carefully kept the way open for his chance at the White House during the past years. Daugherty always liked to think that he was running Harding's campaign and strategy. He did not see Harding's extensive correspondence with others, and he forgot Harding's insistence on his own plan of action. Harding left Daugherty increasingly with his illusion; because if the latter thought he was doing all the work, he would work all the harder. Daugherty, moreover, was becoming financially committed to boosting Harding and was paying his expenses out of his own pocket. Harding had been in debt in 1917 and was still short of money; he needed someone who would raise campaign expenses, as Daugherty could.

In addition, Harding knew that he had enough enemies to make any declared friend useful. "I have no misconception," he wrote to Charles Hard, "about the unalterable devotion of any of the active group in the Cincinnati machine." The old city of Foraker, whom Harding had betrayed, now seemed ready to betray Harding for Leonard Wood and the old friends of Roosevelt. The leaders there, Harding knew, would not give him "a political bank account on which to draw with confidence." They were likely "to make united and effective action impossible in Ohio." [45] Thus Harding needed all the support that he could get, even the support of the once-treacherous Daugherty.

The heat was soon turned on Harding by the supporters of Wood. They demanded to know Harding's intentions. Did he want to run for the White House or for the Senate? Harding stuck to his time-honored policy of being uncommitted. Of course, he disavowed any personal ambition by refusing to make up his mind. His reason for not saying yea or nay was because the end of October was a time when no one could foresee "what program gives the greater promise of party success." Harding did, however, indicate that he preferred to run for the Senate again, although he was honored by those who wanted to back him for the White House.[46] Indeed, his professed reluctance to run for the White House fooled his enemies so much that they based their strategy for Wood on the assumption that Harding would not run.[47]

Thus, at the beginning of November, the strategy in Ohio politics was clear, at least to the individuals involved. Harding wanted to run for both the Senate and the White House. Because he thought his chances for the White House slim, he wanted to warn off any rivals for the Senate seat. The Wood supporters wanted a deal by which Harding definitely gave up Ohio to Wood in the Presidential race in return for their support in his Senate race. Daugherty, however, wanted to commit Harding to the struggle for the White House. If Harding won, Daugherty might reach the Cabinet. If Harding lost, his Senate seat would be vacant, and no one knew who would inherit it—Willis or perhaps Daugherty himself.

Certainly both Daugherty and Willis fought for Harding as a Presidential nominee in the hope of possibly succeeding to his vacant Senate seat. "I have always felt I could depend on Daugherty," Harding now declared to Charles Hard, "though he did give me no little annoyance during the trying period we passed through last winter." [48] The way was to be kept open by the state organization for Harding to run for both offices. By a new law, he would not have to file for renomination in the Senate until the very date of the Presidential balloting at the coming Republican convention in Chicago in 1920. Even though nearly every politician in Ohio wanted Harding to clarify his ambitions, his strategy of evasion won in November, since he had the support of the regular party machine. Those who wished to be his friends in order to be his heirs had to back Harding in his politic vacillation.

The Wood forces, however, were to force Harding into the open, as Daugherty and Willis had tried to do for some time. Although Harding declared privately to Jennings that Wood might prove to be the best Republican "political asset" in 1920, he said that he would not allow Walter Brown and the Cincinnati group to deliver Ohio to Wood. If Wood wanted Ohio's support, he must deal with Harding and those old regulars who still controlled the organization. "It is unthinkable," Harding declared, "that Walter Brown and his crew should be allowed to seize the helm and undertake to pilot the Republican party in our State." Repeating to Jennings his famed personal willingness to withdraw even from the Senate for the good of the party, Harding declared that the good of the party demanded that he keep the Wood supporters out of the state organization and thus become Ohio's favorite son. "I really do not care a rap about higher political honors and do not mean to aspire to them," Harding wrote. And then he added characteristically, "At the same time, I have the personal satisfaction of knowing that I have about as much common sense and capacity as most of the men who are heralded as saviors of the republic." [49]

It was this fear of a take-over by the Wood forces and this sense of his own worth that made Harding declare himself. The state organization had to back someone for the Presidency who would represent Ohio's privileged position at the convention. Otherwise, by default, the state would go to Wood, who was openly seeking the nomination. Wood's first manager had tried to get the Old Guard of the Senate to back Wood, so that his nomination could be arranged without "fuss, feathers, or publicity." [50] But Wood was taking other advice and was threatening to campaign in the open. He was obviously the front-runner for the Republican nomination. And Harding knew that a reluctant candidate could no longer remain reluctant when a front-runner threatened to take his home base away from him.

Thus Harding finally declared that he was definitely running for the White House, on December 17, 1919, although the Wood forces had known this from the beginning of the month because of Harding's moves within the party organization.[51] Daugherty and Daugherty's shadow and familiar, Jess Smith, had also been jumping the gun with this statement for a fortnight, trying to push Harding off into deep water. According to Daugherty, both Harding and his wife hesitated about making the final plunge. Meanwhile, Jess Smith was declaring to the Ohio press that Harding was William McKinley risen again and that Daugherty was his Hanna. But it was Harding's own ambition that finally made him speak up in his own favor, after he had carefully arranged for the official Republican organization in Ohio to endorse him as a favorite son.

He claimed that his reluctance to announce his candidacy was genuinely sincere, but now that the Republicans of Ohio had honored him, he could not ignore "the natural and laudable wish to maintain the large part Ohio has taken in the national councils

of the party, and to invite the attention of Republicans in the
nation to the availability of a candidate from our great State." Of
course, Harding said, had there been a worthier candidate from
Ohio, he would have supported that man. But as "fortune" had
offered him the job of keeping Ohio as the mother of Presidents,
he must accept "the manifest wish of the Republicans of the State."
And as a thing worth doing was worth doing with all one's might,
the reluctant candidate would run hard. But he would run in good
faith and amity toward the rest of the candidates, for he put party
above himself.[52]

So the reluctant candidate became the available dark horse.
Harding was in the position that he had always wanted to be. He
was still in the race for the Senate, but he was also the favorite son
of Ohio, at a time when Ohio was the Presidential state. He still
maintained to those who felt that he had lied previously about his
wish not to run for the White House that only the fear of Wood's
supporters in Cincinnati taking over the state machine had made
him run at all.[53] But this was untrue.

Harding, like any Ohio politician, had been running for the
White House in his dreams ever since he had entered politics.
And once he had entered the Senate, his chance of nomination by
the Republicans in a deadlock had always been good—*if he could
keep the Ohio delegation behind him*. He had taken great care to
appeal to all factions in Ohio, and now he seemed to be receiving
his reward. He even asked for the support of Walter Brown, since
he was now the representative of "an Ohio ambition" in the
national Republican convention.[54] And he at last became committed to Daugherty as his official manager because of Daugherty's
success in rounding up support in the state organization for him.

With Daugherty to do the dirty work, Harding could maintain
the role of a modest and kindly man, the friend of all. It suited the
image each man had of himself and of the other: the dark horse
should play the friendly figurehead, while his manager should play
the incredible schemer. "I am very comfortable in regard to your
speeches," Daugherty informed Harding at the end of the year.
"If I was not I would be crazy." And here he reverted to his old
air of political superiority. "I am far more comfortable as to your

ability to cope with great public questions and public appearances, positions and utterances, than I am for you to deal with those who are engaged in intrigue. I will take care of the latter and together we will make a fair combination in this great enterprise." [55]

8

The Dark Horse

"All of the great patriots now engaged in edging and
squirming their way toward the Presidency of the Republic run true to form. This is to say, they are all extremely wary, and all more or less palpable frauds. What
they want, primarily, is the job."   H. L. MENCKEN

"A 'dark horse' is a person not very widely known in the
country at large, but known rather for good than for
evil. He has probably sat in Congress, been useful on committees, and gained some credit among those who dealt
with him in Washington. Or he has proved himself a
safe and assiduous party man in the political campaigns
of his own and neighboring states, yet without reaching
national prominence. Sometimes he is a really able man,
but without the special talents that win popularity. Still,
speaking generally, the note of the 'dark horse' is respectability verging on colorlessness; and he is therefore
a good sort of person to fall back upon when able but
dangerous favorites have proved impossible. That native
mediocrity rather than adverse fortune has prevented
him from winning fame is proved by the fact that the
'dark horses' who have reached the White House, if
they have seldom turned out bad Presidents, have even
more seldom turned out distinguished ones." LORD BRYCE

A dark horse in the Presidential race thinks that his chances of
nomination are small. The political commentators and the party
bosses also think so. Except for the month before the national

convention at Chicago, neither Harding nor Daugherty nor any informed observer considered that Harding was a dark horse. He was always ahead of the other dark horses, running a little behind the front-runners. As the suspected favorite of the Old Guard of the Senate, Harding was strong, but he lost that favor by his poor showing in the two popular primaries that he entered. The long tradition of boss control in the Republican Party worked in Harding's favor *even when that control no longer existed in fact.* Few thought that Harding was a dark horse before the Republican National Convention of 1920. Only the voting there would prove that he actually was.

When Harding announced his candidacy, the Cleveland *Plain Dealer* summed up the local attitude to his declared ambition:

Sincere friends of Mr. Harding—and he has thousands of them in Ohio—look upon him as a bona fide contender for the nomination. Old Guard leaders look upon him as an instrument to defeat Wood. If a chance of politics makes him the nominee, if indeed it makes him president, the Old Guard will be well satisfied. It knows what kind of chief executive he would make. It knows the forces that would control a Harding administration—knows and is content. . . .

The Harding record has been that of a party regular. No partisan leader ever had to crack the whip to get this Ohioan in line; he gets in line before the rush begins and stays till after the benediction. Regularity is the cornerstone of his party faith. . . . The president has no more insistent critic than the junior Senator from Ohio. . . . The senator is everything a regular should be. *The heyday of his kind was thirty years ago.*[1]

Such was the record and image that Harding ran on. He was William McKinley come again, the favorite son of a state from which ten out of the last thirteen Republican Presidential nominees had come. Harding, standing for America First, would keep Ohio first in America. He had never deserted the Republican Party. As McKinley, his hero of thirty years ago, had seemed, Harding publicly appeared to be "a man democratic in habit, exceptionally free from selfish ambition, without a trace of personal arrogance or egotism." [2] Since the Presidential election of 1896, as Ohio went so went the nation. Because Governor Cox was likely to be on the Democratic ticket in either first or second place, Ohio's Republican favorite son should also be on the Republican ticket. No man could reach the White House without Ohio's vote. Harding had won in 1914 by more than 100,000 votes, although the Democrats had won six of the last seven elections for the Governorship. By personality and geography, Harding should be the Presidential choice of the Grand Old Party in the coming year, especially since he was considered the favorite son of the bosses in the Senate.

So ran Harding's publicity. But it did not convince. The claims of many of his rivals seemed stronger. The front-runner was General Leonard Wood, a rigid New Englander, kept from high command in France only because he was a stalwart Republican. As the old supporter and heir of Theodore Roosevelt, he had inherited much of the Rough Rider's powerful financial backing (he had himself commanded the Rough Riders in the Spanish-American War). Many of the big-money men wanted him in the White House because they feared a social revolution. He declared himself all for strong government and eradicating the Reds. He might easily have won the nomination in 1919 had he followed the advice of his first manager, John T. King, and made a deal with the Old Guard of the Senate. But the Old Guard found him intractable and hard to manage; indeed, a potential Roosevelt.

Wood, angered by King's secret dealings with such manipulators as Senator Boies Penrose of Pennsylvania, sacked King as his manager and replaced him with the aggressive multimillionaire William Cooper Procter of Cincinnati. Procter immediately raised more than a million dollars for the campaign, and he advised Wood to fight everywhere in the primaries for delegates. Wood should storm the nomination, making enemies all the way. The straw vote showed that he was by far the most popular candidate among the Republican rank and file. Using the old Roosevelt machine and large campaign funds, Wood should be a steamroller, as his dead leader had been eight years before. Procter claimed that he did not know much about politics, but he did know how to sell soap. A Harding backer wrote a mock advertisement for Procter:

USE
Ivory (Wood) Soap
It will float
And make pretty bubbles.
But who can use bubbles
In their business? [3]

Harding, at first, discounted Wood's threat. As an old machine politician, he could not see how Wood could challenge the party leaders in the Senate and win. He knew that their chosen nominee —if they could agree—would be the hardest to beat in the national convention of 1920. And he underrated Wood's popular appeal. He wrote to Jennings early in February that he had heard a prominent Senator bet a new hat that Wood's name would not even be presented to the convention. The Red Scare had diminished. "We made presidents out of military men for more than thirty years after the Civil War but there doesn't seem to be any sentiment for a military candidate at the present time. I think General Wood is very much of a fellow himself but I do think his military connection and his militaristic ideas are going to put an end to his candidacy." [4]

As for the next most popular candidate, Herbert Hoover, Harding thought that the boom for him was ephemeral. First, Hoover had not declared whether he was a Republican or a Democrat. Second, he would have few delegates and no support among the Old Guard. And, third, "in its deliberate moments the country does not want a dictatorial and autocratic personality like that we know our friend, Hoover, to possess. There is no doubt about his marked ability." [5]

The third popular candidate, Senator Hiram Johnson of California, was also unavailable. Although he was popular with the people and had the backing of his home state, he was an old Progressive and was credited with giving the election of 1916 to Wilson by sitting on his hands in California in anger at Hughes. He was too independent and radical to get the support of the Old Guard of the Senate.

Harding's chief rival early in the year appeared to be Governor

Frank O. Lowden of Illinois. Married to a Pullman heiress, he had made his name as an efficient business Governor. The Old Guard of the Senate liked him. He showed strength among the corrupt Republican state organizations in the South. He seemed to be the logical candidate to stop Wood, and he was willing to fight in the Presidential primaries against him, as was Hiram Johnson. Harding, indeed, found in Lowden so much of his own way of thinking that he said in Chicago that he would like Lowden to win the nomination if he could not.[6] Later, Harding's wooing of Lowden and his backers was to pay large dividends. For these regular organization men were responsive to the leadership of those who called themselves Republican bosses. By a gentleman's agreement, Lowden and Harding kept out of the primaries in each other's state. "I felt that I should resent any outside candidate coming into my own State," Harding wrote in order to restrain a supporter in Illinois, "and I had much rather treat Governor Lowden with the courtesy and consideration which is due than to attempt any activities and incur the resentment of him and his friends." [7]

In fact, Harding knew that his hope of the Presidency depended on the good opinions of the kingmakers among the Old Guard of the Senate. Three dark horses from Ohio had reached the White House because of the support of powerful Republican bosses. Since he had more support than a Garfield or a Hayes before the convention, Harding hoped to be the fourth. He expected that his five years of making many friends and influencing few in the Senate would now be rewarded.

The trouble was that the bosses in the Senate had lost much of their power and were not agreed. Senator Penrose of Pennsylvania was no Marcus Hanna, and he even lost the Pennsylvania delegation. It went to its favorite son, Governor Sproul, rather than to Penrose's own late choice, Philander Knox, the other Senator from Pennsylvania. Senator Lodge of Massachusetts could not even get the support of his home state for his Presidential ambitions. Few of the other leading Republican Senators had their state delegations in their pockets. Although the legend of a Senatorial cabal in control of the Republican Party survived, real power in the Senate was divided. Harding, however, still believed in the cabal, and he hoped to be its choice.

According to Senator James E. Watson of Indiana, Penrose offered to back him for the Republican nomination. Watson declared that he was opposed by labor and the drys. Penrose replied that this was unimportant: "After a man is nominated they bring out the royal robe and put it on him, and that covers up all the cracks and nail-holes." Unfortunately, Penrose fell sick soon afterward, and Watson did not feel popular enough in Indiana to win it in the primaries against Wood and Lowden and Johnson. So he refused to run, and he ostensibly backed Harding, even though Harding claimed that Watson had it "sewed up." At this time, Watson claimed, he persuaded Penrose to back Harding too, although it seems likely that Penrose was not ready yet to commit himself to one candidate.[8]

The myth that Harding was a dark horse was not believed by the Old Guard of the Senate or the political commentators. They talked openly of Harding or Lowden as the choice of the bosses in the Senate, unless Wood upset them by grabbing all the primaries and making a deal with Johnson. Harding, indeed, was preferred by the commentators to Lowden because of his faithful party service, Senatorial connections, small-town background, and position in strategic Ohio. Republican National Chairman Will Hays thought Harding the most likely choice.[9] Brand Whitlock had been told by Wilson's friend Colonel House of Harding's probable nomination as early as the winter of 1915–1916. Two other Senators had confirmed this to Whitlock in 1919. "The old guard in the Senate," Whitlock concluded *after* Harding's nomination, "had long ago, I fancy, decided on it." [10]

Yet even if the Old Guard had decided to choose Harding rather than Lowden in the early months of 1920—and that is open to question—Wood's determined campaign threatened to prove that the Old Guard no longer controlled the Republican party. Wood and Johnson entered most of the possible open primaries, with Lowden sometimes entering as well. By the close of the primaries, Wood had won 124 instructed delegates, Johnson 112, and Lowden only 72. It was clear that if the people's choice were considered by the Republican delegates to the national convention, either Wood or Johnson should be nominated. This impression was confirmed by the results of the large straw polls held by the *Literary Digest*, which showed Wood as the most popular Republican candidate, following by Johnson and Hoover. Wood had seven times the votes of Harding.[11]

Wood, indeed, by his tactic of frontal assault, nearly wrecked Harding's ambitions. He refused to make a gentleman's agreement with anyone, and, prodded by Procter, he entered the Ohio primary. And Harding, so confident of Wood's impending collapse and of the united support of his home state, found himself, as usual, threatened by the desertion of his old backers. As always, Ohio was the most alluring and most dangerous state for the Presidential hopeful.

Trouble began for Harding in Ohio from the date that he was forced to declare his candidacy. He had to choose among his supposed friends those who would serve as delegates from Ohio at the convention. "How difficult it is," he complained, "indeed, how utterly impossible it is—to start on a campaign of killing off one's friends." [12] In naming his slate of delegates, Harding made one bad mistake. He refused to include a symbolic Negro politician in the Buckeye delegation. Thus he offended the Negro vote.

Although the Wood forces in Ohio, led by Procter and Rud Hynicka of Cincinnati, had not yet persuaded Wood to enter the primaries, Harding came under fire because of his alliance with Daugherty. Ex-Governor Herrick had warned high Republican officials of the proposed Wood strategy: "A large part of the fight will be directed against Daugherty, to Harding's detriment." [13] Harding was also warned and was advised to drop Daugherty. This would leave him with no weak point for attack by the Wood forces.

At first, Harding seemed almost ready to disengage himself from Daugherty. He agreed with Herrick that Daugherty was one of the "embarrassments" that he hoped "to get past without difficulty." [14] Between Christmas, 1919, and the new year, however,

Harding decided that he would stick by Daugherty. Either Daugherty convinced Harding of his necessity as a fund-raiser and fixer or Harding decided that he could not afford to alienate Daugherty for fear of losing him to his enemies in Ohio. There is no evidence of why Harding decided for good and bad to hold on to his new manager. There is only evidence that he did decide to do so, much to his own embarrassment.

At any rate, with Daugherty's support, Harding felt ready by January 5 for "a reasonable show-down" in Ohio with the Wood supporters.[15] By January 9, Herrick had accepted that his pressure would not separate Harding and Daugherty, and he talked of being willing "to wipe the slate and forget the occurrences of the past" with Daugherty in order to help Harding.[16] Although many complaints of Daugherty's unpopularity continued to flow to Harding, he worked out a formula to answer them. Much of the grumbling against Daugherty, he wrote, was "genuinely directed." Not a little was discreet hostility to Harding himself. "Frankly, the matter has caused me a very great deal of embarrassment," Harding declared, "but I came to the conclusion in the very beginning, that I could not enter upon the big political game upon a platform which involved the sacrifice of any friend because somebody was opposed to him. It has always been my political plan to invite the support and cooperation of everybody and to submerge our differences in the attainment of a common cause." [17] Inclusion was always Harding's policy—inclusion behind himself of those who called themselves his friends.

In reality, however, Harding admitted to having only three close friends—Jennings, the absent Scobey in Texas, and his old Marion neighbor Colonel Christian, the father of his private secretary. Thus it was to Jennings, if to anyone, that Harding declared his true feelings about Daugherty. On February 4, he wrote to his trusted friend that he was not "a worshipper" of Daugherty. "He has never asked anything at my hands which it was not perfectly consistent and easy to grant. He may have designs concerning which I know not, but I am sure that you, and others who know me, know that I would not be unalterably tied up to any one individual, in case success should attend our efforts." [18] In this way,

Harding still persisted in saying that he was his own man, as indeed he was.

The large amount of correspondence preserved in the Harding papers for the early months of 1920 shows conclusively that Harding, helped by the younger Christian and Howard Mannington in the Harding for President Club, ran his own campaign for the Presidential nomination. After Harding's death, the self-important Daugherty claimed that it "was a one-man managed campaign, carefully planned" by Daugherty himself. "Harding did not know much about what I was doing," Daugherty wrote. "I never bothered him, just went ahead, and when I learned what the situation was I told him about it." [19] In fact, Daugherty did not know much about what Harding was doing, which was a great deal.

In nearly every state, Harding kept up a correspondence with an old newspaper or business or holiday friend. Colonel Charles R. Forbes, met on a trip to Hawaii, worked for him in the Northwest, influencing delegates toward Harding as a second choice. In the South, George Mendelsohn, an Ohio editor, gave him important information about the feeling of the delegates there, who favored him and Lowden and Johnson, with Wood nowhere. Harding replied personally to every offer of support from every state and was untiring in his work for his own cause. What he left to Daugherty was the raising of a small campaign fund of $113,000 and the use of that fund to influence as many delegates as possible.[20] With this shoestring budget, Daugherty spent wisely, although he could write out a check for as much as $1,250 to the head of the Missouri state organization in order to sound out the sentiments of the state.[21]

Harding's strategy was based on three assumptions. First, he hoped that most members of the Old Guard of the Senate would support him. Much of their influence was based on the "rotten boroughs" of the Southern state organizations, which could be relied on to support the "regular" candidate against the popular one. It was their support, for instance, that had upheld Taft against Roosevelt in 1912. Thus Harding sent Mannington to woo delegates in Alabama, Georgia, North Carolina, and Oklahoma, while he himself went on a speaking tour through Texas and Missouri.

Second, he hoped to be the second choice of as many delegations as possible. So he courted the Lowden delegates and the delegations of such favorite sons as Senator Poindexter of Washington. In pursuit of this goal, he spoke in Kansas and Colorado. Third, he wanted to prove his direct popular appeal and increase his delegate strength by entering the Indiana primary against Wood, Lowden, and Johnson. As Indiana was a neighboring state, he hoped to do well there.

Procter and the Wood forces, however, wrecked his plans. They had been angered by Harding's insistence on running Daugherty as a delegate to the national convention. So they decided to steal Harding's home state from under his nose. When Harding refused to agree to commit Ohio's delegates to Wood as their second choice, they entered Wood in the Presidential primaries. And, of course, Harding was prepared to fight. For all his pretended kindness, he declared to Jennings that he did not intend to be "kicked around by a lot of smooth hypocrites." Just because he was inclined to be courteous and considerate and to hide from "every political crook" what was in his heart, people were misled into thinking he did not relish a scrap. But that was all nonsense. "Really, when it comes down to brass tacks," Harding confided, "I would just as soon have a row as anybody would." [22]

Privately, before the Wood campaign got under way in Ohio, Harding was full of confidence. "I am bound to say," he wrote to Jennings, "that the whole situation looks infinitely more promising than I have any reason to expect. I am beginning to feel now as though I am afraid I will be nominated." [23] In mid-March, he counted on most of the Texas delegation, organized by his friend Scobey and by Colonel Creager, and on support from Colorado and Missouri.[24] But suddenly, his situation in Ohio worsened rapidly. Charles Hard warned him that the Negro vote and the veterans' vote had gone to Wood and that the railroad workers were against him because he had supported the antistrike clause in the Cummins-Esch railroad bill. Even some of the business people in Ohio, whom Harding had always wooed personally and through Jennings, had gone to General Wood, "because they want a bayonet user in the White House when that dreadful American revolution comes off." [25] Although Harding expressed contempt for the "purchasable support" behind Wood, he began to run scared. "We have a pretty stiff fight on in Ohio," he complained to Forbes on April 1, "and it gives me a great deal of annoyance that I am obliged to give the slightest attention to my home State." [26]

Harding was forced to stump Ohio actively in order to stop it from going "to the bow-wows." [27] The Wood forces were strong enough in the Republican Advisory Committee to stop it from endorsing Harding as its choice. Harding stressed his own claims, both as a backer of a "business administration" and as someone who could "coordinate the differences between the White House and Congress." [28] Even the Anti-Saloon League seemed on the point of coming out against Harding, but it was stopped at the last moment by his devoted dry supporter Mary Lee.[29] When the primary results came in, Harding held his home state against Wood by only some 15,000 votes and won only thirty-nine delegates of the forty-eight. Daugherty himself was beaten in his attempt to become a delegate. Union labor had been urged by Gompers, its leader, that "Harding is Your Enemy," while the Cincinnati machine had worked openly for Wood. Harding's chances seemed shattered in his home state by this "conspiracy between the military candidate and his financial supporters and the devil." [30]

Another blow shook Harding almost at once. On May 5, he ran behind Wood and Johnson and Lowden in the Indiana primary, receiving a derisory vote. It seemed that he had no popular appeal outside his home state, not even in bordering states. At this point, he was ready to withdraw from the Presidential race; but Mrs. Harding, who had opposed his running in the first place, now opposed his quitting. "Give up?" she is reported to have said. "Not until the convention is over. Think of your friends in Ohio." [31] Gambling on the certain opposition of the Wood forces even in his campaign to regain the Senate, Harding decided to go on. He believed that he still had the backing of the bosses in the Senate.

His bad showing, however, had lost him the support of the powerful Senators, who now switched to their alternative candidate, Lowden, in order to stop Wood, who was gaining support every day. The Southern delegates began to declare their support for the Governor of Illinois, and Nicholas Murray Butler, the favorite son of New York, made a pact to release his delegates slowly to Lowden when they were needed. Harding obviously did not yet know of this change of plans. He had been made by machine politics, and he had not yet been dropped by a machine at the last moment. He did not know that he was truly a dark horse for the first time.

Still confident of support from the bosses in the Senate, with their influence over the uncommitted delegations, Harding wrote to a supporter on May 12, "There never will be so many uninstructed delegates gathered together in one convention and you will be interested to know that more than one hundred of them are disposed to be favorable to me on the first ballot and I think it likely that we can show a continued growth from that time on." [32] At Chicago, Harding was bound for quick disillusionment.

Harding was not, however, prepared to burn his bridge back to the Senate. When a friend wrote to him about arranging the state convention to support him for renomination to the Senate, he would not say yea or nay.[33] He temporized. In fact, during the balloting at Chicago, he did file for renomination to the Senate at the last possible moment, because his chances of winning the Presidential spot appeared remote. News of this filing did not reach many in the convention, however, because Harding was successful in Chicago on the following day. The report of his faintheartedness was immediately suppressed in Ohio and was recollected only in later years by Daugherty.[34]

Certain intimations of his hopeless situation began to reach Harding in the last weeks before the national convention opened on June 8. He saw the support of the Old Guard waning. "Penrose is getting to be quite serious about the Knox matter," he wrote, referring to Penrose's new choice of a candidate from the Senate.[35] He turned down a contemptuous offer by the Wood forces to unite the Ohio delegation behind him briefly if he would then throw his delegates to Wood and be content with the Senate. And he watched the popular opinion polls give him even less support than Charles Evans Hughes, who was not running for the White House. In the Wall Street betting, he dropped even below Hoover, finding few backers at ten to one. Only one advantage had accrued to him from the battering that he had received in Ohio and Indiana. "Nothing could arise to persuade me," he now declared, "to desert Mr. Daugherty, who had been so devoted throughout the fight." [36]

Once again, however, Harding's chances were to be salvaged by the actions of others. When the leaders stumble, the dark horse may forge ahead. Hiram Johnson, annoyed by Wood's huge campaign expenditures in the primaries, persuaded a Senate subcommittee to inquire into these outlays of money. This strategy very much suited both the progressive Johnson and the Old Guard, each of whom was determined to stop Wood. It was easily discovered that Wood had officially spent $1,773,000, of which Procter had contributed $700,000. Thus the charge that Wood was trying to buy the nomination seemed to be proved, as unofficially he was credited with spending $4,000,000 more. No one in the history of American politics had ever spent so much *before* a national convention.

The Senate investigation, however, also boomeranged on the second most powerful candidate, Lowden. This may well have been Johnson's intention. For among the five Senators who sat on the subcommittee, not one was a supporter of Lowden, while friends of both Johnson and Harding were represented. Although Lowden's campaign expenditures were only $415,000, less than one-quarter of Wood's, the strange switch of the Missouri delegates from Wood to Lowden was investigated. A direct payment of $2,500 each to two of the Missouri delegates by Lowden's state manager was proved.[37]

Thus, on the eve of the national convention, the two front-runners were tarred by accusations of buying their way to the nomination. Hope revived in Daugherty and Harding, although neither was sanguine about the outcome. Reporters found that nobody was talking Harding and that he was not even considered to be among the more promising of the dark horses.[38]

After Harding's success, only Daugherty's wild and famous early prophecy about the smoke-filled room was remembered. He was, however, more candid upon his arrival in Chicago. It was then that he spoke with truth to reporters about his faint hopes: "I won't try to fool you. You can see what we've got here, it's only a shoestring. I'll tell you in confidence what's in my mind. All I'm doing is getting in touch with the leaders and delegates who are for Wood and Lowden, being friendly with them. When the convention comes, those two armies will battle each other to a standstill. When both realize that they can't win, when they're tired and hot and sweaty and discouraged both the armies will remember me and this little headquarters. They'll be like soldiers after a battle, who recall a shady spring along a country road where they got a drink as they marched to the front. When they remember me that way maybe both sides will turn to Harding—I don't know—it's just a chance." [39]

9

The Smoke-filled Room

"About eleven minutes after two on Friday morning at the convention, when fifteen or twenty men, somewhat weary, are sitting around a table, some one of them will say, 'Who will we nominate?' At that decisive time, the friends of Harding can suggest him and can afford to abide by the result."

HARRY M. DAUGHERTY, on February 21, 1920

"With Wood, Johnson and Lowden out of the way, I knew I could count on friends in every one of their delegations, because I had followed in my pre-convention campaigning the rule that has guided me throughout my political career, which is not to hurt any one's feelings or to step on anybody's toes if I could find foot room elsewhere. I figured that if politeness and an honest desire not to humiliate any rival just for the sake of winning a few votes were ever going to produce anything, this was the time. Other fellows, just as competent as I, or more so, had made enemies, and it looked to me that there was no one in sight that the convention could unite on except myself."

WARREN HARDING, on the reasons for his nomination

Four months before the convention, when Harry Daugherty made his famous prophecy—later to be called the theory of the Smoke-filled Room—he was merely elaborating on Harding's own strategy for winning the nomination. Harding then believed that he had gathered the support of most of the powerful Republican

Senators, as his confident letter to Jennings in the same month proved. He believed that a majority of the group including Senators Lodge of Massachusetts, Brandegee of Connecticut, Watson and New of Indiana, Smoot of Utah, Curtis of Kansas, and Wadsworth and Calder of New York would back him. In the case of a deadlock between Wood and the field, he placed his trust in these Senators to influence many delegations to support him. As a machine politician, Harding had faith in the ability of the machine to deliver the vote. While Daugherty was hurrying about, rather unsuccessfully, collecting only some twenty-five firm delegates in scattered states, Harding was trusting in the bosses. And by the boss theory of Republican politics, in which Harding had always believed, Daugherty predicted the outcome of the convention.

When he arrived at Chicago, however, Harding discovered that the bosses did not control the convention. Most of the uninstructed delegates—the largest amount ever seen at a Republican convention —were really uninstructed or were in favor of Wood or Lowden. Thus the bosses were disagreed among themselves, and if they were at all agreed, they backed Lowden. Seven lean years out of office had meant disorganization at the local level because of lack of patronage. Moreover, Harding's stalwart work in the national conventions of 1912 and 1916 was worth little. Of the 1,031 delegates and alternates, only one in five had been delegates four years before, and only one in ten had been delegates eight years before. Most of these old hands came, anyway, from the South and were supporters of Lowden.

As one old supporter of Roosevelt recorded, the convention was "a headless affair. A Mark Hanna was needed to guide the chaotic mass of delegates." But there was no Hanna, only "the awful heat, the steaming crowds, and the strike of hotel waiters," which made life "almost unendurable. There was very little sleep for anyone." [1] To another observer, the convention was "as perspirative as any ever held on the prairie in good corn weather"; Harding's eventual nomination only came about because the delegates wanted to escape the heat and leap on the last train home on Saturday night.[2] Yet another observer thought the convention a leaderless and "rather spiritless affair." [3]

With this breakdown of boss control, the convention was wide open to those who could exploit the situation. Both Wood and Lowden could, through their previous organization and personal appeal. Hiram Johnson was eliminated, for the temper among the delegates was standpat rather than progressive. Meanwhile, the bosses of the Senate, although they lacked real power, could operate on the myth that they had power if the convention deadlocked. For with delegates longing to go home and not knowing how to end a stalemate, self-styled leaders can become genuine leaders. In a moment of chaos, it is the myth and the manner that count, as Genet showed in *The Balcony*.

It was also a situation in which the active intriguer, Harry Daugherty, could come into his own. He had spent a lifetime in the lobbies of Columbus putting together combinations to secure the passage of bills. He had also survived as a minor power in the toughest political school of all, that of Ohio. So he scurried about at Chicago, pleading, cajoling, begging, and selling delegates on the oldest Republican myth of all: when in doubt, turn to Ohio. Harding himself, for one of the few times in his life, gave way to despair. He thought correctly that he had lost the support of the bosses, who had lost the support of the delegates. William Allen White saw him disheveled, with a two-day beard, a little drunk, his eyes bloodshot, the picture of discouragement, nothing like the "oiled and curled Assyrian bull" who had abused Roosevelt four years earlier.[4]

Daugherty, however, had sunk all his money and his political prestige in Harding. And he would not go down without a fight. He begged everyone shamelessly for support for Harding, if not as second choice, third choice or fourth choice would do; just so long as there was a place for Harding at the back of every delegate's mind. The Columbus Glee Club, which serenaded each delegation in its rooms, added to the strategy of the pleasant approach and the "shady spring" before the battle.

Luck held with Harding, as it had held with him for most of his political career. Machiavelli pointed out that half of a man's success depends on his own cleverness; the other half depends on fortune; but his life must end whenever necessity strikes. Harding was both clever and fortunate. Necessity did not strike him down until he reached the White House.

Harding's first luck was the choice of Lodge as the keynoter of the convention and as its permanent chairman. This choice made the Old Guard of the Senate *seem* firmly in control. Lodge devoted his speech to a "hymn of hate" against the League and Wilson. These were Harding's own recent themes. Lodge also spoke as a Harding when he declared, "Let us stand fast by the principles and policies of Washington and Monroe and against— utterly against—those of Mr. Wilson. We must be now and ever for Americanism and Nationalism, and against Internationalism. There is no safety for us, no hope that we can be of service to the world, if we do otherwise." [5] His speech was a far cry from the younger Harding's keynote plea for internationalism four years before, a plea that the Ohio dark horse had forgotten in his new cry for America First.

Harding's second stroke of luck was that the Old Guard of the Senate controlled the writing of the Republican platform. This platform was frankly conservative, against the League and for big business. The Republican candidate would have to run on this platform even if he would not have to stand on it. Hiram Johnson's chances waned as the progressives in the party saw how firmly the standpatters were in control of policy. To Woodrow Wilson, the Republican platform was "the apotheosis of reaction." [6]

Fortune also smiled on Harding in his choice of the man to present his name before the convention on Friday, June 11. In order to unite Ohio behind him, Harding had given the job to his old opponent Frank Willis. And Willis was to be rewarded by the position for which he had long intrigued—Harding's seat in the Senate. Willis' speech nominating Harding at the convention held, in Mark Sullivan's words, "the combined enjoyments of oratory, grand opera, and hog-calling." [7] In a folksy, good-humored way, Willis reminded the convention that Harding was just as they were, a small-town businessman, who liked being friendly; a second McKinley, who would not give them "brilliant maneuvers but safe and sane seamanship" by cooperating with Congress. He even leaned over the rostrum to plead with the delegates as if they were nominating Marion's Man of the Year. "Say, boys—and girls, too— why not name as the candidate the man whose record is the platform of the party?" [8] Such was the image of Harding presented to a convention that a later observer noticed was represented somewhat accurately by Harding himself.[9]

Harding's greatest fortune was the fact that a deadlock between Wood and Lowden really did develop. No one had known the exact strength of the two leading candidates before Chicago, because so many of the delegates were uninstructed. On the first ballot, Wood's strength surprised everyone. He secured $287\frac{1}{2}$ votes, with Lowden getting only $211\frac{1}{2}$, Johnson $133\frac{1}{2}$, and Harding $65\frac{1}{2}$. Wood had secured at least 50 votes more than was expected. The Lowden forces immediately called on the help of the anti-Wood group. Even Daugherty lent Lowden a few votes, while the Senate bosses also helped. Nicholas Murray Butler, the favorite son of New York, was particularly concerned about stopping Wood. On the second ballot, Wood gained 2 votes, Lowden 48, and Johnson $12\frac{1}{2}$. On the third ballot, Wood leaped ahead to 303 votes, three-fifths of the votes necessary for nomination; Lowden stood at $282\frac{1}{2}$; and Johnson had 148. Harding polled only $58\frac{1}{2}$ votes and seemed doomed.

On the fourth ballot, Wood crept ahead again. He reached $314\frac{1}{2}$ votes, while Lowden reached 289. Johnson lost votes and was essentially out of the race; his standpat delegates, won in the primaries, were betraying him. Harding inched forward again to $61\frac{1}{2}$, well behind the leaders, but with a little support. At this moment, with Wood steadily rolling forward and Lowden in hot pursuit, luck and Lodge again intervened on Harding's side. It was Friday night, and Chairman Lodge wanted to get together with the bosses of the Senate to discuss a compromise candidate. If the struggle between Wood and Lowden continued throughout the night, it might develop into a knockdown affair between the two, which would expose deep rifts in the Republican Party. It was the Republican tradition to fight behind the scenes and to have a quick nomination. Only the enemy Democrats were ruffians enough to fight in the open.

Thus Lodge from the chair put the question of adjourning the convention to the vote, on the motion of Harding's friend, Senator Smoot. A few "ayes" were heard in the hall. But the hordes of Wood and Lowden bellowed out their "noes." Lodge, however, was a machine politician of the old school. Ignoring the wishes of the delegates, he walked off the rostrum. The convention was adjourned. When Mark Sullivan asked Senator Smoot of Utah why the Old Guard had forced an adjournment, Smoot brazenly replied, "Oh, there's going to be a deadlock and we'll have to work out some solution; we wanted the night to think it over." [10]

Because the Senate bosses had to meet somewhere in a hotel room to work out their strategy, the myth of the Smoke-filled Room was allowed to grow. In fact, there were many smoke-filled rooms and endless conferences throughout the night. No delegates could have slept much. The air was sultry. There were continual comings and goings of what Wood's biographer described as "smooth, sleek little animals slipping noiselessly to and fro." [11] Combinations were earnestly sought and refused. Plots were laid in many rooms of the Blackstone Hotel. It was only the plot that was thought to be successful that gave notoriety to the rooms of George Harvey at the Blackstone, particularly Room 404. There *is* conspiracy in democratic politics, but that conspiracy is usually made up of so many plots and counterplots that the struggle leads to something resembling democracy.

The first important meeting of the evening seemed a local affair. The Ohio delegation gathered. The nine Wood voters from Cincinnati persuaded four more to desert Harding and join Wood. Ohio's favorite son obviously did not have a chance. It was known, indeed, that Harding would file for renomination to the Senate before midnight, the final hour for filing. The whole delegation might have deserted Harding at this point if he had not recovered his usual political courage. As he had written before in his private correspondence, he enjoyed a fight as much as any man. He now begged the delegates to continue to support him if the deadlock continued. Thirty-five of the delegates agreed.[12] Had Harding been as despondent at this time as many later reports made out, he could hardly have kept his split delegation behind him.

The second important series of meetings were, indeed, those held in George Harvey's rooms. Harvey liked intrigue and was an influential publisher of magazines, but he was also a braggart who wanted to be a kingmaker. He was sharing his quarters with Senator Brandegee, one of the Old Guard; and the Old Guard one by one sought out Brandegee's hospitality to plot a strategy.

Throughout the night, in an ever-changing group, tired Senators came and went. Harvey, along with Senators Lodge, Brandegee, Curtis, and Smoot, was there most of the time. Senators Wadsworth and Watson and McCormick also called, as did less influential Senators. There was no agreement between them, and there was no formal meeting. They did not know what the convention would do, what Wood and Lowden and Johnson would do, or what compromise choice they would make. The smoke-filled room was filled mainly with smoke.

Smoot, as a delegate from Utah, was one of the only two Senators who had voted solidly for Harding and wanted Harding to win.[13] It was he who backed Harding in the endless conversations in Harvey's rooms. And it was he who was responsible for the partisan statement to a reporter early on Saturday morning that Harding had been chosen by the Senate bosses and would be nominated that afternoon, after Lowden had been given a run for his money.[14] The fact that his prediction was correct made Harding's nomination seem a conspiracy. But hundreds of other incorrect predictions were also being fed to reporters. Smoot's was no more than the declaration of his personal hunch. If Wood or Lowden had been nominated that afternoon, other theories of conspiracy, backed by predictions, could just as easily have been proved. It was because there were many millionaires and oilmen at the convention, including the speculator Jake Hamon, who was in control of the Oklahoma delegation, that theories of conspiracy abounded that Friday night in Chicago.

Actually, most of the Senators who met in Harvey's rooms believed that they deserved the nomination more than Harding. It so happened that none of them had the backing of even the delegation of his home state. Lodge was too old at seventy, and Massachusetts was mostly behind its ambitious Governor, Calvin Coolidge. Lodge was himself accused the next day by Daugherty of trying to prevent Harding's nomination, and Massachusetts gave only 1 vote to Harding until the final ballot. Watson voted throughout for Wood. Wadsworth voted for Lowden for four more ballots, and Harding later said that he did not think Wadsworth was for him.[15] Calder voted as Wadsworth did. McCormick stuck with Lowden until the tenth and last ballot. Brandegee's state, Connecticut, cast no votes for Harding until the ninth ballot, nor did Curtis' Kansas, although Curtis was influential in the final break for Harding. The other leading Republican Senators of the Old Guard did not swing their own votes or those of their delegations to Harding until the final two ballots. Even Penrose's Pennsylvanians remained solidly behind Governor Sproul until the last ballot.[16]

In fact, the Old Guard of the Senate did not help Harding much. They talked in circles all through Friday night, even if the circle began and ended with Harding. Wood was unmanageable. Lowden was disliked by Wood's backers because he had stopped Wood. Johnson was too progressive. Thus the choice fell on Harding, who had a little support, and could be sold to the delegates because of the myth of Ohio, the Presidential state. In a deadlock, the tradition was that Ohio's candidate became the nominee. So Harding was logically the most available compromise choice, although not the only one. As the Associated Press reported the next day, most of the leaders of the Senate "appeared agreeable to trying Harding *first* among the large field of dark horses." [17] Only Smoot and Curtis of the leading Senators *liked* that choice, but Lodge and the rest tolerated it. The influential Senators, Wadsworth later declared, "were like a lot of chickens with their heads off." [18]

Because the bosses of the Senate could not agree and because they feared that they could not control the convention even if they did agree, Harding appeared to them as the man most likely to win. Thus they were prepared to throw behind him what little influence they had if he could *show strength* on the next day. None of the other dark horses, Coolidge and Sproul and Butler and Hughes, was as available as Harding, for none of them came from Ohio and the Senate. The true dark horse and the choice of Harvey and some Senators was Will Hays, the national chairman of the Republican Party. If Harding failed, Hays was due to be sprung on the convention. Or so believed Daugherty and Taft and others. It was Hays himself who had rented the Blackstone rooms for Harvey and Brandegee.

The second spreader of the legend of the smoke-filled room was the braggart Harvey. He called in two newsmen early on Saturday morning, and with only two Senators present, probably Brandegee and Smoot, he predicted Harding's nomination that afternoon.[19] It was also Harvey who called in Harding at three o'clock in the morning to tell him that the bosses of the Senate were now behind him and would nominate him. It was then that the ridiculous scene that Harvey's sense of power and drama demanded of the occasion probably took place. He asked Harding whether there was anything in his past that would disqualify him from the nomination. So the would-be kingmaker made the future king humiliate himself, as Lodge was to do again after the nomination.

Instead of replying that his private affairs were his own business, Harding asked for time to think over Harvey's demand. It was suggested later that he considered rumors about his Negro blood and his affairs with Mrs. Carrie Phillips and Nan Britton at this time. This is unlikely. Many a Presidential candidate had had worse stains and known mistresses in his past. Harding probably considered the fact that he had a weak heart and perhaps his declared inadequacy for the position. He replied, however, that nothing stopped him from accepting the nomination.[20]

While Harding, because of his belief in boss control, was sure that he had the nomination in his pocket, neither Wood nor Lowden nor most of the delegates agreed with him. In fact, on Friday night, Hiram Johnson, with his 140 delegates, held the key to the situation. Wood and Lowden and Harding all approached him to offer him the Vice-Presidency if he would throw his delegates to them. He refused them all. Perhaps he hoped that the convention would still turn to him in the deadlock. And even if he knew his case was hopeless, the progressive Johnson could hardly back Wood or Lowden—his opponents with tainted money in the primaries. Nor could he support such a known reactionary as Harding. So Johnson decided to fight it out, unknowingly giving up his chance of entering the White House through a dead man's shoes. This was another stroke of fortune for Harding. If Johnson had been prepared to lie down with his enemies as easily as Harding always was, his strength would have put either Wood or Lowden over the top early on Saturday morning.

Daugherty, meanwhile, had organized his workers throughout the night to remind the delegates of their promises to support Harding as their second or third or fourth choice. If he was not as in control of the proceedings as he later claimed, yet he was indefatigable at drumming up support for the logical compromise candidate from Ohio, acceptable personally to both the Senate and most of the delegates. Harding's cause seemed good that Saturday morning, unless some delegation suddenly broke to Wood or Lowden and unless Wood and Lowden agreed to run on the same ticket. This, Harding claimed at breakfast, could not happen. They hated each other too much. "You see it never pays to become bitter in political warfare." [21]

On the fifth ballot, which led off the voting on Saturday morning, Wood dropped to 299 votes, while Lowden passed him with 303 votes. Johnson dropped to 133½, and Harding advanced to 78. There was one of the traditional attempts of Ohio's delegates to knife their candidate at this point. A delegate rose to shout that Harding had filed for the Senate and therefore was no longer seriously in the Presidential race; the delegate now intended to vote for Wood. Harding's men in the Ohio delegation howled the heckler down, and the vote was counted as usual, 39 for Harding and 9 for Wood. "Cast your vote if you see fit to do it that way," the deserter to Wood was told, "and that's enough." [22]

Harding's new support of 16½ votes came chiefly from previous promises, now honored by those scattered delegates who had agreed on Harding as a second choice in case of deadlock. Moreover, a growing rumor had it that Harding *was* the choice of the Senate bosses, whose mythical control was believed by many delegates. All the world of a convention loves a conspiracy. And the so-called powerful ones are powerful when the mass of people believe them to be powerful. Thus the headless convention of 1920, looking for a conspiracy of the powerful, was prepared to jump on the bandwagon of the man who seemed to be the choice of the great.

Yet Wood and Lowden battled on. Whatever the rumors, victory would go to him who received the votes of 493 delegates. And the front-runners together could block anyone's nomination until they released their supporters, for they held more than two-thirds of the votes of the convention between them. While both Wood and Lowden stood firm, the bosses in the Senate could do nothing.

The balloting continued. On the sixth ballot, Wood advanced again, tying with Lowden at 311½ votes. Johnson was quickly betrayed by his delegates and sank to 110. Harding came up to 89, as the rumors that he was the chosen one grew. At this moment, the planned revolt of four Ohio delegates nearly upended him. The four voters switched to Wood, to give him 13 votes from Ohio. But Harding's gain of 15 votes from other states, chiefly in the South, outweighed this second show of treachery at home.

On the seventh ballot, only Harding advanced materially. Wood gained a ½ vote, Lowden stuck where he was, and Johnson dropped back behind Harding to fourth place. Harding's 105 votes were still scattered, except from Ohio. Most of his 16 new votes also came from the conservative South. His preconvention speeches there were paying dividends, delegate by delegate, although no state delegation had broken for him. Harding's years of making individual friends were helping him now. Texas, which he had counted on in February, had gone to Wood. Now individuals from Texas were jumping onto the Harding bandwagon as it began to roll.

On the eighth ballot, only Harding gained. Wood dropped to 299, Lowden to 307, and Johnson to 87. Harding gained another 28½ votes, again mainly in Southern scatterings. The four Ohio deserters returned to him, which created a good effect. He had been cultivating the Lowden forces for some time, and they were soon expected to break ranks for Harding to end the deadlock. Both Lowden and Wood had stalled; Johnson had lost. Without much help from the Senate bosses other than their rumored and fictitious backing, Harding had gained on his own merits by attracting *individual* delegates in the various states. The fact that the convention was leaderless and that the delegates were bound only loosely by unit rules made these individual breakaways to Harding possible. It was the incoherence and lack of discipline of the convention of 1920 that played into the hands of Ohio's favorite son.

Here Lodge intervened again, this time *against* Harding. The Lowden and Wood forces obviously wanted a recess to see whether they could make a deal in order to stop Harding's bandwagon from rolling on to victory. He had shown the delegate strength that the Senate bosses had wanted to see. He was obviously on the point of attracting whole delegations in a stampede behind him. The psychology of the Harding movement demanded an immediate ninth ballot. Lodge, however, called for a recess, persuading Willis of Ohio that Harding should not try to crash through to victory, but that he should try to make a last-minute deal with Johnson to put the progressives on the ticket in second place and thus unite the party. Daugherty, mad with rage, accused Lodge of trying to defeat Harding deliberately. This accusation may have held some truth. For Lodge could not have relished much the thought of his yes-man in the Foreign Relations Committee becoming his master in the White House.

In the recess of the convention, Wood and Lowden conferred with each other. Faced by losing all to Harding, neither would agree to take second place on the other's ticket. Each would be President or nothing. The hours went by. The end of the recess approached. Will Hays, still hoping to be the dark horse if Harding were stopped, rushed to meet with Wood and Lowden. All three agreed to ask Lodge to extend the recess and adjourn the convention until Monday. Then a deal could be arranged over the weekend to eliminate Harding for good.

In fact, the Senate leaders now decided to stop Harding. As his nomination approached, their lukewarm endorsement of the previous night turned into an attempt to stop him. He had been *too* successful too quickly. In fact, it is likely that Harvey and Brandegee and Lodge had wanted to use Harding only to stop either Wood or Lowden from winning. Now they wished to do what they had always intended to do—to slip in Will Hays as the chosen dark horse of the Senatorial cabal. One of Lowden's managers was a good friend of Hays and could swing votes to him. Hays himself, a colorless but wily politician, was considered eminently manageable. He was later to become Hollywood's first official film censor and a champion of the industry that he was supposed to regulate. Moreover, if Harding were stopped and Hays then failed, who knew to what individual Senator the weary convention might turn?

The chairman of the Connecticut delegation was told by Brandegee to swing the whole delegation behind the theretofore unconsidered Hays. The chairman demurred, saying that the delegates had already decided to jump on the wagon behind Harding. Brandegee said that the Senators had already lined up 600 votes for Hays and that he would win. But Brandegee could not change the mind of the chairman of his own state delegation.[23] Connecticut was to lead the break to Harding. Once again, it was the lack of power of the Old Guard of the Senate that was to lead to Harding's victory.

At this point, Harding would still have had to fight if Lowden had not decided to throw the nomination to him rather than to Wood. Harding's policy of making friends with Lowden and his delegates again proved successful. For personal reasons, Lowden thought that Harding represented his point of view more than Wood did. Moreover, he was frightened of his delegates' switching to Harding without a word from him. He was like a man condemned to death who prefers suicide to execution. By *choosing* to release his delegates, Lowden hoped to commend himself to Harding's favor. For Harding had already made gains among Lowden's supporters in the South, and he would obviously gain more. It was not so much that Lowden liked Harding as that he hated Wood.

Lodge delayed the ninth ballot for a further three-quarters of an hour while plans were being made to stop Harding. The Wood forces wanted the recess continued until Monday, and they thought Lowden had agreed. But through treachery or confusion in Lowden's ranks, the ninth ballot began. Lodge was unable to delay the voting any longer. Connecticut led the break for Harding. "The stubborn independence" of that delegation, according to Nicholas Murray Butler, prevented the Senators' substitution of Hays as their chosen dark horse.[24] The delegates, wrongly convinced that Harding was being put over by the bosses, were ready to desert Lowden for Harding in droves. But it was Kansas that caused the real upset, and here Harding was helped by his friend Senator Curtis. According to William Allen White, Curtis persuaded the delegation that the bosses were behind Harding and that he would win. If Kansas switched, its Governor Allen might be Vice-President. So the delegation deserted Wood on the ninth ballot, and even White, the old Progressive firebrand, swallowed the "awful pill" and marched with the rest of the delegation behind Harding and reaction.[25]

"At Kansas it was all over with Wood," Mark Sullivan wrote. "That settled it. The big break was on." [26] The next state, Kentucky, led by one of Lowden's managers, went to Harding rather than Hays, whose boom had never started. Louisiana and Missouri also jumped on the bandwagon. Butler then deserted Lowden and threw most of New York behind Harding. North and South Carolina, Tennessee, Texas, and Virginia now put the South pretty solidly behind Harding. And Oklahoma, led by the oil speculator Hamon, joined him. At the end of the ballot, Harding led the field with 374½ votes, with Wood at 249 and Lowden down to 121½.

Nothing could stop Harding now as the tired and sweaty delegates jumped aboard. On the tenth ballot, the remainder of the Southern states joined Harding, and Pennsylvania at last came over to give him the nomination—perhaps on the telephoned orders of the absent Penrose. Harding got 692½ votes, and the convention was declared unanimous, despite a chorus of noes from Wood's 156 faithful supporters, from the 81 progressives who stuck to Johnson, and from the 24 Wisconsin delegates who had voted throughout for La Follette. The Wisconsin Senator, who might have bolted the Republican Party at this point, as he was to do four years hence, later refused to lead a third party.

The nomination of the Vice-President further showed how unbossed the convention was. The Senators had apparently decided to nominate the moderately progressive Senator Lenroot to balance the ticket. A delegate, however, rose on a chair and shouted for another conservative, Calvin Coolidge, the Governor of Massachusetts. The remaining delegates yelled and voted for him, then rushed for the last train home. In these closing chaotic minutes, they picked Harding's successor in the White House. Again they were deceived by a myth: that Coolidge was a strong man who had broken the Boston police strike with the famous message, "There is no right to strike against the public safety by anybody, anytime, anywhere." In fact, Coolidge had sent out the message; but while he dithered, the strike had already been ended by the vigorous Mayor of Boston. Myth again was to put a second-rate reactionary in the White House.

"The whole show at Chicago," Dwight Morrow wrote, "was a terrible jumble." [27] In this terrible jumble, the myths of politics *believed by the delegates* were in command. When Wood and Lowden deadlocked, two myths gave Harding the nomination. The first: when in doubt, turn to Ohio (ten of the previous thirteen nominees had come from Ohio); the second myth was that the bosses of the Senate *did* control the convention, when they did not. Thus Harding became the most available man to break the deadlock. The image of him as a small-town self-made businessman confirmed his appeal. And the personal contacts, which he and Daugherty had assiduously fostered before the convention, gave him the increasing strength from *individual* delegates that started his bandwagon rolling on Saturday morning.

Harding was certainly the popular second choice of a majority of delegates at Chicago. He was not the popular second choice of a majority of Senators. In fact, the unbossed convention beat the Senators over both the nominees. It was only after the fact that Harding's fellow Senators claimed that they had seen to his nomination. Daugherty knew that they had not, as did many others. If, at any time, Wood and Lowden had agreed or if Johnson had joined either, Harding would have been finished. He won by his subtle strategy of appealing to all without pride and by treating false friends as though they were true ones. Harding and the delegates believed that he was the Senators' choice. Thus when the delegates chose him, he became the Senators' choice in legend and retrospect. By playing the innocent, Harding outfoxed the conspirators.

Once the nomination was made, Harding was overcome with joy and humility. He begged for help from Butler and Lowden before Daugherty whisked him away. Mrs. Harding, superstitious as always, had already declared to a reporter, "I can see but one word written over the head of my husband if he is elected, and that word is 'tragedy.' " [28] Mrs. Harding knew about Harding's weak heart, and she had seen the White House kill Wilson, "as surely as if he had been stabbed at his desk." [29] She feared not only her husband's death in office, but also her own. She told Senator Watson that she would walk into the White House, but be carried out.[30] She had been against Harding's running at all, although once he was in the fight, she had told him to fight to the finish. Now, with victory, both she and he feared the outcome and the office.

To most of the delegates in Chicago, Harding represented a man like themselves, on the side of the past and of business. The progressive surge had washed back. Johnson and La Follette and the Rooseveltian supporters of Wood feared one another and could not combine. The split among the Progressives, which had begun with Roosevelt's desertion in 1916, could not be healed by Wood and Johnson. Thus the convention was given over to the standpatters. It was the new temper of the times, a reaction toward the temper of the old times. As White wrote, the death of Roosevelt and the collapse of Wilsonian liberalism created in his heart "a climax of defeat. . . . The spirits of the liberals who called themselves Progressives were bewildered. The faint-hearted turned cynics. The faithful were sad and weary, however bravely we shouted. I did not sink low enough to carp; but as I trudged up the aisle of the convention hall, when Kansas took her banner to Ohio for Harding, I was too heartsick to rise and fight." [31]

One last humiliation waited for Harding at the hands of Lodge, who had tried to stop his nomination and was now determined to make Harding think that he owed his nomination to the Old

Guard of the Senate in a smoke-filled room. Leading the official committee to notify Harding of his nomination on July 22, Lodge presented him with something of an ultimatum:

> The makers of the Constitution intended to coordinate the three great elements of Government and strove to guard against either usurpation or trespass by one branch at the expense of the other two. In that spirit, *we all know well,* you will enter upon your great responsibility. . . . *We know that you were in full accord* with the belief of your Republican colleagues that the League of Nations as proposed by Mr. Wilson and upon which he and his party still insist ought never to be accepted by the American people. . . . We stand for the policies of Washington and the doctrine of Monroe, and against the internationalism and the permanent alliance with foreign nations proposed by the President. . . . *Such has been the policy of the Republican party as represented in the Senate and such its policy will remain. We are certain that you who helped so largely to frame this policy will, when the executive authority comes into your hands, carry it out.*

Harding's reply to Lodge's ultimatum was capitulation. He felt himself the nominee of the Senate. "Let me be understood clearly from the very beginning: I believe in party sponsorship in government. I believe in party government as distinguished from personal government, individual, dictatorial, autocratic or what not." Ohio's next President, Warren Harding, would be the weak Chief Executive that Ohio's first President, William Henry Harrison, had intended to be. The Senate, "fit to be the greatest deliberative body of the world," would resume its authority. Its members were "the designated sentinels on the towers of constitutional Government." They had just saved the independent nationality of the Republic from the dream of an autocrat. Harding declared that he understood "the purpose of the dominant group of the Senate." He had been one of them. "We were not seeking to defeat a world aspiration, we were resolved to safeguard America. We were resolved then, even as we are today, and will be tomorrow, to preserve this free and independent Republic." Harding saw only harmony between himself and the Old Guard of the Senate, with whom he had usually agreed and always followed. "With a Senate advising as the Constitution contemplates," he would keep America independent and free while seeking for an understanding between nations.[32]

So Lodge made Harding swear to be the weak President whom the Senate had sought vainly for more than twenty years. Lodge was to be disappointed. For if the office does not make the man, the vanity of office does. Harding wanted to be a good President and a loved one. In the pursuit of this, he was ready to forget that he had once been a junior Senator.

The theory of the men in the smoke-filled room at Chicago who pulled the strings and nominated their puppet Harding was born in Daugherty's early boast, fed by the legend of boss control of the Republican Party, and confirmed by the kingmaking remarks of Smoot and Harvey. After the event, of course, many Senators testified that they had helped to choose Harding, in order to make him beholden to them. In fact, he was beholden only to Smoot and Curtis, to Daugherty and the delegates. He had won the victory chiefly by himself, through his time-tested strategy of hard work in making friends and of extreme care in not making enemies. Harding had won at Chicago through his own political skills and through his cleverness in disguising them.

In an acute article immediately after the convention, Arthur W. Page discounted the widely held theories of conspiracy at Chicago. At most, these were but half- or quarter-truths. "Almost everything that was done was done by compromise between many leaders and as a result of mixed motives and much pulling and hauling." The regular bosses had agreed on only one thing, on stopping Wood, who had offended them by trying to win on the popular vote of the primaries. No boss liked to be told that he was powerless. Yet he *was* powerless unless the headless delegates were looking for a chief. "The propelling force behind Harding was not primarily belief in Harding, it was the belief on the part of the majority of the delegates that it pays to follow the leaders, to remain with the permanent organizations which can give a man patronage, power, or prestige year after year rather than to join organizations gotten up temporarily to back a candidate." Harding was a regular, most of the delegates wanted to be regular, and they believed that Harding was the choice of the regular bosses. After the eighth ballot, "the word passed everywhere that the regulars were going to 'put him over' . . . and this means a lot in politics. To stick fast in the face of apparent defeat is a terrible ordeal." [33]

The joke was that Harding was *not* the choice of the regular bosses, although he and most of the delegates believed so. Thus, in the name of regularity, the delegates had committed a great irregularity. The moment that Harding was chosen, the bosses naturally claimed that Harding had always been their choice, in order to preserve the myth that they had been in control. For the myth believed is the fact in politics. The bosses wanted to be in genuine control in 1924. Thus they spread the false story of the smoke-filled room in order to claim the power that they wished they had. And they were generally believed, because all the political world loves a conspiracy.

The most notable thing about Harding's victory at Chicago was his consistent good luck. Everything broke his way, except for Lodge's attempt to stop him after the eighth ballot. He might well have said the remark that legend has attributed to him: "I feel like a man who goes in with a pair of eights and comes out with aces full." Most of the metaphors of politics are taken from gambling, because luck has to join with skill in order to win. The road to Chicago had really started for Harding on the unexpected death of Theodore Roosevelt. Finesse and fortune took him to the heights. "How wonderfully Our Lady Fortune—whom you call 'Cocotte'!—" one Rooseveltian wrote to another, "gets her work in. Had T.R. lived, he would have been nominated unanimously; instead, the man who snarled at his heels is chosen!!" [34]

IO

The Solemn Referendum

"It is clear that the responsibilities of his position weigh rather heavily on Harding. One might think that the dignity of the presidency had already fallen upon him. There is a new note of authority in everything he says or writes, as if the result of the election were already an established fact. He looks more than ever like a president."   ROGER LEWIS

In his summer home in Maine, Frederick Jackson Turner was correcting the galley proofs of his book on the frontier. The political convention seemed to confirm his thesis that the qualities bred by the frontier were ended. "I am disgusted with the Republican convention," he wrote, "as a Democrat has a right to be; and am hoping that the Dems. will really get religion and find a Moses. Of course the tide will turn, and Harding will grow stronger, but just now almost any one could beat him, judging by the remarks of natives as well as rusticators in this barometric Maine." [1] By September 17, barometric Maine was to rise for Harding by a majority of 66,000 votes, a storm warning that predicted the outcome of the whole election. In the campaign, Harding was to provoke a solemn referendum, not against the League or Woodrow Wilson, but for himself.

Wilson's statement that the election would be a solemn referendum on the League, and the readiness of the opponents of the

League to treat Harding's victory as such, misled commentators on the result. The legend of a referendum favoring isolation was created. And a second myth was also set up: that the vote was against Wilson and not for Harding. In fact, Harding's victory was more personal and positive. He confirmed the pattern of Party politics for the next decade and restored the Republican Party to the position of ascendancy that it had had in 1908, before it was split by the Progressive movement. And he won through his own merits and shrewdness, by appealing to the nostalgia in people for normalcy—defined by a wit as the desire that everything should remain as it never was.

The immediate reaction of the press to Harding's nomination did damn and faintly praise him. He was thought to be the creature of the Old Guard. The Hearst papers called him "the flag-carrier of a new Senatorial autocracy." The New York *Evening World* declared that the Republicans "did not nominate a man; they nominated a group, an oligarchy." *The New York Times*, indeed, was so indignant that it called Harding "the fine and perfect flower of the cowardice and imbecility of the Senatorial cabal." Even the stanchly Republican press could say only that he stood "for representative as opposed to autocratic government," and was a splendid example of the average citizen. The most powerful of the Republican papers, the *New York Tribune*, was not satisfied with the result, which seemed to give over the party to the standpatters. [2]

The press, however, was chiefly owned by Republicans and soon rallied to the Republican standard. As Charles Hard wrote to Harding, it was merely "the usual run of adverse criticism on platform and on candidates." A reaction would soon take place, for "at the bottom, the people desire a return to common sense. They are tired of viewing rainbows and soap bubbles." [3] Soon Hard was proved correct. The Boston *Transcript* found that "the sober second thought of the country" was favorable to the Chicago nominations. The Philadelphia *Inquirer* thought Harding "better than a genius for an administrative job, because he is a practical man of common sense." His resemblance to McKinley and his harmonizing image were widely noted. In fact, the second choice of some soon came to represent the best of all possible worlds. In a parody of Harding's own fudging of issues, the Pittsburgh *Gazette-Times* called him "that type of conservative that merits the further description of progressive." [4]

Above all, the press noted that Harding's nomination had given the Democrats their chance. Harding was a conservative of the old school. "One thing in the situation stands out," declared the Des Moines *Register*, "and that is the opportunity the Democrats have of establishing with some permanence a more logical party division than we have had since the sixties." If the Democrats nominated a sincere progressive, Lord Bryce's famous sneer (that Europeans only asked what the difference between the Republicans and the Democrats was because they never received an answer) might be answered.

The Democrats, however, threw away their chance of putting up their strongest candidate against Harding. That man was William Gibbs McAdoo, a Cabinet member and Wilson's son-in-law. Tall and commanding in a Lincolnesque way, McAdoo had the reputation of being a hive of industry, a progressive, and a stern dry. He had great support in the rural South and West, the parts of the country where Prohibition sentiment was strong. Unmistakably, he could get the endorsement of the Anti-Saloon League against Harding, and thus he might carry enough rural states to give himself the kind of victory that Wilson had won against Hughes. He could appeal to the rural future rather than to the rural past. At least this seemed the best strategy of the Democrats. But the sick Wilson, in an excess of personal ambition that appeared to seek suicide as well as filicide, knifed his own son-in-law by making it clear that he wanted a third term.

In this situation, the iron-willed McAdoo had to withdraw officially. He did not even attend the Democratic National Convention at San Francisco. His managers never knew whether or not he might repudiate their efforts on his behalf. And Wilson, always hoping that a third nomination might come from a deadlock in the convention, refused to endorse McAdoo for the White House.

Equally, the delegates at San Francisco refused to believe that Wilson was well enough to run for a third term. Thus, by his delicacy and refusal to campaign against his father-in-law, McAdoo relinquished his chance of opposing Harding, the man whose speeches McAdoo called "an army of pompous phrases moving over the landscape in search of an idea. Sometimes these meandering words would actually capture a straggling thought and bear it triumphantly, a prisoner in their midst, until it died of servitude and overwork." [5]

Despite his withdrawal, McAdoo came as the front-runner to San Francisco. He would have won, too, had his manager been able to come to an agreement with the urban bosses of the Eastern cities. This group, however, refused to endorse a man who was an out-and-out dry. His candidacy would alienate the wet Democratic vote in the cities, and no politician likes to ensure his own future wake. The ambitious, Red-hunting Attorney General, A. Mitchell Palmer, kept McAdoo from gaining a victory; and, as at Chicago, a second-rate editor from Ohio, James M. Cox, came up from behind to break the deadlock and receive the nomination. As a disguised wet, he received the city bosses' vote; as a progressive in his first term as Ohio's Governor, he received the McAdoo vote; as a reactionary German-hater and Red-hunter in his third term as Governor, he received the Palmer vote; and as a three-time winner in Ohio, he received the politic vote. His running mate was chosen strictly on his little-known character and well-known name, the young Franklin Delano Roosevelt of New York.

The choice of Cox at San Francisco disgusted the press as much as the choice of Harding at Chicago. The Democrats had thrown away their advantage by failing to choose a strong man at a clean and unbossed convention. "The conclusion is inevitable," *Collier's* declared, "that each party went the worst way possible about the job of selecting its candidate for president. . . . The national disinterest—and sometimes disgust—registered while the proceedings were under way revealed how remote it all was from what the people were thinking." [6] It was generally held that McAdoo should have won and would have won with Wilson's support. He was

the choice of most of the delegates. But like the Republicans, the
rank-and-file Democrats were the victims of circumstances. As at
Chicago, the bosses had seized the initiative when the delegates
did not know what to do, and they had "an ascendancy which
was entirely disproportionate to their real influence." [7] After the
conventions of 1920, the radicals and progressives seemed to have
nowhere to go.

Cox was, unfortunately, even more unknown than Harding. As
the proprietor of several Buckeye newspapers, he was worth some
$2,000,000. Like Harding, he was a self-made man and a shrewd
operator and politician. During the Progressive flood, he had been
excessively progressive; during the war, he had been excessively
patriotic; before the convention of 1920, he had been excessively
available at making no mistakes. Although more clever than
Harding, he had one conspicuous disadvantage: he was middle-sized
and cocky, with an ordinary and bespectacled face. His friends
called his manner Napoleonic, but this trait was merely Cox's way
of elevating the undistinguished and the mediocre. Against the
most handsome Presidential nominee since Fillmore, the Democrats
were putting up a faceless executive and millionaire whom
nobody knew.

To many, the trouble in the election seemed to be that there
was no political choice. Both men were self-made Ohio editors
without a national reputation. Both were economic conservatives
and were progressives only under pressure. In New York, the
Commercial declared that "business will be safe with either," the
Globe that each was "a man of mediocre ability and of unimpeach-
able party regularity," and the *Evening Post* that, for the liberal,
"neither the Republican party nor the Democratic has any clear
claim to his vote." *The Nation* found that the choice was between
the Socialist leader Eugene "Debs or dubs." [8] William Allen White
wrote that the only honest vote a Republican or a Democrat could
cast "should be a spite vote against his own party." Whenever he
got to thinking about Harding, he would decide to vote for Cox,
until he began to think about Cox, and then it seemed the only
thing was to vote for Harding.[9] And indeed White did vote for

Harding, in the election as in the convention, and the Emporia *Gazette* remained true to the fellow newspaper owner in the Republican Party.

Although Cox tried to make political issues out of the campaign, his attempts were vain against the clever straddling of Harding, who, as James Reston pointed out later about Richard Nixon, could campaign in Scylla and Charybdis and carry both precincts. With Harding ducking a campaign of issues, the battle between him and Cox took place on Harding's strongest points—style and personality. And here Harding won a resounding victory. If his clever strategy was less one of intention than of natural bent, yet Harding had an instinct for the appealing that approached inspiration.

Harding's chosen strategy was modeled on McKinley's final campaign. Even as a Senator, Harding had rebuilt his front porch in the style of McKinley's famous porch at Canton. Marion neighbors at the time had thought that this act warned of "the presidential bee." And, indeed, after the nomination, Harding chose to campaign from his porch, true to the Ohio tradition. "I am glad you like the home campaign idea," he wrote to Jennings, "because I am thoroughly committed to it and have no notion of changing my plans." [10] Later tradition attributed the idea of the front-porch campaign to Penrose; but then tradition had also wrongly made Penrose responsible for Harding's nomination. "Keep Warren at home," Penrose is supposed to have said. "Don't let him make any speeches. If he goes on a tour, somebody's sure to ask him questions, and Warren's just the sort of damn fool that'll try to answer them!" [11] If this was Penrose's advice, it merely coincided with Harding's own strategy and proved that Penrose, as well as Daugherty, liked to underrate the political skill of the Republican nominee.

The front-porch campaign, of course, was admirably suited to the image behind which Harding had successfully run for office all his life. Newspaper correspondents came to Marion to scoff, and stayed to smile approval if not to cheer. If Harding appeared to be Marion, yet the small town was still considered a good place. The stories there about Harding were generally favorable. As one resident said, "When they look good through a microscope to us there isn't any reason why they shouldn't test out the same way through the telescope." [12]

Daily, Harding seemed to acquire more and more the dignity and air of a President, the reticence and manner. Mark Sullivan found him so distinguished that he would be "a marked man in any metropolis." And Sullivan saw what few saw—and what was true: that although Harding's disposition might be sweet, he had a streak of firmness in him that was close to stubbornness. Once he was set on anything, he was "as sot as the meetin' house." And he was set on "an orderly world, a neat world, a world of carefully graveled paths, and nicely clipped hedges—above all, a world that stays the same from day to day . . . a world that stays put. Harding winces at all the mess the war has made in the world, and he wants to get it all cleaned up and out of the way, and get back to 'normalcy.' " [13] This was also what a majority of the American people obviously wanted.

To this considered image of the dignified gentleman in a small town, Harding added a new factor to successful campaign strategy. His relations with the journalists were excellent, and he knew all about their jobs and their deadlines and their troubles. Thus he went out of his way to make their lives easier. From the press point of view, Harding was one of the most popular candidates and Presidents that the nation ever had. A special bungalow with three rooms was erected for the use of the journalists. Once or twice a day, Harding would wander in, greet them personally by name, borrow a plug of tobacco or a stogie, and say "Shoot!" He would then answer all questions in a friendly way, without evasion; but he would specify which news could be used and which could not.[14] He always handed out copies of his speech to the correspondents *before* he spoke, so that his words could catch the headlines in time. He was ready to pitch horeshoes or exchange stories off the cuff with almost all reporters; and by relying on their discretion and that of their editors, he kept an intimacy with them that made them friendly to him. He set a fashion in good press relations that was not equaled until the time of Franklin D. Roosevelt and John F. Kennedy.

Harding's own behavior and seduction of the press was backed by a brilliant campaign machine, run by Will Hays. The machine had been prepared in skeleton form for over a year and was ready to move into action. It seemed like a Republican year, so money was easy to collect. Hays spent about $8,100,000, nearly four times the sum that the Democrats could raise. The theme that Hays plugged in advertisements was Harding's own old theme: America First. The slogan was, "Let's be done with wiggle and wobble." The image presented was one of extreme nationalism:

> Absolute Control of the United States by the United States. . . .
> Independence means *independence*, now as in 1776. . . .
> This country will remain American. Its next President will remain in our own country. . . .
> We decided long ago that we objected to foreign government of our people.[15]

The style of the Republican campaign was very much the style of its candidate. Its slogan and approach were *his*, not those of many of his advisers. If Harding did not always write his own speeches, his hand was evident in their phrases.[16] And his appeal was deliberate and positive. It was aimed at the majority of Americans, those who had once lived in small towns and on farms, even if they were now living in the city. It was also aimed at attracting the discontented vote of various groups of new immigrants, who both longed for the "normalcy" of a vanished peasant past and wanted to cast an honest vote of spite against the war and Wilson. There was an element of hatred of Wilson that reflected itself in the votes given for Harding. But no one had attacked Wilson more viciously in public than Harding, except possibly Lodge. In his last appearance in the Senate, Harding had begun his campaign with an assault on Wilson as a dictator who, "in the lure of ambition or the intoxication of power," had tried to barter away the safety of the Republic.[17] Harding hated Wilson positively and outspokenly. He had done so for years. Thus he naturally attracted the vote of those who also hated Wilson, *because he stood for definite values, which Wilson did not.*

These values were essentially the values of the fatherland. Harding had always praised the Germans for their love of their country and had expressed a wish that Americans would love their country as much. Thus when Harding praised the virtues of the fatherland, the American immigrant, with two fatherlands, could warm to Harding. Harding spoke not only in praise of nostalgia, but also in praise of love of country. The German-Americans were angy at Wilson over declaring war and over the revenge exacted at Versailles. The Irish-Americans wanted Wilson to endorse Irish independence. The Italian-Americans thought that Wilson had betrayed Italy over Fiume, which Lodge had said was as necessary to Italy as New Orleans was to the United States. The Russian-Americans wanted total isolation from the Russian contagion or else large-scale intervention on the side of the Czar. And the Swedish-Americans wanted neutrality at all costs, for this was the policy of their homeland.

All these groups swung to Harding. Those who had backed Wilson and peace in 1916 now voted against Wilson and war. "A vote for Harding," said the German press, "is a vote against the persecutions suffered by German-Americans during the war." [18] Not one German-language newspaper supported Cox. And more positively, the image of Harding and his soothing words about normalcy conjured myths about the past in every rural immigrant skull. As an analyst of the Boston suburbs in the early years of the century found, both native-American farmer and European peasant tended to make a golden dream of the "old days" and the "old country." This dream shut out the horrors of the slum and factory and supplied the comfort and pride missing in urban life.[19] To this dream of normalcy, the handsome Harding appealed from his front porch in his home town; and for this dream of normalcy, the rural immigrants in the cities were to vote. Harding carried the twelve largest cities by a plurality of 1,638,000 votes, for he carried the country heart of the city-dwellers with him. It was a positive vote for the nostalgia of a farm and for crafts no longer necessary in the age of mass production.

Cox did not appeal to this vision. His temperament and style were different. "Cox belongs to the city and has the urban type of mind, if there is such a thing," declared one reporter. "He has the alert-mindedness, the nervous energy, and the quick responses *which at least are popularly attributed to the city*. . . . Farmers and provincial people of tranquil minds like and understand Harding. They like his serenity, his sober dignity and reticence, and most of them, as a matter of course, are going to vote for him in the coming election." [20] Country memories, however, were still prevalent in the slums of the cities, and these nostalgias also were to be translated into votes for Harding.

Cox's campaign style also differed from Harding's. Instead of loftily campaigning on a dream of the past, he tried to hit at Harding with the filth of the present. He spent the first month of the campaign taking a leaf from Hiram Johnson's book and accusing the Republicans of trying to buy the election with a huge slush fund. Then he switched to major issues—the League of Nations and progressivism. He tried to speak in every state in the nation, in a whirlwind of activity. He even campaigned against Harding in Marion. He was estimated to have spoken directly to two million people. And yet Harding grew stronger every day. Although Cox's activity knocked him off the front porch briefly, so that he undertook a short speaking tour in the Midwest and a few other areas, Harding usually remained on his chosen ground and let the visitors come to him.

Harding's strategy of quietism was highly successful. He simply ignored his energetic opponent. One observer could not remember a single occasion when Harding mentioned the name of Cox, except in answer to a direct question. While Cox "was campaigning all over the lot, in a sweat, in his mental shirt sleeves with his coat off, ringing fire alarms," Harding appeared as "a quiet gentleman who had no beads on his forehead, no dust on his shoes, no red in his eye." These are the pictures, the observer continued, that win and lose campaigns. "They are not produced by accident. They are produced sometimes by the instinct of a man like Harding. The only certain way to produce them is by the conscious art of political strategy." [21]

The front-porch campaign also prevented Harding from making mistakes. He did not tire himself or talk loosely. It was a Republican year, and everybody knew it. He had only to avoid errors and he would win. So he waited in Marion, while little Cox, in Mark Sullivan's opinion, overdid the violence. Cox came to seem in the public mind "a little like a frontier 'bad man' shooting up the meeting." The people thought that the Republicans were running a future President, in "a very orderly and dignified way, with great decorum and ceremony," who simply and rightly ignored Cox's challenge to "get off that front porch, and cut out that pink tea—I'm here with the rough stuff." [22] Even the disillusioned Mencken decided to perform the revolting duty of voting for the numskull Harding rather than Cox, for Harding was an open and unashamed capitalist like Mencken, and his striking inability to speak intelligible English obviously concealed "a very tolerable gift for practical politics." [23]

One of the favorite games of the campaign, which rivaled "the Ouija in popularity," was to ask the two Ohio editors what they thought of one another. Both were kindly about each other's personalities, but they obviously thought more of themselves. Harding's statement about Cox was another of his more successful attempts to link the aggressive Cox to the autocratic Wilson and to offer himself as the opposite of both. Claiming that Cox was the nominee of the party bosses, Harding declared himself proud to be the nominee of the Senate: "We seek again a government of laws and not of men." Instead of seeking for a superman to guide them, such as Wilson or his supporter Cox, the American people should choose a President "near the normal." And here Harding used his knowledge of what was dear to the small-town heart to boost himself.

The community of endeavor which "made" the little city I love to call home is, I take it, not unlike the same thing that has made the thousands of communities which in the aggregate compose our United States. No superman did it; no one man did it. We worked together, counseled one another.

Now make the application. This wonderful land of ours is but the aggregate of communities, the sum total of cities, villages, and farms. As a group of us have done in one little city, so must all of us do in the congeries of cities and villages and farms that compose the nation. Not in the glory of the superman should we seek our guidance, but in our neighborly counsel, one with another.

What Cox thought of Harding was, actually, the chief reason for Harding's appeal to middle-aged and elderly voters. "Senator Harding," Cox declared, "has always stood for the forces of reaction. He venerates the past. He now wants us to turn the hands of the clock back to the time of Hanna." [24] What Cox did not realize was that most of the American people, in the reaction from war and rampant industrialism, also wanted to turn the clock back to the time of rural peace and quiet.

As the campaign continued and Cox sought vainly to engage Harding on a battle of issues, he became angrier about his opponent. He felt "not unlike a duelist whose opponent has chosen to settle the dispute by a quiet game of solitaire." Cox, indeed, claimed that he had no settled conviction about Harding, because he did not know what Harding meant when he talked and he doubted whether Harding did.[25]

Harding did. He knew very well how to cloud difficult issues into comforting smoke screens of words until no one knew whether he stood to left or right, to North or South, or above or below them. Gamalielese, which Mencken found so bad that a sort of grandeur crept into it, was more cleverly praised by *The New York Times* as a misty language in which the great majority saw "a reflection of their own indeterminate thoughts." [26] When Harding had not made up his mind, he knew how to make comforting noises about it. Like Marshal Kutuzov at the Battle of Borodino, he saw his function as that of encourager, not of controller. When his lieutenants rushed up to him bringing bad reports of how all the issues were hurting him, he would nod and say, in multitudinous polysyllables, the equivalent of "I know, I know." And the lieutenants would rush off comforted to tell the public, who, however differing their opinions, could feel sure that the man in command understood them.

For Harding played politics in the old style of dignity and sonorous nonsense, which pleased rather than enlightened. Politics was not a matter of issues to him, but a matter of party. He ran on his party platform, and not until he had power would he decide on anything so unpleasant as issues. He asked for a vote of faith in past methods, while Cox tried to cadge votes from such petty things as the good progressive laws that he had put in during his first term as Governor of Ohio. Harding asked for a judgment between men, not between measures; between parties in the past, not between promises in the future. And he was confident about the result, for, like Oliver Wendell Holmes's katydid, he "say'st an undisputed thing in such a solemn way."

On the League, Cox tried for a showdown. He went personally to visit Wilson and stayed to endorse the League. Later on in the campaign, seeing the unpopularity of both, he pointed out that he personally was no Wilson and that he wanted the League only with reservations, particularly on the dangerous Article Ten. Harding, in Hoover's words, skillfully "carried water on both shoulders." Since his own party was split over the League, he sometimes spoke almost as an Irreconcilable and sometimes openly supported a world court or a world association of nations. Thus he left the question open.

Toward the end of the campaign, however, he talked of "not interpretation, but rejection" of the League, and he attacked Article Ten as something that, "in its sinister possibilities," was "the most dangerous proposition ever presented to the American people." This later declaration prevented Senators Borah and Johnson and many of the rural progressives from bolting the party. But Harding's outspokenness under pressure was quickly nullified by the open declaration of thirty-one prominent Republicans in favor of the League but with reservations. The signers of the declaration included Taft, Hughes, and Elihu Root. The party had come to the aid of its nominee, and he would gratefully name one of the thirty-one as his Secretary of State. Wilson's "solemn referendum" on the League was denied by the failure of either party to come out for or against the League, although Cox was for the League in a mild way, and Harding against it if an alternative could be found.

Many of the newspapers considered correctly that the election would not be a referendum on the League. The New York *Globe,* which supported Harding and the League, declared that Harding would be forced to enter the League. "The voter need not rely on his promises or try to reconcile his inconsistencies. The choice is between the situation which will be created by Harding's election and that which will be created by Cox's election, not between Harding's promises and Cox's promises." [27] After his election, Harding would have to conciliate the thirty-one and enter the League. He had, after all, made a promise, when rejecting the League, that after his election, he would "advise with the best minds in the United States," especially in the Senate, and enter "an association of nations for the promotion of international peace." When Harding found that the other nations would not accept this association or "Bush League," he would have to enter the proper League after all.

So those Republicans who wished to vote for Harding and yet favored the League rationalized their choice. In truth, only the German-Americans and the Irreconcilables were passionately against the League. Most people were simply fearful and wished to reject it only because it was new. As Brand Whitlock observed, Harding would undoubtedly be elected, and the people were not voting for him on account of the League—they didn't know anything about it or give a damn for it one way or the other. "The people, indeed, do not know what ideas Harding or Cox represents; neither do Harding or Cox. Great is democracy." [28]

It was, in truth, not an election of ideas, but of personalities. In the wings stood Wilson, hated, but obviously finished. Harding attracted by his dignity and reserve and appeal to rural nostalgia. Cox attracted somewhat in the cities by his energy and go-getting qualities, but he attracted very few. Raymond Robins went to see Harding in behalf of some progressives from Chicago and said that the experience was like going up some steps and through the front door of a magnificent and imposing façade—only to find oneself in the backyard. Such urban progressives voted for Cox, but they were lukewarm about his politic progressivism. The rural progressives, however, stuck with Johnson and Borah and La Follette, and they went to Harding over the issue of staying out of Europe. They swelled the more positive Harding vote of the immigrants with golden dreams of the "old country" and the great mass of regular Republican voters that had kept their party the normal majority party since the Civil War.

As the campaign was little more than a solemn referendum between the images of two Ohio editors—the one representing country peace and the other urban drive—personalities could and did play a prominent role. The official view of the campaign was that it was a gentlemanly one, with Cox and Harding polite to each other. The popular view, however, was that it was a campaign of unequaled viciousness and filth. It somewhat resembled Sherwood Anderson's view of *Winesburg, Ohio*, all white paint in front and barnyard behind. Forty years later, when the present writer asked an old Ohio countryman whom he intended to vote for, he replied that he had not been interested in politics since 1920. "That was an election," he said. "Of course, Cox was up to his elbows in filth. And Harding was a nigger." Old folklore dies hard.

Cox had, indeed, made his newspaper fortune of $2,000,000 quickly, by methods which were never explained, starting from nothing. He was a sharp businessman. As his campaign biographer noted with pride, "Governor Cox is the only man ever nominated for President who owns wealth—real wealth." [29] For this reason, he could arouse little sympathy among the old progressives. He was also divorced from his first wife. These facts, in the small puddle of Ohio politics, made Cox a victim of whisper and innuendo. But he escaped almost scot-free compared with the smears on Harding.

Ever since Harding had become involved in politics, he had been accused of having Negro blood in him. The swarthiness of his skin was the only obvious hint of this. The Hardings explained this story, which had moved with the family from Blooming Grove to Marion, by saying that a neighbor long ago had been caught stealing by the Hardings and had spread the rumor in revenge. The rumor that the Hardings were "part niggers" had followed the family for a hundred years, all because of the spite of this one thief.[30]

Nothing other than rumor seemed to be the basis of this story until a racist but respectable professor at Wooster College, Ohio, decided to investigate Harding's genealogy. This man, William Estabrook Chancellor, was to help in producing a detailed book on Harding, claiming that his great-grandmother, Elizabeth Madison, had been a Negress and that his great-grandfather, George T. Harding, had Negro blood. According to Chancellor, "Warren and his brothers and sisters were reared and treated as colored people." At Blooming Grove, not one man or woman denied that the Hardings were colored. "The Hardings themselves agreed that they were so called by everyone." Eight old people at Blooming Grove swore that they had seen the black-skinned Elizabeth Madison. Her presence there was explained by the fact that Blooming Grove was a fugitive-slave district. Half the residents there had Negro blood.

Although Chancellor's evidence was superficially convincing and may even have contained a stain of truth, his bias against the Hardings militated against fairness in his assessment of the evidence. Chancellor himself came from old, slave-owning Virginian stock. He claimed that Warren Harding was "big, lazy, slouching, confused, ignorant, affable, yellow and cringing like a Negro butler to the great"; that he had been a deserter from the army and had had delirium tremens several times; that he was a Republican only because all Negroes were Republicans; that he was loose in sex morals, like all Negroes; and that if he became a good President, "we should, all of us, seek to marry our sons to colored girls; though, of course, not our girls to colored men." Such marked racial bias confirmed that Chancellor's mind was disturbed and that his evidence was prejudiced and untrustworthy.[31] He was dismissed from his post at Wooster College.

Although Chancellor's work was not published until after Harding's election, his material was made available to the Democratic Party during the campaign. Wilson and Cox forbade its use, but it was used. In the corridors of a New York hotel, strangers handed out small pictures of the White House with the caption "Uncle Tom's Cabin?"[32] Fistfights broke out on a train bound for Chicago when similar pamphlets were handed out. Smear material claiming Harding was a Negro infiltrated the Midwest. And the Republicans were worried, particularly in Ohio:

> We have had Chancellor of Wooster interviewed [wrote the head of the Ohio Republican State Campaign Committee to Charles Hard]. He backs water quite handsomely. He admits that he has absolutely nothing. He says further that the typewritten propaganda being circulated by the Democratic Party is absolutely false. He thinks that the "color stain" if anywhere is in the paternal side. The typewritten copy circulated fixes it in the maternal. He thinks that there might be something to it, but that the admixture of blood was so far back that nothing could be proven.
>
> You have no conception of how the thing is flying over the state. It is everywhere. *It is affecting the woman vote.* . . . We have fought this thing through before, and we must fight it out again.

Charles Hard's own comment scribbled on the letter was that the "negro blood" story did Harding much harm all over the country. "One morning Harding wanted to go over to Wooster and beat Chancellor up. It took some little time to get him to cool off." [33] Harding, indeed, continued to express disappointment, even when he was President, that he could "not deal with the situation as becomes a man and a gentleman." [34]

The news correspondents of Marion were filing up to five thousand words a day on the story; but little of it was printed, because of decent editors. Harding was ready to come out with an official denial, but he was restrained by his wife. In the end, he remained true to his philosophy of simply ignoring the unpleasant. It also fitted in with Boies Penrose's more worldly-wise advice, "From what I hear, we've been having a lot of trouble holding the nigger vote lately." [35] Democrats even alleged that the Republicans were deliberately spreading the story to keep the Negro vote in line.

In fact, the story did not hurt Harding except in the Deep South, which was Democratic anyway. "No man," declared one observer, "ever suffered from abuse of the degree of nastiness which finally marked that campaign. Nor has any man gained more politically from abuse than Harding did; nor has any man gained more from patience and silence under abuse of the most provocative kind." [36]

The more the smears, the more the kindly light of Harding's noble resignation seemed to shine above them. Nobody really believed that such a fine-looking, hawk-nosed, gray-eyed specimen could have Negro blood. The accusation was a vile plot by rabid Democrats, as indeed it was.

The interest of the episode was that anyone should have thought it even an issue that Harding could have been a mulatto. Americans were, on the whole, a mongrel race. Negroes were among the oldest Americans. Harding himself was said to have wondered whether or not one of his ancestors had jumped the fence. Recent ethnologists have estimated that nearly three-quarters of the Negro people and one-fifth of the Caucasian people have mixed origins. In 1920, of course, such a conclusion would have seemed a shocking heresy. The flood tide of racism was at its height after the war, with the Ku Klux Klan stirring again in the South and with the grim warnings of Madison Grant and Lothrop Stoddard about the Passing of the Great White Race Under the Rising Tide of Color. Harding campaigned at a time when racism was an issue, and the failure of this issue to hurt him was a tribute to his good sense, to his good looks, and to the good taste of the American people in the North and the West. A smear has two sides; often it smears only its users.

The other bogey of the election was the women's vote. It proved to be a chimera. Before American women voted for the first time in a Presidential election in the North and the South, no one knew how they would behave. It was Cox's belief that the women's vote would have given victory to the Democrats if the Republicans had not spread stories that entry into the League meant that American boys would have to fight in foreign wars.[37] This was another illusion. In fact, the novelty of votes for women produced two results: a larger Republican vote and more indifference to voting. In Baltimore, for instance, more than one-third of the registered Republicans were female, but less than one-third of the registered Democrats. An analysis of the election in Chicago revealed the same pattern: Republican women tended to go to the polls more than Democratic women.

In general, fewer women voted than men, and they voted much

as their male relatives did. The women's vote did not exist as a separate vote; or, if it did, it merely increased the normal Republican majority. Even if Harding had voted against the Nineteenth Amendment, women voters would not have punished him at the polls. Indeed, only the predominantly male delegates at Chicago would have punished him, by thinking wrongly that he was no longer available. As Frank Kent later observed, the only sound principle for the candidate to observe in regard to the woman voter was not to worry about her. There was no such thing as sex solidarity in politics.[38]

The final vote in the election of 1920 is usually taken as a proof that there was no interest in the personalities of the campaign. The fact that, for the first time in a century, less than one in two American voters bothered to cast their ballots for the Presidency is taken to mean that only a minority cared enough about Harding or Cox to support them. Such an interpretation suited the progressive view of history, and there were many disillusioned progressives in 1920. "Disgusted. Not going to vote for any of them," was frequently recorded on the straw votes collected by the *Literary Digest* just before the election.[39] Thus the interpretation of the election as a negative vote for Harding was born.

In fact, the election result showed a large positive *male* vote for Harding. For several reasons, his landslide victory was smaller than it should have been. First, the early result of the election in "barometric Maine" indicated a huge Republican victory. Second, every straw poll and every commentator predicted a large Republican win. It did not seem worth the voter's while to go to the polls. There was less interest in the election than normal only because *everyone knew that Harding was going to win.* He had become enormously and personally popular during the campaign.

Indeed, the size of Harding's victory showed his appeal. He won 60.2 per cent of the popular vote, while Cox won only 34.4 per cent, and the jailed Socialist leader Eugene Debs won 5.4 per cent. Harding carried every state outside the South, and he even won 40.3 per cent of the vote there. The reason for the low turnout of 49.3 per cent of the eligible voters to the polls was entirely a question of the women's vote. Women were not used to voting and did not vote. In Illinois, the only state where the votes of men and women were counted separately, 74.1 per cent of the men voted and only 46.5 per cent of the women. But the total vote in Illinois was 10.7 per cent above the national average. In the South, where woman suffrage was unpopular, women ignored the election almost completely. A careful analysis of the vote showed that men probably voted in much the same numbers as they had since 1904, while the women's vote represented about 35 per cent of eligible women voters.[40] Outside the West, women were not used to voting, and it would take decades of political education to bring them to the polls as frequently as men.

Thus the low turnout of voters for Harding was not due to their indifference to him, but due to the fear of women in exercising their new right. Harding did well to win handsomely in an election that had had few popular issues and little excitement. He was so predictably the victor that the wonder was that anyone bothered to vote for him at all. As it was, he won the largest personal victory in a century, gaining 16,143,407 popular votes and 404 electoral votes to Cox's 9,130,328 popular votes and 127 electoral votes. He carried even Tennessee and Oklahoma. As Joseph Tumulty said, "It wasn't a landslide; it was an earthquake."

The size of Harding's victory stunned the commentators, who were prepared to attribute it to everything except the main cause—the Republican candidate's immense appeal to rural nostalgia. The anti-League newspapers said that the vote had been a solemn referendum against the League. The pro-League newspapers said that it had been no referendum on the League, and if it had been, at least ten million pro-League Republicans had voted for Harding with the expectation that he would change his stand and favor the League. The whole League idea, indeed, had originally been a Republican one, Theodore Roosevelt's own; it still had much support among Republicans.[41] The truth was that both parties were split on the League question, and few were prepared to allow considerations of the League to influence their choice of a candidate for the White House. As a later historian of the phenomenon of isolationism noted, the election of 1920 was important in its history,

not because of the way people voted, but because of "the dangerously simple popular interpretation of the result" as a solemn referendum against the League.[42]

More plausible were those who thought that the vote showed
only how much Wilson was hated. *The Nation* called "the Mario-
nette" Harding's election "the gift of Mr. Wilson, and of no one
else." The League of Nations debate had appealed only to the
intellectuals. The people had voted "with the profoundest shame
that such a choice should be laid before the American electorate." [43] William Allen White thought Harding's victory was
neither personal nor political, but "a barbaric yawp of enraged
democracy at the incompetency of the Democratic Party." [44]
Hatred of Wilson and of the Democratic conduct of the war was
a factor in the Republican victory, particularly in the large protest
vote of the German-Americans. But commentators failed to give
Harding credit for his popular appeal.

Harding had always been careful to woo the German-American
vote in Ohio. He married into a German-American family. He
spoke the language that German-Americans and other recent
immigrants understood, the language of patriotism and home and
country. He seemed, as a prominent Democrat sneered, like five
million other men of the country. "No higher compliment," another commentator remarked, "could have been paid him." [45]

Because so many male voters identified themselves with this
small-town editor who made good, Harding received the greatest
plurality for a century. If one of the functions of a democratic
President is to make the average voter identify with the man in
the White House, Harding was a master at conveying this sense
of identification. In political skill, he was well above the average;
but part of his political skill consisted in conveying a sense that
he was no better than the average man could hope to become.
Walter Lippmann noticed that Harding's image represented a
definite philosophy. Harding thought that he was marked for
leadership because there were no marks on him. He was the
normal man demanded in abnormal times. The Presidency had
grown too big for one man, and the country did not want a

superman playing the dictator. Thus a President should represent the harmonizer among a group of best minds in the Senate and in the Cabinet.

"That the glory of the normal should be presented to a weary nation as the purest Republican doctrine according to the Fathers," Lippmann concluded, "is one of those paradoxes which, Mr. Chesterton says, always sit beside the wells of truth." It was primitive Democratic doctrine, based on the thinking of William Jennings Bryan and the South, that anybody could govern, that leadership was dangerous, and that excellence was somewhat un-American. The Whigs and Republicans, from the days of the Hamilton whom Harding admired, had officially called for the leadership of great men, although they had sometimes chosen as Presidential nominees mere regents of the Senate.[46]

The glory of the normal needed a man like Harding, whose manner made the normal seem glorious, to become a successful political philosophy. What confused the commentators was the fact that the small town was under attack in novels and urban newspapers and census returns for the first time in American history. It seemed unpopular, and Harding represented its ideal to perfection. Therefore, his huge majority could not have been *for* him. But the fact that the small town was a declining institution compared with the booming cities obscured the more potent fact that its ethic was still dominant in both city and country at the time of Harding's election. And Harding, from a lifetime of experience, knew how to represent and appeal to that ethic.

In a time of strikes and inflation and postwar discontent, Harding knew how to voice the dream of the rural past and of normality. He was "shrewd unto vacuity," a political artist, while Cox was a mere political artisan.[47] His confident manner and dignified bearing and stance on petty or major issues persuaded a great many voters that he could bring back the time of the golden past, before the slum and the machine. He was a town boomer who radiated confidence when confidence was badly needed. This was his chosen and deliberate role. By sure instinct, he brought about his own success. For in himself he represented many of the myths most dear to America's rural heart and past. He was the embodiment of the small-town myths that had displaced the myths of Turner's frontier, as the village had displaced the wilderness, and before the city would displace the village.

Thus Harding won his great victory. And soon he would be forced to solve great problems. He had now to choose among the best minds, and their advice was conflicting. Nearly all of them wanted to be in his Cabinet, and places there were few. He had to start on the impossible task of choosing among his friends and yet preserving party peace. "The new President will prefer harmony," the *New Republic* pointed out, "but he will not know how to get it." [48] And Woodrow Wilson commented on Harding's victory, "How can he lead when he does not know where he is going?" [49]

Part Two

THE REALITY
OF POWER

"If you are as happy, my dear sir, on entering this house as I am in leaving it and returning home, you are the happiest man in this country."

EX-PRESIDENT BUCHANAN TO PRESIDENT LINCOLN

"I haven't had a happy moment in this job."

WARREN HARDING

II

The Best Minds

"God, I can't be an ingrate!"   WARREN HARDING

With the reality of power to come, the burden of choosing a Cabinet came to rest on Harding. And here he was temporarily disillusioned by one of his own pet myths: that the best minds of the country would help him to arrive at the ideal choice. He was to discover that superficial party harmony among the best minds had ended the day that the election results were in. And even that harmony had been disturbed by the quarrel over the League. Now the best minds quarreled for place and power. As a shrewd observer during the election had written to Harding's friend Charles Hard, "the factional troubles are a closed incident for the present. I presume after the election is over that these gentlemen will pull one another's hair, especially those who are seeking the pie counter." [1]

The best minds did indeed offer a great deal of conflicting advice about which of the best minds should grace Harding's Cabinet. And here the Old Guard of the Senate received their first shock. The man whom they liked to think was their second-rate nominee showed that he intended to choose his own collection of best minds. He would not accept the dictation of Lodge or anyone else over the composition of the Cabinet. It would be *his* Cabinet;

he had been elected President by the vast majority of the American people. A friendly Ohio editor had told him that he was "not under obligation to any body for his nomination *except to . . . people from Ohio.*" Procter had verified that the Senators had "tried to work in a couple of other candidates before they came to Harding." [2] In fact, whatever his public expression of gratitude to the Senators, Harding privately knew that they had not helped him much at Chicago. And he showed this knowledge by appointing no incumbent Senators to the Cabinet, except for the bad appointment of Fall of New Mexico.

Harding, indeed, soon found out that the role of listening to the best minds and choosing amidst their conflicting advice gave him a superiority, a sense of being *above* petty considerations of place and power. "I am just beginning to realize," he wrote to Jennings, "what a job I have taken over. The man who has a Cabinet to create has one tremendous task. I find I am called upon to be rather impersonal about it and put aside some of my very intimate views of men and give some consideration to the public estimate of available timber." [3]

Harding's sense of isolation and withdrawal grew. He felt himself more and more unique, the only President, the chosen of the nation, and his old friends, sensing this new feeling, also drew back. He described this change of personality to his fellow Masons at Columbus. "There is an aloofness of one's friends [to the President-elect], and that is one of the sad things; and in me there is a deepening sense of responsibility. I have found already there is intrigue and untruth that must be guarded against. One must ever be on his guard. This everlasting standing on one's guard spoils a man. I wish for an atmosphere of truth and sincerity in government . . . an autocracy of service." [4]

Harding, aloof and suspicious inwardly, although outwardly as cordial and receptive as ever, chose his Cabinet by his own criteria. These he listed in order for reporters. The first consideration was the proposed Cabinet officer's fitness for public service. The second was *the attitude of the public* toward the appointment. Harding, who wanted to be the best-loved if not the best President, resolved to have a popular group of best minds about him.

The third consideration was "the political consideration." Harding, as determined a partisan as ever, declared shortly, "This is going to be a Republican cabinet." [5] And there was a fourth and unmentioned consideration: Harding's *personal* choice of friends to whom he felt gratitude and in whom he trusted.

It was during this period of choosing the Cabinet that a newly discovered letter of Thomas Jefferson was shown to Harding. Two of Jefferson's phrases must have struck chords of sympathy in Harding's heart. "My theory has always been," Jefferson had written, in the true style of the American boomer, "that if we are to dream, the flatteries of hope are as cheap, and pleasanter than the gloom of despair." Also, Jefferson had foretold Harding's belief that good business meant good men. "Men are disposed to live honestly, if the means of doing so are open to them." [6] By giving some men the means of serving their country in the Cabinet, Harding also believed that they would be disposed to live honestly.

The first and most important choice, that of Secretary of State, was easy to make. Harding refused to take the elder statesman of the party, Elihu Root, for this position. He was too old at seventy-six, and Harding did not want him, although Root had strong backing in the Senate. Nicholas Murray Butler claimed that Harding offered him the position, but this claim is unsubstantiated. Since Harding saw Charles Evans Hughes on December 10, *before* seeing Butler, and told him then that no one else had been asked to be Secretary of State, Harding should be believed, especially since Hughes accepted the offer of Cabinet rank at once.

After Hughes's appointment, Harding resisted strong pressure from the Old Guard to put some "amiable and colorless futility" in the place of Hughes, who had publicly supported the League of Nations. This "futility" would take orders from the Senate. Lodge and the Foreign Relations Committee were in a state of "revolt" against Harding's independence. But Harding stood firm and stuck by Hughes, whom he much admired. In February, he told reporters of Hughes's appointment and declared that it was the policy of his Administration to give Hughes full control over foreign affairs. He would not be another Wilson and dictate to his own Secretary of State. Nor, the implication was, would the Senate be allowed to dictate.[7]

Harding's next major appointment was also a slap at the Senators, who had expected to control him. He chose as Secretary of Commerce the most popular administrator in the country, and the man least liked by professional politicians, Herbert Hoover. Hoover had made a large fortune in mining enterprises around the world. He had gained the reputation of being an international philanthropist and efficiency expert by his brilliant handling of relief programs in Belgium and Europe. Harding's first two qualifications for Cabinet office—fitness for public service and the attitude of the people—were amply filled by the appointment of Hoover. Moreover, the new Secretary of Commerce came originally from Iowa and was a resident of California. Thus he gave the West and the progressives Cabinet status.

Nothing shows Harding's determination to be independent more than his appointment of Hoover. He even ignored the advice of Daugherty over the matter. Daugherty wrote to Harding that "a great many prominent persons in Washington" had insisted on seeing him to try to stop Hoover's appointment. None of the progressives, according to Daugherty, were friendly to Hoover; they would be embarrassed if he were appointed. Particularly hostile were the powerful Insurgent Senators, Borah and Johnson and Norris, and Harding's personal backers, Senators Curtis and Smoot.[8]

Harding, however, was not to be deterred from his picking among the best minds, even if other best minds and friends disagreed with him. "I am sorry," he replied to Daugherty, "that so many people impress you as hostile to Mr. Hoover to a place in the Cabinet. Of course, I do not want the administration to start out with a quarrel with the Senate or any considerable faction in the Republican Party. I do hold him in very high esteem and think *his appointment would appeal to the cordial approval of the country*. The more I consider him the more do I come to think well of him. Of course, I have no quarrel with those who do not think as I do, but *inasmuch as I have the responsibility to assume I think my judgement must be trusted in the matter*." [9]

Hoover, in his own memoirs, says that Harding asked him to join the Cabinet soon after the election result. According to Hoover, he was offered the choice between the Department of Commerce and the Department of the Interior. If that is true, then Harding could have made no deal with the oil interests at Chicago to give over control of the Department of the Interior to a representative of the oil interests. Hoover wrote that he *chose* the Department of Commerce. He then heard nothing for three months, because of Senatorial opposition, including that of Penrose and Lodge. Harding stuck by him and secured the promise of Penrose's and Lodge's support in return for accepting their nominee for the Secretary of the Treasury, the billionaire financier from Pittsburgh, Andrew Mellon. Harding told Hoover that he had declared, "Mellon and Hoover or no Mellon." [10]

Over the selection of the Secretary of the Treasury, Harding was prepared to listen to others. Throughout his life, he held a superstitious awe of the mental processes of the very rich self-made man. And Mellon was reputedly the second-richest man in the world. He practically owned Pittsburgh, and his banking interests had underwritten $1,500,000 of the campaign deficit of the Republicans. Both the financier's personal prestige and the financial situation of the Republican Party dictated the choice of Andrew Mellon as Secretary of the Treasury. He was also highly desirable to the business world, who divined correctly that Mellon would reduce taxes on the rich and cut the national debt.

A conspiracy of the financial press soon persuaded Harding and the country that the unassuming Mellon was indeed the greatest Secretary of the Treasury since Alexander Hamilton, Harding's boyhood hero. Harding shared in the popular American belief that a few great international figures controlled the economic destiny of the world. The thing was to employ one of them in the service of the nation, and the result would be prosperity for all and not merely for himself. Harding died still firmly holding the belief that the very rich really did have the best minds of all. He termed Mellon "the ubiquitous financier of the universe" and considered his appointment to the Cabinet a stroke of good fortune.[11] It proved, however, the ill fortune of his country that Mellon was still Secretary of the Treasury at the time of the Great Depression. Another powerful banker was selected for an important part in Harding's Administration. Harding sincerely believed that government spending should be cut and that businessmen and bankers were the only people who knew how to cut it. Charles G. Dawes of the Central Union Trust Company of Illinois had long been a financial power in the Republican Party. He had become a general in the American Expeditionary Force in France, but only as a businessman in uniform in charge of military buying and spending. He was chiefly known for his uncommon oath "Hell 'n Maria," which he claimed was merely a corruption of his boyhood curse "Helen Maria." [12] As a backer of Lowden, his appointment to office would satisfy a segment of the Republican Party.

Harding had called Dawes in early to discuss Cabinet posts. If Mellon had refused the Treasury, Dawes would probably have received the office, despite his professed unwillingness for the position. "I fully appreciate," Dawes wrote to Harding, "that you are not making up your cabinet along the lines of least resistance— that, when your cabinet is announced, it will be your own cabinet." [13] Harding replied that he had always felt "very strongly disposed" toward appointing Dawes as Secretary of the Treasury, but that he was still fitting "the machinery of administration together" to suit his own "wishes and ideas concerning an organization for service." [14] In this process of fitting the machinery together, Dawes came out as a lesser cog than Mellon. He was later offered, and he accepted, the post of Director of the Budget, in charge of cutting government spending in all departments. Harding promised Dawes his full support in his campaign for economy at Washington, and he was reported to have chosen Dawes as his successor in the White House. [15]

To counteract the image of government by rich bankers, Harding needed to put a conservative workingman in the delicate post of Secretary of Labor. He found a perfect specimen in "Puddler Jim" Davis, an old-time ironworker turned banker. James J. Davis did not have one of the best minds, but he had the right frame of mind for a businessman's government. He believed, as Harding did, from the experience of their own lives, that poor boys could make good and rule the country. The rich were rich because they had taken their chance. Davis proved personally what Harding believed: that equality of opportunity existed for the poor as well as for the Mellons. "I have been a puddler of iron," he said "and I would be a puddler of men." As he also declared in a funeral tribute to Harding, that typical and admirable American of common sense, "There is not a bright boy belonging to the American working class who cannot obtain a collegiate education or its equivalent with little difficulty. There is no American man so humble in our time who is not virtually better off than the proudest of a few centuries ago." [16]

For the equally delicate post of Secretary of Agriculture, Harding chose the editor of a farm journal in Iowa, Henry C. Wallace. Wallace was a moderate progressive from the discontented prairie belt. He could be counted on to soothe the farmers, whose anger at falling farm prices in the summer of 1920 had helped Harding to his gigantic victory.

With the choice of Hughes and Hoover, Mellon and Dawes, Davis and Wallace, Harding felt that he had done his duty by the various interests and groups in the country. In the most important positions in the Cabinet, he had put men of proved public service, either generally popular or favored by large sections of the community. The remaining appointments to the Cabinet could be made on a political or a personal basis. They were to be a group of the best party men or of the best personal friends—men of good minds if not of the best minds. The Cabinet was, for Harding, a mixture of both a committee and a club.

The first and most important appointment was a debt of gratitude. Harding offered Daugherty the Department of Justice and the post of Attorney General. In a private conversation with William Howard Taft, Harding said that he could see through Harry Daugherty when Daugherty did not suspect it, but that Daugherty was loyal and a good lawyer. Taft replied that Harding was entitled to have such a friend in the Cabinet.[17] Thus it was as a *faithful servant*, not as a *hidden master*, that Harding asked Daugherty to serve in the Cabinet. Finley Peter Dunne, who met Harding and Daugherty in Florida at the time of the appointment, described the relationship in such terms. "Harding's middle name was Gamaliel. But no Paul ever sat at the feet of another Gamaliel more humbly than Daugherty did at the feet of this one. I believe that if Harding had refused him the appointment he would have gone into a corner and cried. But then he would have wiped away the tears and come back and served as faithfully as ever."

It was to Dunne that Daugherty declared his intention of running the Department of Justice as well as he could. "There'll be no politics or graft in my office," he declared, apparently sincerely.[18] And he was hurt, as Harding was hurt, at the storm of party and newspaper criticism that greeted his appointment. Instead of choosing a best mind, *The New York Times* sneered, Harding had been content "to choose merely a best friend." [19]

Harding's thin-skinned attitude toward criticism and his streak of stubbornness immediately showed themselves. "It isn't fair," he said. "This premature criticism is a serious menace to popular government. Unhappily it is a tendency in our journalistic practice. I don't like it. It amounts to jumping on a man before he has had opportunity to demonstrate his ability or intention." Harding had already begun to identify his personal preference with popular government. And his continued remarks should have warned both himself and Daugherty of trouble to come. "After there has been malfeasance in office, then go after that man. Go after him hard. But don't make any imputation in advance of action." [20]

Harding's other appointment, which brought disaster to his Administration and a flood of adverse criticism from the newspapers, was the choice of Senator Albert B. Fall of New Mexico as the Secretary of the Interior. There is no question that Fall was Harding's own choice. He had long been friendly to Fall and had perhaps considered him as a possible Secretary of State. Before his death, Roosevelt had been a supporter of Fall and had chosen Fall to put him in nomination for the Presidency in 1916. To personal liking of Fall, Harding added the political consideration that the old followers of Roosevelt would like to see Fall in an office that was normally reserved for a man from the West. Knowledge of Fall's connections with the oil interests in New

Mexico and the evident readiness of Fall to accept the Department of the Interior should perhaps have warned Harding. The newspapers were only too willing to do so, once the lanky, mustachioed oil operator was selected. In the face of criticism, however, Harding showed his usual stubbornness. He was too vain a man to think that he could be mistaken about the qualities of his friends or his picked best minds. "Few men ought to know more about men than Mr. Harding," a journalist commented ironically. "Few have had more friends. . . . Four years from now President Harding will know who his friends are." [21]

The rest of the Cabinet appointees were mainly political. Will Hays was given the chief patronage department, the office of the Postmaster General. He would now be expected to reward the faithful whom he had organized for victory. The post of Secretary of War went to a rich man and ex-Senator from Massachusetts, John W. Weeks. Like Mellon, he had contributed heavily to the Republican campaign. He had had some experience in Congress in war finance and could be passed off as a reasonable mind. Finally, when Lowden refused the minor post of Secretary of the Navy, the job went to another millionaire, Edwin Denby, a surprise choice who "didn't even know enough about Harding's thought of him to be a sad Cinderella." [22] A rich man approaching fifty years of age, Denby had joined the Marines as a private when war had been declared. His appointment was expected to boost morale while the battleships of America were scrapped for the sake of economy. Instead, his indolence involved him in disgrace over the Teapot Dome.

The process of choice by which Harding arrived at the final selection of his Cabinet was described by Mark Sullivan. The prospect of his high office had already begun to make Harding circumspect. In the beginning, Sullivan said, Harding had wanted to fill the Cabinet with old political friends and associates. "If Harding had chosen his Cabinet the day after his election, it would have been much more nearly a Cabinet of politicians than it now is. Harding, as his position grew upon him, and as he rose to it, went through a process of growth readily apparent to those about him. He realized increasingly that his responsibility was less and less to his party and more to something broader. Out of that four months of growth there are at least two casualties, two men who, by every warm impulse of Harding's heart, were destined for the intimacy of his official family, but who fell outside as sacrifice to a newly elected President's increasing responsiveness to considerations other than personal." [23]

As with Baron Clive's defense of his division of the spoils in India, Warren Harding could justly be amazed at his own moderation. He had denied places in the Cabinet to all his friends in the Senate save Albert Fall and to all his political friends save Harry Daugherty. He had resisted the advice of the Senate in his choice of Hughes and Hoover, and he had kept the most important posts from the hands of the party nominees. He could feel proud of his own independence and could feel misunderstood by the popular press. He had already come a long way from being a regular wheelhorse of Buckeye politics or the Old Guard of the Senate.

The newspapers, indeed, did receive the news of Harding's Cabinet with mixed feelings. But, above all, their main note was one of relief. There was certainly somebody for everybody. Only Fall and Daugherty were considered beyond the respectable pale. *Collier's* summed up the general feeling that Harding's appointments had been "spotty; some very good and some very bad." [24] Altogether, the newspapers were ready to give Harding the benefit of the doubt until he and his Cabinet could prove themselves in office.

In other appointments, however, Harding showed how little he had escaped from the Buckeye notion that now the victory was won, it was time to think of the division of the spoils among friends. It was in these posts of importance outside the Cabinet that Harding placed the intimate and the unfit. It was petty administration by crony. Harding wanted, in the manner of the *grand seigneur*, to distribute largess to his favorites. He was vain and human enough to wish for the reputation of the good man who did not forget his old friends. "God," he is supposed to have said, "I can't be an ingrate!"

Thus the old Marion doctor Charles Sawyer became "the

suddenest brigadier general in all history" and the White House physician. Harding's companion in drinking and parlor stories, Ed Scobey, became Director of the Mint. The Reverend Heber Votaw, who had married Harding's sister, took over as Superintendent of Federal Prisons—a more important job than the one the young Harding had begged for another sister in the Ohio State Kindergarten for the Blind. Daniel Crissinger, a local banker and friend from Marion, became Comptroller of Currency and later Governor of the Federal Reserve System. Another Marion boy, Henry Hane, became a bank examiner. The adventurer Colonel Forbes refused the Governorship of Alaska, but landed first the Bureau of War Risk Insurance and then the Veterans' Bureau. Elmer Dover, Marcus Hanna's old secretary, became Assistant Secretary of the Treasury, in control of Customs and Internal Revenue, where he swore to "Hardingize" the service.

Other appointments went as payments for favors. Twenty-three of the major diplomatic jobs were reserved for party and personal friends, such as George Harvey and Myron Herrick. And Leonard Wood, Harding's enemy, was sent away to the Philippines, Harding's old concern in the Senate. "No single appointment," Harding assured Wood, "has given me more concern than this particular one." [25] The Philippines were indeed important, but more important was the removal of political rivals from the domestic scene. To the vanquished belong the hinterlands. Over minor matters of patronage, Harding did not apply at first the principle of the best minds. He applied three other rules: that efficient friends and party regulars came first, that patronage was the grease of the party system, and that he should be consulted personally. Few Presidents have occupied themselves more in office with the question of postmasters and political appointees. Harding did not even trust Daugherty enough to let him choose all his underlings alone.

Harding quickly found out that there were too few jobs for too many people. And he inherited a vexing problem from Woodrow Wilson, whose early years in office had been spent replacing Republican postmasters with Democratic ones. In 1917, however, Wilson had decided to listen to the recommendations of the Civil

Service Reform League and had issued an executive order requiring the post offices to be given to the best candidates on merit. In two thousand subsequent cases, the post offices had been divided fairly equally between Republicans and Democrats, after candidates had taken an examination.

Harding, however, when he came to office, was under heavy pressure from Republicans who had promised spoils to their supporters after their victory. On the other hand, progressive reformers insisted that Harding should make all offices open to the winner of a civil-service examination. Harding compromised, as usual, caught in the dilemma of reconciling politics with the merit system.[26] He issued an order making post office appointments open to one of the first three candidates in the examination. In practice, this usually left appointment to the office in the hands of the party machine or the local Senator or the Cabinet officer or the President. "I have been strongly urged by the leading Congressmen of my own party," Harding told the reformers, "so to arrange it that only Republican postmasters will be appointed." [27] In fact, after his executive order about one candidate from the first three receiving the position, in less than half the cases did the winner of the examination get the job. Equality of opportunity to become the local postmaster did not exist for the local best minds.

In many cases, there was no competition for political jobs. By executive order, Harding appointed the postmaster at Marion. In Westerville, he asked Mary Lee to take the civil-service examination, but promised her the post office in advance: "It will not be necessary for you to study up in order to prepare for the test. Most of the grading is based on business reputation and general standing in the community. . . . Please do not have any worries about coming into the realization of the promise made to you. I should be disappointed in the discriminating power of the Executive if he could not choose a post office appointee. . . ." [28] Harding was even prepared to intervene personally with the Postmaster General on behalf of a friend of thirty-five years' standing, who, although too old to take the civil-service examination, should have the post office at Bedford, Virginia.[29]

Usually, however, Harding adopted the method of keeping local Republican political machines and most Senators sweet by turning over minor patronage to them. "If a considerate attitude toward one of your friends," he wrote to Senator John Sharp Williams of Mississippi, "is the price of your continued friendship for me I am disposed to retain a reverent regard for your request." [30] He arranged for Scobey and Colonel Creager to take over the Republican machine in Texas by giving them the patronage. This was in response to a preconvention agreement that Scobey could make promises of office to certain delegates if they would eventually support Harding at the nominating convention. Although Harding did not give Scobey all the patronage he wanted, he went "a long ways" toward doing so.[31] He even proposed to use an executive order to put one of Scobey's men in office, a method of "helping without cheating." [32]

Yet Harding could be as relentless at breaking promises over patronage as any Wilson. "I am not particularly interested," he wrote coldly to Daugherty about the patronage of New Mexico, "in carrying out the political contracts which were made in that State in 1920." [33] And in Ohio good friends were ignored by the score, including the faithful Jennings and the powerful Newton Fairbanks. As a disappointed office seeker wrote to Fairbanks, anyone who, like Harding, "ignores his party in appointments to offices usually comes out the short end of the horn. That was the chief charge against Woodrow. He ignored the men who helped him and appointed men whom he wanted to appoint on the theory that his friends would stick by him and he would make new friends among the men whom he appointed and their friends. The net result of the performance was that he alienated the men who made him and the new friends he made either did not interfere in politics or had no appreciable influence in politics. After all, people are still human and ill treatment does not bring friendships." [34]

Harding's excuse for his seeming ingratitude was a reasonable one. He hated criticism about bad appointments and sinecures for political friends. He claimed, indeed, that he gave so many jobs to Buckeye men that "the constant cry here in Washington is that 'Ohio gets everything.'" He supposed that no one could be

President and keep half the people in his home state satisfied about patronage. "I have long since," Harding confessed, "given up the expectation of making everybody happy." [35]

Harding, indeed, as he continued in office in the White House, grew increasingly dissatisfied about the traditional views of patronage. He reverted to his original idea that perhaps the best minds should get the best places, even in the lower ranks of government. Several significant incidents in the battle over patronage showed that Harding grew more and more in stature as President after he had made the preliminary mistake of giving powerful jobs to some hack politicians from Ohio.

The first incident showed Harding's increasing suspicion of Daugherty. Daugherty recommended a candidate to be postmaster at Columbus. Harding then checked with Jennings to find out his opinion of Daugherty's candidate. Jennings replied that Daugherty's man was a "rough neck" of the butcher type and had been accused of shady dealings.[36] The result was that the term of the existing postmaster was extended, and a new one was not chosen before Harding's death. The discredit and venality of the Prohibition appointees—officially under Daugherty's ultimate control—did not serve to convince Harding that Daugherty picked good men.

The second disillusionment that Harding suffered was through his attempt to build up a vital Republican Party in the South by giving declared Republicans the jobs. The Grand Old Party in Dixie remained venal and inefficient. "Alas," Harding confessed to Lodge, "I grow discouraged whenever I contemplate the question of patronage in a state like that of Georgia. I sought to encourage the organization of a new party down there, and I thought we had brought into it a number of people who would give us some hope of Republican success and at the same time help us to bring high-grade men into the public service." [37] But low-grade men and turncoat Democrats continued to run the Republican Party below the Potomac.

The third disillusionment was the attempts by the politicians to put unqualified men into positions that Harding had decided should be run only by the best minds. When Daugherty asked for a place on the Shipping Board for an Ohio friend, Harding replied that he had promised its chairman that the board would not be an "institution for the distribution of political patronage." Harding's pride in doing a good job as President came before his wish to help his friends' friends. "We simply cannot have that sort of administration," he declared.[38] His campaign for economy meant the elimination of the superfluous jobholder. It was not the plan to create a body, he wrote to the head of the Washington Commission to the Brazilian Exposition, merely to give paid positions to appointees who were rendering no service.[39]

Harding particularly disliked bad recommendations to office made by powerful local Republicans. The discredit for making these bad appointments landed on himself, and Harding loathed criticism. Once he offered to publish the list of endorsers of a particularly bad candidate for office, and they all withdrew their endorsements. "It's a damned shame," he complained to a friend, "that so many men not only lack the courage to say 'no' when an unfit candidate seeks their indorsement, but also have the cowardice to unload the responsibility on the appointing power." [40] To Daugherty, Harding sent a confidential memorandum about one appointee in whom he had "come to cancel" his own satisfaction. "This is one of the frequent disappointments which come of accepting organization recommendations in a political situation." [41]

As canniness and disillusionment were thrust on Harding, so he inclined more and more to a system of choice by merit and best minds. The Cabinet was split over the spoils system, with Hughes and Hoover and Mellon and Wallace favoring appointment by merit and with Daugherty and Davis and Fall favoring appointment by political favor. When, however, the showdown came between Elmer Dover of Ohio and Andrew Mellon, Harding chose to keep the best mind of Mellon rather than the spoils system of Dover. Dover had tried to sack long-term employees in the civil service in order to put in Buckeye friends. Mellon insisted on efficiency as the only criterion in the Treasury Department. When he threatened resignation if Dover's policies were carried out, Harding was too fearful of losing the greatest Secretary of the Treasury since Alexander Hamilton to allow Dover to continue the policies of patronage. Dover resigned, and Mellon stayed, and the Treasury Department was exempt from the spoils system.[42]

In fact, as Harding grew more and more into the role of President, so his belief grew in his own judgment and in the judgment of the best minds that *he* had chosen to help him. When ex-Senator Fall chose to resign before the oil scandal of Teapot Dome, Harding's faith in his own judgment was hardly altered. He shifted Hubert Work, who had taken over Will Hays's place as Postmaster General, to the Department of the Interior, and he placed ex-Senator New of Indiana in the Cabinet—to the fury of the whole Republican machine in Indiana, including both of its Senators. The gradual discovery of the inefficiency and corruption of many of his personal and Buckeye appointees made Harding want to choke such disloyal friends, but it did not shake his faith in himself as a chooser of men. He had, after all, made the brilliant choices of Hughes and Hoover and Mellon for the highest positions. All he had to do was to extend the principle of the best minds down to the lower ranks of government.

Thus Harding, by the end of his short term in the White House, was growing out of his traditional belief in the need for political patronage and into his new belief in the need for the best minds to rule everywhere. His vanity as a President demanded an efficient government, and he could be an ingrate if his reputation were at stake. His pride was greater than his sense of obligation. The gathering scandals of 1923 at last persuaded Harding that the myth of the Best Minds was a true one. They might disagree, but they should be chosen for office rather than best friends. Of course, if they coincided, as in the case of ex-Senator New, this was best of all.

Before his last trip to Alaska, Harding was found in a discouraged state by his speech writer, Judson Welliver. Welliver talked to Harding of a vacant position on the White House staff and wanted to know whether Harding wished to choose a friend for the vacancy. Harding replied that the whole idea of making political capital out of political appointments was "pretty illusory." He had come to believe in the reality of the best minds. "This government ought to be run by the best man," he declared. "Go pick your man and I'll appoint him." [43]

12

Honeymoon of Disharmony

"Really, I think we are getting along measurably well.
I find I cannot carry out my pre-election ideals of an
Executive keeping himself aloof from Congress."

WARREN HARDING, July 14, 1921

At the Inauguration Ceremony on March 4, 1921, Harding looked
healthy and tanned and strong as he rode to the Capitol beside
the emaciated and haggard Wilson. He ran lightly up the Capitol
steps in the flush of his enthusiasm, leaving the stricken Wilson
to take the back elevator to the President's room. A few minutes
before twelve o'clock, it was Senator Lodge, at the head of a
committee, who appeared to announce that the Senate and House
were about to adjourn and awaited President Wilson's pleasure.
Seeing his old enemy and about to be succeeded by his old enemy's
Senatorial henchman, Wilson smiled slightly. "Senator Lodge, I
have no further communication to make," he said. "I thank you.
Good morning." Then he left the room, leaning on his stick, a
private citizen once more.

Shortly afterward, President Harding delivered his Inaugural
Address in his solemn and ponderous style. "Surely," he said,
"there must have been God's intent in the making of this New
World Republic." He repeated his belief in the wisdom of an
inherited policy of noninvolvement in Old World affairs. A

world supergovernment was contrary to the American ideal. "This is not selfishness; it is sanctity. It is not aloofness; it is security. It is not suspicion of others; it is patriotic adherence to the things which made us what we are." Harding took the view that internationalism had been rejected by public mandate; but he said that America was still ready to cooperate in any program to prevent war and, particularly, to increase trade. This declaration boded ill for the League of Nations.

"Our supreme task," Harding continued, "is the resumption of our onward, normal way. Reconstruction, readjustment, restoration—all these must follow. I would like to hasten them." America should put its house in order and get "a rigid and yet sane economy." This could be done by reducing abnormal government spending and abnormal war taxation. Harding warned of wage reductions to come, because prices would reflect "the receding fever of war activities." But the American people must be prepared to give and take. And there was hope, as the forward course of the business cycle was unmistakable.

"I speak for administrative efficiency," Harding declared, "for lightened tax burdens, for sound commercial practices, for adequate credit facilities, for sympathetic concern with all agricultural problems, for the omission of unnecessary interference of government with business, for an end of government's experiment in business, and for more efficient business in government administration." [1] Thus, blithely confident in the old ways of American capitalism, Harding threw aside the idea of deficit spending and federal pump priming, which had given the United States its period of greatest prosperity during the First World War. Harding gladly returned to the old sad cycle of inevitable boom and slump, which only government investment could end. It was a return to "normalcy," in which the radical left wing for once agreed with the mass of the American people. "After Wilson's lofty and deceptive rhetoric," wrote Joseph Freeman, "it was refreshing to have an inaugural address which frankly proclaimed capital's intentions to exploit the world market." [2]

Three major problems occupied Harding in his first months in office. He had three pledges to redeem: the first was to return the country to promised economic normalcy; the second was to work out a scheme of international peace without entering the League of Nations; and the third was to cooperate with Congress from the White House. The reality of power made Harding run into immediate trouble.

Economic normalcy proved to be what G. K. Chesterton called successful capitalism, "not normalcy but abnormalcy." [3] The United States had never known a period of continual boom. And by the summer of 1921, the economy of the country was falling into the pit of a slump. In 1920, agricultural prices had collapsed; and the next year, manufacturing prices followed their example. Real wages, which had averaged $620 in 1919, dropped to $522 within two years. Instead of bringing back the good old days, Harding seemed to have brought with him a severe depression.

To Hoover, the new Secretary of Commerce and one of Harding's financial experts, the slump was a good thing. It was "the result of inflation and disasters from the war" and "the necessary reaction from the foolish post-war boom." It was the fourteenth industrial depression since the Civil War, and America had "come through the thirteen others all right." With greater resources and no less courage, skill, and intelligence, America should meet the disaster in the same ways as before. The system of boom and slump was natural and could not be avoided. For, by Republican faith, private enterprise and government economy must be right. [4] It did not seem possible to Hoover to doubt a system that had failed fourteen times in fifty-five years, although he would certainly have doubted a company that had done so once.

Harding's solution to the slump was to treat it as naturally as did Hoover. He did not try to increase government spending or to make work for people, but he backed Dawes to the hilt in his successful campaign to reduce the budget by more than a billion dollars in one year. He did not increase the spending power of the veterans; in fact, he spoke against a bonus bill for them in a message to Congress and received a letter of "personal thanks" for his "extremely courageous action" from J. P. Morgan of Wall Street. [5] He did, however, allow Mellon to increase the spending power of the rich. To the fury of the farmers and the unions and the veterans, Harding signed Mellon's revenue bill providing for the repeal of the wartime excess-profits tax and a cut in surtax for the rich from 65 per cent to 50 per cent. Taxes on the poor were hardly touched. "Brazenly and impudently," La Follette declared in the Senate, Mellon had laid down the principle that "wealth will not and cannot be made to bear its full share of taxation." [6]

Harding, of course, concurred with Mellon's views. Saving money in large quantities, he had written to a correspondent, was one of the most useful contributions people could make to putting the world right. In fact, the only way to straighten out the tangled finances of the war was to establish again the world's stores of working capital.[7] And this Mellon's financing did, by leaving in the hands of the rich and the stockholders and the corporations more capital to invest. Harding was guilty of giving Mellon his head in increasing the fortunes of the rich without distributing more to the poor. This surplus capital was, in turn, to find its way to the stock market and start the speculative boom that was to end in the Great Depression and in the fracture of the image of Mellon the great financier.

As the depression continued throughout 1921, Harding was worried enough to call a Conference on Unemployment on September 26. He blamed the depression on an "inevitable reaction" after the boom of the war. "To such heights there is necessary ascent and inescapable descent. With the world involved, there is no escape for any of the world from the valleys of depression." With startling resignation, Harding told the conference that he could do nothing to stop the depression other than to continue his policy of getting the government out of business. "Liquidation, reorganization, readjustment, reestablishment, taking account of things done and the sober contemplation of things to be done, the finding of firm ground and the open, sure, and onward way—all these are part of the inevitable, and he who thinks they might have been avoided by this plan or that, or this policy or that, or this international relationship or that, only hugs a delusion."

Nakedly, Harding declared that the unemployed were unemployed because of their own faults. "There is always unemployment," he declared. "Under most fortunate conditions, I am told, there are a million and a half in the United States who are not at work. The figures are astounding only because we are a hundred millions, and this parasite percentage is always with us." Unemployment in 1921 was admittedly excessive, but that was in the nature of things. "There has been vast unemployment before, and will be again. There will be depression after inflation, just as surely as the tides ebb and flow."

Harding pointedly observed to the conference that it was *not* asked to solve the problem of why there had to be inevitable slumps. "We have builded the America of to-day on the fundamentals of economic, industrial, and political life which made us what we are, and the temple requires no remaking now." Unrestricted private enterprise was normalcy. Therefore, slumps were normalcy, too. Harding did admit that relief should be given to mitigate unemployment, but he had little enthusiasm for any proposed relief from the public treasury. In other words, the conference was to solve the problem of unemployment without saying how slumps could be prevented and without spending any federal money to put people to work again.[8] The conference was a failure.

Harding never showed the extreme backwardness of his economic thinking to more disadvantage than in this speech. He spoke as unintelligently about the shibboleths of free enterprise and as heartlessly about the problems of the jobless as any Babbitt in his Rotary Club. Cox's opinion of him should perhaps have disturbed him more: that for a beggar he would cheerfully empty his purse on the way to the Senate and then just as cheerfully vote for some measure against the welfare of the masses.[9] Harding thought that personal charity was the substitute for public welfare, and he excused his cruelty to millions by his kindness to individuals.

Samuel Gompers, the powerful head of the American Federation of Labor, told an interesting story of Harding's basic antipathy to workingmen. At their first meeting, Harding put his arm on Gompers' shoulder and said, "Mr. Gompers, I want your help." At their second meeting, however, Harding dropped his mask of interest in labor's problems and declared bluntly, "The whole trouble with the labor movement, Mr. Gompers, is that you and a lot of other labor men are not advising workmen to accept necessary reductions in wages and give an opportunity for a revival of industry." With that statement, he cut short the interview and left Gompers with the sure impression that the President was only on the side of business.[10] Harding, however, avoided a showdown with the labor unions until his second year in office.

To the discontented farmers, Harding gave the same answers of economic inevitability. On April 21, 1921, the National Farmers' Union presented Harding with a memorial stating that "the farmers are overwhelmed with debt. They are unable to buy necessary fertilizer. They cannot obtain needed credit and there are in hundreds of thousands of cases no markets open to them. This condition they had no part in bringing about. Like the starving child or the undernourished mother in the city they are the innocent victims of a misused economic system, manipulated, we fear, by shortsighted and selfish interests." In an oblique reference to Harding himself, the memorial continued, "Some citizens, who have not felt the sting of adversity, are insisting that things are all right and they will correct themselves. They are living in the enjoyment of great wealth and are wondering why anybody should complain. They know of nothing that should be reformed except the income tax schedule and this they think should be scaled down." But the farmers and the industrial workers wanted government action and reform. They wanted *all* to prosper, not the rich men in the cities to prosper at the expense of the farmer and the worker. "In the war America was a great brotherhood; why in peace should this brotherhood be unscrambled into fragments, each contending with the other for mastery and threatening ruin to the whole economic fabric?" [11]

To this appeal for deliberate action in bringing real economic harmony to the country, Harding replied with resignation. He liked harmony in politics, but he bowed to the law of supply and demand in economics. Parties should stick together, but interests and companies should compete. "Government paternalism," he declared, "whether applied to agriculture or to any other of our great national industries, would stifle ambition, impair efficiency, lessen production and make us a nation of dependent incompetents. The farmer requires no special favors at the hands of the government. All he needs is a fair chance." [12] Later, he told his own Secretary of Agriculture, Henry C. Wallace, that unity among farmers was hopeless, "because of the peculiar economic circumstances of their industry. Every farm is an economic entity by itself. Every farmer is a captain of industry. The elimination of competition among them would be impossible without sacrificing that fine individualism that still keeps the farm the real reservoir from which the nation draws so many of the finest elements of its citizenship." [13]

These platitudes of free enterprise did not satisfy the new and expanding farmers' organizations, which now had powerful allies in the Senate. La Follette and Norris had organized a farm bloc of twenty-seven insurgent Senators who could cause any administration trouble. "Now, Bob, be good," Harding had begged La Follette on his last visit to the Senate before his Inauguration. "I'll be busy, making you be good," La Follette had warned prophetically. [14]

Norris, as chairman of the Senate Committee on Agriculture, was quick to introduce a bill to create a Farmers' Export Financing Corporation. Both Hoover and Mellon opposed the bill, while Wallace supported it. "Do you appreciate, Mr. President," a farmers' lobbyist wrote to Harding, "the extremely serious condition of the farmers of America? They have just lost between five and six billion dollars in the slump in prices of farm products. They have been continuously exploited by our present banking and credit system. They are seeking relief through this export financing corporation." Did Mellon, the ex-banker, have the President's ear or did the Secretary of Agriculture? [15] Harding's reply came through George Christian; he said that Harding listened to all his Cabinet. The farmers were not suffering the slump alone, nor did the bankers exploit them. All was harmonious, in fact, despite these protestations of disharmony. [16]

Norris, however, and the farm bloc in the Senate were not satisfied with Harding's theories of harmony and economic individualism and inevitability. Although the Norris scheme for helping agricultural exports was blocked by the Administration, an alternative plan of a billion dollars' worth of loans through the War Finance Corporation was passed. Speculation in wheat was restricted, and the packing and stockyard industry regulated. A Commission of Agricultural Inquiry was also set up by both Houses of Congress. Its findings and recommendations did little to solve the farm problem. Indeed, Harding came to the conclusion that prosperity could not return to the farm "by legislative formulas but must be the result for the most part of the interplay of economic forces." [17] Nothing much could be done to help the farmer and nothing much should be done.

This superstitious reverence for the blind forces of economics blocked Harding and his Congress from doing anything useful to help alleviate an economic crisis. In fact, Harding did the only thing that he had ever done: he boosted America in the same way that he had once boosted Marion. By talking frequently of the boom to come, if only Americans stuck to the tried-and-true ways of their fathers, the boom would come. It always had, and it always would.

Harding, indeed, by his imperturbable manner, did do something to restore business confidence. Normalcy, Will Hays pointed out, was not an economic condition. It was "a psychological condition . . . a state of mind." At any time and during any Presidency, the state of mind of the country at large was influenced by the state of mind of the man in the White House.[18] While Mellon and Hoover made the businessmen confident with tax cuts and nationalist commercial policies, Harding made the people at large confident by talking of good times coming as surely as good times had once been. Normalcy meant being confident in Harding's wish to let business right itself. And as industrial conditions improved in 1922, normalcy appeared to work for the factories if not for the farms.

In fact, technological advance put an end to the depression, even if Harding's manner also helped to change the business mood of the country. Frederick W. Taylor's theories of scientific management and mass production through the use of assembly lines increased output wherever they were employed. This revolution would have taken place even more quickly in a planned economy, for in depressed industries the innovations were not introduced because of lack of capital. But in the booming industries, Taylor's ideas were added to the findings of the new research teams, and efficiency was improved. Safeguards were installed to protect workers and to prevent the waste of trained labor. Electrical power was brought into increasing use. Although the shipbuilding and textile and coal-mining industries fell back, the automobile industry forged ahead—by the end of the decade, it was to be America's leading industry.

Henry Ford displaced Harding as the most popular man in America. He became the rural folk hero, with his country ways and his Model T and his million cars a year. The cars, in their turn, stimulated new work in the steel and rubber industries, in the construction of highways and garages and hotels. The building industry also boomed, and improved roads made frequent holidays possible on the seacoasts of America. The revolution in communications, which Harding had once welcomed, proliferated in the expanding industries of the radio, the airplane, the movies, advertising, and chemicals. Harding had never stood pat on the expansion of private industry. Now its new discoveries helped to put an end to the depression of his first year in office. The inventors and innovators had saved the economy, not the tried-and-true ways of old-fashioned capitalism.

Harding's second major problem was how to repudiate the League of Nations and yet live in peace with the world. Technically, the United States was still at war with Germany. Thus, on April 12, 1921, Harding sent a message to a special session of Congress. "To establish the state of technical peace without further delay," he declared, "I should approve a declaratory resolution by Congress to that effect, with the qualifications essential to protect all our rights." The resolution was passed, for the Senate was only too pleased to *initiate* legislation on foreign affairs, even if this meant sharing its powers with the House of Representatives.

Congress had now taken over the right of accepting the advantages and reparations and rights accruing to America from the armistice and the Treaty of Versailles without entering into any of the obligations of that treaty. If Congress could declare war, why should not Congress declare peace? This action by Congress established a new precedent and seemed to give it more power over the President. Harding was, however, still in charge of making a formal peace treaty with Germany—something that was done before the end of the year. Through the clever drafting of Hughes, the treaty used much of the language of the Congressional resolution and was thus approved by the Senate.

In his message, Harding also declared his final opposition to the League. Although Hughes had been given full control over foreign affairs and still supported the League with reservations, he found that it would be useless to press Harding to fight the Senate over the matter. The Senate was fresh from its defeat of Wilson, and it would certainly humiliate Harding. The President himself did not want to make the fight. So Hughes was forced to betray the promise that he had made before the election that a Republican administration would enter the League. And Harding again endorsed the position of the Old Guard that the election had indeed been a referendum against the League—which it had not. "There will be no betrayal of the deliberate expression of the American people in the recent election," Harding declared. "The League Covenant can have no sanction by us." [19]

Thus Hughes's policy and Harding's hope of a world association were crushed by the Senate within six weeks of the Inauguration. Hughes decided to swallow his pride and continue to serve. In a letter to a friend, he excused his own and Harding's conduct by saying that if Harding had proposed entry into the League, "he would have wrecked the Administration by involving it in a most bitter fight and he would not have succeeded." [20] America's role in the League was reduced to the sending of "unofficial observers" to its sessions, powerless, helpless eagles without beaks or wings or talons.

The final repudiation of the League and the signing of a separate peace with Germany dashed the last hopes of those who thought that the World War had been fought to engage *all* the nations of the world in putting an end to war. It was obvious to them that

America's refusal to stand by the Allies would encourage a resurgence of German nationalism. "German diplomacy," declared the New York *World*, "for the last two years has recognized only one aim, which is the nullification of the Treaty of Versailles. For all the practical purposes of Berlin the first wedge has been driven into the Treaty of Versailles, and the business of finally wrecking it can be carried on as prudence and opportunity dictate." The Louisville *Courier-Journal* was even more outspoken: "We have now incontinently deserted our associates, ingloriously disowned our obligations; we are international welchers, brazenly withdrawing from the game which we voluntarily entered, our IOU's repudiated, our pockets full of swag." By keeping the spoils of war and refusing the involvements of keeping the peace, the Republicans had made "a sharp deal," indeed. "To-morrow," declared the New York *Globe*, "it will be the memory of shame." [21]

The refusal of Harding and Hughes to fight for some American endorsement of the League may have been politic in view of Senate hostility, but it was dangerous in view of European disillusionment. By putting America first, Harding had put the world last. He refused as President to recognize the end of isolation that he had hymned in 1916. He was still enough afraid of the power of the Old Guard of the Senate to duck a head-on battle with his former colleagues. If they had defeated Wilson, what would they do to him? So in a desperate search for an alternative that would honor his frequent promises for a world association outside the League, Harding again looked to the Senate for a policy. And he found it in the mouth of Borah, the Irreconcilable who had first begun the campaign to scuttle the League.

Borah did not think that national independence and international cooperation were conflicting ideas. In this way, his philosophy represented the ideal compromise for Harding. It reconciled the Irreconcilables to membership in the human race. When the League of Nations put out an active program for world disarmament, Borah saw a clever strategy to spike the League's and America's guns at the same time. He proposed in the Senate a resolution calling for a conference between the three leading naval powers—America, Britain, and Japan—in order to reduce their naval building by half within five years. This plan would preserve American independence, cut government spending, and lessen the probability of war. It could appeal to the nationalist and Republican and pacifist and progressive alike.

Although Harding tried to block Borah's resolution in the Senate in order to steal the credit for holding the disarmament conference, the resolution eventually passed both Houses of Congress at the end of June, 1921, as a rider to a naval appropriations bill. By this time, Harding had been provoked into action. He stated that he did not like "having the Executive hand forced by Congress in the realm of disarmament." [22] But his hand had been forced. He issued informal invitations to a disarmament conference on July 10. And he accepted a cut in the naval building program. Security at home must give way to economy at home and agreement abroad.[23]

Harding was showing early resistance to Senate dictation; but, as yet, the Irreconcilables had beaten him on the issues of the League with reservations and the rebuilding of the American Navy and the timing of a conference on disarmament. Although Harding later claimed that he himself had first thought of the disarmament conference when voting against the League of Nations, the idea was Borah's. Harding also claimed that he called the conference in the winter of 1921 only because Britain was on the point of doing so; but it was also true that he was forced to call it quickly, before Borah and the Senate raised a public outcry against him.[24]

The Senate, public opinion, the Administration, and British action—all played a part in the calling of a conference on disarmament. It seemed a politic thing to do. It would take the public mind off the depression. Moreover, with both Japan and England matching the proposed American expansion of its Navy, world tension would be eased by the scrapping of warships. Harding now showed his independence of the Senate by including France and Italy and China and other smaller powers among those invited to the proposed conference at Washington and by asking for a discussion on land armament as well. When murmurs of a Senate revolt came to him, he adopted the policy McKinley had used at the signing of the Treaty of Paris and invited Senator Lodge and

Elihu Root and a prominent Democratic Senator, Oscar W. Underwood, to serve with Hughes as America's delegates at the conference. By engaging prominent members of the Old Guard from both parties in the work of negotiations, Harding hoped to get the support of the Senate *in advance* for any treaty made at the conference. This subtle maneuver was intended to put an end to the twenty-year war between the Senate Foreign Relations Committee and the White House. Some Irreconcilables, indeed, attacked the appointment of Senators as delegates to the conference, since it would block the Senate's function as a check on the executive branch by getting its leaders to advise and consent to the first draft of a treaty.

Harding's nationalism was shown by his insistence that the conference should be held at Washington. He had promised not to travel abroad and not to be deceived as Wilson had been at Paris. America could not go to the world. The world must come to America. Despite British pleas for a preliminary conference in London, Harding and Hughes stood firm. The conference was scheduled to meet in Washington on November 11, 1921. And the Senate, as a proof of its power and as a final snub to Wilson, passed a resolution urging the American delegates to hold an open conference, with full press coverage and no secret negotiations. Versailles might be full of hidden passages, but Washington should contain only open corridors.

Thus, on the threshold of the Washington Conference on Disarmament, Harding had already made it clear that he was not the creature of the Senate and that he had never been. The skirmishes between the White House and the Irreconcilables continued, with the Senate usually winning, but with Harding and Hughes gaining little victories and experience all the time. Harding went far in his strategy of appeasing and pleasing the Old Guard, but he would not accept dictation. If he did not always know what he wanted, he knew that he did not want to seem the servant of what others wanted. He wished to *choose* between the policies of others.

As the acute writer of *The Mirrors of Washington* observed in 1921, "A man as handsome as Harding, as vain of his literary style as he is, has an ego that is not capable of total self-effacement.

He will bow to impersonal authority like that of the party, or invoke the anonymous governance of 'best minds,' calling rather often on God as a well-established authority, but he will not let authority be personal and be called Daugherty, or Lodge or Knox or whomever you will." [25] As soon as he got to the White House, Harding discovered that cooperation with Congress was an illusion and that if he was to be a good President, he must try to lead. And his vanity allowed him to see himself only as a good President. If a man thinks well of himself, he can act better than he is by nature.

After Harding had been in office six months, Mark Sullivan commented on the change in his image. The Senators had thought that "Harding would make a good President—under Senatorial tutelage. They didn't foresee his capacity for generating his own motive power continuously and abundantly. On this point—of his capacity to stand on his own bottom—Harding was not merely underestimated. He was totally misapprehended. It was only a year ago that the phrase 'creature of a Senatorial oligarchy' was the epithet of the opposition party, supposed to be potent to deprive Harding of votes." After six months, however, "if that phrase is recalled at all, it is to point a joke on those who once believed it." According to Sullivan, Harding had always "undersold" himself. He was a ram in lamb's wool. And he had changed his personality. Harding the President bore no relation to Harding the Senator, because of the "different point of view in the man's own conception of his relation to life." Where Harding the Senator had felt it was his duty to follow, Harding the President felt it was his duty to lead. With the Senate split up among the quarreling standpatters and Insurgents and Irreconcilables, with Penrose and Knox dying and Lodge slipping and the bosses generally losing control, it was time for the President to be firm. "From assuming that the Senate was going to boss Harding, the pendulum has swung to where the country, and the Senate itself, begs Harding to boss the Senate." [26]

In the White House, Harding quickly found that the Senate would not cooperate with him just because he was the first man to step directly from Capitol Hill uptown to 1600 Pennsylvania Avenue. He had irked the Senate by his independent choice of a

Cabinet, and the Old Guard was ready to slap him down. The Insurgents never had liked him, as he was so obviously a believer in big business. The Irreconcilables, despite his stand against the League, feared that he might be more the creature of Hughes than of themselves. And even if the regular Republicans could be relied upon to support the President, a combination of Democrats with either Insurgents or Irreconcilables could block any Administration measure.

Harding's first dealing with Congress showed how little he trusted his old colleagues from the very beginning. By a brilliant stroke of political strategy, he read out the names of his chosen Cabinet directly to the Senate, who then ratified them through the various committee chairmen in his presence. This subtle action, based on an old precedent, meant that none of Harding's appointees could be blocked by a Senate committee. Indeed, Harding's strategy was proved correct, for La Follette had intended to contest Fall's appointment as Secretary of the Interior and was caught off his guard.[27] Fall's name was received with cheering by most of his brothers in the Senate.

In the debate over the Soldier's Adjusted Compensation Bill, which sought to give a bonus to veterans, Harding intervened personally on the side of economy. "This menacing effort to expend billions in gratuities," he told Congress, would imperil the restoration of normalcy. Tax reduction to revive business, the refunding of the war debt, and a settlement of foreign loans—these were necessary. "We may rely on the sacrifices of patriotism in war," Harding said with some toughness, "but to-day we face markets, and the effects of supply and demand, and the inexorable law of credits in time of peace. . . . A modest offering to the millions of service men is a poor palliative to more millions who may be out of employment." [28]

The genuine tears that Harding had shed seven weeks before on a Hoboken pier seemed to have dried. For these had been tears over 5,212 transported coffins of American dead who had fought in the World War, veterans indeed. "Never a death," Harding had then cried, "but somewhere a new life; never a sacrifice but somewhere an atonement; never a service but somewhere and somehow an achievement." [29] Yet Harding's idea of atonement for the service of the living veterans did not include putting money in their pockets. Tears for the dead were becoming, but the hard facts of economics had to be seen with dry eyes.

Congress was more receptive to showing gratitude—and to placating the veterans' lobby of five million votes—than was the President. The bill for a veterans' bonus passed both Houses the following election year, and it was firmly vetoed by Harding, who was not running for reelection until two years later. Harding preferred reducing the national debt to increasing it in order to pay for a bonus to veterans. Although the House of Representatives rejected the veto, the Senate narrowly sustained it. The veterans, however, were due to collect their bonus from Congress in the end. They had, after all, borne the brunt of the war on soldier's pay. If the rich were to be allowed to keep their war profits, the military should at least be allowed to receive a small cut themselves. By approving Mellon's budget to help the rich, Harding made his refusal of the veterans' bonus appear to be a mean and biased action. He was, apparently, in favor of the wealthy at the expense of the brave.

Harding further came to grips with Congress over his two pet projects. The first was a ship-subsidy bill that aimed at helping private companies to buy cheaply and operate profitably the transport ships made by the government in the war. The second was the creation of a Department of Public Welfare. Both were turned down by Congress, on the very grounds of government economy that Harding had used in the debate over the veterans' bonus. As Harding quickly discovered, Congress would always use the argument of economy against any extension of the power of the Chief Executive, just as he used the argument of economy to prevent Congress from pandering to the voters. It is a fine thing to impose the saving of public money on others, but a hard thing to accept it oneself.

A makeshift tariff bill also passed Congress, but it was a stopgap measure that reflected no policy and many special interests. It pleased few except the protected beneficiaries in industry. Everyone knew that it was merely a temporary measure, to be in force only until the best minds of the Cabinet and the Senate could work out a proper tariff. Otherwise, the large Republican majorities in Congress revealed themselves as futile and bickering groups of men at cross-purposes. They had successfully combined against President Wilson. Now they could not combine to help President Harding.

In this situation, Harding moved in to try to act the part of the leader. His intervention over the bonus bill and the disarmament conference gave him the taste for power. The press of the country and his friends egged him on. And he himself grew more critical of the Congress, in which he had served. "The trouble is," he confided to Jennings, "three men out of four in either House or Senate are thinking ten times as much of their own political fortunes as they are the welfare of the government. I believe, however, I can be helpful, largely because of the fact that I have refrained from assuming anything like a dictatorial attitude." [30] By keeping on the appearance of the harmonizer and conciliator, Harding intended to lead.

His new role did not escape the notice and the jeers of the Democrats in the Senate. Harding's old tormentor, Senator Reed of Missouri, now sneered at the Republican majority in the Senate. "No more pitiable spectacle of complete legislative subserviency, of legislative truckling, of legislative crawling upon the belly at the feet of a master and licking the boots of authority" had ever been seen by the Senator. Another Southern Democrat thought that if the President had changed his mind about the wickedness of executive encroachments, he ought to make a public apology for his past attacks on Wilson and his old professions of humility. As the Philadelphia *Record* commented, " 'Personal government' is an admirable thing by a Republican President; it is only when the President is a Democrat that it violates the Constitution and destroys our liberties." [31]

Office had changed the humble Senator into the pushing President, even if he was not as successful in controlling the Republican majority in Congress as his critics claimed. Over one matter, however, he and Congress concurred. That was over the restriction of immigration to America. "Melting Pot or Dumping Ground?"

George Creel asked ominously in *Collier's*.[32] And the answer came back: Old American Reservation.

Overriding Wilson's veto, Congress had insisted that immigrants should pass a literacy test, despite the unanswered questions of Senator Wagner of New York: "If the literacy test was not applied to the Irish and the German, why should it now be applied to the Jew, the Italian or the Slav of the new immigration? Like our ancestors, they are now flying from persecution, from ignorance, from inequality; like our ancestors, they expect to find here freedom and equal opportunity. Are we going to deny them an equal opportunity?" [33] Instead, Congress had listened to the false and racist findings of the Dillingham Commission and the Laughlin report, which asked for the restriction of immigration on the basis of "superior" and "inferior" national blood and background. Moreover, the fact that 119,000 Jews had immigrated to America during the year 1920–1921 encouraged latent anti-Semitism. Congress now had "scientific" facts and figures to confirm its prejudice in favor of keeping America for a majority of Anglo-Saxons. Acting swiftly, both Houses of Congress agreed on a temporary law to restrict immigration. A yearly quota of 3 per cent of the foreign-born in the United States at the time of the census of 1910 would be allowed to enter. This would not restrict immigration from Northern Europe, while it would restrict it from the rest of the world. The Jews, having no official nationality, would find it difficult to enter at all.

The bill was sent to Harding to sign. It was a bill that reflected the fear of a majority of rural old-stock Americans, who felt in danger of being swamped by the immigrant masses that provided cheap labor in the large cities. Harding was one of those rural old-stock Americans. He had always shared in their fears, for the Marion *Star* had reflected opinion as much as it had led opinion. As early as 1886, Harding had written in an editorial, "Foreign immigration made America . . . and is now promising to ruin it." [34] As a Senator, Harding had voted in favor of the literacy test for immigrants, although he had excused himself to the irate manufacturers of Ohio, with their desire for cheap labor, by saying that he had cast his vote "as one takes a dose of castor oil." [35]

Thus when Harding was faced with signing the quota bill of 1921 he did not hesitate for long. In response to rural and small-town and old American fears, he wanted to restrict immigration to the land of opportunity. "There is a very general feeling," he wrote to a racist correspondent, "that we tighten up on the restrictions until matters are adjusted to a normal gait once more." [36] In response to this general feeling, Harding forgot the support he had received from the Italian-Americans and the minority groups in the election of 1920. He was on the side of Old America, and he was even prepared to defy that holy of holies, big business, to keep out more aliens. Fear of the urban masses from Southern and Eastern Europe and fear of displeasing the majority of rural Americans were even stronger in Harding than fear of annoying Mammon.

Those who presented briefs to Harding in order to get him to veto the bill were wasting their time:

> In the past [Louis Marshall declared on behalf of the American Jewish Committee], we have welcomed the immigrant. We have made it possible to enlist him in the development of our resources and in the creation of our great industries, in the construction of our railroads and of our vast public works; to bring into our citizenship men and women of admirable qualities, who have known how to live and to die for the country of their adoption. This measure casts an undeserved slur upon our foreign-born citizens. It tells them that they are men and women of inferior race, that they are not assimilable, that they are undesirable, that even though they are citizens and performed the duties of citizenship they are not wanted. This is an unfortunate manifestation of a spirit of arrogance and of racial prejudice that bodes ill for the future if it is to be at all encouraged.[37]

Harding, however, showed the spirit of arrogance and racial prejudice. Otherwise he would not have signed the bill. Efforts to restrict immigration had been blocked not only by Wilson, but also by Theodore Roosevelt and Taft before him. Republican precedent, the demands of big business, and the urge to win the votes of the new immigrants dictated the use of a veto to Harding. Yet he signed the bill. For he remained true to his rural prejudice against the new immigrant and the large city.

Near the end of his life, when he had decided to run for reelection in 1924, Harding seemed ready to modify his position on immigration. He talked to Judge Gary, the powerful steel king, and was reported as attacking the new immigration law. Albert Johnson, the chairman of the House Committee on Immigration, immediately took Harding up on this, for Harding had previously declared that he did not want an excess of labor or an excess of immigrants. It was the quota system of immigration, Johnson claimed, that had turned the five million jobless of 1921 into the "*Labor in demand*" of 1923. Did Harding want another depression? [38] Harding's secretary quickly replied that Harding had been misquoted. In all probability, Harding would have signed the bill of 1924 that permanently restricted immigration to America, just as his small-town successor, Calvin Coolidge, did. He always thought of America first, and when he thought of America first, he included as 100 per cent Americans only those whose families had first come to America.

In the Annual Message to Congress delivered on December 6, 1921, Harding asserted his increased authority. He wanted bipartisan support for whatever treaty was the result of the Washington Conference on Disarmament. He acknowledged the large amount of work done by Congress, but he said that he did not agree always with the result of the roll calls. He thanked Congress for approving Mellon's budget and Dawes's budget system of government economy. And he wanted Congress to pass a law to set up tribunals to mediate in strikes.

On one matter, however, Harding was frankly puzzled. He wanted the normal Republican policy of high tariffs to protect American industry. But the war had changed the whole economic situation: "Everything relating to trade, among ourselves and among nations, has been expanded, excessive, inflated, abnormal, and there is a madness in finance which no American policy alone will cure. We are a creditor Nation, not by normal processes, but made so by war." Suddenly, America not only had a surplus of exports over imports, but also was owed $3,000,000,000 privately and $10,000,000,000 publicly. Unless European goods were allowed into America at favorable rates, Europe could neither pay for its purchases nor pay the interest on its debts. Yet Harding preferred not to think about this dangerous situation, which was in fact only to be alleviated by tourism and the private investment of a billion dollars a year by Americans in European stocks.

Harding wanted traditional Republican economic policy, even if the position of the United States in the world had changed. He wanted high tariffs *and* European trade, although high tariffs made European goods uncompetitive on the American market. He wanted America to sell more than it bought and yet to receive repayment on its war loans in dollars or gold. He did not see that this was impossible. After all, to become rich, surely Europe had only to imitate the American example.

"With all my heart I wish restoration to the peoples blighted by the awful World War," Harding declared, "but the process of restoration does not lie in our acceptance of like conditions. It were better to remain on firm ground, strive for ample employment and high standards of wage at home, and point the way to balanced budgets, rigid economies, and resolute, efficient work as the necessary remedies to cure disaster." The way to set this good example was to increase the tariff and to give the President the power of doing so through a commission. Harding hastily added that he disavowed "any desire to enlarge the Executive's powers or add to the responsibilities of the office" even if few of his hearers in Congress believed him. There must be a protective policy, and Harding wanted the power to negotiate one. If this policy made it hard for America's debtors to pay, yet America and America's unemployed came first.

Particularly important was the need to protect the American farmer. For, Harding said—true to his rural beliefs—"the base of the pyramid of civilization" still rested on the soil. The President confessed himself appalled by the drift from the farm to the city—although he had been one of the drifters himself. He wanted the war of the country and the city to end in the prosperity of both behind a high-tariff wall: "We have a just pride in our great cities, but we shall find a greater pride in the Nation, which has a larger distribution of its population into the country, where comparatively self-sufficient smaller communities may blend agricultural

and manufacturing interests in harmonious helpfulness and en-
hanced good fortune." As for Europe, it should look after itself.
And, if necessary, America would send its charity there, even to
starving Red Russia. For humanity came before everything.[39]
Although not, apparently, the chance to earn a living rather than
accept a handout.

So Harding sketched out his program to Congress and put the
seal on his policy of economic nationalism and America First. And
Congress was ready to give him a little of what he wanted, for
it had begun to recognize that the man in the White House and
his Cabinet possessed the approval of both the press and the people.

The Presidential honeymoon with the press normally lasts some
six months. But Harding stretched out the idyll for more than a
year. If he had any political genius other than the art of saying
nothing well, it was the art of good press relations. Many journalists thought that his informality during the campaign would be
replaced by stiffness once he reached the White House. On the
contrary, Harding restored the biweekly White House meetings
with the press that Wilson had begun and had given up. Moreover, the atmosphere of these press conferences was not one of
a teacher addressing inquisitive pupils, but of a give-and-take
between equals. "To Wilson," wrote one commentator, these conferences "were a painful necessity. To Harding they were an
opportunity to mingle with his own kind of people and with rare
exceptions he enjoyed them." [40]

In the words of a local journalist, Harding regarded "the persistence of the Washington correspondents in the light of what
he, as publisher of the Marion *Star*, might expect of one of his
men." He had a keen appreciation of the fact that journalists represented the public. His reward was that most of the correspondents
"laid aside their axes and fine tooth combs." They were "ready
to do their share toward making permanent the program of mutual
helpfulness thus established by Mr. Harding." [41] By continuing
to take the journalists into his confidence and by relying on their
discretion, Harding received a more favorable press reception over
a longer period of time than any other President before him.

For the first time, journalists were shown how the Presidency worked. They were told many secrets off the cuff, and they usually respected these confidences. There were unfortunate leaks, which embarrassed such sticklers for propriety as Hughes. But these leaks did not often come from Harding or his trusted correspondents; they came from loose-tongued members of the Cabinet. The throwing open of the Washington Conference on Disarmament to newsmen was a particularly happy stroke of Harding's. Never before had diplomacy been conducted in full view of the members of the press, and they praised Harding to the skies for the experiment.

Although Harding had a bad time with the press in the June of 1922, when he exploded with rage because he thought that the newspapers were giving too much space to his critics in Congress, his relations with the press continued in the manner of a settled marriage. The press forgave this unusual outburst on the part of their favorite President, who seemed to forget for once that he was only a President now and could no longer edit the news to boost himself. "America has not reached the stage of normalcy," a correspondent observed, "that will also permit her President to be editor-in-chief of her newspapers." [42] Yet on the whole Harding remained always the friend of the journalists, for he continued to take a lively interest in the Marion *Star*. When William Allen White called on him for the last time in the White House, Harding would discuss only newspaper matters. "There is nothing in this job here," he declared. "As a matter of fact, I go to press at the White House every afternoon at three o'clock." [43]

Harding's relationship with the press provides an accurate measure of the man. He had always been a booster, and he expected the press to boost him. He would help newsmen in every possible way in order to get their help in return. He was thin-skinned toward criticism, and he had always disliked those who knocked people in power. He himself had normally praised the great, and now that he had become great, he expected to be praised. And because he sought the praise of the press, he made genuine efforts to do things that he thought the people would like. He also made the office of the Presidency more open and democratic than it had ever been.

The result was double-edged. During Harding's life, he was praised for his humanity. After his death, he was blamed for his indiscretion. His intimacy with journalists provided each one of them with a personal story of Harding's failings. Each story could be added to the wall of gossip that was built around the man after his death. In the White House, however, the susceptible Harding became a little more inured to misrepresentation and criticism. "I have had my viewpoint about journalism broadened," he said ironically, "while twisting around occasionally in the executive chair." [44]

Thus, by successfully wooing the press during his life, Harding invited damnation by the press after his death. He had never bothered to hide his petty weaknesses, as most Presidents had done. He let the reporters into the smoking room of the White House. Thus each of them knew some minor frailty of the President—a poker party here, a bet there, an occasional drunkenness, a compromising action. While he was alive, Harding's dignity kept these stories quiescent. But when he died just as scandal broke out in his Administration, the journalists remembered the stories and put them all together to make a picture of an affable and stupid and weak-willed nonentity of a President, the creature of the dark forces of corruption behind him.

This myth of Harding as the mere front of a conspiracy was as false as the myth of Harding as the creature of the Senators at the Chicago nomination. Yet nobody more likes to be wise after the event than a reporter or a politician. The fact was that during his life, Harding successfully persuaded the press that he was doing a good job as President. At least the journalists reported this in the main, and if they were lying, they should not have been in their jobs any more than Harding should have been in his. The presumption is that the press really did think Harding was performing adequately in the White House, and he made them think so, even if he was not. For he was a genius at public relations. Only after his sudden death did the reporters claim to have seen through him all the time. *De mortuis nil nisi bunkum.*

Nothing showed more clearly the difference between the views of Harding alive and Harding dead than the stories of how hard he worked as President. A reporter, William H. Crawford, was asked to spend a week in the White House with Harding directly after the Inauguration. He reported that Harding was no union man, because he violated "the eight-hour law twice every day, his usual day lasting about seventeen hours." Harding rose at seven o'clock in the morning; he met people and signed papers until midnight.[45] Later, Colonel House recalled that one of the permanent White House staff had told him that Harding was the hardest worker of any of the Presidents. This view was confirmed by Louis Ludlow, who said that regular men at the White House declared that "Mr. Harding put in more hours of toil per day, on the average, and more hours in the aggregate, than any other President within their recollection." [46]

Senator Watson, who patronized Harding and was jealous of his friend's position, put forward the case for the lazy President, which is still believed about Harding. "The simple fact is," Watson declared, "that my dear old friend just did not like to work, and he ought never to have taken upon himself the enormous burdens incident to the presidency and entailed upon the president immediately following the most titanic struggle that ever cursed the earth. He simply was not adapted to the place and daily shrank from its exacting and gruelling toil." [47] To Watson's version, a host of journalists added their memories of the President, who played golf three times a week, went to poker parties in friends' houses, and had stag dinners and stag breakfasts as often as possible in the White House.

These conflicting versions of Harding were, in fact, two sides of the same truth. Harding chose to show himself as a casual man. There was a hint of laziness in the stoop of his shoulders and the drawl of his voice. Those who wished to prove his sloth took this manner to be the fact. But the truth was that Harding worked hard and played hard and "was vigorous in whatever he did." [48] Hughes told Taft at Harding's funeral that he had never comprehended how Harding stood the wear and tear of such long stretches "of work or exercise or social enjoyment to the 'wee sma' hours.' " [49] Ike Hoover, White House electrician and usher for forty-two years from the time of Benjamin Harrison, explained Harding's ability to work and play so hard by revealing that he slept *least* of all ten Presidents that Hoover had known.[50] In fact, President Taft had worked less than half the time when he was in the White House that Harding did.

Ike Hoover also pointed out that Harding, even when he played, plowed through much work. "He was on close terms with a great number of Senators and Congressmen and discussed official business with them on all occasions. Meals, golf, card games, travels, walks, every place was a field of action." Hoover continued with an illuminating observation that proved that, however much Harding allowed people to go their own way, he had first to be convinced by his friends. These friends argued with Harding as they had with no other President "and *generally* had their way, convincing him that whatever they did was right." Yet they had to convince him, and once he was convinced, they had the job of getting done whatever they wanted and Harding now wanted. The President "never *seemed* to be very concerned with the fate of a measure under consideration, depending more on these so-called friends to take care of his interests." [51]

The subtlety of Harding's method of procedure was not to be used again until Eisenhower came to office. By pretending to be casual and lazy, a golfer and a sport, Harding allowed others to take the burden of pushing through measures. If they succeeded, he would take the credit. If they failed, the fault was theirs. He stood above the ploys of the mere politicians. For he was President. He did not want to be the fount of authority, but the forum before which special interests pleaded their cases. He wished to appear relaxed and confident in order that everybody should believe that he had things under control. If his friends then thought that *they* had things under control, so much the better for their deluded vanity.

When Harding wanted something for himself, he certainly tried to get it. He allowed others to go their own way over matters that did not interest him in order to gain their support for what he wanted. It was this stubbornness about his own ambitions that had put him in the White House. Perhaps one of Harding's greatest gifts was to make other people feel superior to him, when all the time he knew that he was superior or equal to them. For in their illusion of importance, they might well perform an important action that would tend to help Harding himself.

Harding worked hard and played hard and slept little. Thus he strained his strong physique and his weak heart. He pushed himself too long in office. He was not lazy enough, although he worked hard at seeming so. His folly was to attend too much to the minute and the inessential. It took Christian, his secretary, some time to learn how to keep much of the unnecessary work from his chief. For there is a Parkinson's law for Presidents as well as for petty clerks. Any President can expand his work to take up all his time. Harding did so. He did not stop to ask himself what he should work at doing and whom he should see. He just did the work that came along and saw the people who came along. He chose to be undiscriminating in the name of being democratic. The result was that democracy later judged him harshly for his failure to be an aristocrat in his actions and in regard to his friends.

Immediately, however, Harding's policy of seeing everyone and doing everything paid handsome dividends. When he was not working at his desk, he hurled himself into an orgy of public relations—as Lyndon Johnson also was to do when he became President. From the moment of Harding's arrival, the White House was thrown open to the public. Both the President and Mrs. Harding literally shook hands "with tens of thousands of persons, in a steady streaming line through the White House gates." [52] The White House had been effectively closed for more than a year during Wilson's sickness. Harding knew well the psychological effect of throwing open the gates to the people and was prepared to stand the strain. As one observer noted, the White House under Wilson had seemed to the local people in Washington an isolated house, cut off from the Capitol, its great gates closed and chained and locked, guarded by policemen, "in a void apart," exhaling "a chill and icy disdain." As soon as Harding entered, however, "this miasmatic vapor" was dissipated. The Washington atmosphere became "that of Old Home Week or a college class reunion." The populace wore a grin, and all went to meet the President. It was one of the things that made Harding immediately popular and gave him "a stock of good opinion," which, his observer guessed, he would need to draw upon.[53]

The later impression of Harding as a kindly and generous man of little courage, the mere creature of Daugherty and his Ohio Gang, was put to the test on three occasions during Harding's first year in office. On these occasions, Harding appeared as a politic and even vindictive man of some courage, opposed to the actions of Daugherty and the Ohio Gang. The matter of the pardon of Eugene Debs and the jailed radicals of the First World War, the matter of Harding's speech on the Negro question in Birmingham, Alabama, and the matter of Harding's dealings with the Department of Justice destroy the popular image of Harding as a mere figurehead, generous to a fault.

The moment that Harding reached the White House, pressure was put upon him to pardon Debs and other prisoners jailed because of antiwar activities. There were three categories of wartime, or "political," prisoners—those who had personally dodged the draft through conscience or cowardice; those who had verbally opposed the war on principle; and those radicals, such as the International Workers of the World, who had proposed the overthrow of the wartime government. These groups could be categorized as conscientious objectors, political objectors, and revolutionaries. All were in jail only because of the repressive Espionage and Sedition Acts, now repealed.

The case of Debs was unique. He had been sentenced to ten years in jail in 1918, under the terms of the Espionage Act, for "actively and purposely" obstructing the draft. According to Daugherty, he had admitted his guilt at his trial, although he himself denied ever mentioning the draft in his incriminating speech. While still in jail, he had been nominated again by the Socialist Party of America for the Presidency and had received nearly a million votes. Wilson had refused to pardon him, saying to Tumulty, "This man was a traitor to his country and he will never be pardoned during my administration." Harding, however, had wired the Farmer-Labor Presidential candidate during the campaign that he himself favored a general amnesty. Once he reached the White House, he was expected to honor the promise he had made.

Norman Thomas, the onetime newsboy of the Marion *Star* and coming Socialist leader, wrote to Harding immediately. Calling up Marion memories, Thomas begged the President to consider the case of the "political" prisoners: "The best known and perhaps best loved of these is Gene Debs, but his case is not different from that of scores of others. They took a position in the war which you and the majority of Americans condemned. That they took it honestly and sincerely is obvious. There is no proof that they in any way hurt the military forces of our country. Is it not a splendid thing that a country should have men brave enough to speak their minds even when they are in a minority?" [54] To his appeal was added that of the Central Labor Bodies Conference, which pointed out that nearly all the conscientious objectors, 13,600 military offenders, and 135 "political" offenders had already been released. Only Debs and a few hundred others remained in jail. From all over the world, the voices of the great joined in the appeal for clemency, including those of George Bernard Shaw, H. G. Wells, Henri Barbusse, Clarence Darrow, and Upton Sinclair. John Cowper Powys wrote:

> These are the days of hungry common sense.
>   Millions of men have died to bring these days;
> And more must die ere these good days go hence;
>   For God moves still in most mysterious ways.
> Ah Debs, Debs, Debs, you are outweighed, out-priced,
> These are the days of Caesar, not of Christ.[55]

Although the powerful American Legion protested against the pardoning of Debs and other conscientious objectors, the World War Veterans, an organization with half a million members, asked for the release of these men: "Is it not strange, Mr. President, that veterans of the World War should ask for the release of men who opposed war? These men were moved by the same ideals as moved us. They differed from us only as to the methods of achieving those ideals. We realized that it would be necessary first to fight to end war." [56]

Committees of the liberal and the radical, the godly and the reformers came to see Harding about the Debs case. He refused to declare a general amnesty for all war prisoners as Britain had done. He promised that the Attorney General would review all their cases separately, with the case of Debs heading the list. The radical Lincoln Steffens was received sympathetically by Harding, who made his usual and clever appeal to sympathy. Harding said that he *personally* favored a general amnesty, but that "they" wouldn't let him do it. By "they," he meant Hoover and "Puddler Jim" Davis. If Steffens could convince these two to support a general amnesty, Harding would go along. Of course, Steffens failed, and thus Harding said that he could not issue such an order.[57] He gained Steffens' sympathy without releasing the prisoners. He did not point out that it was *he* who had chosen Hoover and Davis to sit in his Cabinet and that it was *he alone* who had the responsibility for pardoning the prisoners. Harding chose to accept responsibility only when it favored him. He willingly claimed to be under the influence of others when he wished to avoid a nasty situation.

In fact, Harding took some time to pardon Debs, and he issued no amnesty. In October, he promised a committee to release Debs soon. By December, he was protesting through Christian that he would do "the wise and just thing" when he chose to do it, unswayed by public opinion. Daugherty's view of a general amnesty was not encouraging. Of the 197 wartime prisoners still held, only 10 to 15 were really "political" prisoners. Most of the rest were revolutionary "Wobblies," whose crimes were not "political." According to Daugherty, "the crimes of these men were more horrible than outright murder." If any were pardoned, Daugherty suggested that they should take a loyalty oath that they recognized their guilt, regretted their crimes, swore their gratitude, and promised to behave well in the future. Only Debs, according to Daugherty, should not be required to take the oath if Harding pardoned him: "He is such an habitual violator of the laws of this country and has such a chronic disregard for his country and is so ignorant of his obligation to society that he might go upon his honor, if he has any."

So Daugherty wrote of one of the most principled and frank men in the United States. And so he proposed to make the pardoned prisoners humiliate themselves for their release. He was wrong in saying that they had committed crimes more horrible than murder. A few of them had been convicted for industrial sabotage, but most for mere revolutionary *talk*. In many cases, the actions of the judges and juries had been hopelessly biased and unfair, bound up with the spirit of ruthless brutality of war. Harding, at least, was kinder than his Attorney General, although hardly the merciful lamb of legend. Steffens told him that anyone who accepted Daugherty's oath was not fit to be pardoned. Harding crumpled the paper and replied to Daugherty that "this sort of a pledge would be of little avail. It would have the savor of bargaining for amnesty and I doubt if that would meet with any marked degree of approval." [58]

Thus Harding decided on a limited act of clemency on Christmas Day, 1921, although Daugherty declared that such an act would desecrate the holy festival. He did not want to offend the businessmen and the American Legion by releasing radical prisoners and "Wobblies." On the other hand, he wanted to pacify the liberals by releasing Debs. Thus some of the war prisoners were released, and some deported. Harding personally saw Debs and was friendly to him. After the interview, Debs told reporters that Harding *appeared* to be "a kind gentleman" and that they understood each other perfectly. The President, however, made it clear in a tough statement that he was not being merciful but merely politic. The grant of clemency, a spokesman for the White House said, "does not question the justice of any action of the courts in enforcing the law in a time of national peril, but . . . the ends of justice have been fairly met in view of changed conditions. The vast majority of the so-called political prisoners still imprisoned are of the I.W.W. group, are rarely American citizens and have no good claim to Executive clemency."

The pressure on Harding did not die down. It was pointed out that of the seventy-six "Wobblies" still in jail, none had done a violent act and all were "political" prisoners. They had received a total of eight hundred years of jail time for *speaking* against the government and the war. In England, the maximum sentence for such a crime had been six months. Britain and Italy and Belgium had long ago freed such prisoners. For three years, the United States had been the only known country holding such people in jail. Harding was unmoved. "He would never as long as he was President," he declared, "pardon any criminal who was guilty of preaching the destruction of the Government by force." [59] Individualism, as always, would be preferred to collective action. "There will be no general amnesty: there will be no wholesale release," Harding wrote. "I do not believe that to be a consistent course. We are granting Executive clemency, now and then, to individuals from the general group." [60]

Harding liked giving charity to the unfortunate and opposed the principle of welfare for the masses; federal welfare would deny his beliefs in ambition and opportunity. In the same way, Harding liked pardoning individuals to prove his own goodness, but opposed a general amnesty; the latter would cast doubt on the fairness of American justice in the war. Harding enjoyed being thought good in the particular case; he was not interested in being thought a philosopher of abstract justice.

Moreover, the "Wobblies" had really offended Harding. They had attacked the ark of the covenant—the Constitution—and the principle of capitalism, and Harding felt himself the sworn defender of both. In the name of American government and American business, Harding refused to let his generous impulses conquer his sense of duty. When a Wives' and Children's Crusade, made up of the families of "political" prisoners, picketed the White House, Harding ignored their pleas for an amnesty. He also refused the plea of fifty-one members of the House of Representatives. Indeed, he turned down the appeal of Senator Lodge himself. In 1922, Harding did not appear to be merciful, but, rather, repressive.

The appearance was the fact. Harding revealed that politics came before mercy in his mind. On September 26, 1922, in the aftermath of widespread strikes on the railroads and in the coal industry, he wrote to a Catholic priest that he had delayed the pardon of several of the "political" prisoners. "These decisions have been delayed because I felt it undesirable to pardon men with I.W.W. tendencies in a time when the nation was greatly threatened by the existing industrial strikes." [61] In other words, Harding was using the unjust sentences of wartime to keep labor agitators in jail.

By December, 1922, there were still sixty-two jailed "political" prisoners. By April, 1923, there were fifty-two. Even the conservative Civic Federation, every one of whose members was "a safe and saner from Constitutionville," demanded the prisoners' release. " 'Political prisoners!' " jeered a journalist to Harding. "It was President Wilson who made possible this phrase in the United States. Don't you see that it would be good politics to make the phrase historic rather than current?" [62] On June 19, 1923, Harding commuted conditionally the sentences of twenty-four "Wobblies" and had two deported. At the time of his death, five years after the war had ended, twenty-one wartime "political" prisoners were still being held in jail. Some of the blame for this violation of American civil liberties must be placed at the door of the Red-baiting Attorney General, Harry Daugherty. But Harding certainly must carry most of the blame, for he was not ignorant of the cases. In the matter of the "political" prisoners, the quality of Harding's mercy was strained.

Over the Negro question, Harding showed definite, if misguided, courage. On entering the White House, he seemed to wish to give the American Negro no more than the symbolic representation in a Republican Administration that the Negro had always had. In a memorandum to all Cabinet officers, Harding stated that they should find "a couple of suitable places for colored appointees," for the Administration wanted to place "a few representative colored Republicans into administrative activity." [63] Harding did not, however, attempt to repeal Wilson's shocking surrender to the Southern bloc in the Senate, which had insisted upon the segregation of Negroes in federal buildings for the first time.

Yet the fact that two in five voters in the South in the election of 1920 had cast their ballots for him did tempt Harding as a politician. He saw that he might make the Republicans the majority party all over America and break the Democratic Solid South if he could get a few more Negroes to vote there and not lose the increasing Republican vote among the whites. As William Howard Taft reported in the Philadelphia *Public Ledger*, "Mr. Harding is anxious to strengthen the Republican party south of Mason and Dixon's line. He thinks that the time is ripe for dissolving the Solid South. The victories of the Republicans in Maryland, Kentucky, Missouri, Tennessee and Oklahoma and the fact that the majorities of the Democrats in most other Southern States were greatly reduced and the total Republican vote much increased furnish the basis for his hope." [64]

The strategy of Harding's foray into the Solid South demanded a mixture of courage and caution. He had to provide a new policy for Republicans there, one that would allow them to register more Negro votes and yet uphold the majority opinion that the Caucasian and Negro races should live apart. In other words, the Negro should remain a social and racial inferior, while advancing to the status of a political equal. With this adroit plan, Harding went to Birmingham, Alabama, on October 26, 1921, to deliver an unexpected speech on the racial question. Not since the Inaugural Address of Taft had any President spoken out so openly on the question, and never before in the heart of the Deep South.

In front of an audience of twenty thousand white Southerners, carefully segregated from an audience of ten thousand Negroes, Harding began by praising the new industrial achievement of the South, which had brought it economic prosperity. He continued by mentioning Lothrop Stoddard's racist work *The Rising Tide of Color*. This proved that the racial problem was worldwide, not merely American. The World War had also proved the patriotism of the colored man, and there should be a gradual adjustment of relations between the white and the black race. The formula for this adjustment was the only one of practical justice. The black man should have political and economic equality with the white man, but he should recognize his social and racial difference. "Politically and economically there need be no occasion for great and permanent differentiation, for limitations of the individual's opportunity," Harding asserted, "provided that on both sides there shall be recognition of the absolute divergence in things social and racial."

After this bold statement, Harding quickly defined his policy of segregation for the Negro before that of opportunity. "Men of both races may well stand uncompromisingly against every suggestion of social equality. Indeed, it would be helpful to have that word 'equality' eliminated from this consideration; to have it accepted on both sides that this is not a question of social equality, but a question of recognizing a fundamental, eternal, and inescapable difference." Like slumps, Harding thought that racial differences were in the order of things. Yet he was too much a believer in old American values to think that class differences should even exist.

As for political equality, Harding tacitly approved an unconstitutional literacy test applied with fairness. "Let the black man vote when he is fit to vote; prohibit the white man voting when he is unfit to vote." The Negroes should educate and improve themselves apart and should develop racial traditions and ambitions that would lead to "natural segregations." These natural segregations were already proceeding in the Southern states, "satisfying natural inclinations and adding notably to happiness and contentment." When Negroes had equal opportunities in separate education, they would develop their own leaders in favor of segregation. Racial partnership was needed. "Racial amalgamation there cannot be." Harding declared he would accept "that a black man cannot be a white man, and that he does not need and should not aspire to be as much like a white man as possible in order to accomplish the best that is possible for him. He should seek to be, and he should be encouraged to be, the best possible black man, and not the best possible imitation of a white man."

Everybody would benefit from such a system of political and educational and economic equality, allied with permanent social segregation. The South would benefit as a whole, and so would American democracy:

Just as I do not wish the South to be politically entirely of one party, just as I believe that is bad for the South, and for the rest of the country as well, so I do not want the colored people to be entirely of one party. I wish that both the tradition of a solidly Democratic South and the tradition of a solidly Republican black race might be broken up. Neither political sectionalism nor any system of rigid groupings of the people will in the long run prosper our country.

I want to see the time come when black men will regard themselves as full participants in the benefits and duties of American citizenship; when they will vote for Democratic candidates, if they prefer the Democratic policy on tariff or taxation, or foreign relations, or what-not; and when they will vote the Republican ticket only for like reasons. We cannot go on, as we have gone for more than a half century, with one great section of our population, numbering as many people as the entire population of some significant countries of Europe, set off from real contribution to solving our national issues, because of a division on race lines.

At this point, Harding made another appeal to the reactionary sentiment among white Southerners. He asked for vocational training schools for Negroes, who should not try to overstock the professions. Harding pointed out that immigration had been restricted and that the American birthrate was falling rapidly. This meant a great increase in the opportunities for manual labor. America would be forced to turn back upon its "older population to find people to do the simpler, physically harder, manual tasks." There was small chance that America would ever again "have such armies of laborers landing on these shores as have come in the past." Thus the Southerners would *have* to treat the Negroes well, or else Northern factories would offer the Negroes reasonable wages at unskilled jobs. The Negroes would take over the place of the new immigrants in the North and would be the cheap labor of the booming factories.[65]

Such were the policies and prophecies of Harding in the Deep South. In them, he revealed himself as the racist and segregationist that he was. On the other hand, he spoke bluntly for once, in an effort to break up the Democratic South. He failed. The white Southerners would neither allow the Negroes to vote nor would they join the Republican Party in large quantities. Harding's only success was his correct prediction that *de facto* segregation would increase in the South and that the Southern Negroes would become the new immigrants and cheap labor of the North. The great Negro dispersion over America—the problem of the sharecropper becoming the problem of the slum-dweller—had already begun.

The most interesting result of Harding's speech at Birmingham was the reaction of the press. The Southern newspapers, on the whole, admired both Harding's courage in speaking out in the South and his support of segregation. Most of them agreed that the President had merely declared the fact of a doctrine already held by "the best thought [of] Southern leaders, white and black." Such distant newspapers as the New York *Globe* and the Los Angeles *Times* agreed that Harding's speech was the most frank and intelligent one on the race question in generations.

Of course, Southern Senators strongly objected to Harding's demand that literate Negroes should be allowed to vote. Senator Watson of Georgia said that political and social equality *were* linked and could not be divided. "So far as the South is concerned," said Senator Heflin of Alabama, "we hold to the doctrine that God Almighty has fixt limits and boundary lines between the two races, and no Republican living can improve upon His handiwork." In Norfolk, the *Virginian Pilot* complained that the President had only been repeating the usual policies of race harmony through segregation. "We have been admiring the view . . . for a long time now, and it does not help much to be told to admire it some more."

Yet, in the main, Harding received nothing but applause from all but rabidly Democratic politicians and newspapers. His policy of making a virtue of segregation and pressing for the slow political and economic advance of the Negroes seemed to win approval in all parts of the country—except among the Negroes themselves. This group praised Harding's demand for political equality. "The President's insistence that men of both races," declared the New York *Age*, "may well stand uncompromisingly against every suggestion of social equality was undoubtedly necessary in order to keep the uneasy consciences of the whites from balking at this bugbear. The fact that the whites have done so much in the past to bring about a quasi 'social equality' by the mixing of the blood of both races has rendered them unduly sensitive on this point." In general, the radical Negro leadership rejected Harding's plan, and the conservative leadership supported it. W. E. B. Du Bois expected the Negro, and all believers in humanity before race, to repudiate at the polls the President's "inconceivably dangerous and undemocratic demand" for social inequality.[66] Privately, however, some Negro educators wrote to Harding to praise him for "the most notable and courageous expression on the race question made by any President of the United States since Lincoln."[67]

Harding's speech at Birmingham showed that he was prepared to risk controversy to pull off a political shift of power in favor of the Republicans. In fact, he failed both to build up Republican support in the South and to bind the Northern Negroes more firmly behind the Republicans. He offered the Negroes too little for themselves and too much for the South. There is no doubt that a majority of Americans held his racist and undemocratic assumptions about the Negro people. It was sad that Harding's political courage did not also make him stand up against the current prejudices of American life.

In his dealings with Harry Daugherty, Harding showed his increased feelings of power and stature, although he also showed his lack of shrewdness in preventing Daugherty from acquiring opportunities to take graft. Suspiciously, one of Daugherty's first actions as Attorney General was to ask for powers from the President "with regard either to the allowance or rejection of non-litigated claims for property taken under the [Trading with the Enemy] Act in the hands of the Alien Property Custodian or the Treasurer of the United States, or with regard to the voluntary return of certain classes of this property at the instance of the President without awaiting the filing of formal claim therefor."[68]

In other words, Daugherty wanted to be sole arbiter—with Harding's acquiescence—of the sale or return of tens of millions of dollars' worth of German-owned property seized during the war. This would give him a marvelous opportunity for accepting retainers to favor one suit or another. In his later investigation by Congress after Harding's death, he was accused of accepting

$40,000 worth of bonds from the representative of the American Metals Company—a German-owned concern worth six and a half million dollars that was turned over with suspicious ease to a Swiss corporation that claimed to own it by verbal contract. The bonds were in Daugherty's name in his brother's bank in Ohio, but the records of how the bonds reached the bank were conveniently burned by Daugherty. The verdict of two hung juries on Daugherty was that he was not proven to be a grafter. His confidant, Jess Smith, had received $200,000 worth of the bonds, but he had later committed suicide. The records of how Daugherty had acquired his share of the bonds, and a moderate fortune on a salary of $12,000 a year, were destroyed. If Daugherty was not a grafter, as he claimed, it was unfortunate that he had immediately asked Harding for authority over Alien Property—a department that had already brought scandal to the Wilson Administration. If Daugherty had wished to keep a clean reputation, he should have left such opportunities for corruption alone.

Also under the Department of Justice was the Prohibition Bureau. It was headed by a dry from Ohio, Roy Haynes, whose appointment was a sop to the powerful Anti-Saloon League. Haynes had a staff of fifteen hundred agents to enforce the Volstead Act and end the liquor trade in America. These agents, with the backing of the Anti-Saloon League, were exempt from civil-service examination under the terms of the Volstead Act. This was done because the dry leaders, "without the patronage provision for Congressmen . . . didn't think the bill would pass." [69] The result was that the first group of Prohibition agents were spoilsmen, grafters, and incompetents of the first water. Daugherty's Buckeye friends at Washington openly dealt in protection to bootleggers, illegal withdrawals of bonded liquor, pardons and paroles for ready cash, prosecutions dropped for a price, and even in federal offices for sale. Dry-law enforcement became open robbery. George Remus, the so-called King of the Bootleggers, who was said to have made $40,000,000 from his trade, was one of the few sent to jail as an example, despite spending huge amounts of bribes in Washington. "I tried to corner the graft market," he said sourly, "only to find that there is not enough money in the world to buy up all the public officials who demand a share in the graft." [70]

Daugherty, however, and his Ohio friends kept the scandals moderately hidden from Harding in his first year of office. They concentrated on supplying the President with a little good liquor for his personal use, and thus they involved him in a minor infraction of the law. Yet on the one occasion that news of Daugherty's operating came publicly to Harding, he was brutal to his old campaign manager. He did not mind so much what Daugherty did under the counter, but he hated to be criticized for Daugherty's shady operations once they became known.

In the case of Lee Gibson of Arkansas, a convicted criminal was pardoned on Daugherty's recommendation *before* he had served one day in jail. "I am writing to express a marked degree of displeasure," Harding wrote to Daugherty, "that the records in this case did not plainly show that the petitioner had been given a further stay of sentence and that I was *mistakenly* led to pardon a convicted man who had not served any portion of his sentence. . . . I have been subjected to unfair criticism, because I was not fully informed in this particular instance." [71] Daugherty ate humble pie, put the blame on his pardon attorney, promised to reform, and claimed that he had made an honest mistake through hurry. Harding forgave him.

Thus Harding reached the end of the year of 1921. Early in the new year, he suddenly sat down and wrote a long and confidential letter to his old friend Malcolm Jennings. It was a letter of extraordinary and appealing frankness, in which he set down exactly his own opinion of himself as a President. Florence Harding later wrote to Jennings, wondering whether he had caught the tinge of sadness in the letter. "I realized," Florence Harding wrote, "Mr. Harding was opening up his heart to you in a very confidential way. It seems to me sometimes he feels the burdens upon him, and I must say all the days are very trying, though I don't want to leave the impression there are not some attractive features." [72]

In this very confidential letter, Harding turned to his one old friend who had not been corrupted by coming to Washington to profit from the Presidency. First, he thanked Jennings for letting him know that he was not now thought to be so much of a duffer as he had been when he received the nomination:

> I think perhaps it has been of some advantage to start into office so poorly appraised, because one does not need to accomplish very much to find himself somewhat marked up in value. I heartily agree with you that the party is not nearly so strong as it was last year. I may say to you, in the confidence which covers our correspondence, that the party is not much more than twenty-five per cent as strong in my own estimate, and there are a good many people in Congress whom my experience has led me to mark down to about ten per cent of their normal appraised value. In simple truth, I get discouraged sometimes about the stability of popular government, when I come in contact with the abject surrender of public men to what appears to be about one-half of one per cent of the voters to whom they look for their commission to public service. What the country needs more than anything else is a House and Senate for ten years which gives at least as much thought to the welfare of the Republic as is given to individual candidacies for re-election. Nothing so disheartens me as to have an extended conference with men in responsible places, hear them admit of the correctness of a policy or position and then frankly say it is impossible to go through with the policy or maintain the position and be assured of re-election. I have concluded that I would vastly prefer a limited career with the consciousness of having done the right thing, than to hold on to the constitutional limit by playing to the favor of those who do the fake work under our political system. My own disappointment with the public estimate of me lies in the fact that so many seem to think I can take a whip and show Congress where to head in. It was possible for my predecessor to follow such a course during the war when men ofttimes put aside their petty interests to perform what was believed to be a patriotic service. Conditions are not quite the same now. Probably I am lacking in the domineering traits which Mr. Wilson possessed and found himself able to exercise for considerable time. In the end he came to failure because of the practices followed....

You refer to the Debs commutation of sentence as one lessening the approval of me. Probably you are right. We should have gotten away from the subject as a matter of discussion if there had been less explaining and publicity by the Department. I realized full well that I would encounter no little criticism. It was one of those situations where one is bound to encounter criticism whichever course is decided upon. The matter was given very serious and earnest study. I may say that the esteemed lady whom you delight to address as 'Duchess' [Mrs. Harding] was very much opposed to any clemency being shown to Debs. However, I was persuaded in my own mind that it was the right thing to do. It is fair to say in behalf of the Attorney-General that he advised against Executive clemency. I did not think it wise to make a martyr of Debs. I recalled that he had been several times a presidential nominee, but personally he is of a very clean and lovable character, and I am sure I have heard men in Congress say things worse than the utterances upon which he was convicted and the men in Congress, of course, went scot-free. I could pick you out a half dozen Members of House and Senate who deserved quite as much to be in the penitentiary as did Debs. . . .

The Conference on the Limitation of Armament is going to achieve very gratifying results. There have been disappointments, of course. It was not to be expected that we could escape them. The French have not been as helpful as we had a right to expect. I think the spokesmen for France, in their hearts, have been in harmony with practically everything we have attempted to do. Unhappily, their course has been modified by the exigencies of politics at home. I do not see how we can find overmuch fault about them changing their course to meet political conditions when we have ourselves to face the possibility of defeat by the envious, the jealous, the contentious and the opposing political elements here at home. I do not think we shall fail in the Senate. If we do fail we will have pretty thoroughly established the fact that our government is of such character that no Executive can very successfully undertake to negotiate any foreign relationships or join upon any foreign policy which is calculated to promote our peace at home and throughout the world. No one can hope to show that we have entered upon any entanglements, certainly upon no alliances, and we have only done the very natural things which led to the ways of understanding and peaceful relationship. If the Senate can block this program after such great care has been taken in working it out, and after the perfect miracle of cooperation on the part of the British and Japanese it will not be worth anybody's time to bother with such a project again. I hope this frank statement does not give you the impression that we are expecting to lose in the Senate. I do not think we will.

The one particular grievance of the noisy ones will be removed before the Senate is officially acquainted with what has been done, and I do not think the vociferant supporters of George Washington will have a leg to stand and howl upon. . . .

I note your criticism of the Birmingham speech. There were some unfavorable reactions. In the main, the newspaper comments throughout the South, particularly in papers worth while, were all of a favorable nature. Now and then a petty little partisan squirt or some blackguard sheet cried out in opposition, but the leading papers of the South were more than hearty in their commendation. I doubt now myself if it were worth while to have made the effort. The impelling reason was the claim of the negro politicians for the performance of the things written into our platform and promised in the campaign. The negroes are very hard to please. If they could have half of the Cabinet, seventy-five per cent of the Bureau Chiefs, two-thirds of the Diplomatic appointments and all the officers to enforce prohibition perhaps there would be a measure of contentment temporarily, but I do not think it would long abide. Personally, I would be rejoiced if they would divide their political allegiance. Moreover, I am pretty well convinced that the public man who thinks he is going to break the solidarity of the South is dreaming. Maybe it will come by natural processes in a long while, but I have my doubts about it. . . .

Thus the changed man in the White House summed up in an impulsive letter to his oldest friend what he thought of himself in his job. He knew that he had changed, and he was proud of it. The Senator had become the President, and there was no connection between the two: "One gets a very different view of Congress from the Executive Office than I have ever entertained heretofore. Indeed, one gets a very different view of all the problems of government. Responsibility has a strange effect. I am not boosting myself, but I do not believe anyone could come to the Presidency without being imbued with the desire to serve above and beyond most selfish aims. I find even myself growing less a partisan than I once was." [73]

13

The Break with Normalcy

"I am not sure that there is very much satisfaction about being President at any time. Of course, if one is a glutton for trouble he ought to be delighted with the office. Curiously enough, most of the men whom I know, who have been seekers after the Presidency are those who care the least about encountering trouble, and if any of them ever comes to realize his ambition he will experience a rude awakening."   WARREN HARDING, July 13, 1922

The Washington Conference on Disarmament began as dramatically as possible. Its opening was put off for one day in order that the delegates might attend the burial of an unknown American soldier at Arlington National Cemetery. On this Armistice Day of 1921, men all over the Western world paused to consider the futility of war. The following morning, President Harding opened the conference with an emotional speech on the need to avoid the horrors of another World War: "How can humanity justify or God forgive? . . . Our hundred millions frankly want less of armament and none of war." [1] He left the details of disarmament to Hughes.

Hughes's opening speech, which he had not shown to Harding for fear of a leak to the press, was a triumph of skill and diplomacy. He was playing from a weak hand. He had already been told that the thrifty Congress would not approve the policy of a large American Navy. Thus, by proposing to scrap many of the

American warships already under construction, he was merely proposing to do what Congress would certainly do. This was not known by the foreign delegates.

Thus when Hughes proposed that America should scrap 845,740 tons of warships he was scrapping a fleet that was already on its way to the scrapyard. In return for sacrificing fifteen planned ships and fifteen old warships already built, he proposed that the British should scrap four planned battleships and nineteen older ships, and the Japanese seven proposed warships and ten old ones. This would leave the American and British and Japanese navies in a ratio of 5:5:3. There should be a moratorium on building large warships for ten years. By making his proposals open and detailed, Hughes hoped to force the British and Japanese into agreement under public pressure. In one speech, Hughes aimed to sink more British battleships than "all the admirals of the world had destroyed in a cycle of centuries." [2]

After months of negotiation, Hughes won most of his points. But his greatest victory was less in terms of foreign than of domestic policy. American public opinion supported Harding and his Secretary of State. Even the jealous Senate was somewhat appeased by the open diplomacy and involvement of its leaders. As Heywood Broun pointed out, it should have been grateful to Woodrow Wilson. "His was the horrible example which made the open session possible." [3]

Yet the result of the Washington Conference seemed more successful than it was. It led only to the scrapping of battleships, which were expensive and obsolete craft. It did not restrict the construction of submarines or destroyers or torpedo boats, although the construction of aircraft carriers was limited. The conference did not, in the end, deal with the question of armament by land or take up the question of air power, much to the anger of the French, who feared German rearmament. In fact, Harding personally supported German rearmament, writing to the Undersecretary of State that "Germany's commitment anew to a policy of limited armament on both land and sea will be *a helpful thing in tranquillizing Europe*." [4]

Another major defect of the Administration at the Washington

Conference was its failure to make any progress with the idea of a world association of nations. Harding floated trial balloons on the issue and was bitterly opposed by a combination of Irreconcilables, against all involvement, and Democrats, against the man who would not join the League. Even if the association of nations were agreed upon, with periodic consultations between friendly powers, it would have to be "no more entangling than a rainbow" to satisfy the Senate.[5]

The third hidden failure was the concessions made to Japan under the separate Four Power Treaty between America, Britain, Japan, and France. Under this treaty, the official Anglo-Japanese alliance was ended, but America was forbidden to fortify Manila or Guam. Essentially, this arrangement handed over Harding's old concern, the Philippines, to the Japanese at any time that they wished to attack it. Moreover, the disarmament agreement meant that Japan's fleet in the Pacific would always be stronger than America's unless America concentrated all its fleet there.

Two other agreements at Washington were also dangerous. The first was the limitation of the French fleet to the same size as the Italian fleet, at a ratio of $1.75:5$ compared with the American fleet; this was done without giving France guarantees against German rearmament. The second was a Nine Power Treaty on the subject of the Far East, which did not give China guarantees against future Japanese aggression or European penetration. Thus the conference did nothing to achieve disarmament by land or air, although it did help in delaying an armaments race after the First World War, in proving that America was concerned with the rest of the world, and in contributing to an international climate of peace. As Harding said at the concluding session of the Washington Conference, the great powers had "challenged the sanity of competitive preparation for each other's destruction." He confessed that he himself had once believed in armed preparedness, but now believed in the "better preparedness" of the public mind and of conferences of peace.[6]

The three treaties were hailed with joy in the press of the United States; but they still had to be accepted by the Senate, jealous of the Chief Executive and fearful of involvement. William

Jennings Bryan had already warned Harding that the Four Power Treaty should contain a reservation—namely, the American right to act independently.[7] Harding had replied, with his growing irony at the pretensions of the Senate, "Very likely the thing which you suggest will be adopted as a reservation by the Senate. I fear the Senate would be very unhappy if it did not have opportunity to write a reservation. . . . Of course, you know, as I do, that there is nothing in any of the treaties which involves us in any way, which commits us to make war, which includes us in any alliance, or otherwise endangers our freedom of action." [8]

In his message to the Senate on the subject of the treaties, Harding was more careful to court favor. He referred to his former membership in the Senate and its "proper jealousy" over its part in framing foreign agreements. He admitted that this had been in his mind when he asked Senators Lodge and Underwood to serve as delegates to the Washington Conference. This was designed to allow the Senate to participate in the negotiations. "The Senate's concern for freedom from entanglements," Harding asserted, "for preserved traditions, for maintained independence, was never once forgotten by the American delegation." It was thus the Senate's turn to accept the fact of the Chief Executive's responsibility and to approve of "shared authority" in the making of the treaties. Otherwise, if the treaties were rejected, the Senate would "discredit the influence of the Republic, render future efforts futile or unlikely, and write discouragement" when the world was ready to acclaim new hope.[9]

The subtlety of Harding's strategy was shown by the fact that the vain Lodge became the chief defender of the three treaties, which he had helped to frame, while Underwood prevented a complete revolt among the Democrats. Lodge had been steadily wooed by Harding. When Lodge had asked that a warship go to Boston for reconditioning rather than to another yard, Harding had involved his whole Cabinet in his reluctant refusal, on the grounds that Newport News had put in the lowest tender.[10] Harding would not oppose Lodge on his own, and he flattered the Senator's vanity by frequent conferences with him. As a result, Lodge fought the treaties through in their agreed form, although the Senate could not resist a final slap at the executive branch. A reservation was adopted to the Four Power Treaty: the United States would have, under its terms, "no commitment to armed force, no alliance, no obligation to join in any defense." Thus the Treaty was no more than a declaration of isolation and of hope. Here Lodge ignored Harding's plea that such a reservation was "utterly needless" and tended "to discredit the influence of our government in undertaking the most conservative action to increase international peace." [11]

Harding became bitter about this last humiliation by the Senate, when he had done everything to conciliate that body. When Finley Peter Dunne reminded him that Wilson had made the same complaint about Harding and the Old Guard, Harding replied sharply, "That was different." [12] In fact, it was. Wilson had tried to override the Senate and had failed completely to make a radical departure from traditional American foreign policy. Harding had tried to include the Senate in a "most conservative action" and had won nine-tenths of what he wanted. The difference between the Senate under Wilson and that under Harding was that Wilson's Senatorial enemies were usually reactionaries, while Harding's were usually progressives. Only on the subject of foreign affairs did both Presidents find that the jealousy of the Senate made them the same enemies.

As the year 1922 progressed, Harding grew to resemble Wilson more and more in his anger at the Senate's claim to control foreign policy. He refused to write a personal letter to Lodge to recommend his reelection in Massachusetts, and he was curt about Lodge's proposal in the Senate that an economic conference should be called to deal with conditions in war-torn Europe. "On the face of things," he wrote to Lodge, "it is equivalent to saying that the executive branch of the government, which is charged with the conduct of foreign relations, is not fully alive to a world situation which is of deep concern to the United States. As a matter of fact, the European economic situation has been given most thorough and thoughtful consideration for many months. Without questioning the good faith of the proposal, I am very sure it would have been more seemly, and the action of the Con-

gress could be taken much more intelligently if proper inquiry
had been made of the State Department." [13] The fool that the
Old Guard of the Senate thought was in the White House was
learning every day to reproach his old masters for their folly.

The seeming success of the Washington Conference, with its
guarantees of disarmament through "a parchment peace," marked
the high point of Harding's Administration. It was the ideal
peace of the rural dream—a peace that seemed to cost nothing and
involve no one. When the commentators summed up Harding's
achievements after one full year in office, in the spring of 1922,
the success of the disarmament meeting led the list. It was followed
by his campaign for economy in government, brought about by
his Director of the Budget, Charles Dawes.

In fact, the popularity of Harding and his Administration was
briefly at the flood, while Congress was accused of preventing
the government from being one of the best of all time. "Congress
is the liability of the Republican party to-day," declared the Boston
Transcript, "the President and his Cabinet its great asset." In one
year, Harding's image of sweet reason had changed the public
mind from an approval of the Republican majorities in Congress,
as a check against the dictator in the White House, into a disapproval of them for not helping their own President to get the
country back to normalcy.

Even the antagonistic William Allen White admitted that Harding was doing "a better than fair job." The President did rule
through all the Best Minds, Incorporated, and he played no favorites, even among the Best Fellows, Limited, his social friends. In
fact, Harding merely listened to the better minds and chose between them. There was no "best or first." The President had "few
friends and several advisers." White, the old supporter of Roosevelt, admitted that perhaps the theory that *any* man could be
President might be right: "It would seem as if democracy were
based upon the theory that if you put one red shot and two hundred black ones in a double-barreled shotgun, and fired both
barrels at the National Convention of Elks, you could take the
man hit by the red shot and make a president of him." And then
the rural White admitted why, in the case of Harding, he approved

of the dogma of the average man in the White House. Harding was "a country man, not an urban citizen." [14]

This prejudice of White's explained why Harding remained generally and easily popular. His studied policy of appearing reasonable and of appealing to the best in all men disarmed critics. Harding followed the policy of the medieval kings: he could do no wrong; if wrong was done, it was always the fault of his advisers or enemies. As a rural gentleman in Washington, he could and did seem a dignified man of common sense, helped by the best minds, but set upon by city tricksters. His successes were his own; his failures were those of his enemies, for his heart was good.

The continuing support of Harding in rural areas—despite rapidly falling farm prices—was further explained by another article of White's in the summer of 1922. Twenty-six years before, White had written a famous piece, "What's the Matter with Kansas?" This boosting praise of the American economic system had been widely reprinted by Mark Hanna and had been a factor in McKinley's defeat of Bryan. Now White tried to repeat his feat with an article called "What's the Matter with America?" It revealed obliquely why the new McKinley in the White House retained the loyalty of those who had supported the old.

According to White, the state capitals had become "a replica of the city halls, with the little band of protesters recruited from the small towns and rural districts." A "moron majority" from the large cities had taken over control of American democracy. The new immigrants, who bred so fast, were more dangerous than their "fellow half-wits in Europe," for they were exploiting the genuine democracy of America, the government of which was "nuts for them." [15]

So the old progressive, William Allen White, now spoke almost in the voice of the reviving Ku Klux Klan. And he explained the enduring popularity of the rural and standpat man in the White House, who had stopped immigration and boosted business and wanted to return to the times of McKinley, when the old-stock Americans had ruled the land from the cracker barrel in the grocery store. Harding appealed to those farmers and townsmen who felt that their status was declining in the face of new urban values and riches. It was useless for Heywood Broun to write "What's the Matter with White?" and point out that the old-stock rural Americans were "perfectly capable of rolling their own" moron majority and that the new immigrants were no more moronic than the old ones. White and Harding and most of the old-stock Americans did believe wrongly what another critic accused them of believing: that "men are not created equal, but that their grandfathers are." [16]

So Harding stood on the threshold of his second year, with business beginning to improve in the cities and with the country-dwellers still in favor of this representative of rural nostalgia and exclusiveness. He had been a fortunate and skillful President. But, as the acute Uncle Henry of *Collier's* warned, it was going to be harder on Warren than it had been on other Chief Executives because his Presidential honeymoon had lasted longer. And that ancient custom was "about as personal as the hearty breakfast they give a condemned man." [17]

Harding's immediate trouble was an old one. His relationship with the Senate grew worse and worse. He felt himself every inch a President—except in his dealings with Capitol Hill. As he told the National Press Club at the close of his first full year in office, he felt as if he had been "President for twenty years. Life since I came to the White House has been so full there is scarcely an impression left of the life before. There is only one distinct one. I recall my previous conception of the Senate as compared with the one I have to-day, but no unkindliness is meant by that." [18] The unkindliness was all on the side of the Senate, and Harding was puzzled by the hostility of that once-friendly body.

Hostility toward Harding was especially bitter in the farm bloc of the Senate. By the end of 1921, according to Senator Capper of Kansas, American farmers had lost $8,000,000,000 in crop values compared with the values of 1919. The poverty of the farmer led to his growing power in Congress. The bipartisan farm bloc took over the leadership of the Senate from the moribund Old Guard. In the Senate itself, rural areas were heavily over-represented at the expense of urban areas. Thus the Senate was the logical place for the farmer to make his stand.

The farmer's interests, at bottom, were not opposed to those of the industrial worker. They were allied. For with money in his hand, the farmer could buy the goods from the factories in the shops of the small towns. In this way, as Henry C. Wallace pointed out, the prosperity of the city depended upon that of the country. In a timely and prophetic warning, Wallace declared, "Forty per cent of our people are directly dependent upon what they grow from the soil, and the purchasing power of that 40 per cent cannot long continue so seriously out of relation to the purchasing power of the other 60 per cent. If we do not recognize the national danger in this condition and take prompt measures to cure it the cure will come through the operation of brutal economic forces which will lay upon the 60 per cent who do not live on the farms a burden as heavy as that which the farmers are now bearing, and a burden which will cause them even greater suffering." [19]

It was the failure of the Harding government to keep up the purchasing power of the farmers and the small towns that prevented the American economy of the twenties from having a healthy consumer base. Harding was prepared to call a National Agricultural Conference, as he had called a Conference on Unemployment, but he was not prepared to spend government money to help the farmer. He was interested in balancing the national budget and in reducing the national debt, not in balancing the budget of the farmer to equal that of the factory worker or in paying the debt of the cities to the farmer for the food that he produced. While Harding looked after the nation's finances, the farmer should look after his own. As Harding said at the opening of the National Agricultural Conference, "It cannot be too strongly urged that the farmer must be ready to help himself." [20]

The conference came out with the slogan "Equality for Agriculture." The slogan was coined by George N. Peek, who was to be the first administrator of the later Agricultural Adjustment Act, which would make a law of the principle put forward at the conference: The government should subsidize farm prices in order to give the farmer a fair return for his labor. But that legislation was a decade away. Harding rejected such Socialist doctrine;

it conflicted with the memories of his idealized youth. "After all there is no remedy," he wrote to a banker, "which will eliminate periods of hardships which attend the inevitable hazards of farming. I can remember, in my early youth, there were many relatively barren years on the farm, but in those days nobody expected relief through the government. Farmers accepted their fortunes as they came and would economize and deny and seed again and look forward to a helpful harvest. While I believe in every possible help which is consistent with sane government I do fear that in our modern agricultural life we have become too prone to expect the government to cure every ill which is encountered." [21]

The remedy which the conference suggested and which Harding liked was the raising of the tariff to protect American agriculture. On September 21, 1922, the act setting the highest tariff rates in American history received the President's signature—the Fordney-McCumber Act. For once, country and city, Capitol Hill and the White House were agreed. The products of both farm and factory were protected. America First was the theme in all things. Special interests with the ear of the government were given full control over the American market, without any fear of outside competition. The consumer had to pay more. While each Senator fought to protect the industry of his home state—and usually succeeded—even the Secretary of the Treasury ensured his own profits. The Mellon interests that controlled the aluminum market immediately put up the price of aluminum, behind a tariff wall of five cents a pound, and made, according to a later estimate by the Democrats, an annual profit of $10,000,000 on capital of $18,000,000. The Fordney-McCumber Act did set up the Advisory Tariff Commission, through which the President might scale down the tariff to permit increasing trade with European countries; but Harding did not make any significant use of this commission.[22]

The effect of the tariff on world trade was disastrous. It not only prevented Europe from selling to America, but also, through retaliatory European tariffs, prevented America from selling to Europe. Harding's declaration of economic isolation was even more dangerous than his acceptance of political isolation. The prosperity of America no longer depended on the home market. Economics was a worldwide affair. Moreover, as a wealthy creditor nation, America had to play a role in the balance of payments of the world. By insisting on collecting its debts without allowing payment for them in goods, America caused a continuing problem to European governments, one that would bring down their economies with the later crash of the American stock market and the sale of American private investments abroad.

Harding, by temperament, was unable to approve of new measures for new economic situations. Change scared him. When the coal strike forced him to set up a government agency to distribute coal at a fair price, he hated what he was doing. The action tended in a direction that he viewed with "much reluctance." [23] As a newspaper owner, Harding had hated interference with his business and his profits; and even in the White House, he remained a newspaper owner. He refused to see that newspapers could flourish only if people had enough money to buy them. He merely thought that people spent unwisely if they did not buy newspapers. As he wrote of the American farmer, "He throve mightily at the height of war inflation, and he invested, as a rule, no less highly, and generally with the average farmer's usual lack of good judgment. Half the disappointment of the country is not to be traced to the inability of people to earn. The sore spot is always a symptom of inability to expend wisely." [24]

With this businessman's approach, Harding could not hope to come to an agreement with the farm bloc of the Senate. He might seem to be a rural gentleman, but they knew him to be a town entrepreneur. As Carol Kennicott discovered in Gopher Prairie, the small towns existed to fatten on the farmers, not to serve them; "to provide for the townsmen large motors and social preferment" at the expense of the farmer. [25] Despite the rural values that he praised, Warren Harding from Marion was on the side of business against the farmer when the chips were down. He might preach harmony, but he practiced the support of big business.

Thus the farm bloc in the Senate tried to make Harding be good, and they failed. Harding successfully presided over the liquidation of the American government's attempt, under progressive and wartime pressure, to regulate the business of the country. The railroads had already been returned to private hands, and Harding took the opportunity of appointing economic conservatives to the Interstate Commerce Commission, which had been meant to be a progressive check on the railroads. Harding's first appointment to the commission was John J. Esch, coauthor of the transportation act that had returned the railroads to private ownership. As La Follette said, this was a travesty of justice, since Esch could now judge what he had made law. An out-and-out progressive on the commission was rapidly replaced, since Hoover made it his business to inform Harding of what the members of the commission thought of private enterprise.

With the other regulatory commissions set up in the progressive era, Harding pursued the same policy. These boards were turned over to those whom they were meant to curb. The Federal Reserve Board and the Federal Trade Commission were given into the hands of small-town men of limited capacities or of bankers and corporation lawyers. As Senator Norris pointed out later, this process of staffing the federal commissions with businessmen was "the nullification of federal law by a process of boring from within." If trusts, combinations, and big business were to run the government, why did not the Republican Administration allow them to do so directly, rather than through the costly machinery meant to protect the people against monopoly and business control? [26]

Senator Norris also began his long delaying action over the government-owned nitrogen plants and dams at Muscle Shoals in the Tennessee Valley, which Woodrow Wilson had set up for the manufacture of cheap explosives for the American Armed Forces. The Harding government wished to sell them. The folk hero Henry Ford put in a low offer for them, promising to make cheap fertilizers from nitrates for American farmers and to continue to supply explosives to the American government. His propaganda was so efficient that even the farmers of the Tennessee Valley backed Ford's offer. Harding and his Cabinet and a majority of Congress also backed Ford, but Senator Norris did not.

Norris sneered at Ford's proposal as "the most wonderful real-estate speculation since Adam and Eve lost title to the Garden of Eden." [27] He wanted Muscle Shoals to stay in the hands of the government. He wanted to set up what Franklin Roosevelt was to set up, a Tennessee Valley Authority, to provide cheap electrical power for country people. Single-handedly, by the devious use of Senatorial procedures, Norris kept Muscle Shoals from the hands of Henry Ford and in the hands of the government as a nucleus for its later scheme to control the turbulent Mississippi River.

Thus Harding did little or nothing to improve his relations with the discontented farmers and their representatives on Capitol Hill. He might appear to be what William Allen White called him, "the ordinary American, a country man, never urban." [28] Yet his philosophy seemed to be the philosophy of Wall Street. He did not understand the farmers, although he tried to ally himself with them by negotiating to buy for himself the ancestral farm at Blooming Grove and an adjoining farm. He did not see that he could make this purchase only with the money of Marion, the county seat that fattened on the farmers. He had not made his money from the land as a farmer did. He had made commercial money in order to buy up the land as a gentleman did.

In fact, despite his lip service to the values of the farm, Harding confessed to Jennings a curious willingness to force farm boys to follow his path and go to the cities. He would do nothing to put money in the pockets of the farmers, and he knew very well what would happen, as a result, to the rural areas. "Of course," he wrote to Jennings, "the agricultural world cannot go on with such a disparity between agricultural compensation and the present wages to industrial workers. If the adjustment does not come in any other way many of the men will leave the farm and diminish agricultural production and turn to employment in the industrial centers." [29] This would indeed help big business, which had been denied the cheap labor of immigrants from Europe and now needed the cheap labor of immigrants from the farm.

If Harding was no friend to the farmer, he also seemed no friend to the industrial worker. Under union pressure, he had allowed the employees of the Marion *Star* to join the unions. If he had not done so, he would have been threatened with union opposition at the polls of Ohio. Although Harding was proud of never having had a labor dispute on the *Star*, he also was a believer less in unions than in the benevolent paternalism of employers. To him, a manufacturers' association or a Chamber of Commerce was the most natural thing in the world, while a labor union was something of a conspiracy against business.

The hostility of labor toward business grew as it became evident that the government was a businessman's government. Attorney General Harry Daugherty was extremely reactionary. He openly supported the American Plan, a scheme for keeping or instituting the open shop in industry or for setting up company unions run by employers. Harding backed Daugherty in this view. In reply to a letter from the head of Marion's largest company, Harding declared his support for the broad principle that "every American citizen, whether union or non-union, should have the privilege of working where and when he pleases and should be guaranteed protection by the government in the exercise of this right as an American citizen." [30] Of course, this support of the open shop was intended to shatter the growing strength of the labor unions, which had 4,000,000 members by the end of the First World War. Within the decade, union strength was to be reduced to 2,700,000 members because of the American Plan, often backed up by the full powers of the Department of Justice.

Faced with reduced wages and falling union membership, the leaders of American labor decided to fight. In January, a strike of textile workers began in New England; it was called in opposition to wage reductions and an increased working week. The strike dragged on for six months and involved 100,000 workers; but it was won—a rare success for labor in 1922. This strike was followed by a strike of 650,000 miners organized by John L. Lewis and the United Mine Workers of America. The strike was called because of wage cutting and the introduction of an irregular working week. A third strike—that of railroad shopmen, involving some 400,000 workers—followed the coal strike; this walkout was also because of wage reductions. In fact, the strikes were not only against falling wages, but also against inefficient management in declining industries. Textiles, coal, and railroads were doing badly in 1922 because of the lack of both capital and modern techniques. The employers were forced to cut wages because of their own inefficiency.

In the face of these strikes, Harding's first gesture was one of conciliation to labor. It was initially the gesture of a public-relations man—it recorded Harding's sympathy with labor without doing much to help the workingman's cause. The most notorious black spot on American industry was the twelve-hour day, seven days a week, in the steel plants. According to Herbert Hoover, it was "barbaric" as well as uneconomic. Hoover arranged for Harding to call a conference of steel manufacturers at the White House, including the most powerful of them all, Judge Gary. Gary's biographer claimed that Gary himself opposed the twelve-hour day and had reduced such shifts to only fourteen men in every hundred among the steelworkers.[31] On the other hand, Hoover and the press thought that Gary viewed the ending of the twelve-hour day as "unsocial and uneconomic." [32] Harding refused to intervene against the steel industry. He merely asked for the appointment of a committee of steel manufacturers, under Gary's leadership. This committee, not unexpectedly, declared itself—after one year of solemn deliberation—opposed to the ending of the twelve-hour day.

Harding himself, however, had gone on record, in a public letter to Gary, as saying that institution of the eight-hour day and the six-day week in the steel industry "would have a tremendously helpful effect throughout the country." This was only a pious hope. But when the report of Gary's committee finally came out in 1923, Hoover drafted another public letter for Harding that expressed the President's disappointment. Harding was now prepared to be bolder, for he had decided to run for a second term in the White House, and he needed labor's support. This second letter of protest led to a massive public outcry against the steel manufacturers, and they backed down. Before the President's death, the twelve-hour day in the steel industry was abolished, giving Warren Gamaliel Harding the credit for the only act that he ever performed to help labor against inhuman exploitation by American industry.

Harding's first letter to Gary, hoping that he would end the twelve-hour day, did not persuade the leaders of labor that the government was on the side of workingmen. Harding complained against "the evident propaganda to make this administration seem unfriendly to organized labor." [33] But the propaganda was the truth, as events were to show. The coal strike was growing ugly. At Herrin, in Southern Illinois, armed miners killed some twenty strikebreakers who were trying to resume work there. The coroner's jury returned a verdict that blamed the officials of the Southern Illinois Coal Company for causing the deaths of the strikebreakers. No one was convicted for the murders.

The Herrin massacre sent a shock of fear around the business sections of the country. Pressure for government intervention was overwhelming. Harding could no longer let striking miners lie. He called John L. Lewis and the mineowners to conferences in the White House. He carefully did not seek to punish the killers of the strikebreakers at Herrin for fear of antagonizing the miners, who had suffered for fifty years from the brutality of the private armies of the coal operators. "I suppose," Harding excused himself to his business friend Malcolm Jennings, "nobody felt worse than I did about the Herrin matter, but there is not anything that the federal administration could do except talk about it, and I have a very strong aversion to a government official indulging in excessive talk and inadequate action." [34]

Harding's solution of the strike, however, did favor the mine operators. He may have complained privately that they were "so stiff-necked you can't do anything with them." But publicly, when the miners refused to go back to work on their old terms pending arbitration, Harding threatened to call out federal troops to seize the mines and protect strikebreakers. This would have meant total victory for the mineowners. John L. Lewis and the United Mine Workers had to capitulate and accept their old terms, on the understanding that a federal commission of inquiry would investigate the conditions in the coalfields.[35] In fact, the miners lost everything by putting their faith in the commission. Although it

found for the miners on the whole, its recommendations were ignored by Congress, and Lewis' men were worse off at the end
of the golden twenties than they had been at the beginning.

Although the coal strike was ended, the railroad strike continued.
The Esch-Cummings Transportation Act of 1920 had created a
Railway Labor Board to rule on wages and railroad affairs. This
board had increased and then cut the shopmen's wages. When the
shopmen struck, the board had ruled that they should lose their
seniority rights. Although most railwaymen stayed at work, sabotage and violence resulted, and the railways ground to a halt. Harding, after consulting with the reactionary Daugherty, commanded
"all persons to refrain from all interference with the lawful effort
to maintain interstate transportation and the carrying of the
United States mails." The shopmen ignored the President's message. Then Hoover intervened to bring about a solution, but he
could not persuade the railroad owners to accept any concessions
or to restore the seniority rights of the strikers. The situation
seemed to have reached an impasse.

At this time, the *New Republic* published an accurate appraisal
of how Harding saw himself in the struggle of labor against
capital. He wanted to be "a friendly neutral." The effulgence of
his general goodwill fell "upon the man in overalls as well as
upon the man in frock coat and top hat." He wanted both to
prosper. Yet this position was impossible, for Harding lacked the
intelligence to see both sides of a question. "In spite of the best
will in the world . . . defect in intellectual power will inevitably
range a man on the side which makes the most definite appeal
to his unacknowledged prejudices and preconceptions." [36] Harding *was* a businessman, and, in the end, he backed business, even
if he was not prepared to go "to the brutal test of strength."

His bias was rapidly shown by his address to Congress on the
strike crisis, on August 18, 1922. He had received secret information from labor spies that the railroad shopmen knew that they
could not win unless the other railroad men joined them. In the
reports, the spies had quoted a labor official as calling the President
"this old skunk at the White House"—and Harding hated being
called names.[37] Daugherty had also tried to persuade Harding that

the railroad strike was part of a vast Communist plot to call a general strike and take over the United States.[38] It is doubtful that Harding believed such lunacy but he had certainly been fired into militance. He had discarded his resignation of the previous week, when he had written: "Perhaps the battle between capital and labor must be fought again, as it has many times before. Neither defeat nor victory has ever been proven decisive for any considerable period of time." [39]

To Congress, Harding appeared as the strong man on the side of business and government intervention. While proclaiming that the government had always remained "a just neutral," he declared the government's willingness to invoke laws against attempts by the railroad shopmen to stop strikebreakers from keeping the trains running. "There are statutes forbidding conspiracy to hinder interstate commerce. There are laws to assure the highest possible safety in railway service. It is my purpose to invoke these laws, civil and criminal, against all offenders alike." Harding even asked for a new law to enable federal courts to judge the Herrin massacre, because two aliens had been killed there. He declared himself against "mob warfare," which had been directed "against men merely for choosing to accept lawful employment." Although Harding said that he approved of labor unions in principle, he denied them in practice any weapons to stop the employers from breaking them through the open shop and the employment of scabs.[40] Press opinion was that the President's speech was the most scathing indictment ever laid upon any body of workers in America, "the voice of a patient man who has decided to use force." [41]

Daugherty took Harding's speech as approval of strong action. He went to Chicago and found a federal judge, James H. Wilkerson, who owed his appointment to Daugherty and Harding. The Attorney General evidently knew his man, for when Daugherty had presented the government's brief of crimes committed by the striking shopmen, Wilkerson issued a brutal temporary injunction against the strikers. It forbade them from interfering in any way with strikebreakers on the railroads. They could not even picket peacefully or incite others to picket. Although the injunction was unconstitutional and denied the strikers their rights under law, it broke the strike within two days. The railroad shopmen were utterly defeated. And Daugherty expressed his determination to continue the fight for big business with every weapon in his power, saying that so long as, and to the extent that, he could speak for the government of the United States, he would use the power of the government "to prevent the labor unions of the country from destroying the open shop."

Daugherty's action caused an explosion in the Cabinet. Hoover and Hughes thought it was "outrageous in law as well as morals." Although Daugherty claimed later that Harding had backed him in his action, Hoover wrote that he had denounced Daugherty openly in front of Harding and that the flabbergasted Daugherty had been rebuked by Harding and made to withdraw the illegal parts of the injunction.[42] Albert Fall also claimed to have denounced Daugherty. In all, Daugherty suffered badly for his temerity, although a Red conspiracy to get him out of office hardly began at this point, as he later asserted.

In fact, Harding could now have easily shed his unpopular Attorney General, with the feeling that his political debt of gratitude had been canceled by Daugherty's recklessness. But he chose to stick by Daugherty, despite denunciations of the Attorney General's illegal action by labor and in Congress. Harding's incredible loyalty to Daugherty had no limit. Perhaps it was because of the President's vanity and refusal to believe that he could have chosen his friends and Cabinet wrongly. Or perhaps it was because the forced resignation of Daugherty might seem to be an admission on the part of the President that the scandals increasingly blamed on the Department of Justice were true. As in the case of the accusation that he was a Negro, Harding chose to ignore rumors and smears, in the hope that they would smear only their users. He had used smears against the President when he had been a Senator, and he knew how often the smears were false.

The angry farm bloc in the Senate had decided to take their revenge on the government by attacking Harding at his weakest point. A Cabinet is only as strong as its most inferior men, and these were obviously Daugherty and Fall. The attack on Daugherty began in response to the scandals in the Department of Justice, not in response to his action over the railroad strike, as he later claimed. In June, 1922, Daugherty was accused of failing to prosecute war profiteers. One of these, Charles W. Morse, had once been jailed and had used Daugherty to secure a pardon from President Taft. Morse had again employed Daugherty over litigation in 1916 and 1917, when he was growing suspiciously rich on shipping deals with the government. He and his board of directors were not being prosecuted vigorously for their war profiteering. Congress wished to know why and threatened to investigate and perhaps impeach the Attorney General.

Harding's reaction to the assault of Congress on his Cabinet was not to question Daugherty's behavior, but to see the assault as another tactic of Capitol Hill in its war on the White House. He saw the attack on Daugherty as a repetition of the Ballinger affair, when muckraking members of Congress had forced the resignation of Taft's Secretary of the Interior. He hated "the tendency of the Congress to investigate the heads of its own administration. There might be partisan excuse for such a course if the Congress were of a different political faith, but to have a Congress overwhelmingly in majority in the same party seeking to destroy public confidence is a most unusual manifestation. There is no explanation for it, of which I can think, except the unfortunate tendency to get away from the party system and party responsibility." [43]

The attack on Daugherty by Congress grew. It was led by Congressman Oscar Keller of Minnesota, and it ended in a formidable list of charges, which were filed with the Committee on the Judiciary of the House of Representatives. Among the charges were that Daugherty or his subordinates had failed to enforce the antitrust laws, had refused to prosecute war profiteers and bootleggers, had obtained pardons for favored criminals, had secured the Chicago injunction against the strikers by undue influence on the local judge, had employed corrupt people in the Department of Justice, had set federal agents to shadow critics in Congress, had diverted funds to illegal uses, and had failed to prosecute the Standard Oil Company for trespassing on government oil lands.

Daugherty's reply was in three parts. He denied completely those charges for which he had to admit responsibility. He shifted the onus of the blame onto subordinates or onto other departments whenever he could. And he claimed that the trusts and bootleggers were being prosecuted, but that charges took a long time to prepare and to reach the overcrowded courts. Moreover, he questioned the motives of his critics. "Back of this so-called bill of impeachment," Daugherty declared in his rebuttal of the charges, "stands arrayed certain radical leaders of certain organizations seeking to serve notice upon every future Attorney General that if he dare enforce the laws of the United States against such organizations he does so under the pain and penalty of being haled before the Senate of the United States, sitting as a high court of impeachment under the Constitution." [44]

Harding refused to believe the charges against Daugherty, although he was receiving increasing evidence that his minor appointees and Daugherty's Ohio friends were betraying him. Doctor Sawyer, the old Marion physician, hated the convivial Charles R. Forbes of the Veterans' Bureau, and he took it upon himself to prove Forbes's corruption to Harding. Harding, who had been proud of the work Forbes had apparently done in building hospitals for the veterans, was angry. The suicide of Forbes's second-in-command confirmed his suspicions. By one account, he called Forbes in to see him and tried to choke him. At any rate, he forced Forbes to resign. He did not live long enough to see Forbes sent to jail for two years for graft involving perhaps $2,000,000,000.

There was also the question of the increasing notoriety of the Ohio Gang. Daugherty later defended the Buckeye men as "real Republicans." The invidious phrase was manufactured, according to him, by renegade Republicans seeking to take over the party in Ohio.[45] But the Ohio Gang was real enough. The lobbyists and friends of Daugherty from Columbus moved to the richer pickings of Washington. Chief of these was Jess Smith, Daugherty's familiar and accountant and worshiper. He was given office space in the Department of Justice, near Daugherty's own office. He was thought to be Daugherty's mouthpiece and his agent for unofficial business. He lived with Daugherty in a house on H Street, lent by the wealthy proprietor of the Washington *Post*, Ned McLean, also an Ohio man. Smith was also the clown in charge of another little house on K Street, which was the center of the operations of the Ohio Gang, with its parties and its profiteering, its contacts and its blackmailing.[46]

Daugherty's chief agent in terrorizing into silence those who knew too much about the Ohio Gang was his chosen head of the Federal Bureau of Investigation, William J. Burns. Burns had been a notorious private detective, chiefly distinguished for strikebreaking activities. He ran his federal service as a private "government by blackmail," according to Senator Brookhart. Those who spoke out against Daugherty and the Ohio Gang were immediately investigated by Burns's men in order to force them to be dumb. Complaints against Burns were legion, and some reached the White House. There is in the Harding papers a letter from the news editor of a Brooklyn newspaper to George Christian claiming that Burns had used his agents against Brooklyn reporters and had called him "a G— D— liar" and "a damn big stiff." [47] Such action by a federal employee against the newspapers was hardly likely to increase President Harding's popularity.

How much Harding knew about the activities of the Ohio Gang is open to question. He did go from time to time to poker and drinking parties at the house on H Street. He also invited the Ohio Gang to parties at the White House. Alice Roosevelt Longworth once went to Harding's study while an official reception was going on below. "No rumor," she reported, "could have exceeded the reality; the study was filled with cronies, Daugherty, Jess Smith, Alec Moore, and others, the air heavy with tobacco smoke, trays with bottles containing every imaginable brand of whisky stood about, cards and poker chips ready to hand—a general atmosphere of waistcoat unbuttoned, feet on the desk, and the spittoon alongside." [48] Cabinet members sometimes attended these parties, but they excused themselves early. They were, after all, breaking the prohibition law and wasting their time.

Harding does not seem to have been involved in the actual misdemeanors of the Gang. The Gang involved him as a private person in its petty drinking and betting in order to *appear* to involve the President in its peddling of government influence. The truth of the matter was probably described by the Boston manager of the Hearst newspapers. He said that Harding was made a fool of. The President liked a game of cards and liked the girls. He would go over sometimes to the little red house of the Gang and play poker and drink. The grafters in the Gang would say, "Hand over your money to us and come around to the little red house this evening and we will show you our influence with the President." Those seeking government favors would be allowed to peek over the stairs and see the President enter the house. They then gave up their money, which never reached Harding.[49] It is not necessary for a lobbyist to *have* influence over the government. He must merely *seem* to have it.

Harding's guilt over the peculations of the Ohio Gang was in choosing to associate with such men of easy virtue. He must have known from his Ohio days how lobbyists sell to the gullible their acquaintance with the great. He chose to remain friendly with questionable Ohio operators, and for the conviviality of the poker table, he sacrificed the good name of his Administration. He had, after all, put Daugherty in office. By keeping his Attorney General, he made himself responsible for Daugherty's scandalous behavior. Harding wished to be a good President, but he did not choose to see an obvious fact: a President is thought to be only as good as his associates.

Evidence of the level at which Harding felt friendly toward Daugherty is found in an exchange of letters between them. Daugherty had promised to make a speech outside Washington, but no longer wished to do so. He wanted Harding to write him a letter saying that urgent affairs kept the Attorney General in Washington. "I don't want you to lie for me as I would be delighted to lie for you," Daugherty wrote, confessing his chosen role as the evil genius behind Harding's mask of innocence, "but you can do this in a second and I will forgive you what you owe me on account of the bet you made Saturday morning." Harding's reply was formal and stiff and distant, although he did what Daugherty wanted: "I will be glad if you will make your excuse in order to be ready to meet the possible problems which I may be called upon to refer to you." [50]

The letters reflect the relationship between the men. Daugherty was always trying to keep the friendship on the basis of equality, that of cronies or of brothers. Later, Daugherty was to claim that Harding "was like a younger brother" who appealed to him "for advice more than to any or all other men put together." [51] For Daugherty's political career now depended entirely on his master. On the other hand, Harding was withdrawing more and more into the aloofness of the Presidency and was seeking the advice of the best minds, such as Hoover and Hughes and Mellon. Harding, unfortunately, could not definitively break off his friendship with Daugherty for fear of being thought ungrateful. He was prepared to risk his reputation rather than be thought mean to his old friends.

Death came too soon to Harding for historians to judge whether he would have shed his Attorney General in the end. Certainly, he gave Daugherty less and less of his time and confidence and favor. Daugherty's subordinate in charge of pardons told the Senate that Harding, in the latter part of his Administration, would not pardon anyone unless the criminal had served some part of his sentence in jail, "no matter what the situation was." It was probably Harding's command to Daugherty that he should disassociate himself from Jess Smith and his known peculations that led to Smith's melancholia and suicide. And, significantly, Harding wrote to Daugherty himself, on December 4, 1922, about someone accused of corruption. In this letter, he seemed to make an oblique attack on Daugherty, who had asked to be responsible for alien property. "There appear to be commercial and financial vultures," the President wrote, "wherever there is a piece of property to be disposed of and not infrequently we find it impossible to escape their damning influence." [52]

The damning influence of the commercial and financial vultures was already evident to Harding in the matter of the private leases on the naval oil reserves. Ever since Fall's appointment as Secretary of the Interior, the dedicated conservationists, led by Gifford Pinchot, had been watching him with suspicion. They feared the actions of such an adventurer and rancher. They noted that Fall and Denby had persuaded Harding to sign an executive order that transferred control over the government oil reserves to the Department of the Interior. A private oil company owned by

Edward Doheny soon began to drill on one of the three great oil reserves set aside by Taft and Wilson as a strategic store for the future needs of the American Navy. When Fall then proposed to take over the Forestry Service from the Secretary of Agriculture and to give over the Territory of Alaska to exploitation by private business, Pinchot began a detailed campaign against Fall in the press. The opponents of the Administration were quick to seize upon details of scandal in the Department of the Interior.

On April 7, 1922, Fall leased the entire oil reserve at Teapot Dome, Wyoming, to Harry Sinclair and his Mammoth Oil Company. The story reached the conservationists three days later. They passed it on to the farm bloc in the Senate. Fall was forced to admit to the lease in public and to another lease, on the California oil reserves, granted to Edward Doheny. Thus all three naval oil reserves were given over to Sinclair and Doheny in return for a percentage payable to the government. There was no competitive bidding. The naval oil reserves were to be tapped by private interests for private and public profit. Only part of the oil was to be stored aboveground for the Navy.[53]

On April 28, La Follette asked for the appointment of a Senate Committee to investigate the matter of the oil leases. His resolution was approved. Although the committee was led by Reed Smoot, Harding's friend and a standpatter, Thomas Walsh of Montana was a member of the committee, and he had a sharp nose for corruption. He was to prove after Harding's death the venality of Albert Fall, who had accepted a cash payment of $100,000 from Doheny and at least $233,000 in bonds from Sinclair.

Meanwhile, Harding was well acquainted with the matter of the leases of the naval oil reserves. Although he had made speeches in favor of conservation in his Presidential campaign, he had never supported exclusion of private interests from public lands. He supported "rational, natural, and becoming development" of national resources through private and public funds, although he opposed "further doling out of natural resources to favored groups."[54] He had arranged for Fall to take over the naval oil reserves, and he approved of Fall's policy in leasing them to private interests. As he wrote to the Senate, in a letter accompanying the documents that Fall handed over to the investigating committee, Fall's leasing policy was submitted to him "prior to the adoption thereof, and the policy decided upon and the subsequent acts have at all times had my entire approval." Even if he had not been fully informed, Harding was too angry at the Senate not to defend his Secretary of the Interior against its inquisition. Harding was continually being warned against Fall by private correspondents. One observer in New Mexico called Fall "an *absorber*, and all for his own selfish ends—he would absorb the presidency if he could, and many think he has absorbed the *President* to quite an extent." [55] Harding replied that he did not for an instant share his correspondent's views. Why should he, when Fall had been supported by the dead Roosevelt, the archexponent of conservation?

In fact, Harding was prepared to back Secretary Fall's policy to the full, as was Harry Daugherty. When one of his own friends and campaign contributors, Colonel Darden, tried to drill illegally for oil in the Teapot Dome, Harding told the colonel that he was "obliged to protect the government's interests" and that he "hoped to avoid taking drastic measures in doing so." [56] When Darden continued to drill there, Harding was prepared to back Fall in sending the Marines to clear out Darden's men. "Friendship," Harding declared, "does not justify the defiance of government authority." [57] In the end, the Marines were sent in, and Darden's men left.

A copy of a Daugherty letter remains in the Harding papers that says that Daugherty knew "absolutely nothing" about the Teapot Dome; but Daugherty did interview Darden over the affair, and thus he must have learned about it, despite his later denials of any knowledge. The evidence shows that both Harding and Daugherty knew of the Teapot Dome and were prepared to use the Marines *against their own friends,* under the mistaken impression that Fall had leased the oil reserves to Sinclair and Doheny at the best possible advantage to the government and at none to himself. "I have both a very high regard for your ability," Harding wrote confidentially to Fall on July 14, 1922, "and an unfaltering belief in your integrity. I had these impressions when I asked you to come into the Cabinet, and I have had no reason of any kind to modify my earlier impressions concerning you as either friend or public servant." [58]

Despite this letter, Harding accepted Fall's resignation on January 2, 1923. Fall's reasons for resigning did not seem to have anything to do with the proposed investigation by the Senate. In fact, Harding was so little worried by this aspect of the affair that he reportedly offered Fall a seat in the Supreme Court. Fall refused, for he had already accepted a lucrative post in the oil business under Harry Sinclair.

Secretary Fall had obviously done what he had meant to do in the Department of the Interior—to hand over the naval oil reserves to those who would pay him well for them. He had failed in his second ambition—to absorb the President. Harding was listening more and more to the advice of the best minds of Hoover and Hughes and Mellon and less and less to the advice of cronies such as Daugherty and Fall. It was as though the President had at last learned to suspect the suspicious. Moreover, Fall saw that he would be defeated by Secretary Wallace in his effort to get hold of the national forests and Alaska Territory. He had already been defeated by Hughes in an attempt to declare an aggressive policy against Mexico, where Fall had interests. In fact, Fall had made his money from the lease of the oil reserves, and now he wanted to turn his talents for wheeling and dealing to private affairs.

Thus, with little definite proof of scandal, Harding had grounds for suspicion of his friends. So much was alleged by Congress against Daugherty and Fall that something had to stick. Harding knew enough of the pasts of both men to have private doubts about their purity in office. His consolation was probably that they were too clever to be caught. And even if he did not suspect his friends, blinded by a loyalty that discounted a whole lifetime of political shrewdness, he might have pondered over the message that was sent by the famous Jacob Coxey of Ohio, who had once led an army in protest against Washington: "Do not think for a moment that all Profiteers and grafters are confined to the Democratic Party; (they are like the invisible Government), they look upon the Government as a good thing to feed upon, (knowing no party), as the buzzard does a dead horse, only there is something to be said in favor of the buzzard as he waits until the life has left the body of the horse, while the Profiteer, grafter and invisible Government sucks the life out of the body of the Government during its existence." [59]

Florence Harding's serious illness in the summer of 1922 did not add to her husband's peace of mind. And his sense of fore-boding and disillusion was increased by the result of the midterm election of 1922. Although most midterm elections show a swing away from the government, this one was a massive repudiation. The new radical farmers' organizations—the Non-Partisan League and the Farmer-Labor Party—destroyed Republican control of the prairie states. The number of Republicans in the House fell from 300 to 221, and in the Senate from 59 to 52. In the rural belt, only the old progressive Republicans were sent back to office. Else-where, the standpatters and the supporters of normalcy were routed. The vote was not so much a vote for the Democrats as a protest vote against the worst agricultural depression in the century. Riding on the protest, La Follette of Wisconsin was returned to the Senate by a huge majority.

The election meant a victory for the Insurgents and the farm bloc. They now held the balance of power between the two major parties. Independent newspapers considered the election "a terrific rebuke to Old Guard Republicanism" and "to the normalcy which came dangerously nearly degenerating into reaction." The radical-ism that showed in the voting exceeded sectional bounds and ate "into the very fiber of both the old parties." [60] Harding himself lamented the insurgency of the vote, which refused to endorse the regulars of either party. "The popular American mind has a way of expressing itself and doubtless it is well that it should," he wrote. "I would be much more satisfied with the situation if it always ex-pressed itself for or against a political party and that we might have party sponsorship and party triumph and party ability to do things." [61] He hated those Republicans "who have their individual vote-catching platform and who bear the party banner and rarely if ever respond to the party call of duty." [62]

Harding's response to the election was an immediate effort to put through some progressive legislation in the lame-duck session of Congress, before the new radicals took their seats. Norris tried to pass a law abolishing lame-duck sessions, but the bill passed only in the Senate. In his Annual Message to Congress, on December 8, Harding began with the remarkable admission that the return to normalcy was impossible and that progress must be resumed: "There never again will be precisely the old order; indeed, I know of no one who thinks it to be desirable. For out of the old order came the war itself." Reconstruction had already gone forward faster after the First World War than in any other period in history. Economic conditions, despite the strikes, were improving, and agriculture must not be allowed to fail. But still more must be done. Harding wanted an extension of cheap credits to farmers, and he favored cheap transportation. Behind the new tariff wall, American "self-containment" would allow prosperity to come to the land. And when America was rich again, then it could again engage in more liberal world commerce.

In a bid for the support of the rising nativist feeling in America, Harding asked for bills to provide for the registration and education of aliens. Speaking in words that the Ku Klux Klan could approve, Harding said, "There is a call to make the alien respect our institutions while he accepts our hospitality. There is need to magnify the American viewpoint to the alien who seeks a citizenship among us." America should come first, to those within her shores and without. "We ask no one to assume responsibility for us; we assume no responsibility which others must bear for themselves." Harding once again took refuge in the crudest form of isolationism and Americanism.

While allaying nativist sentiment, Harding also made an effort to steal the rural progressives' thunder. He proposed to abolish child labor, enforce the Volstead Act strictly, set up a commission to investigate the high cost of living, give up the unpopular Railway Labor Board, and restrict the issue of tax-exempt securities. In another matter, too, he struck a new note. He had, from his earliest days, been an enthusiastic advocate of the revolution in communications. He had been one of the first in Marion to buy a motorcar. He had long supported the efficiency of the railways.

He had written enthusiastically about the educational possibilities of the movies, although he himself preferred to see in Washington illegal and smuggled films of prizefighters. Now he spoke up for the coordination of the methods of transport in the United States—the use of the waterways, highways, and railroads to supplement one another and provide cheap freight rates for the farmer. His voice spoke for the future, not the past: "It would be folly to ignore that we live in a motor age. The motor car reflects our standard of living and gauges the speed of our present-day life. It long ago ran down Simple Living, and never halted to inquire about the prostrate figure which fell as its victim." [63]

Such was Harding's attempt to assert the leadership of the White House before the radicals and the Insurgents made a shambles of even the few laws demanded by the President. The press widely hailed Harding for assuming leadership of his party and of Congress at last:

> Political leaders in and out of Congress agree that the "Republican joy ride" is over [declared *The New York Herald*] and that President Harding is determined to compel the participants in it to pay for the damage done by them to his party machine. . . . Senators and Representatives who have talked with the President say he made to them what amounts to a new confession of faith. He has not hesitated to express the opinion that no man who enters the Presidency can long remain reactionary. With engaging frankness the President has informed some of his "hard-boiled" party associates who refused accurately to interpret the recent election results that his view-point on matters of public concern has undergone a material and even drastic change during recent months.[64]

Harding had been "sanely progressive" before, when the tide was flowing that way; and now that he was the leader of his party and was probably going to run again for the White House, he would be "sanely progressive" a second time. In response to popular discontent, Harding was always ready to do a little to allay it, as long as this did not result in "disturbing legislation." [65] If he was going through a temporary slump in his popularity, he was a good enough politician to know that a rise in farm prices and in wages would make him popular again. Until that happened, he was prepared to advocate some cautious change in the laws and in his dealings with Congress. Normalcy had failed. The people had declared so in the elections. Thus, as William Allen White pointed out, Harding had to "decide to turn back to abnormalcy and lead the people as their ruler; not as a mere 'subordinate branch of the government.' We can't go back a quarter of a century. Something has happened; chiefly, Roosevelt and Wilson and really, 'How you goin' to keep them down on the farm—after they've seen Paree!' " [66]

14

Death Without Conclusion

"If I were trying to record much less answer all the attacks made on me, this shop might as well be closed for any other business. I do the best I know how, the very best I can; and I mean to keep on doing it to the end. If the end brings me out all right, what is said against me will not amount to anything. If the end brings me out all wrong, ten angels swearing I was right would make no difference." ABRAHAM LINCOLN, quoted by WARREN HARDING at the dedication of the Lincoln Memorial

Commentators noticed the new strength and purpose in Harding's manner. "Office seekers wear nose guards an' shin protectors when they go to the White House nowadays, an' even then they come out bruised to the color of a California plum," observed Uncle Henry in *Collier's*. "Harry Daugherty carried a whole window frame away with him last time, an' Secretary Fall is still collectin' accident insurance." Harding's very face had changed from "the soft contours of a Floatin' Island" to granite. Every new furrow in his forehead was "a lost faith." But was the change in the President's image a permanent one? "It's all right as a snapshot," Uncle Henry warned, "but I'm afraid the people are goin' to demand a time exposure." [1]

Harding had a success to announce at the closing session of the Sixty-seventh "do-nothing" Congress. (He was dead before he had to deal with the problem of the Sixty-eighth.) His Administration had succeeded in signing an agreement with Britain to fund the British war debt. American loans were to be repaid, although Britain had not yet succeeded in funding its loans to Europe and had failed to pass on its debtors to the United States. Nothing could have made Harding more popular in the eyes of Congress than this agreement to be paid back by Britain. As Harding said, the agreement "means vastly more than the mere funding and the ultimate discharge of the largest international loan ever contracted. It is a recommitment of the English-speaking world to the validity of contract." [2] America's chief debtor, despite its shaky economy, had agreed to pay. And thus Harding stood in triumph in front of his discredited first Congress, which even Senator Lodge admitted had been "more criticized and more fiercely attacked" than any other he had known.

Once Congress was safely in a recess for nine months, Harding continued his attacks upon it. He stressed the danger of factionalism in American life. In front of the new statue of his chosen hero, Alexander Hamilton, Harding reminded his hearers of Hamilton's "seemingly inspired fear of factionalism." The President continued, linking all opposition to himself in a national conspiracy of evil, "We have our factions which seek to promote this or that interest without regard to the relationship to others and without regard for common weal. We have the factions of hatred and prejudice and violence. We have coalitions which would invade the Constitutional rights of others or subvert the Constitution itself. We have our factions challenging both civil and religious liberty, and without them both made everlastingly secure there can be no real human liberty. We have the fatal factionalism which contemplates obstruction to the execution of the laws." [3] Harding had now identified his philosophy of harmony with his own wishes. He wanted only agreement with his policy, not the conflict of pressure groups or the disobedience of the dissatisfied. He had conveniently forgotten that, as a Senator, he had believed that his particular faction was saving the Constitution.

Over foreign policy, prodded by Hughes and Hoover, Harding was prepared to take another bold step forward. He was bidding openly for the League vote of 1920, which had felt itself betrayed by the President's subsequent actions. The unpredictable Borah had suddenly introduced a resolution in the Senate on February 14, 1923, calling for the outlawing of war. War between nations would be declared a crime, and "a judicial substitute for war," modeled on the Supreme Court, would arbitrate compulsorily in international disputes. Hughes and Harding took Borah's declaration to mean that a significant number of the Irreconcilables were veering away from extreme isolationism, under pressure from their constituents. Lodge's near defeat in Massachusetts in 1922 seemed a sign of the times.

Thus Harding, seeking to capture internationalist voters, asked for the Senate's consent on February 24 to join the World Court, already set up at The Hague by the League of Nations. Careful of the Senate's jealousy, reservations on such an American action were suggested by Hughes. These reservations drew careful distinctions between the World Court and the League of Nations, and they committed the United States only to membership in the Court.

The reaction of the Senate Foreign Relations Committee was curious. It opposed entry into The Hague Court because the Court did not have powers of *compulsory* arbitration. Such a stand, Hughes wrote to Harding, was "really amusing, in the light of the historic record of the Senate." [4] Hughes did not for one moment believe that the Senate opposition was in good faith, nor would it support a new world court with compulsory powers. It was merely a tactic to stop the United States from joining an organization already set up by the League. Such suspicious men as Borah considered The Hague Court "an international political tribunal masquerading in the guise of a judicial tribunal . . . under the thumb of the European Premiers." Or even more picturesquely, Borah quoted Arthur Brisbane as saying that the World Court was to the League of Nations "what plain water is to H_2O." [5]

Against such jealousy and suspicion, Harding stood firm. He pointed out that entry into The Hague Court did not mean entry into the League. Hughes's reservations made this clear. Harding denied that he was being inconsistent, for he had always supported peaceful arbitration through an association of nations *outside* the League. Membership in The Hague Court involved no political obligations, as its judgments depended for enforcement merely on friendly national governments and public opinion. As Harding wrote to a nationalistic friend:

> . . . you know me well enough to have confidence that I would urge nothing which would bring about the slightest restriction of the rights of this nation or any of its nationals. I believe, with all my heart, in the proposition which I submitted to the Senate. I think it was desirable in the fulfillment of our part in the world and I think it was necessary, as a political gesture, to give evidence that we are keeping the faith. If it were not for the vanity of some public men and the obstinacy which has been developed in contest there would not be a question about it. I have long since come to that conviction, which is inevitable when one serves as Chief Executive, that we can not be wholly aloof from the world and ought not to be, and I also have the very profound conviction that it is an unseemly thing for this nation to say to the world we are unwilling to have to do with anything which is not our own specific creation or a creation erected under our explicit specifications.[6]

So the ex-Senator, changing into the President, declared himself ready to fight his old masters. He had come to despise the Senate as a reactionary and obstructive body, needlessly jealous of its own powers at the expense of the public good. He would not submit to the Senators any longer. "The great hubbub" over The Hague Court, he wrote to Jennings, was "largely bunk. Most of it emanates from members of the Senate who have very little concern about the favor with which the administration is regarded, and the remainder of it come from those who are nuts either for or against the League. The League advocates have somewhat embarrassed the situation, but I do not fear the outcome. A good many people have urged me very strongly to drop the matter, but I do not find myself ready to accept that sort of a sneaking program." As for Borah himself, who had backed a similar idea and had then backed down, Harding conceded his ability and brilliance, but found him "utterly lacking in practicability, stability and fidelity. He attracts ample attention in the press because the newspapers of today are always looking for the unusual and find him a good copy-maker as a spokesman for the persistent opposition to whatever is." [7]

As the Irreconcilables spoke out louder against the proposal, so popular and press opinion began to back the President. There were ominous threats of a split in the Republican Party on the part of those who thought that the anti-League issue had won the election of 1920, while the Court issues would lose the election of 1924. These Irreconcilables also feared that Harding might not run again in 1924 and would hand over the White House to Hughes or to Hoover, the two best minds who obviously had the most influence over the President. Moreover, Harding's proposed speaking tour of the West on his way to Alaska would provide him with an opportunity to rally the people to the World Court, as Wilson had tried to do over the League in 1919. "We mean to stand by the guns," Harding wrote to Jennings, "and give such a fight as is necessary to defend a righteous and wholly justifiable position. . . . I am sure that it was not only the wisest political gesture which I could make but I think it was the perfectly right thing to do." [8] So spoke the clever politician, who saw in the World Court both a winning and a just issue.

In face of the President's determination, the Republican revolt died down. Harding stated categorically that the Administration did not propose to enter the League "by the side door, the back door, or the cellar door." But he was equally determined to recapture the popularity that the Washington Conference had given him among people and press. The World Court was the logical succession to the Conference on Disarmament. A tribunal should follow the laying up of warships. It not only was good for peace, but also was sound Republican doctrine. Since the days of Roosevelt, all the Republican platforms except the one in 1920 had specifically favored the establishment of a world court. Now that the World Court did exist, America should join it. This was back to international normalcy, after the excessive action of Wilson and the excessive reaction of the Senate.

In his final speech on the matter of The Hague Court, in St. Louis on June 21, Harding adopted his old policy of trying to reconcile the Irreconcilables. But this time, he did not yield his position except on the one issue that matched his own prejudice. He wanted the judges of the World Court to be elected by themselves, not by the League. In other words, he wanted the World Court to have as little to do with its founder as possible. Two conditions were indispensable for America's joining the Court: "*First,* that the tribunal be so constituted as to appear and to be, in theory and in practice, in form and in substance, beyond the shadow of doubt, a world court and not a league court. Second, that the United States shall occupy a plane of perfect equality with every other power." [9] Harding also declared his intention of satisfying a majority in the Senate before joining the Court. He would not be another Wilson.

With these terms, Harding hoped to unite all factions in the Republican Party. "It is finesse instead of combat," one independent newspaper commented, "the compliance of a doctor, rather than the defiance of a crusader." [10] Even if America could not join the World Court on these terms—as some opposition newspapers suspected—Harding was searching for a genuine compromise with the Senate *without conceding his wish* to join the World Court. "My soul yearns for peace," he had declared at St. Louis. "My heart is anguished by the sufferings of war. My spirit is eager to serve. My passion is for justice over force. My hope is in the great court. My mind is made up. My resolution is fixed." [11]

The reasons why Harding took a stand on the issue of the World Court are complex. In part, he was seeking a good campaign issue: a poll in *Collier's* showed that more than four in five of all voters favored the Court.[12] In part, he was showing how much he was now relying on the advice of Hughes and Hoover, the two internationalists in the Cabinet. In part, he was proving his independence of the Senate. And, in part, he was showing something of a change in character, even a spiritual change. While he remained the small-town gentleman playing a part too large for him, the very largeness of that part seems to have pushed out the time-serving politician in him and let in the statesman. He had, at last, the power to do something about his vague feeling of goodwill to all men. If the way to the White House is paved with good intentions, the way in the White House is also occasionally paved with good executions.

In an interesting letter to Brother Joseph Dutton, an eighty-year-old American priest who was running a leper colony in Hawaii, Harding showed something of his increasing aspirations. He did not feel that Brother Dutton's sense of satisfaction could be increased by a letter of praise from the President; but he wanted Brother Dutton to realize that many people regarded his life as a perfect example of self-abnegation, sacrifice, and service. Dutton had set up a model that the President wished might be raised up for the view and emulation of many others, for it was in the selfless service of all their brothers that all men must at last find the great satisfactions and consolations of life.[13]

The question of whether the President was prepared to serve again was answered openly by Harry Daugherty in March, 1923, when he declared that the President would run the following year. This announcement had merely been a confirmation of the probable, and Harry Daugherty had made it less to strengthen Harding's position than his own. His critics had grown vociferous, and Daugherty wished it made clear that the probable President of the United States *for the next five years* would be standing ready to protect his old friend and political manager.

In fact, Harding had always been ready to run again. It was the normal thing to do, and Harding believed in the normal. Although he disliked the unending hard work of the Presidency, he daily felt himself more and more capable of the office, except in occasional moments of weariness. He also liked to draw out his guests by protesting his unwillingness to be President, but this was only an old political trick of his: he liked to be called for, not to call. Eight months before Daugherty's announcement, Harding had confided in Jennings his views on a second-term candidacy. Although he claimed to be doing no fence building, he wrote, "If I do well none of the opposition will amount to a continental, and if I do not do well I ought to be unanimously opposed." [14] By the spring of 1923, Harding thought that he was doing well.

There had been talk of Harding's second term since the beginning of the year. Senator Watson declared Harding's renomination inevitable, and most of the newspapers agreed.[15] If Harding did not seek a second term, he would be confessing to the failure of his first term. And neither his own vanity nor his party could countenance such a development. But the timing of his official decision to run was taken out of his hands by the personal decision of Daugherty.

Since Fall's announced resignation and the investigation of the Department of Justice by Congress, Daugherty's resignation was expected daily. On January 12, 1923, William Allen White declared, "Soothsayers in Washington pretend to see the shadow of Daugherty coming out of the front door of the White House with his resignation accepted, stalking into the oblivion whence he came. He is expected to follow Secretary Fall. Shadows of coming events cast themselves into the whispering gallery of politics." [16] With the threat of exposure coming nearer, Daugherty proved more and more difficult to see. He was rarely in his office and would answer no questions. After Jess Smith's suicide, Daugherty suffered some sort of nervous breakdown. He went to Florida to recuperate. There, pressed by reporters and conscious that his enemies had the President's ear, he declared that Harding would run again. He was under pressure from "the unjust criticism" of public figures by "the scallawag and the blatherskite." [17] These criticisms of himself were being given wide publicity. He wanted to counter by putting himself on the front page as the President's manager, in order to scare the opposition.

He was successful. "One blast from the bugle horn of Harry Daugherty," declared the *Literary Digest*, "sets the wild echoes flying in every corner of the land." [18] Although most commentators declared themselves puzzled by the suddenness of Daugherty's declaration, Daugherty pretended to Harding that he had made a slip of the tongue about a second term for the President. "I have never mentioned [it] to you," he wrote to Harding, "and you have never mentioned the matter to me. I hope it has not embarrassed you. I never speak for you without having first received explicit authority. . . . Just what happened was that the newspaper men had importuned me to give them a visit. . . . It was my personal opinion. It is my personal opinion. It was said without any expectation of exploitation." [19] Always the supreme political animal, Daugherty was ever seeking vindication, even for his calculated indiscretions. He was always prepared to do wrong as long as he was thought right.

Harding's reaction to Daugherty's outburst was one of tolerance and kindness. To Jennings, he confessed that he was a little embarrassed by Daugherty's announcement. He did not want his tour of the West and of Alaska to have the appearance of a series of campaign speeches for a second term: "I really want to speak as President, and am convinced that I can do so." Again, as in 1916, Harding wrote off Daugherty as a spent force. The Attorney General had "really been seriously ill." He was improving, however, and should be able to go on with the work of his office. Yet Harding doubted whether Daugherty could ever become again "as active politically as he has been in the past." [20] Just as he continued to provide a job at the Mint for the faithful pensioner Scobey, Harding wanted to keep Daugherty in the Department of Justice to sweeten his declining days.

General agreement that Harding would become the nominee of the Republican Party for a second time was owing to the lack of a serious challenger to the President. Without a rival folk hero and without a slump, Harding's chances of a second term in the White House looked good. Yet although the prosperity in the cities continued, a folk hero did arise. His name was Henry Ford.

There was an extraordinary boom for Ford for President in both major parties in 1923. *Collier's* held a poll as to the most *popular* choice for the next President. Ford beat Harding, 88,865 votes to 51,755 votes with McAdoo a bad third with 19,407 votes. Ford ran ahead of the President even in Ohio. Ford began giving interviews on the subject "If I Were President." A summary of his life appeared in *World's Work*. The boom for the maker of the Model T was under way.

The reasons for Ford's popularity give an insight into the continued favor in which Harding was held. Ford declared that he was no politician, and Harding had always hidden the fact that he was. Both were country boys who had made good. Ford had revolutionized American life by producing a million cheap cars a year; Harding had done his little bit in the communications revolution by running a successful newspaper and boosting the revolution. Despite his business success, Ford still spoke in the language of the country store and the old American Way. So did Harding, although he did not go so far as Ford, who declared that big cities were illogical, uneconomic, unsanitary, and necessarily insolvent. Both men promised a businessman's government with a rural heart. In this way, both appealed to the mind of the small town. It so happened that Ford appeared to be the stronger and more successful of the two. Thus he was briefly more popular, with his promise to be "a scientist" in government and to give the American people all they wanted. "Many will say that he is already the Chief Executive of the United States," one journalist wrote, "although he holds no official title." [21]

The fact was that, in 1920, the American people had split minds. Half lived officially in the country and half in the cities, although most had rural memories. These Americas wanted to be led by a man who praised the old ways while pushing on the new machines. They wanted a Santa Claus in the White House, a traditional figure who handed out presents of material prosperity. Harding fitted the bill very well, but Ford fitted it better. While Harding represented a pleasant President, Ford seemed to be a scientific expert. He would run America as he did his car plant, turning out sleek and shiny models of prosperous businessmen and workers by the million. If his silly paper, the Dearborn *Independent*, had not shown up Ford's anti-Semitism and total lack of political judgment and if Coolidge had not wooed and won Ford's endorsement after Harding's death, one of the more illiterate and inane millionaires in the land might have reached the White House. There is no connection between the ability to make a car and the ability to run a government. It was fortunate for America, indeed, that Harding was not to be succeeded by someone who was both his political and even his mental inferior.

With the Ford boom under way, Harding sought to appeal to the rural vote, which was swinging toward this religious and rural manufacturer. According to Wayne Wheeler of the Anti-Saloon

League, Harding took the pledge to abstain from liquor in order to win dry support.[22] He spoke out increasingly strongly on the need of American citizens to observe the dry law, which had, in fact, been moderately successful in action during 1921 and 1922. The cities of America were becoming openly wet, with Governor Alfred E. Smith leading the opposition in New York; but the rural areas were still militantly dry. On his Western tour, Harding spoke out in Denver, urging citizens to obey the law. "The country and the Nation will not permit the law of the land to be made a byword." [23]

As for the farm revolt, Harding refused to panic. When he was warned by Jennings that he should speak entirely on the farm problem during his Western tour, he refused to do so. He was President of the whole country, not a candidate for reelection. Those who presumed to give him such advice had "a bargain sale appraisal for the President." [24] He knew that a boom in farm prices might well come before the election of 1924, as, indeed, it did. And this would make the farmers conservative and Republican again. Walter Prescott Webb has pointed out that farmers are only radical in adversity, and Harding, too, with his belief in the ebb and flow of prices by inevitable processes, knew that the tide must sweep in his way in the end.

"Why is America country-minded?" William Allen White asked himself in Emporia, Kansas, as Harding prepared to go on his Western tour and to Alaska. The answer came truthfully and significantly: "In America most of us are Emporians in one way or another. Some of us live in towns ranging from five thousand to a quarter of a million, others were born in or around these towns, and still others of us cherish golden dreams of going back to some Emporia. People say to us Emporia dwellers: 'Why do you live in Emporia?' and the answer seems simple: 'Everyone does—more or less.' . . . We are Emporians all, *because we desire to belong to the governing classes*." [25] The old-stock Americans, who made up the middle classes of the small towns, saw in the President a replica of themselves. As long as a Harding could rule, the small townsmen in their old towns or in the new cities could see in him the living proof that opportunity was equal and American democracy true.

Farm prices might be temporarily down, but while such a President ruled, the new and the mob and the urban would be kept at bay.

Before he left on his Western tour, Harding had a premonition of betrayal and of death. According to White, he exploded with the words, "My God, this is a hell of a job! I have no trouble with my enemies. I can take care of my enemies all right. But my damn friends, my God-damn friends, White, they're the ones that keep me walking the floor nights!" [26] He also accepted an inflated offer for the Marion *Star*. In 1917, he had put a "steep" price on the *Star* of $140,000, and the negotiations had broken down because the price was too high.[27] In the spring of 1923, he had told the American Society of Newspaper Editors that he had been offered for the *Star* "a good deal more than it is worth" by two Ohioans who were setting up a chain of syndicated newspapers. Harding had claimed, however, that he would hang onto the *Star*, because he "would rather be a newspaper publisher than anything else in the world," until his estate was settled in a legal manner.[28] Yet a month later and six weeks before his death, he sold the *Star* for $550,000—perhaps twice its true value, even considering an agreement that the President would write an occasional editorial during the next ten years. Harding possibly sold the *Star* to cover losses suffered in the stock market under an assumed name. He also made a will, settling his affairs.

These actions by Harding argue a temporary sense of his approaching end, either in scandal or in death. He had worked himself too hard, his heart was weak, and the accusers of his Cabinet were vociferous. He hoped that the trip through the West and to Alaska would put him on his feet again, both physically and in the esteem of the people. In fact, he was to come back to Washington dead—and mourned more than any other President since Abraham Lincoln.

The trip was carefully prepared. Harding's old Ohio enemy, then his adviser, Walter Brown, was sent ahead by the efficient politician in the White House. His mission, according to Harding, was "to visit every one of the cities in which speaking engagements or any sort of stop or stay is contemplated and check up thor-

oughly on the local arrangements and make certain that nothing is
unprovided for, and especially to make sure that there have been
no cases of unmindfulness which are likely to leave a trail of disappointment or wounded feelings behind us." [29] Brown had already
proved his worth to Harding in heading a joint committee of Congress as the President's representative; this committee was charged
with modernizing the machinery of government. Only slow progress had been made by Brown against the opposition of "the rutted
chaps" in Congress, but Harding was pleased with him and wanted
him to be the next Senator from Ohio. In the case of Brown,
Harding's policy of making friends with his enemies had again
succeeded.

Despite his bad health and his growing weariness and an attack
of influenza, Harding allowed Brown to plan many speaking engagements. The holiday trip became "unavoidably a very arduous
one." On the Presidential train traveled the new Secretary of the
Interior and Herbert Hoover and Dr. Sawyer and George
Christian and the faithful Jennings, summoned at last from Marion
to be with the man who was feeling betrayed by the rest of his old
friends. Harding rose early and went to bed late, using alcohol
occasionally as a relief against fatigue. "Time and again in answer
to pleas from places along the road, he arose early in the morning
and remained up until after midnight." [30] He made eighty-five
speeches in six weeks, many of which he composed himself in long-
hand. The climate on the Presidential train and on the voyage to
Alaska changed all the time, from heat to cold and back to heat
again. Only on the voyage to and from Alaska did Harding get
any rest. And even then he seemed unable to sleep, preferring cards
and company to quiet.

Hoover had been taken along on the trip as a kind of conscience
to the President. Later on, Nicholas Murray Butler claimed that
Harding had tried to tell him of his worries, while William Allen
White claimed that Harding had seemed disturbed after meeting
with Fall's wife on the trip. Yet only to Hoover did Harding make
the beginnings of a confession on the ship to Alaska:

One day after lunch when we were a few days out [Hoover wrote
in his memoirs], Harding asked me to come to his cabin. He plumped

at me the question: "If you knew of a great scandal in our administration, would you for the good of the country and the party expose
it publicly or would you bury it?" My natural reply was "Publish it,
and at least get credit for integrity on your side." He remarked that
this method might be politically dangerous. I asked for more par-
ticulars. He said that he had received some rumors of irregularities,
centering around Smith, in connection with cases in the Department
of Justice. . . . I asked what Daugherty's relations to the affair were.
He abruptly dried up and never raised the question again.[31]

In the West, Harding did campaign for the radical rural vote by
supporting one demand of the Farmer-Labor Party. In Borah's
Idaho, he put forward a scheme to push up farm prices by coopera-
tive marketing. Soon, he asserted, the farmers would be called "the
aristocracy of America," for farming was "the most independent
occupation in the world." It was only marketing that needed cooperation in order to get a fair price from the organized city con-
sumers and middlemen.[32] In Alaska, Harding promised sound
business development, but no quick panacea for its economic troubles.[33] In Vancouver, he praised the Canadians for being such good
neighbors that there was no need to defend the frontier: it was a
prime example of the Anglo-Saxon concept of liberty and peace.
And in Seattle, where Daugherty met him for an hour before he
spoke, Harding faltered during his speech and suffered some sort
of collapse.

The sick President was hustled onto his special train. Hoover
took the opportunity to redraft a speech for Harding, with the sick
man's approval, making a firm stand on the issue of the World
Court. When the train reached San Francisco, Harding was put to
bed in his hotel. Dr. Sawyer made a wrong diagnosis of his case,
saying that he was suffering from a digestive upset caused by eating rotten crabs. As there were no crabs eaten on the train, this
erroneous diagnosis of ptomaine poisoning was later interpreted
as a doctors' plot to hush up the truth about Harding's death.

Other doctors in attendance on Harding made another diagnosis.
Dr. Ray Lyman Wilbur, a heart specialist and President of Stan-
ford University, met with other doctors and quickly discovered
that Harding's illness was a heart attack. Harding had long suffered

from an enlarged heart and high blood pressure, and he had also been prone to nervous depression. Between 1889 and 1901, he had gone five times to Battle Creek Sanitorium in Ohio in order to recover from fatigue, overstrain, and nervous illnesses. In his later correspondence, he complained frequently of symptoms of heart disease—sensations of shortness of breath and faintness. He confided to Senator Watson before he became President and to Hughes when he was President that his blood pressure had sometimes been as high as 175. He had put on weight, until he weighed nearly 240 pounds, and had been able to sleep only when propped up by pillows. Dr. Emanuel Libman, a well-known diagnostician who had noted the President's appearance late in 1922, had predicted that he would be dead within six months from "a disease of the coronary arteries." Harding's condition was aggravated by an attack of influenza, followed by an exhausting trip and continuing worry because of scandals in his Administration. "He was a corpse," one journalist wrote, "essaying a *pre mortem* tour." [34] It is small wonder that Harding was ready to die.

His actual death took place in his hotel room at San Francisco. His heart attack was followed by pneumonia. He complained of fatigue and breathlessness, but he made a surprising rally. Mrs. Harding sat by his bedside, to read to him a favorable article by a journalist—"A Calm Review of a Calm Man." The article claimed that Harding was suffering from unjust criticism because of his refusal to boost himself. In fact, he was doing a good and hardworking job in a calm way.[35] "That's good!" Harding said. "Go on, read some more." Then a blood clot reached his brain. While his wife ran to call the doctor, he died of thrombosis.

After Harding's death, five doctors, led by Wilbur and including Dr. Sawyer, certified the cause of death as thrombosis. No autopsy was performed. The President's body was embalmed almost immediately. Mrs. Harding refused to allow a death mask to be made. A year later, Dr. Sawyer died unexpectedly of thrombosis while Mrs. Harding was in his house. Within six months, Mrs. Harding died too. These deaths, as inclusive as the end of a Shakespearean tragedy, provided blood for rumor to drink. When Gaston B. Means, a perjured ex-investigator from the Department of Justice, hinted that Mrs. Harding had poisoned her husband, in a book published in 1930, the theories of conspiracy about the President's convenient death became hallowed by spurious notions.[36]

In truth, the rumors that Harding had been killed by his wife, with or without the collusion of Dr. Sawyer, or had committed suicide proved only one thing—the readiness of the American people to believe in conspiracy. Conspiracy was supposed to have put Harding in the White House; therefore, it was only logical that conspiracy was supposed to have put him in his grave. In point of fact, Harding was a sick man, liable to die soon. As his nephew later testified, even at the time of his nomination, Harding's health had worried his father and his brother and his three nephews—all of whom were doctors. He had shown heart-disease symptoms in Washington and had strained his heart in Alaska when he had walked up 190 steps to visit an invalid.[37] Harding had every reason to die of natural causes, of a bad heart and overstrain and worry. As Hoover wrote, "People do not die from a broken heart, but people with bad hearts may reach the end much sooner from great worries." [38]

Some three million people turned out to watch the dead President carried past in his funeral train to Washington and then home to burial at Marion. There was an extraordinary and national outpouring of grief, which revealed how strong the dead man's hold on the rural heart of his countrymen had been. Even the slums of Boston, where the foreign-born peasants lived, were empty at the hour of the President's burial, and the churches were filled. Briefly, by his death, Harding seemed to have brought a harmony of grief to all Americans. A collection of obituary editorials published in the year of his death repeated the same theme over and over again: Harding was the "typical 'self-made' average American, and the fact that he got where he did is high tribute to every home town in his native land." [39] Harding had proved that the small townsman could still make good, and he seemed to have given his life in service to the democratic ideal of his country. He was truly mourned, for the myth that he represented was most dear to the hearts of his countrymen.

In a real sense, Harding had killed himself in office. He had not shirked the work. He had tried too hard to do too much of it, when his health was poor. He had desired to be a good President, but he had not known how. In a famous, if apocryphal, story, he complained that there must be a best mind who knew the answer to a given problem, but he did not know this man's whereabouts, and that there must be a book that solved the matter, although he could not read it if there were.[40] Harding worked too long at doing the inessential and at trusting the untrustworthy. As the best mind of all, Charles Evans Hughes, said of him in a funeral oration before the House of Representatives, "President Harding had no ossification of the heart. He literally wore himself out in the endeavor to be friendly. It was pain to him to refuse a courtesy; personal convenience could never be considered if it was an obstacle to any act of grace. He dealt personally with a vast correspondence, not being content with mere acknowledgments, but writing friendly letters with the touch of a keen human interest. His generous receptivity multiplied the appeals. He sought relaxation in the intimate contacts of old friendships, and this led him even in his diversions often to give himself to an undue exertion instead of rest." [41]

"That is the way things go. If a man in politics complains about the way the winds blow he had better stay out of politics and out of the wind."

HARRY DAUGHERTY

15

The Evil That Men Do

"How often do we criticize harshly when we ought to
bestow a garland. We do it in private life and leave a
wound where praise would be more becoming. We do
it in public life, and withhold from sacrificing public
men the one compensation which might atone."

WARREN HARDING

The legacy of Harding's death was chiefly the myths about his life.
He left little permanent trace. The Supreme Court, to which he
had appointed four conservatives, including William Howard Taft
as Chief Justice, did interpret the Constitution in a most conservative way for two decades; but eventually it was to become one of
the most progressive forces in American life. Harding's Cabinet
did remain much unchanged by the cautious Coolidge, who was
reluctant to shed even the liability of Daugherty. Harding had set
a fortunate precedent in inviting Coolidge to attend Cabinet meetings in order to prepare him for stepping into the White House,
and he had also set a model in the treatment of the press by the
White House. Some credit must be given him for the Washington
Conference, although his acceptance of political and economic
isolationism proved disastrous in the long run—if any President can
be blamed for the continuing of his bad policies after his death.

For one appropriate act, Harding deserves to be remembered.
He had always stood on the platform of the Constitution and had

declared his intention to preserve it. The latter he did, in literal fact. Three previous Presidents from Ohio, Hayes and McKinley and Taft, had tried to get Congress to appropriate enough money to construct a fireproof hall for the government archives. They had failed. By the time Harding came to office, both the Declaration of Independence and the Constitution were in danger of falling to pieces through exposure to light and bad handling. By executive order, Harding had these documents transferred from the files of the Secretary of State to the Library of Congress. And under his prodding, Congress at last appropriated enough money to build "a special marble and bronze shrine" for the two documents. This was done, according to Harding, "to satisfy the laudable wish of patriotic Americans to have an opportunity to see the original fundamental documents upon which rest their independence and their Government." [1] In truth, Harding was the preserver of the Constitution; and today, those who visit its glass-and-bronze shrine in the National Archives might think of him.

Harding's wife was accused of destroying his papers by those who believed in a conspiracy. She did take all her husband's correspondence with her from Washington; and for the remaining eighteen months of her life, she did work at destroying some of his papers. But 325,000 documents still remain. They are now available for the research of qualified scholars at the Ohio Historical Society, where they were deposited after being held for forty years by the Harding Memorial Association—a group of Harding's friends in Ohio. In collecting and sorting out Presidential papers, Mrs. Harding was only following the personal or family custom of many Presidents. The precedent was set by George Washington himself, who took his Presidential papers with him into retirement. All Presidents followed his example until Franklin Delano Roosevelt. The papers of Van Buren and Fillmore and Pierce and Grant and Arthur were all carefully edited and partially destroyed, while those of the Adams family and Garfield and McKinley and Taft and Wilson were kept for restricted eyes. [2] Mrs. Harding and the Harding Memorial Association only did what was *usual* with the Presidential papers of Warren Harding, although they were later blamed for destroying and restricting the use of these papers.

The interring of the bones of a public figure means the birth of gossip. Harding's memory suffered from this more than that of any other President. He suffered at the hands of both his friends and his enemies. It was convenient for Republican politicians to bury all the scandals of his Administration with his body. It was Daugherty's purpose to prove that his dead master had been a political figurehead, an impractical politician of no willpower, the creature of Daugherty. This, Harding had never been, however much it soothed the vanity of Daugherty and the President's other friends to think so. Nor was Harding the lecherous and lazy fool that gossip made him out to be.

Like many other Presidents, Harding had had extramarital affairs. His bad luck was that one of his ladies, Nan Britton from Marion, provided the material for a book after his death called *The President's Daughter*. In this work, Miss Britton proved to all except the most charitable that she was the mother of Harding's daughter.[3] Although an Ohio jury found against her claim to have been libeled in a refutation of her book, most of Harding's friends believed her. The wonder was that the affair was held so much against the dead man. Grover Cleveland had been elected to the Presidency *after* admitting to siring a bastard son. Yet Warren Harding was not allowed to lie quiet in his grave once he had been accused of siring a bastard daughter. Victorian times were more forgiving than the emancipated 1920's. The recent discovery of a collection of Harding's love letters to another mistress, Mrs. Carrie Phillips, has shown that the people of the permissive 1960's still seem as interested as those of past ages in the lechery of the great.[4]

The gossip about the Hardings was not diminished when President Hoover finally agreed in 1931 to dedicate the large and noble and hollow-centered memorial put up at Marion in memory of its dead President. Hoover was advised that in his speech in front of the worthies of Ohio politics, he should "aim at under, rather than over-statement."[5] His dislike of the furious Daugherty, who was sitting in the audience in front of him, conquered his discretion. After praising the dead Harding as a man of peace and a man of the people, Hoover talked of Harding's "great disillusionment" on his Western trip. The dying President had weakened "not only from physical exhaustion but from mental anxiety." Warren Harding, in the words of his old Secretary of Commerce, "had a dim realization that he had been betrayed by a few of the men whom he had trusted, by men whom he had believed were his devoted friends. It was later proved in the courts of the land that these men had betrayed not alone the friendship and trust of their staunch and loyal friend but they had betrayed their country. That was the tragedy of the life of Warren Harding. . . . There is no disloyalty and no crime in all the category of human weaknesses which compares with the failure of probity in the conduct of public trust." [6]

In fact, Daugherty had not been *proved* guilty of crime in the courts of the land. After Harding's death, he had refused to resign. He had preferred to stay where he was and to use the weapons of the Department of Justice against his enemies. The whole Cabinet quaked at the thought of the revelations he would make if he were dismissed from office. Yet Coolidge, in the end, had grasped the nettle and asked for Daugherty's resignation on the technical ground that a Cabinet officer should not testify before a Senate committee that was investigating him. Later, Daugherty had survived two trials for graft because of hung juries. He had done so only by putting the blame on the dead Jess Smith and by refusing to testify on the grounds that he might incriminate the dead President. "The Ohio Gang never surrenders," Bruce Bliven wrote; "and neither does it die. It piles its corpses on the breastworks, and holds the fort." [7]

After his dismissal, Daugherty survived for more than two decades, getting along "on the principle that the Lord tempers the wind etc., and the devil takes care of his own." [8] His pride lay in the fact that he had been *technically* cleared by the courts of law.

As a lobbyist, he had never drawn the distinction between politics and the law. He thought that one trade should merely whitewash the other. He would have agreed with Mr. Dooley that the Supreme Court follows the election returns. "Law and politics, you know," he was quoted as saying, "go hand in hand." [9] In his own case, the master politician from Ohio had administered the law of the land in Washington, and nothing was ever proved against him, despite all the thunderings of prosecutors and the liberal press and Congress. "Getting a man's goat is a great game," declared the unrepentant operator. "I never had a goat farm and they could not get a goat where there was none." [10]

The rest of the profiteers under Harding's regime fared less well. Sinclair and Doheny went to jail over the question of the oil leases; Denby resigned; and Doheny's son, who had carried the bribe to Fall, committed suicide. Of those connected with the scandal in the Veterans' Bureau, two committed suicide and two went to jail. Of the Ohio Gang, two were jailed and one committed suicide and one died awaiting trial. Daugherty's brother's bank crashed in the Great Depression, with debts of $2,600,000; the owner was convicted of operating it in a disreputable way. A fortunate pardon freed him from jail. "Ohio immunity," as Samuel Hopkins Adams observed, "was still potent in 1930." [11]

With the trials of Daugherty and Fall and Forbes and their associates continuing during the years after his death, Harding was not allowed to rest in peace. Once these scandals were brought to court and forgotten, new gossip arose in the memoirs of the various members of the White House staff. A mail clerk wrote of destroying Nan Britton's letters to Harding in the White House. A White House maid told of Harding and his wife's drifting apart and of Mrs. Harding's icy calm at her husband's funeral. A White House secretary told of Mrs. Harding's choosing which of the "political" prisoners should be pardoned; she quoted Mrs. Harding as saying, "Well, Warren Harding, I have got you the Presidency; what are you going to do with it?" The White House housekeeper testified to Mrs. Harding's domineering over her husband. And a medium, Madame Maria, even declared that she was once "the hub round which the national government revolved" through her power over the superstitious Mrs. Harding, to whom she had declared that her husband would meet his death by poisoning at the hands of an enemy near to him.[12]

Harding and his wife could not reply to these innuendoes, whether false or true. They—the representatives of decency in Marion—were subjected to the gossip of that overblown small town, Washington. Many of the stories about the Hardings were absurd, but they claimed the foundation of fact. Yet, curiously enough, Harding's reputation as a shrewd politician and as a President at least as competent as Hayes was blasted more by writers of fiction than of fact. When Sinclair Lewis wrote *Main Street* and *Babbitt*, the comments were that Main Street and Babbitt had come to the White House. Because Harding had many of the trappings of the small-town booster, people tended to confuse him with Babbitt, whom, after all, Lewis had created from the mere sum of his superficial characteristics.

Scott Fitzgerald began a Broadway fashion by modeling a bad play on Harding's presumed incompetence. In this play, *The Vegetable*, the supremely average Jerry Frost becomes President, appoints his friends to office, declares Idaho independent to be rid of its Senator, and is impeached. His defense is, "I don't want to be President. I never asked to be President. Why—why, I don't even know how in hell I ever *got* to be President!" [13] The play flopped, although other versions of the same theme had successful runs on Broadway twice in the next forty years. Samuel Hopkins Adams also set a profitable fashion for best-selling novels on supposed life at Washington. In his inferior and notorious novel *Revelry*, he parodied the dead Harding in the character of the easygoing and incompetent President Willis Markham, with his "streaky cut of bacon, the Cabinet," and his real center of government, the little house of his poker-playing circle, "The Crow's Nest." In the novel, the President is betrayed by his cronies and dies, accidentally taking poison by his own hand. The moral is spelled out by a wise Senator: "Friendship in politics undermines more principles than fraud, and gratitude is a worse poison than graft." [14]

It so happened that Harding's term of office coincided with the first full-scale onslaught by the American intellectuals on the values of the small town, which the President represented so perfectly in all its inconsistencies and grandiloquence. With such a splendid specimen of the "booboisie" to assault, Mencken did not spare his darts, nor did Sherwood Anderson spare his bitter memories of Ohio. The expatriates who fled with Harold Stearns to Paris thought that they were fleeing from the incompetent and the stupid in American government. To them, the memory of the early twenties was a memory of a materialistic America that was led by the crass and the venal. In their shame at this memory, the American intellectuals chose Harding as the gullible scapegoat of his time.

Nothing shows more the swing in American opinion on the subject of Harding than the second change in attitude of William Allen White, whose running commentary on Harding's career reflected the malleable nature of intelligent small-town feeling. When White was still a progressive, he thought Harding a vile reactionary. Once Harding was President, White thought him the decent representative of small-town life, an average man doing a better-than-average job. But as the effluvia of the scandals rose to drown the dead President's good name, White wrote in 1926 to the old Ohio progressive Brand Whitlock, "God, what a story! The story of Babylon is a Sunday School story compared with the story of Washington from June 1919 until July 1923, and so far as that goes, considerably later. We haven't even yet got back to our Father's house. He can't see us even from afar off. It's invisible. And the whole thing is epitomized by the rise of Harding. If ever there was a man who was a he-harlot, it was this same Warren G. Harding. But I suppose it ought not to be written now. It would hurt too many hearts. I don't know. I could write it and I dare to write it, but it would be a bitter and awful thing." [15]

White made his attitude clear enough in his later history books of the period and in his autobiography. He never gave Harding after his death the credit that he had given the President during his life. In this, he set or shaped the fashion of nearly all historians and journalists. Harding's name has become a byword as the worst American President, the prime example of incompetence and sloth and feeble good nature.

The verdict of Harding's own time was different. And it cannot be the verdict of any historian who has looked at the evidence of the papers preserved at the Ohio Historical Society. Harding was a hardworking and shrewd Ohio politician. He was always his own master. He used compromise and humility as political tactics. He listened to the opinions of others in order to flatter their vanity and educate himself. He was a man of mediocre intellect, but of great presence, ambition, and political talent. He was exceedingly

fortunate in rising so high, but he was helped by his own persistence and strategy of harmony. He was a good friend, and he was
a formidable opponent in an election. He resembled in his abilities
President Hayes, whom he thought had been misjudged because
of partisanship and prejudice.

Harding's defects lay in his lack of education. He had a fuzzy
mentality, what Woodrow Wilson termed a "bungalow mind." He
never questioned the easy assumptions of right and wrong of the
shoddy Ohio towns in which he grew up. He knew nothing of the
science of government, only of the gutter politics of Ohio and the
Senate. It was no training for the White House. As an economist,
Harding was limited to the kind of observation that he made on
Social Justice Day in Marion: "It is our duty as a whole people
to see if we cannot make every job in the country a small business
of its own." [16] As a statesman, he was limited to the principle of
America First. As a philosopher, he was limited to the concepts
that friends should come before principles and that loyalty to party
should come before loyalty to an abstract ideal. Harding believed
in the nineteenth-century system of corrupt politics and unrestricted business opportunity, because this was the university of his
youth and middle age. Although, in the White House, he began to
learn painfully the duties and the role of a modern President, his
education came too late. The office can make the man, but only
when the man is ready to shed his old friends as well as his old
misconceptions.

Harding clung foolishly to the Daughertys of the world because
he was too weak to give up the nostalgic joys of his life, the parties
of cronies, and the stories of the small-town smoking room. He
was not ruthless enough to be President—perhaps he feared the
example of the ruthless Wilson. "He was a mother's boy," observed
Hudson Maxim, "—that was the trouble with him. Not enough of
a brute—too much of a gentleman." [17] Unfortunately, Harding
viewed his own tolerance of his old friends in office as an amiable
weakness, not as a national disaster. *The New York Times* noticed
that Harding seemed to take comfort when he spoke before the
Lincoln Memorial and described the great Republican as "a very

natural human being, with the frailties mixed with the virtues of humanity." [18]

Harding was the representative of normalcy in abnormal times. In office, he had to discard this nostalgic program of returning to a time that never was. He came to realize that the President in the White House was no more the harmonizer between farm and city, between labor and capital, between West and East, between poor and rich than was the rural businessman in the small towns of the Midwest. The President might seem to symbolize the whole nation, and the rural businessman to represent the individual flowering of the American dream; but both had to fight daily for a successful living. Both might cry for harmony and the good old days, but both had to grapple with the pressure groups of the new. Both might boost American industry while praising the American farmer, but both knew that one was growing rich at the expense of the other. Harding was the frock-coated businessman with mud on his boots whom most Americans thought that they wanted in the White House. Only after his death did they see that he was out of his place and out of his time and fortunately in his grave.

Because a man is available, he should not necessarily choose to be chosen.

NOTES

In these explanatory notes, I have included a full notation of all the sources employed except for the Harding papers in the Ohio Historical Society, which are cited as *HP* and *OHS*. I should like to acknowledge particularly the aid of Kenneth W. Duckett, Curator of Manuscripts at the Ohio Historical Society. He was unfailingly generous with his time and help in finding sources on Harding, although he is in no way responsible for my use of those sources. It is my hope that this book will relate the life of that misunderstood President, Warren Harding, to the rural and small-town and political myths of his time. And I trust that my own researches will be supplemented in due time by the researches of three scholars who are in the process of writing detailed biographies on Harding—Dean Albertson, Ralph Downes, and Francis Russell. The long-delayed opening of the Harding papers has rightly encouraged work on this significant, if mediocre, man.

Preface

1. Brand Whitlock to William Allen White, October 8, 1926, in *The Letters of Brand Whitlock*, A. Nevins, ed. (New York: 1936), p. 389.
2. Quoted in Merriman Smith, *A President Is Many Men* (New York: Harper, 1948), p. 2.
3. Press release of Harry Daugherty on December 17, 1919, *HP*.

1 / The Country Boy

1. Hayes, Garfield, McKinley (nominated twice), Taft (nominated twice), and Harding were residents in Ohio when nominated for President by the Republican Party. Grant and Benjamin Harrison (each nominated twice) were raised in Ohio, although nominated from other states. All the four Vice-Presidential nominees were also nominated from other states, although native sons of Ohio.

2. Senator C. C. Dill at the memorial service for Senator Frank B. Willis, quoted in Charles A. Jones, "Ohio in the Republican National Conventions," *Ohio Archaeological and Historical Quarterly*, XXXVIII, January, 1929.

3. The obsessive interest of the members of the Harding family in writing genealogies and in joining the Daughters of the American Revolution is explicable because of the accusation of Negro blood so frequently leveled against them. The best of the genealogical resurrections was written by Wilber J. Harding, *The Hardings in America* (Keystone, Iowa: 1925), and is based on the painstaking work of the Reverend Abner Morse of the New England Historical and Genealogical Society—a society that President Harding himself was proud to join. The wish to prove noble descent in the Harding family is rather touching, with statements such as "'Hardin' is doubtless a Gothic word," common in Norman England, and noble by the eleventh century.

4. See Dr. George T. Harding, Jr., to Charles E. Hard, March 22, 1926, Hard papers, *OHS*. See also V. Hampton, *Religious Background of the White House* (Boston: 1932).

5. Sherman A. Cuneo, *From Printer to President* (Philadelphia: 1922), p. 23.

6. I am indebted to a description of the rural life of some of the Presidents by Edward T. Booth, *Country Life in America as Lived by Ten Presidents of the United States* (New York: Knopf, 1947).

7. Quoted in Sidney Hyman, *The American President* (London: Odhams, 1954), p. 205. His chapter on "The Laws of Natural Selection" for the Presidency is penetrating.

8. See Thomas Jefferson's *Notes on Virginia*, and the excellent examination of the antiurban feelings of intelligent Americans in Morton and Lucia White, *The Intellectual Versus the City* (Cambridge, Mass.: Harvard, 1962).

9. Alexis de Tocqueville, *Democracy in America* (2 vols.), P. Bradley, ed. (New York: Vintage, 1945), vol. 1, p. 300.

10. Jack Warwick, "Growing up with Harding," *Northwest Ohio Quarterly*, XXVIII, Winter, 1955–1956, and XXX, Summer, 1958. Also useful on Harding's childhood is Ray Baker Harris, "Background and Youth of the Seventh Ohio President," *Ohio State Archaeological and Historical Quarterly*, LII, July–September, 1943.

11. *Speech of Warren G. Harding at the Marion Centennial*, Marion, Ohio, July 4, 1922.

12. Frederick E Schortemeier, *Our Common Country: Mutual Good Will in America* (Indianapolis: 1921), pp. 250–254.

13. William Allen White, "The Other Side of Main Street," *Collier's*, July 30, 1921.

14. *Ibid.*

15. Louis Reid, "The Small Town," in *Civilization in the United States,* H. Stearns, ed. (New York: 1922), pp. 285–296.
16. Sherwood Anderson, "Towns, Ho!" in *The Sherwood Anderson Reader,* P. Rosenfeld, ed. (Boston: Houghton Mifflin, 1947). See particularly pp. 743–757, 800–801.
17. See note 11.
18. Warren Harding to the Iowa Diamond Jubilee Committee, January 10, 1922, *HP.*

2 / The Self-made Man

1. Quoted in Dixon Wecter's excellent *The Hero in America* (New York: Scribner, 1941), p. 316.
2. Quoted in C. B. Galbreath, *The Story of Warren G. Harding* (Dansville, N. Y.: 1922), pp. 9–10.
3. Frederick E. Schortemeier, *Our Common Country: Mutual Good Will in America* (Indianapolis: 1921), p. 149.
4. *Ibid.* pp. 119–120. Harding was not above playing personalities. In the *Star,* he called one of the rival Marion editors "a sordid soul . . . gangrened with jealousy" and "a sour, disgruntled and disappointed old ass." The other editor he called "a lying thief." In return he was termed "a moral leper."
5. Anonymous, *What a Country Boy Did with 200 Pounds of Type* (Columbus, Ohio: 1920), p. 11.
6. See the Harding papers, and see also the copy of Harding's will in the Library of Congress.
7. See note 5.
8. See Clinton Rossiter, *Conservatism in America: The Thankless Persuasion,* 2nd ed. rev. (New York: Knopf, 1962).
9. *The Woman's Journal,* March 6, 1880.
10. Warren Harding, "How We Advertize" (undated handwritten speech, probably 1916, delivered to a group of Ohio editors), De Coppet papers, Princeton University.
11. "The Railways and Prosperity," *Address by Warren G. Harding at the Annual Dinner of the Railway Business Association,* New York, December 10, 1914.
12. See note 10.
13. See Robert and Helen Lynd, *Middletown* (New York: 1929). This work gives the best understanding of the small-town ethic that formed Harding's thinking. All social histories of the period are deeply in its debt.
14. *Address of President Harding at the Joint Banquet of the Conventions of Postal Associations,* October 13, 1921.
15. See David Riesman, *The Lonely Crowd* (New Haven, Conn.: Yale, 1950).
16. See C. Wright Mills, *White Collar* (London: Oxford, 1951).
17. See Report of the President's Research Committee on Social Trends, *Recent Social Trends in the United States* (New York: McGraw-Hill, 1933). See also Henry May's excellent "Shifting Perspectives on the 1920's," *Mississippi Valley Historical Review,* XLIII, December, 1956.

18. See Daniel Boorstin, *The Image: What Happened to the American Dream* (New York: Atheneum, 1962), p. 61.
19. C. B. Galbreath, "Warren Gamaliel Harding," *Ohio Archaeological and Historical Quarterly*, XXXII, October, 1923.
20. Schortemeier, *op. cit.*, pp. 19–21, 42–51, 300–301.

3 / The Presidential State

1. *Address of the President of the United States on the One Hundredth Anniversary of the Birth of General Ulysses S. Grant*, Point Pleasant, Ohio, April 27, 1922.
2. Frank Kent, *The Great Game of Politics* (New York: 1923), pp. 156–162.
3. Sherwood Anderson, *Winesburg, Ohio* (New York: 1919), p. 40.
4. See Jones, *op. cit.*, "Ohio in the Republican National Conventions," and Malcolm Moos, *The Republicans: A History of Their Party* (New York: Random House, 1956), for Ohio's role in Republican National Conventions.
5. Brand Whitlock, *J. Hardin & Son* (New York: 1923), p. 109.
6. Howard D. Mannington to Horace Potter, April 29, 1920, *HP*.

4 / The Political Innocent

1. Herbert Croly, *Marcus Alonzo Hanna: His Life and Work* (New York: 1912), p. 474.
2. See Charles Glaab, "Jesup W. Scott and a West of Cities," *Ohio History*, LXXIII, Winter, 1964.
3. See James Rodabaugh, "The Reform Movement in Ohio at the Turn of the Century," *Paper Read Before the Mississippi Valley Historical Association*, April 21, 1944.
4. See "The Whole World Loves a Presidential Nominee," *Literary Digest*, July 17, 1920.
5. Frederic C. Howe, *The Confessions of a Reformer* (New York: 1925), p. 173.
6. Norman Thomas to Samuel Hopkins Adams, quoted in the latter's *Incredible Era: The Life and Times of Warren Gamaliel Harding* (Boston: Houghton Mifflin, 1939), p. 25. Adams' book is the most convenient collection of the myths about Harding's career.
7. Harry Daugherty to Ray Baker Harris, November 30, 1937, Harris papers, *OHS*.
8. See Adams, *op. cit.*, p. 38.
9. Harry Daugherty to Warren Harding, March 7, 1913, *HP*.
10. Harry Daugherty and T. Dixon, *The Inside Story of the Harding Tragedy* (New York: 1932), p. 5. This work is Daugherty's attempt to whitewash his career. Again and again, he repeats how indispensable he was to Harding both in Ohio and in Washington.
11. Adams, *op. cit.*, p. 51.
12. A Columbus journalist, quoted by George MacAdam in "Harding," *World's Work*, October, 1920.

13. See particularly F. E. Scobey to Harding, December 29, 1913, *HP*. An extract from the letter reads, "I am also in receipt of some of your 'Parlor Stories,' and your suggestion to pick the parlor is appropriate. What kind of a 'parlor' do you think I wanted to tell these stories in? Have you the same opinion of San Antonio that you have of Paris? You usually have some right cute, up-to-date stories, but will say as far [as] the list you have sent me this time you have surely fallen down. Perhaps before you write the next time you will have an opportunity to see Nick Longworth and get a list that a man can tell."

14. See the letters of H. P. Crouse to Harding on July 20, 1895, and July 10 and 25, 1896, *HP*.

15. See the Foraker-Harding correspondence, particularly Foraker to Harding, April 30, 1895, *HP*.

16. *The Autobiography of William Allen White*, (New York: Macmillan, 1946), p. 618.

17. State Senator C. D. Wightman to Harding, November 18, 1899, *HP*.

18. Howe, *op. cit.*, p. 172.

19. See John Hopley, of the *Evening Telegraph*, Bucyrus, Ohio, to Harding, March 29, 1900, *HP*.

20. M. A. Hanna to Harding, November 17, 1899, *HP*. Although a supporter of Foraker, Harding was careful never to oppose Hanna or any Ohio boss. As he declared, "The *Star* has neither assailed nor opposed Senator Hanna. It has simply declined to abuse the opposition to him."

21. See MacAdam, *op. cit.*

22. Franklin Rubrecht to Harding, April 11, 1899, *HP*.

23. See note 20.

24. Adams, *op. cit.*, p. 68.

25. Marion *Star*, January 22, 1908.

26. "If you are a candidate to succeed yourself," Harding wrote to Foraker on November 6, 1908, "any influence I may have will be gladly exerted in your behalf. My faith in your honesty and integrity has never been impaired in the slightest degree, and my reverence for your ability is abiding."

   There is an excellent article by Earl R. Beck on "Joseph B. Foraker and the Standard Oil Charges," *Ohio State Archaeological and Historical Quarterly*, LVI, April, 1947.

27. Warren Harding to H. R. Kemerer, July 22, 1909, Harding papers, Library of Congress.

28. Warren Harding to William Howard Taft, July 17, 1910, quoted in Ray Baker Harris' unfinished biography of Harding, MS in the *OHS*.

29. See MacAdam, *op. cit.*

30. Warren Harding to Carolyn Votaw, January 22, 1910. Quoted in the Harris MS, *OHS*.

31. Warren Harding to H. R. Kemerer, November 15, 1910, Harding papers, Library of Congress.

32. For Harry Daugherty's account of his role in the 1912 convention, see Daugherty to Harris, May 4, 1937, Harris papers, *OHS*.

33. Alice Roosevelt Longworth, *Crowded Hours* (New York: Scribner, 1933), p. 203.

34. *Proceedings of the Fifteenth Republican National Convention*, Chicago, June 18–22, 1912, p. 378. (My italics.)

35. For a favorable explanation of Burton's action, see Forrest Crissey, *Theodore E. Burton: American Statesman* (Cleveland: World, 1956), pp. 224–238.

36. Mark Sullivan, *Our Times* (New York: 1935), vol. 6, p. 33. Harry Daugherty read through and corrected Mark Sullivan's influential account of how Harding rose to the Presidency. The result was that the myth of Daugherty as the mastermind behind Harding was perpetuated in Sullivan's seemingly impartial account.

37. See Crissey, *op. cit.*, p. 235.

38. Warren Harding to Fred. W. Wile, February 13, 1922, *HP*.

39. Joseph B. Foraker, *Notes of a Busy Life* (2 vols.), (Cincinnati: 1916), vol. 2, p. 462. Foraker also disliked primaries, like the rest of the old-style politicians, and admired the old bosses as individuals who had fought their way to the top. His case for the old regime (vol. 2, p. 459) is worth quoting:

> "The only important difference between the old and the new systems is . . . that the so-called bosses who control the organization and through its agents control nominations are now more invisible than ever, and for that reason less responsible than they were. They do nothing but recommend, and they do not do that openly; the people nominate, and if a mistake be made *the fault is theirs!*"

40. Warren Harding to N. H. Fairbanks, July 16, 1914, Fairbanks papers, *OHS*.

41. J. B. Foraker to Harding, August 24, 1914, quoted in the Harris MS, *OHS*.

42. N. H. Fairbanks to B. L. Barr, March 4, 1914, Fairbanks papers, *OHS*.

43. For the Democratic version of the campaign, see James M. Cox's informative autobiography, *Journey Through My Years* (New York: Simon and Schuster, 1946), pp. 178–179.

44. Quoted in H. Pringle, *The Life and Times of William Howard Taft* (2 vols.), (New York: Farrar, Straus, 1939), vol. 2, p. 888.

5 / The Guardian Senate

1. Quoted by William Miller in "The Realm of Wealth," *The Reconstruction of American History*, J. Higham, ed. (New York: Humanities, 1962), pp. 146–147.

2. See Arthur B. Tourtellot, *The Presidents on the Presidency* (New York: 1964), p. 238. This is an extremely useful compendium of the views of the Presidents.

3. *Ibid.*, p. 212.

4. Quoted by Arthur Schlesinger, Sr., in *The Rise of Modern America, 1865–1951*, 4th ed. (New York: Macmillan, 1951), pp. 221–222.

5. Forrest Crissey, *Theodore E. Burton: American Statesman* (Cleveland: World, 1956), p. 233.

6. "The Railways and Prosperity," *Address by Warren G. Harding at the Annual Dinner of the Railway Business Association*, New York, December 10, 1914.

7. George B. Christian, Jr., to Harry Kemerer, December 23, 1919, *HP*. Kemerer

wanted Christian's job, which may explain Christian's abrupt reply. A journalist during the campaign of 1920 made the following observations: "The only difference between Harding and Christian is perhaps a quarter or a fifth. The secretary is that much narrower, that much shorter; otherwise, he is the small pea shelled out of the end of the same pod; as devoid of angles or guile as a buckeye, as pleasant as a lozenge, intelligent, alert, receptive, and as poised as the center of population."

8. George B. Christian, Jr., to Stratford L. Morton, April 21, 1923, *HP*.

9. Wadsworth's remarks on Harding are quoted in the Ray Baker Harris MS, *OHS*.

10. H. F. Alderfer, *The Personality and Politics of Warren G. Harding*, Ph.D. dissertation, Syracuse University, 1935, p. 170. This thesis is the only good biography of Harding extant, although it is chiefly based on newspaper sources. It should have been published.

11. Quoted in Frederick Schortemeier, *Rededicating America: The Life and Recent Speeches of Warren G. Harding* (Indianapolis: 1920), p. 20.

12. *Speech of Senator Harding to a Delegation from the Ohio Convention of the Congressional Union*, June 24, 1915, reported in *The Suffragist*, July 10, 1915.

13. See Harriet Taylor Upton, *Random Recollections*, unpublished MS, Women's Archives, Radcliffe College. Mrs. Upton was later appointed vice-chairman of the National Executive of the Republican Party. She wrote that she always "felt free" in the White House when Harding was President: "Nothing was so small that he did not want to listen."

14. T. J. Steuart, *Wayne Wheeler: Dry Boss* (Chicago: Revell, 1928), pp. 111–112.

15. *Congressional Record*, 65 Cong., 1 Sess., p. 5648. (My italics.)

16. George MacAdam, "Harding," *World's Work*, October, 1920.

17. *Address of President Harding Before the Tenth Annual Meeting of the Chamber of Commerce of the United States*, Washington, D.C., May 18, 1922.

18. *Congressional Record*, 64 Cong., 1 Sess., pp. 1679–1681.

19. *Proceedings of the Sixteenth Republican National Convention*, Chicago, June 7–10, 1916, pp. 14–28.

20. His full remark about his keynote speech to Finley Peter Dunne was: "It's rotten. I wrote a good one, but my friends in the Senate made me put things in—the tariff, reciprocity, public lands, pensions, and God knows what, and now it's a rag carpet."

21. See "An Impression of Harding in 1916," *Ohio State Archaeological and Historical Quarterly*, LXII, April, 1953.

22. *The Autobiography of William Allen White* (New York: Macmillan, 1946), p. 522.

23. Warren Harding to Theodore Roosevelt, June 28, 1916, quoted in the Harris MS, *OHS*.

24. *Congressional Record*, 65 Cong., 1 Sess., pp. 1437–1438, 1492.

25. Warren Harding to Theodore Roosevelt, June 12, 1917, quoted in the Harris MS, *OHS*.

26. Henry Cabot Lodge to Theodore Roosevelt, *ibid.*, April 23, 1917.

27. *Congressional Record*, 65 Cong., 1 Sess., pp. 3323–3329. (My italics.)

28. *The Memoirs of Cordell Hull* (2 vols.), (New York: Macmillan, 1948), vol. 1, p. 127.

29. *Congressional Record*, 64 Cong., 2 Sess., pp. 4277-4279, 4387-4391.

30. Richard Barry, "America's Need for a Supreme Dictator—An Interview with Senator Harding," with penciled notes by Senator Harding, 1917, MS in the Library of Congress.

31. *Congressional Record*, 65 Cong., 2 Sess., p. 3087.

32. *Ibid.*, pp. 5747-5748.

33. *Ibid.*, pp. 5749-5750.

34. *Ibid.*, pp. 7564-7568.

35. *Address of Senator Harding at the Ohio Republican State Convention*, Columbus, Ohio, August 27, 1918.

36. *Congressional Record*, 65 Cong., 3 Sess., p. 1808.

6 / *America First*

1. Warren Harding to O. A. von Lueblow, February 22, 1917, Harding papers, Library of Congress.

2. *Ibid.*, March 21, 1917.

3. *Congressional Record*, 65 Cong., 1 Sess., pp. 253-254.

4. *Ibid.*, 2 Sess., p. 4890.

5. Malcolm Jennings to Harding, September 10, 1919, Jennings papers, *OHS*.

6. *Address of Senator Harding Before the Baltimore Press Club*, Baltimore, Md., February 5, 1920.

7. *Address of Senator Harding Before the Ohio Society of New York*, New York, January 10, 1920.

8. Claudius O. Johnson, *Borah of Idaho* (New York: 1936), p. 233.

9. For an excellent presentation of the battle over Article Ten of the League of Nations Covenant, see John C. Vinson, *Referendum for Isolation* (Athens, Ga.: University of Georgia, 1961).

10. For a full transcript of the meeting of the Senators with Woodrow Wilson, see Henry Cabot Lodge, *The Senate and the League of Nations* (New York: 1925), Appendix IV.

11. See Warren Harding to Charles E. Hard, September 13, 1919. Hard papers, *OHS*.

12. *Congressional Record*, 66 Cong., 1 Sess., pp. 5219-5225.

13. For a dramatic account of the collapse of Wilson, see Gene Smith, *When the Cheering Stopped* (New York: 1964). The works of Arthur Link are definitive on Wilson's Presidency.

14. *Congressional Record*, 66 Cong., 1 Sess., pp. 8791-8792.

7 / *The Reluctant Candidate*

1. Joseph G. Butler, Jr., *Recollections of Men and Events* (New York: 1927), pp. 308-309.

2. Warren Harding to Malcolm Jennings, January 28, 1916, Jennings papers, *OHS*.

3. Newton Fairbanks to Harding, May 8, 1916, Fairbanks papers, *OHS*. Harding, in his usual way, claimed that he had remained neutral so as not to offend Herrick. In fact, he did endorse Daugherty, at least in the opinion of his hearers.

4. Warren Harding to Malcolm Jennings, August 26, 1916, Jennings papers, *OHS*.

5. *Ibid.*, March 29, 1916.

6. *Ibid.*, April 24, 1916. (My italics.)

7. Malcolm Jennings to Harding, March 13, 1917, Jennings papers, *OHS*.

8. Warren Harding to Malcolm Jennings, December 31, 1917, Jennings papers, *OHS*.

9. *Ibid.*, March 8, 1918.

10. Warren Harding to Charles E. Hard, March 4, 1918, Hard papers, *OHS*.

11. *Ibid.*, November 14, 1918.

12. *Ibid.*, November 23, 1918.

13. Warren Harding to Malcolm Jennings, November 30, 1918, Jennings papers, *OHS*.

14. Warren Harding to Harry Daugherty, November 29, 1918, *HP*.

15. Harry Daugherty to Harding, November 26, 1918, *HP*.

16. *Ibid.*, November 29, 1918.

17. Warren Harding to Charles E. Hard, December 7, 1918, Hard papers, *OHS*.

18. Warren Harding to Harry Daugherty, December 12, 1918, *HP*.

19. *Ibid.*

20. Harry Daugherty to Harding, December 17, 1918, *HP*.

21. Warren Harding to Harry Daugherty, December 20, 1918, *HP*.

22. Warren Harding to Charles E. Hard, undated, but certainly mid-December, 1920, Hard papers, *OHS*.

23. *Ibid.*

24. Harry Daugherty to Harding, December 30, 1918, *HP*.

25. Warren Harding to Charles E. Hard, January 6, 1919, Hard papers, *OHS*.

26. Harry Daugherty to Harding, January 9, 1919, *HP*.

27. "Theodore Roosevelt: The Most Courageous American," *Address of Warren Gamaliel Harding Before the Ohio Legislature*, Columbus, Ohio, January 29, 1919.

28. Charles E. Hard to Harding, February 24, 1919, Hard papers, *OHS*.

29. Harry Daugherty to Harding, April 2, 1919, *HP*.

30. Warren Harding to Harry Daughterty, April 4, 1919, *HP*.

31. Charles E. Hard to Harding, July 1, 1919, Hard papers, *OHS*.

32. Warren Harding to Harry Daugherty, July 25, 1919, *HP*.

33. *Ibid.*

34. Harry Daugherty to Florence Kling Harding, July 19, 1919, *HP*.

35. Harry Daugherty to Harding, September 6, 1919, *HP*.

36. *Ibid.*, September 13, 1919.

37. *Ibid.*, September 16, 1919.

38. Warren Harding to Harry Daugherty, October 4, 1919, *HP*.

39. Charles E. Hard to Harding, August 21, 1919, Hard papers, *OHS*.

40. Warren Harding to Charles E. Hard, August 26, 1919, Hard papers, *OHS*.

41. Harry Daugherty to Harding, October 24, 1919, *HP*.

42. Warren Harding to Harry Daugherty, November 3, 1919, *HP*.
43. See *HP*.
44. Harry Daugherty to George Christian, Jr., November 2, 1919, *HP*.
45. Warren Harding to Charles E. Hard, October 21, 1919, Hard papers, *OHS*.
46. Warren Harding to George H. Clark, October 30, 1919, *HP*.
47. See Walter Brown to Colonel William C. Procter, December 2, 1919, Brown papers, *OHS*, for how Harding's "reluctance" was taken as genuine by the Wood supporters.
48. Warren Harding to Charles E. Hard, November 3, 1919, Hard papers, *OHS*.
49. Warren Harding to Malcolm Jennings, November 4, 1919, Jennings papers, *OHS*.
50. See H. F. Alderfer, *The Personality and Politics of Warren G. Harding*, Ph.D. dissertation, Syracuse University, 1935, p. 6.
51. See note 47.
52. Letter of Senator Harding to J. Clare Hughes, released on December 17, 1919, *HP*.
53. See Warren Harding to E. S. Landes, February 5, 1920, *HP*.
54. Warren Harding to Walter Brown, December 15, 1919, Brown papers, *OHS*.
55. Harry Daugherty to Harding, December 26, 1919, *HP*.

8 / The Dark Horse

1. Cleveland *Plain Dealer*, December 18, 1919. (My italics.)
2. Publicity handout for Harding, December 18, 1919, *HP*.
3. M. W. Harvey to Harding, December 17, 1919, *HP*.
4. Warren Harding to Malcolm Jennings, February 4, 1919, Jennings papers, *OHS*.
5. Warren Harding to Francis B. Loomis, January 13, 1920, *HP*.
6. See William T. Hutchinson, *Lowden of Illinois: The Life of Frank O. Lowden* (2 vols.), (Chicago: University of Chicago, 1957), vol. 2, p. 423. Hutchinson has done meticulous work on the Lowden campaign.
7. Warren Harding to Everett Harding, January 26, 1920, *HP*.
8. *As I Knew Them: Memoirs of James E. Watson* (Indianapolis: 1936), pp. 207–211. According to Robert Bowden, *Boies Penrose: Symbol of an Era* (New York: 1937), pp. 256–261, Penrose had backed Harding early in 1919 and had become disgusted with his poor speeches and lack of popular support. He had then vainly tried to make Senator Philander Knox run, but Knox seemed disqualified because he had voted against the Eighteenth and the Nineteenth Amendments, which Harding had luckily supported. Penrose had then turned to Senator Watson, but finding him unresponsive, he had returned to Harding.
9. See Hutchinson, *op. cit.*, vol. 2, p. 450. See also Wesley M. Bagby, *The Road to Normalcy: The Presidential Campaign and Election of 1920* (Baltimore, Md.: Johns Hopkins, 1962), pp. 39–40.
10. *The Journal of Brand Whitlock*, A. Nevins, ed. (New York: 1936), p. 611 (entry for June 13, 1920). In a letter of April 4, 1920, however, Whitlock admitted that Lowden would suit the bosses almost as well as Harding and that Wood's candidacy seemed likely to wreck them both.

11. *Literary Digest*, June 5, 1920.

12. Warren Harding to C. L. Newcomer, December 13, 1919, *HP*.

13. See Herrick's confidential analysis of the Ohio situation for William H. Hays, the chairman of the Republican National Committee, December 16, 1919. Herrick sent a copy of his analysis to Harding.

14. Myron Herrick to Harding, December 25, 1919.

15. Warren Harding to Charles E. Hard, January 5, 1920, Hard papers, *OHS*.

16. Myron Herrick to Harding, January 9, 1920, *HP*.

17. Warren Harding to William Davis, January 23, 1920, *HP*.

18. Warren Harding to Malcolm Jennings, February 4, 1920, Jennings papers, *OHS*.

19. Harry Daugherty to Ray Harris, June 29, 1938, Harris papers, *OHS*. From 1920 until his death, Daugherty never stopped perpetuating the myth of himself as the Svengali of Harding.

20. Daugherty's own official contribution to this sum was $12,500, although he later claimed to have spent $50,000 on the campaign. Other large contributors were Carmi Thompson, an Ohio magnate, $13,950; Colonel Darden, an oilman, $6,000; and—unofficially—the Sinclair Oil Company, $15,000, although Harry Sinclair was one of Wood's powerful backers.

21. Testimony of W. L. Cole at the *Hearings Before a Subcommittee of the Committee on Privileges and Elections* (2 vols.), U.S. Senate, pursuant to S.R. 357, "Presidential Campaign Expenses," 66 Cong., 2 Sess., Washington, D.C., 1921, vol. I, p. 18.

22. Warren Harding to Malcolm Jennings, January 20, 1920, Jennings papers, *OHS*. It was in this letter that Harding told Jennings that he and Scobey and Colonel Christian were his only three "genuinely devoted friends."

23. *Ibid.*, February 14, 1920.

24. Warren Harding to Charles R. Forbes, March 16, 1920, *HP*.

25. Charles E. Hard to Harding, March 19, 1920, Hard papers, *OHS*.

26. Warren Harding to Charles R. Forbes, April 1, 1920, *HP*.

27. A. R. Johnson to Harding, March 31, 1920, *HP*.

28. Warren Harding to Robert L. Long, April 5, 1920, *HP*.

29. See Mary Lee to Florence Kling Harding, April 23, 1920, Lee papers, *OHS*.

30. A. R. Johnson to Harding, April 30, 1920.

31. *The New York Times*, November 22, 1924.

32. Warren Harding to Thomas P. Dewey, May 12, 1920, *HP*.

33. B. Buckley to Harding, May 13, 1920, *HP*.

34. Harry Daugherty to Ray Harris, July 7, 1936, Harris papers, *OHS*.

35. Warren Harding to Harry Daugherty, May 19, 1920.

36. Warren Harding to A. R. Johnson, May 17, 1920.

37. See note 21, *op. cit.*, vol. I, pp. 590–618, 631–650, 842–850, 919–932.

38. *The New York Times*, June 6, 7, 1920.

39. Chicago *Tribune*, June 7, 1920.

9 / The Smoke-filled Room

1. H. H. Kohlsaat, *From McKinley to Harding* (New York: 1923), p. 226.

2. James Morgan, *Our Presidents*, 2nd ed. (New York: 1926), p. 291.

3. David Starr Jordan, *The Days of a Man* (2 vols.), (New York: 1922), vol. 2, p. 777.

4. *The Autobiography of William Allen White* (New York: Macmillan, 1946), p. 584.

5. *Proceedings of the Seventeenth Republican National Convention*, Chicago, June 8–12, 1920, p. 32.

6. New York *World*, June 18, 1920.

7. Mark Sullivan, *Our Times* (6 vols.) (New York: Scribner, 1936), vol. 6, p. 51.

8. *Proceedings, op. cit.*, pp. 168–170.

9. See H. F. Alderfer, *The Personality and Politics of Warren G. Harding*, Ph.D. dissertation, Syracuse University, 1935, p. 61.

10. Sullivan, *op. cit.*, vol. 6, p. 58.

11. Hermann Hagedorn, *Leonard Wood* (New York: 1931), p. 355.

12. See Ray Harris, *Warren G. Harding: An Account of His Nomination for the Presidency by the Republican Convention of 1920* (Washington, D.C.: 1957), p. 15. Harris spent years collecting affidavits from those people most concerned in the drama of Friday night, June 11, 1920, at Chicago. His account is the best single demolition of the legend of the smoke-filled room. Also useful is Wesley M. Bagby's account in *The Road to Normalcy: The Presidential Campaign and Election of 1920* (Baltimore, Md.: Johns Hopkins, 1962).

13. The other Senator was Phipps of Colorado. He was the lone voter from his state for Harding, however, until the fifth ballot, when one other delegate joined him.

14. Harris, *op. cit.*, p. 17.

15. See H. Holthusen, *James W. Wadsworth, Jr.* (New York: 1926), p. 89.

16. See note 12. The Harris work is invaluable on the positions of the Senators themselves.

17. *The New York Times*, June 12, 1920. (My italics.)

18. Sullivan, *op. cit.*, vol. 6, p. 61.

19. See Bagby, *op. cit.*, p. 89.

20. See Sullivan, *op. cit.*, vol. 6, pp. 62–64. Harvey's unreliable testimony is the basis of this account. Sullivan, however, checked the MS of *Our Times* with fifty prominent Republicans present at Chicago, and none of them denied Harvey's story. Harris thinks the story unlikely, saying that Harvey was alone with Harding, but Bagby, *op. cit.*, pp. 89–90, says that Brandegee was present and that the episode took place later than in Sullivan's account.

21. See Dr. George T. Harding, Jr., to Ray Harris, July 26, December 13, 1937, Harris papers, Library of Congress.

22. *Proceedings, op. cit.*, p. 199.

23. Bagby is excellent on this second plot—to *stop* Harding—in a smoke-filled room.

24. Nicholas Murray Butler, *Across the Busy Years* (2 vols.), (New York: Scribner, 1939, 1940), vol. 1, p. 278.

25. White, *op. cit.*, pp. 586–587.

26. See "Inside Story of the Republican Nominations," *Literary Digest*, July 3, 1920.

27. See Harold Nicholson, *Dwight Morrow* (New York: 1935), p. 233.
28. Chicago *Tribune*, June 11, 1920.
29. Henry L. Stoddard, *It Costs to Be President* (New York: Harper, 1938), p. 81.
30. *As I Knew Them: Memoirs of James E. Watson* (Indianapolis, 1936), p. 227.
31. White, *op. cit.*, pp. 587–588.
32. *Proceedings, op. cit.*, pp. 254–261. (My italics.)
33. Arthur W. Page, "The Meaning of What Happened in Chicago," *World's Work*, July, 1920.
34. William Roscoe Thayer to Albert J. Beveridge, June 13, 1920.

10 / The Solemn Referendum

1. Frederick Jackson Turner to Mrs. William Hooper, June 30, 1920, Turner papers, Huntington Library.
2. See "How the Press Size Up Harding," *Literary Digest*, June 26, 1920.
3. Charles E. Hard to Warren Harding, June 15, 1920, Hard papers, *OHS*.
4. See note 2.
5. William G. McAdoo, *Crowded Years* (Boston: 1931), p. 389.
6. *Collier's*, August 14, 1920.
7. *World's Work*, September, 1920.
8. See "Cox's Chances," *Literary Digest*, July 17, 1920.
9. See *Selected Letters of William Allen White*, W. Johnson, ed. (New York: Holt, 1947), pp. 207–208, and Everett Rich, *William Allen White: The Man from Emporia* (New York: Farrar, Straus, 1941), p. 278.
10. Warren Harding to Malcolm Jennings, June 24, 1920, Jennings papers, *OHS*.
11. Robert Bowden, *Boies Penrose: Symbol of an Era* (New York: 1937), p. 261.
12. Anonymous, *Behind the Scenes in Politics* (New York: 1923), p. 189.
13. Mark Sullivan, "The Stump and the Porch," *Collier's*, October 9, 1920.
14. Sherman A. Cuneo, *From Printer to President* (Philadelphia: 1922), pp. 101–103. Cuneo knew Harding and Daugherty throughout their careers. When his book was announced, Daugherty was scared; he obviously had a great deal to hide in his past. "If Cuneo writes a life of you, it will be the death of all of us," Daugherty wrote to Harding, who was unworried. Harding obviously knew his man better. "No publisher will undertake to bring out such a document without my consent or approval," he replied.
15. Republican advertisement in *Collier's*, October 30, 1920.
16. Charles E. Hard kept a memorandum of a conversation with Harding in the White House, on April 18, 1921. Harding had seen a framed excerpt from a speech of his on November 18, 1920, which ran: "Our great assurance at home lies in a virile, intelligent, resolute people, in a land unravaged by war, at enmity with no people, envying none, coveting nothing, seeking no territory, striving for no glories, which do not become a righteous nation. This Republic cannot, will not fail, if each of us does his part." Harding's comment to Hard was, "That was pretty good—if I did say it." Yet even if he did not write it himself, the theme and the use of the word "become" could only

have sounded right in his mouth. Even when others composed Harding's speeches, he worked them over to suit his literary style.

17. *Congressional Record*, 66 Cong., 2 Sess., p. 7099.

18. See Samuel Lubell, *The Future of American Politics* (New York: Harper, 1952), p. 135. Lubell's work gives an important analysis of the ethnic element in the vote for Harding.

19. See S. B. Warner, *Streetcar Suburbs* (Cambridge, Mass.: Harvard, 1962), p. 11.

20. Roger Lewis, "The Two Ohio Editors Again," *Collier's*, October 16, 1920. (My italics.)

21. See note 12, *op. cit.*, pp. 61–62.

22. Sullivan, *op. cit.*

23. Baltimore *Evening Sun*, October 18, November 29, 1920.

24. "What Harding and Cox Think of Each Other," *Literary Digest*, October 9, 1920.

25. Lewis, *op. cit.*

26. Baltimore *Evening Sun*, March 7, September 9, 1921.

27. See "The League Issue Splitting the Parties," *Literary Digest*, October 23, 1920.

28. *The Journal of Brand Whitlock*, A. Nevins, ed. (New York: 1936), p. 639 (entry for October 31, 1920).

29. Charles E. Morris, *Progressive Democracy of James M. Cox* (Indianapolis; 1920), p. 12. See also Roger Babson, *Cox—The Man* (New York, 1920).

30. See Alena Hartwell, *Hardings: History of the Harding Family* (Boston: 1936). Evidence of Helen Harding Meredith.

31. Anonymous, *Warren Gamaliel Harding, President of the United States* (The Sentinal Press, 1921), based on the researches of William Estabrook Chancellor. All the copies of the book except two were allegedly bought up by agents of the Department of Justice and destroyed, at the orders of Daugherty. This is, in fact, only partly true. Many copies still exist in private hands in Ohio, as well as one each at the New York Public Library and Princeton and the Ohio Historical Society. Alderfer, who investigated Chancellor's evidence, believed that much of it was true. For two recent examinations of the evidence, see Francis Russell, "The Four Mysteries of Warren Harding," *American Heritage*, April 1963; and Warren Boroson, "America's First Negro President," *Fact*, January–February, 1964.

32. Henry F. Pringle, *Alfred E. Smith: A Critical Study* (New York: 1927), p. 337.

33. George H. Clark to Charles E. Hard, October 13, 1920, Hard papers, *OHS*.

34. Warren Harding to R. B. Creager, February 1, 1922, *HP*.

35. Walter Davenport, *Power and Glory: The Life of Boies Penrose* (New York: 1931), p. 233.

36. See note 12, *op. cit.*, p. 48.

37. James M. Cox, *Journey Through My Years* (New York: Simon and Schuster, 1946), p. 275.

38. Frank Kent, *Political Behavior* (New York: Morrow, 1928), pp. 281–282.

39. "How the Straws Say the Election Will Go," *Literary Digest*, October 23, 1920.

40. See Hugh L. Keenleyside, "The American Political Review of 1924," *Current History*, March, 1925.

41. For this thesis, see particularly Samuel Colcord, *The Great Deception* (New York: 1921), and Roland Stromberg, *Republicanism Reappraised* (Washington, D.C.: Public Affairs, 1952).

42. Selig Adler, *The Isolationist Impulse* (New York: Abelard, 1957), p. 114.

43. *The Nation*, November 10, 1920.

44. William Allen White, *Forty Years on Main Street*, R. Fitzgibbon, ed. (New York: Farrar, Straus, 1937), p. 107.

45. Arthur Dunn, *From Harrison to Harding* (2 vols.), (New York: 1922), vol. 2, p. 413.

46. Walter Lippmann, *Men of Destiny* (New York: 1927), pp. 107–111.

47. See H. F. Alderfer, *The Personality and Politics of Warren G. Harding*, Ph.D. dissertation, Syracuse University, 1935, p. 179.

48. *New Republic*, November 10, 1920.

49. R. S. Baker, *American Chronicle* (New York: Scribner, 1945), p. 485.

11 / The Best Minds

1. Albion Z. Blair to Charles E. Hard, September 30, 1920, Hard papers, *OHS*.

2. Alexander P. Moore to Walter Brown, June 22, 1920, Brown papers, *OHS*. (My italics.)

3. Warren Harding to Malcolm Jennings, December 14, 1920, Jennings papers, *OHS*.

4. *Speech of Senator Harding at the Masonic Temple*, Columbus, Ohio, January 6, 1921.

5. *The New York Times*, February 22, 1921.

6. A copy of a letter of Thomas Jefferson to Monsieur de Marbois, June 16, 1817, shown to Harding on January 17, 1921, *HP*.

7. See M. Pusey, *Charles Evans Hughes* (2 vols.), (New York: Macmillan, 1951), vol. 1, pp. 405–408.

8. Harry Daugherty to Harding, February 6, 1921, *HP*.

9. Warren Harding to Harry Daugherty, February 9, 1921, *HP*. (My italics.) This is a copy of a letter from Harding, made by the Harding Memorial Association. The original has disappeared, but there is no reason to suppose that this copy or other copies made by the Association are inaccurate.

10. *The Memoirs of Herbert Hoover* (3 vols.), (New York: Macmillan, 1952), vol. 2, p. 36.

11. See Harvey O'Connor, *Mellon's Millions* (New York: John Day, 1933), p. 123.

12. See Bascom N. Timmons, *Portrait of an American: Charles G. Dawes* (New York: Holt, 1953), for a eulogistic portrait of Dawes.

13. Charles G. Dawes to Harding, January 25, 1921, *HP*.

14. Warren Harding to Charles G. Dawes, January 31, 1921, *HP*.

15. See Timmons, *op. cit.*, p. 202.

16. See Joseph M. Chapple, *"Our Jim"—A Biography* (Boston: 1928), p. 282.

17. H. Pringle, *The Life and Times of William Howard Taft* (New York: Farrar, Straus, 1939), vol. 2, p. 955.

18. F. P. Dunne, "A Look at Harding from the Side Lines," *The Saturday Evening Post*, September 12, 1936.

19. *The New York Times*, February 22, 1921.

20. *Ibid.*, March 6, 1921.

21. Lowell Mellett, "What Every President Knows," *Collier's*, March 5, 1921. Later in the article, Mellett tells an interesting story about Woodrow Wilson. Apparently, Wilson also believed in the legend of the small town, declaring that "the real public opinion of the country . . . was formed in the small towns where the free and the brave gathered about the stove in the corner grocery of an evening, spat tobacco juice in the sawdust box, and talked things over."

22. Mark Sullivan, "The Men of the Cabinet," *World's Work*, May, 1921.

23. *Ibid.*

24. *Collier's*, June 18, 1921.

25. Warren Harding to Leonard Wood, February 14, 1921, *HP*.

26. See *The New York Times*, April 1, 1922.

27. See Bliss Perry, *Richard Henry Dana, 1851–1931* (Boston: Houghton Mifflin, 1933), p. 171. The president of the National Civil Service Reform League said that "the only good the examination does, at an enormous expense of time and money, is to keep out some of the dunces who are too stupid to get a place on the list from which an appointment can be made. Otherwise the old political system prevails."

28. Warren Harding to Mary Lee, June 29, 1922, Lee papers, *OHS*.

29. Warren Harding to Harry S. New, May 2, 1923, Harding papers, Library of Congress.

30. Warren Harding to J. S. Williams, December 11, 1922, *HP*.

31. Warren Harding to F. E. Scobey, March 21, 1921, *HP*.

32. *Ibid.*, May 12, 1921.

33. Warren Harding to Harry Daugherty, August 10, 1922, *HP* (copy).

34. W. W. Bride to N. H. Fairbanks, June 17, 1921, Fairbanks papers, *OHS*.

35. Warren Harding to Mary Lee, April 16, 1923, Lee papers, *OHS*.

36. Malcolm Jennings to Harding, November 15, 1921, Jennings papers, *OHS*.

37. Warren Harding to Henry Cabot Lodge, October 20, 1921, *HP* (copy).

38. Warren Harding to Harry Daugherty, November 28, 1921, *HP* (copy).

39. Warren Harding to F. A. Harrison, February 9, 1922, De Coppet papers, Princeton University.

40. Henry L. Stoddard, *It Costs to Be President* (New York: Harper, 1938), pp. 126–127.

41. Warren Harding to Harry Daugherty, February 11, 1922, *HP* (copy).

42. There is an excellent chapter on the question of Harding and patronage in H. F. Alderfer, *The Personality and Politics of Warren G. Harding*, Ph.D. dissertation, Syracuse University, 1935.

43. *Ibid.*, p. 251.

12 / Honeymoon of Disharmony

1. *Inaugural Address of President Warren G. Harding, Delivered Before the Senate of the United States*, 67 Cong., Special Sess., S.D. 1, Washington, D.C., 1921.

2. Joseph Freeman, *An American Testament* (New York: 1936), p. 232.

3. See G. K. Chesterton, *What I Saw in America* (New York: 1923).

4. Herbert Hoover, *Address Before the National Association of Real Estate Boards*, Chicago: July 15, 1921, *HP* (copy sent to President Harding).

5. J. P. Morgan to Harding, July 15, 1921, *HP*.

6. Harvey O'Connor, *Mellon's Millions* (New York: John Day, 1933), p. 127.

7. Warren Harding to Earl R. Obern, March 28, 1921, *HP*.

8. *Address of President Harding at the Opening of the Conference on Unemployment*, Washington, D.C., September 26, 1921.

9. "What Harding and Cox Think of Each Other," *Literary Digest*, October 9, 1920.

10. Samuel Gompers, *Seventy Years of Life and Labor* (2 vols.), (New York: 1925), vol. 1, pp. 552–554.

11. Memorial to President Harding presented by A. C. Davis on behalf of the National Farmers' Union and other agricultural organizations, April 21, 1921, *HP*. Harding was never very sympathetic to organized groups of farmers or workingmen. As he wrote to Jennings on November 19, 1919, "Neither farmers nor labor men ought to have any right to organize to plunder the remainder of the human forces. It is a very curious thing, however, that certain branches of the organized farms have a very radical representation here at Washington and I find myself very frequently nauseated by such utterances as I note in the press coming from that source."

12. Frederick E. Schortemeier, *Our Common Country: Mutual Good Will in America* (Indianapolis: 1921), pp. 92–93.

13. Warren Harding to H. C. Wallace, October 14, 1922, *HP* (copy).

14. B. and F. La Follette, *Robert M. La Follette* (2 vols.), (New York: Macmillan, 1953), vol. 2, p. 1020.

15. Benjamin C. Marsh to Harding, June 26, 1921, *HP*.

16. George Christian, Jr., to Benjamin C. Marsh, July 5, 1921, *HP*.

17. See Chester C. Davis, "The Development of Agricultural Policy Since the End of the World War," *Farmers in a Changing World* (Washington, D.C.: 1940), p. 300.

18. See Mark Sullivan, "One Year of President Harding," *World's Work*, November, 1921.

19. *Congressional Record*, 67 Cong., 1 Sess., pp. 172–173.

20. C. E. Hughes to George W. Wickersham, March 28, 1923, quoted in M. Pusey, *Charles Evans Hughes* (2 vols.), (New York: Macmillan, 1951), vol. 1, p. 434.

21. See "A Peace of Disentanglements," *Literary Digest*, September 10, 1921.

22. Philadelphia *Public Ledger*, June 30, 1921.

23. There are two good books by John C. Vinson on the role of the Senate in international relations during this period, *William E. Borah and the Outlawing of War* (Athens, Ga.: University of Georgia, 1957), and *The Parchment Peace* (Athens, Ga.: University of Georgia, 1955).

24. See *They Told Barron*, A. Pound and S. Moore, eds. (New York: 1930), p. 246.

25. Clinton W. Gilbert, *The Mirrors of Washington* (New York: 1921), p. 17.

26. Sullivan, *op. cit.*

27. La Follette, *op. cit.*, vol. 2, p. 1024.

28. See 67 Cong., 1 Sess., S.D. 48.

29. *Address of President Harding on Hoboken Pier*, Hoboken, N.J., May 23, 1921.

30. Warren Harding to Malcolm Jennings, August 13, 1921, Jennings papers, *OHS*.

31. "Why Harding Takes the Helm," *Literary Digest*, August 6, 1921.

32. *Collier's*, September 3, 1921.

33. Quoted in J. Huthmacher's illuminating "Urban Liberalism and the Age of Reform," *Mississippi Valley Historical Review*, September, 1962.

34. Marion *Star*, May 27, 1886. For the general attitude toward the new immigrants, see John Higham's brilliant *Strangers in the Land* (New Brunswick, N.J.: Rutgers, 1955) and Oscar Handlin's illuminating *Race and Nationality in American Life* (Boston: Little, Brown, 1957).

35. Warren Harding to Malcolm Jennings, February 10, 1917, Jennings papers, *OHS*.

36. Warren Harding to Hulbert Taft, May 2, 1921, *HP*.

37. *Brief of Louis Marshall to W. G. Harding, HP.*

38. Albert Johnson to George Christian, Jr., May 2, 1923, *HP*.

39. *Address of the President of the United States to Congress, December 6, 1921*, Washington, D.C., December 6, 1921. Harding's wish to trade with Europe and yet to protect American industry made him make this remarkable statement to Bruce Bliven: "The United States should adopt a protective tariff of such a character as will help the struggling industries of Europe to get on their feet."

40. There is an excellent chapter on Harding's relationships with the press in James E. Pollard, *The Presidents and the Press* (New York: Macmillan, 1947), pp. 697–712.

41. See Robert T. Barry in *Editor & Publisher*, March 12, 1924.

42. *Ibid.*, June 10, 1922.

43. Nicholas Murray Butler, *Across the Busy Years* (2 vols.), (New York: Scribner, 1939), vol. 1, p. 351.

44. *Editor & Publisher*, April 28, 1923.

45. William H. Crawford, "A Week in the White House with Harding," *World's Work*, May, 1921.

46. These views are quoted in the Ray Baker Harris MS, *OHS*.

47. *As I Knew Them: Memoirs of James E. Watson* (Indianapolis: 1936), p. 226.

48. *Starling of the White House*, as told to T. Sugrue (New York: Simon and Schuster, 1946), p. 174. Starling was head of the Secret Service detail charged with guarding the President.

49. Quoted in Ishbel Ross, *Grace Coolidge and Her Era* (New York: Dodd, Mead, 1962), p. 84.

50. Irwin H. Hoover, *Forty-two Years in the White House* (Boston: Houghton Mifflin, 1934), p. 268.

51. *Ibid.*, p. 251. (My italics.)

52. Washington *Post*, May 29, 1921. Because of the friendship of the Hardings with the McLeans, who owned the Washington *Post*, it came to be known as "The Court Journal."

53. Edmund G. Lowry, *Washington Close-Ups* (Boston: 1921), pp. 13–16.
54. Norman Thomas to Harding, March 12, 1921, *HP*.
55. See *Debs and the Poets*, Ruth Le Prade, ed. (Pasadena, Calif.: 1920).
56. Message of the World War Veterans to President Harding, November 13, 1921.
57. *The Autobiography of Lincoln Steffens* (New York: Harcourt, Brace, 1931), pp. 843–844.
58. See Harry Daugherty to Harding, December 17, 1921, *HP;* Warren Harding to Harry Daugherty, December 19, 1921, *HP;* and Lincoln Steffens, *ibid.*
59. Memorandum on a statement of President Harding on July 19, 1922, *HP*.
60. Warren Harding to Gilson Gardner, May 22, 1922, *HP*.
61. Warren Harding to Rev. John A. Ryan, September 26, 1922, *HP*.
62. Gilson Gardner to W. G. Harding, April 20, 1923, *HP*.
63. See Warren Harding to J. J. Davis, April 7, 1921, *HP*.
64. Copy of an article of William Howard Taft, copyright, 1921, by Public Ledger Company, *HP*.
65. *Address of the President of the United States at the Celebration of the Semi-centennial of the Founding of the City of Birmingham, Alabama*, Birmingham, Ala., October 26, 1921.
66. "The Negro's Status Declared by the President," *Literary Digest*, November 19, 1921.
67. J. Wilson Pettus to Harding, November 25, 1921, *HP*.
68. Harry Daugherty to Harding, March 10, 1921, *HP*.
69. Bliss Perry, *Richard Henry Dana, 1851–1931* (Boston: Houghton Mifflin, 1933), p. 173.
70. See A. Sinclair, *Prohibition: The Era of Excess* (Boston: Atlantic Monthly, 1962), p. 185. Sinclair's book gives a full interpretation of Harding's attitude toward prohibition and of the enforcement of the dry law under his regime.
71. Warren Harding to Harry Daugherty, September 2, 1921, *HP* (copy). (My italics.)
72. Florence Kling Harding to Malcolm Jennings, March 2, 1922, Jennings papers, *OHS*.
73. Warren Harding to Malcolm Jennings, January 6, 1922, Jennings papers, *OHS*.

13 / The Break with Normalcy

1. *Address of the President of the United States at the Opening of the Conference on Limitation of Armament*, Washington, D.C., November 12, 1921.
2. *Manchester Guardian Weekly*, November 18, 1921.
3. Heywood Broun, "Scrapping the Scrappers," *Collier's*, December 24, 1921.
4. Warren Harding to Henry P. Fletcher, November 25, 1921, *HP*. (My italics.)
5. See the comment of the New York *Evening World* in "What the Harding Plan Means to the League," *Literary Digest*, December 10, 1921.
6. *Address of the President of the United States at the Concluding Session of the Conference on Limitation of Armament*, Washington, D.C., February 6, 1922.

7. William Jennings Bryan to Harding, January 26, 1922, *HP* (copy).

8. Warren Harding to William Jennings Bryan, January 31, 1922, *HP* (copy).

9. See 67 Cong., 2 Sess., S.D. 125.

10. Warren Harding to Henry Cabot Lodge, February 16, 1922, *HP* (copy).

11. *Ibid.*, February 23, 1922, *HP* (copy).

12. F. P. Dunne, "A Look at Harding from the Side Lines," *The Saturday Evening Post*, September 12, 1936.

13. Warren Harding to Henry Cabot Lodge, December 27, 1922, *HP* (copy).

14. William Allen White, "The Best Minds, Incorporated," *Collier's*, March 4, 1922. Later, blessed as always by the penetrating vision of hindsight, White repeated his theory of the red shot and the Elks Convention to point out the moral that Harding *failed* because of his "weak heart and thick head" [see *Masks in a Pageant* (New York: Macmillan, 1928), p. 421]. This was a direct contradiction of his use of the theory in 1922.

15. William Allen White, "What's the Matter with America?", *Collier's*, July 1, 1922.

16. H. Broun, "What's the Matter with White?", *ibid.* Also see the comment of S. Strunsky on White's article.

17. *Collier's*, April 15, 1922.

18. *Speech of the President of the United States Before the National Press Club*, Washington, D.C., March 4, 1922.

19. See "The Farmer's Need and the Farmer's Power," *Literary Digest*, February 4, 1922.

20. See Chester C. Davis, "The Development of Agricultural Policy Since the End of the World War," *Farmers in a Changing World* (Washington, D.C., 1940), pp. 300–302. It is ironic how deeply conservative Republicans would pay lip service to the qualities of the American farmer, but would do nothing to help him economically. After Harding's opening speech at the National Agricultural Conference, his conservative Solicitor General, James M. Beck, wrote to congratulate him on January 24, 1922 (*HP*): "Although a city-bred boy, who knows nothing of farmers or farming, I am deeply impressed with the fact that the most serious sign of the times is the movement from the farm to the city. Curiously enough, modern scientific history now believes that the downfall of Rome was not the corruption of the Caesars, but the fact that alien slave labor destroyed the farmer and drove him to the cities." Yet Beck would do nothing through government spending to make it worth the farmer's while to stay on his farm. (Beck's figures were even wrong; by 1920, more Americans were in the cities than elsewhere.)

21. Warren Harding to Samuel Hill, December 4, 1922, *HP*.

22. For a detailed account of the actions of Congress under the Harding regime, see John D. Hicks, *Republican Ascendancy, 1921–1933* (New York: Harper, 1960). Also useful is Karl Schriftgiesser's *This Was Normalcy* (Boston: Atlantic Monthly, 1948).

23. Warren Harding to Jonathan Bourne, August 25, 1922, *HP*.

24. Warren Harding to Malcolm Jennings, October 30, 1922, Jennings papers, *OHS*.

25. Sinclair Lewis, *Main Street* (New York: 1920), p. 261.

26. See George Norris, "Boring from Within," *The Nation*, September 16, 1925.

27. Quoted by R. Neuberger and S. Kahn, *Integrity: The Life of George W. Norris* (New York: 1937), p. 207.

28. White, *Masks in a Pageant*, p. 426.

29. Warren Harding to Malcolm Jennings, October 30, 1922, Jennings papers, *OHS*.

30. See Charles B. King to Harding, August 7, 1922, and Harding's reply, August 10, 1922, *HP*.

31. See Ida M. Tarbell, *The Life of Elbert H. Gary* (New York: 1926) pp. 292–295.

32. *The Memoirs of Herbert Hoover* (3 vols), (New York: Macmillan, 1952), vol. 2, p. 103.

33. Warren Harding to C. G. Smith, June 19, 1922, *HP*.

34. Warren Harding to Malcolm Jennings, July 13, 1922, Jennings papers, *OHS*.

35. In George W. Pepper's autobiography, *Philadelphia Lawyer* (Philadelphia: Lippincott, 1944), he claims the chief credit for settling the coal strike, although much of the credit or discredit should go to the pro-business Secretary of Labor, James J. Davis. Pepper tells one amusing, if apocryphal, story. When he asked Philip Murray, one of Lewis' lieutenants, what he meant by "collective bargaining," Murray is said to have replied, "It's a bargaining where you collect something."

36. *New Republic*, August 9, 1922.

37. See the anonymous reports of the meeting of the presidents of Shopcrafts and Brotherhoods, August 11, 1922, *HP*.

38. See Harry Daugherty and T. Dixon, *The Inside Story of the Harding Tragedy* (New York, 1932), pp. 132–136.

39. Warren Harding to Charles B. King, August 10, 1922, *HP*.

40. "Strike Crisis," *Address of the President of the United States, Delivered Before the Joint Session of the Two Houses of Congress*, Washington, D.C., August 18, 1922.

41. See "The President's Plan for Industrial Peace," *Literary Digest*, September 2, 1922.

42. See note 32, *op. cit.*, vol. 2, pp. 47–48.

43. Warren Harding to James T. Williams, June 13, 1922, *HP*.

44. For the full charges brought by Congressman Keller and for Daugherty's answer to them, see *Reply by the Attorney General of the United States, Hon. Harry M. Daugherty, to Charges Filed with the Committee on the Judiciary of the House of Representatives, December 1, 1922, by Hon. Oscar E. Keller, Representative from Minnesota*, Washington, D.C., December 1, 1922, *HP*.

45. Harry Daugherty to Ray Harris, November 18, 1932, Harris papers, *OHS*.

46. The fullest account of the activities of the Ohio Gang is to be found in Samuel Hopkins Adams, *Incredible Era: The Life and Times of Warren Gamaliel Harding* (Boston: Houghton Mifflin, 1939).

47. Joseph J. Early to George Christian, Jr., February 24, 1923, *HP*.

48. Alice Roosevelt Longworth, *Crowded Hours* (New York: Scribner, 1933), p. 324.

49. See *They Told Barron*, A. Pound and S. Moore, eds. (New York: 1930), pp. 253–254.

50. See Harry Daugherty to Harding, May 17, 1922, and Harding's reply, *HP* (copies).

51. Harry Daugherty to Ray Harris, May 24, 1934, Harris papers, *OHS*.

52. Warren Harding to Harry Daugherty, December 4, 1922, *HP* (copy).

53. There are several accounts of the Teapot Dome scandal. The most useful of these are to be found in John Ise, *The United States Oil Policy* (New Haven, Conn.: Yale, 1928); Burl Noggle, *Teapot Dome: Oil and Politics in the 1920's* (Baton Rouge, La.: Louisiana State, 1962); and J. Leonard Bates, *The Origins of the Teapot Dome* (Urbana, Ill.: University of Illinois, 1964).

54. Frederick E. Schortemeier, *Our Common Country: Mutual Good Will in America* (Indianapolis, 1921), pp. 173–194.

55. M. Allis to Harding, June 1, 1922, *HP*.

56. Warren Harding to Harry Daugherty, June 30, 1922, *HP* (copy).

57. *Ibid.*, July 24, 1922, *HP* (copy).

58. Warren Harding to Albert Fall, July 14, 1922, *HP* (copy). Other than this slight correspondence, the Harding papers are notably bare on the subject of the Department of the Interior or the Teapot Dome.

59. Jacob S. Coxey to Harding, June 2, 1922, *HP*.

60. See "The Democratic Tidal Wave," *Literary Digest*, November 18, 1922.

61. Warren Harding to Jonathan Bourne, November 9, 1922, *HP*.

62. Warren Harding to Malcolm Jennings, October 30, 1922, Jennings papers, *OHS*.

63. *Address of the President of the United States to the Congress*, Washington, D.C., December 8, 1922.

64. See "Harding's Fight to Keep the Reins," *Literary Digest*, December 23, 1922.

65. Harding excused himself to his friend Jonathan Bourne for not taking too strong a line with Congress or asking it to do too much. He knew very well how easily a rebellious Senate could make him powerless. "It would be easy enough to fight," Harding wrote on December 4, 1922, "there is ample provocation, but we have so dissipated the party spirit and are so lacking in effective organization, that I have to proceed tactfully to avoid paralyzing the activities of the government. Under the rules of the Senate, as you are well aware, it is very easy to paralyze all activities. If Congress were to refuse to pass the supply bills, which refusal might readily attend very much of a fight, the government would be stalled in its activities unless I turned to an extra session of Congress. I would be willing to make a very considerable sacrifice in order to save the country from the extra session. If there is any one thing we need in the United States at the present time it is a period of relief from the threat of disturbing legislation."

66. William Allen White, *Forty Years on Main Street*, R. Fitzgibbon, ed. (New York: Farrar, Straus, 1937), p. 109.

14 / Death Without Conclusion

1. See "After Two Years of Republican Rule," *Literary Digest*, March 17, 1923.

2. *Address of the President of the United States to the Congress*, 67 Cong., 4

Sess., H.R.D. 554, Washington, D.C., February 7, 1923.

3. *Address of the President of the United States at the Unveiling of a Statue of Alexander Hamilton*, Washington, D.C., May 17, 1922.

4. Charles E. Hughes to Harding, March 1, 1923, *HP* (copy).

5. Quoted in John C. Vinson, *William E. Borah and the Outlawry of War* (Athens, Ga.: University of Georgia, 1957), p. 80.

6. Warren Harding to Jonathan Bourne, April 30, 1923, *HP*.

7. Warren Harding to Malcolm Jennings, April 16, 1923, Jennings papers, *OHS*.

8. *Ibid.*, May 5, 1923.

9. See *Speeches and Addresses of Warren G. Harding, President of the United States Delivered During the Course of His Tour from Washington, D.C., to Alaska and Return to San Francisco, June 20 to August 2, 1923*, Washington, D.C., 1923. This speech was delivered at St. Louis on June 21, 1923.

10. See Adrian (Michigan) *Telegram*, quoted in "Courting the Court's Critics," *Literary Digest*, July 14, 1923.

11. See note 9.

12. *Collier's*, August 11, 1923.

13. Warren Harding to Brother Joseph Dutton, May 10, 1923, Harding papers, Library of Congress.

14. Warren Harding to Malcolm Jennings, July 13, 1922, Jennings papers, *OHS*.

15. See "The Loom of the Harding Boom," *Literary Digest*, February 24, 1923.

16. William Allen White, *Forty Years on Main Street*, R. Fitzgibbon, ed. (New York: Farrar, Straus, 1937), p. 111.

17. Harry Daugherty to Alice Robertson, March 5, 1923, *HP*.

18. "Harding's Chances for Another Term," *Literary Digest*, March 31, 1923.

19. Harry Daugherty to Harding, April 16, 1923, *HP*.

20. Warren Harding to Malcolm Jennings, April 16, 1923, Jennings papers, *OHS*.

21. See article by Charles W. Wood in *Collier's*, August 20, 1922.

22. See T. J. Steuart, *Wayne Wheeler: Dry Boss* (Chicago: Revell, 1928), pp. 205–206.

23. See note 9. This speech was delivered on June 25, 1923.

24. Warren Harding to Malcolm Jennings, June 11, 1923, Jennings papers, *OHS*.

25. William Allen White, "Blood of the Conquerors," *Collier's*, March 10, 1923. (My italics.)

26. *The Autobiography of William Allen White* (New York: Macmillan, 1946), p. 619.

27. See Warren Harding to Malcolm Jennings, March 19, 1917, Jennings papers, *OHS*.

28. See *Editor & Publisher*, May 5, 1923.

29. Warren Harding to Walter Brown, June 5, 1923, *HP* (copy).

30. Malcolm Jennings, "Washington—Alaska—Marion: A Journey and Its Ending," *The Rotarian*, November, 1923.

31. *The Memoirs of Herbert Hoover* (3 vols.), (New York: Macmillan, 1952), vol. 2, p. 49.

32. See note 9. This speech was delivered at Idaho Falls on June 28, 1923.

33. Donald Richberg wrote an interesting poem on Harding watching the glaciers of Alaska:

The world moves on
And leaves him standing there
Quite satisfied,
Completely unaware.

Proudly—with face
Turned toward the crimson West—
He cries: "The dawn!"
And adds: "Old ways are best."

O, head of oak!
No wonder that you sigh
At youthful haste
As glaciers pass you by.

34. Strickland Gillian in the Washington *Post*, November 20, 1942. For a correct analysis of Harding's health, see the work of Ray Harris, the testimony of Hoover and Hughes and Watson, and S. N. Behrman's piece on Dr. Libman in *The New Yorker*, April 8, 1939. Also useful is K. Walker and R. Downes, "The Death of Warren G. Harding," *Northwest Ohio Quarterly*, XXXV, Winter, 1962–1963.
35. See Samuel G. Blythe, *A Calm Review of a Calm Man* (New York: 1923).
36. See Gaston B. Means, as told to May Dixon Thacker, *The Strange Death of President Harding* (New York: Guild, 1930). Curiously enough, it was Mrs. Thacker's brother who helped Daugherty to write his whitewashing book. Since Means was a confessed perjurer and since Mrs. Thacker later signed an affidavit that all the evidence in the book was backed by nothing except Means's word-of-mouth stories, the book cannot be relied on for any historical fact. Means was employed by Burns and Daugherty; he did know some details of the scandals in the Department of Justice, but neither he nor his readers could tell fact from fiction. The muckraker Clement Wood, who wrote an exceedingly inaccurate and fictional biography, *Warren Gamaliel Harding: An American Comedy* (New York: 1932), claimed in a persuasive appendix that Means did tell something of the truth and that he proved this to Mrs. Thacker. According to Wood, the Macfadden publishing interests owned affidavits proving that Means's testimony was substantially correct. Wood, however, could not produce these affidavits, some of which he asserted proved that Mrs. Harding poisoned her husband.
37. See the testimony of Dr. Warren Harding, Jr., in *The Moffat Papers: 1919–1943*, N. Hooker, ed. (Cambridge, Mass.: Harvard, 1956), pp. 138–139.
38. See note 31, p. 51.
39. See *He Was "Just Folks,"* Cash Asher, ed. (Chicago: 1923), pp. 19ff.
40. White, *The Autobiography of William Allen White*, p. 616.
41. *Memorial Address in Honor of the Late President, Warren G. Harding, Delivered by the Hon. Charles E. Hughes, in the Hall of the House of Representatives*, Washington, D.C., February 27, 1924.

15 / The Evil That Men Do

1. See Robert Connor, "Shall the Constitution Be Preserved?" *Ohio State Archaeological and Historical Quarterly*, XLIV, July, 1935.

2. See Buford Roland's illuminating "The Papers of the Presidents," *American Archivist*, XIII, July, 1950.

3. Nan Britton, *The President's Daughter* (New York: 1927). The book seems authentic in its wealth of haphazard detail. Miss Britton is still alive, and she visited Harding's home in Marion only a few years ago. No one noticed her until her name was discovered in the visitor's book.

4. For extracts from Harding's 108 letters to Mrs. Phillips, see *The New York Times*, July 10, 1964. It is to be hoped that these letters will soon be made available to qualified scholars, as have the rest of the Harding papers in the Ohio Historical Society, without restriction on their use. They are said to contain material of historical and psychological importance to biographers of Harding. The extracts from the letters which have been printed show little more than Harding's adolescence in matters of the heart. The heirs of Warren Harding have instituted a lawsuit for $1,000,000 against those responsible for the publication of part of the letters, and they are also attempting to recover the letters, which were bought by American Heritage from the estate of the deceased Mrs. Phillips. Until the fate of the letters is decided, they cannot be published by historians, for the copyright belongs to the family.

5. This was the advice of Harlan Fiske Stone, quoted in A. T. Mason, *Harlan Fiske Stone: Pillar of the Law* (New York: Viking, 1956), p. 270.

6. *Address of President Hoover on the Occasion of the Dedication of the Harding Memorial*, Marion, Ohio, June 16, 1931.

7. Bruce Bliven, "Not Proven Guilty: The Ohio Gang in Court," *New Republic*, October 27, 1926.

8. Harry Daugherty to N. H. Fairbanks, April 3, 1924, Fairbanks papers, *OHS*.

9. "How Daugherty Helped Harding into the White House," *Literary Digest*, April 9, 1921.

10. Harry Daugherty to Ray Harris, November 18, 1932, Harris papers, *OHS*. Clinton W. Gilbert correctly appraised Daugherty as early as 1922 in *Behind the Mirrors*. "Your professional politician," he wrote, "for that is what Daugherty was, always is an object of doubt. And for this reason he always seeks what is technically known as a 'vindication.' Conscious of his own rectitude, as he measures it, he may come out of office cleared in the world's eyes, and with a fine title, to boot, ready for life upon a new level."

11. Samuel Hopkins Adams, *Incredible Era: The Life and Times of Warren Gamaliel Harding* (Boston: Houghton Mifflin, 1939), p. 421.

12. See Ira Smith and Joe Morris, *Dear Mr. President: The Story of 50 Years in the White House Mail Room* (New York: Messner, 1949), pp. 110–114; Lillian Parks and Frances Leighton, *My Thirty Years Backstairs at the White House* (New York: Fleet, 1961), pp. 170–171; Mary Randolph, *Presidents and First Ladies* (New York: 1936), p. 229; Elizabeth Jaffray, *Secrets of the White House* (New York: 1927), pp. 87–88; and Madame Marcia, "When an Astrologer Ruled the White House," *Liberty*, April 9, 1938. Such exposés

played the part of the old courtiers' memoirs of Europe, which they matched in inaccuracy and fell behind in style.

13. Scott Fitzgerald, *The Vegetable* (New York: 1922).
14. Samuel Hopkins Adams, *Revelry* (New York: 1926), pp. 41–42, 318.
15. William Allen White, *Selected Letters of William Allen White*, W. Johnson, ed. (New York: Holt, 1947), p. 260.
16. See "Harding the Sentimentalist," *New Republic*, October 20, 1920.
17. Quoted by Clifton Johnson in *Hudson Maxim* (New York: 1924), p. 250.
18. Quoted in Dixon Wecter, *The Hero in America* (New York: Scribner, 1941), p. 269.

INDEX

GOLD
MOUNTAIN

by
CHARLOTTE PAUL

ace books

A Division of Charter Communications Inc.
A GROSSET & DUNLAP COMPANY
1120 Avenue of the Americas
New York, New York 10036

GOLD MOUNTAIN

An ACE Book,
by arrangement with Random House, Inc.

The quotation from "Barb'ra Allen" appearing on page 94 is used with the kind permission of J. Fischer & Bros., owners of the copyright.

First Ace Printing: April 1977
Second Ace Printing: May 1977

Printed in U.S.A.

To my sons, Hiram and John,
because they've always wanted
to be in a book

author's note

This is not a history book. It is a love story. But as anyone who has ever been in the Snoqualmie Valley could see with half an eye, this mountain-enclosed area of big trees and cold rivers has been very much in my mind and heart while I was writing it.

I came to the Snoqualmie Valley four years ago and hadn't been here two weeks when I attended a club meeting where the main address was delivered by a little white-haired lady with a long memory and a twinkle in her eye. She was the third white child to be born in the valley, and the stories she told that afternoon were the first I put down in a notebook which in the next two years grew to weigh three pounds and measure four inches cover to cover.

When the old-timers of the valley came to realize that their memories really interested me they were coöperative to the extreme. I've talked to people who were born here seventy-five years ago, and to others who came here as little children when the whites were outnumbered by the Indians. Two of my informants have died since I began my research, and most of the others are in their eighties, though a couple of them won't admit it. I could write a history book, but I haven't. This book is fiction; the people in it are not "real." But in spirit, in setting, in every detail, from the way people made a living to the way they felt about it, I think it is far more real than a history book would have been.

"You're going to get into hot water," the wife of an old settler warned me when I began this book. "Either you're going to change things around, and people hereabouts will say, 'Why, he didn't do that and I didn't do that.' Or else you'll write just what they did do, and then they *will* be mad!"

But I think she underestimated her neighbors, for two of the "young men" who gave me material read this book before publication, and their only complaint was that they might not be around to receive their autographed copies.

I'd like to express heartfelt gratitude to those who helped me most in the writing of this book: Mrs. Olive Quigley, Grandma Pickering, Tom Bird, Mrs. Charles Carpenter, Chief of the Snoqualmie Tribe, Jerry Kanim; George Foster Kelley, W.W. Stephenson, Albert Prenatt, Otto and Deo Reinig and Elva Polley. I am indebted also to the late Mrs. Alice Rachor and to Herbert Knowles, who has also passed away.

Charlotte Paul

Snoqualmie, Washington
1953

GOLD MOUNTAIN

CHAPTER ONE

i

THE STEAM WHISTLE on the riverboat *Viking* shrilled a warning. Two Indians in blue jeans, black hair to their shoulders, feet bare, were stuffing the boiler with lengths of wood. The engine belched mightily. In a moment the paddle wheel would turn and the round-nosed little scow with the crackerbox cabin would begin the struggle upstream. Time to go, the whistle wheezed, like a fat woman calling in her children.

Captain White and his son Carl stood among the crates, boxes, sacks, bedrolls and livestock that crowded the *Viking*'s deck, and looked back toward town, checking the progress of the last stragglers. Carl was tall and slender, with a polish to him, a fineness of feature, so different from his father that people often wished they could have seen his mother. The riverboat captain, like the men who were waiting on deck and those approaching along the rutted wagon road, was as solid and as rough as a log cabin, built for weather but no extra trimmings.

"Here they come," Carl said.

"The whistle always brings 'em."

Tall, short, fat and lean, the group of men moved toward the boat like a wave rolling slowly but inevitably toward shore. They were dressed as the captain and his son and every other man was dressed in this tree-shadowed valley: rough work clothes, heavy boots, dark felt hats pulled down to the eyebrows. At the gangplank they fell silently into a single file. They were aboard, Carl took hold of the plank, the captain headed for the wheel, when one of them burst out, "Say, who's that pretty little gal?"

To a man, they turned to look. It was a girl, all right, a young girl for all the fact that her red hair was piled in an old-maidish bun on top of her head and a handful of straw and ribbon and artificial flowers had been impaled on top of that by a pair of grown-up hat pins. It was mid-September and hot enough for July, but she was wearing a blue serge traveling dress, the kind a little girl might borrow from her mother for a game of dress-up. Her hands were covered with bright pink gloves, one of them holding a shiny wicker suitcase. Dress, hat, gloves, suitcase—it was clear she was figuring on making the trip on the *Viking*.

Captain White called to Carl, "It might be her. I had a notion she might be coming in this trip."

"Her?" a toothless logger squeaked to the man next to him. "Her who?"

The next man shrugged. "Somebody's wife."

"I ain't heard of nobody sending for his wife."

"Kinfolk."

"Ain't heard of nobody expecting kinfolk."

"You don't have to hear everything."

The man laughed delightedly. "What've we got in this whole crazy valley? Besides Indians and wild animals? Fifty white families and a couple dozen loggers and shingle weavers? I don't miss nothing, neither do you."

"Might be the new schoolteacher. They're waiting on one at Gold Mountain."

The toothless mouth gaped as the man turned to look more directly at the girl. "That scaredy-looking little thing?" he whispered hoarsely. "You forgot what happened to the last one?"

They stared, but they didn't move. The girl seemed to be taking two steps backward for every one forward. She was in trouble—they sensed it, wanted to know all about it, were so eaten by a desire to see her close up that they pretended not to care whether they ever saw her at all. In the whole crowd of men on the *Viking,* only Carl White thought of walking back up the gangplank toward the strange little girl with the red hair and the dress that was too old and too big for her.

"Now," the toothless man breathed, cracking his friend's ribs with his elbow. "Now young White's on the job. *He* knows how to talk to girls. He learnt how in Seattle."

ii

She was afraid. A dozen steps would take her to the gangplank. Twelve steps, more or less, and the trip was begun. For a moment shorter than the tick of a clock she felt she could do it. Walk! Her mind commanded and her small body bent forward, tensed with awareness of the movement it was about to make. The hand on the suitcase tightened, one foot lifted. But the impulse died. She stepped backward, timidly set the suitcase down. With a sense of shame she saw her hands were shaking.

It was clearly time to go. The other passengers had all walked across the gangplank and were looking back at her now. "Come aboard if you've a mind to," they seemed to challenge her. "This here tub's good enough for us." And worst of all, one of them, a tall young man with dark hair and a serious face, was coming straight toward her.

How wrong I was, she thought, to believe I could do this without being afraid. It was an old, bitterly familiar feeling. It had come on her the moment she began to walk down the road to the riverboat. As always it began with a tightness in her throat, settled into a knot in her stomach, spread through her body as if it were a disease the blood could carry. Fear—sickening, paralyzing fear. It had crippled her at every important moment of her life, ever since she was a little girl.

The young man was near. The men on deck had fallen silent, watching them. They're all laughing at me, she thought. "Run!" the inner voice shrieked. In senseless panic, her hand groped for the handle of the suitcase. But he was right beside her. It was too late.

She looked up at him. He wasn't a logger—she saw that in her first frightened glance. He was wearing calked boots and rough work clothes but there was a gentlemanliness to him. And he wasn't laughing at her.

"I beg your pardon," he said, inclining his head in a gesture that somehow made her feel he had bowed. "But are you Miss Katherine Duncan?"

The last of her strength went into a gigantic effort to face him calmly. Voiceless, she nodded.

"I'm Carl White, the captain's son. He sent me out to see if I could help you aboard."

But I'm not going. . .The words were loud in her own ears, but looking into the thin, serious face of the captain's son she didn't say them. He made her feel proud. She thought, it isn't as shameful to be afraid if you keep other people from knowing it, and instantly the fear lessened. "Thank you."

He looked down at her thoughtfully. "You *are* the new schoolteacher?"

She answered with a lift of the chin and a quick squaring of her shoulders.

He smiled. "Excuse me." His voice was so gentle that she blushed. "But I wouldn't have been sure, if there had been anyone else on the pier."

She was still too much afraid to be angry. Besides, his words could be taken in many ways. Only a girl without confidence in herself would imagine they were anything but a compliment. And he was bowing, a real bow this time. I am a gentleman, his manner said, and you are a lady.

Katherine Duncan's hand flew to her hat. A pat or two reassured her that it was in place. Quite suddenly her fear wasn't as pressing as the necessity of acting the kind of person he took her to be. The new school-teacher. . .Men on deck were watching. The young captain's son, so close she could see the shadow of tomorrow's beard on his cheek, was waiting. Her mouth straightened primly and one pink-gloved hand settled protectingly over the other. Thank God I bought the pink ones, she thought. Black gloves tell the world you're poor.

"I didn't know where to buy a ticket," she said. He nodded solemnly. The lie had been accepted. Her confidence grew immeasurably.

"They do things differently in the valley," he said, "than in Seattle."

There was the faintest emphasis on "They." Katherine caught it, wondered why, and yet admired him for disclaiming a place she already hated. There was a hint of an apology in his voice as well. She could not be asked to push past Indians and step over a crate of chickens in order to buy a steamboat ticket. He took her for a lady from Seattle.

She smiled happily. "I'll follow you," she said, and he picked up the wicker suitcase so quickly that she was saved the mistake of reaching for it herself.

"If you'll excuse me," he murmured, turning towards the *Viking*. Katherine followed, with just the slow and careful step she knew he would think proper. The new schoolteacher, she chanted silently, the new schoolteacher. . .Head high, she walked past the watchful men and sat down carefully on the bench nailed to the outside of the cabin. She felt as if she could see herself just as they did, from the storeboughten hat to the dress that was warm but dignified. I was right, she thought, to pin my hair up on top of my head. The new schoolteacher. . .

She sighed. Carl White did not know how close the new schoolteacher had come to running away. Nor could he know her other, deeper secrets. That the new schoolteacher had never been in school herself for longer than a month or two at a time. That she had lied mightily about that, as well as about her age, in order to get the teaching job in Gold Mountain. That she was alone, utterly and irrevocably alone, as only a seventeen-year-old girl who has run away from home can be.

iii

It hadn't been easy to find a teaching job. The city of Seattle wasn't much more than thirty years old, but teaching certificates were already required, and she had to admit that she could not qualify. "Previous experience?" they inquired next, and she could only explain that she had never taught before. "Almost eighteen," was still seventeen years old to the people who hired teachers. They were impatient or sympathetic, but never impressed when she said she had had "about eight years" of schooling. A few months in Kansas, a year or so in Nebraska, a few weeks in Montana and Nevada and California and Oregon—it couldn't be made to sound like an education, no matter how earnestly she added, "But my mother taught me, too." Squeezing her conscience, she had lied desperately but not well. Twice she had ended up pouring out the truth to the very person who might have hired her if he hadn't known it.

One of them told her to go back home. Katherine listened to him sermonize on what her duty was to her father and wondered where his own sense of duty lay, that he could exhort her to go back without asking what she had fled from. But the second man was elderly, with a bright and penetrating glance. Like everyone else he turned her down. But he added, "I got an idea you're still determined to go out on your own and teach school."

"I can't go back. The reasons—"

"Are your own business," the man broke in, waving one hand impatiently. "Sooner or later you'll know whether or not they were good ones and that'll be your own affair, too." He studied her for a moment, eyes narrowed. "You know, a female is a deceiving thing. You look like the kind that would cry if someone frowned at you. I'd say you'd never stick with anything. But here you are, asking me for a job, and you've been turned down six, seven times already." He chuckled. "You know, don't you, that you're no more of a schoolteacher than I am a wet nurse."

Katherine's mouth set stubbornly. "I think I *can* be a teacher, because I want to so much."

"Ahh. . ." The white head nodded slowly. "Ever thought of teaching out in the country?"

The country. Log cabins, sod houses, snakes, and doing your washing in the river. If she tried, she couldn't tell him what "the country" meant to her. The mud hut in Nebraska in which she had been born, the first child of a dreamy Scot named Peter Duncan and his Boston wife, Naomi Fairfield. That home had been a hole in the side of a hill. A roof of cottonwood poles stuck into the dirt and covered with matted slough grass. Furniture made from wooden boxes begged from the general store and the only heat from a fire of grass and dung. It had been the children's job and as eldest, hers especially, to bring that fuel in from the prairie. There had been a new "home" every year, always different, seldom better. In every one of them Katherine had learned to hate "the country" and her father, who talked dreams and promises but sent his children out to collect cow chips. She shook her head. "I've lived in the country all my life."

He smiled. "A long, long time," he said gently. "Then you're just the one to be a country school-teacher."

"No!" she said. There was a shameful catch in her voice. She swallowed hard and added more steadily, "I want to better myself."

He patted his stomach serenely. "Well, my dear, as I said, your reasons are your own. I don't even care to hear them. But if you want to get started in teaching, you may have to come down a little. *I* began teaching in backwoods Missouri. Whatever you don't like about the country, we had it there in doubles. Never had a schoolhouse, never got paid in money. Got my first knife wound from one of my fourth grade pupils. By the time I had a school in town, I was a good teacher. You could be too, if you've got the gumption."

He pulled a sheet of lined letter paper from the pile

on his desk. "Now here's a job," he said, "out in the Snoqualmie Valley. School at Gold Mountain needs a teacher, the letter says." He squinted at the signature. " 'Julian Sparks.' If I was a youngster and dead set on teaching, I'd write to him."

"Where—where is the Snoqualmie Valley?"

The old man gestured vaguely. "Due east, toward the mountains. Gold Mountain's the first prairie town below the pass. Wagon trains from the east stop there to mend their wagons, oftentimes to bury their dead." He smiled. *"They* won't ask how old you are or whether you graduated."

Katherine whispered, "I don't even know how to get there."

"How are you going to teach children to think," the old man retorted, "If you are afraid to think for yourself?"

So she had written to the man named Julian Sparks. The reply came quickly.

"Dear Miss," it began. "If you are determined to begin your teaching career in the Snoqualmie Valley—your reasons for which are mysterious to me—Mr. Bengston says to come ahead. There are always children here to be taught. Until now our children have been more than a match for their teachers but trust your experience will have prepared you for same.

"Gold Mountain is about thirty miles east of Seattle by wagon trail, but most whites find it more comfortable to come in by boat. You will travel from Seattle to Snohomish City by the *Nellie,* which I trust still leaves Seattle every three days. The riverboat *Viking* is the comfortable way to continue upriver to Black River, the end of the line by reason of the gigantic waterfall above it. Someone there will loan you a horse, if you get that far, and direct you to the hop ranch, where you will be expected by

Yours truly,
Julian Sparks.

P.S. Bring an umbrella, if you have one.''

Katherine read the letter until her fingers smudged the penciled words.

What was the use of wondering who was this ''Mr. Bengston'' who had decreed that she come? In a moment of rebellion she had sworn to be all that was respectable and respected. In hate and misery she had recalled the envious conviction of her childhood, that schoolteachers wear clean clothes, live in homes with glass windows and never need gather cow chips to start a fire. ''You can't stop me from being a teacher,'' she had cried, ''and I won't go back to the country, no matter what you say!'' She had stunned her father, but the facts were not as easily defied.

In the city she would be a housemaid or a store clerk for two or three dollars a week. Or she could teach school—in an unknown wilderness called Gold Mountain and at the command of a mysterious ''Mr. Bengston.'' Once a teacher, she had reasoned, I can get away from the country forever. Once a menial, I could never better myself. . . . Katherine was already dreaming of leaving Gold Mountain when she wrote Julian Sparks that she would come.

But she did not buy an umbrella. More important, she decided, were the hat and gloves, and a suitcase so that she would not have to carry her belongings in a paper parcel. She would be a schoolteacher and a lady. Whoever, whatever, this Mr. Bengston was, she must impress him from the first minute he saw her. Her success—her escape—depended on it.

iv

The Valley was wide at first, the gray-black river flowing deep and slow. As the flat little *Viking* groaned her way upstream, the heavily timbered hills pressed closer on one side, and fell away at the other. Vine maples tangled with nettles that were shoulder high, hiding whatever might be on the slopes above.

"It ain't wild, like it used to be," the captain had assured her. "Nowadays there's a settler nearly every quarter section." But as the hours passed Katherine saw little that proved him right. A few homestead cabins were visible in clearings above the river, their doors and windows opening onto the waterway that was their only road. Here and there cedar canoes were moored to a log piling or an overhanging alder. The farther upstream the *Viking* pushed, the darker the wilderness. Teklatuak, Tolapus, Kalakwahtie—these were settlements whose existence was proved only by a muddy landing, a log cabin trading post, three or four bearded men and a shrieking handful of children waiting for the mail.

Katherine sat quietly on the bench, back straight and hands resting in her lap. There was comfort in being sedate, as long as no one guessed the panic beneath. The men kept a respectful distance, staring her only when they thought she didn't see it. They going home. She was going into exile. Every k and gurgle of the paddle wheel pulled her farthe way from the neat, secure little world she had dreamed of finding in the city. She hated the

Valley without seeing it. "I'll go back," she promised herself, "the very first chance I get."

The captain's son spoke to her from time to time. "Are you comfortable, Miss Duncan?" or "Would you like to rest in the cabin, Miss Duncan?" The very ordinariness of it was soothing. Every time he appeared at her side, bending toward her in his solemn half bow, she felt grateful to him for giving her something to live up to. She wanted to ask, "Do you live in the Valley?" and dared not for fear that was too intimate a question. Above all, she longed to inquire about this Mr. Bengston, but if he were truly the man who had sent for her, wouldn't that show childish ignorance? At length she planned a fitting question. "Have you worked on the *Viking* long?"

It had sounded proper enough when she had recited it to herself, but Katherine watched his face anxiously for reassurance.

"Only occasionally." For the first time he smiled, and Katherine found herself smiling back. "I don't intend to shove freight on a riverboat for the rest of my life."

"Then you're not in this"—she gestured toward the squat, horseshoe-shaped cabin—"with your father?"

"I'm studying law in Seattle."

Katherine looked at him in open admiration. An attorney. He would live in the city, in a home his children wouldn't be ashamed of. She knew the answer she wanted to hear when she asked, "Then you don't plan to be an attorney out—out here in t Valley?"

He frowned. "I intend to live in town. I don Gold Mountain and I never will." Katherine he had spoken more vehemently than he intended He smiled apologetically. "Before long," he added quietly, "I'll be practicing law in Seattle."

With this, spoken like a confession, he seemed to ask her to understand him. She responded impulsively, "In two years I'll be in Seattle, too!"

Even as she said it she blushed. But he was nodding matter-of-factly, showing her the courtesy of believing just what she said, hearing nothing more. His dark eyes were solemn, his posture a little stiff. Unexpectedly her mind raced back through memories of the men she had known—the admirable, the despicable, the exciting or the dull—and whispered silently that no one she had ever known had been as fine as he.

He bowed and excused himself. A few minutes later, when her pulse had quieted and she had patted hat, skirt, bodice to make sure the watchful men on deck would see nothing amiss, she realized that she still knew nothing about Mr. Bengston.

v

Shadows were lengthening before the afternoon sun when Carl White stopped at her side to say, "Black River is just around the bend."

The end of the run—Katherine suppressed a little gasp of fear. When she stepped off the *Viking*, the last link would dissolve between herself and the world she had sworn never to leave. The men on deck were stirring sleepily. They stretched, scratched themselves, pulled their hats down hard. Katherine stood up, letting one hand hold the other steady. "Thank you."

"They expect you to come to the hop ranch?"

"They"—yes, of course it was "they," Julian Sparks and "Mr. Bengston." But it struck Katherine as strange that the captain's son should seem to know. "Mr. Sparks wrote that someone would loan me a horse."

Carl nodded. "I'll get one for you. Wait for me at the hotel. I'll borrow two horses and ride up to the hop ranch with you."

"Oh. . ." It was pure relief, but Carl stiffened instantly. "If you'll allow me. The country is strange to you."

Katherine said quickly, "Please—please do."

Once Carl had left her Katherine peered anxiously toward the settlement they were approaching. A muddy bank, crowded with several dozen people. Behind and above them a clearing so wide it could only be man-made. At first she could see nothing more. As the *Viking* chugged closer, she made out faces and figures of the waiting people. There were children of all sizes, all of them barefoot, even the boys with hair so long it had to be pulled behind their ears to be kept out of their eyes. She saw men in denim work pants rolled high over thick-soled boots, a dark shirt open at the throat and a broad-brimmed hat jammed squarely down to the eyebrows. Young and old, they were bearded, though she could not tell whether they were recognized beards or just the usual growth between shaves. The women were dressed in calico and wore dark shawls.

There were Indians, too. If you counted them, Katherine thought, they might outnumber the whites. Old men, dressed only in breech clouts and blankets of gray and red, their hair long and hanging about their faces; younger men in the trousers and shirts and boots of the white man. The women stood with feet planted wide, arms crossed under their blankets, while the children ran around them like a pack of noisy dogs. Most of the Indians were on the north side of the river opposite the village, as if they neither wanted, or were wanted by, the *cheechacos* who were resisting the wilderness on the south side. The whites shouted, guffawed, bellowed greetings across the strip of water between themselves and the boat. The Indians watched, silent and motionless.

Slowly the *Viking* sidled up to the crude wooden landing, and the town of Black River came into view. Katherine's heart jerked in fear and disappointment. Of course she could have guessed there wouldn't be more than this. How many crude settlements had she lived in—and hated—already? Here there were three—no—four, rain-darkened structures. One a store perhaps, another some kind of warehouse. The third a hotel, with a weatherbeaten sign bearing just that one word. And the fourth, a doctor's house. "Dr. Martin Meade, Operative Surgery and Surgical Diseases a Specialty."

The *Viking* settled, her motor gasped to a stop. The men were elbowing forward to the gangplank. Carl walked past, a gray canvas mailbag thrown over his shoulder. "At the hotel," he said quickly. "Ask for Hilke Orvaag." Then he was gone.

Katherine waited as long as she dared. The crowd on the bank had studied the boat, the cargo, and now they were studying her. Slowly, trying not to look right or left, she walked down the plank to the landing and up the muddy slope.

She dared not walk too slowly, and therefore have no excuse for not taking time to look at them. But she would not walk fast, and show how much she wanted to get away from them. The new schoolteacher . . .Their voices hushed as she walked by. Or became louder, as the speaker turned his head to look at her but kept on talking to prove that he wasn't really looking at all. Far behind her at the river's edge she

heard a man shout, "Where's that load of stuff for
Nils Bengston?" and Carl White's reply, "I'll get to it
when the rest of the freight is out of the way."

"Nils is sure in a hurry."

"Tell him to send his own crew down to unload it if
he can't wait his turn."

The man swore loudly. Someone laughed. Her
heart hammering, Katherine walked down the rutted
wagon road to the hotel.

vi

Hilke Orvaag was a round little man with bright blue
eyes, tremendous blond eyebrows and almost no hair
above that. He fed Katherine and Carl an early supper of cold venison and apple pie, produced a black
horse for Carl and a big bay for Katherine, and
threatened to clip Carl's ears if he didn't have the
horses back by morning.

"I gave my word to my wife, we ride over to Squak
tomorrow," he said with a heavy accent. "So tonight
I tell people I loaned you the horses. Starting eight
o'clock in the morning I tell that you steal them."
And he gestured dramatically with two fingers of
each hand—snip, snip, snip at the ear lobes.

The trail from Black River to the hop ranch and
Gold Mountain went east along a narrow strip of
prairie between the woods and the river. To their left
the Snoqualmie ran swift and shallow over a series of
riffles, sparkling under the late afternoon sun.
Ahead, so directly their goal they could sight it off the
end of the trail, was a great dome-shaped mountain.

"Old Hi," Carl called over his shoulder.
"Bengston's ranch is on the prairie right at the foot of
it."

"The hop ranch?" Katherine tried to make it sound like a statement instead of a question.

"Biggest in the world." Carl was ahead and she could not see his face, but his voice was cold. It made her uneasy. Whoever this "Mr. Bengston" was whose wish had brought her to Gold Mountain, Carl did not like him.

Below two Indians were standing knee-deep in the river, fishing with spears. On the opposite bank a raft of logs rode the surface at the mouth of a creek, and a sawmill was visible in a little clearing beyond. Carl pointed toward it. "Smith's mill," he said curtly, "but I hear Nils Bengston just bought him out."

Bengston again. . .She began to speak and stopped. She would find out soon enough,

The trail bent towards the woods, plunging them from sunshine into darkness. The trees were so tall and the foliage so interlaced that the sky disappeared except for the thin crack of light directly overhead. "It's like falling into a hole," Katherine thought, her teeth chattering, "and never getting out." It had been warm in the sun. Here among the timber it was damp, and the smell of cedar was a cold smell. The forest seemed to press in on the road. Wherever a log had fallen across the trail, it had been hacked away to the width of a box wagon.

The horses lowered their heads and breathed heavily as the way grew steadily steeper. It was a sharp climb. Muffled by distance and the heavy timber came the steady, thundering roar of a waterfall.

They reached a clearing and Carl motioned to rein in. Below them the river crashed over a precipice for three hundred feet to pound into a rocky basin below. Its force beat the water white, raised billows of foam which blew upward into a soft mist. Rocks, derelict logs, tangled in the frothy white water below.

Carl pulled his horse close to Katherine.
"Snoqualmie Falls," he shouted. "Hop ranch is
about two miles ahead."

Katherine nodded. Two miles, only two miles, before "Mr. Bengston" and "Yours truly Julian
Sparks" would see and judge the new schoolteacher.
For a time the presence of Carl White had made her
forget how much she dreaded that meeting. Panic
shot through her. "Two miles," she repeated
stupidly.

Between Black River and the Falls the Valley
had been narrow and crooked and lost in timber. It
widened now. The ridges on the south, of which Old
Hi was a part, were four or five miles from the craggy
chain of hills which defined the Valley to the north.
Straight ahead to the east, blue and gray and misty in
the gathering shadow, were the mountains through
which Snoqualmie Pass led to the dry piney land of
the eastern territory.

Here in the upper valley of the Snoqualmie the
forest crept down off the hills but ended abruptly in
open, grassy prairie. Katherine thought, how different it is from the sunburned prairie of Kansas or
Nebraska. It was drought time in the Middle West,
but here the grass was green as new leaves, darkened
by deeper green patches of sallal and Oregon grape.

As they rode, Carl called over his shoulder to name
the landmarks. There to the left, the little village of
Three Forks. A cluster of grayed shacks, hugging the
riverbank. Closer now was Old Hi, dark green with
timber, pink-gray with bare rock. Katherine listened
half-heartedly. Fear was coming back full force;
Carl's voice became a wordless monotone. She took
a deep breath, fighting the rising sickness.

For the hundredth time she looked down at her
dress. For the hundredth time she was sorry it wasn't

alpaca or delaine. Gingham, calico, petticoats of bleached muslin and everything that went under that cut from boiled flour sacks—that was the contents of the wicker suitcase. She looked at her pink gloves, seeking some relief in the fact that they were still clean. The hat—her hand touched it anxiously. It isn't much, she thought, but at least it isn't a sunbonnet. Sunbonnets, shawls, black gloves—the sure signs of a person who's had very little meat with her cornmeal.

"The ranch is right up ahead," Carl called, and Katherine felt her heart pound like a frightened child's. Unconsciously her hands adjusted themselves over the saddle horn like those of a lady at a tea party. How will I look to them, she wondered, how will I look? A seventeen-year-old who doesn't stand five feet three with her shoes on. Freckles from ear to ear and hair so miserably close to red she'd had the same nickname wherever she went. A tip-tilted nose and green eyes. "You were bound to favor your mother," her father's sister had said, but not as if it were something to be proud of. It wasn't her aunt who would look through and through her now. It was the people of the Valley whose children she would teach. It was everyone who might be idling at the hop ranch. It was Julian Sparks, whose letter had brought her, and Nils Bengston, whose word had the power to send for the new schoolteacher.

New schoolteacher, new schoolteacher. . .the words beat in her head. They were coming in sight of some buildings now. Farm buildings, cabins, lean-tos, even tents. And in back, a strange kind of shed that seemed to stretch endlessly into the field. There were people, too. Grouped in the barnyard, watching the riders approach. Indians—there were hundreds of them. Some whites, with hands in pockets. In her panic their figures blurred together before her eyes.

She straightened her back until it ached. She lifted her chin. Carl smiled reassuringly, but her return smile felt like a grimace. Her hands were icy, and the pulse was beating wildly in her throat. Is my hat right, she thought desperately, or has it tipped a little too much over one ear? My skirt, is it covering my ankles properly? The new schoolteacher, the new schoolteacher. . .Nausea rose in her throat, receded. She gulped hard, forcing herself, to look straight ahead. Her dress, her gloves, her skirt, her hat, her chin. The new schoolteacher, the new schoolteacher. . .

A boy detached himself from the crowd, ran down the road towards them. He was carrying—dear Lord, Katherine whispered in despair. Yes, it was a slingshot. Carl didn't seem to notice. I'm the new schoolteacher, Katherine thought numbly. She watched with icy fascination, her mind screaming that she was lost but her face frozen into an expression of pleasant dignity. No, no, he wouldn't. . .But he did.

She heard the whing of the stone, felt the horse jerk back, gather his strength, then wildly plunge forward. She was out of the saddle, grabbing for the horn, missing it. The big bay, crazy with shock, bucked again. Too stricken to cry out, Katherine went over the side.

But her foot, one foot, caught in the stirrup. The horse pounded ahead, free, or almost free. Katherine followed, bouncing like an Indian travois through the dirt. She didn't think for a moment about the hooves. "My skirt!" she sobbed out loud, fighting to hold down her petticoats.

Someone grabbed the reins and the horse stopped

abruptly. Carl's frightened voice said, "Katherine, Katherine, are you all right?"

There were other voices, too, mingling in excited whispers. She had to look up. She couldn't bury herself in the dirt. Slowly, with an impulsive wish that she had been killed after all, she raised her head.

A hundred people were standing in a circle around her. One of them, an old Indian in a logger's shirt and nothing else, was holding her hat and grinning appreciatively. The hat was mashed and torn. Carl was beside her, lifting her to her feet, supporting her with a strong arm.

"I'm all right," she said stiffly. It was obvious that they all knew who she was. "Really, I'm perfectly all right!" she repeated, a little irritably because it was so clearly untrue. Frantically her hands worked at straightening her skirts. No use trying to arrange her hair. Every pin that had held it in a grown-up knot at the top of her head was gone; the hair hung loosely down her back.

A man laughed. It was a deep, confident, amused sort of laugh. A man wouldn't laugh like that if he were the kind to wonder what he'd do should the same thing happen to him. A laugh with power, with . . . conceit behind it. Katherine wheeled around angrily.

He was standing only a few feet away, thumbs hooked easily in the edges of his trouser pockets. He was big, very big. His blond head, held erect with such easy pride, was inches above those of the tallest. Sun had burned the hair to straw color, made the skin as dark as an Indian's. His eyes were blue—and amused.

He had stopped laughing. Or at least he stopped laughing out loud. But there was mockery in the way he looked at her. Down his nose, his head a little to one side, his eyes so bright they seemed to be winking at her. He was measuring her, but not seriously. More like a rich farmer who had ordered a draft horse and got a burro. At the corners of his eyes the laugh wrinkles were deep. He was used to laughing. Being bigger than everyone else, Katherine thought angrily, he can whenever he wants to.

She lifted her chin. It had seemed like the end of the world to be dragged into camp at the end of a stirrup, but anger was healing the wounds of embarrassment. She would like to have ignored him. But his bodily presence was too overwhelming. He compelled her, by his very bigness, to look at him.

The memory of a day in the fourth grade in Montana shot crazily across her mind. The moment when shaking with rage she had faced the school bully, crying, "Oh, I'd beat you up if I were bigger!" He had laughed, but instead of slapping her he had kissed her. How she had hated him, then!

"One of the Greene boys," the big man said good-humoredly, pointing to the boy who had hit her horse. But he talked to Carl, not to her. Katherine thought, he sees no reason to explain anything to a woman. "Those Greenes'll have hell filled up by the time the rest of us are ready to go in." He laughed. He was looking at Carl. But his eyes pulled her into the area of his glance, held her there.

Carl's polite voice seemed to break across a heavy current. "Miss Duncan, may I present. . ."

The big man stopped him with a wave of the hand. "I know who she is."

"Hasn't it occurred to you, Nils," Carl said coldly, "that the lady might not know you?"

Katherine felt the antagonism curling behind Carl's words. It was there, too, in the brown face of the man named Nils. But again, the strength belonged to the man who didn't care. Nils laughed. What a silly idea, the laugh said, everyone here knows who I am, and who cares about a skinny little schoolteacher?

Despite his name, it didn't occur to her for a moment that this man who had so little use for her was the one who had sent for her. I'll show you, Katherine thought, and her mouth set stubbornly. "I'm not at all interested in knowing you," she said clearly, "unless you're Mr. Julian Sparks, whom I was to meet here."

"Uncle Julian?" Nils looked at Carl, silently asking, what sort of nonsense is this freckled-faced friend of yours talking? "That addleheaded old man?" he asked out loud. "This time of day, he's usually in his rocking chair, sleeping off his supper."

Carefully, Carl took Katherine's arm. "We'll find him."

Katherine hesitated. What silly notion held her here, aching to say more to this blond giant? "Would you have laughed if that horse had killed me?"

For the first time he looked straight down into her face. He shook his head. "No," he said deliberately, "I would have buried you."

Katherine was trembling all over. "Still laughing, I suppose?"

He grinned. "No, I would have felt real sad." He chuckled. "If you'd been pretty."

The pressure of Carl's hand grew stronger. "Please come," he was saying, and she obeyed blindly. She turned her back to Nils, clutching hard Carl's guiding arm.

"Uncle, come here!" Nils' voice bellowed suddenly behind her. "New schoolteacher wants to see you."

Still holding Carl's arm, Katherine looked back.

An old man was shuffling across the barnyard towards Nils and the crowd. Long white hair hung in strings around his wrinkled face. His mouth moved as if he were talking to himself. Katherine turned to Carl. "Is it possible," she whispered, "that the big man is Mr. Bengston, and that is Julian Sparks who wrote me a letter?"

Carl nodded. "Uncle Julian is bright enough, but he's old and he's been saying yes to Nils Bengston for the past nine years. In his clear spells he writes a beautiful hand."

The old man had reached Nils' side and was squinting toward Katherine. "She going to stay here?"

Nils replied brusquely, "Not in my house." With an imperious wave of the arm, he called her back. "Back up," he commanded, "and let Uncle Julian take a look at you."

Katherine felt the anger begin in her throat, spread with a hot flush to the roots of her hair, rush painfully to the very ends of her fingers.

"The riverboat goes back toward Seattle in the morning," Carl was saying. "You don't have to stay. . ."

"No!"

"Don't worry about breaking your word. If Nils decides he doesn't like you, he'll send you back anyway."

"I'll stay!"

"Katherine, there have been six different teachers in Gold Mountain in the past two years. No one stays."

Her voice shook but it had never been stronger. "Is there a hotel in Gold Mountain?"

"Yes, but that's three miles farther on."

She faced him. "Carl, will you ride along with me?"

He nodded. "But you needn't ride. That was a bad fall. I'll borrow a team and wagon from Nils."

"No!" she said, almost crying. Head high she turned and walked back, through the crowd and to her horse. Skirts and petticoats were torn and dusty. Her hair hung below her shoulders, blowing and tangling with the rising wind. The pink gloves, the beautiful, silly pink gloves, were caked with mud. "I'll ride," she announced. The old Indian with the logger's shirt and naked thighs held out the remnant of her hat. She shook her head. Carl at her heels, she walked past old Uncle Julian, past Nils Bengston, and did not look at either of them.

"I'll help you mount," Carl was saying, and she heard herself reply in a loud, clear voice, "No, thank you, Mr. White." Her teeth were chattering. She took a good grip on the saddle horn and with the strength of anger and desperation, flung herself up onto the giant horse without a hand from anyone.

"You'd better let me lead," Carl was calling, but she paid no attention. Leaning forward in the saddle she lifted the reins and kicked the bay into a gallop. The new schoolteacher, she thought, the new schoolteacher. . .Following her, enveloping her in a cloud of sound, was the rumbling laughter of the man who would have been sad, if she'd been pretty.

CHAPTER TWO

i

NILS BENGSTON LAUGHED UNTIL the schoolteacher and the captain's son were out of sight. Then the laughter faded into a wide yawn, and he lifted both arms to stretch. "I hate schoolteachers," he said matter-of-factly.

Old Uncle Julian looked at him wearily. "You sent for her."

Suddenly the picture of the little teacher bouncing in the dust and grabbing for her petticoats came back to him, and Nils grinned. "I'd send for a dozen more, if they'd all be delivered upside down."

The old man was looking down the trail to Gold Mountain, as if he could still see her if he squinted hard enough. "What did you think of her?"

Nils shrugged. "What's the difference?" He looked out toward the hop fields stretching east and south across the Valley. "Go to bed, Uncle. I'm going to take a look around while there's still light enough."

The old man's voice took on a persistent whine. "It *does* make a difference. Your own daughter goes to school now. School is important. When I was a boy in Pennsylvania. . ."

Nils broke in irritably, "Maybe it is, to old men and weak-minded women. I got a hop ranch to think about." He took a long, deep breath, expanding his tremendous chest and thumping his hands together happily. "By golly," he said, smiling to himself, "and it's the biggest hop ranch in the world."

"Big talk," Uncle Julian said tartly. Ain't yet picked the first crop. You're land poor. I never saw anyone with more brass and less hard money."

"I'll end up the richest man in the territory."

"Or the poorest," the old man snapped, but he was smiling.

"Go to bed," Nils repeated, walking away.

"You should have asked her to stay here just the same."

Nils turned back. "Who?"

"That scared little schoolteacher."

Nils wheeled around and headed for the field. Uncle Julian watched him. Such a big man, he thought, and getting bigger. When I was twenty-nine I was still waiting for a good idea. Such a strong-minded man. The teacher should have been invited to bunk in at the ranch. Any other settler would have shown that much courtesy, whether he admired schoolteachers or despised them—Nils knew it himself. But Uncle Julian was wiser than to ask Nils why he hadn't. He knew, and knew he dared not say, why Nils didn't warm up to having whites in the house. The old man shook his head, talking softly to himself. Nils was ashamed of his Indian wife, when she was there; still more ashamed, since he had deliberately made her his wife, if she were not at home to act a wife's proper part. He's mixed up in his own mind, the old man mused, and sometime I'll tell him what ails him. Sometime, when I'm good and ready to die.

ii

Nils held the hop cone as gently as a mother whose new baby has just been given to her for the first time. The touch of it went through him to his boots. It lay across his palm, perhaps six or seven inches long, its overlapping bracts feeling rough even against his calloused skin. The green it had been was now ripening to yellow. Carefully, very carefully, he pressed down on it, conscious of holding back his strength. He watched it unblinkingly, as if he could feel and smell it with his eyes as well. It rustled. The sound was faint, but he knew he couldn't be mistaken. He pressed harder. A drop of transparent liquid oozed out onto his hand. And the smell of it—he knew the smell was right. Sharp, aromatic. Something to stab right up through the nostrils into the back of the head. Nils crushed the catkin to a sticky wood pulp and triumphantly threw it over his shoulder.

He had figured it out right. He had won. He *was winning*.

It was a wonderful feeling to stand alone like this in the hop field, with the last of the sunset dropping off at the edge of the prairie. Alone he could taste his triumph more sharply. No Indians to threaten. No foremen to take down. No quarreling children or wide-eyed, docile Indian women. He'd built up this little empire by being a good deal more daring or far-sighted than the next fellow, and if anyone had got stepped on in the process, it was a natural process and who could prove God hadn't intended it that way? Nils grinned to himself, wiping the sticky hop liquor off on his pant leg. It was all his, and standing right in the middle you couldn't see the end of it in any direction.

The biggest hop ranch in the world—a broker in Seattle had told him that. Maybe it was true and maybe it wasn't. Nils wanted to believe it but he knew the world and himself well enough to be skeptical for that very reason. Whether it was or not, he muttered with a clenched jaw, it's big all right. And it's going to make me a very rich man.

The vine rows stretched for two miles, clear across the Valley from east to west. Their perfect pattern— seven feet from pole to pole, either way—anticipated the harvest season when the wagons would have to go through for loading. The poles, split from fresh cedar, stood eighteen feet high. And yet the vines had grown to the top of them, crawled out along the connecting strings and spilled over, heavy with the hops that would make him a rich man. Nils felt his pulse quicken, as it always did when he had a chance to view his property alone.

His foremen would trail him from kiln to shed to hop field, supposedly inspecting the ranch but in reality studying him. There were so many ways to fail. The hop louse or bad prices or unseasonable weather or not enough pickers at the right time. Their deliberately expressionless faces, their quick side-ways glances, said, "This time Nils Bengston has outreached himself, and he's scared." Or else they said as loud as words that Nils Bengston was lucky again, and how they envied him.

Either way, Nils despised them. He paid them twice what they asked, used them and needed them, and despised them. Or tried to. Looking over the laden vine rows extending in all directions to fade in the gathering shadow, Nils could smile at the idea of disdaining anyone. The crop was good, the crop was ripe, the pickers were ready, the sky was clear, hop prices were high and by the end of the month they'd be talking about Nils Bengston from here to San Francisco. Nils laughed out loud. No one would ever know how scared he'd been.

In the distance the Indian pickers were shouting over one of their gambling games. Those might be the Yakimas. Hundreds of them had ridden through the

Pass, leading a thousand or more cayuses they would
sell to the Indians who had come down from Canada.
They had camped on a stretch of prairie along the
riverbank toward Three Forks—men, women, children, ponies and dogs. Every night the sound from it
and all other Indian groups had been the same. The
rhythmic chants rose to the night sky with the smoke
of many fires. Horses, wagons, saddles, blankets,
jewelry, rifles, bed quilts, shawls, clothing, cash—
they were all lost or won as the big wood chips
clattered dully to the ground. During the next three
or four weeks each Indian hop picker—and there
were a thousand two hundred of them—would receive a stack of silver dollars. How many of them,
Nils mused, will go home penniless?

He smiled, feeling a little envious. They had no
ambition. They would willingly paddle five hundred
miles or more in their long canoes, or make the hard
ride over the mountains, just for three weeks' work.
What could that bring, at a dollar a box and two
boxes a day about the best a man could do? Fifty
dollars perhaps. There wasn't an Indian on the place
who would accept it in paper money either. Only
silver dollars were "real." Silver dollars that might
buy a pony from the Yakimas, whiskey from the
whites if they could find some stupid enough to sell it
to them, or else be gambled away in a night. Was it
wrong for Nate Tarpee to sell them bluing when they
came to the Gold Mountain trading post begging for
whiskey? "New kind of fire water," Nate had said,
"but don't drink it here." Nate hadn't cheated them.
You can't cheat people of money they care so little
for themselves.

"Money is nothing," Nils thought, "unless you
use it to get more." The thought hit him suddenly,
rippling pleasurably through his body. He burst out

laughing. "I don't want much," he told himself, "just to be about ten miles and five thousand dollars ahead of the next fellow."

It was almost dark now. Old Hi bulged upward against the pale gray sky, a black mass that seemed to lean over the fields below. Looking down toward the buildings grouped together near the river, Nils could just make out the outlines of the long sheds in which most of the Indians slept, and across the field from them the farmhouse and barns and kilns. He pushed his hands deep into his pockets and let his shoulders drop forward easily. Slowly he walked down the row towards the farm.

He felt too good to go inside. A white woman would be full of questions if her husband came in at midnight. Not Mary. She hadn't questioned him in nine years. That much could be said for an Indian woman.

Nils checked himself uneasily. He had labeled her, setting her somewhere below the whites, in thinking of her not simply as Mary but as his Indian wife. And he'd been doing it more and more, as if time were pulling them in opposite directions. He was being careful, now, not to call her an Indian. So very careful, and so irritated by a sense of guilt when he did. For she was still Mary, the mother of his daughter Julie, and not even the change in her could alter that fact. Years ago, Nils thought, nothing I said about her could have sounded disloyal, because there wasn't any disloyalty in me. Nor "loyalty," exactly, for you don't start being loyal to the person you love until you discover that sometime you might not be. He shrugged impatiently. Mary had been gone so much during the past year, to stay with her own people for weeks at a time. The Indian camp below the Falls was only three or four miles away. Once it had been near; now it seemed like a distant, separate place. Nils was uneasy during Mary's lengthening absences, but he didn't blame her. He blamed himself, because he had done nothing about it. He should resent her leaving but didn't. He should miss her. . . He swore softly. It was a fine night, the hops were ripe, such thoughts spoiled his mood. He walked faster.

In the barnyard a short square figure pulled itself free of the shadows. Indian Doc, so proud to be wearing one of Nils' old wool shirts, so unconscious of having nothing under or below it. Doc's age couldn't be figured, Nils knew, but only estimated from the wrinkled face and sagging eyes, the scrawniness of his little bent-over body. Poor Doc was a perennial refugee from his own people. For should one of his patients pass to the great beyond—and Nils knew better than most whites how often one did—the doctor was legally obliged to go along. Nils had tucked old Doc behind, over, and even under his own house so many times he had almost run out of hiding places. A lucky thing for Doc and maybe for me, Nils thought with a grin, that Indians have short memories on this particular subject. Even the kinfolk of the departed forgot their intentions after a time and eventually would even bring him another patient.

"What is it, Doc?" Nils asked. He liked the old man. He had done so much for Doc he couldn't help liking him.

Doc's eyes were weakened by age, but they peered up earnestly. His brown face had shriveled into a mask of a thousand wrinkles, with little clumps of scraggling white whiskers bursting out unexpectedly along the cheeks, under the chin, above his mouth. His long hair was white and hung in uneven lengths about his face, so thin that the ears stuck through.

Looking at him Nils always wanted to laugh but he had frequently punched the nose of someone who did.

Silently, Doc extended a hand. There was just enough half light to see what it was. The new teacher's hat.

Nils burst out laughing. She had been so prim, sitting up there on Hilke Orvaag's big bay. The new schoolteacher, eh, and yet the biggest part of her were those green eyes. She hadn't looked so prissy after the horse threw her and she was grabbing at her petticoats like a hen trying to right herself when you carry her by the feet. A schoolteacher . . . Nils snorted out loud. "What are you going to do with it?" he asked in Chinook, gesturing toward the little hat in Indian Doc's hand.

Grinning, the old man explained he would make it a present to Julie.

An unreasonable anger flashed thorugh Nils. Any Indian woman would wear the wreck of a hat proudly, but Julie was his daughter. He snatched the hat from Doc's hands, walked to the horsebarn where a long nail protruded from an outside wall, and with one might gesture impaled it on the nail. Instantly he felt better.

He stepped back. The hat was a silly little blot against the wall. Nils grinned. Carl White wouldn't like to see it stuck to the barn wall. Old Carl had certainly been wearing his heart on the outside that afternoon. But he's the kind that's always in love, Nils thought, and woe to the little teacher with the big green eyes if some more elegant or more helpless female touches his fancy before she's had enough of him herself. Carl doesn't want a woman with feeling; he wants a woman with manners.

Perhaps I'm not doing him justice, Nils thought.

Perhaps Carl has it in him to love a woman, as I
dreamed of loving Mary nine years ago.

iii

He had just hit twenty when he first saw Mary, that
summer of 1875, his first year in the Valley. Had there
ever been another summer like it? Could he ever
again be as brave, as lonely, as blind?

There had been two dozen families in Gold Mountain. The old Tarpee brothers, the first whites on the
prairie, who had paddled canoes from Seattle in 1858
and struggled up the hill past the Falls to lay claim to
ground in the area later called Gold Mountain; the
Tines, Agatha Tine weighing three hundred and fifty
pounds, scaring her husband, loving children; Pete
and Lars Anderson, both of them old prospectors
who had had a great deal and lost it, and now hunted
and fished like the braves with their squaws at home
to do the dirty work. The settlement of Gold Mountain had been named after the Andersons' empty
dream. Tom Stump and his family, who never
explained where they'd come from the same way
twice; Gifford Greene and his many sons, most of
them near babies then; and a dozen odd more, many
of them kinfolk to each other. They were all there and
all beginning to marry into the neighbor's family
when Nils arrived, an independent-minded
nineteen-year-old with a winter's wages at logging in
his pocket and a lot of ideas his father said were too
big for him.

"I made it from the bottom up," George Bengston
had told his son. "You don't have to. Logging's the
natural business for this country, not crops or cattle
or mining. Logging and fishing, that's what God put

out here and we was intended to use it. I couldn't stand the smell of fish so I turned to the trees. This logging is going to get better all the time and some day it will be yours, anyway. You know how many feet I'm shipping out of Port Angeles this month? Stay here. Mine now, yours tomorrow."

"I'll take wages for the winter," Nils had said. "I want to get away from the Duwamish country and go farther in, where's there's as much land as I want."

"How you going to get it?"

"I don't know."

"What you going to make with it when you do?"

"I'll find out."

His father grinned. "Mule-headed as his old man," he said, and turned to count out a winter's wages.

Who wants to start life where someone else has left off, Nils thought—never to be Nils Bengston but simply George Bengston's heir? So at nineteen he had found a spot where there was all the land he wanted, land so remote only a couple of dozen families had registered claims. All he had to do, then, was to figure out how he was going to get it.

He had begun, as they all had, by filing his claim to the quarter section allowed him by the homestead law. He hadn't known how this bight of land between Old Hi and the river was going to yield enough to satisfy him, or how this achievement, common to every settler in the Valley whether he be lazy or crooked or miserly, could be alchemized into something so much bigger it would set him above everyone else. But he wanted to be rich, he wanted to be strong, he wanted to be better—how often that wonderful feeling had burst through him in those days, telling him there was nothing he couldn't do. That he could grab life and squeeze and squeeze and never come to the end of his strength. There is no limit, he told himself, no limit at all while you're still alive, and let any man try to show me otherwise.

He had never, even at nineteen, expected it would all come at once. Nils was forward looking. That was his advantage and he knew it. He had seen so many other settlers exhausted, or at least satisfied, simply by getting to the Valley and proving up a claim. Their minds could stretch no further. Their blood wasn't hot as long as their bellies were full.

Nils was only nineteen and there were older heads on the prairie before him, when he planted apple trees. No one else had done such a thing.

"What for?" Tom Stump asked suspiciously, as if what Nils was doing might take something from him. "You don't have to do that to make your claim good. They don't ask that. And what are you going to do with all them apples? I wouldn't break my back clearing ground for no apple trees."

The truth was that Nils didn't know what he would do with the apples. He was just getting the land to give him something back. In time, he found what foresight was worth. He dried the apples and sold them at a good price in Seattle. But that had been years later, years after he first saw Mary.

How beautiful she had looked to him then, Chief Tom's daughter whom the whites called Mary. It had been in July, when the Valley Indians got into their long cedar canoes and paddled fifty miles downriver to Tulalip for the games. Nils had come down the hill to old Smith's water-powered sawmill and the sound of voices attracted him to the sloping bank at Black River. He watched idly, conscious of the warm sun on his back and the hum of crickets in the nearby field.

The Indians were getting into their canoes, five or

six to a canoe, with the squaws, as usual, in position to paddle. Women and children, young men too proud to paddle and the old ones who were to stay behind, crowded the bank. The *klootches,* the girls, talked gaily as they loaded the canoes with baskets and the thick bedrolls woven out of split cattail leaves. They were dressed in full elegance. Beaded moccasins, brighter, newer blankets, with some of the younger men in the highest style wearing white man's work clothes. They would be gone for many days, Nils knew, for it would take two or more to reach the meeting ground at the mouth of the river; and the games there, attended by tribes paddling in from every direction, would last almost a week. Everyone, even the women, would enter the games. Many a young woman would win over the braves in the canoe races. There would be big salmon barbecues on the shore, dances, ceremonials, speeches. Nils watched them embarking for this holiday. Suddenly he felt lonely.

Their voices sounded so happy, so full of anticipation. They blurred together in a warm hum. And then a young girl's laughter broke free, rising above all the others. It was a ripple of pure glee. Nils felt his throat tighten. He looked from brown face to brown face, unexpectedly anxious to know who it was.

It wasn't hard because she was standing up in a canoe, laughing because she was rocking it from side to side, while the fat mother or aunt or grandmother at her feet was scolding her and trying to look at the river and the cattail mats and the baskets and the girl all at the same time.

Nils guessed who she was, for he recognized the squaw at her feet as Rosa, second wife of Chief Tom. No one but Chief Tom's daughter would dare such tomboyishness with her. So this was the girl the

whites called Mary and often remarked that she was
pretty for a Siwash.

Nils felt a stab of hate for Tom Stump and others
like him, who were ugly and ignorant but made kings
of themselves by calling the Indians "Siwash." Mary
was beautiful. Her body was straight and slender.
Her black hair, in heavy plaits down her back, shone
in the sun. Her face was delicate, with a narrow,
rather short nose and a laughing mouth. It was the
laughter that hit Nils so hard. He watched until the
last canoe was loaded, sliding out onto the water to
disappear soundlessly around the bend. Until he was
alone on the riverbank with the old men, listening for
the ripple from a moving paddle, a sound they all
knew existed but none of them could hear.

He had been so proud of Mary. He had been different from the whites who couldn't see that one Indian
might be better than another. "If he's got red skin,"
Tom Stump always said, "he's no good. I never have
to look any further." Indians were the creatures who
worked for you, whom luckily you didn't have to
fight, as your father and grandfather might have earlier in territory to the east. Whom you married without ceremony if you were lonely and there weren't
white women at hand, and would send back to the
tribe should the time come, before you were too old,
that there were some of your own kind to choose
from. Such were the feelings of the Tom Stumps.

But Nils had promised Mary to love and keep her
for the rest of her life. Such a vow was not part of the
Indian ceremony, and Mary had smiled without understanding as it burst from his mouth. Nils had
insisted on a legal marriage. It was his first statement
of loyalty to Mary. "Legal" meant white, and the
early settlers had laughed because he and Mary had
ridden all the way to Squak to catch a traveling

preacher. "She don't care, she don't know the difference," the older men had assured him, and only respect for their age and great knowledge on everything else had kept him from hitting them. His was a real marriage, a marriage on paper. Anything less would have been an insult to his feelings, as well as to Mary.

Those first two years with Mary could have been a dream. Even after the dream ended, Nils would remember Mary as she had been, and his heart would ache with nostalgia. An aimless, hopeless longing that brought nothing back. When he was awake the memory could not touch him. But at night in a dream he would see Mary as she had been, slender and laughing, running to him, touching him, promising she was real. Over and over he dreamed it and woke with hopelessness tight in his throat.

It was like dreaming of someone whose death you have been mourning. In daytime you knew she was dead. But sleep knocks down your guard, and she comes back to you, alive, beautiful, the product of your heart's refusal to believe she's gone. And she can prove she is alive. She touches you, speaks to you, laughs, even says, "See? I'm alive . . ." until you wake suddenly, ashamed because you might have cried out in your sleep.

But Mary hadn't died. The Mary of today had once more come back from her own people and was in the ranch house, waiting patiently. While the Nils of today lingered outside, dreading to go in.

In those first years Nils had lived like an Indian, not only because of Mary but because there were far more Indians than whites and it was they who worked for him, traveled with him, surrounded him. His house was the rough log cabin he had put together on his first homestead, but in the summer he and Mary moved into a house of mats tied over a framework of green willow poles. Mats Mary made as her great-grandmother had taught her, by pulling the sharp thread down the center of the cattail reed, weaving the dark green strips. He ate as the Indians ate—the roots of the ground, the wild animals of the woods, the berries. The Indians had no gardens, but for each tribe there were certain woods and prairies where they hunted food for their own people.

"How do you know where your places are?" Nils asked Mary.

She smiled patiently. "How do I know my own man from a hundred others?"

"But if there isn't enough?"

She replied simply, "It is provided."

He had loved to watch Mary settle the reed basket on her back for berry-picking. It was held in place by a wide strap around her head. Solemnly she would adjust it on her forehead, shift her shoulders from side to side until the basket rested comfortably across her shoulder blades. Suddenly she would become aware of him, and looking up, laugh like a little girl. As she picked the wild berries, she threw them over her shoulder into the basket. Nils had seen her returning with so heavy a load that she had to brace her neck against the basket's weight by putting both hands palm-flat across the back of her head. Even then, she would look up and laugh at him. The young Mary, Mary at fifteen and sixteen, had laughed a lot.

They dug roots that were like a thin, long carrot, and dried them as Mary dried the blackberries. They dried and smoked deer meat and salmon. Mary knew, as they all did, what were the proper times for spearing fish, the proper times for hunting.

"Indians know when the fish is sweet," she had explained. "Indians know when the deer is fat."

Mary had disdained a white like Tom Stump, who pulled salmon out of the river by the wagonload when they were coming up to spawn and then let half of them rot on the riverbank. "There's more in the water," Tom said.

"He eats soft meat," Mary remarked coldly.

Nils had watched Mary's people and learned from them. He saw them making a winter house, splitting a giant cedar with an elkhorn wedge, tying the overlapping cedar slabs together with long, slender cedar limbs that had been softened by heat from the campfire and later dried as hard as stone. Within these houses many familes lived, each in its own section but always with a center area "for playing," as Mary told him. Each family had its own fire, with a trap door in the roof above to be pushed open with a long pole if the smoke were heavy.

"If it rains?" Nils had asked.

Mary shrugged. "We open it only a little."

"And get only a little bit wet?"

That had made her laugh delightedly.

Even in love Nils did not forget his destiny. He was cutting timber on his homestead and making money from its sale. He had cleared land for pasture. But his most pressing desire was for more land. He added another hundred and sixty acre tract acquired through preëmption. By mortgaging what he already had, he raised enough money to buy nearly four hundred acres from the Territorial University, to which certain lands had been allotted by the government. From year to year he bought homesteads others had proved up, for there were always settlers who quit because of hard luck or wanderlust. Or could be made to quit, Nils thought coldly, if they've borrowed money from you and can't pay it back.

With a few silver dollars in his pocket from the sale

of timber, Nils bought up his neighbor's hogs.

"What for?" Tom Stump had whined anxiously, afraid all over again that someone was getting ahead of him. "You can't eat that much meat, what with deer plentiful, and the deer feeds itself."

"I'm going to dress them all in calico," Nils replied, "and send them to school."

In the fall Nils hired dozens of Indian farm hands and another dozen Indian women to cook for them. For three days the butchering went on, until every hog had been killed, cleaned, soaked in brine and hung over a slow fire of alder. Once cured, the meat was stored in the smokehouse for the winter. While Tom Stump and others like him couldn't think as far as thirty miles away, Nils had looked into the price of bacon and ham in Seattle.

"In the spring," he promised Mary, "we'll fill up the canoes with meat and paddle out to the city."

That first trip, above everything else in those first years, remained perfect in Nils' mind. There had been eleven canoes that year. Most of them Mary's cousins and half brothers had made, burning long hollows into the cedar logs with rocks heated red-hot in a camp fire. "Long time to build canoe," the Indians said, and Nils had smiled at their understatement.

Heating a big rock in a campfire, pushing it to the log with a stick, fighting to lift and move it to the right spot, Then scooping out the charred wood, scraping and digging with rocks roughly shaped like curved hoes the size of a man's hand. Then starting again to heat the rocks, to burn away another inch here, a few inches there. Thus the canoes for Nils' retinue had been made.

Nils could picture Mary as she had measured the progress the boys and men were making on a canoe.

She would lean forward, one knee on the ground, her
braids falling against her smooth cheek. She placed
one palm gently against the inside of the canoe, the
other at the same spot on the outside. Her dark eyes
had looked dreamy. She gazed, not down at her
hands or at the wall of the canoe, but straight ahead.
Thus she judged the thickness of the canoe.

"I can't see how you can measure that way," Nils
had protested. "You can't feel through it."

"We all know how," Mary replied simply, meaning that only a white man needs a measuring stick.

Mary had described that springtime trip to Seattle
with "We leave when the salmonberries just begin to
bloom. We come back when the berries are half
gone." It was a peculiarly Indian way of telling the
passing of time, though Nils hadn't thought of it that
way then. The canoes slid soundlessly down the
river. They were natural to it. Unlike the unwieldy
riverboats, they skimmed the treacherous riffles,
darted easily away from the uprooted trees or derelict logs that occasionally broke across the course of
the river. They hadn't talked a great deal, he and
Mary. The canoes moved forward, past the dark
timber. The sun brightened the shiny water. Mary
would turn, every now and then, and smile.

They shot game for food. At night they cooked it
over a campfire built in the shallow declivities Mary
scooped out of the sand. And then they prepared a
bed of cattail mats, and while the glowing embers of
the campfire held back the dark, they undressed, and
lay together, body against body. They were near
exhaustion after those long days on swift water, but it
was a peaceful tiredness that released their desire for
each other rather than numbed it. They made love
with drowsy passion, and often fell asleep with their
bodies still joined. After a time, Nils would awaken,

and watch the last live coal glimmer and die, and the velvet darkness close in. Then he covered himself and Mary with sheepskin robes and they slept, pressed together, until first light. Like wild creatures, they awoke then, and went to the river's edge to drink and to bathe their faces in the icy water.

At the Sound they abandoned their river craft and moved the load of smoked meat into the longer, heavier salt-water canoes. Their food then was salmon and clams, baked on the wide beach over fires of driftwood.

Seattle that spring of '77 was growing like an adolescent with a childish mind and big feet. The crooked wooden shacks still leaned over the water but throughout the city the new buildings were of brick. Civilization's goal—to forswear the materials of nature in favor of those man makes for himself. Lake Union was no longer an outpost, where a man might shoot a twelve-foot cougar without much notice taken of it. Logs still bumped against each other in the bay but more ships than ever before were tied up at the foot of Mill and Main and Madison Streets. It was still an Indian town, but the Chinese were moving in. The railroad builders, hammering together the line between the coast and the mountains; the little slant-eyed cigarmakers and cooks and slave workers. Walking along Washington Street, Nils had counted twenty-seven Chinese houses in a half a block. Angeline, the great Chief Seattle's daughter, was selling little bunches of pitchwood to the whites from whom she still would not beg.

"It's changing and that's good," Nils had thought. "There's going to be a market here for anything I have to sell." And he doubled his price for the smoked meat.

Little Jake Stokes had been the man he sold it to,

his neighbor Agatha Tine's husband before the big, heavy-drinking Martin Tine. Agatha had told Nils to see him. "He's a real good little man," she said fondly, folding her arms across her soft, enormous stomach. "He always said we would spend the rest of our lives together if I'd stayed under three hundred pounds."

"He was your first husband?" Nils asked.

Agatha's moonlike face broke into a series of concentric circles. "No," she chuckled, chins quivering, "just the one before this one."

Behind his meat counter in Seattle, Jake listened to Nils and his dark eyes brightened. "I can see you ain't figuring on giving the meat away."

"You're the one who's going to sell it across the counter," Nils retorted. "Are *you* figuring on asking the least you can?"

"Do you really think you're giving me a fair price?"

Nils was only twenty-one. He felt he knew a good deal less than this bright-eyed little butcher but he'd be hanged if he'd show it. "There's no such thing," he said boldly. "There's only a selling price. Far as I'm concerned, that's to the penny what the buyer's got."

"If business weren't so good," Jake said with a narrow smile, "I'd try to tell you a few of the things you don't know. But why should I? The town is filling up. They're asking a dollar a dozen for eggs and people are buying them. So I can meet your price and still make money."

"In that case," Nils said flatly, "I'll go into partnership with you."

Jake's smile dropped. He swore softly. But before Nils and Mary left Seattle, the partnership was formed. Nils would buy cattle east of the mountains.

He would drive them through the Pass, pasture them in the Valley, sell them in Seattle. Jake Stokes signed his name to it all, even to putting up the money with which Nils was to buy the first herd.

That partnership was Nils' first big triumph. Money from the sale of cattle would mean cash for more land. Land meant cash, first from the sale of timber, next as pasture for more cattle. A dollar makes two makes four makes eight . . . Nils lay on his back on the hotel bed in Seattle, arms folded behind his head, figuring. Life was moving faster now. He had made a little plan and its momentum was carrying him on to a bigger one. Nothing could stop him. Nothing. He laughed out loud, inexpressibly happy.

He hadn't been thinking of Mary. Strange, in those days, to have forgotten Mary even for a moment. A dull whimper startled him. She was squatting in the corner, her back against the wall. Nils saw that for some reason she was terrified.

It had been hard to discover why, for fear made the laughing Mary dull-eyed and inchoherent. For an hour Nils paced the barren hotel room and questioned her, fighting his impatience, feeling ashamed of it. At last he came to understand. Mary wanted to run from Seattle.

There was bad sickness among the Seattle Indians. She had seen them that day, lying in their huts, too feverish to move away from the bodies of their dead ones. She had seen them run into the cold bay, come out near-dead to collapse on the beach. The Indians were fleeing, not even waiting to bury their dead. The pox . . . Mary hadn't called it that, but Nils guessed from her halting Chinook.

"We'll go home," he said gently, lifting her up in his arms. "The sickness will never touch you. I will keep you safe forever. Don't be afraid."

They had walked back to the Valley along the old Indian trail, expanded now to the width of a covered wagon. Brown sugar, black syrup, flour, parched coffee, were in the packs the Indian workers carried, fifty to seventy-five pounds to a man. Unlike a good squaw, Mary carried nothing. She had wanted to, though she was carrying a child by then and just beginning to show it. Nils had refused. For a few days in Seattle he had thought of her less than he should. He grasped this white man's way of making up to her, and carried her pack as well as his own.

Mary had never again made the trip to Seattle. He tried, the next spring, to insist. But nothing he said would convince her that the city was not pox-ridden. Terror of going with him had driven her into blank, stupid silence. Finally, angry to the core, he had given up and gone alone.

He apologized for her, to himself. He knew that after they had left Seattle the smallpox had spread among the Indians to a killing epidemic. The largest part of the surviving Duwamish and Skagit Indians had fled, not even bothering to bury their corpses or with proper ceremony send them floating out to sea. In Mary's mind that made the city accursed. Nils apologized further with a white man's reasoning, closing his eyes to the fact that no Indian woman would consider it reason at all. That second spring Mary had Julie. Nils told himself that she would have come with him to Seattle if she hadn't had to stay home and take care of the baby.

And what a baby little Julie had been. Very round-faced, all Indian as far as hair and skin were concerned, but with a most un-Indian little nose and bright blue eyes. Nils was absorbed, heart, mind and muscle, in his new business ventures that winter Mary had been carrying. He rarely thought of the baby's coming.

The day Julie was born he was up in the Pass, driving a herd of white-faces through two feet of snow.

When he reached the cabin, Mary waited on him silently. She removed his boots, set out a hot meal, carried wood to the fire. Suddenly, through a haze of exhaustion, he had seen the change in her.

"Why didn't you say something?" he shouted.

Mary led him to the wooden box in which the baby slept. And what had seemed inevitable but rarely unimportant became, with that first glimpse of Julie, more important to him than anything else.

From the first, Julie was Nils' papoose. It was Nils, not Mary, who carried the baby, strapped to his back or in his arms, and later a special seat tied with leather thongs to the front of his saddle. Mary relinquished the baby mutely.

Was it then, Nils had often wondered, that she began to change? Or was it as time passed, and no more children came, and she saw that the one little blue-eyed girl, as different from herself as the color of her bright eyes, was the last she would have?

Mary had once been quick-moving and laughing. Each year, even each month, she became duller. Little by little, she grew fat. Nils found himself wishing again and again that they might talk together— was it talking that he missed, or spirit? He had turned to Mary so often, hoping to see her dark eyes sparkle as they had before; to see her head lift with some strong emotion, to feel that she either loved or detested him. But she was merely placid. Dutiful, silent, hard-working, fat. Where had the Mary of that old dream gone?

The Mary of the dream, whose warm naked body had once responded so joyfully. The Mary who had slept with him on the riverbank and turned to him eagerly when the slightest pressure of the hand that cupped her breast told her that he wanted her.... Nils clenched his fists. *That* Mary had been gone for a long time, and no one had taken her place.

There had been women. The "good" women who flirted, who teased, who hinted, too respectable to recognize that the only significant difference between them and the "bad" women on the Seattle waterfront was that they demanded payment in the form of a wedding ring and the biggest hop ranch in the world, while their modest sisters would settle for two dollars cash and a few swallows from his whiskey bottle, if he happened to be carrying one.

On several occasions Nils had climbed the narrow staircase to a second floor bedroom where he fell onto the passive form of a faceless woman and expelled his hunger simply because he couldn't contain it any longer. The satisfaction had been brief. Even while he was thrusting feverishly, he was aware that this was a pathetic imitation of the real act of love. Afterwards, he fled the room and the woman, already regretting the loveless exercise and sickened by the fact that the next man to use that room and that woman might pass him on the stairs.

These dreary visits outraged Nils' fanatic need for bodily cleanliness and did nothing to quiet his yearning for tenderness. The alternative was to take a wife, for marriage to an Indian was not considered binding and as Mary's long absences became noticeable, several Gold Mountain settlers had hinted that it was time to send her home permanently. The ratio of men to women was so out of balance that competition was keen for every marriageable female, "marriageable" meaning white. But scarcity wasn't what kept Nils from looking over the ranks. It was plain, simple loyalty to Mary, to the dream Mary and to the child she had given him rather than to the mute and passive

Mary of today. More than one single young woman had attracted and aroused him in spite of himself, but he had always retreated, throwing up a barricade of indifference he didn't feel and laughter he didn't mean. He would stick with Mary, by God, as long as she was his wife, and this, he swore, was a resolve nothing could shake.

But it was being shaken, wasn't it? Mary had come back. For a while Julie would have a mother and he would have a wife. And here I am, he thought, out in the dark, mourning for an Indian girl who doesn't exist any more, trying to fill my life with a million dollars' worth of hops. While in the house Mary was waiting for him.

Her dark eyes would tell him nothing, ask nothing. He would see how fat she was, the way she dragged her feet in the old felt carpet slippers she always wore. "That's the trouble with them squaws," Tom Stump often said, "they're old before they're twenty." Hang the old miser, Nils thought, for ever saying anything I'd find myself remembering later. How old was Mary, since Julie was seven and had been born when Mary was fifteen? Only twenty-two years old. Only a few years older than that new little schoolteacher. And yet Mary's done with childbearing and squats in the corner waiting for old age. While the teacher is big-eyed, as daring and as skittery as a child.

Nils hurried toward the cabin. Mary would be waiting. He had no business out here, measuring her against Carl White's girl.

CHAPTER THREE

i

IT WAS NIGHT WHEN Katherine Duncan and the captain's son rode into Gold Mountain. A crooked cluster of buildings hugged the black ribbon of the wagon road. Through the windows of the general store the smoky gleam of a kerosene lamp quivered against the shadow. Loud voices hurtled through the open door of a saloon. Elsewhere people slept; windows were dark.

In front of the store a peeled log lay across two or three fenceposts. Carl dismounted quickly and hitched the reins around the log. He nodded toward the building. "Nate Tarpee's trading post. It doesn't look like it, but it's a hotel, too."

Anger had carried Katherine all the way from the hop ranch, but it had exhausted her, too. She meant to dismount briskly. She had even planned how to ask for a hotel room without betraying the fact that she had only once before done such a thing. But somehow with her hair hanging down her back, pretense seemed silly. She nodded wearily.

Carl was at her side, hands extended. "Here," he said, "let me help you down." She hesitated, reciting her refusal. Would it be proper for the new schoolteacher. . . With a sigh she slid toward him, let him lift her off the horse and set her on her feet. Across the slit of darkness they looked into each other's faces.

"I'm grateful to you," she whispered at last.

Without replying he took her arm and gently pulled it through his own. He led her into the trading post. Behind a rough-hewn counter a man with thinning hair and a long nose was unpacking a box of patent medicine.

"Nate Tarpee," Carl said. "Nate, the new school-teacher, Miss Duncan."

Katherine saw the storekeeper narrow his eyes in speculation. Her self-confidence crumbled. She would have to say something . . . But Carl's voice went on smoothly. "Just for a day or two. Until she knows where she is to board out."

Nate Tarpee set down the bottle of tonic, pulled a key from his pocket and studied it carefully, both sides. "Yup," he said. He squinted at Katherine. "She got a valees?" he asked Carl, his eyes still on Katherine.

"It's coming up tomorrow with a load for the hop ranch."

"Well I don't know what kind of trappings we got for her to sleep in. Bertha's in bed and her stuff'd go around this girl three times anyway."

"Never mind, Nate. . ."

"Don't know what I've got to feed you, either. I can make coffee. Out of anything. Barley, wheat. Done it many's the time. But Bertha's the cook, and Bertha's in bed."

"It's all right, Nate. . ."

"Well, come on then." Nate picked up one of the lamps, ordered Katherine toward the stairs with a jerk of the head. Whistling softly, he walked around the counter and across the room.

Carl faced her, holding out his hand. "Good-bye, Miss Duncan."

He was leaving. Katherine looked at him dumbly, stricken by the realization that she had been depending on him and that soon he would be gone. She felt suddenly that this was more than she could bear. She had to go back with him. He had suggested it himself. The *Viking* would leave in the morning; in two days she would be back in Seattle. She could be a housemaid for the family on Madison. She could be a clerk at the "San Francisco Store." As Peter Duncan's daughter she had known nothing but hard work anyway. With her mother, who could remember life in Boston, she had despised what she was and dreamed of being a gentle woman. But what was the use of reaching for gentility, if that old childish fear of change was going to plague her all along?

For the first time Katherine saw the men at the other side of the store. They were in chairs tilted back against the wall, bootheels caught in the side rungs and thumbs hooked under their belts. Silently they surveyed her. The new schoolteacher. . .

Carl's posture was all formality. Lifting her chin, Katherine tried to copy him. "Thank you," she said stiffly.

"Coming?" Nate called from the stairs.

Katherine looked up at Carl in a last-minute plea for help. She saw his eyes, his whole face, change. "Listen," he said urgently, barely touching her hand. "The trip downriver and back usually takes a week. I'll be back here Monday. I'll help you get down to the boat and you'll be in Seattle before you know it."

That seemed impossibly far away. Katherine wanted to say, "No, now right now!" but she nodded.

"Remember, I'll be back Monday." He turned toward the door.

In desperation Katherine took a few steps after him.

He stopped. "Is there something I can do. . ."

Katherine held out her hand mechanically. "Good-bye," she said in a strangely hollow voice. He shook her hand, and she realized that they had done just that only the instant before. Along the wall the silent watchers were measuring her, perhaps laughing at her. In confusion she turned and followed Nate Tarpee up the stairs.

The room was directly above the store entrance, with windows opening on Gold Mountain's rutted street. Nate pulled a candle from his pocket, lit it from the lamp and, softening the end over the lamp's flame, set it on a saucer on the washstand.

There was a bed covered with a crazy quilt, a hand-made table, a chair with a hand-hewn back and a seat of rawhide. On the washstand a big crockery pitcher covered with hand-painted roses stood next to a cracked white bowl. Beside it lay a bleached flour sack and a bar of orange-colored soap.

Nate was watching her closely. Katherine looked around the room, feeling that he expected it of her. Perhaps she should say something. She murmured, "This is your hotel?"

Nate chuckled. "Was for five years. If I had been the first white in the Valley I'd of done all right. Any time there's two of us the other fellow gets the best of me. I only run the place. It belongs to Nils Bengston."

Katherine felt a flush creep into her cheeks.

"Lock your door," Nate said, and went out whistling.

Katherine ran to the window. The bottom slid open easily. She dropped to her knees and leaned out, trying to make out the hitching post, the two horses, Carl. But there was nothing there. In a last spurt of panic she peered through the darkness in the direction Carl must have taken. Straining, she heard the rhythmic clop of horses' hooves in the distance. It was a muffled, lonely sound. She clutched the window sill, listening. The sound grew fainter.

Slowly she pulled herself to her feet and went across the room to the bed. The straw mattress crackled as her body pressed into it. I'll get up right away, she thought, and take off the dusty serge and wash my face with that orange soap . . . Tears came to her eyes. I'm afraid, she thought, I'm afraid and I'll never go to sleep . . . The hotel was silent as an empty barrel. From the saloon below came the sound of a man's drunken singing. A door slammed, shutting it off. Everything was still. The bed rocked gently on a sea of silence.

ii

It was the terror of her dream that wakened her. She was in Nebraska again. Or was it Kansas or Minnesota or Montana or Nevada? A little girl in a dirt house. Her mother was beside her. She couldn't see her mother's face, but she heard her crying. Somewhere her father was saying, "Naomi, I promise, the next place will be better. I'll get you a house with glass windows." Glass windows, glass windows, a house with glass windows—the words mixed together with the sound of her mother's crying. Katherine, the little girl, sobbed, "She wants a house with glass windows. *My mother* wants a house with glass windows. . ." Her father's voice stopped. He wasn't talking now, he was laughing. Deep rumbling laughter that came from all around and in back of her. She began to run. The laughter followed. She turned to beat it with her fists, and the laughter grew. Then she saw him. Nils Bengston. . ."Stop!" she screamed. "Stop. . ."

Katherine awoke. She stared at the rafters, trembling with fear, wondering if she had called out loud. The hotel was still. On the washstand the stub of candle sputtered in a pool of wax. She had slept only as long as it takes to burn a candle; yet she was wide awake.

Katherine got up slowly, every movement of her body hurting. It had grown cold. Shivering, she pulled the quilt off the bed, wrapped it around herself and stumbled to the chair by the window. She lowered herself painfully. I'll sit up for a while, she thought, before I try to sleep again.

Which house had she seen in her dream? It had seemed real, and yet with the dream still vivid she could not say. It reminded her of the game her younger brothers and sisters had played. "Which house do you like best?" Felicity would begin.

"That one back in 'Brasky," Angus would answer.

"*He* don't even remember that one," from the scornful Teddy. "He *couldn't* remember it."

"Yes, I do!"

"*He* wasn't borned yet."

Katherine had always held herself aloof. A new home, a new baby every year—that way, she had once reflected bitterly, her father always has children young enough to believe him. When he told them they were going to pack up and this time it would be a wonderful place, their eyes sparkled. Yet in that next "wonderful place" they still had to sleep three in a bed, more for warmth than for lack of straw or cornhusks for the mattresses.

Once, when they couldn't buy flour, Teddy had been given the chore of grinding wheat through the hand coffee mill. For a week his thin shoulders had been hunched over the job, his eyes blinking with every hard crack of the kernels. Once ground, the coarse meal had to be put through again. At the end of a week he had finished, and saw with his own eyes what so much hard work had brought forth—no more than a two-gallon jarful. The next week his father was describing another place. "I can get it on a trade," he said, "and there's a good spring on it. I'll tell you what we'll do. . ." And Teddy was sitting on his lap, his arm around his father's neck. Only Katherine, the oldest, knew enough to doubt him.

Only once had her father been rejected by his younger children. Felicity had been a little girl of six or seven. There seemed to be nothing but corn in those days. Parched corn, in little, shriveled, pointed ears with rows as irregular as an old man's teeth. Like Indians they ground it into coarse meal, which most of the time came to the table as a thick, hot mush. Black syrup, grease, baking powder—that was all they could trade for then. When the year's cash spendings had been added, they came to thirty dollars.

Come Sunday the family sat down to hear their father's weekly grace. "Dear God," he concluded at last, still looking heavenward over their bowed heads, "bless this poor house. Bless my faithful wife. Bless these children. In the name of Jesus, Amen."

He lowered his eyes. There was a moment of silence as the children watched intently to make sure he was through. He *must* be, their hopeful eyes said, or why would he say "Amen"? With a clatter they picked up their spoons. A hush fell as they bent over their steaming bowls. And at just that moment, without as much as a whisper to cover it up, Felicity added her bit to the grace. As clear as a bird call her sweet voice said, "And darn the mush!"

The other children's spoons stopped in mid-air.

"Felicity!" her mother gasped.

Color shot to the little girl's face. Tears came to her eyes. The defiance was out of her and she was hungry. She picked up her spoon, slowly dipping it into the mush.

"Naomi, I *promise* you . . ." Peter Duncan had made this plea again and again, each time as if his promise were totally unsullied. Katherine recalled the weary patience on her mother's face as she nodded. "Of course, Peter."

She doesn't believe him, Katherine had thought. She couldn't, after what he's done to her. He would sense it himself, and quickly go outside to find the little children. Through the cabin's open door Katherine and her mother heard him, saw the thin, dirty faces of Angus and Felicity and Tommy and Petie shine with belief in this, their father's favorite fairy story of all.

"We'll have a garden with so many things growing in it you can pick something whenever you get hungry. We'll get new clothes for you, and anybody who goes to school gets to have a pair of shoes. We'll have a real wood house, made out of boards. A house with glass windows. . ."

Katherine's mother sat lifelessly at the bench beside the rough-hewn table. He hands lay in her lap as they had fallen when her husband released them—palms up, motionless. Her face, which matched Katherine's so closely, was gray with fatigue. "You shouldn't be angry with your father," she said at last. "You can't blame him. He believes it. He wouldn't say it to me if he didn't."

"A house with glass windows!" At the very thought Katherine had tasted the full strength of her bitterness. Such were the houses of rich people. The respectable, the stay-in-one-place people. Windows were for storekeepers and doctors and school-teachers.

Naomi Duncan shrugged. "We don't *know* he won't get it."

"Oh, Mother!" How bitterly she had resented her mother's loyalty. "Don't we? Don't we know that he won't?"

They had looked at each other in silence, the mother needing the illusion, the daughter refusing it. The mother lowered her eyes. "Boil water for tea, will you, dear," she said quietly. "It seems I never want my tea as much as when I'm carrying a baby."

Katherine turned toward the stove and reached blindly into the box beside it for a handful of quick-burning grass. Grass and cow chips, the makings of a poor man's fire. Why, she thought angrily, they aren't even from our own cows.

When I grow up, I'll be a schoolteacher. I'll be clean and respectable and someone else will lay the kitchen fire.

"Glass in *all* the windows, papa?" said Angus' little squeaky voice outside. "Front, side n' back?"

Katherine had had to close her eyes tight against sudden tears. Her mother didn't cry. Then she wouldn't, either.

Katherine hugged the quilt tighter against the night cold. Through the window Gold Mountain was no more than a hole in the dark. She was alone. She felt alone, as she never had before her mother died. From the time she was old enough to know hunger from contentment and a sod house from a house with glass windows, from that moment she had been lonely. But it had been a feeling consciously shared with her mother. "I want to be just like you," she had whispered to her mother so often, and that meant to dream of the things her mother yearned for, to despise the things her mother hated.

Her mother had had a fine education. Thus the girl Katherine had wanted schooling more than anything else in the world and had resented her father for pulling them farther and farther from the civilized places where she could get it. Her mother had been a lady, whose finest dresses had once been fashioned by a French designer from New Orleans. Yet life made by her father's hands was rough, poor, wild. Knowing nothing else, she had not learned to be a lady, and she blamed him for that, too. Katherine stared sightlessly through the window of Nate Tarpee's hotel, and thought, I *will* be a lady, as Carl White believed me to be.

Carl had expected her to be displeased by the Valley. Katherine sighed. That was a tribute to be cherished. Like everything else about the captain's son—his strong sense of propriety, his courtesy, his assumption that dirt and coarseness would shock her—it was something to live up to. He had seen in her the quality her mother never quite lost, the air of having known something better.

Only once, Katherine reflected, once in eighteen years of marriage had Peter Duncan offered his Boston wife something of the life she had lost by marrying him. He had swapped houses and homesteads, mortgages and cattle and logs, as gaily as a boy trading jackknives and almost as fast. They had moved from desert to timberland and back again, buying sight unseen, lucky one time, hungry the next. Throughout Peter Duncan acted as if his promise were still good. The next place would be better, and at last, on the last trade he ever made, it was.

In return for a homestead on the Skagit and a quarter section of timber, he took a house in Seattle. That was only a year ago, Katherine thought with surprise, too little time for so many changes.

A year ago the whole family had been together, and her mother had been well. Her face had been radiant as she took her first look at that beautiful house in Seattle. "Be sure and wipe your feet, children," she had said absentmindedly, like a little girl watching her elders divide up the barley candy. The house stood at the top of the hill overlooking Elliot Bay. It was made of real wood boards, cut at a sawmill—not a peeled log or a handsplit shake about it. More than that—it was painted white and stood two floors high, with an upstairs porch supported by six pillars sheltering a wide veranda below. And windows—glass windows—in every room.

Angus and Felicity and Tommy ran ahead. Naomi Duncan followed with Petie in her arms. Katherine and Teddy held back, disbelieving to the very last.

"An easterner built it," Peter Duncan told them excitedly. "A real easterner from Virginia. Wanted it like the houses he was used to. He ordered it built, but he didn't even move into it before went to Frisco with a brig of timber, hit a bad storm, and went down. I bought it off his son." He glanced at the children, estimating his audience. "I made a smart deal, too."

But he didn't look at me, Katherine remembered, when he said it.

The hallway had been as wide as a parlor. The newel posts were made of fancy carving, the hall windows contained leaded red and green glass. Above the parlor fireplace statues of naked ladies faced each other. Angus was at the glass windows, rubbing a stubby, uncertain finger down each pane. Teddy was in front of the fireplace, his mouth wide open. "It's yours, Naomi," their father kept saying, "yours, just like I promised."

After eighteen years in which nothing had been elegant or useless or beautiful, Naomi Duncan could only reply, "I wonder where you do the washing."

"A smart deal," her father had called it, but in time they found its weaknesses. Katherine had planned to give up her job in the dry-goods store and go back to school. Teddy had been talking about shipping out on one of the San Francisco boats. The night they moved into the beautiful white house, Peter Duncan admitted they would all have to work to keep it.

"Unless," he said vaguely, "we use what we got put away in the strongbox."

But the strongbox and its little burden of cash had come to be their only security. Katherine, Teddy, even little Tommy and Felicity, had worked to add to it. So Teddy laid aside his ambition to go to sea and Katherine told herself once more that it wouldn't be long before she could start training to be a school-teacher. They all worked. Angus swept out the grocery at the corner of First and Marion, and took his pay in sausage and coffee beans and lard. Teddy split shakes and traded them for flour at the Busby mill. Felicity hired out to a wealthy family at the top of Madison, and Tommy ran errands for the San Francisco store. Carrying Petie, their mother did char work at a Mill Street hotel and Katherine went back to her job in the dry-goods store. Peter Duncan signed up to dig coal at the Newcastle mine.

He worked harder than any of us, Katherine thought. Why then should I blame him for what happened? Because he was so long in making the dream come true, or because he made it come true at all?

Katherine, Teddy, their mother and little Petie

were the only ones at home when the house caught
fire. It had happened so fast. The kitchen full of
smoke, her mother's cry, Teddy's running footsteps
and shaky call, "Katie! The house is on fire! Where's
the strongbox?" Katherine had picked up Petie, run
down the great curving stairway. Teddy was clinging
to the carved lady who topped the newel post, his
face stiff with fright.

"Run and call the fire department!" Katherine
shrieked, only an inch from his face.

Naomi Duncan was in the hallway, staring at the
smoke billowing through the kitchen door. "I don't
understand," she said dully. "How did it start?"

Katherine put her arm across her mother's back,
gripping the thin shoulder. "Come on, Mother,
hurry!" Petie was being squeezed by her other arm,
and whimpered.

Her mother looked at Petie, then Katherine. "Did
the lard spill onto the fire?"

"Please!" Katherine shifted Petie to a new position and pulled her mother toward the front door.
"We've got to get out."

Naomi Duncan shook her head but she moved as
the pressure of her daughter's arm directed her, in
stumbling steps toward the door. They met Teddy on
the porch.

"A boy that was outside is going after the fire
truck!" He was gasping for breath but he ran past
them and into the house.

"Teddy, come with us!"

The boy kept going. "The strongbox," he called.
"It's in here somewheres!"

Katherine led her mother along the walk to the
street. Hurriedly she set Petie down on the dirt. Then
she turned to her mother, shaking her as hard as she

dared. "Where is it, Mother? Think! Quickly!"

Naomi Duncan's thin, weather-browned face was vacant. "Is Teddy all right?"

"The strongbox, Mother. The box with all our money. Teddy's looking for it. Where did you put it, Mother?"

His arm across his eyes, Teddy hurtled through the door and across the grass. "I can't find it," he sobbed, shaken with a fit of coughing. "I looked all over and I can't find it."

Katherine's grip bit into her mother's shoulder. "Where, Mother?" she begged. *"Where?"*

Naomi Duncan looked at her helplessly. "I can't remember."

Katherine felt her throat tighten. "It's no use, Teddy, no use at all."

In the street four or five housewives had gathered, and a dozen children. Others were moving up the hill as fast as their ages permitted. A little boy pulled out of the crowd, running so hard he fell against Katherine, and clutched the folds of her calico skirt. "I called the fire department," he gasped. "They're coming. Bang, bang, cloppety, cloppety, clop. . ."

Katherine nodded mechanically. As mechanically her right hand patted her mother's shoulder. Little Petie was playing contentedly in the dirt, dreamily tasting what was stuck to the end of his finger. Teddy was staring back at the house, his eyes watering from the smoke. He seemed to be trembling on the finest balance, as if one desperate word might send him running down the hill or just as easily back toward the flames. Suddenly he broke into a run.

"Teddy!" Katherine screamed, losing all control of her voice. It was a maniac's voice, rising hysterically and breaking into a sob. "Teddy, Teddy. . ."

On the porch he flung up both hands, as if the

gesture were supposed to tell her something, and disappeared through the door. Naomi Duncan stared after him. Smoke was beginning to pour out. Fat, round pillows of smoke puffed around and past each other and flattened into a cloud under the veranda roof. She pulled against Katherine's arm. "I'll get him," she said hoarsely.

Katherine clung to her mother. "It wouldn't do any good." Her jaw was so tightly clenched she could hardly swallow. "He'll come out," she said fiercely, "he'll be all right."

Over and over she said the empty words, holding her mother tightly with both arms. The crowd stared at them. The little boy who had called the fire department was dancing from one stranger to another, crying, "I ran all the way down the hill and all the way up the hill and told the firemen to come. I ran all the way down the hill and all the way. . ."

Please God, Katherine prayed, let Teddy come out safe.

In the distance, the fire bell clanged. Katherine turned to watch the crest of the hill over which they would come. The dashing, brightly painted wagons, the kingly fire horses with their arched necks and tremendous withers. Just a year before, she and Teddy and two or three of their smaller brothers and sisters had stood in front of the bakery at Third and Union and cheered as they pounded past in the annual Seattle fire cart race. Where were they now, when everything they owned was burning down and her brother was lost in the flames?

Teddy staggered to the door. He was swaying crazily and coughing. In his arms was the strongbox.

"Teddy!" Katherine cried. "Run!"

The boy stumbled forward, clutching the metal box with all his strength. He was doubled over it, his

long thin arms overlapping across his ribs. Reaching
them, he gasped, "I got it." Cough after cough shook
his loose frame. His eyes squinted against the sting of
the smoke.

And yet, Katherine mused, he had been grinning,
as a man might. . .

The fire cart's bell clanged louder. The crowd
turned toward the sound. Some smiled excitedly. As
if to mock the sound, new spurts of flame exploded
through the front windows.

Fast and hungrily the blaze licked into the
framework, and still the building stood. Flames pouring through the windows swept skyward to gnaw
furiously on the walls, and yet it did not fall. The big
white house had been queen of the hill. Her windows
looked out toward the glistening Sound, down on the
rooftops of her inferiors. Katherine thought wonderingly, "She's larger, whiter, more elegant than all
the rest, even now."

Teddy was hugging the precious metal box. Her
mother stared impassively down the hill.

"It's coming!" a boy shrilled. The heavy thud of
horses' hooves grew louder. The hill was steep. As
cart and horses came into view, they slowed down.
The horses snorted, their heavy necks arched against
the strain. Their hooves beat up a cloud of thick
brown dust.

"Never mind, Katherine dear," Naomi Duncan
said.

"Hurry up!" Teddy screamed. "Hurry!"

Little Petie pulled excitedly on Katherine's skirt,
his baby mouth rimmed with dirt.

"Oh, if father had only. . ." Looking at her
mother's face, Katherine bit back her words. If father
had only—what? He was twenty miles away, digging
coal at Newcastle.

The spectators kept their distance from the Duncans. Their eyes traveled from the fire cart to the burning house, then turned curiously to the woman and her three children, as if to measure the size of the disaster in their faces.

"Never mind," Naomi Duncan repeated meaninglessly.

The firemen raced the horses up the sloping lawn before the house. Shouting, cursing, the men connected hose to water tank. More people—the idle, the old, the curious—had followed the clamor of the fire bell and gathered now in a semicircle around the dying house. Shopkeepers and children, housewives, with their aprons on, cluttered the dirt street. They fought to catch breath, gaped at the house, stared at Katherine and Teddy and their mother, and the baby playing so happily in the dirt. Poor woman, the glances of the housewives said. Such an elegant home, even if they were too poor to put anything into it. And they say the house was all they had in the world.

Katherine's mother looked straight ahead. How can she stand so still and quiet, Katherine thought miserably, when her reward for eighteen years of wretchedness is burning down before her eyes? How strange we must look. Poor people off the Kansas prairie. Wearing patched-up cottons and scrawny from years of trying to fill up on potatoes and beans. They're wondering—How did we ever get such a house? Silently Katherine patted her mother's shoulder.

Thin streams of water spurted from the hose. The firemen sweated with the heat of the blaze. At the cart others pumped furiously, sweat dripping from their foreheads. "Harder!" the firemen at the house shouted. "Build up the pressure!" But the water was

mere spit against a holocaust. It hit the building peck-
ishly, like an insect trying to kill a bear. Steam rose
from spots the water dampened. The flames recoiled,
curling sideways from the helpless stream, then burst
out stronger.

"It's burning down, it's burning down!" a little boy
squealed, dancing down the road. "Look, look,
look!" he sang, dancing by.

The firemen were yelling at each other, "Stand
back! Everybody stand back!" The crowd was
numb. Housewives with soapsuds drying at their
wrists, children who had raced to see the fun and now
stood frozen next to their elders, merchants who had
run out leaving their shops unlocked—they were all
voiceless with the knowledge that the final moment
was about to come.

"She's going!" a man called.

The great white house trembled in her final
agony. In a moment no longer than a gasp, her walls
leaned inward, hung crazily at an angle. Then, the
crash. The thundering, sickening crash as the whole
building crumbled to the ground and the flames leapt
up to engulf it.

"Aaahh. . ." the crowd moaned, sick with awe and
delight. The fire horses whinnied, reeling backward.

"Mother!" Katherine put her arms around her
mother. The sobs she had been stifling ached in her
throat. She looked into her mother's face. The eyes
were dry, the mouth straight, but there was a dull-
ness to it, as if she had always known this would
happen.

Teddy rattled the strongbox angrily. He had forgotten he was fifteen years old and tears poured
down his cheeks. "This was all I could get," he
sobbed. "I tried to think of what to take and I

thought, this has all our money in it, this is what to take.''

''You were right, Teddy.'' Katherine felt choky, but now that he was crying, she mustn't for sure. ''You did the right thing.''

''But Katie!'' Teddy, ''It feels like it's empty!''

The two children turned to their mother. She didn't seem to see them. ''Open it,'' Katherine whispered to her brother, ''if it isn't locked.''

Together they loosened the catch and pulled up the lid of the strongbox. Teddy's hand trembled as he picked up the piece of paper inside. ''Their wedding license,'' he said, crying like a baby. ''That's all there is.'' A wedding license, handwritten by a traveling preacher in Nebraska, to unite Naomi Fairfield with Peter Duncan.

Katherine looked helplessly at her mother. Dear God, she thought, she knew that, too.

Her mother's face seemed as flat and empty as her voice. ''I was just thinking how lucky we are this happened on a schoolday,'' she murmured. ''The children have their good clothes on.''

Katherine led her down the hill and made tea for her in the kitchen of a neighbor's house. ''Drink it while it's hot, Mother''—and Naomi Duncan obeyed. Like a frightened child she let Katherine undress her, wash her and tuck her into a strange bed. Katherine had seen then, for the first time, that her mother was again carrying a child, and her indignation against her father boiled up uncontrollably. She sat by her mother's bed, smoothing her hair, gently rubbing her back where it ached most, until she saw that her mother was asleep.

Two days later Peter Duncan returned from Newcastle. He began calling ''Naomi, Naomi!'' before he had closed the door behind him. He ran past the children, dropped to his knees beside their mother's chair and threw both arms around her. "Don't worry," he murmured, "I'll take care of you."

Perhaps that was the moment, Katherine thought, that I decided to leave home. She had turned away from the sight of her mother in her father's arms and walked out of the house. Until then she had believed that she could not leave. Her mother needed her, but stronger now was the urge to escape. I've got to get away, she had repeated over and over as she walked through the streets of Seattle. Away from promises and hunger, a new house and a new baby every year. Away—from him.

While her mother was ill, she could not leave. "She needs me"—it became her only excuse, for actually she was afraid of the decision she had to make. Fear was a familiar sensation. Fear of being laughed at, fear of being disliked and, most of all, fear of the unknown. The only relief came from bursts of temper, and these, like Felicity's "Darn the mush!" had changed quickly into shame at hurting her mother. All her life the world had been too big and had changed too fast. Like her mother, she wanted to draw its boundaries closer, to tidy and straighten them. "When mother is well," she had said. And then quite suddenly, only a month after the fire, her mother died.

Dry-eyed, Katherine dressed the body, painstakingly brushed and braided her mother's hair. Aunts and uncles from Oregon, the settled, steady Duncans whom Katherine had seen once and almost forgotten, came to Seattle in answer to their brother's letter. From the moment they walked into the shack Peter Duncan had found for his family, Katherine resented them.

"Your aunts, Nellie and Rebecca. Your uncles Ian and Angus." Peter Duncan ticked off the children with quick little jerks of his head. "Starting at the top, Katherine, Teddy, Felicity, Tommy, Angus, and we called the little one after me, Petie. They've grown some since you last saw them."

"We've been in and out of three houses since then!" Teddy's voice was changeful, and it betrayed him now, rising to an angry squeak at the end.

Aunt Nellie, the plump one with a sweet smile, nodded sympathetically, "You poor dears."

Katherine saw Teddy shy away from her kindness. "That's all right, we got along fine."

"We did not!" This from Felicity, in an indignant squeal. "One place had snakes and it was awful."

"Ugh, snakes," said Angus.

"You poor dears," their plump little aunt repeated.

"She makes me sick," Teddy hissed into Katherine's ear. "How long is *she* going to stay?"

Katherine studied her relatives. Her aunts, looking scrubbed and starchy, her uncles wearing dark suits and shiny black shoes, the symbols of prosperity. Their politely blank faces turned toward her father. They seemed to be waiting. They've been talking together, father and the relatives, Katherine thought. About *us*.

"Children, your aunt Rebecca and your aunt Nellie have very kindly offered. . ." Peter Duncan hesitated, turning to the relatives. They were smiling, hands folded in their laps. Aunt Nellie nodded brightly ". . .have kindly suggested that we move down to Oregon and live with them for a while."

Katherine felt a warning twinge in the pit of her stomach. That was it, of course. What else could have put those empty smiles on their faces, those "you poor dears" into their mouths?

"All of us?" she asked flatly.

Teddy's voice broke in. "Not me!" he said. "I'm not going." There was anguish in it. Nothing any of them say, Katherine thought, is going to be right with Teddy. Nor with me.

Her father looked at his eldest son. "Peter and Felicity will live with Uncle Ian and Aunt Nellie," he continued mechanically. "Tommy and Angus with Uncle Angus and Aunt Rebecca."

The little children are to be taken away from me. He's already arranged that. And still he isn't facing me, Katherine thought, because there's more to it than that.

"You didn't say anything about me!" Teddy was standing as tall as his thin body would allow. His sandy hair bristled like the scruff on the back of an angry dog.

"I figured you and me and Katherine would stay together, maybe go down to California. They tell me there's real opportunity down that way."

"I won't!" Teddy looked all around the room, meeting every frown, defying it. "I've been wanting to ship out on the San Francisco boat. I would have last year if it hadn't been for the house." He turned to Katherine. "*You* know that. I can get on the boat now. You don't get me to go to California or Oregon or any place. I'm old enough to leave home and that's what I'm going to do." His voice softened. "Listen, Katie, you do it, too. You always wanted to teach school. Aren't you old enough, now?"

"Katherine has to go to California with me!" Peter Duncan's voice trembled. He's unsettled, Katherine thought wonderingly, because Teddy has bested him in front of his brothers. And he's afraid. He looked from one child to the next. "I'm going to be saving for a home, for all of us," he said. "Soon as I get it we'll all move back together again."

Aunt Nellie nodded briskly. "Of course you will, Peter dear."

"All in good time," Uncle Ian added.

And Aunt Rebecca murmured nervously, "The best of care. . ."

"Things will go real well in California," Katherine heard her father say. "More money down there, more jobs. We'll forget all our hard luck. This time things will be better."

This time. . .The old phrase, the old, old promise that was a lie. Katherine heard it with a feeling of wonder. He was smiling at the younger children, trying to cajole them into smiling back. But they stood in a motionless line, their faces solemn. He reached out to touch them affectionately. Even little Petie ignored his father's hand. He turned away to study the strangers who were ready to take him home. The silence in the room was heavy.

Peter Duncan faced his eldest daughter. "Well," he said huskily, "we'll let Teddy work on the San Francisco boat, if that's what he wants to do. But we'll go south, Katherine. You and I."

She wanted to cry out—No! I won't be trapped as my mother was, with each year growing wearier, more hopeless. I won't be beaten down to crying, as my mother once cried, "If I could just know, know so sure that nothing could change it, that I could always start the washing on a Monday morning." *He* always knew where the land was rich, the best of it waiting to be claimed. *He* knew where a man could make a fortune, in silver or gold or lumber or cattle. *He* knew the place, the place sunk deep in nowhere, where the houses are elegant and the saloons are cheap and this time everything will be better. In how many crude, heatless cabins had her mother listened to what he knew? How much had his dream comforted her when she carried the washing down to the river and found nothing more than a dirty trickle?

Of his own accord her father had wrenched from her the only reason for taking her mother's place. The little children, her mother's little children—this round-cheeked little aunt and the thin sparrowy one would tub them and kiss them and see to their buttons. So it was for himself, not for them, that he was pleading. Take care of *me*, his soft gray eyes begged, your mother always did.

Katherine's voice felt thick in her mouth but it came out loudly. "No," she said, facing them all, "I won't go to California."

The words fell into a pool of silence. They echoed soundlessly, like ripples rolling toward the shore. The fixed smiles still fitted tightly over the faces of the relatives. Teddy was grinning widely, for in a way she had vindicated him. The little children were staring at the strangers, clinging to each other's hands.

Finally her father answered. "But I'll be all alone."

Katherine thought, he knows that will get their sympathy. It tells them he is helpless and lonely, that his daughter is selfish. He doesn't say things, her mother had always apologized, unless he honestly believes them. Was this the "honesty" for which her mother had forgiven everything, even his failure?

Then, at last, anger had come to her. She felt it break loose and clung to it triumphantly. Now, now was the time, and it might be short, for she could never stay angry long. Now was the time to defy him, to escape everything she hated and let this split second of frantic courage catapult her so far that she could never turn back. "You ruined my mother's life!'' she cried at him. ''But you're not going to ruin mine. I'm going to leave. You heard what Teddy said. I'm going to be a schoolteacher. I've always wanted to be a schoolteacher. Mother taught me how. She wanted me to teach school. She didn't want me to be a failure—'' Katherine gasped for breath, added wildly, ''like you!''

''My, my,'' plump little Aunt Nellie murmured. Thin Aunt Rebecca pursed her lips and shook her head.

Her father's face was white. ''That's no way to talk.''

Katherine kept on desperately. ''You're taking my mother's children away from me. All you're worried about is who's going to take care of *you!*''

She turned toward Teddy. ''He wants someone to *believe* him,'' she sobbed. ''I won't!''

Sounds and faces blurred together after that. Teddy was hugging her, whispering, ''Don't be scared, Katie. I'm going to run away, too.'' One of the uncles said, ''Quite a temper for such a little girl.'' ''She favors her mother,'' both aunts seemed to say in unison, clicking their tongues. Her father was standing with his back to them all, staring out across the Sound. Felicity dragged Angus by the hand to present him solemnly to Aunt Nellie. ''Angus wants to know,'' her clear voice said, ''if maybe now he's in the third grade, does he get a pair of shoes?''

Katherine had broken free of Teddy's arm and run from the room. There had been pitifully little to take along, for her few clothes had been lost in the fire. A shawl given to her by a neighbor, her past week's wages from the San Francisco store, a little castoff clothing. She stuffed it all into an old paper sack. While the voices of her aunts and uncles babbled in the next room, Katherine ran out the back door.

That night, for the first time in her life, she had

walked into a hotel and asked for a room. The clerk
squinted at her curiously. A little girl with red hair
hanging down her back, an old shawl over her head
and a paper parcel under her arm. She held out a
fifty-cent piece. He looked at it, shrugged and took it.
As Nate Tarpee had done tonight, he warned her,
"Be sure to lock your door."

The night wind was rising. It came in gusts, rattling
the poorly fitted windows of the Gold Mountain
Hotel. The candle flame flickered and went out.
Katherine sighed. In the dark she felt her way from
the chair to the washstand and slowly began undres-
sing for bed.

iii

The new day brought Uncle Julian with a riding horse
and a set of instructions. He delivered them both
absentmindedly, with a look of perplexity in his pale
eyes.

"Miss Duncan, Nils sent over this pony. It's
yours." He scratched his head. "Now, let's see. The
schoolhouse. That's going to be the old Wright cabin.
It's over near the first hop shed. Wright's dead now,
they tell me. Don't know what become of his wife.
Seems to me she was a cousin to Nils' wife, though
maybe not. She was a Klickitat. Nils' Mary's
purebred Snoqualmie. Wright, he went gold hunting."

"Mr. Bengston has a wife. . ."

The old man's glance sharpened as he peered
wisely at Katherine. "It's no wonder you didn't
know it. She's over at the Indian camp more than she
is at home. And Nils don't talk about her, out of
loyalty."

Katherine interrupted briskly. "You were telling me about the schoolhouse, Mr. Sparks."

"Yes, yes. . ." Uncle Julian's old eyes clouded. "Old Wright. Did I say he's likely dead now? He went gold hunting, after Nils bought him out. Died because he couldn't find anything. Or maybe because he did. Who knows?" He chuckled, looked at Katherine apologetically. "I'm an old man, Miss Duncan. I talk too much. Well, now, about where you're to live. The Carlsons'll put you up. They'll have more children in school than any other family in the Valley, so they're bound to help out."

"Who decided that?"

"You sound like you know already." Uncle Julian's old eyes brightened. "Nils, of course."

"Always."

Uncle Julian nodded good-humoredly. "He's the decidingest man in the Valley. That's all right. He decided there'd be a teacher and he decided you'd do. You owe him that much."

Katherine snapped, "I don't care to owe him anything."

Uncle Julian's head went back in a quick, dry laugh. "No, of course not. But my dear young lady, you're going to, anyway. It's Nils who pays the teacher, right out of his own pocket."

"No. . ." Katherine stared at the old man. Nils hated schoolteachers, they had told her. Nils ridiculed schools and said they were made for ugly girls. He could keep the school from opening, they said. Why, then, was he providing the building and paying the teacher, unless it was to add to his power?

"I'll have to live at Carlsons'," she said doggedly, "because I don't know the Valley well enough to find a place by myself. I will *pay* them myself. But I won't take that horse!"

"She's a good little mare."

Katherine shook her head. "I won't accept her."

Uncle Julian's eyes narrowed. "From Nils?"

"Exactly. I don't care for his—manners."

"Ha, ha, ha." The old man's laughter trailed off weakly. "My dear young lady," he said wearily, "neither do I. Nils hasn't got as much manners as a bear has tail. But for some reason he's sent you a horse to ride and I'd take it, if I was you. Except for these little beat-up villages at Gold Mountain and Three Forks and Black River, there isn't a homestead within a mile of the next one. Carlsons live up toward the Pass, a good six miles or more from the schoolhouse. You'll want to get down to see the riverboat come in, too, and that's a good fifteen. On top of that, the woods can be a scary place for a woman, and if she's walking it takes a long time to get out of them. On a horse you can let out a scream, close your eyes, grab ahold of the pummel and ride for the clearing."

Katherine looked at him uncertainly.

He winked, a long slow wink. His shaggy white eyebrows seemed to quiver with it. His nearly toothless mouth was curved into a friendly smile. "After a week of walking, you'll be begging Nils for this horse," he said gently. "Look, daughter, wouldn't it be better to take it now and stay as high and mighty as you please?"

iv

"God bless Richie and Martha and Tom and Susan and Jane and Hiram and John." Jeb Carlson sighed, lifted his head, saw Katherine in the extra place next to the twins and hurriedly remembered his manners.

"And bless Miss Duncan." He sat down heavily, as a man does who has been trying to pull stumps all day with only one ox.

The brown-eyed one named Hiram looked solemnly at the girl he had been told would be his teacher. "He almost forgot you," he said. "I wonder what would happen if he did?"

Katherine swallowed her smile. "Happen where?"

Hiram, who was seven, looked at her impatiently, as if he already doubted that she was prepared to teach. "In heaven, of course."

"Faith," Jeb Carlson called down the table, "tell your son not to ask so many questions."

Mrs. Carlson looked up wearily. "Hush, Hiram," she sighed. Her shoulders sagged forward again over the task of cutting up a smaller boy's meat.

"Oh, that's all right," Katherine spoke anxiously. These children were to be her pupils. Considering the number of them, it appeared they were going to be most of her pupils. Only John, who was five, would not be present when she opened school. They were all looking at her now, eyes round and solemn and hopeful. Catching Martha's eyes, Katherine smiled. Martha giggled.

"It is the duty of the children," Jeb Carlson's voice roared suddenly from the end of the table, "to keep their eyes down and their mouths closed."

The silence was instant, but lasted only a second. Hiram's voice broke it. "But Pa," he said matter-of-factly, "how can we eat that way?"

Jeb reared to his feet.

"Please, Pa," his wife's voice pleaded.

Jeb sat down, slowly shook his head. "Children are a blessing. It would serve *that* one right if he was blessed with another one just like himself later on."

"Please pass the beans?" Susan's reedy voice seemed to rise to a question. Suddenly conversation was over and eating began.

Roasted smoked venison, new potatoes baked in the coals, white biscuits with wild honey that tasted of red clover, a pudding of dried apples and ground cinnamon. Katherine recognized the unaccustomed plenty. There was even butter on the table, firm from being cooled in the spring behind the cabin. She knew how seldom a family with one cow and seven children had butter on the table. The food was good. In the children's eyes Katherine could read the thought that it was good if only because it was so plentiful.

"Let the food that gives us strength give us strength to follow Thee. Amen."

With the last syllable of their father's final grace, the children swung their legs over the bench and raced for the open door.

"Hiram!"

The square little boy with brown eyes stopped as if reins had been jerked on him. "Yes, Pa."

"What were you whispering during grace?"

"Thank you God for the butter."

Jeb Carlson said, "Well. . ." Then he sighed. "It would be more to my liking if we said one grace at a time. But it was good, wasn't it, Son?"

Hiram nodded, moving experimentally toward the door.

"But you should have bowed your head."

"Pa, I was looking at *her*."

Jeb Carlson glanced quickly at Katherine.

"Let him go, Jeb," Faith Carlson said wearily. "He's only seven."

Hiram disappeared around the corner of the cabin. After him Jeb Carlson went, carrying a bucket.

Katherine heard him calling the cow. "Co boss, co boss. . ."

Mrs. Carlson turned to her. She smiled faintly, as if she'd got out of the habit of it. "Hiram isn't the only one, I'll be bound. How old are you, dear? Seventeen?"

Katherine was caught off guard. She was nodding even while she was reminding herself to lie. She smiled. "Yes, seventeen," she said weakly. "But I told them twenty, to get the job."

Mrs. Carlson pursed her lips. "It don't make no difference out here, anyways. After some of the teachers we've had. . ." She hesitated, looked at Katherine, decided to hold her tongue. Nodding to herself she went to the hearth, lifted the steaming teakettle from the iron hook and poured water into a pan. "I don't often talk," she apologized, "but it's a pleasure sometimes. See that teakettle? It's made of copper, hammered by hand. My grandfather made it. My grandmother gave it to me just before we left Ohio. I've lost most everything else we had, but I did keep this kettle."

"How did you lose. . ." Katherine began the question even as she knew the answer. How had her own mother lost so much—her pendants and earrings, first, then her good clothes, cut and sewn by a French dressmaker at the time of her marriage; her cherished pictures and fancy work, and the furniture shipped upriver from New Orleans. And finally her looks, even hope. . ."You lost everything coming west?"

Mrs. Carlson nodded. "Coming west." She laughed suddenly. "Grandma's teakettle saved my life. A sneaking Indian came into our cabin once in Dakota. I hit him over the head with it. We always said if christening alone would do it, I'd turned one redskin into a Christian." She looked expectantly at

Katherine, grinning like a naughty boy. "That there teakettle was full of boiling water."

Together they washed and dried the dishes, set a bowl of dough to raise overnight, swept the split cedar floor with a broom of twigs, put potatoes to soak for a new batch of yeast. Mrs. Carlson banked the fire under the blackened coffee pot. "Someday," she said, "I'm going to cook on a stove. They say it really saves your back." She straightened up slowly, her hands behind her pressing against the pain. "You were real helpful, dear. Shall we go outside and set for a while? I always sleep better if I've had a look at the mountain."

They settled themselves on the bench against the cabin wall. Mrs. Carlson's rough, red hands folded contentedly in the hollow of her skirt. "Isn't it beautiful?"

Beautiful—it was hardly a farm wife's word, yet she spoke it naturally. Reluctantly Katherine followed Mrs. Carlson's gaze.

The mountain's rocky dome over four thousand feet above cut up into the darkening sky. Its great bulk hung over them, black where the timber was heavy, pink where the setting sun colored the steep cliffs. The forest that blanketed so much of the Valley continued up the sides of the mountain, but irregularly, as if the huge rock had burst through it, pulling the cover of timber up its sides. As the sun dropped, the light changed and the shadows moved, like clouds changing their shapes before the wind.

"See? It never looks the same twice. I love that mountain." Mrs. Carlson smiled dreamily. "I wish you could have seen the way it looked to us the day we got here.

"We'd come all the way from Dakota. It'd been hot all the way, and so dusty you couldn't spit. We'd had sickness. We'd lost a wagon in one river and our milk cow got stampeded off with a bunch of buffalo. Half the children were sick from eating moldy grits.''

She sighed, her eyes on the jagged outline of the mountain top. "When we come through the Pass, we were half-starved, half-dead, and you know what was in harness pulling our covered wagon? One old ox and a yearling heifer. Pray often and shave once a day, that's what Pa kept saying. That's what he did. Jeb's prayers got us through.

"You might say we were lucky, not being the first wagon through the Pass that year. It's only sixty miles but sometimes the first over in the spring take two—three weeks. Every tree that's fallen across the trail has to be cut out to let the wagons through. Either that, or stack branches deep enough on each side of the log so the wagons can drive right over them. And every washout has to be filled in.

"We were lucky, too, to keep our dog, him being such a good hunter. All the wagon trains before us that year had lost every one of their dogs, most often in a certain place where the road makes a switchback up above the south fork of the river. Right there our hound got a scent and took after it. Pa'd heard about trains losing their dogs so he took off right after him. It was a cougar, all right. He was eleven feet long. Pa missed him on the first shot but got him on the second. God was on Pa's side or he wouldn't have got that second shot. He was praying so loud I could hear him way back at the wagon.''

She gestured toward the rim of mountains which enclosed the Valley at the east. "From here you can't see the road because of the trees," she said, "and when you come down from the Pass the trees keep you from seeing the mountain. You're coming down so fast the wagon wants to ride up on the ox's rump.

They put their feet down with a slide and a jerk, the way a man does going downhill when he takes it all in his knees. You're dead beat and sick and maybe scared, because there's always talk about those eastside Yakimas and how they might send war parties through the Pass. Then suddenly, like stepping out of night into day, you hit the prairie. And there's this mountain, Old Hi, looking over you.

"The river was running along at the foot of it, singing like. The fields were as green as new grass. The trees were in full leaf and the air smelled of wild clover. We'd come two thousand five hundred miles, and all but one of us had lived through trials you'd of thought would kill us every one. There it was.

"I said to Jeb, 'We'll stay right here.'

"He said, 'Faith, we talked of going on to the coast.'

" 'No, Jeb, right here,' I said.

" 'Leastways, we ought to ride on to the settlement. Gold Mountain's only three miles ahead.'

" 'Jeb,' I said, 'I come two thousand and five hundred miles but I just can't make that last three.'

" 'I like it here, anyways,' Jeb says, grinning at me, and so we put our claim in to this very spot right here.''

Mrs. Carlson's eyes filled with tears. "I looked up at the big old mountain and I cried and said, 'I didn't think we'd make it, I just didn't think we'd make it.' '' She turned to Katherine. "*You* like it here, don't you?''

Katherine felt helpless in the face of such a plea. She hated the place, but could she throw that at a woman who had entrusted her with her love for it? "I want to live in the city,'' she said, turning away from Faith Carlson's warm, earnest face.

"Oh. . .'' Mrs. Carlson's voice flattened as if

Katherine had dropped a weight on it. "Then you'll
be leaving the Valley as soon as you can. Anyway,
try to do a good job of teaching while you're here. It's
been hard on the kids, the kind of schooling they've
had. One teacher beating them almost to death, the
next one running away because the kids beat *him*
almost to death. You don't get educated that way."
Mrs. Carlson grasped Katherine's arm, shaking it
with every word. "Miss Duncan, I want my children
to read and write and believe in God!" For a long
moment she held Katherine's arm. At last her grip
relaxed and she patted Katherine in a motherly way.
"Just try and do a good job," she said with a sigh,
"even if you don't stay long."

v

Katherine lay with her head toward the open window. The flat shutter of cedar boards, hinged over the
opening to be dropped down on cold or rainy days,
was propped wide by a stick of kindling wood. Cool
night air poured through the opening, blowing
against her cheek. She pulled the comforter up under
her chin.

The cabin was of cedar shakes, split by hand. The
long boards were ribbed with the grain, for they had
been made by a man with an adze and a sledge
hammer. Those that had been smoothed showed the
cut marks where the draw knife had bitten into them.
A big kitchen and a fieldstone hearth, a room at each
end for sleeping, and out back a lean-to for firewood
and the milch cow—everything was made by hand,
cut from the giant cedars that had once towered over
the pasture land. Katherine touched the rough wall
gently, running the tips of her fingers with the rough

grain. The homestead house was two years old, but it still had the sweet spice smell of cedar.

In bed with her was Martha. Across the room, but so near she could hear their breathing, were the twins, Susan and Jane. The boys were tucked into the other room with the Carlsons, the smallest in a trundle that pulled out from the larger bed. And they were all asleep. The night air was heavy with sleep.

But Katherine was wakeful. Martha, sleeping beside her, was her pupil. Across the room there were two more pupils. They already worshipped her, as she could remember worshipping every teacher she had ever had. They promised this worship with every sigh and solemn glance of their big eyes.

Thoughts at night are so different from thoughts in daytime—Katherine wished them away. Thinking alone in the dark is like dreaming with a fever.

Carl will be back Monday. I will leave on Monday, Katherine thought. There is no contract, no promise to keep me here. Nils Bengston himself has said he didn't want me.

Martha's thin body rolled against her. Katherine pulled back, resenting the touch. And then she sighed, a sigh as shaking as a sob. Gently she reached over and caressed the little girl's head.

CHAPTER FOUR

i

THE SCHOOLHOUSE HAD BEEN a homestead cabin. It was small, because the man who had built it had spent his strength on a two-thousand-mile wagon trip from Dakota and could think of nothing but abiding by the rules of the Homestead Act and getting in out of the rain.

His wife had insisted on a rough plank floor and two windows with split-cedar shutters. These were the adornments. The hearth where a lonely woman from Dakota once cooked had long since crumbled away. Chimney and fire pot had fallen together in a heap of stone as the clay which bound them gave way to the weather. The great cedars overshadowing the cabin had been cut, dragged by ox to the river, rafted, pushed down a chute beside the Falls and steered to Smith's mill at Black River. Around the cabin now were the civilized hop rows. Poles as tall as young saplings lined up in columns so long the ends of them melted together in the distant haze. The vines crawled to the top of them, spilling over with the weight of the ripening pods. In the wind the hop leaves rustled, whispering.

Such was the "school," Katherine thought, which Nils Bengston allows to exist. Only one concession had been made. There were three benches, narrow, splintery and backless, but still long enough to seat ten children apiece. And there were tables, matching the benches in length and roughness. Some former teacher whom Nils had "allowed" and then for some reason ceased to tolerate had abandoned a large slate.

Katherine inspected the school carefully. She had spent two days riding from one homestead to another announcing the opening of school and listing the pupils. Three days remained before the morning she had designated as opening day. Alone in the dusty cabin, with the sun shining peacefully and her pony grazing in the clearing, she felt secure. The spirit of Nils Bengston might whisper, I've provided the school, I've hired you as its teacher. Now go ahead with the childish nonsense or quit and admit it's as childish as I say it is. But the days and hours which had yet to pass protected her. Thus far she had won, because the hour had not come when she might lose.

Like a good housewife, Katherine looked around to see what must be done. Eventually the hearth would have to be rebuilt, or they would all be too cold to study. As for school supplies, there were none. If former teachers had used books during their short tenures in the Valley, the books had disappeared as hastily as they had, and as completely. The cobwebs were thick. Their dainty lacework sagged with a burden of dust. But they hid no readers or geographies or spellers. Chalk, pencils, papers, maps, tablets, all the physical bits and pieces of the schoolroom Katherine loved the very feel of—they would have to come later. First there was soap and water.

Katherine pushed back her sleeves, knotting them securely around her elbows. Picking up the bucket she had brought from Carlsons', she walked to the river. There was danger in worrying about how to teach a dozen strange children with nothing but a jagged piece of slate and a headful of untried ideas.

But I don't have to do it right now, she told herself. At this moment, at this very exact little moment alone at the schoolhouse in the sunshine, I don't have to think about anything but scrubbing the floor.

She worked rapidly. There was peace simply in the quickness of movement, in concentrating so thoroughly on each lift of the arm and bend of the back. She carried the crumbled hearth outside, stone by stone. With a handful of sword fern she swept down the heavy cobwebs. She whipped the soft soap into a fine suds, even in cold river water, and scrubbed the tables and benches. The world which had always seemed too big grew smaller as she worked.

She began to hum. In a moment she was singing, keeping time with each forward push on the scrub cloth. She hardly thought of Monday. The schoolhouse was damp and soapy-smelling, the benches and tables were in place and the slate propped into position at the front of the room. The work was done and Katherine had dumped the last bucket of water and rolled her sleeves down before she remembered that Monday was also the day Carl White was to return.

"I'll be back Monday," he had said. "I'll take you back to Seattle then."

How could she have forgotten that promise, to which she had clung so desperately during that first long night in Gold Mountain? In a week, Monday had become only Opening Day, the day she became what everyone in the Valley had called her from the first—Teacher. It was a title, as "General" or "Captain" or "Lawyer" was a title. Taking her hands in his, Carl White had promised to save her from this.

Katherine stopped humming. She had been singing one of her mother's favorite songs, but suddenly she couldn't remember what it was called. She dropped the hard maple bar across the school door, and un-hitched the pony's reins from the alder limb. Wearily she pulled herself into the saddle. She hadn't felt tired until now.

ii

From the doorway Katherine studied the clearing around the school. Pride and panic tore her. She saw there were more children here than she had listed and certainly twice what she had expected. She had gulped down Mrs. Carlson's black coffee and wheat mush, and ridden out while the dew was still heavy on the prairie grass and the woods were cold and dark as night. Hours early, she had thought, but three little children had been earlier. The towheaded Ander-sons, Tillie and Judy, and their little brother Lars. They watched her owlishly as she propped the shut-ters open. They followed her from bench to door-way to yard. With self-conscious briskness she straightened things she had already put to rights and tidied where nothing could be more clean.

Soon other children came. Most of them rode ponies, two or three children to a horse. They gathered in the rough open space which the hop rows still ceded to the school. They whispered, pointed, giggled. When Katherine gained courage to approach them, they ran like fawns, peering at her silently from around the corners of the schoolhouse. She retired to the cabin, trying to walk casually, yet with so straight a back that they could not feel she was retreating. And there she remained.

At last the watch Mrs. Carlson had pinned to her blouse read half-past eight. It was time for school.

The voices outside were shrill with excitement. Daring had come with the appearance of some older boys. With teacher at a safe distance, the meekest was a lion and the weak attacked the strong with impartial enthusiasm. Eight or ten children were wrestling, in lightly chosen groups of two and three.

Besides the watch, Mrs. Carlson had given Katherine a cow bell. Katherine picked it up, walked deliberately to the door. Her pulse was wild, as if beating time to the thoughts she had told herself to remember. Show no fear. Demand respect. Keep calm. She lifted the bell, brought her arm down with one great, determined sweep. The sound startled her. She blinked but kept swinging.

When she stopped, the schoolyard seemed paralyzed. The children were standing as they had been caught by the sudden clangor, staring at her speechlessly. The wrestlers looked up, still tangled together in the dirt. The big boys still leaned against the cabin, observing everything, mocking everything. Mouths were open with the last shout, fists were clenched for the last fight.

Gratefully, Katherine picked out the Carlson children. "Hiram," she said clearly, for the other names she had known so well at breakfast had fled her mind. "Hiram, would you please lead the line into the schoolroom? The others will follow, one at a time."

The little square boy named Hiram bounced forward, his round brown face twisted with a wide grin. Looking proudly from right to left, he marched toward the door. No one moved. At the door he turned, waving both arms like windmill blades in a cyclone. "Well, come on," he squeaked. "Or your ma'll give you a licking when you get home."

Miraculously the line formed. The children marched in. Even the big boys followed, two of them so tall they looked down on Katherine as they passed.

She had planned this day. She had lived through it a dozen times during sleepless nights beside Martha. She closed the door behind the last pupil. The wooden thud of door against frame hung in the hollow silence. A sigh shuddered through her body. She fought it down, and saw that her fists were clenched hard. Painfully she relaxed them. It was time to face the school, and herself as teacher. She turned around.

"Good morning, children," she said. Her voice was level, but a little too high. "We'll begin the day with the Lord's Prayer."

Several voices were distinct as they recited it. Several were puzzled. Their faces turned from one side to the other, their eyes lingering anxiously on the moving lips of others. All but the biggest boy mumbled dutifully and kept heads bowed.

"Now, the roll call. We will start over here. Each one stand in turn and give his name."

As each child rose to speak, Katherine nodded. "Thank you," she said quietly, writing the name into the notebook under "Present." Tommy Tine—that must be Agatha Tine's son. The Carlson children—Richie, Martha, Tom, Susan, Jane, Hiram—and right beside him, five-year-old Johnny, whom she had been too muddled to notice before.

"My brother wants to go to school, too," Hiram piped up hurriedly.

"He's only five, isn't he?"

"But he's smart!" Hiram's brown eyes were earnest.

"He should be six. Five is too young."

"I'm seven. I'm just starting. You didn't say I couldn't come because I was too *old*."

"He may stay," Katherine said weakly. "Next, please."

Bertha and Bobby Smith. The three identical Andersons—she had seen two at their homestead, but their round, pink faces were so much alike she couldn't tell which was the extra child. Then the Stump children, with hollow cheeks and a kind of hopelessness in their eyes. Sammy, Gerald, Susie and three smaller ones who whispered their names so fearfully she could not hear. Levi Barker—he was one of the taller boys, and he kept off by himself, surveying her solemnly from the end of the farthest bench. Liza Tarpee, eleven years old with pigtails. Emil Greene, who looked twenty. The last was a little, dark-haired girl. She had been in the schoolyard of course. At the end of a bench she sat quiet as a frightened grouse. "Julie," she said softly, as she took her turn. "Julie Bengston."

Katherine saw the darkness of her skin, the dull blackness of her thick braids. And yet her eyes were blue. Despite herself, Katherine thought—as blue as her father's. No other Indian or half-breed had thought to come to school. Only Nils Bengston's daughter would have come, to take her place among children whose parents scorned the "Siwash," to go to school while the hops were being picked.

"Julie Bengston," Katherine forced herself to repeat it. The little girl was watching her solemnly. She is so quiet, Katherine thought, so watchful. Even here at school Nils has his way of being present.

iii

To Katherine the day had gone well, simply because it was almost over. The list of activities she had recited for so many days had not forsaken her. The picture she had formed of herself as teacher, standing before a roomful of respectful children, with praise for one and a deserved sharp word for another—the truth wasn't too ridiculous compared with it.

Even the complications of her own feelings hadn't kept her from being teacher. The sight of Emil Greene, who had only last week stoned her horse into running away with her. The little half-Indian girl Julie. The memory of Faith Carlson's hopeful smile begged her not to desert them. The room was barren and bookless, but she had managed to be teacher, anyway.

"I'll teach you another song. Everyone stand, please."

The girls jumped to their feet obediently, grinning for approval. The boys looked from side to side, hesitated a moment, then awkwardly followed.

"It was upon a high, high hill,
Two maidens chose their dwelling,
And one was known both far and wide,
Was known as Barb'ra Allen. . ."

Katherine sang it slowly, as her mother had always sung it and as her grandmother had taught it to her. The children watched, their eyes wide.

"Now slowly, from the beginning."

The children's voices followed hers, resting tipsily on some notes, falling hard on others. "It was upon a high, high hill. . ."

The school door swung open, hitting so hard against the wall that bits of dry bark and dirt fell in a cloud to the floor. Nils Bengston, the man who had laughed at her, stood in the doorway with his hands in his pockets.

Katherine stared at him despairingly. She had made herself teacher in a day. She had created order and found comfort in it. But here he stood, the man who mocked a schoolteacher and yet paid her out of his own pocket. Suddenly she felt bare, helpless and a little angry.

His big hands rested easily on his hips, the thumbs hooked over the trouser pockets. Ignoring Katherine, he turned his head slowly to survey the room. His blue eyes flickered as they rested on one child and then another. The children didn't move. Teacher and classroom were held immobile. He was in command, and he knew it. But he wasn't laughing now.

"Go on home!" he said suddenly. "All of you. Go on. Get!"

The motionless, silent children broke loose like a herd of frightened colts. Without a questioning glance at their teacher, they pushed past each other to the door. Four or five were already shouting in the schoolyard before Katherine recovered herself. She walked stiffly, but quickly, to the door, and turned her back to it. "I have not dismissed school," she said, fighting to keep her voice level. "Go back to your places, children."

The children hesitated. Right in front of her, so close the dry dung smell of his clothing swept down on her, was the big Greene boy. His eyes were surly but uncertain. Pressing against her skirt was little Johnny Carlson, who had begun to squeeze by but suddenly reached for her hand, as if she might lead him to safety. The Stump children stared fearfully at Nils Bengston. Solemn as a preacher, little Julie Bengston looked on, waiting.

"I said, school is over. All through for today, and tomorrow, and the day after that." Nils menaced the crowding children with a gesture of his arm. They squeezed more tightly together, pushed harder against Katherine. His voice was low but cold. "No more school for a month and maybe not then. Now get out of this shack and run home or I'll sell every one of you to the Yakimas."

Their open mouths and scared eyes said it wasn't true, but they stampeded anyway. The Greene boy and Johnny Carlson and all crushed against Katherine, ripping her fingers loose from the door jamb.

"You'll get hurt, teacher," Nils Bengston said flatly.

Katherine looked at him numbly. But I won't move, she promised herself bitterly. I just won't move.

The Greene boy put his hands out to push her aside. His fingers had only grazed her shoulders when Nils Bengston picked him up by the shirt collar and the seat of his pants and threw him against the wall. Nils turned back to Katherine. "Didn't you know," he said quietly, "that you're not as big as he is?"

The Greene boy struggled to his feet. Whimpering loudly he crouched against the wall. Katherine stared at Nils. There was a hard knot in her throat and she was trembling. She noted crazily that his brows and lashes were very dark for so blond a man and that he had a long, thin scar along his jawline. Slowly, in the slow motion of a bad dream, she stepped away from the door.

The children fell out of the room. At the door the Greene boy turned to stick his tongue out at her, then vanished with a heathen yell. The schoolyard cleared.

"Yi, yi!" the oldest Smith child shrieked, whipping up the pony on which the three of them sat. The horse wheeled and disappeared down the trail. "Yi, yi!" came back from the distance, mingling with the faint clatter of hooves on the gravelly riverbank. Only little Julie Bengston remained. She walked past her father without a word. Her face smooth of expression, she crossed the yard and took a place near her father's horse. There she squatted, looking the other way.

"Aahh. . ." Nils Bengston exhaled deeply. He turned away from Katherine, as if there were no longer any necessity of facing her. "Miss Duncan, you started your school too soon. You can open it next month when the hops are in."

His tone was matter-of-fact. Katherine found her head clearing. As flatly as he, she replied. "If children are kept out of school to pick hops, they can be kept out to trap furs, or bring in the hay, or help with the butchering. In the end they are lucky to get three months of school a year."

"That's school enough for boys," Nils said easily, "and three times too much for girls." He looked appraisingly at the benches, the walls, the floors. "Quite a hard-working little housekeeper, aren't you? The shack looks tidy enough for church. At least, I suppose it does. Last time I was in church my mother carried me in her arms. They'd never have got me into the place if I'd been any bigger." He grinned, pleased with his joke.

Katherine's resentment sharpened. "I opened school today because it is the proper time to do it," she said in a voice which sounded three times louder than her own. "I will keep it open."

Nils continued to study the vista of hops. She waited, her chin higher than it need be and her back so straight it ached. At last he turned to face her. He was still smiling. He shook his head. "No," he said quietly, "next month."

"No one person has the right to rule the lives of everyone else! Keep your own child away from the school if you wish, but let the other parents decide such things for themselves."

Nils frowned. "Don't be a nuisance, Miss Duncan. For a week I've been looking for more hop-pickers. The crop is heavier than anyone had figured and every five, ten, or a dozen who might be picking and aren't are making it harder for me. So there's nothing for anyone to decide. I decided already." He laughed suddenly. "Julie will be here, though. Julie don't pick hops. So you and she can keep the school open, if you want."

Katherine could feel anger pounding in her throat. "Mr. Bengston," she said, "I understand you own a large part of this valley. I've been told that you are a very powerful man. I've been reminded that you pay my wages out of your own pocket and I'd better do exactly as you say. But I'm a schoolteacher, Mr. Bengston. You don't own *me*."

"I wouldn't know what to do with you," he said, grinning, "if I did."

Katherine gasped involuntarily. Mockery was the hardest blow of all. "This week I rode to every homestead and talked to most of the mothers and fathers in the Valley. They want their children to go to school, whatever your wishes may be. They promised me."

"And what would all their promises mean," Nils said quietly, "if I asked them to promise something different?"

"I'll go around to each one of them again!" Katherine's voice rose in desperation. "I'll tell them the school *is* open!"

Nils studied her silently. "You're not yet twenty," he said, "or I'm a poor judge. But a woman don't even have to be full size to be a troublemaker. This school is a little thing to me, Miss Duncan. I could have the building tore down tonight, if I wanted to. The riverboat's due in Black River and I could have you put on that and taken back to Seattle if I wanted to, too. But I've plenty on my mind and I don't want to be bothered." He walked past her to the door. As if it were an afterthought, he turned and added, "Just remember, though, that I can get rid of you any time you start to get too pesky. So you let me do the deciding around here or you'll be out of the Valley before Thanksgiving."

The tears, the cursed, give away tears, were beginning to come now. Katherine shook her head desperately. She had meant to reply angrily that he couldn't send her back to Seattle, because Carl White was coming and she was leaving that very night anyway. Leaving the gloomy, wild, tree-covered Valley and the dark mountains pressing down on it. Leaving the leering Greene boy and the blue-eyed Indian girl, the Nelsons, Carlsons, Stumps and Smiths, and Mrs. Carlson with her worship of Old Hi and the pain she wouldn't admit. Leaving them all, with Carl White at her side to help her.

"Maybe some day you'll learn that the people here aren't like so many children you can lock up in the woodshed!" she sobbed. "I'm not only going to stay right here and teach school, but inside of two years I'm going to see that a real schoolhouse is built. You won't own the building, and you won't own the land that it's on. It will have books and tablets and pencils, and you won't own them, either! It will be a *real* school!"

Nils' eyes brightened with surprise. And then he

shrugged. Like an Indian on the hunt, he walked soundlessly across the clearing, picked Julie up and placed her carefully behind the saddle. He didn't spend a glance on Katherine as he mounted and rode away.

Katherine closed her eyes, forgetting even now to wipe away the tears. She heard a sound and opened them. Hiram Carlson was standing before her, looking curiously at her face.

"I was hiding behind that cedar tree," he explained. "But I didn't know you were going to cry."

Katherine groped for the edge of her skirt, pulling it up roughly to wipe her eyes.

"He's big, isn't he?" Hiram reflected. "Bigger'n Pa. He must be twice as big as you are. Miss Duncan, can I ride home behind your saddle like Julie does?"

Katherine nodded fiercely. "I'll have to close up the school," she whispered. With a feeling that there had never been anything else to do about it, she made her big decision. More loudly, she added, "and straighten up for school tomorrow." Hiram took her hand. With the little boy silent beside her, teacher arranged the benches, closed the door and shutters, and barred the door securely on the first day of her teaching.

iv

Carl's hand reached instinctively for Katherine's, then hastily retreated. From vantage points at the other side of the clearing, two or three Carlson children were watching eagerly. There might be others in the cabin behind them. He brought his hands to his sides. "If it's a question of the fare. . ."

Katherine shook her head. "I hadn't even thought of that. Though it's true. I don't have enough money for the trip to Seattle."

"If you're hestitating because you don't have a position or a place to stay. . ."

Katherine smiled. "I should apologize to you," she said softly. "Because I haven't even thought of those things, either."

"Katherine. . ."

She looked up at him curiously. He had spoken her name so earnestly, throwing aside the little game of politeness they had enjoyed together. In real life you don't live by rules, she realized suddenly, you live by situations. And so he is calling me by my first name, as I have thought of him almost from the first. "Yes, Carl."

They looked into each other's faces. They were properly separated by at least two feet of the Carlson's rough cedar bench, and more than properly chaperoned by a half dozen interested Carlson children. No one, Katherine thought, no one in the world can say I'm not being a perfect lady. No one need know how inadequate such ladylikeness seems to me now.

"Yes, Carl," she repeated, forcing herself to look down at her hands.

"Then you won't take the *Viking* tomorrow?"

"Not tomorrow," Katherine said slowly. "I don't feel I can leave right now. I've been here only a week."

"But isn't that enough?"

"Enough?" Katherine echoed the question uncertainly. Yes, of course it had been more than enough. And yet at the end of it she had shouted at Nils Bengston that in two years she would have her own schoolhouse. How could she explain that to Carl?

She sighed. "I'll stay," she said, "for a while."

"Some day I'll have something better to offer you," Carl spoke jerkily, as if he were bowing at the same time. "I'm sorry I don't right now."

Katherine flushed. The implications were almost too serious to be thought of. Life in Seattle, where a lady walked on planked sidewalks and kept her skirts out of the dirt. Churches and schools and houses with glass windows.

"Will you come to the town meeting tonight?" she asked quickly.

Carl nodded. "If you'll let me accompany you."

Katherine looked at him wonderingly. His speech was too perfect. It left her groping for the perfect answer. She nodded. How handsome he is, she thought. So much finer a type than Nils Bengston.

"Would it be all right," Carl said huskily, "to take a walk?"

Katherine heard the plea in his voice and felt her color deepen. It seemed as if this were a play in which all other actors knew their lines but her own had escaped her. She managed to nod. She rose, smoothed her skirts and put her arm through his. He withdrew at her touch as if the intimacy shocked him. As quickly he pulled her arm hard against his side.

They walked in trembling silence, across the clearing, past the woodshed, into the dark clump of willows along the riverbank. The action of the play came alive in Katherine's mind. She saw them strolling together, knew how solemn and adoring his eyes were, knew, as Carl stopped, that he would put his hands on her shoulders, lift her chin, kiss her. His mouth was on hers. She submitted anxiously, placing her hands gently at the back of his head.

Carl stepped back. "Please," he said stiffly, "please accept my humble apologies."

Katherine nodded. He was correct, of course. She should be grateful to him for pretending she had resisted. But the taste of his kiss lingered on her mouth, and even deeper was the feeling of what another could have been. She was trembling, and prayed he wouldn't notice. The lady of the play came forward and spoke for her. "Shall we go back to the cabin?" she said primly. "The meeting will begin soon."

They walked with arms at their sides, a casual distance between them. Carl's eyes were cloudy, but Katherine saw in them only a gentlemanly degree of shame and a much greater sense of his own propriety. He is always so *right*, she thought enviously. He belonged to the world I've always peered at from the outside. But with every solemn step, Katherine's mind played traitor to her, and whispered, why, oh why, did he apologize?

Nils was amused by the sight of Uncle Julian calling the meeting to order. The old goat, Nils thought, sitting up there on Nate Tarpee's stool and banging the store counter with his fist. The old man's eyes watered heavily as he blinked at the crowd. The perfect judge, Nils thought. At his age he won't know one side from the other.

The lobby of the hotel and trading post was filling up. Benches had been placed in rows facing the counter. Nils was proud to have thought of that, for it gave the whole affair an offical look. Flour barrels and coffee sacks and stacks of cured skins and kegs of nails and drums of kereosene had been pushed to the side. The round-bellied wood stove remained alone among the alien benches. The two or three sodden prospectors who usually killed the day in chairs along the wall had been shaken from their posts and were standing in the doorway, hands in pockets and hats jammed down over their ears, staring suspiciously at the unusual crowd. Women! their sharp little eyes said. Farm women were sitting in the store at eight o'clock at night with their good bonnets on and their hands folded proper in their laps.

"Town meeting?" one of the men shrilled at Nils. "I bet I had more fun at a funeral."

Nils leaned back, his powerful shoulders resting lightly against the wall. Uncle Julian was looking his way, no doubt wondering when to begin. Nils shook his head. The Carlsons weren't here yet, and their pesky little boarder. It wasn't his plan to hold the meeting without them and he was sure they'd come. "Important town meeting," he had told Jeb Carlson as he rode from homestead to homestead late that day. "It's your duty to come." Duty—that was the word that would bring the Carlsons. And that little green-eyed schoolmarm, too. In all her life, Nils reflected wryly, I bet she's never done anything just because she wanted to.

At last Jeb and Faith Carlson walked in. Right behind them was Carl White. Nils saw him holding the door wide with one arm and knew even before she appeared that the schoolteacher had come, too. Katherine Duncan entered slowly, holding her skirt with two fingers of each hand. Her reddish hair piled on top of her head was half covered with a shawl. I know where your hat is, Nils thought to himself. You'll be leaving soon. I'll remember to give it to you.

The man at Nils' elbow whispered, "Is that her?"

"You know everyone else in the room. What a brainy cuss you are, Tommy, to figure that out."

"I just wanted to be sure."

"Good. I'm sure, too. Sure that the best part of making you a schoolteacher is that I won't have you around as a foreman." Nils caught Uncle Julian's watery eye. The old man's eyebrows rose. Nils nodded.

"Aahh," said Uncle Julian, loudly. "Ah, well. . ."

The assembly looked at him patiently. He wet his lips. As if surprised to find them wet, he brushed them with the back of his hand. The room was as still as an old well. "Silence, please," Uncle Julian said. He blinked at Nils, his head cocked a little to the side as if he were trying to hear some whispered instructions. "Friends," he said, "we are gathered here tonight. . ."

Nils leaned back, watching the faces as old Julian spoke. Though we are far from being an incorporated town, he was saying, we must look forward to the time when we are a real town. We must act, as townspeople do, together.

Several listeners nodded vigorously. Other faces were stiff with suspicion. They know who's behind this, Nils thought. But let them.

"We must join in our common purpose, dedicated to our common future. . ."

Wonderful words the old man knows, Nils reflected, when he warms up. But will he remember what I told him at supper tonight?

"The future of our children. . .The sancity of . . . ah . . ." Uncle Julian blinked. He's coasting downhill and almost at the bottom, Nils thought. Uncle Julian sucked in a long breath. "We are here tonight," he said rapidly, "to meet the new schoolteacher."

Nils saw Katherine Duncan start and then control herself. He saw a surprised smile flicker across her face. Everyone in the room was looking at her. She turned to Carl, murmuring a question. Uncle Julian looked dreamily around the room, his thoughts a thousand miles or fifty years away. Mrs. Carlson patted Katherine Duncan's arm, "Well, now, dear, that is nice, isn't it?"

The time had come. Nils pushed his back away from the wall and walked to the front of the room.

"Uncle Julian has made quite a speech," he said genially. "But it seems like he come to the end of it. So I'll help him out. Folks, meet the new school-teacher." With a sweep of his big hand he indicated the young man who had been at his side. "Tommy Hutchins."

There was a moment of frozen immobility. It broke, and everyone swiveled to stare at the young man. Tommy Hutchins smiled nervously. Nils saw Katherine Duncan's white face, its primness shattered by disbelief. Carl put his hand on her arm, and spoke to her. Her mouth tightened, and she shook her head.

"What're you up to, Nils?" It was the voice of three-hundred-pound Agatha Tine and it was pitched as if she were calling the cows.

"Katherine, please let me take you out of here..."

Low as it was, Carl's plea carried across the room. But still the girl was shaking her head. Nils grinned and faced Agatha. "I'm seeing to it that the children of this Valley have a schoolteacher."

Faces turned questioningly to Katherine Duncan. Seconds passed, and still she didn't move. They gave her up and began to talk together.

Jeb Carlson got to his feet. "See here, Nils," he said awkwardly, "from all I heard so far people hereabouts are well enough satisfied with the teacher we already got."

Nils nodded. Young Tommy Hutchins was twitching at the back of the room, the color high in his face. Nils ignored him and said, "I'm glad to hear that. But I'm not sure Miss Duncan is as satisfied with us."

Katherine's head jerked up. For the first time Nils saw life come to her eyes. Jeb Carlson looked down at her, his face clearly puzzled. "Well, I. . ." he began, and sat down.

"Tommy, come up here and be introduced." Nils waved imperiously. The young man squeezed past the benches and faced the crowd.

"You all know Tommy," Nils said. "He's been around for a year. Tommy's got an extra fine education. Finished a year of high school in Port Angeles, he tells me. He's working at the ranch during the harvest but he'll be looking for a job after that."

Katherine Duncan's wide eyes were back on Nils' face. They looked black in her pale face. She's scared off, Nils thought, just as I knew she'd be.

"Being a man," Nils said deliberately, "Tommy is better fit for teaching, too. He don't look it but he can pick up a grizzly and hit a she-cougar over the head with it." Nils laughed. Several men echoed him, grinning at Tommy. Nils saw that Tommy was succeeding in meeting all eyes except those of the little schoolmarm. "So," Nils concluded, dropping the easygoing manner, "Mr. Hutchins will open the Gold Mountain school, the first Monday *after* the hops are picked."

The room was utterly still. Faces showed disagreement but no resistance. They don't like it, Nils thought, but they know who's paying, so as long as the teacher keeps still they don't even know how to protest. He felt disdain for their weakness. Pious and spineless, he thought. They were made to be pushed around.

Agatha stirred. "Well, if that's all there is to it, someone better go out front and give my horses the bad news that it's time they pulled me home." Grunting she got to her feet, rubbed her stomach and surveyed the group. "I will say this, though, before I go. If I was that little Miss Duncan, I'd be glad to leave a place where there wasn't one single mother or father that would get to their feet and speak for me."

"You talk too much, Agatha," Nils said. "If Miss Duncan had wanted to, she could have spoken for herself."

"I think I will!"

It was a weak voice, and not a very steady one. Nils wheeled around. Katherine Duncan was standing up, her back as stiff as an English general's. At the school she had cried, as a proud but angry child cries, bitter with shame at her own tears. But her eyes were dry now, and so big and bright they seemed to eat up her face. Nils was amused. Carl White put a high price on outside polish. What would he think of his sweetheart if she raised a ruckus?

"Miss Duncan?"

Nils knew she would ignore him. He grinned as she turned her back to him and faced the open-mouthed homesteaders.

"I have taught school in Gold Mountain for just one day," she said. "You are the parents of the children I taught. Is there any one of you who is dissatisfied with what I've done so far?"

The women shook their heads energetically. The men who owed Nils money or back rent or hayseed looked uncomfortably from the little teacher to Nils. Nils thought, how they wish they'd never come. Agatha Tine, upright as a new silo and just about as round, blurted out, "Dear, you done fine."

Nils leaned back on his heels and pushed his hands into his pockets. It was time to take the meeting back into his own hands. "I'm a parent," he said softly, "and I ain't satisfied."

Katherine looked at him squarely. "The parent of one child. But Mrs. Anderson is here, and she has three children in school. Here is Mrs. Carlson and Mrs. Smith, with nine school children between them."

Nils nodded. You can never tell about the little ones, he thought admiringly. "These Kansas farmers believe in planting often."

He watched her face for the color he knew would come to it. Little Miss Prissy, he thought, wanting to laugh out loud. Go ahead and talk. Everyone in the room but you knows how useless it is.

"I think the majority should decide."

From out of his daydream old Uncle Julian echoed fuzzily, "The majority . . . yes, The majority . . ."

Mrs. Carlson said, "She's doing fine. She should stay." ·

Carl pulled on Katherine's sleeve. "There is really no use. . ."

Nils felt a flash of irriation at the way Carl's hand fell so possessively on the teacher's arm. "You're right, Carl," he said curtly. "You always know when to give up."

Carl's eyes darkened. "This is a ridiculous meeting, Nils."

"You're right again," Nils snapped. He had expected to enjoy the evening, and except for Carl's presence, he had. "Let's end it." And he brought his fist down on the counter.

"Just a minute."

The teacher had pulled free of Carl's anxious grasp. She was standing with her arms across her breast, like a farm woman facing up to the mortgage owner.

"You called these people together, Mr.

Bengston," she said. "Was it some kind of a joke, or do they have something to say about who their teacher is to be?"

Nils' annoyance at Carl lingered. "I'm paying the teacher," he said flatly, "and I never buy anything I don't want."

Katherine gasped. Instantly Nils felt better. Looking at her white face and the funny, stubborn set to her jaw, he even felt like laughing. Surely she'd had enough. Now she can leave in a huff, all bristling with righteousness and hurt feelings, and Carl will be right there to tell her she was right. And to kiss that childlike mouth of hers. "Well?" he asked irritably.

"Well, well?" Uncle Julian muttered, peering toward the door as if he thought it might have been moved since he last walked through.

Katherine breathed deeply. "Mr. Bengston, I need the job."

Nils shrugged. "And so," with a gesture of the thumb over his shoulder, "does Mr. Tommy Hutchins."

"It was my understanding that I was to receive fifty dollars a month, for every month the school was open."

Nils grinned. "Have you figured out what I owe you for today?"

Her eyes sparked but she continued levelly. "I assume Mr. Hutchins has been promised the same sum."

"He's worth it."

"But you would like to spend less for—for a schoolteacher." Katherine turned to address everyone in the room. "*I* will do an equal amount of work for forty-five dollars a month."

Like exclamations rippled across the crowd. Uncle Julian murmured. "When I was a boy in western Pennsylvania. . ." Tommy Hutchins said, "Look, Nils, I thought you said this afternoon that the thing would be all settled before we came."

Nils grinned mightily. This wasn't what he had planned but this was good. "It was, Tom, it was. Only thing is, that girl has gone and unsettled it." He stepped aside and with one big hand pushed Tommy Hutchins forward. "You're the one who wants the job," he said, enjoying himself thoroughly. "Go ahead and bid for it."

The faces moved curiously from Katherine to Tommy Hutchins. "In western Pennsylvania," Uncle Julian began chasing the shadow of an old memory.

Tommy Hutchins pulled himself up. "I would teach for forty-two fifty if I got room and board with it."

"Forty dollars a month," Katherine flashed, so quickly the heads hadn't turned her way, "and room and board."

Tommy Hutchins looked at Nils. Nils shrugged, keeping his eye on Katherine. "Well," he said to Tommy out of the corner of his mouth, "what are you going to say now?"

Mrs. Carlson pulled Katherine down and whispered in her ear. Tommy opened his mouth to speak, but Katherine spoke first. "Forty without board and room," she said quickly. "I'll work for the board at Carlson's."

Tommy Hutchins stammered, "Thirty-eight dollars a month, but that's only because I need a job."

"So do I!" Katherine retorted. "Thirty-seven dollars and fifty cents!"

Tommy looked to Nils, but Nils' face was blank. The Carlsons and Smiths and Andersons were whispering and taking no pains to hide their smiles.

Agatha was patting her stomach as if she'd just enjoyed an entire roast grouse. One of the loggers was
chewing hard and looking about uneasily for a place
to spit. Tommy tapped Nils' arm. Nils ignored it,
studying the ceiling.

Katherine's voice was louder now. Like a man who
runs the last few steps up the mountain, for fear he
won't get to the top, Nils thought. "Am I to understand," she said, "that I am to be the teacher at Gold
Mountain?"

Tommy looked sullenly at Nils. Nils grinned.
"Well, is she, Tommy?"

"I guess she is. . ."

The voices broke loose. Everyone pushed to his
feet. A bench fell backward and hit the floor with a
splintering crash. Some walked out without a word to
anyone, still wondering what they had come for.
Others collected in a friendly group around
Katherine and one by one shook her hand. At the
door they turned back.

To see how I'm taking it, Nils thought, and the
laughter that had been begging for release all through
the meeting poured from his throat. Hands in pockets, he laughed until the last shocked face had
turned away and the last good farmer's wife had
pulled down her bonnet and departed. Then he
turned to Tommy Hutchins.

"Man," he exclaimed, "you let her take your job
away for fifty cents a month."

Tommy said stiffly, "I din't like the way things
were going."

"Neither did I!" and he laughed some more.

Tommy hurried out of the empty store. Nils
beckoned to Uncle Julian. "Let's go home, old
man."

Uncle Julian nodded. "That's the first time I ever

saw you let someone else take things out of your hands.''

''You have your sharp spells, don't you?'' Nils grinned. The old man often sensed the difference between what Nils was saying and what he was thinking. Ordinarily, Nils considered this faculty to be a damned nuisance. Tonight the little redheaded school teacher's spunk had put him in such a good mood that he didn't care what the old man made of it. All the while Teacher had been slugging it out, toe to toe, with that chicken-hearted Tommy Hutchins, Nils had been thinking—By God, we're alike, Katherine Duncan! You're half my size. I could pick you up and toss you over the cow barn. But ounce for ounce, you're as much of a fighter as I am. Once more Nils' enjoyment of the scene took over. ''Listen, old man,'' he said between bursts of laughter. ''I could have sent her packing. Maybe someday I will.''

''Heh, heh. . .'' Julian wheezed when he laughed, making a sound like a child pumping a broken reed organ. ''But you didn't.''

Still laughing, Nils strode to the door and out into the dark street where his horse was waiting patiently at the hitching post. A wagon was just leaving, the Carlsons' wagon, with that damned Carl White holding the reins and Teacher sitting beside him. Nils watched them until the night swallowed them up.

Carl and his sweetheart, he thought peevishly, and his good mood broke into a thousand pieces. A hundred to one he won't kiss her without asking her first. Lovemaking by the rule book. With Carl for a husband she'll never know what it is to be weakened, and lost, and helpless with love. . .

Nils flung himself into the saddle and turned down the dark trail toward the ranch. Hard as he rode and as angrily as he tried to erase the image from his mind, he could not black out the mental picture of Carl holding Katherine in his arms, of Carl with his mouth against Katherine's, of Carl's hand searching Katherine's body.

CHAPTER FIVE

i

OLD UNCLE JULIAN THOUGHT he knew how the little schoolteacher felt. Only children and old people see that Nils is kind. And God knows you have to love him to understand his weaknesses. He sighed. The sun filled the barnyard and the old rocking chair was as comfortable as a bed. He would go to sleep presently with the calls of the hop-pickers—"Ticket! Ticket!"—coming to him from the distant field like occasional bursts of an old familiar song.

"Ticket!" the Indians called when their reed baskets were filled to the top. Down the row the white field bosses would come, carrying on their shoulders the slanting wood trough with the boards which stuck out as handles at both ends. A ticket for a full box, to be cashed in at the end of the day for two big, round silver dollars—that was what they worked for: "Ticket. . .ticket. . ." Indians called in high, nasal voices. Pick fast so they don't settle and pack them lightly in the box—the Siwash know the tricks of it, Uncle Julian thought with a smile. Chinese pickers packed the hops down neatly—and starved.

"Ticket. . ." The old man closed his eyes against the sun, still smiling. The crop is free of the hop louse and the price is holding up. Nils is getting rich today. I wonder how many of the little teacher's pupils are out there helping him do it?

It had been amusing, that town meeting the night

before, though Uncle Julian couldn't quite remember why. He had a general feeling that several very funny things had been said and occasionally they came back to him. But he couldn't force himself to catch them firmly, at least not in a rocking chair in the sunshine right after a good meal. Anyway he couldn't remember things any more, not the things that happened today or yesterday. Today's events appeared before him briefly, and retreated, mocking him from a safe distance. His mind felt tired.

The new teacher—that was it, of course. Gold Mountain was a fine spot for a girl her age, and one with such a scaredy look in her eyes. How could such a girl handle a pupil like the Greene boy?

Uncle Julian sighed again. He enjoyed sighing, for the act was a voice of nostalgia. It was a physical bridge to the days an old man can only sigh over, the days he could remember so sharply that he could smell and feel and hear the odors and touch and sound that went with them. Teachers, he thought, are getting to be women. It was hard to convince himself that it really mattered, one way or the other, what would happen to the little green-eyed Duncan, she being a woman. There were always women and there was always trouble. In his seventy-two years of ricocheting from one to the other, old Uncle Julian had even ceased to distinguish between the plain ones and the pretty ones, for whom in earlier years the agony had seemed worthwhile.

A teacher was a teacher. You have to have them, Uncle Julian supposed, as soon as your country begins to fill up with farmers. Farmers don't travel light, carrying little more than a gun and marrying the women at hand. Farmers marry white women and white women want their children to better themselves. It had been that way in western Pennsylvania, where he was born. It had been that way in Ohio, where he was married. And now, with the new century only sixteen years away, it was changing to be that way even in the Washington Territory.

Uncle Julian didn't resent it, as some of the others did. He didn't go shouting that the hunting was no good any more and the good land was grabbed off and there were getting to be too many laws. He didn't resent anything any more, short of having someone steal his gun or call him a liar. He'd had eight years of schooling himself, sixty-odd years before in western Pennsylvania, and he didn't really agree with Nils, even if Nils was the boss of Gold Mountain, that you don't teach school unless you've failed at everything else and you don't go to school unless you're too lazy for anything else. Nils' mind was young and his fist was quick but an old man had his own thoughts. Who had told him to write to this new teacher, anyway, if it wasn't Nils himself?

Of course, Julian knew, Nils was full of soft spots when it came to getting something for his daughter Julie. Despising schoolteachers on the one hand and on the other going out looking for one to teach Julie—that was Nils. That had been Nils, for years.

"Why you so set on teaching her to read?" that lardhead Tom Stump had asked Nils. "Ain't she half-breed?"

Uncle Julian, for all his habit of not remembering, had no trouble recalling what Nils had done to Tom. Beat him to sleep, and left him all bloody for his wife to pick up and drag home.

There had been other "town meetings" besides the one the night before. If Nils sometimes let the Carlsons and Hansons and Smiths have the first word, he always had the last one. Or had until last night, when that little girl with the red hair on top of her head got up to say her piece. Uncle Julian chuckled. Tom Hutchins was a weakling, and Nils had even less use for weaklings than he did for schoolteachers. Others had been surprised that Nils let the school-marm beat down the man he'd picked, but then, others didn't half know Nils, for lack of trying. Nils liked strength wherever he found it. He admired temper, though he himself was so strong he didn't need it—he bent things to his way without it. Some might think he had failed at the town meeting... Julian chuckled softly. Nils didn't know failure. Unless...The old man squinted thoughtfully. Unless there was failure in the end of his marriage to Mary.

For Mary had left him again, and this time old Indian Doc brought word from the Indian camp that she wouldn't return. Some sense of his own failure had kept Nils from going after her, Julian judged. He hadn't loved her as he once thought he would—that was Nils' failure, and he didn't try to deny it by searching Mary out and forcing her to come back. There was honesty in doing nothing, and there had been honesty in Mary's leaving without a word to her daughter Julie, as if the child had always belonged only to her father.

"Will you stay here?" Uncle Julian had heard Nils ask, "or will you go to your mother?"

The little girl's eyes begged her father for the right answer.

"I'll get," Uncle Julian had murmured. "Leave you two to talk it out."

Nils' big hand pushed Julian back into his chair. "Stay here," he said gruffly. "Keep me from saying the wrong thing."

Julie whispered at last, "Maybe she'll come back?"

"It don't look like it, this time." Nils squatted on

his heels so as to look into her face. "Julie, baby, I know how I feel about you. I got to know how *you* feel. I can take you to Mama. What do you want to do?"

They wouldn't believe it, Uncle Julian had thought at the time, those people who are afraid of Nils. They wouldn't admit that Nils Bengston, who takes what he wants, would have the conscience to give up what he loves most.

Julie's face was only an inch from her father's. Solemnly, she said, "She doesn't seem like my mother any more."

Nils straightened up slowly. "All right, Julie. We'll stay here together." He turned to Uncle Julian. "No need to tell the whole Valley Mary's gone." And later, after Nils had taken out separation papers at the courthouse in Seattle, he warned Uncle Julian all over again to keep his private affairs, and Julie's private affairs, to himself.

"I'm no talker," the old man had snapped the day Nils admitted that Mary had left for good. Uncle Julian would have said a good deal more, but just then Julie reached up for her father's hand. Nils swung her up into a tight, silent embrace, and his face, looking blindly toward Julian over the little girl's shoulder, was so shattered by defeat—or was it loneliness?—that Julian's retort dried up in his throat. Nils was a giant of a man, and meant to be strong. If he ever goes down, Uncle Julian had reflected, I hope I'm far away from the sight and sound of it. Uncle Julian was a small man. Perhaps that was the reason why, when he first saw Nils, he had been more impressed by his size than by anything else. Sixty years of living had taken Julian from Pennsylvania to Ohio to Utah to California to Oregon City to Seattle. In those years, when the world was opening

up for people who got there first, he had never been
the first at anything, but he'd been there second often
enough to try his hand at a good many occupations
and to live well. In Seattle he had an old man's job at
the bakery, and a little house and a plump wife, both
of which were as comfortable and unbeautiful as old
shoes. Julian wasn't proud of anything except that he
had reached the age when he was no longer expected
to do anything first or even well.

He met Nils Bengston in a market decorated with
the sign, "Stokes, Grady, and Bengston. Meats.
Founded 1869." Stokes, a wiry little man with bright
black eyes, was wrapping up a piece of beef for him
when the back door slammed open against the wall.

"Take it easy, Nils," Stokes said without looking
up. "It took a dollar's worth of hardware to fix that
door the last time you broke it."

A silver dollar clanked onto the marble counter
and rolled to fall against the meat. "There's your
money, Jake," a big voice said, "but isn't that the
second time you've collected a dollar for fifty cents
worth of hardware?"

Jake Stokes grinned wryly. "From you, Nils? Collect twice from you?"

Julian had really looked at Nils then. Nils was big.
He carried himself as if he knew how big he was, but
at the same time as if he'd never had to stoop for
anyone where he came from.

"My partner," Stokes said briefly, pushing the
silver dollar aside with the back of his hand.
"Bengston."

Julian nodded.

Nils faced him squarely. "Well," he demanded,
"what's yours?"

Julian wondered why he felt forced to answer.
After all, there had been nothing out of the way about

the question. I'm twenty-five years older than you are, Julian had an impulse to say, as if that would establish his right to answer Nils or not to answer him. But he replied, "Julian Sparks," adding, a little pettishly, "though you won't remember it."

"Glad to meet you, Mr. Sparks," Nils said, surprising him with his deference. They shook hands.

Julian picked up his package of meat. "You live in Seattle?"

"Snoqualmie Valley. Ever heard of it?"

Julian shrugged. "I might have."

Stokes laughed. "You see, Nils?"

Nils' grin didn't entirely vanish, but his face seemed to harden. "That's all right. I don't want too many getting interested until I can see a little clearer what's in the bottom of the pan. Well, everything's cleaned up so I'm heading back."

"Good-bye, Nils."

Nils waved his hand. "Good-bye, old-timer," he said, "when you get tired of buying your meat in somebody else's butcher shop, come out to the Valley." And the door slammed behind him.

Old-timer. That had hit Julian hard. Fifty-eight years old and a big Swede from the mountains makes me old with the wave of his hand. "Anything ever happen to trim that fellow down a little?"

"Not yet," Stokes said dryly. "And with his brains and muscle and luck, maybe it never will. That guy," he added slowly "*might* end up the richest man in the Territory."

And he called me old, Julian thought irritably.

ii

During the next five years Julian had been reminded

occasionally of Nils and the Snoqualmie Valley, by a word now and again from Stokes. "Nils was asking," Stokes had said once, "if you was an educated man."

"Now why," Julian exclaimed, "did he want to know that?"

Stokes shrugged. "If he asked, he had a reason."

Then Julian had been in the post office one day, sending a letter from his wife Kate to her sister back east, when a long, thin man with a wide-brimmed hat pulled down hard over his ears strode past, carrying a leather pouch by a strap over one shoulder.

"Headed for Snoqualmie," the postmaster volunteered. "Goes by horse to Black River, Squak prairie, then on to Snoqualmie. Been carrying the mail out that way for almost three years now."

"They get mail out there, eh," Julian had mused, remembering with a tinge of malice how Nils Bengston hadn't wanted too many people in the Valley. "Good number must have settled down there since I last heard about it."

The postmaster smiled. "There's not a settler between Cedar River and Squak," he said, "Nor between Squak and Snoqualmie. You could carry all the mail in your pants pocket, if the government would allow it."

"How many folks are there?" Julian insisted.

The postmaster narrowed his eyes thoughtfully. "Whites, you mean?"

Julian nodded.

"Twenty-five, thirty. That is, both in Squak Valley and Snoqualmie Valley, put together."

What was that fellow Bengston doing these days? Julian had wondered. But he hadn't wondered long. In two minutes he was thinking instead that Kate had baked a wild blackberry pie that afternoon. Kate was a good wife. Kate, and old age, had brought him peace.

And then only a few months later Kate died.

She died quietly, not ailing at all beforehand. "Julian, would you get me a glass of water?" she had asked him, and he had been so surprised by the request that he did it instantly, with a shiver of premonition making his hand tremble as he lifted the dipper and tried to carry it across the room without spilling too much on the floor.

She tried to drink, gasped and fell forward. He wasn't sure how long she lived. Maybe a few minutes, maybe an hour. After he had carried her to the bed and covered her with the old crazy quilt, he stood looking at her, stunned into helplessness. It hadn't been original, Julian knew, to get drunk. Hadn't men always met the challenge of disaster that way, if they were lucky enough to have the price? An hour after Kate was buried, Julian was on the waterfront, and as far as he ever knew he stayed there until Nils found him.

Nils came to life like the brightest figure in a delirium. He had known him instantly, even known his name. But looking up, the face seemed to ripple like lake water under a gust of wind, and the mouth moved grotesquely, without speaking. Julian kept murmuring, "Where's Kate?" And then the warm, quivering blackness closed in.

When he awoke he was in a hotel room, and Nils was with him.

"I got drunk," he said weakly.

"You're more than that. You're sick," Nils said. "Lie down."

He had awakened many more times. Not out of a

drunken stupor, but into those brief moments of clarity which break through the heat of fever. Sometimes Nils was there, sometimes he wasn't. Nils was a compassionate giant, bringing cold water, smoothing the covers. Even in delirium Julian had felt surprise at Nils' kindness.

In their first conversation, Nils said, "You better come out with me to the Valley."

Julian shook his head weakly. "I've got a house in Seattle."

"You want to go back to it?"

Of course he didn't want to. He groped for another reason. "I've got a job. In the bakery."

"A job, a job. . ." Nils' blue eyes narrowed disdainfully. "I'll give you a job."

And so Julian had exposed the bottom reason, the one he hadn't wanted to dig down to. "Young man," he said, "young man, I've done my part of breaking ground and neighboring with the Indians and proving claims. You aren't the kind to figure anyone else has ever done anything, but maybe I've done more than you will ever do. And I'm not trying to pioneer any more. I'm sixty-three years old, and I'm tired." He closed his eyes and pretended to go to sleep.

But of course he had gone with Nils. It was nine years since the summer day he had tied his old saddlebags on the back of one of Nils' horses and followed him across the hills to the Valley. He'd been too sick and confused, right up to then, to wonder why Nils bothered to take him along. For there had been a reason. Nils had definitely offered him work, for all his self-sufficiency implying that he needed him.

On one of their stops Julian had asked him why. "What do you need with an old man like me? What do you figure I'll do worth paying for?"

''There are going to be accounts to keep, letters to write. You've had education. You talked like it. And you're the kind I can trust.''

Or the kind you can bend around your finger? Julian thought, and remembering Nils' compassion, felt ashamed of himself. Heaven knows, Nils had saved his life. ''I don't need to get paid,'' he said impulsively, ''as long as I have a place to sleep and enough to eat.''

''You'll get paid,'' Nils said, adding flatly, ''just what you're worth.''

Julian snorted. It was all right with him if this ambitious young man had no use for gratitude. That would ease the pain of owing him something. ''You don't say,'' he chuckled. ''And how do you figure I'll be worth anything?''

In nine years in the Valley Julian could remember only that one occasion in which Nils had seemed to say something he didn't want to say. ''I might as well tell you,'' Nils replied. He forced himself to look straight at Julian, but his eyes showed what it cost him. ''You went to school didn't you? You can read and write and keep figures?''

Julian nodded. ''You asked me that a couple of times before. Like I said, yes, I done some of it.''

''I can't read or write.'' And then Nils jumped onto his horse and rode through the timber as if a pack of wolves were upon him, leaving Julian to mount and follow as best he could.

iv

Uncle Julian laughed softly. For nine years he had written Nils' letters and read Nils' newspapers, a barricade between Nils and the chasm of his own ignorance. The people to whom it mattered had never discovered that the big man of the Valley could neither read nor write. Those who knew were illiterate themselves and, except for Agatha Tine, put so little value on education that it would never strike them to miss it in Nils. But Nils missed it. Strange, Uncle Julian thought, and laughed again. The teachers we've had in Gold Mountain have never known. Maybe they haven't lasted long enough to guess.

Three months—that was a fair average, the old man reflected. The last one, now, the one before this little Scotch-English girl from Seattle. Uncle Julian had put her on the riverboat at Black River himself. He could still see her, teetering up the gangplank with a wicker suitcase in one hand, her bonnet askew over one big red ear, and with the other hand threatening him with an umbrella. She'd scolded him every step of the way, and he the one who had taken her down the hill on the back of his horse. A face like a weasel with a bellyache, the old man thought contentedly—that was Miss Clara Beane. God was good to help them get rid of her.

God, the Greene boys and the old Indian graveyard. Bless those idiot Greenes for thinking of that.

It was an old graveyard, which some earlier generation of Snoqualmies had placed close to the river. Searching for a high spot, they had stretched out the bodies of their dead in the tops of the cottonwood trees. To one of them, perhaps one of their finest braves, they had given special honor. He had been carefully placed in his cedar canoe, bolt upright, staring bravely ahead, with a long musket braced to lie across his lap. It hadn't been hard for the Greene boys, and maybe some of the others, to figure out that if they hid in the graveyard and made the right sounds at the right times, Teacher Beane would be scared out of her leggings when she walked past.

Julian had laughed when he heard about it. In fact he wasn't sure that he hadn't made the mistake of laughing in front of Clara Beane. But what matter, Julian thought. There's been eight or nine school-teachers in the Valley already and none of them ever lasted. And none of them will, as long as Nils is the power here and Nils put so little value on learning.

There was the teacher who claimed he had been to high school. Nils' daughter was six then, and Nils had hired him on the spot. Julie and the three little Wright children, whose home was the schoolhouse now, and a couple of little Indian boys, who were Julie's cousins on her mother's side, were in that first class. School was held in the back of the Gold Mountain trading post. That teacher lasted three weeks, Julian recalled. At the end of that time the pupils got up and walked out.

Little Julie had led them straight to Nils. In a solemn group they approached him, Julie in the fore.

"That teacher," Julie explained, "told us zero times two makes two and zero times three makes three and zero times anything makes something."

Nils had hesitated. Being puzzled, he laughed. Just as suddenly, he grew angry. "See what I mean about those schoolteachers?" he had shouted at Julian. "How stupid can you get when you're educated? I know better than that and he's taking my money. Sixty dollars a month because he went to high school. Who talked me into getting a schoolteacher, anyway?"

Of course no one had. It had been Nils' idea and as

they both knew there would have been no school-teacher if it hadn't been. Julian shrugged. "Send him away."

"*Send* him! Don't you suppose he'll have sense enough to be gone when I get there?"

He had. In fact, as Julian remembered vividly, Nils had never caught up with him though he'd saddled up and ridden all the way to Squak prairie. "If anyone ever talks schoolteacher to me again," Nils said later, "I'll chase him up Old Hi and break his head over the point of it."

But the next year there had been another teacher in Gold Mountain. Perhaps Nils had consented because some of the other settlers had children and wanted schooling for them, or perhaps because Julie had asked. The new teacher had stayed until the morning he took a stick to little Jimmy Wing, one of Julie's cousins. Teacher had hardly touched Jimmy when Julie and the six or seven other girls in the school attacked. They scratched his face, pulled his hair, pushed him over and took off his shoes and pants. Then they hit him with the shoes until both eyes were blackened and he was cut and bruised in a dozen other places. No one had to ask that teacher to leave the Valley. Like Clara Beane, he had boarded the *Viking* at Black River the first time she touched land.

Julie came home from school that last day with a vest button proudly clutched in one hand. Solemnly she handed it to Nils. Julian watched Nils laugh until he cried.

Uncle Julian settled his hands comfortably about his stomach. His mind whispered that it was time to go to sleep. Yes, when this little teacher left, they'd have to look for a man teacher. A man, maybe, who could stand up to Nils. Not an old man, like himself, or a weak one, like that youngster Tommy Hutchins.

I drove Miss Clara Beane to the riverboat myself, the old man thought wistfully. And she shook her umbrella at me. I wonder who will make the ride with Miss Katherine Duncan. He smiled, because he had suddenly remembered her name. I can remember, he thought, at times. His head fell forward. His mouth drooped open with the first gentle snore.

In the hop field, an Indian called, "Ticket! Ticket!"

CHAPTER SIX

i

KATHERINE HAD TAUGHT school in Gold Mountain for only six weeks when she saw the wisdom of Uncle Julian's advice to bring an umbrella, if she had one. The golden fall ended with the cry of the last hop-picker. It began to rain.

There was the persistent, quiet rain, which dripped musically into the rain barrels at the corners of the cabin. There was the furious rain, whipped to lashing gusts by winds which seemed to come from every direction. Wind dashed the lowering clouds against the mountains, and they broke into rain. Wind came down the Pass, carrying the rain with it. Some days it did not seem to rain, but the clouds would settle so deep into the Valley that mist dampened the clothing and beaded itself along the eyebrows and hair.

Katherine kept the school open, though so few children had come during hop season that it was hard to say whether she or Nils had won. Agatha's boy Tommy hadn't missed a day, nor had Julie Bengston. The Carlson children had been as faithful as they could, but even they had picked hops for two weeks.

"I'm real sorry, teacher," Faith Carlson said. "No one wants the school open more than me and Jeb. Most of all I hate to have the children pick hops because it's one more time we let Nils Bengston have his way. But we've got to have a little hard money set aside for the winter." Like an Indian family, all the

Carlsons except five-year-old Johnny had worked during the harvest.

Johnny had cried because he couldn't go along with the others. It was Hiram, the seven-year-old, who quieted him. "Listen, John," he said soberly. "I've got to pick hops but you get to go to school. While I'm gone you can be the boss of the school in my place."

"The boss?" Johnny squeaked, the tears drying as if they had never been.

"See?" Hiram exclaimed. "See my little brother happying out his cheeks?"

For a few hours the pickers were working the rows so close to the schoolhouse that their calls broke into the lessons. Three of the Stump children appeared suddenly at the open window. Their pale faces lined up on the sill, like tomatoes set out to ripen. Katherine smiled at them. They stared in silence. Suddenly a woman's voice shrilled, "Where you kids at?"

"We'd ruther be in school," the biggest child whispered, and the three dropped from sight and scampered back into the field.

Katherine had steeled herself against trouble with Julie Bengston. But there was none. The little girl was distant but attentive. Her mother had gone off and left her for good, the settlers were whispering, though Katherine knew none of them dared discuss it openly with Nils. It served him right, they said vaguely, as if Mary's leaving Nils were his just punishment for refusing to leave her, as they had so often advised him to do. Katherine suffered during such conversations, for she could not think of Nils without antagonism so uncontrollable that the walls of her comfortable little world were wrecked by violence and she was left exposed and helpless. She

didn't want to think about Nils at all, or even about
Carl White, for thoughts of him were disturbing in
another way. She loved and admired him, but when
he sent word that he would have to miss a few of the
Viking's trips into the Valley she had been light-
headed with relief. Carl would raise the question of
her leaving the Valley, and for some reason she didn't
want to be forced to answer it. She had begun a job;
she wanted to finish it. She wanted to be Teacher, and
only Teacher, to let hard work build such a high
enclosure that her feelings about Nils or Carl or
anything else would be shut out completely.

Katherine had told herself that her promise to
build a real school in two years was spoken in anger
and no one, least of all Nils Bengston, would take it
seriously. Building a new school was a goal for the
teacher who was in the Valley to stay. Not just for the
winter. Not for only a few months, or a year, or a
year and a half until Carl White took her back to
Seattle for their wedding.

But there were lesser goals, and these Katherine
allowed herself to think upon, like a woman who has
refused the cake but reaches for tiny flakes of frost-
ing. First, she had won over Nils and held the job.
She had kept the school open. Next, the fireplace, so
that school would be possible in cold weather. The
bigger boys had rebuilt it in a day and chopped and
stacked two months' firewood.

With these things done, Katherine began to make a
list of accomplishments to come. Not, she promised
herself, because she planned to stay forever. To
prove it she headed the list "School year of 1884-
85." This notebook was at the Carlson home, tucked
under the rafter above her head. When the work was
done at night she sometimes sat alone at the long
table, her back to the dying fire and a bit of candle

melting slowly in a cup in front of her. It was a time to write a little, to think a great deal. She went to bed when the fire was out and the cold began to creep into her fingers.

Books—those were at the top of the list for "School year of 1884-85." With the schoolroom filled once more after hop-picking, she talked to the children about the books they might have at home.

"We ain't got a book," the oldest Stump child replied, flushing miserably.

"Lots of people ain't!" Hiram Carlson offered loyally.

"Haven't," Katherine corrected.

"Haven't," Hiram echoed.

Little John nodded wisely. "Lotsa people ain't got what haven't."

But when the children explored the forgotten corners of their homestead shacks and lean-tos, they found books, and they carried them to school as proudly as yearling hunters dragging home their first venison. There were five Bibles, all with birth and wedding and death dates written in the front. "Containing the Old and New Testaments; translated out of the Original Tongues; and with the former translations diligently compared and revised"—such was the title of one of them, but under it, in a clear round hand, was written: "Mary Anderson. Born at Fort Lincoln on July the 14th, 1878. Returned to God August the first, 1878. We held services on the trail in Montana territory."

On the shelf next to the Bibles was *The French Student's Companion* by a professor in the Albany Female Academy. There was a first reader, a history book, a copy of the journals of Lewis and Clark. Then a book called *Chauncey Judd: or, The Stolen Boy. A story of the Revolution*. It was rain-spotted but the bold figure of a minuteman, one hand under his coat and the other ready at his musket, still embellished the cover. *Golden Thoughts in Pen and Pencil*—this one contained two petunias, pressed and dried so long ago that they crumbled into dust when Katherine opened the book. Down the row a large volume in gold-embossed leather stood out from the rest. *Poetical Quotations, from Chaucer to Tennyson,* Katherine read, "published in Philadelphia in 1876." This last had come from Tommy Tine, carried to school in a careful wrapping of washed gunny sack. Yet Tommy had never been to school before and fat, good-natured Agatha could neither read nor write. To whom had this elegant book belonged, published in a far-distant eastern city only eight years before? How little, Katherine thought wistfully, how very little any of us here know about each other.

* * * *

The same thought struck her one afternoon after school, when the children had left and she sat down at the rough hewn cedar table that was Teacher's desk and began to outline lessons for the next day. A half dozen books were stacked at her elbow, the latest donations for the school, and she hadn't gone through them. She picked up the one on top. A small, thin book in faded green binding with stains on every yellowed page. The gold lettering on the cover was almost washed away, but she made out *Laus Veneris, and Other Poems,* by Algernon Charles Swinburne.

She opened it carefully, curious as to who had owned such a book. Across from the title page, a name was written in elegant script, faint but still legible:

Property of Julian Webster Sparks
November 17, 1853

Old Uncle Julian, who mumbled and forgot what he had said ten minutes earlier! The old man had been young, he had read poetry, and loved it enough to treasure this little volume for more than thirty years. What disasters and disappointments had struck Julian Sparks since the day he had written his name on the fly leaf? Storm, flood—at least that judging by the weather-beaten and watersoaked condition of the book. Musing, Katherine turned the pages, and began to read.

She sat for a long time, swept up by the beauty and the rhythm. Only half conscious of what she was doing, she began to read aloud:

"There will no man do for your sake, I think
What I would have done for the least word said.
I had wrung life dry for your lips to drink,
Broken it up for your daily bread."

A faint sound, a movement glimpsed out of the corner of her eye. . .Startled, Katherine looked up. Nils Bengston was standing at the open door.

She blushed like a guilty child, closed the book quickly and stood up. "Uncle Julian gave the school a book of poetry. I've been reading it."

Nils Bengston nodded slowly. "I know."

Katherine thought nervously, what new complaint about the schoolteacher will he make of this—

Teacher sitting all by herself reading a love poem out loud?

"Uncle Julian's, eh. . ."

The thoughtful tone of voice was so out of character in a man Katherine thought of as a rude and laughing blond giant that she looked up into his face with frank curiosity. "Yes," she said. "Uncle Julian's. Does that surprise you?"

"I don't surprise easy," Nils said quietly. "You never know about people."

Katherine could not help smiling. "That's exactly what I was thinking earlier today. Word for word. You never do know about people, do you?"

For a moment a sense of peacefulness filled the room, as warm as the sunlight pouring through the open window. A brief and totally unexpected moment, in which Nils spoke softly and there was a trace of sadness in his eyes. And then it was gone, and Nils, the domineering boss of Gold Mountain, the man too big to be challenged, was towering over her, measuring her, weighing her, as if she were a calf at an auction and he had just decided not to make a bid.

In spite of the grim mouth and the veiled expression in his blue eyes, Katherine felt drawn to him. There was tension between them, a current of feeling she could not identify. Hostility? Anger? She didn't know, but it held her as surely as if she had been hypnotized.

Nils broke the spell. With a gesture at the book of poems, he said, "Go on reading." It was a command. Having issued it, he whirled around and disappeared through the open door.

Katherine looked at the book, as if the last thing she expected to see in her hand was Uncle Julian's book of poems. She dropped it on the desk and ran to the door.

Nils Bengston was already in the saddle. "Mr. Bengston!" she called. "What was it you wanted?"

With a mighty shrug, he answered, "Nothing. Just riding by." With that he slapped the reins and began to ride away.

"But Mr. Bengston. . ."

He flung an answer over his shoulder but she couldn't hear it. Some sort of complaint, Katherine thought angrily as she went back into the schoolroom. Nils Bengston would never "just ride by." Nils Bengston does nothing for no good reason.

She picked up the little waterstained book and tried to read. It was no use. With every beautiful image, with every note of love, she kept seeing Nils Bengston's face in that brief moment when it was suffused with sadness. How long had he been standing there? How much had he heard? "I had wrung life dry for your lips to drink. . ." She closed the book, put it aside, and forced her attention back to the chore of preparing lessons for the next day.

* * * *

Thus the Gold Mountain school had acquired a shelf of books, however useless some of them might seem to be when the job was to teach the alphabet to a clutch of little Swedes and an Indian girl. Next on

the list Katherine had written "School supplies."
She ordered them from Seattle, and when the day
came that they would arrive on the *Viking* Katherine
saddled her pony and rode down the valley to get
them. There would be pencils and tablets and grammars and spelling tablets, but also there would be a
baseball and bat.

It was a long ride in the rain, and Katherine was
wet through by the time she was halfway back to Black
River. But thinking of the order, she smiled happily.
The grammars and tablets were for all the good little
children, the Carlsons and Nelsons and Andersons
and the rest. But the baseball and bat were for the bad
boy, Emil Greene.

They had told her that if the Greene boys came at
all, they wouldn't stay in school longer than a week.
Emil alone had come, but Emil had stayed.

"I ain't coming to school no longer," he had told
her almost every afternoon.

Each time she had agreed, "Good-bye then,
Emil."

"You can't make me come to school. "I'm sixteen," he added after school one day.

"I couldn't make you come to school if you were
only six," she replied steadily.

"Well, then," he muttered.

"Well, then, good-bye, Emil."

He hesitated, looking down at her as if he were
trying to make up his mind whether or not to break
her in two. Katherine forced herself to smile.

Emil growled, "I guess you didn't hear about me."

Katherine's heart jumped. For a moment panic
won out and she stared at him dumbly.

"About all the things I done," he said louder, stepping toward her.

"Can you handle a shingle bolt?" Katherine

asked. It was a wild stab but it reached him.

Emil stared at her. "Sure! Sure I can. Ask 'em over at the mill. Ask them there what kind of a shingle weaver I was this summer. They'll all tell you."

"You do look strong," Katherine said quietly. "Well, good-bye, Emil," and she turned and walked back into the schoolhouse. Emil, somewhat subdued, had been in school as usual the next morning.

She had been proud too soon of conquering the bad boy. The first morning she laid a fire in the new hearth, smoke poured back down the chimney, filling the cabin and setting the children to coughing. Tears in her eyes, Katherine rushed to open the door. Someone was laughing loudly. Even in her flurry Katherine identified the voice as that of Emil Greene.

She lined the children up in the schoolyard, in rows just like those they kept at their benches inside.

"She's got to close the school, she's got to close the school. . ." That was Emil Greene's hoarse whisper from the back row. The others, still blinking with smoke, watched their teacher dutifully.

"Someone has stuffed something up the chimney," Katherine said matter-of-factly. "Is there anyone here strong enough to climb on the roof and pull out whatever it is?"

Levi Barker, one of the older boys, raised his hand. Emil Greene stared resentfully at Levi, looked back at his teacher and then bolted toward the school. The children waited in heavy silence while Emil pulled himself onto the roof and removed a great wad of dirty rags. Their eyes were round and wondering. Emil threw the rags to the ground, jumped down and returned to his place in line. The children's eyes rested expectantly on Katherine. Emil's sullen face said—now for the lecture.

Katherine ignored him. "While we're out here," she said, "I'm going to tell you about a plan I have. We're going to have a baseball team. Tomorrow I'll send to Seattle for a ball and a baseball bat."

Emil Greene hadn't missed a day of school since. Katherine laughed, telling Carl about it later.

But Carl had seen nothing laughable about it. "Baseball is a man's game."

"Don't you see, Carl, the game itself isn't important. It's taming that wicked Greene boy, keeping him in school. . ."

"You can't make a silk purse," Carl retorted flatly, "out of a sow's ear."

"Why not?" Katherine asked, and felt ashamed because her voice was anything but genteel. "In a way my school is filled with sow's ears."

"I suppose you'll be on this—this baseball team?"

Katherine had smiled, knowing she was tormenting him but for some reason enjoying it. "You can look for me," she said softly, "on second base."

Carl had been irritated. It was irritation she knew would vanish at the merest touch of her hand, or at any sort of an apology. Yet she had neither touched him nor asked to be forgiven.

Their meetings were less frequent now, for Carl was spending more time at school and had been working as well as an apprentice in a Seattle law firm. It was a month since that last meeting, a month since he had said good-bye, his lips still tight with disapproval. A simple little, "I'm sorry, Carl," a look of acquiescence instead of defiance—but she hadn't been able to give in that much.

And so he had gone back to the *Viking* with only a tense, "I hope things go well during the next month," riding across the Carlsons' clearing without even turning to wave as the trail bent toward the woods. He hadn't kissed her good-bye. And yet, like a naughty child, she still wanted to laugh.

The rain had stopped. Humming to herself, Katherine leaned back in the saddle and let the pony take her down the familiar trail. In among the giant cedars the air was warm and aromatic. Carl had said he wasn't coming for several weeks. When he did, she would be careful not to offend him and he would be too polite to remind her that she ever had. Meanwhile, no need to worry about their next meeting. There was plenty of time, plenty of work. On Monday she would take the tablets and the baseball bat to school. It would be weeks and weeks before the snow would be heavy enough to keep the children away from school. Things were going well. "School year 1884-85"—she had failed at nothing on her list, so far. Impulsively she reached forward and ran her hand along the pony's neck. She had all but forgotten to whom the pony belonged, and how defiantly she had once refused it.

ii

By the middle of December even Katherine had to admit that the school should be closed. There was no arguing with the early snow, which mere determination could not clear from the wagon roads and trails. There was real danger to the children who pushed through drifts half as tall as they were, to arrive at school wet and shivering and an hour or more late. For those who lived in the true wilderness, like Levi Barker, the journey was impossible.

"I could talk back to Nils Bengston," Katherine said to the Carlsons. "But I can't do anything about the weather."

"I don't think you were supposed to," Faith Carlson said.

"No. But if I can't teach school, what will I do?"

"You can stay here with us." Faith and Jeb Carlson said it almost together.

Katherine shook her head. "Thank you. But we need hard money, don't we? We always do. I can't live here without putting in my share."

"Just until you can start school again."

Katherine gestured toward the nearest shutter. It was tightly barred with a length of split cedar. But the east wind had driven the fine snow around the edges and through the invisible cracks. It lay in a feathery white ridge along the sill. "How can we know when that will be? Remember you were telling me about the school principal who had to work on the railroad half of the year? And last year the teacher at Squak earned a living splitting hop poles. I can't do those things. But I'll have to think of something different."

"You got spunk, Miss Duncan," Jeb Carlson said.

Katherine smiled. "No," she said, "but maybe if I stay here long enough I'll learn to get it."

It was Agatha Tine who helped her find a job. "It's just like Faith Carlson to ask you to live off them," Agatha said. "But they ain't got shoes to go around. Why don't you come down here. I'll give you room and board if you teach Tommy and me to read." She chuckled. "If you can teach me, don't think you won't earn it."

"I'd help the Carlsons out more by paying them room and board than I would by moving out."

Agatha grinned. "Good girl. All right, then, you're out for a job. A paying job. Can you cook?"

"I was the oldest of six children, not counting the ones that died."

"That's right," Agatha laughed. "The way you

talk sometimes, I keep thinking you're one of those delicate city girls. Someday people around here are going to forget about the wrapping and look inside the package. Maybe some of them will be surprised." She settled herself comfortably, hands clasped across her stomach.

"There's that shingle mill Nils opened up on the South Fork last spring. There's fifteen, twenty men working there now, and three days ago their cook took a notion and made off for Alaska, along with what cash he could find in among everyone else's belongings." She stopped, her bright little eyes fixed hard on Katherine.

"Would I have to ask Mr. Bengston for the job?"

Agatha nodded slowly. "He's the one."

Katherine spread her hands in her lap, studied the rough skin, the burns from hot skillets, the fingernails broken from carrying cordwood, the cracks and chapping from using the coarse yellow soap she and Mrs. Carlson made. "I don't like to," she said, "but I will."

"He's not the skunk you think he is," Agatha said. "*I* know Nils."

"And *I* don't care to," Katherine said flatly.

Chuckling, Agatha rolled across the kitchen to the pantry shelf. "Before you go back to Carlsons I'm going to fill up your saddlebags. There's some jars of veal meat, some real dates Jake sent me out from Seattle, some pickled crab apples and a nice smoked slab of bacon. Faith won't want to take them. Tell her I gave them to you. Tell her they're for Christmas. Tell her I'm on a diet." Holding her stomach she laughed uproariously. "Now she'll believe *that*, won't she!"

Old Indian Doc was in the barnyard when Katherine rode into the hop ranch. She dismounted quickly, conscious of the glass windows in the ranch house and the faces that might be behind them. Since the day her runaway horse had dragged her into this same yard she had come no closer to it than the trail to Black River which ran past a quarter mile south. There, right in front of her on the barn wall, was her hat, the little bit of vanity she had bought instead of an umbrella and lost along with her pride that terrible day three months before. Rain had softened the straw and made the dyes in the ribbons run together. When snow came it had settled on the ribbons and frozen fast; it glistened in the wintery sunlight, mocking the shape of the hat that was to have made her look like a lady.

Nils had put it there—Katherine was sure of it, and for a moment she forgot everything but how much she hated him. Like an angry terrier, she grasped the tasseled ends of her shawl, pulled it off her head and shook it so hard snow sprayed in her face.

The old Indian approached her. Looking from Katherine to the old hat and back again, he giggled, covering his toothless mouth with his hand.

Katherine looped the reins around the hitching post. "Mr. Bengston?" she said stiffly.

The Indian spoke rapidly in Chinook, but he pointed toward the house. Nils and Julie and old Uncle Julian lived alone now. Katherine had heard a dozen contradictory reports on how they were getting along without Mary to cook and wash for them. She wanted to ask if Uncle Julian and Julie were there, too; she felt weak at the prospect of facing Nils alone. But Indian Doc had turned his pointing finger to the silly, snow-encrusted hat on the barn wall, and was repeating some question she couldn't understand. "Oh, leave me alone!" she snapped at him, like a crotchety grandma slapping at a mosquito.

Strengthened by annoyance, she made her way to the house.

At her knock, the door opened suddenly and Julie was in front of her, her face bright with an unusual smile. "Teacher!" she breathed.

Katherine smiled, fully as glad to see Julie as Julie was to see her. "How are you, Julie?"

"I'm doing the washing all by myself," the little girl said breathlessly. "Mama isn't here any more."

"Julie!"

It was Nils' voice, a sudden roar from a corner Katherine couldn't see.

Katherine flushed. She had never seen Nils' Indian wife, and hadn't expected that her absence would make this meeting with Nils any worse or any better. But it was worse, somehow, for there had been pride in Nils' angry command. Pride was a feeling she understood. Despite herself, Katherine felt a twinge of sympathy.

"Let her in, Julie!"

The little girl hesitated, confused by her father's manner, but she opened the door.

The great fieldstone fireplace filled the end of the room. Elsewhere Indian mats were spread, with a hand-split table and three or four handmade chairs with cowhide seats making up the white man's furniture. On a stool next to the fire sat Nils, elbows on his knees.

Katherine advanced to the middle of the room. She had planned what to say, but she had not expected to recite it standing up. Nils' blue eyes were curious and amused. It was Julie who darted across the room, pushed a chair forward and said, "Please?"

Nils grinned, "My, ain't she polite?" But he didn't move.

"Thank you, Julie." Katherine sat down carefully, collecting herself while she shook the snow from the hem of her skirt. Nils' gaze was so steady, so—uncompromising. She forced herself to meet it directly. "Mr. Bengston, the school is closed temporarily because of inclement weather, as you know."

Nils nodded. "Is that what you call it?" he said mockingly, pointing at the snow heaped up against the bottom half of the windowpane. "And so you're out of a job."

Katherine flushed. That miserable color in my face, she thought angrily. It's the one thing I can't control. "I see you already know."

Nils laughed out loud. "Who would know better than me?"

Of course he would remind her that the school building was his, the wages came from his pocket, the job had come from him in the first place; and yet for weeks Katherine had almost forgotten it. In a way, it wasn't true any more. The building and money were his, yes. But the school, the children's acceptance of the school, their love of school, even to his own little daughter Julie—this was something Nils Bengston couldn't touch. Katherine felt pride stiffen her backbone. "You also know, then, that I need another job, until spring, when I'll reopen the school."

It gave her some satisfaction to see that Nils was surprised. "Go on back to Seattle," he said bluntly. "You've never belonged out here anyway. Your friend Carl will help you find work."

"I'll stay here."

She said it quickly because she was growing angry at him, as always. She resented it. Anger, like love, was a personal thing, it came from the heart.

"This is no place for you," he repeated. His voice

was harsh. "You belong in Seattle, where men bow when they meet a lady and you wouldn't have to ask for work from a man who won't get off his chair for nobody."

Katherine said in a rush, "I'd like to go to work cooking for the men at the shingle mill."

Nils stared. He pulled the cigar from his mouth, studied each end of it, tossed it into the fire. At last he looked back at her.

"Would you please tell me what the wages are?" Katherine knew she spoke with telltale haste, but she managed to hold her head up and keep her hands sedately folded in her lap.

"Ten dollars a week for cooking three meals a day," Nils said slowly. "And your board and room."

"It's not far to Carlsons'. I'll sleep there."

"If you don't put breakfast on the table by six o'clock tomorrow morning, you don't get the job."

A shiver of triumph was beginning to run through her. It rose to a wonderful light-headedness. She stood up, adjusted her shawl and walked to the door. She felt his eyes on her every step of the way.

At the last moment she remembered Julie. "Good-bye, Julie," she said, giving the little girl the smile she dared not turn on her father. "And thank you, Mr. Bengston."

Nils was still watching her silently, and he still hadn't moved. At the door, Katherine turned back impulsively. "I surprised you, didn't I?" she said lightly, and hurried out.

iii

Fried ham, wheat mush, platters of fried eggs, hot cakes and molasses, baking powder biscuits, fried potatoes, pie, coffee . . . Katherine got up at four o'clock every morning, reciting victuals as if they were part of a dream she hadn't had time enough in bed to finish. Her eyes burned and her mouth was dry with lack of sleep. She washed quickly, gasping as the cold water assaulted her face. She hadn't time to arrange her long hair in the elaborate dress she had worn as Teacher. She brushed it fiercely, and let it hang in long braids down her back.

With the shawl wrapped around her thin body and securely knotted at the waist, she picked up the lantern and Mrs. Carlson's big, black umbrella, and hurried to the shed to saddle her pony. She moved quickly but in the trance of half-sleep, like a serious-minded ghost with an important tryst. She was never fully awake until she was in the saddle, the lantern in one hand and the umbrella in the other, and the pony was walking through the woods toward the shingle mill.

After breakfast she began the baking. Apple, blackberry, prune, pumpkin pies—many of the loggers would eat a pie a day. Then there was bread, made from the sponge of sourdough she kept in a crock in the cooler, and doughnuts for the men to soak in their coffee. She cooked beans every day, with chunks of fat pork dropped in first at the bottom of the iron kettle. Nils brought meat to the kitchen in the form of halves and quarters. Because she wouldn't ask him to cut it for her, Katherine had been left alone with two hundred pounds of hog and the choice between cooking it whole or going after it with a carving knife and carpenter's saw. She cut it herself, tears of anger, despair and weariness dropping onto her hands.

As a schoolteacher she had gained hard muscles and a few pounds. As a mill cook, the muscles grew even harder but there wasn't much else to her except bone, freckles, heavy red hair and eyes too big for her face. The day she met little, wiry Hi Barker from the trading post he said, "Nate's just about to put me on the grain scale. He's been betting I won't make a hundred. You better get weighed, too, teacher. It looks to me like you're gradually disappearing."

"She don't dare eat what she cooks," said Nate. "She knows what's in it."

At first it seemed to Katherine that the three meals at the shingle mill overlapped. If she did not pound the big copper dinner gong on time, the men walked in anyway, threw themselves onto the benches and banged the table with their fists. In the kitchen she would stack pork chops on platters, tip the bean pot into a big bowl, scoop up the gravy, praying that it was cooked all the way through. They shouted if the food was late. They had as much or more to say if it was raw.

By the end of the first week, Katherine's dread of that shouting, her deeper dread that Nils might walk in, had made a thorough mill cook out of her. The food was on the table at six in the morning, twelve noon, and six at night. Always, thought Katherine, the hands of the clock are straight up and down or just straight up.

On her way to the door to ring the gong she glanced methodically at the table, checking off each item. Milk pitcher. Mustard pot. Jelly jars. Pickles. Like a starter pointing the gun that would open the horse race, she picked up the mallet and beat the dinner gong.

The whine of the great circular saw would die away. The donkey engines would cough, spit and stop. Covered with grease and sawdust, the shingle weavers and bolt haulers and kneebolters and

packers pushed past her to the table. Sawdust coated
their hats, stuck in a fine red dust along their eyebrows. They smelled of sweat and cedar wood, odors
imbedded forever in the very fabric of their clothes.
There was no shouting now. Katherine went back to
the kitchen. Not a voice was raised except to call for
the coffee pot or another bowl of beans. When they
had finished, they kicked back the bench and walked
out.

They moved quickly before the meal. Afterwards
they dragged their feet, thumbs hooked under their
suspenders and the top pants button open for comfort. They worked from seven in the morning until six
at night, for twelve and a half cents an hour. Two
days wages paid for food and bunk.

Every week new men came to camp, others left.
"You can tell how long a man will stay," her father
had said, "by the size of his turkey." Katherine
smiled whenever she thought of Peter Duncan's old
rule. A "turkey" was the bedroll, the carpetbag, the
sum of a man's moveable possessions. In its size and
kind you read his character. She had come to the
Snoqualmie Valley with a wicker suitcase, three
dresses, a red flannel petticoat and a heap of under-
things made from bleached muslin and boiled flour
sacks. How long was *she* going to stay?

When the last man had eaten and gone, Katherine
took her only rest of the day. She scalded the teapot,
carefully measured two pinches of tea into it, poured
in the boiling water. Putting pot and teacup on the
table at her elbow, she dropped wearily into the
kitchen chair and closed her eyes. The steam engines
would start up again. Their chugging was deep and
rhythmic. Then the scream of the saw as it bit
through the wood. A shout, occasionally, from one

man to another, too muffled to mean more to her than a sound. In time, the noise was peaceful. She drank her tea slowly, holding the cup in the palms of both hands so as to warm her fingers.

It was unusual for anyone to come into the dining room except at mealtime. When Katherine heard the thump of boots one morning after breakfast, she set the teacup down quickly. Whoever it was, he was headed for the kitchen. It couldn't be Carl. The boat wasn't coming upriver, in this weather. And why would Nils come, since there were plenty of supplies? But the thought of Nils was disturbing. She stood up, nervously wiped her hands on her apron.

The man appeared in the doorway between dining room and kitchen. It was an Indian she had never seen before. His clothes were ordinary enough— jeans and a heavy shirt and boots—but his hair was long, stringing out below his dirty felt hat like a black mop dropped carelessly over the top of his head. He was grinning foolishly, and mumbling a combination of Chinook jargon and English swear words. He moved toward her, hands outstretched.

Katherine backed away. Fear made her heart pound and her mind go blank. "No, no," she said, "get away. . ."

He seemed to be talking steadily. His gestures grew more dramatic, but even more senseless, as he advanced.

"I'll scream!" Katherine cried, but it didn't inter-rupt the mumbling flow for a second. Who will hear me, she thought desperately, with the engines puffing and the saws whining? Down in the mill a man had to shout to be heard by someone only three feet away. Perhaps a scream would excite him even more, bring him on her in one leap. If she could talk to him . . .

Her throat ached but she said, "Please, if you want something, the boss is over in the mill. Go see the boss. . ."

Her words sounded foolish, even to herself. She was pleading with him, but clearly he wasn't listening. Instead he seemed to be pleading with her. She backed away still further. He followed her. Her back hit the edge of the table. Keeping her eye on the Indian, she reached behind her, groping for a weapon. "You want money?" she asked him. "Go away. I'll get you some money."

He was only a few feet away now. Katherine felt along the surface of the table, searching frantically but afraid to turn her head. The Indian was a giant mass, a grinning, chattering mass, barring her way to the door. "No, no!" she shrieked, losing the last of her self-control. She ran from him, toward the stove. Skillet and bean pot and kettles blurred together in her eyes. There was the meat block, the knife with the big bone handle lying next to the ham. She had dropped it there only an hour before. She grabbed blindly, and turned to meet him. But he hadn't followed. He was standing just where she had left him, and at last she had silenced him. He was staring at her in sheer amazement.

Her confidence returned. With pulse pounding in her neck and throat she moved to drive him out of the kitchen. The object was heavy in her hand. She stepped toward him, waving it in the air. Miraculously, he backed up. Boldness swept through her. "Get out of here!" she screamed, advancing like an angel with a fiery sword, "or I'll kill you with this!"

He looked more puzzled than terrified, but he moved back.

"I'll stab you!" she shouted, in a frenzy of courage. "You come near me again and I'll kill you!"

He stumbled, halting abruptly in the doorway. As suddenly, Katherine's courage disintegrated. He had stopped, he wasn't leaving, he might come at her again—she lost her wits entirely. The weapon in her right hand was forgotten. Her arm seemed paralyzed by it. Right at her elbow was a stack of flapjacks, still warm on the griddle at the back of the stove. With her left hand she scooped them up and whirled to take aim. He was standing there, his mouth gaping. "Get out, I said!"—and she put her body behind the throw that sent the whole stack of hot cakes across the room.

They were out of her hand when she saw him duck, falling to the floor as if he'd been shot between the eyes. They had landed with a soft splash before she saw what she had hit. It was Nils Bengston. Nils had walked in, unheard because of the rumpus. And Nils had got the hot cakes squarely across the face.

The silence throbbed like a pulse beat. Nils lifted one big hand and brushed the spatter out of his hair, off his cheek. The Indian was sitting flat on the floor, legs straight out and eyes round, like a frightened baby. Nils looked down at him. "Well, hello there, Jimmy. You begging again?"

The Indian replied with a burst of jargon.

Nils nodded sympathetically. "Too bad. The lady didn't understand." He turned to Katherine. "I see you haven't met Jimmy. He's never done anything bad, except beg for food. He's always hungry." Nils rubbed his cheek with the back of his sleeve. "I'm glad you decided to give him pancakes, instead of beans. You might have given them to him in the kettle, hm?"

The Indian got to his feet. Nils gestured toward the door, issuing a curt order in Chinook, and he fled.

Katherine looked up at Nils. She was still trembling. "He just wanted . . . something to eat," she said, feeling hysteria bubbling through her.

Nils nodded. His eyes were bright. "When I come in, you were yelling you'd stab him to death." He pointed to Katherine's hand, still clutching the weapon with which she had been ready to defend herself. "Were you going to do it with *that*?"

She lifted her arm, stared at the object she had been clutching so hard. It was the big soup ladle. The carving knife with the heavy bone handle lay untouched on the meat block. The ladle, it seemed, had been handier.

She looked back at Nils. He was smiling, with his eyes sparkling and his teeth white in his tan face. The whole thing suddenly seemed funnier than anything that had ever happened to her before. Katherine began to laugh. Nils laughed, softly at first, more loudly as he watched Katherine's face. For a long time, with the saws whining outside, with the soup ladle hanging crazily at Katherine's side, they looked into each other's face, and laughed together.

iv

Katherine tried to listen carefully, for she knew this was a real proposal of marriage. How often Carl had regretted that he couldn't take her away from the Valley. How romantically he had promised, "Some day. . ." It had been all wishing, and she had agreed without reservation because in it all there was nothing to say yes or no to. Now Carl was holding her hand, and his words were so exactly what she had expected to hear some day that she almost forgot she must reply.

"I hope I'm not presuming," he was saying. "We

do understand each other, don't we, dear?''

She nodded. "Oh, yes, Carl," she said very warmly because she was afraid she hadn't been listening closely enough and might have missed some question. She felt ashamed of her absent-mindedness. To make up for it she pressed his hand harder than she meant to.

"You will, then." Carl pulled on the reins. The big work horses stopped obediently and the wagon settled into the ruts. Carl's arm encircled Katherine. He bent over and kissed her cheek. "Have I told you that I love you?"

"Yes, oh yes. . ." She spoke fervently, but she was glad he couldn't see her face. The truth was that she couldn't remember. Hadn't he said he loved her? Hadn't she said she loved him? Surely their kisses, prim as they were, had meant as much without a name tag. She thought suddenly, he sounds a little silly, and was immediately ashamed of herself again. "I love you," she said, "very much."

He kissed her, and for a moment the dreadful urge to doubt him, and to doubt herself, was stilled. She lay passively against his shoulder, accepting his kisses but lacking any desire to kiss him back. Her lips lay beneath him as sweet and virgin as a child's, for she had learned it was only the sweet and virgin that he wanted from her. Desire in the girl he was to marry, the shiver of awakening passion that had once—only once—made her cling to him—he had been shocked by it. She had felt it, and drew away, furiously ashamed. After that she never forgot the part he expected of her. In his arms now, she felt nothing. I wonder, she thought, if this is all there is to it? And she knew instantly that it wasn't.

He was talking to her. Katherine flushed. He was waiting for an answer, and once more she hadn't heard the question. She looked at him, seeking reassurance. The serious face, the dark, thoughtful eyes, the kind mouth and gentle hands—of these things the Carl she had loved seven months ago had been made. They were Carl's now. September until March—he couldn't have changed. Had she?

"I'm sorry, Carl," she said hastily. "What did you ask me?"

"You were thinking of something else."

He was accusing her, and of course he was right. "I'm sorry," she repeated. "I'm to open the school again Monday morning and there are so many things to think about." She felt guilty at using such evasion. This was Carl, whom she had just promised to love.

Carl pulled her around gently to face him. "Katherine, I've asked you to come to Seattle with me. I've asked you to marry me this week, and live in the home of my parents until I have finished my training and can pay for a home of our own. Is this your answer, that you've been thinking about the school?"

Katherine felt a wave of unhappiness as she looked at him. No, he hadn't changed. He had known her mind as surely as he ever had. How could she defend herself, except with another lie? She should be clinging to him joyfully, telling him he had made her utterly, completely happy. But she was uneasy.

His proposal hadn't made her happy. It had only confused her. Worst of all, she felt a twinge of pity, because she knew how clearly he could see it. Her face was full of it. Embarrassment, confusion, a sense of duty and a wish to please, but not ecstasy, not love.

"Not now, not so soon," she whispered. "It's only that I wasn't expecting. . .it so soon." She put her hand on his arm, and then wished that she hadn't, for it was such an obvious gesture of comfort. "Later," she said. "Carl dear, I do love you. I always have, from that first awful day at Snohomish City when I was going to run away from the boat instead of getting on it, and I bumped into you. You remember. Did I ever tell you that you stopped me from running away? I would never have come to the Valley at all, if it hadn't been for you." She was talking too much. She knew it and stopped abruptly, looking anxiously into his face.

It was different. It was shadowed with new wisdom she hadn't seen in it before. We are both changing, she thought, and I believed it was only I.

He smoothed back her hair, as grave and careful as a mother. "Later, then," he said quietly. He picked up the reins and slapped them along the horses' backs. The spring wagon rolled forward, creaking softly. "Now," he said, keeping his glance away from her and straight down the road they were traveling, "tell me all about school, and your plans for reopening it."

So Katherine began to talk and talk, though suddenly all she really wanted to do was to cry.

CHAPTER SEVEN

i

KATHERINE PACKED HER LUNCH for the box social with utmost care. It would go to Carl, of course. If it were filled with gold nuggets, no one in Gold Mountain would think of outbidding the man who had spoken for her. For Carl, then, or for the new school building, to which the bidding money was to go, her hands moved delicately, appreciating their task. Besides, Carl was watching. He sat on a three-legged stool by the open door.

"I'm so glad you got here in time." Katherine shook the Indian reed basket, squinted critcally at the inside. "This will do," she added absently. "I haven't got a box."

"It was luck that I made the trip this week at all."

Katherine glanced up quickly. But his face showed no hint of displeasure. She smiled, and meant it. Carl so often seemed displeased that she was relieved whenever she found she had only imagined it. "Perhaps I should have written you about the social."

"No matter," he said stiffly, "since I arrived without invitation anyway."

She flushed. Then he *was* angry. Had there been a time during the past year when she had completely measured up to the standards he set for her? She must be a lady, he often reminded her, suggesting that there were ways in which she wasn't. In the way she sometimes let her hair fall loosely down her back. In the speed with which she had learned to mount and ride a horse, like a young Indian. In her costume, which had been without a proper bonnet or gloves, without lace, ruffle or finery, for the whole year. In all these outer things he saw a loss of dignity. "But no one in the Valley finds anything wrong," she had often protested, and he shamed her with his reply, "They don't know any better. *I* do."

She picked up a clean dish towel, shook it hard and spread it as a lining inside the basket. For the hundredth time she resolved not to apologize to Carl. "I didn't think of it as a party," she said. "There have been so many different affairs, all through the summer, for raising school money. This is just another one of them."

"It may seem that to you. But at a box social men bid for the lunches, and their supper partners are the girls whose boxes they win."

Carl was being deliberately patient. It inspired Katherine with a ridiculous desire to stamp her foot. "Of course." Her hands worked furiously with the lunch basket.

Carl came to the table. "We are engaged," he said quietly. His hand touched her elbow, asking her to look at him. She turned. "If I hadn't come, would you have gone to the social and sat as a partner with another man?"

"I am the teacher," she said stubbornly, but her voice had lost its boldness. Carl was hurt. According to his code—and hers, too, for hadn't they always looked at things in the same way?—she had slighted him. Besides—and this was worse—she had been something less than a perfect lady.

"I'm sorry, Carl," she said. Now she had apologized, as she had done so often, and so often sworn never to do again. His face softened; she knew he would never refer to it again. But she would remember. Once more she had apologized, and the apology had curdled in her mouth.

"I've made apple turnovers," she said, "and some little venison pies. There are some sandwiches of smoked pheasant. Mr. Carlson hung several birds in the smokehouse when he cured that last deer. Eggs are scarce." She knew she was prattling like an old woman, but she went on, "Our best hens are getting broody so I couldn't make spiced eggs, as I had planned. Then there is honey bread, and a little pot of fresh creamed cheese."

Carl lifted one hand. "Whoa!" Katherine halted with the last sharp intake of breath. He was smiling. He was neither scolding her nor pressing her with the question which seemed harder to answer every time he asked it. She felt such a wave of relief that she faced him and lifted her face for a kiss.

His arms went around her, and he held her tightly against the musty wool of his lapel. She felt him tremble. Once she had been ashamed of feeling too much; now she felt nothing at all. His hands pressed her anxiously, as if he sensed her detachment and was trying to bring her closer. With curiosity she noted the heavy beat of his heart. The Carlson children will be running into the house about now, she thought, yelling that it's time to go. . . ."Carl," she whispered uneasily.

"You've been in the Valley for over a year now," he said. He spoke hurriedly, as if he had to say it all before she left his arms. "I've asked you many times to come to Seattle and marry me. You've always answered, not just now, later." His arms tightened convulsively. "How much longer do I have to wait?"

Here was an intensity of feeling she had often

longed for. And yet the question turned her cold. Guiltily, she hid her face against his shoulder.

"Katherine," he pleaded, "Katherine. . ."

Her mind ran blindly from the necessity of answering him. She lifted her face, and he kissed her hungrily. From the distance a child shouted. Another answered from some spot near the cabin. The children were coming in.

Carl released her so suddenly he seemed to have jumped backward. "Your hair," he said hastily, "is—is disarranged."

Katherine stood still, feeling awkward and numb. Her hands went to her hair and dutifully smoothed it back from her face. Why be disappointed in him, she asked herself, when a moment ago I was disappointed in myself? Now that the children were here, there would be no chance for questions she couldn't answer, kisses she didn't share. Gratefully she went to the cabin door, and waved the children to come in.

ii

The box social was held on a Sunday at the schoolhouse. Since the day was warm even for the middle of September, the men moved the benches out into the yard, and those who could sit still at such gatherings took places in the shade of the big cedar and alder trees. Katherine's desk, a table one of the settlers had discarded when his family got too big to find places by it, was set in the center of the yard. By four o'clock it was covered with the lunches.

Some were in Indian baskets, like Katherine's. Two or three women had been able to boast and packed their lunches in shoeboxes the like of which everyone had seen, but few bought, at Nate Tarpee's store. One lunch was put up in an old sewing basket, another in a clean flour sack with a girl's satin sash tied around.

Puffing enormously, Agatha Tine lowered herself from her spring wagon, and trundled across the clearing to deposit a lunch packed away in a milk can. "Whoever gets these eats is going to have to share with me," she wheezed. "So nothing else was near big enough to hold it all." She spotted Nils in a nearby group of men. "How about it, Nils? You bid for my lunch and I'll promise to eat with one hand. Anyways, I finished off a meal just before I come." Laughing, she moved toward the benches under the trees.

Old Uncle Julian blinked up at her, hands and chin resting comfortably on the piece of cherry wood he was using as a cane. Next along the line was Faith Carlson, with little Johnny, now six years old, stretched out asleep with his head in her lap. Agatha looked appreciatively from one to the other. "This is where I belong," she said, turning to lower herself onto the bench. "In among the old men and the lucky women."

Faith frowned. "I don't know as you have to holler it. Nobody knows but Jeb and he says it don't show."

Agatha chuckled. "What kind of an eye has a man got for things like that? Why not holler it? I'd be proud."

Faith nodded wearily. "I *am* proud. I'm just too tired these days to show any of my better feelings."

The crowd at the box social represented Gold Mountain prairie so thoroughly that it was easy to see who was absent. The tight little groups of men, the lines of women on the benches, turned to identify each newcomer and to catalogue the missing. There's Nate Tarpee and his wife Bertha, their silent glances said. She don't get out much but they say he don't encourage it, the way she likes her chaw of ter-backer. . .There's Hi Barker, bless him, and his son Levi. Could it be he come without his fiddle, or is that it over there under the wagon seat?. . .Look at that wagonload of Stump young 'uns. She's nursing one right now, but what do you bet she's already carrying another. It'll show when she stands up. If Tom does what he did last time, he'll put in the first bid for every lunch, and never raise his voice otherwise . . . Let's see, Andersons, Nelsons, Smiths, Carl-sons . . . And there's Nils Bengston holding little Julie by the hand while he talks to that crowd of shingle weavers. Right next are a dozen loggers Nils has working in his woods. Now what would bring them traveling no-goods to a box social if it wasn't orders from Nils? . . . Teacher was the last one here. She's got real pretty the last year. Who'd of thought that scary-looking little girl would finish out her first year, least of all start a second by raising money for a new schoolhouse? The captain's boy's been courting her all year. Oh yes, there he is, right behind her, and don't he dress like a gentleman from Seattle!

Agatha leaned toward Faith Carlson. "Who's the sweetheart of the social going to be today?"

Faith smiled. There was always one girl at a box social whose box lunch caused a special flurry of bidding. She wasn't always prettiest, and whether or not she was a clever cook had nothing to do with it. But the eyes of the young men would be caught by her, and they would make a game out of paying her attention. Some would start it, others would follow, until the girl was in an agony of blushes and laughter. The older girls, who could remember when such court had been paid them, would smile, their hands lingering possessively on the arms of their own men. They would be critical or tolerant. They would laugh softly or sigh with nostalgia. While the others, the men and women who had long ago got over envying the young, laughed with the game. Faith looked over the crowd with an expert eye. "The boys seem to like that oldest Anderson girl."

A girl whose head was covered with pale yellow ringlets had been surrounded by four or five boys. They were teasing her, each fortified by the presence of the others. She giggled, tossing her blond head.

Agatha said, "That's Belle, ain't it?" She studied the girl critically. "Yep, there's bound to be some real lively bidding when her box is sold."

"If they know which is hers. You aren't supposed to tell."

Agatha guffawed. "Ain't you the innocent, Faith Carlson. What do you suppose keeps the young men busy before the bidding starts, if it isn't going around asking every pretty girl which box is hers?" She punished her stomach with a hearty slap. "For myself, I think that little redheaded Katherine Duncan is far and away the prettiest female here. She's ragged as the rest of us, but she's got style!"

"She's the teacher!" Mrs. Carlson sounded genuinely shocked.

"Sure she is," Agatha retorted, "but God gave her a pair of big, beautiful eyes and the kind of hair men can't wait to get their hands into. Teachers are supposed to be old maids but that one don't look to be built for the part."

"Miss Duncan is engaged."

Agatha's little eyes rested speculatively on Carl White. "Yes, I know. He told me, way last spring, but I don't see no ring on her hand. And you still ain't heard them talk about a wedding date." Agatha squinted wisely. "What's that mean, to be 'engaged'?"

"To be promised," Faith Carlson snapped. Her pain had grown worse with this pregnancy and Agatha's good nature irritated her.

"Huh! When I first come to the Territory a girl was 'engaged' just as long as it took the preacher to get to the house after she has said yes."

Nate Tarpee walked to the middle of the clearing and whopped the table with his fist. His long black hair had been carefully parted and plastered down with water. In one hand was a wide-brimmed black hat. He banged the table again, and the hum of voices quieted. Surveying the crowd, he twirled the hat several times at the end of a long forefinger. His face was expressionless as he flipped it into the air, ducked his head forward and straightened up, hat squarely on his head. Someone laughed. Frowning with mock fury, Nate turned toward the sound and shook his fist. At that, everyone laughed. Nate's long, sallow face cracked into a grin. "Well," he boomed, "now that you're awake, let's open up the bidding."

Nate made a good auctioneer. Having a sharp eye and a sure instinct, he knew which lunch belonged to Belle Anderson, which one the teacher had put up. He set them both aside for the last. He talked constantly, shouting, gesturing, pleading, confiding. When the bids were quick, his words rolled from his tongue so fast they shed their meaning. "It's for the school, itsfortheschool. . ." he chanted. "Be good to the school. Buy this lunch and be good to your stomach."

The men bid lightly, with a grin and a shrug of the shoulders, for most of them had already set aside a certain amount of money for the school and they enjoyed the game of letting Nate Tarpee tease it out of them. The lunches brought two dollars, four dollars, sometimes six or seven. At last only two remained. Nate Tarpee picked up the one every male under forty knew belonged to the pretty Belle Anderson. It was said that Belle had been spoken for by a young woodsman from Black River. Tim Naughton, his name was, and he was here now, the center of a tight knot of his fellows.

The lunch was wrapped in a white cloth and tied around with a wide pink sash. Nate held it high, turning it to examine the side, top, and bottom.

"Two dollars!" someone shouted. "Two dollars for the ribbon, five for the whole lunch!"

Another man yelled from the back of the crowd. Everyone laughed. Nate ignored them all. He turned the lunch around once more, even more slowly than before. He sniffed it loudly, rolling his eyes. The loggers began yelling. In their center, young Tim Naughton grinned self-consciously.

"All in good time, men, all in good time," said Nate.

"One million dollars!"

"The shirt off my back."

"If you could eat with your eyes, old Nate'd be full up."

"Start the bidding, you bow-legged swindler."

Nate bowed and a woman giggled. Belle Anderson, her face a bright pink, looked at everyone in the crowd but Tim Naughton.

"I have here," Nate began, "a rare jewel."

The bidding went fast at first. Secure in the fact that Belle's intended would have to win the lunch in the end no matter what it cost him, every man in the crowd got into it. "Two dollars!" one man called who hadn't but a dollar in his pocket. "Three!" another shouted, though he'd won a lunch three minutes before and had already pulled his supper partner behind a wagon and kissed her. "I'll give four!" said a third man, gesturing coarsely at the other two.

The bids leaped up a dollar at a time. There was so much loud joking, with two or three men blowing kisses toward the blushing Belle and several more challenging each other over the heads of the crowd, that the voices were almost indistinguishable. At five dollars the pace slowed and the bids went up fifty cents at a time.

Nate nodded, pointed, called, his ear alert for the highest number. "Eight dollars!" That was from Tim Naughton himself, and it stood out boldly from the bids of those less serious than he. It would be the last bid. Nate knew it so he bellowed. "Now we're getting started. Now we're bidding. Eight dollars! That's fine for an opener. Do I hear ten? Do I hear ten?"

The answer burst out suddenly from the midst of the shingle weavers. Chuck Dwelley, his name was, and he had already lost two fingers though he was only twenty-four years old. "Down in Squak," he drawled, "we wouldn't think of taking a lady's box lunch for less'n twelve. So that's my bid."

The shingle weavers, brothers for every piece of finger that ever went down the chute, grouped behind their challenger. Around Tim Naughton the loggers closed in and began talking together in quick, low voices. The older men and women looked excitedly from one camp to the other. It was clear everyone else was out of it now.

Nate Tarpee rubbed his hands together. Belle Anderson blushed anew. The tittering of the other girls went on feebly for a moment, then stopped.

"Twelve!" Nate announced with a great show of

disinterest. An ordinary bid, his long face said, a very ordinary bid in any auction *I* ever steered. . . "That don't seem like. . ."

"Fourteen!" Tim Naughton interrupted. The loggers wheeled around, watching the weavers.

Chuck Dwelley laughed. "Is that all?" he said. "A girl would sure be unlucky to get herself a logger. I'll make it twenty!"

Man, woman and child caught a sharp breath and stared at the shingle weaver. His hands were in his pockets, he was resting back easily on his heels. His friends were lounging in the same position. No one in the crowd had ever heard a higher price offered for a pretty girl's lunch. Whispering started up. Who would have guessed that young fellow from Squak even knew Belle Anderson. Or did he? Everyone knew that to push the bid from fourteen to twenty, without even leaving an open door at all the figures in between, was an act of daring. But the weavers were looking at the loggers and grinning. We work in the mill, you work in the woods. You say we get high pay for staying under a roof and juggling little shingles and we say you're ignorant roughnecks without a brain between you. Twenty dollars, their grinning faces said. Why, that's nothing to a weaver!

Young Tim Naughton was frowning uneasily. His friends looked at him. He murmured something, shrugged his shoulders.

"Twenty," Nate warned, the hand that was high over his head keeping the bidding open. His eyes were on Tim Naughton.

Every logger in the little group pushed his hands into his pockets. Hurriedly they pulled out their money. A stack of three silver dollars. A handful of coins. A greenback, creased where it had been folded into a tight little square.

"Do I hear another bid?" Nate shouted. "Just one more before the end."

A logger waved at him frantically.

The shingle weavers laughed. "Mr. Auctioneer," Chuck Dwelley called, "is it allowed to raise my own bid?"

The loggers were sorting out the money, awkwardly counting it into Tim Naughton's hand. One of them reached back into his pants pocket, fishing anxiously through its empty depths. In the distance Belle Anderson bit her lip and turned alternately pink and white. Tears filled her eyes.

"Going, going. . ."

"Hold up!" the loggers yelled. Tim Naughton advanced, his hands cupped under the pile of money. "Twenty-seven dollars and thirty cents!"

Nate whirled, pointing his forefinger into Tim's face. "Going going gone!" he shrilled, so rapidly the all-important words melted together.

Chuck Dwelley drawled, "Hey, wait a minute. . ."

Tim Naughton dropped the money on the table and grabbed the lunch. The men cheered and the women laughed as he loped across the clearing to Belle Anderson's side. She was laughing now, though her cheeks were wet.

The shingle weavers thumped Chuck Dwelley's back, and doubled over with laughter at how they'd cost the loggers every cent they owned.

Carl stood up. "They've had their fun," he said to Katherine. "We'll buy your box outright, and save the bidding." He held out his arm.

A lady walks on her fiancé's right arm. It was the mannerly thing to do. But Katherine was conscious of Agatha, grinning wryly. Of Mrs. Nelson, arms akimbo, frankly judging her every gesture. She thought of the loggers and the shingle weavers, who laughed easily and mocked everything. Of Old Uncle Julian, who called Carl "the gentleman from Seattle." And Nils was still there, close by the table. She got up, pretending not to notice Carl's arm. "Yes, let's walk a bit."

"Katherine. . ."

She turned guiltily. Was he insisting for the sake of courtesy, or to claim her in front of everyone? "Oh, yes," she murmured. Her color rose unhappily as she slid her hand through his arm. She would not have minded so much if Nils had not been there. In silence she let Carl guide her through the crowd to the table.

Nate was leaning forward to pick up her basket. The weavers and the loggers had wandered off, and many of the others had left to claim their partners. The fragrance of coffee drifted across the clearing. The women were boiling it on the schoolhouse hearth. Some of the men had gone back to playing horseshoes. There was a metallic clink of shoe against pin and a quick burst of laughter.

"No need to put this up for bidding," Carl said to Nate. He dropped a five dollar bill on the table and picked up the lunch basket.

Nate shrugged. "It don't matter to me. You'd of got it anyway." He picked up the bill. Yawning, he stuffed it into the canvas sack which contained the rest of the money.

"I'll bid ten."

Katherine's hand jerked from its hold on Carl's arm. She turned toward the voice and faced Nils Bengston.

He was smiling, not at her but over her head at Carl. There was no smile in his eyes. "Ten dollars," he repeated. "You ready to go better than that?"

Carl's voice was cold. "See here, Nils, I've bought

the lunch. The bidding is closed."

"The bidding was never opened." He looked at Nate Tarpee. "O.K., Nate, you're the auctioneer. Take back that lunch and put it up right."

Nate shrugged uneasily. "Nils, you already bought a lunch. It cost you six-fifty. What do you want with another?"

Nils answered Nate, but he looked down at Katherine. "We got to build that new school, don't we?"

Katherine pulled her glance away from Nils. Her hands were trembling. She let one clutch the other, trying to steady them. She had better luck with her voice. "This is ridiculous!" she said quite clearly.

Nils chuckled. "Twelve dollars, then," he said. "That'll do more for the school than Carl's five, won't it, Teacher?"

Carl stepped forward. "Miss Duncan's lunch is not for sale!" He jerked a ten dollar bill from his wallet and threw it on the table. "Fifteen, then, to close the bidding. It's all I have."

Nate stammered, "Going going gone. . ."

Carl said to Nils, "You can outbid me, but Miss Duncan would refuse to be your supper partner anyway."

For an instant Nils looked thoughtfully at Carl. Then he grinned, dismissing him entirely. "I'm glad we got your friend to loosen up a little," he said to Katherine, "for the sake of the new school."

Carl exploded. "Damn you, Nils!"

Katherine, not Nils or Carl, heard the first shout. It came from the oldest Smith boy, who had been too sick with a fever to come to the social. He was here now, riding a pony bareback and with nothing much on but a cotton shirt and a pair of jeans. His face was flushed with fever and the effort of riding hard.

"Prairie fire!" he gasped as the pony galloped into the clearing. "It's burning across our place, headed north and west!"

Katherine looked dumbly from Nils to Carl. Nils could have forgotten them. Anger, amusement, deviltry were wiped from his face. "Prairie fire!" he shouted. He cupped his hands to his mouth. "Prairie fire heading this way! Every man get home fast, pick up every bucket you got and ride for the Smith place!" He began to run.

All around them, the men and boys began running, too. As Nils reached his horse and leaped into the saddle, the first box wagon was headed for the trail.

"Jennie, Tommy, Max. . ." a mother called. "Jennie, Tommy, Max. . ."

"Into the wagon," Jeb Carlson shouted, carrying Johnny over one shoulder and dragging Hiram with his free hand. Faith Carlson limped painfully behind, her body heavy with the new child.

"Prairie fire . . . prairie fire . . ." Young Tim Naughton was racing toward his horse, the bright pink sash from his sweetheart's lunch draped idiotically across his chest.

Hi Barker ran toward his wagon, Levi right beside him. "Wagon's too slow," Hi called to his son. "We'll unhitch the team and ride on their backs. Them draft horses will pass up every cayuse on the trail."

"But Pa, your fiddle's in the back."

Hi Barker hesitated, then said gruffly, "if we don't stop the fire, I won't be here to play it," and he began to loosen the harness.

Prairie fire at the Smith place—Katherine thought suddenly, Why the next homestead north and west of the Smiths' is the Carlsons'! She whirled on Carl. "Quick, unharness the team. Faith and the children would be better off waiting here anyway. We'll ride as the Barkers are doing. We'll get there faster.''

"Fighting a prairie fire is no job for a woman.'' He tried to take her arm. "Here, I'll help you into the wagon. When we reach Carlsons', I'll go out with the men.''

Katherine shook herself free of his protective arm. "Where do you think I come from?'' she blazed at him. "A—city? I've seen prairie fires. The more hands on the bucket line the better. I'm going to help.'' She grabbed his sleeve. "Please, Carl,'' she pleaded, trying to pull him toward the wagon. "Take the harnesses off the horses. We can go faster!''

"A woman, racing bareback on a workhorse? Katherine, you're the teacher here!''

Katherine peered into Carl's face. He just could not see. She looked desperately around the schoolyard. Not ten feet away the Greene boy, her seventeen-year-old pupil, was tightening the cinch around his pony's belly. She ran to him. "Emil, may I ride behind?''

The boy grinned. "Sure, Teacher.'' Katherine grabbed the rim of the saddle, and he boosted her onto the horse with one hand.

"Katherine!'' Carl called, running toward them. "Come back immediately!''

"Should I wait, Miss Duncan?'' the Greene boy asked, in the voice of an obedient school boy.

"You may go,'' his teacher gasped, throwing her arms around his waist, "and Emil, the faster the better.''

iii

It was the river that saved Gold Mountain. The trading post and the hotel. The blacksmith shop, the boarding house and the grist mill. Lean-tos, cabins, the lop-sided shack and the abandoned building rotting under its false front—they were all preserved for the next generation because the river happened to run only a hundred rods away.

But the homesteads south and east of the settlement were not as well protected. The Smith cabin burned to the ground. The wind rose, blowing down on the prairie from the east, and by the time the men had collected buckets and raced to the fire the Carlson place was in flames.

The homestead lay at a sharp bend in the Middle Fork, so that the river ran along two sides. The fire, a crackling, darting line of flame that was over a quarter mile long, swept forward at an angle from the other side.

The Greene boy kept his pony at a full gallop most of the way. Katherine held on around his waist, hugging him as a frightened bear cub hugs it powerful mother. The smoke was heavy when they were still a mile away. As they neared the Carlson place, Emil Greene began slapping the reins on each side of the pony's neck. "Yi, Yi!" he hollered at the sweating cayuse. "Yi, yi. . ." The smoke was sharp and he began to cough. Katherine felt it sweep into her nostrils, down into her throat. She lowered her head, half burying her face in the boy's back.

They could see the fire from a spot where the trail followed a curve of the river. Emil pulled the pony up. There were other horses here, some free, some loosely tied to the trees nearest the water. "Looks like we don't dare ride in further," he said. He sounded like a conscientious fifth-grader apologizing for the way he'd done his lesson. "Better leave the pony and run for it."

They hit the ground at the same time, and began to run. The smoke became more unbearable with every step. Katherine stopped. She grabbed Emil's arm and motioned to lie down on the ground. With a quick jerk she opened a tear in her petticoat, quickly ripped a long strip off the bottom and tore the material in two. "Here, tie that across your face." They knotted the pieces of petticoat at the backs of their heads, and ran on.

The meadow Jeb Carlson had cleared so painfully with one ox was a field of fire. The new barn he had built only two months before was in the center of it, a peak of flame. But a strip of pasture still lay between the fire and the house. Along its edge the bucket line had formed, the last man standing up to his knees in the river.

It was Tim Naughton, the silly pink satin ribbon still tied around his chest. The ends of it were wet from dragging in the river. "Other end of the line!" he gasped. "Need help at the other end of the line." He lifted his hands like a baseball player, caught the empty bucket the next man threw. With one sweep he bent down and filled it. The next man leaped across the intervening space and lifted it from his hand. Tears from the smoke streamed down his face and he ran as awkwardly as a wounded bull moose, but he held the bucket gingerly, scarcely spilling a drop.

"Other end," Katherine said, blinking to take her direction. The line from the river was single. Nearing the fire, it fanned out. From there on there was no set pattern to it, for the front of the fire was broad and there were very few men to police it. With Emil beside her, Katherine ran as Tim Naughton had directed.

The last man at the far end was Nils Bengston. His

face glistened with sweat. Soot had streaked his
cheeks and settled on his blond hair like black
hayseed. He glanced at her briefly, then at Emil.
"There," he said, jerking his head toward buckets
which lay on their sides behind him. Katherine recognized them as the ones Jeb Carlson had kept in the
new barn. Someone—Nils?—had got into the barn
and pulled them out. She picked one up and took a
position some ten or twelve feet to Nils' left. Emil
grabbed another, ran back to exchange it for a full
one.

They moved rhythmically. The instant the weight
of a full bucket pulled on his hand, the man up front
lowered his head, ran through the smoke. Aiming as
carefully as he could he threw the water along the
edge of the flame. Back to the man at the head of the
water line, he dropped the empty bucket, reached for
the full one.

Nils ran to Katherine. "This wind is tricky. You
stay well back of me." He was shouting, though he
was so close she had to tip her head to see his face.
"You pass the buckets. I'll go up to the fire and empty
them."

She nodded. Smoke was so thick she could not
speak without choking. She reached out blindly, and
Nils dropped an empty bucket into her hands. Suddenly he grinned. "Good girl," he seemed to be
saying. She turned and ran to Emil, dropped the
empty bucket, took the full one from his hands.

It was harder to run with a pail of water than she
had expected. She was fighting for breath when she
reached Nils. His big hand touched hers as he took
the water from her. Lightly, the handle of the empty
bucket fell across her palm. She turned and ran back.

There was no time to it, no day, night or hour. The
first wave of exhaustion passed, and Katherine felt

strong and light-headed. Then weariness swept back, and she worked grimly, pleading for a little more breath. She and Nils and Emil raced toward each other through the yellow smoke, met briefly, turned and ran apart.

They did not shout it to each other, but they knew that the fire was gaining. With each frantic glance over her shoulder, Katherine saw they were closer to the house. The wind was tricky, as Nils had said. For a while the creeping fire would lie low along the ground, and then with a sudden gust from the east it leaped forward. Then the pitiful buckets of water were useless against it.

More men arrived to fight the fire and the line closed in a little more with each new addition. The rhythm of the bucket line remained unbroken. Swing to the right, grab a good hold, swing to the left, let go when he has it, pick up the empty one, roll it down the line, swing to the right. . .

"She's breaking through!"

Katherine heard Nils shout. She stopped in her race toward Emil, and turned back. With her eyes all but closed against the smoke, she could just pick him out, a dark giant in an eddy of smoke. In confusion she ran toward him. Before she reached him she saw there was fire at her right where the next man in line had been standing only a second before. She wheeled around, trying to get her bearings from the position of the house. The house was lost. She stared helplessly, like a child suddenly separated from its mother. The wind, fierce and capricious, turned the smoke aside for an instant, and she caught a glimpse of the house. It was directly in back of her, as she thought. But between them was a roaring wall of flame.

She turned back. "Nils!" He appeared almost miraculously. He was bare to the waist. The shirt in his hands was charred and his arms were singed. "You moved," he gasped. "I looked for you. Make for the river."

Obediently she began to run. His arm stopped her, thrown around her hard and jerking her backward. "No!" he cried against her ear, "not that way. It broke through and the house is going." He whirled her around roughly, with one hand pushed her forward. "I got to get Emil. You can make it alone. But run, girl, run!"

She ran. Her long skirt sagged where she had torn it. One foot caught in it and she fell to the ground. She jumped up, beginning to run again. The skirt caught on a snag and she went down once more. She could hear the fire behind her, hissing like a wildcat. With the wind behind it, it was moving as fast as a horse could run. She struggled to her feet. Panic turned her feet to lead. You can make it, he'd said. Her feet in their high button shoes raced with a will of their own. Across the field, through the long dry grass, down the slope—with a sob of relief Katherine felt the gravel of the riverbank press into the thin soles.

She looked back. The fire could have been no more than a few feet behind her. She watched with sick fascination as it ripped down the grassy slope, sputtered and died in the stretch of wet sand only a few feet away. People were shouting, some of them very near. She meant to turn and look for Nils, to see if he had found Emil Greene and carried him to safety. She should look for Jeb Carlson, for the Barkers, for Carl. But she didn't do any of these things. For a second or two she looked straight ahead, a strange dizziness creeping through her brain to lodge in a great black mass at the back of her eyes. Then she fainted.

* * * *

It might be a dream, Katherine didn't know. She sensed that she had been asleep, and now she seemed to be waking up. But the dream pursued her, clung to her, drew her back among the frightening images she wanted so much to run away from. She could save herself if she could open her eyes. She *did* open her eyes, only to realize that she was only dreaming they were open.

The strange part was that she could feel, and she knew absolutely that what she was feeling was happening in the real world. She was being lifted, she was being carried. The ice cold darkness of the dream was receding; warmth and comfort were all around her. Still she couldn't open her eyes; the lids were too heavy. But it didn't matter anymore, because she was awake now, truly awake. She couldn't open her eyes, but she could see. Where she was, what was happening, who was carrying her. She saw it all. How wonderful, she thought sleepily. What a lovely feeling, to see right through my eyelids.

Drifting through a mist of semi-consciousness, Katherine knew that she was in Nils Bengston's arms. Her clothing was soaked through and wet strands of hair clung to her cheeks. In a flash of memory, she saw the dark pool below the riverbank where she had fainted and fallen. Where Nils had found her, and picked her up out of the river. Now she was wrapped in his heavy Indian sweater, cradled in his arms, and he was carrying her, away from the river, away from the dream.

Pressed against his body, she felt his warmth and the strong beat of his pulse, and against her cheek, the steady rhythm of his breathing. I wonder where we're going, she thought drowsily. To Carlsons'?

Suddenly the nightmare of the prairie fire detached itself from her dream. The burning haystacks, the cabins and barns engulfed by hungry flames, the terrified whinny of horses cornered by a wall of fire—they were all real.

She opened her eyes. The darkness was so thick that Nils' face was a pale and featureless blur though it was only inches from her own. With tremendous effort, she turned her head. Instantly Nils' arms tightened around her. "You're all right, Teacher. Stay still. We're almost there."

She tried to speak and couldn't muster a sound. All her strength had gone into opening her eyes; none was left to bring her voice up out of her throat. So she sank back into a peaceful No Man's Land, somewhere between waking and sleeping. In this pleasantly dreamy state she became a third person, a silent spectator, curious and watchful, but completely separate from the other two.

This other Katherine watched Nils carrying Katherine across a dark field, almost running, as if the weight of her body was no burden at all. A dark shape became a log cabin; she saw Nils duck his head in order to get through the cabin door. Then he was lowering her onto a bed of cedar boughs. The pungent aroma of cedar surrounded her. Minutes later, a fire was burning in the fireplace, opening up the darkness, bringing warmth.

Nils returned to her bed and began to unbutton her shirtwaist. She pulled away and tried to sit up. "It's all right, Katherine," he said quietly. "It's all right."

She fell back, too weak to resist the gentle but confident hands that were pulling off her shirtwaist, removing her long watersoaked shirt, untying the strings of her petticoat. She kept her eyes closed, consciously trying to shut out the vision of her own nakedness, but the other, separate Katherine, Katherine the curious spectator, looked on while Nils stripped off the last covering and Teacher lay naked on her bed of pine boughs.

Nils looked down at the slender body, rose-pink in the firelight. Then he turned quickly, opened a large chest and pulled out a coarse woolen blanket. As deftly as he had undressed her, he wrapped Katherine up as if she were a papoose he was going to strap to his back.

"Now go to sleep."

She was already half asleep and drugged by the heat of the fire, but Katherine heard the hoarseness in his voice, and saw his hands close into fists, and open, and close again, as he walked away from the bed and sat down on a stool in front of the fire.

Some time later she awoke. The sound of her own voice crying was echoing in her dream-ridden mind.

"You were dreaming. . ." That was Nils Bengston's voice. Nils Bengston's hands were drawing the blanket up under her chin. "Go back to sleep. . ."

After that she awoke only once, and briefly. Long enough to see that Nils was still there, and to watch him put another log on the fire.

In the morning she was awakened by sunlight streaming through the cabin window and the aroma of boiling coffee. Nils brought her a cup, and handing it to her said gruffly, "Careful. It's hot."

She took the cup from him. Holding it in both

hands she inhaled the wonderful fragrance. "Back home in Kansas, we never had real coffee. We used barley, mostly, but we didn't always have that." It was a curiously personal thing to say to this arrogant and domineering man, even if he had saved her life. She was sorry almost immediately that she had revealed so much of her inner and most secret feelings.

"This was old Julian's cabin when he first came here, before he moved into the house. I keep coffee here, and blankets, because I come here sometimes. When I want to get away by myself."

He stopped abruptly. Katherine knew from the change in his voice and expression that like herself, he had said more than he wanted to and regretted it as quickly as it was said.

"Your clothes are dry," he said with a curt gesture in the general direction of the wooden chest. "There, on top of the chest. I'll go outside while you put them on. But hurry up. I want to get back to the ranch."

"Yes, Mr. Bengston. And thank you, Mr. Bengston. . ." But he was already outside and did not hear her. Or might not have heard her even if he were still in the room, because her voice was little more than a whisper and it trembled with a sudden foolish need to cry.

iv

Everyone agreed later that Katherine was lucky not to be drowned. Lucky that Nils reached the spot on the riverbank only seconds after she dropped. They said the Smiths and Carlsons were lucky, too, lucky to be alive. Both families lost their homes, their barns and sheds, and everything in them except the livestock. Nate Tarpee moved a few barrels and

sacks around and found room for the Smiths in the
back of the trading post. The Carlsons moved into an
abandoned homestead shack that was part of Nils
Bengston's shingle mill.

"It's lucky the good weather is holding," Faith
Carlson said. "It's hard to hold a good house-raising
in the rain." But she didn't call it "luck" that her
pain had grown worse. Patiently she lied to herself,
saying that these later pregnancies were always hard.
But she let Katherine tend to the cooking and mind
the children. Only when Jeb came near the cabin did
she force herself to get up, and with a second, even
harder effort, force herself to smile.

The dates for the house-raisings were set. Every
family in the Valley joined in. The men cut logs, split
the shakes, trimmed and shaped and cut with adze
and frow, axe and drawknife. The women brought
food and clothes for the children and squares for the
quilting bee. The last of the hops had been picked,
dried, baled and pulled by four-horse teams to the
storehouse near the Black River boat landing. So the
crews of foremen were free, and Nils brought them
along to help with the building.

The day the Carlsons moved into their new cabin,
Mrs. Carlson was too sick to sit up. She rode to her
new home in the back of the box wagon, carefully
wrapped in layers of borrowed quilts. "I'll be up by
Thanksgiving," she promised the children. They
looked at her solemnly, a puzzled little crowd in a
semicircle around the big new bed.

"Promise?" Hiram asked.

"Promise," she said.

He turned to his little brother. "She promised,
John," he explained. Relieved, the little group broke
up and raced outside.

Katherine hid her face by busying herself at the

kitchen table. With hands that had grown quick and sure, she laid a cooking fire. If Faith Carlson could so promise, if Faith could smile fearlessly at her husband, what grounds were there for her own uneasiness? Pray constantly, the two of them said, and shave once a day. There was comfort in work and in that way, Katherine thought ruefully, she had more to take comfort from than most.

She measured the lard out into the big brown mixing bowl, quickly cutting it into the flour. Clothes had to be made, for they all had but one covering apiece. Nate Tarpee had given them yarn for sweaters and there were castoffs from all over the Valley to be cut down to size for the children. On top of this, there was another week of school, and then Thanksgiving.

The children would be frightened if they did not have a real Thanksgiving. To let the holiday pass, or even to let it be a little less or a little different, would be instant notice that their mother was gravely ill. No, she would have to manage it. The pumpkin pies, made with honey. The mincemeat ground from venison and fruit rinds. The roast pheasant, the ham, the pickled apples. . .

A bit of flour sprayed across her skirt. With the back of her arm, she brushed it off. This was her only dress and she hadn't even an apron. She thought suddenly, I wonder what Carl would think if he saw me.

Her throat tightened, as it always did nowadays at the thought of Carl. She hadn't seen him since the day she had disobeyed him, riding away on the back of Emil's cayuse. She had heard later that Carl worked in the bucket line. "Carried more water than any two of the rest of us," Jeb Carlson told her. "And then he got back on his horse and rode down to Black River." Carl had gone back to Seattle on the

Viking, but he hadn't returned with her next trip nor with any trip since. On the day of the fire Nils Bengston had tried to make him wait, Jeb told her, but Carl wouldn't listen.

"What did Nils say to him?" Katherine asked, for she couldn't, wouldn't, ask Nils himself. "What could have made Carl go off like that?"

Jeb shook his head. "Couldn't of been anything Nils said. I was standing right there. Nils was arguing that Carl ought to stay and take care of you. 'She's down there on the beach, stretched out cold,' Nils told him. 'Somebody ought to take care of her. It ought to be you.' But Carl wouldn't answer him, except to say the *Viking* was due to pull out."

"Then Carl knew where I was."

Jeb nodded. "Yes, he knew." Having told her, because she had asked him and he was a truthful man, Jeb was uneasy. "It ain't like Carl to run off without doing what he ought," he said. "He saw me standing there, he knew I'd go down and watch over you."

But it hadn't been a good excuse, and as time had passed it hadn't improved. Katherine pushed angrily on the dough for the Thanksgiving cookies. According to his code, Carl had been justified in his anger, but there was no code in the world that made it right to run away. If he had come back, if he were in the room right now, she would not apologize. For the first time, she would not bring them back together at all if their only meeting ground was her apology. Once she had cared for him enough to say anything to save his pride. She didn't now. Another step had been taken, another moment had come, another bit had been stolen from the imperfect whole. To be perfectly honest, she thought with a curious feeling of elation, I am deeply relieved.

CHAPTER EIGHT

i

IF HI BARKER SAID it would rain before Christmas, it would rain. Katherine had never doubted it. The crickety little fiddler had an instinct for changes in the weather. While other prophets tested their rheumatic joints and said it was sure to storm, Hi cocked his head to one side, sniffed, listened as if there were sounds too high or low for anyone else to hear, and told you exactly what the weather would be.

The first time Levi came to school with one of his father's predictions, Katherine nodded absently and dismissed it. The children were wearing jackets and there was a fire in the hearth, but Hi Barker said they were in for a hot spell. Katherine was fanning herself with a spelling tablet the next afternoon, schoolhouse shutters and door wide open, when she remembered Hi's words. She laughed, thinking that he must be some kind of wizard. A not-quite-human, music-making sprite, but a good one. No wonder they had named the mountain for him.

Rain before Christmas—that had been Hi Barker's reply the very day the worst blizzard of years broke across the Valley. Now it was the day before Christmas, and the snowdrift that had piled up to the eaves on the east side of the Carlsons' barn was reduced to a dirty gray mound, forlorn in the middle of a mud puddle. Gone was the snow-white Christmas many farmers from the Middle West had been anticipating so sentimentally. It didn't look like Christmas in Minnesota now. There was no reason to be reminded of that last holiday in Kansas, or the days when you took a sleigh to grandma's house across the glittering prairie of Nebraska. No turning back, even in memory, from the new and sometimes brutally unfamiliar country. The giant trees, the swollen river, the hard, wind-driven rain, the damp and the dark—this could be no other place than the timber country of western Washington.

Katherine lifted a log from the pile next to the hearth and laid it on the fire. The children were all outside—there wasn't a youngster in the Valley who would think of staying in the house because of so ordinary thing as rain—and when they came in for supper they would have to be dried out somehow. Christmas Eve. Katherine looked at the room wistfully. Whatever there was of Christmas in it, the children had made themselves.

Richie and Martha had cut the tree and nailed it upright between two pieces of firewood. All of them, even little tow-headed Johnny, had made its decorations. Scraps of ribbon, bits of red calico, a little string, paste made from flour and water—they had used these precious things. On the tree were strings of holly berries and popcorn, "snowballs" of cotton, and stars that looked like almost anything but stars, cut from lined theme paper Katherine brought home from school.

"Stars of Bethlehem," the brown-eyed Hiram called them, and once started on cutting them could not be stopped until every scrap of paper was gone. Then he insisted on putting all of them on the tree. He could reach only the lower branches. The older children obligingly hung their decorations up above. With its lower limbs white with stars and stars alone, and its upper ones so crowded with berries and cotton and popcorn that the green scarcely showed through, the tree looked like an overdressed woman with her petticoats dragging. The children admired the tree unreservedly, except for Richie who seemed a little puzzled. Hiram quizzed Johnny remorselessly as to which of the stars were best and why.

"I like that one," Johnny would reply, so eager to please that he pointed to four or five.

"That's un-possible." Hiram picked up Johnny's stubby hand, pulled up the pointer finger and adjusted it properly. "Now show me the absolute best."

Johnny giggled, looking delightedly at what Hiram was doing to his hand. "You tickled!"

Hiram frowned. "John, pay good attention!"

Instantly John sobered. Without a glance at the tree he flung his arm out dramatically. "That one!"

Hiram seemed impressed by his little brother's posture, but puzzled as he analyzed his choice. He squatted a little so as to sight down Johnny's finger toward the tree. "This one?" he asked, touching a paper star with one finger.

Johnny nodded energetically.

Hiram looked critically at the star. "The absolute best?" he mused. He shook his head slowly. "No, John. This one has too many points. We'll have to start over again."

Little Johnny looked longingly over his shoulder.

"Pay good attention, John!" Hiram warned. "Now, think hard. Which do you think is the absolute best?"

The Christmas goodies were lined up on the shelf next to the fireplace. The children had had a hand in

their making, as could be seen at a glance. Cookie
cutters were a luxury no Valley homesteader owned
unless they were inherited treasure saved somehow
during the long voyage west. Since sugar went into it,
cookie dough was a treasure in itself. Katherine had
divided it between the children and let them cut
shapes out of it freehand. Richie's angel was easily
recognized. Martha's Christmas trees were symmet-
rical, almost, or as Martha put it, "Perfectly even, on
one side." The triangles, circles, rabbits, dogs and
reindeer which the other children made were all clear
enough, until one got down to the handiwork of
Hiram.

After earnest discussion he had convinced Johnny
that six was a little too young for shaping cookies.
Johnny hadn't agreed at all until Hiram presented the
wooden potato masher and told him he "was allowed" to crush the rock candy into the crystals
which were to be sprinkled on the cookies. Johnny
pounded contentedly while Hiram preëmpted his
share of the dough, and made stars out of all of it.

Stars out of cookie dough were an even greater
problem than stars out of theme paper, and when
they were baked most of them looked like blistered
circles. But Hiram went to the shelf every quarter
hour to admire them. His happiness was unmarred
until he was told that eventually they would have to
be eaten. Then his tears were so overpowering that
he had to run outside so no one would see him cry.

The matter of Christmas presents had troubled
Katherine the most. Since the fire there hadn't been
an extra board or nail or length of goods around the
place. Jeb had been cutting timber for Nils; not a cent
of his wages or Katherine's could be spent for anything but necessities.

How many Christmases, Katherine reflected,

have I prayed for a doll and found that my only
present was a suit of long woolen underwear? There
is no poverty worse than the poverty of owning nothing silly. She had bought suits of underwear, seven
of them, at Nate Tarpee's store, paying half and
promising the rest when school reopened and she
would receive wages. But she had made rag dolls,
with embroidered faces and white petticoats
starched stiff as crinoline. She had bargained with
Indian Doc, whose knotted old hands were deft at
wood carving. If he carved and painted small war
canoes for the boys, she would give him a plug of
chewing tobacco. Nate had given her the tobacco.
"But don't tell Berthy," he said. "It's the last in the
place and she had her eye on it."

Thus Katherine believed the problem of Christmas
presents had been solved, until the day she found
Martha in tears because she had nothing to give her
mother.

"I know just how she feels," Tommy sobbed sympathetically. "Because I feel so bad myself."

Faith Carlson was in bed, as she had been almost
continually since the fire, but she slept fitfully.
Katherine herded the children out of the cabin and
into the woodshed.

"Now," she said to the assembled seven, "we will
decide about the Christmas presents for your
mother."

Their faces were sad and wise. Only little Hiram
and Johnny screwed up their foreheads thoughtfully,
as if presents were actually a matter of choice, not of
money.

"We can't buy anything," Richie said.

Tommy wailed, "I feel so *bad*!"

Katherine said quickly, "But you can *make* something."

Tommy quieted and his eyes widened with interest. Richie looked doubtful, but he watched her hopefully. Martha exclaimed, "Oh, Miss Duncan, could we make something for the new baby?"

So for some time they discussed the new baby.

Most of all, Johnny wanted to know where it was. Hiram silenced him with a superior, "Inside of Mama, of course. Where do you think you came from?" Johnny was too astonished to say anything more. Each child decided what his present would be—a toy made from spools, a dress, a shawl, a pair of booties, a crayoned picture, a stuffed bear, and from Johnny, a riding horse.

Hiram exclaimed, "Oh, John! You can't *make* a riding horse!"

Johnny's mouth trembled threateningly.

"That's all right, Johnny," Katherine put in. "Maybe you can't, but somebody makes them."

Richie got up from the keg he'd been sitting on. "I'm going to get started." The other children followed, all of them happy with their secret projects.

Like the tree and the cookies, the presents were now awaiting the day of celebration. Tonight being Christmas Eve, there would be prayers and songs and a simple supper so that every edible involving sugar or raisins or honey or butter or other precious materials could be saved for the next day. Katherine sighed. Thanksgiving, with their mother sick abed, had been hard enough, perhaps because Faith had promised her children to be well by then. She had made no promises about Christmas, and the children seemed to know they should not ask her to. There was to be a new baby in February—they understood and accepted her illness as one of the adult mysteries connected with it.

Only Richie could remember that the other children had been born without these long months of pain. Katherine saw that he was afraid, saw that like her own brother Teddy he would keep it to himself. Faith Carlson had succeeded in deceiving her husband. Perhaps, Katherine thought, because she tried so hard. She seemed to collect her strength all day for the time when Jeb would come in from the woods and ask her how she felt. Even her color improved and her eyes brightened. With Jeb to see her she actually looked different. Tomorrow, Jeb would be home all day.

Faith appeared at the bedroom door. Her face was gray. She steadied herself with a hand at each side of the door frame.

Katherine started. "Faith, whatever. . ."

Mrs. Carlson walked slowly across the room. In her full muslin nightdress her body looked grotesquely out of proportion to her small head and narrow shoulders. The pillow had flattened the hair at the back of her head and the braids had been loosened by her tossing. She reached the rocking chair and lowered herself heavily. "Don't worry," she said unevenly. She was gasping for breath. "I want to be up for Christmas Eve. And I'm going to get up tomorrow morning and stay up all day." She took several long, quick breaths. "Except for going to the church service at the trading post. I don't think I could . . . stand the trip in the wagon. Too bouncy. . ." She tried to smile.

"Really, Faith, you shouldn't."

Faith said wistfully, "Oh, Katherine, not for Christmas?"

Of course Christmas was different. Gay, sentimental. A time to love and a time to forgive. Katherine turned her back to Faith and busied herself with putting the plates out for supper. Carl had neither written to her nor come to Gold Mountain since the day of the box social and the fire. The Carlsons, bless them, had never questioned her.

Being a good deal less sensitive, Agatha Tine had. "Where's that elegant fiancy of yours?" she asked, pronouncing the words with a little pout. "Jilted you, did he?"

"He is very busy," Katherine had replied, "finishing his law course."

Agatha grinned. "Proud, eh. Well, when he gets done with that course," and she winked broadly, "come on down and tell me how your engagement is coming along."

Katherine reached angrily for the mush bowls. With far more speed than was necessary she set them out along the deal table. Agatha had been right, of course. She was "engaged," but forgotten. She had a "fiancy," but no one to love. She turned, and taking the spoons from the shelf, dropped them on the table with a clatter.

"Daddy's coming!"

That was Hiram and Susie, heralding their father's coming with simultaneous shrieks. Another child called, "Is Daddy coming?" and three others, standing out in the yard in the rain, yelled, "Yes, Daddy's coming!"

Katherine kept her back to Faith. She knew what Faith would be doing and could not bear to see it. She would be smoothing back her hair, hastily replaiting her braids. She would straighten her shawl and feel anxiously at the ruching around her throat. When the sound of his voice meant he was nearing the door she would sit up straight, moisten her lips, smile. . . .

Katherine made herself pick up the pile of spoons

and one by one set them beside the bowls. Christmas, she thought, Christmas, alone.

ii

The wind rose as the sun went down. It whined through the cedars so angrily that the knock on the door was almost lost in the sound of it. Frowning, Jeb pushed his chair away from the table. "Now, who, in this storm. . ."

Katherine felt a warning jerk at her heart. If it were. . .

Jeb opened the door. Wet through, his jaw clenched and body tensed against the raw wind, was Carl.

Katherine's hands flew to her hair. It was loose around her shoulders, for she hadn't had time to braid it. Her dress—panicky fingers felt of the skirt, reminding her that this was the one she had cut from a faded cotton of Mrs. Nelson's.

"Come in, come in!" Jeb was saying, his hand on Carl's elbow. He peered into the darkness. "Where's your horse? You *did* ride out from Seattle?"

"I put him in your barn." Carl was shaking with cold. He still hadn't looked directly at the group around the supper table.

Jeb smiled. "Lucky for us you were putting something in instead of taking something out," he said jovially, "We can't hear a sound in this wind."

Katherine meant to rise, but sat frozen to the bench. How will I look to him? she thought. What will he think when he sees me.

"First of all you warm up, and then you'll have some hot food." Jeb turned toward the table. "Faith . . . Katherine. . ."

Carl turned his head slowly. "Mrs. Carlson," he said politely, inclining his head. "Katherine. . ."

He was looking at her at last. She tried to smile. Like a sleepwalker she got up and went to him. The children's heads swiveled slowly as she passed. She extended her hand. "I'm glad to see you, Carl," she said, and flushed because her voice was only a whisper.

"I'm glad to be here," he said stiffly. His hand felt cold, but no colder than her own. Quickly she looked away. "Come over by the fire, and dry out. . ."

During the hours that followed Katherine blessed the number and noisiness of the many Carlsons. But at last all the children were in bed and asleep, and Jeb was saying good night as he helped Faith to bed and closed the bedroom door. Silence was heavy as Katherine and Carl looked at each other, adjusting to the reality of being alone together. It was the moment Katherine had yearned for; yet from her first glimpse of him in the doorway tonight she had dreaded it.

Carl's dark eyes were intent upon her face, asking something of her. In confusion, she turned toward the hearth. "I'll put more wood on the fire."

Carl jumped forward. He took the log out of her hands and dropped it onto the heavy andirons. Dusting one palm against the other, he turned to her.

Like a docile child, she waited for his kiss. He looked down at her, only a shadow of space between them. Her body tensed. The faintest shiver flicked through her, as if someone had blown suddenly at the back of her neck.

Carl cleared his throat. "Katherine, there are several matters we must talk over."

The moment lost its intimacy. Carl walked away, turned with his hands clasped together behind his back. It's to be a business meeting, Katherine thought, not a love scene. She nodded. "Yes, Carl."

"When I last saw you. . ." He hesitated, searching for a word, the right word.

"Yes, Carl."

There was a trace of mimicry in her voice, though she hadn't meant it. His pose cracked and he stepped forward and took her hands. "Katherine," he said huskily, "don't mock me."

She flushed. His dark eyes were hurt and all the pride was gone from his face. It was a kind of loss he couldn't stand as well as other people. Suddenly she had to comfort him. "Carl, I wasn't mocking you. I couldn't."

"There is so much to talk about," he said. "All the things I've been thinking about, the questions that have been tormenting me since that day."

She said softly, "That day of the box social and the prairie fire."

He drew his breath in sharply. For a moment his eyes searched her face. Her hands relaxed, he sighed, and the relaxation seemed to spread through his body. "Yes," he said quietly, "that day." He dropped her hands and turned to stare into the fire.

The unspoken question hung in the silence. It might have been a physical object which Carl had dragged from hiding and flung down between them. Do we love each other and are we to marry? It was that simple, so terribly simple that neither of them could say it. In all the time since she had last seen him, Katherine had never voiced it to herself. It hit her now, brutal and clear. If they understood each other, as she had once imagined they did, that was the question they must answer together. If somewhere during the struggles of the past two years that understanding had been lost, then it was the question she would have to answer for herself. Instinctively she tensed, ready to defend herself. "Well, Carl?"

He burst out, "Why did you ride off in—that way? Why have you refused to leave the Valley, when originally you wanted nothing more than to get away from it? How can you have allowed yourself to—to lower your standards of conduct, and appearance . . ." He wheeled to face her. "Katherine, how . . ."

Katherine lifted her chin. This at least is familiar, she thought. He stepped forward and pulled her into his arms. It was so unexpected that she clung to him, comforting him with little mechanical pats on the arm. "My dear, my dear," he said hoarsely, "don't try to explain anything. I know now that it doesn't matter."

While he kissed her Katherine thought, Why, he has forgiven me! She wanted to protest. In his arms, how could she?

He released her. Before she could speak he pulled a little box from his pocket and opened it quickly. A diamond solitaire in a setting of yellow gold sparkled with the reflected firelight.

His eyes were on her face. Dumbstruck, she looked at the ring, then at him.

Carl laughed. "I wish you could see your face! It's a picture. You really *were* surprised." He picked up the ring and dropped the box into his pocket. Smiling he lifted her left hand and carefully slid the solitaire onto her finger. "You should have had this a long time ago."

Katherine thought, courtly compliment, or a rule of etiquette? And then Carl unknowingly answered her. "It isn't proper to be engaged without it."

Katherine let him take her in his arms, and waited obediently for the proper kiss.

Determined as she was, Faith Carlson was too ill to get up Christmas morning. The children opened her presents for her, and spread their handiwork for the "new baby" all over the coverlet. Jeb asked if her pain was worse, and she denied it. "All of you go ahead to church," she insisted. "The sun's shining. It's a nice day. It'll be three months before Brother Bill gets back this way again and I don't want the children to miss him."

So Katherine put clean shirts on the boys and fresh pinafores on the girls and Jeb loaded them all in the back of the wagon. Katherine sat next to Jeb. Carl, who had slept overnight in front of the fireplace, rode behind.

It had been his own idea to attend services with the Carlsons. "Brother Bill is close to illiterate," he told Katherine privately, "but the church service does give us an opportunity to appear together."

As on other special occasions, Nate Tarpee had moved bales and barrels to create space for the church service. The store's peculiarly varied assortment of chairs, benches and stools was lined up as "pews" facing the "pulpit," which was Nate's store counter. Out of consideration for Brother Bill the bottles of whiskey, the beer keg and mugs, the boxes of cigars and tins of pipe tobacco, had been stowed in the back room. Even the big brass spittoons, the post's special refinement, had been removed from sight, though Nate had always held that this worked a hardship on many members of the congregation, among them his wife Bertha. "More people would come to church," he complained, "If they could spit."

Most everyone came anyway, for though Brother

Bill disapproved of many of their pleasures, he was widely admired. Two or three times a Baptist evangelist had appeared and held mass baptisms in the river; it was generally felt that his kind of religion "didn't take," simply because some of his conversations were notably ungodly. A Catholic priest came occasionally to the Valley; except for two Irish families in Three Forks, his followers were Indians. Best known and widely loved was Brother Bill, whose last name of William was heard so little (some of his devoted followers didn't know it) that few remembered it was the reason for his being called "Bill" and that his first name was really Theodore.

Brother Bill was a Methodist, though more than half of the people who came to hear him were not. For one hundred and sixty-nine dollars a year he walked a circuit of some hundred and fifty miles. Nils Bengston, who said the man was a fool to earn a living that way, had once proved it by figuring that Brother Bill received twenty-five cents a mile. "A quarter for every mile," Nils put it, "and not a cent for preaching." Brother Bill was tall, though not as tall as Nils, and he was built wide and heavy. And he had a temper. People in the Valley said it was just as well that he and Nils had never been in the same room together, and unless Nils got the fear of the Lord in him, they weren't likely to.

Brother Bill slept in barns, and sometimes preached in them. His friends along the circuit fed him and gave him a bed, if they had one, but there wasn't a single settlement big enough to provide him with a church. At one time the people of Black River had thought they could at least give him a horse and buggy, and began a collection for it. When he heard of it from Hilke Orvaag, Brother Bill devoted the last thirty minutes of his two-hour sermon to refusing it.

There were so few trails wide enough for a buggy that he would be forced to neglect parts of his district that were the hardest to reach. The easy way was not the true way to serve God. And he had another reason. If he had a horse and a buggy, he explained, the young men would want to borrow it Saturday nights to go visit their sweethearts. Knowing young men and their girls and the distances which separated them, he was sure the horse and buggy would never be returned on time for an early start on the Lord's work. So he had continued walking. He followed Indian trails, wagon roads, pack and sled trails, sometimes nothing but blazes. Fallen logs, swamp, rivers and creeks impeded his progress. He once admitted that he had often followed bear trails rather than crawl through the brush on his hand and knees.

No one knew whether Brother Bill had heard Nils Bengston's cruel calculation of the value of his service. But the first people in the Valley—the ones who had seen Brother Bill limp into Black River when the only family in town was the one that kept the post office, those people—who heard the third sermon Brother Bill had ever preached—knew that one hundred and sixty-nine dollars a year seemed like enough to Brother Bill because at first he had covered the same circuit for nothing.

"How are you going to live?" the people at Black River had asked him that first Sunday. "We can't pay you."

"Like Sherman," Brother Bill had replied with a grin, "when he marched to the sea!"

iv

"And Lord don't let no bitterness come into our

hearts. Open up our eyes to what's right, like you always done. In Jesus' name, Amen.'' Brother Bill looked up from the final prayer. His straight black hair was hanging in his eyes. Blinking a little he smiled, and the service was over.

The congregation stirred slowly. The men reached for their hats and quickly jammed them down to their ears, as if they had just found they were undressed. The women rose, breathed deeply as if to inflate their bosoms.

On the bench where the Carlsons sat, Katherine began helping little Johnny into his jacket. She saw Carl get to his feet but she had no inkling of his intention until he cleared his throat. It had become his way of declaring that he was about to speak. She looked up at him, suddenly frightened. "Carl. . .''

But he had begun. "Miss Duncan and I wish to take this opportunity. . .''

Katherine looked at little Johnny Carlson, at Mrs. Nelson's broad face, at the familiar shelves and the old stove, at Brother Bill. Everything was so familiar, yet so unreal.

". . .to announce our betrothal. . .''

Carl's hand was on her elbow. She didn't move, and the hand became demanding. Slowly she got to her feet. She was conscious of the fact that one hand was still clutching stupidly at the other to hide the ring. Around her the faces jumbled together in a patchwork of odd-size mouths and eyes and teeth. She felt her mouth stiffen into a smile. Over her head Carl's voice said, "Thank you." He released her elbow, and she dropped to the bench. She was trembling.

Brother Bill began to speak. The smiling faces floated before her. Now Brother Bill was standing at the trading post door like a city minister, shaking the hand of each person who passed through. On the plank sidewalk outside, the churchgoers lingered. Carl's eyes were on the crowd outside. He seemed to be counting them. "A good gathering."

He held out his arm, properly bent so that her hand might rest on it without the intimacy of actually touching his body. Like a pair of dolls, they walked to the door.

Brother Bill shook her hand solemnly. She heard herself say, "Thank you," and realized in amazement that she was smiling. Carl moved forward. She stumbled, caught herself, and felt the wooden smile clamp harder over her face.

Mrs. Nelson was the first to congratulate her. "We'll be real sorry to lose our schoolteacher," she said in her flat, loud voice. "My, ain't that a big stone."

"We all want the best for you, Miss Duncan."

"Going to give up being a schoolmarm, eh? Well, who can blame you?"

"Congratulations, that's what I say, congratulations!"

"I sure wish Mary was here to see that there diamond."

She was acting a part but somehow she had got into the wrong play. In the flurry of their well-wishing, the dreamlike confusion evaporated like a mist. This moment was real, sickeningly real. The night before Carl had put a ring on her finger, and she had not refused it. How could he know her feelings, if she had been too much of a coward to tell him?

Carl was saying, "You're right, Mrs. Nelson. We've always planned on living in Seattle."

"I suppose you already set your wedding date?"

Carl patted Katherine's arm possessively. "This is

the last trip I'll make to the Valley without taking her back with me.''

''Well, well,'' Mrs. Nelson said, looking sternly at Katherine, ''I was hoping maybe she'd finish out the school year.''

''Great guns, Nellie,'' someone behind her objected, ''wasn't you ever young and in love?''

Katherine looked at her hand, as still on Carl's arm as if it had been put out for display. She had never felt such cold, bottomless despair. Who arranges our lives, she thought, that at this particular moment I know for sure that I don't love Carl, that I never will?

v

The moment Katherine walked into the Carlson cabin she knew something was wrong. The children's voices had been loud enough to give Faith plenty of warning. She should be sitting in the rocker by the fireplace, tidying herself for Jeb.

Katherine found her lying in bed. Her eyes seemed sunken, staring at Katherine without understanding. Katherine touched her cheek. The skin was tight and hot. Faith whispered. Katherine leaned over her and heard her repeat, ''I'm dying.''

''No!'' Shocked, Katherine pulled up the quilt and tucked it around her. Faith was stoical. It was unbelievable that she had given up. ''You're going to get better,'' Katherine said flatly, and ran outside.

The horses were still harnessed to the wagon. Running across the clearing, Katherine called, ''Don't unhitch them, Jeb.''

Jeb stared, one hand on the breastband.

''Faith. . .'' She stopped, gasping for breath.

"Faith isn't . . . well. I'm going for the doctor."

Jeb protested, "Nearest one is Doc Meade. I can't let you drive fourteen miles to Black River. I'll go."

Katherine shook her head emphatically. "You go in and sit with Faith."

Jeb stammered, "The sky looks bad. It could storm. If it does, that hill by the Falls. . ."

Katherine put a foot on the step, jumped quickly onto the wagon seat. "It won't storm," she said, as flatly as she had told Faith that she would not die. "Stand back, Jeb," and she took the reins into her hands.

"Anyways I ought to saddle up your pony," Jeb said. "If a storm breaks you can't get a wagon up that hill."

Katherine pulled the horses around sharp. "It won't storm," she repeated doggedly. "And you know Doc Meade can't ride since he broke his leg."

"Katherine. . ."

Katherine leaned down and looked directly into Jeb's puzzled face. "Jeb, you *have* to stay here. It's you she needs now, not me."

She saw his jaw tighten as he understood. "Gee ap!" she called, and slapped the reins hard along the horses' backs.

Jeb had not hurried the horses on the way home from church, and so they were fresh. The wind and the sun had dried up the worst of the mud—that was another blessing. Katherine glanced anxiously at the sky. It was clouding over. If it rained . . . She shook her head angrily. "Gee ap," she urged the horses, "gee ap. . ."

She rode through Gold Mountain with scarcely a glance to right or left. Straight ahead was the old Indian trail through Squak and on to Seattle, the trail Carl had taken only an hour or so before. To the right was the wagon road past the hop ranch to Three Forks and down the hill past the Falls to Black River. She turned onto it.

The woods were dark. For the first time she realized she had come away without a gun or a lantern. There had been so many cougars. . .Grimly she held the horses to a walk. Cougars or not, it wouldn't do to tire the team out now.

She passed the hop ranch, and was in the woods on the other side when a man's voice yelled, "Whoa there!" It was Nils Bengston, in a heavy, gray-white Indian sweater, his head bare and a gun across his arm. He was holding two dead grouse by the feet. It struck her that hunting was a strange and lonely way to be spending Christmas.

"I can't stop."

His grin faded as he ran toward her. "What's wrong?"

Even as she was explaining, he dropped the birds and the gun into the wagon and vaulted in after them. With a sideway thrust of the shoulders he shoved her out of the driver's seat. Somehow the reins got into his hands. He snapped them and the horses broke into motion. Five minutes later he said curtly, "I'll go with you."

They scarcely spoke all the way to Black River. In every clearing they looked up at the sky. Clouds were piling up, and the wind was rising.

"Will it rain?" she asked him.

He shrugged. "It's bound to."

"If it would only hold off until we get back up the hill. . ."

He grinned. "It would help. I'd hate to carry that horse doctor all the way up."

"It's turning cold."

"That all the coat you've got?" He gestured to-

ward the old brown jacket she was wearing. It had
belonged to one of the Anderson boys, the only coat
among the castoffs that hadn't been too big for her.
Katherine nodded, pulling her shawl over her head
and drawing it more tightly around her shoulders.
Nils' face had such an unusual softness to it that she
looked away quickly, frightened that he might see
too much in her own. His next words saved her.
"Just as well Indian Doc finally pulled your hat off
the nail. It wouldn't have looked stylish with that
outfit, anyway." He laughed.

Nils could always laugh. Katherine glared at him
and felt better.

They had just turned into Black River when rain
began to fall.

"It's raining!"

"That's happened here before." But she saw the
way he turned to study the blue-gray clouds piling up
to the east.

Katherine said anxiously, "But it isn't raining
hard."

"It will." He pulled the horses up in front of the
weathered board house that was Dr. Meade's. In one
motion he dropped the reins into her hands and
leaped to the ground. "I'll drag him out fast, if he's
here."

Nils went in without knocking. In only a few minutes the door opened again and Dr. Meade came out
with Nils behind him. He was a squat, sandy-haired
man with long uneven mustaches and a big nose. An
old satchel was in one hand and he was buttoning his
coat with the other. Despite a bad limp, he moved
quickly. "Hullo, Teacher," he said gruffly, pulling
himself into the wagon by the strength of his arms.

Nils spoke to the horses, turning them back. The
doctor settled himself with a grunt, balancing the

satchel on his knees. "Mrs. Carlson pretty sick, is she?" His frown pulled his eyebrows parallel to his mustache.

Katherine nodded. "She has a high fever. She hasn't been right since the fire but today it was different."

"Pains coming regular?"

Katherine whispered, "I didn't like to ask."

The doctor guffawed, appealing to Nils as his thumb gestured toward Katherine. "What do you think of a girl who will start out alone on a twenty-eight mile trip with a snowstorm about to break, but she doesn't have the nerve to ask the woman if she's going to have a baby?"

Katherine stammered, "The baby isn't due until February."

The doctor shook his head slowly, "When it comes to that, the doctor's guessing and the mother's guessing. The time to come is something only the baby knows."

The rain was much harder now. The wind beat it against their faces. Katherine leaned forward, crossing her arms across her chest in self-protection. The half-dried mud puddles were beginning to fill up. In the deepest ones the wagon wheels caught for a moment, rolled forward with a loud sucking sound as the team jerked hard against the traces. "You said snowstorm," Katherine said to the doctor accusingly.

He shrugged. "What do you think, Nils?"

Nils grinned, though the rain was streaming down his face. "I think August will be hot and dry."

They turned into the woods, and the rain was suddenly softer. But the trees were crying with the rising wind. Here the mud was worse, for the sun had shone too briefly to reach in and dry it out. The wagon lurched into each treacherous rut, swaying awkwardly as the horses pulled it out. No one tried to talk. They braced their feet to steady themselves and swayed with each dip of the wagon. Looking sideway Katherine saw that the doctor's face was calm, or at least resigned. Nils could almost have been smiling. Shivering, she hunched her shoulders, clutching at the ends of her shawl.

The road had turned out of the woods and was climbing the hill beside the Falls when it began to snow. Katherine felt the first big, wet flake on her cheek and brushed it off with the back of her hand. They were all soaked through. Now without the protection of the heavy timber they would freeze as well.

"Snow," she said grimly.

"Snow," the doctor agreed. "What did you expect?"

The ascent was steeper now. The horses were straining to keep the wagon moving. In every rut it stopped. Harness squeaked and the wagon groaned as the animals lowered their heads and fought the weight. At last it would rock forward and roll unevenly for a few feet more. The snow was falling fast. With the wind behind, it made an impenetrable white wall. Nils was blinded by it but he ducked his head low, slapped the reins frantically and yelled at the team.

The hill seemed to rise endlessly. Hidden by the swirling snow, the Falls thundered at their left. At last the burden was too great. The horses stopped, rebelliously lifting their heads. Their bodies were streaming.

Nils stood up and handed the reins to the doctor. "They pulled us longer than I thought they could," he shouted against the wind. Snow was covering his bare head and had frozen in a white crust along his eyelashes.

"You drive, Doc, we'll push." He jumped to the ground.

Katherine was shivering so hard she hardly understood Nils' meaning.

"Hey, you!" he bellowed, motioning to her to get down.

Katherine got to her feet. Numb and dazed by the cold, she picked up her skirts and stepped from wagon to step to muddy ground. She could see Nils' head and shoulders at the other side of the wagon. He grinned at her. "What's the matter, Teacher," he shouted. "From all I can see of you it looks like you fell in a hole." The wind screamed against them. "Get ahold of that step and push! Like this—one, two, three, shove. . ."

Katherine grabbed the metal step. Nils called, "One, two, three, push. . ." and she threw herself forward. With the first step she felt her shoe go ankle deep into the soft mud. "One, two, three, push. . ."

Nils' voice was fainter. The wagon moved suddenly. Katherine lost her balance, clutched desperately at the cold step. "One, two, three, push. . ." Nils' voice seemed to come with an effort. "Keep it up . . . like that. . ."

Katherine counted silently. One, two, three . . . One shoe had come loose. She looked down at it helplessly, counted, pushed. With the next forward lurch of the wagon, she felt the shoe sink even deeper into the mud. The wagon seemed to be rolling. Frantically Katherine pulled her foot free of the shoe, and ran along beside it. The wagon settled into a new rut, stopping so suddenly that she threw herself against the hard metal step. She looked over her shoulder.

The shoe was ten steps down the hill. "Again, one, two, three. . ." Nils called. Katherine pushed.

The wind ripped one end of the shawl from her shoulders and slapped it against the wagon wheel. The wheel turned and the shawl went around the axle, jerking Katherine backward and almost throwing her under the wagon. Gasping, she righted herself and grabbed the step. The shawl was gone.

"My shawl!" The wind drove the words back into her mouth. She kept pushing. There was nothing to do but keep pushing. The shawl dragged under the wagon for a time. Katherine saw the corner of it as the wheel went over it, burying it forever in the mud. One, two, three, push. . .

Foot by foot, they moved the wagon up the long hill. Throwing her weight forward, gasping for breath, counting, moving, shoving again—it became a series of mechanical actions. Katherine did them with her eyes closed. At the top of the hill Nils called "Whoa!" She collapsed against the wagon, her eyes still closed. "Well," Nils' voice said. "So that's what you're doing. Sleeping."

She opened her eyes. He was right in front of her, and he was smiling.

"Lost your shawl?"

She nodded wearily.

He looked at her feet. "One shoe come off?" he asked, in a strange voice.

She pointed down the hill. "A mile back."

His smile made her heart jump. "We don't see much of each other," he said quietly, "unless the going is rough."

She would have refused if he'd asked her, but he didn't. He swept her into his arms and lifted her onto the wagon seat. "Doc, you move over and put your arms around this girl and warm her up," he shouted at the older man, "or I'll do it myself."

The doctor moved and Katherine leaned against him gratefully. Nils climbed up and took the reins. Face hidden in the doctor's coat, eyes closed, Katherine thought—it's true. When things have gone badly, it hasn't been Carl who helped me. It's been Nils. Nils, Nils.

vi

For three days the doctor stayed on at the Carlson place. Except for the children, who moved around the cabin like frightned mice but slept well at night, there was very little rest for anyone. Jeb Carlson lay in bed fully clothed, but jumped to his feet at his wife's every move or sound. Katherine sat in the rocking chair by the hearth, napping only when she couldn't stay awake. No one saw the doctor sleep at all. Nils went home at night, returned each morning.

All of them, even little Johnny, seemed to know when the crisis came. The doctor had gone into the bedroom and closed the door. They waited outside, eyes on the pitiless door. Hiram came to Katherine so silently that she started at the pleading touch of his hand.

"Mama's going to die!" he sobbed suddenly. He was the little bull calf who never needed sympathy, the proud little rooster who turns to no one, but he let Katherine pick him up and hold him in her lap.

"No," she whispered, her throat aching. "No, no, no. . ." The chair squeaked softly as she rocked back and forth.

When the doctor opened the door at last, he was

carrying a baby. It was concealed by yards of white cotton flannel but the newborn baby's wail was unmistakable. Jeb jumped in.

"The baby's alive," the doctor said gruffly. "Your wife is, too. Better go in and see her." He turned to Katherine. "Ever take care of a premature infant? Know how to keep its bed warm enough? Heat up some fieldstones, wrap them, line the crib with them. Know anything about the milk?" He threw the questions at her.

Katherine rose slowly, with Hiram clinging to her hand. "Doctor, will they really. . ."

The doctor sighed and for the first time Katherine saw him smile. "The baby will live, if you're a good nurse. And so will the mother," he added, shaking his head, "though I'll never know why."

Nils stepped forward. "I'll go out and pick up some fieldstones. And if there's anything else. . ."

The doctor exploded, "Well, isn't anyone going to ask me whether it's a girl or a boy?"

"Well, what is it, a boy or a girl?" Nils yelled back.

"It's a boy!" the doctor roared.

"Well then it ain't likely to turn into no schoolteacher," Nils said calmly, smiling at Katherine, and went out to get the fieldstones.

vii

Katherine turned her hand slowly from side to side, watching the wintry sunshine pierce the diamond solitaire and flash out again. It was the first time she dared rest, except to fall asleep for an hour or so out of necessity. And it was the first time she had thought about her engagement ring. Only four days earlier Carl had opened the box and proudly slipped it on her finger. Yet she knew that in those four days they had been separated forever.

She leaned back against the barn wall, tilting her face to the sun and closing her eyes. Being new since the fire, the barn smelled sweet with cedar pitch, and even sweeter when warmed by the sun. Exhaustion, now that Faith and the baby were safe, was a pleasant sensation. The doctor was packing his bag and would soon leave for Black River. Nils was in the barn, hitching up the team so as to drive him there. Jeb was asleep, the children were playing. It was good, just for a few minutes after one job was finished and before the next would begin, to be all alone in the sunshine, doing nothing, thinking nothing at all.

Thinking had grown more complicated. Until recently it was Carl she consciously closed out of her mind. Whether it was because she couldn't make up her mind how she felt about him, or because she knew and lacked the courage to tell him, she hadn't wanted to think about Carl. Now for the past four days she had been near Nils, bound to him by their intimate common purpose of saving Faith and her baby. They had spoken very little but Nils' presence had been as comfortable as the crackle of the cedar logs in the hearth and the sight of a well baby sleeping peacefully in his cradle. As two people working together on a life or death task, they were anonymous, and Katherine had not been afraid of him. But the job was done. The urgency had dissolved. She was once more the schoolteacher and Nils was the dominating king of the Valley who hated schoolteachers in general and ridiculed her in particular. If you liked Nils, you bowed down to him. In old Uncle Julian Katherine felt she saw what happened to anyone who admired Nils. Nils didn't need anyone; he was built to have people need him. A woman who loved Nils

would be lost forever, as her own mother had been
lost through the gentler domination of her father.
Katherine had pulled free of her father just in time,
saving nothing but a scared little redhead with just
enough grit to keep the world from knowing how
desperately scared she was. In a year that rebellious
child had made herself into Teacher. Teacher was a
whole person. If she loved Nils, if she even thought
of him. . .

Katherine's body stiffened defensively, the wonderful sleepiness jolted out of her. She mustn't think
about Nils. Once it had been the existence of Mary,
his Indian wife, which branded such thoughts as
wicked; even when people whispered that Mary had
been no wife to Nils for many years, that only Nils
would be too proud to admit it. Now it was a matter
of fact, not of hope or pride or wishfulness. At last
Nils and Mary were divorced. It had been listed in
the *Post-Intelligencer,* printed proof of something
everyone in Gold Mountain had known for years.
Not Mary, then, but Carl's ring, winking in the sunshine, stood between Katherine and Nils. She stared
at it, fighting down the sense of disloyalty it aroused.
She couldn't marry Carl. Why had she refused to
recognize the real reason, unless she was afraid of it?

At the other side of the barn Nils' voice spoke to
the horses. Katherine's right hand flew to cover the
ring, like a frightened mother bird protecting her
young. In a moment, the doctor would come out of
the house, Nils would leave, and she hadn't said a
word of thanks to him in four days. She should get
up, walk around the barn, speak to him. She recited
the actions, like a person who lies in bed in the
morning and dreams that he has already accomplished the dread chore of getting up. The horses
snorted, the wagon creaked as they jerked it into

movement. Nils' voice said, "Who. . ." and then, as she had known all along he would, he came around the barn.

He stood between her and the sun, looking down at her with his hands on his hips, and to Katherine his face was in shadow. She said quickly, "I've been wanting to thank you, Mr. Bengston."

But he had his own ideas of what they were going to talk about. "I see you got a new ring."

The protective right hand pulled back, disclosing the diamond. Katherine flushed. How silly I'm acting, she thought angrily. As if I hadn't known it was there. She forced herself to look up into his face. "An engagement ring."

"I don't go to church. But I heard about it."

It was hard to make out Nils' expression, with the sunlight in her eyes. But it wasn't amused, as it should have been—didn't Nils laugh at everything?

"Yes." She didn't love Carl, but Nils thought she did and had accepted the ring on her finger as proof of it. Katherine uttered silent thanks that she had not taken it off and returned it to Carl. "Yes, it's beautiful."

"Carl knows the right way to treat a lady." His voice sounded strained. "But I bet he don't know how to love one."

Color flooded into Katherine's cheeks. "That's nothing for you and me to be talking about!" She meant to be outraged, but her voice caught, and she knew she sounded more like a little girl trying not to cry.

"There isn't any polite way to love someone," Nils said. "And you can't love out of duty, or because you promised you would."

"I don't know the—the subject of your remarks," Katherine said stiffly, "but I don't want to hear them. I had intended to thank you for helping Faith and Jeb. That's what I'd like to do." She stood up. "Thank you very much, Mr. Bengston. You've been helpful."

Instead of leaving, Nils came so close Katherine had to look up to see his face. She was trembling—would he notice? "Please leave!" she burst out. "I wanted to thank you, and have it ended that way. Why do you always have to spoil everything?"

"When you really love someone," Nils said quietly, "it eats into you. You can't stay away. You can't move a foot or a hand without thinking about him. If he's away from you, you drive yourself crazy trying to remember exactly how he looks, and how he moves, and what he says. Let him—or her be a thousand miles away, you look for him all the time."

Katherine fled to the protection of anger. "If you're talking about yourself, I'm not interested. And if you're talking about Carl White, or about me, I say you're presuming. You've been very kind and I hate to leave you in anger but. . ."

Nils raised his hand. "*I'm* leaving," he said. "I won't be back, unless you send for me."

"I'm sure there will be no reason for that!" She was shaking so badly she knew he must see it. Now was the time for Nils to laugh—she was braced for it. But he didn't. His eyes rested on her thoughtfully and his mouth relaxed. She glimpsed the man who had pulled her out of the river, carried her to old Julian's cabin, undressed her and wrapped her in blankets with gentleness she had never known a man to possess. "Nils," she murmured. "Oh, Nils. . . ."

He hesitated, looking down at her as if her voice had arrested him in flight. Then the moment ended. He simply turned and walked away. Katherine sat down on the bench. The doctor came out, climbed into the wagon, and Nils and he drove away. The sun dropped slowly toward the dark trees. Shivering, Katherine got up and went inside.

CHAPTER NINE

i

NILS WATCHED THE MEN loading a wagon with the last of the season's hops. The oxen blinked patiently as each nine-hundred-pound bale was dropped. The wagon's heavy timbers groaned, the double yokes jerked down on the oxen's necks. The hops had been picked by hand, spread and turned in the kilns by hand, pressed into bales by hand. The men were sweating to load them and the ox teams, four beasts to a wagon, would sweat to get them down the Valley to Black River. From riverboat to seagoing vessel, thus the third crop would go. From the ranch of Nils Bengston into the beer bottles of England. Nils frowned. Other years had been better. But curse those who were prophesying that every season would be worse than the last.

There had been more than a thousand Indians at the pay table this year—did *that* sound as if there were nothing to pick? The great herds of ponies, the horse races and sing gambles and games of two-card Monte; the young Indians in jeans and the half-naked old ones, with long hair and moccasins and a blanket—they had been the same this season as before. The silver dollars had been stacked just as high, and the Indians had as usual spent a good many of them for bottles of Jamaica ginger. Again this year Nate Tarpee had succeeded in selling the Indians several bottles of bluing, with instructions not to drink it until they were back at camp (or at least, out of the store). Where were they looking, what did they see, these cussed long-faces who sniffed for the scent of failure like hounds after bear?

His foremen came to him with anxiety so thin on their faces that their grins showed through. They said the hop louse had hit the ranches up north. They said the crops were so sickly two of the owners figured on planting potatoes next year. They said they'd heard hop prices weren't going to be as good as they had been—the English dealers were buying in the East. They said—Nils muttered angrily. They said what they'd always said, because they had always hoped it was true—that this time Nils Bengston had out-reached himself. And they were as mealy-mouthed as ever.

The driver cracked a long whip over the heads of the oxen, bellowing a string of profanities. The animals lowered their heads and moved with a slow, thudding gait.

The last of the crop—but it had been a good crop, if a smaller one. The weather hadn't been right all year. It had been dry at the wrong time and rainy at the wrong time. Why didn't they think of that, instead of screaming "Hop louse!" when not one of them could show him a vine eaten by aphids? As usual the long-faces were the ones without an acre or a dollar of their own. They were the ones whose wages always go for what they have already eaten. Theirs were the flat bellies during the winter.

Nils thought, But *I* had eight hundred acres of hops this year, and they yielded sixty to seventy-five boxes to the acre. There is so much livestock here that we grew a hundred and fifty acres of hay alone. Potatoes, carrots, turnips, onions, pears, prunes, plums, berries—we raised, we sold them all. The year's apple crop alone was bound to hit above five thousand bushels. Could anyone match that?

Thinking of the apples made him smile. They came from the trees he had planted when he was a heedless kid of nineteen. He'd been as poor as Tom Stump, who laughed at him for borrowing money so he could buy the tiny trees. Tom hadn't been the only one who laughed. Tom wasn't the only one who was still poor while he, Nils, was rich. What had he seen that Tom and the others were blind to? Nothing, perhaps, except that you can't get rich and be safe at the same time.

The loan that bought the apple trees had come from his father. It was the first loan, the smallest one, and the last he'd asked of him. There had been Seattle banks willing to take a chance on him when he wasn't yet twenty-one years old and none of them since had had to press him for payment. Every mortgage had been bigger than the last, but he had grown steadily richer. The others would have stopped years before. They would have paid off their debts and settled down forever with what they had. They were too easily satisfied. Nils grinned. Half the people in the Valley owed him money. What would they think if they knew he was so heavily indebted himself that one crop failure could ruin him?

Some would worry about him. Some would be gleeful, right down to the holes in their shoes. Most of them wouldn't believe it, and this was the remarkable fact that gave him courage whenever he was forced to think of the possibility of failure himself. He had bought worthless stump land and made it rich as pasture. He had bought timber, a sawmill at Black River and a shingle mill at Gold Mountain. He owned buildings in three villages, farms all over the Valley, a hotel and a store. He had handled them all as he had those first little apple trees whose fruit brought him the first cash he had; he spent all income immediately as a down payment on something bigger. No, most people wouldn't believe Nils Bengston could fail. He didn't believe it, either, because he never had.

He wasn't like poor old Captain White, who had staked his life out on a tub of a riverboat. They were building a railroad now. It had already reached Union Bay on Lake Washington and they were saying it would get to Bothell by Thanksgiving. Snohomish Junction would be next, then Squak, then Black River. In a year or two there wouldn't be a living on the river. Ten years from now the little children wouldn't know the sound of the riverboat whistle, bleating as she came around the bend like an old ewe with the sniffles. Riverboats willl soon be gone, Nils reflected, but there'll never be a time when men won't want their beer. No one could be safer, then, than the owner of the biggest hop ranch in the world.

ii

Julie came up so quietly that Nils was startled by the touch of her hand. "Well, Julie," he said, sweeping her off the ground so that her eyes looked directly into his.

She could laugh, though seldom with anyone else but him. There had been times when they were alone together that she had laughed until she rolled on the ground, her knees pulled up against her chest in a spasm of utter delight. But when she was solemn, as she was now, her face was a smooth, tan circle. The mouth barely moved to speak and only the blue eyes, the light and variable eyes of the white man, could give her away. They were shining now.

"I have come home from school."

Nils felt his smile stiffen. Since those days spent at the Carlsons he had seen Katherine only when a meeting could not be avoided. He had had time, in the long months since, to prepare himself for the sight of her. Yet he winced at the mere mention of the school. I *have come* home from school. Julie said it so precisely. It reminded him that before Katherine came she had learned to say it the wrong way—from him. I just come home. That's what he would have said. Nils frowned. Well, what was the difference?

He hugged Julie impulsively. "You like school, baby?" The words were out before he remembered she had asked him not to call her baby.

"We're going to have a new school."

"I've been hearing that for two years," Nils said brusquely. He hugged Julie tighter, bargaining for an extra minute before he would put her down and she could look at his face. I know Katherine is in the Valley. I know what she looks like, I know the sound of her voice. I have seen and memorized everything about her and set it aside. After all this time, he thought, I shouldn't be licked just by thinking about her.

Julie gasped. "A school with glass windows." She sounded as if he were squeezing the words out of her. Nils lowered her to the ground. "With glass windows? Is that what your teacher said?"

Julie nodded solemnly. "So we don't need to light the lanterns, even in winter. The windows will let in light, and whenever we want to, we can look out at the mountain."

"Did your teacher say that, too?"

"Which part?"

"About the mountain."

Julie nodded again. "Teacher loves the mountain."

Teacher. . ."What else?" Nils said quickly. "What else is going to be in that new school of yours?"

"Real desks," the little girl said. "Everybody's going to have his own."

"Is that so?"

"Pencils and new books."

"Yes. . ."

"A regular big wood stove with a round tin chimney."

"You don't say."

"Teacher says maybe we will have a globe."

"What the deuce is that?"

Julie said patiently, "A big, round ball—that's the earth. All the countries are painted on it."

Nils muttered, "Oh, I seen those. Well, what else?"

Julie's voice dropped to a whisper. "Teacher didn't say for sure, but I think there's going to be two toilets. One for girls and one for boys!"

Nils stared at her in his effort not to laugh.

Julie asked anxiously, "Don't you believe it?"

Nils nodded. "Oh, yes, I believe it."

"Father, will you come to the program?"

"I don't know nothing about it!"

Julie clutched his hand. "But we just decided about it today! There's going to be a program at the school."

"What kind of a program?"

"Mostly we're going to recite and sing." She tugged at him eagerly. "I'm going to say 'Tell me little housewife playing in the sun.'"

Nils said roughly, "I never heard it." He took Julie's hand in his. "Let's go to the horsebarn. I've got to look at the teams."

"Father, *everybody's* coming. Teacher's going to tell about the new school. If you aren't there, she'll wonder. . ."

Nils broke in angrily, "She won't wonder about a thing! I got something else to do, something important."

Julie pulled her hand free. Her eyes rested on him for a moment, then she turned and walked toward the house. Nils knew she would not mention the program again.

He wanted to call her back. Julie would obey, but he knew how proud and how tongue-tied they both would be. She could not understand his indifference and he could not explain it. What was the poem— "Tell me little housewife playing in the sun. . ."? Julie would recite it for the others. Others would listen, others would clap their hands and smile because she had done so well. Then Katherine would tell about the school. The others would be there to hear her. The glass windows, the real desks, the big wood stove with the round tin chimney. Others would promise to help her, others would applaud. Perhaps even Carl would come out from Seattle, for the first time since the Christmas Sunday when he had made public his claim to Katherine. But he, Nils Bengston, would be missing, the man who loved her as no one else could.

iii

Elsewhere in the Territory people were talking about

statehood. In Black River they were talking about the railroad. But in Gold Mountain, they were talking about Teacher's new school.

Every few weeks there was some sort of an event "for the new school." There were box socials, school programs, a quilting bee one week and an auction of the quilts the next. With each the school fund grew, sometimes only by a dollar or two. Those who had no money gave butter or eggs or a calf. Nate Tarpee squeezed such donations from one family, wheedled another into buying them, and turned the proceeds over to Katherine.

"Pulling ourselves up by our bootstraps," Agatha called it. "Make something and sell it back to ourselves. I'll never be able to look at that school without seeing hams and butter and box lunches and quilts, and little teacher running around with a shiny nose and her braids coming loose."

Late in the fall of '86, more than two years after Katherine had arrived in Gold Mountain, help for the school came from an unexpected source.

It was Brother Bill's day to preach in Gold Mountain. After the service he approached Katherine. "I've been hearing about the new school."

Katherine smiled. "Every three months for two years?"

Brother Bill looked down at her sternly. "Doubt is a sin." He cleared his throat and pushed the long black forelock out of his eyes. "Someday I hope Gold Mountain will have a real house of worship, as well as a real school."

"Why, of course!"

Brother Bill's homely face cracked with surprise. "Of course?" he echoed.

"I've thought of it often."

"Once the school is built. . ."

Katherine nodded energetically. "That's what I've planned, too."

Brother Bill studied teacher's bright, small face. There was such intensity in the big eyes. He sighed, and a wide grin took the place of the ministerial frown. "Now who was going to commit the sin of doubt," he said. "If I'd thought I would have known that you'd have a plan like that." He forgot his sternness altogether and boyishly stuffed his hands in his pockets. "You're going to need a good carpenter. I was building houses in Seattle long before I knew whether Genesis come first or last. I know you'll help with the church. So I'll put up your schoolhouse."

Katherine said conscientiously, "Money for the school has come in very slowly. It may be years before we can collect enough for a church."

The cowlick had thrown the long lock back in Brother Bill's eyes, but he ignored it. "It looks like God wants the schoolhouse first. He'll show us the right time for the church."

Thus it was decided that Brother Bill would be the school's head carpenter. The lumber would be cut at Nils Bengston's water-powered mill at Black River. Brother Bill would be coming around about the first of February and again about the first of May. On this second next hike around the circuit he would stay long enough to get the school building well started. Others could finish.

That night Katherine took down her notebook from the rafter above her bed. By candlelight, she turned to a new page and printed carefully: "School year 1887-88. Classes will be opened in the new school building."

Over the winter there were more events "for the new school," as weather permitted. Brother Bill reappeared in February. With Katherine he wrote the list of materials which would have to be bought in Seattle. Nails, school desks and the big tin stove with the round chimney—these would be transported by the *Viking*. Windows and doors would come from the Dave Denny mill in Seattle. They would be shipped across Lake Washington, through Squak slough and Squak lake to the village of Squak; it would be fifteen miles along a rough wagon road from there to Gold Mountain.

"It will take some good ox teams to haul that lumber up the hill from Bengston's mill," Brother Bill said. "Who's got them?"

"I don't know." The untruth seemed doubly wicked when told to Brother Bill. Katherine blushed. "The only good teams are at the hop ranch."

Brother Bill frowned. "I'm not on the best terms with Nils Bengston."

"He donated the land for the school." She said it quickly, but having begun his defense she could not abandon it. "He has also given one hundred dollars in cash and some of the lumber is to be free. He's been very helpful." Her voice faded. Nils had offered nothing to her directly. For more than a year they had scarcely spoken to each other. Whatever he had been willing to do for the school had been promised through Julie.

Brother Bill asked, "Is the school to be built with money that comes out of a saloon?"

Katherine's face burned. Brother Bill's antagonism to Nils was reasonable and she should not be hurt by it. "Not from a saloon. . ."

Brother Bill was at his full height. "What else is money that comes from the growing of hops?"

Katherine could not answer. Soon Brother Bill had gone, the list of building materials in his knapsack.

Weeks later Katherine realized that he had not said he would ask Nils for the oxen.

Then *she* would have to ask him. For weeks the thought disturbed her. She had vowed to stay away from Nils, just as she had vowed not to abandon her school and her children in order to run away from him. And yet this was a chance to see him, not across a room, not riding past, not from a window. May came, and still she had neither gone to the hop ranch nor sent her request by Julie.

Before she did, a cattleman riding east from Squak brought a message to the school. It was a note from Brother Bill, who wrote he would be there in three days, and figured on starting work on the school immediately.

She would have to talk to Nils herself. The excuse was reasonable. There wasn't time any more to ask her conscience what was "loyal" to Carl, and what wasn't.

Katherine dismissed the class hurriedly. Heart pounding, she watched the last child disappear down the trail. The shutters were already closed, the door was barred. She raced across the schoolyard to where her pony was grazing. The bridle hung from the saddle horn. She did not wait to put it on him. With one leap she was in the saddle and had the halter rope in her hand. She spoke to the pony, turning him toward the hop ranch. She and Emil Greene had not gone half as fast the day they rode to fight the prairie fire.

iv

Nils saw her coming. He had just come from the hop fields, where crews were setting the poles. The sight of her went through him like a tremor. He'd go to the barn. Whatever brought her here, someone else could talk to her. But he didn't move. In the field he had been testing the soil, rubbing it through his fingers; his hands were caked with dirt. He thought of how dirty his hands were. They felt separate from the rest of him, as awkward and as uncertain as he. He'd go into the house. Under Julie's bright gaze, and with Uncle Julian, a wise old witness, he could meet Carl White's girl and show no more than he should. Still he did not move. Katherine was near now. She was reining the pony in, with the other hand throwing the unruly red curls back from her face.

Nils walked toward her on wooden legs. She should say something. He looked up into her face and panic hit him at what he saw. Dear heaven, he thought, we feel the same. Whether she's Carl White's girl or whether she isn't. And she doesn't know what to say any more than I do.

He put his hand on the pony's neck. "He was always a good horse," he said huskily. "A lot of horse for an Indian pony."

"He's a fine horse."

"I'm glad you didn't send him back." What a stupid thing to say! She'd had the beast for almost three years. She'd even thanked him once, in that proud little way of hers. "Uncle Julian figured you might."

"I didn't," she said, half whispering.

Her mouth was trembling. We can't keep looking at each other, Nils thought angrily. Our faces are too bare. "You need a horse." His hand fell awkwardly on the bridle. She hadn't waited to put it on the horse. His throat constricted at this sign of her eagerness. "You ride real good. As good as a man." It looked as if there were tears in her eyes. Nils stepped back abruptly and thrust his hands into his pockets. "You come for something," he stated brusquely, turning away from her.

Her voice was small as a child's. "I came to ask for the loan of your oxen."

"What for?" He kept his eyes on the trail as if he were watching for someone.

Her answer came out in one breath. "Brother Bill's coming three days from now. He's going to start building the school. He needs the teams to haul the lumber up from the mill."

Nils' old resentment of the evangelist stirred. It was a good feeling. "My oxen wouldn't take a step for no preacher!"

"Oh, but I'm sure Brother Bill could. . ."

"Not him!" Nils frowned. "Three days from now, eh? He figures on hauling the lumber Sunday."

"Well, no, I'm sure Brother Bill wouldn't work on Sunday."

Nils' gaze jerked back to Katherine's face. He had been holding back so much. Gratefully he poured his feeling out against Brother Bill. "Why not?" he roared.

Her eyes flickered.

"Why not?" he repeated.

"It's the Sabbath. He will be holding services. On Monday he'll begin work on the school."

Her mouth wasn't trembling and her eyes had cleared. She never backed away from a fight, Nils thought. He could bear to fight with her. He grinned suddenly. "He ought to have the lumber ready," he said. "So I'll haul it myself. On Sunday."

Katherine began to object, and stopped herself. But the unspoken question lingered on her face.

"Well?" Nils said. "Anything wrong with that? According to Brother Bill I'm headed straight for hell anyway. I might as well haul a little lumber on the way down.''

''We planned to hold the service in the schoolhouse this time. There'll be a dedication prayer afterward outside where the new building is going to be.''

As Nils thought that over his grin widened. ''You mean you wouldn't want me and my oxen to come rolling in and break up your fine prayer meeting.''

Her chin was high and her nose was in the air. God bless her spirit, Nils thought, and his feeling for her came back so hard and sudden it hurt.

''Exactly!'' she said, stiff as the preacher himself.

He wanted to sound mean. He wanted to get riled. *They* wouldn't work on Sunday. He would. He'd haul the lumber on the Sabbath and make hypocrites out of them all for accepting it.

Nils cursed them silently, the good, the nice and the penniless. He grasped at anger and felt it shrivel into nothing. ''Katherine. . .''

Her eyes went real wide. How green they were—he had almost forgotten. And that crazy splatter of freckles across her nose. His size had always given him confidence but now it seemed like a weight he could not move. A sense of hopelessness swept through him. ''You'll get the lumber. It will be there by Monday morning.''

''Thank you.''

She was looking down at him in a way he couldn't endure. He felt himself move toward her, saw her lean toward him, felt the shock of her soft mouth against his. But he hadn't moved, and neither had she. Carl White's girl. . .but he always took what he wanted, wasn't that what they said about him?

''Why don't you get out of here!'' Nils blurted out. ''Haven't you got no place to go?''

He shouted the last words over his shoulder as he walked toward the barn. He walked fast, looking straight ahead. The pony gave a snort of surprise; she must have pulled him around suddenly. Then the sound of the pony's hooves, trotting away down the dirt road. "If I was only sure," he cried out loud, "if I only knew. . ."

v

Three days later the people of Gold Mountain gathered to break ground for the new school. Solemnizing the occasion, Brother Bill gave an extra long sermon. Then the congregation rose. With Brother Bill in the lead they walked across the clearing to the spot where the new schoolhouse—the real school with glass windows—was to be erected.

Brother Bill had just raised both hands and asked them to bow their heads in prayer when a string of oxen appeared at the bend in the road. They were pulling one of the hop ranch's long flat wagons and it was piled high with lumber. The driver was Nils Bengston, bareheaded, his work shirt open at the throat, and laughing.

Every bowed head twisted sideways as the devoted tried to peek at Nils Bengston while Brother Bill prayed. The evangelist's voice faded as he reluctantly lowered his hands.

"Hello, Bill!" Nils shouted. "I got your lumber."

The oxen seemed to move more slowly with every step. Brother Bill looked from his flock to the wagon and back again. "We'll have our prayers," he said sternly, "when he's gone." Two or three of them nooded. The rest were looking at Nils. It was doubtful that they had heard the minister at all.

Brother Bill held his position, his hands at his sides and his shoulders square. The minutes ticked away painfully during the long silence attending Nils' approach. The oxen came so slowly that he was certain several times that Nils had stopped them. At last Nils actually did pull the oxen up.

They were so close the animals could have butted the edge of the group but Nils yelled anyway. "Now where's this stuff supposed to go?"

Brother Bill felt a tickle of sinful anger. "About three hundred feet straight ahead," he said, his eyes on a spot just over and beyond the heads of the congregation.

Nils clucked at the oxen, but they didn't move. He slapped them with the reins. The beasts didn't seem to notice.

Someone in the group called, "Speak to 'em, Nils. You know how."

Oxen traditonally obeyed nothing but swear words. Bill knew it and so did everyone else. Brother Bill glared at the man. Nils was standing up in the wagon, his feet planted wide apart and his bare head tilted back with silent laughter. He was daring all of them—anyone could see it. Brother Bill fought for command. "I'd like to remind everyone that this here is a prayer meeting!"

Nils answered, "Sorry, Bill." He jumped from the wagon, gently patted the neck of the lead ox. "Please," he said. "Please, for God's sake?"

Brother Bill roared, "I will not have blaspheming on the Lord's Day!"

Nils yelled back. "Well if you'll tell me what day you *will* have it, I'll come back and unload this lumber for you!" He crossed his arms and leaned against the ox. "All I said was please."

"You're breaking up our meeting!"

Nils shrugged.

Brother Bill's body stiffened. His temper was his worst sin. He knew its slow rise and terrible strength. "Mr. Bengston," he said, lowering his voice, "you aren't helping me to lead this meeting."

"Brother Bill, you ain't helping me to unload this lumber."

"Can't you make them oxen move?" the evangelist retorted, voice rising.

"Why sure! If I can talk to them the way they's used to."

Brother Bill pressed his lips together frantically. A man chuckled, a woman giggled. He faced the congregation. "We'll go back inside the schoolhouse, until. . .later."

Like a distraught cowdog Brother Bill loped around the fringe of his flock, motioning them toward the old cabin. It was a warm day, and the shutters were open. As the congregation filed in Brother Bill hastily closed them on the side near Nils.

Nils called, "Whatever you're going to say in there, you better say it out loud!"

Brother Bill closed the door with a bang.

They had been whispering. The sound died as they faced their preacher. He saw that some were ashamed, some indignant, and one or two of the men were all but laughing. He thought of the days before he got the call, when the only way to treat a man who laughed at you was to lick him with your bare hands. He thought of the times he'd done it, of the days when money could make him forget how unhappy he was and a bottle of liquor could make him forget anything. His long, rough fingers combed through his hair. "Let us pray," he said unsteadily. "Father in Heaven. . ."

A jumble of swear words broke into the prayer.

Nils was shouting at the oxen in a way the oxen understood. Brother Bill raised his voice. Unencumbered by the fear of God, Nils' was stronger.

Hastily Brother Bill ended the prayer. "We will sing!" he called, loudly enough to inform Nils himself. He sought a hymn that would be fast and loud. "Onward Christian Soldiers!" he announced, and began singing without waiting for anyone else.

For a moment they stared at him dumbly. Their preacher was straining his throat with "Going as to war, With the cross of . . ." Outside Nils was cursing the oxen at the top of his lungs. One by one the group began to sing.

Brother Bill's throat ached. His arms beat the air desperately, urging them to sing louder and louder. When they came to the end of the three verses they knew, they sang right on into the first and went through them all again.

Their faces were red with the effort, their bodies strained forward. Their eyes shone as they followed Brother Bill's flailing arms. They went through the hymn a third time. Some stopped for breath, gasped two or three times and went on singing. The fourth time the tune was lost in the shouting. Sweat stood out on their red faces. "Onward! Christian! Soldiers! Marching! As! To! War!"

Brother Bill's arms stopped their frantic directing. One by one the singers gasped to a halt. Brother Bill listened, body rigid and arms in mid-air. There wasn't a sound from outside. Still they waited, the group as motionless as he. In a moment they heard the slap of board on board. The oxen had moved. Nils was unloading the lumber at the far side of the clearing.

Brother Bill sighed. "I will declare Thy name unto my brethren," he said quietly. "In the midst of the church will I sing praise unto Thee." He ran his fingers through his hair and grinned. "That's from the book of Hebrews." Half his followers were still gulping for air. But they were smiling, too.

vi

Brother Bill began the school in May and the men of Gold Mountain worked on it through the summer, a few hours here, a few there, as time permitted. Thanks to the box socials and twenty-five cent ham dinners and all the other projects Teacher had organized for two years previously, there was money for everything. "School Year 1887-1888" would indeed begin in the new building, just as Katherine had once written in her notebook. By the first of September they would need nothing but books. To raise money for them Katherine planned one last project, and it was to be different from any of the others.

The railroad had moved forward slowly, from Union Bay to Bothell to Woodinville to Squak. It would be in Gold Mountain early in 1888, if what the railroad men said was true. Trains were already running to Black River, and track had been laid along the south bank of the river all the way to the Falls. The people of the Upper Valley had already learned which section foremen would take them up the hill on a hand car for twenty-five cents apiece.

With summer came the Valley's first sightseers. On a warm Sunday fifty or sixty people from Seattle would come out for a look at the Falls or just for the ride itself. Among them were sportsmen, city people who astonished the Valley by fishing and hunting simply for the fun ot it. Hilke Orvaag, complaining that he couldn't feed the Sunday tourists unless he built new tables, gave Katherine a new idea. She and the mothers of the school children would prepare a Sunday dinner, serving it out-of-doors to the people who came out on the excursion train. As teacher, Katherine wrote the railroad with the idea of persuading its director to post signs in the passenger cars on the day of the dinner. She was unprepared for the response.

Ever since the road had been extended as far as the Falls, the company replied, some sort of promotion had been under discussion. They had now definitely secured the services of a professional tightrope artist, for a performance the first Sunday in August. A special excursion train would proceed not only to Black River but all the way up the grade to the end of the track in a clearing above the Falls. There the excursionists would enjoy the spectacle of a famous daredevil making the perilous crossing on a wire stretched across the river. If the mothers of Gold Mountain could be prepared to serve dinner to, say, eight or nine hundred people, at, say, fifty cents a plate. . .

Everyone in Gold Mountain worked for the school that first week of August. The men split logs to make the long plank tables on which the dinner was to be served. They set them up under the maples where the land above the Falls sloped gently towards the river. Hogs were butchered and the boys went out after deer. In every kitchen in Gold Mountain women baked bread, pies and meat. On the big day they loaded it all into box wagons and drove down the prairie to the picnic site.

When the excursion train came around the bend and squeaked to a halt, the women were waiting behind the tables in a close and silent line, like badly outnumbered soldiers sworn to hold or to die. They

had baked two hundred pies and as many loaves of
bread. If all the roasts of venison and baked hams and
chicken and beef and sausage had been weighed together, it would have come to a quarter of a ton.

Their faces were drawn. Even Agatha's moon-
shaped face had a thin look about it. But their aprons
were unspotted and starched so stiff they rattled.

As it turned out, the train had brought a thousand
people, and they found nothing wrong with the food.
In fact it took them less than an hour to eat it all up.
Then the promised entertainment began.

A wire had been stretched out across the river and
tightly fastened to platforms raised four or five feet
above the ground on either side. The platforms were
reached by simple wooden ladders. As the time for
the act drew near, the crowd thickened along the
river banks. Hundreds of Indians had collected silently, their eyes flicking from the dinner tables to the
indefinable white man's folly above the river. Farmers, loggers, prospectors of the Valley mingled with
them, as curious about how Teacher's big doings
were getting along as they were about the performance.

At last a well-dressed man climbed to the top of the
south platform and began to talk. The crowd recognized him instantly as the barker. They listened but
with the air of people who believe only what they see.
One false step, the city man was shouting, and this
man could be dashed to his death on the rocks three
hundred feet below. Gold Mountain knew that.
Another reason to doubt that he would actually get
out on that wire, their glances said. The performer
bowed automatically every time the barker raised his
voice. The Valley people waited patiently for the
proof.

At last the barker stepped back. The tightrope walker leaned down and someone below the platform handed him a straight-backed kitchen chair. With this in his hand, he slid one foot cautiously onto the wire.

There wasn't a sound but the rumble of the Falls. Among the spectators there was hardly a movement. The man moved along the wire. With each step away from the riverbank the silence among the watching people grew more intense. The river swept under him, crashing over the precipice. He hesitated, swaying slightly, then took another step.

In the middle of the river directly over the Falls, he stopped. Crouching, he tested the wire, pushing down on his insteps so that he bounced gently. Then he straightened up, facing first one bank and then another in an appeal for applause. The clapping was faint and died out abruptly, as if the spectators had forgotten what they meant to do.

The performer bowed, his face stiff with the showman's practiced and meaningless smile. He tested the wire again, sliding a little from side to side. Then he struck a pose. Now, now I'm about to do it, the posture said.

He held the chair with one hand and with the other began to unbutton his coat. Before the awestruck crowd he removed the coat and hung it on the chair. Then, very slowly, the shirt. Finally the trousers. One foot, then the other, hung in the air for a long and terrible minute. All his clothes were now draped over the back of the chair. He stood before them, swaying slightly, naked but for a pair of pale blue tights.

He posed again, lifting one free hand. A long "Aahh. . ." rippled across the crowd. Quite suddenly, as if he wanted to stay their applause, he balanced the chair on the wire and sat down.

While he rocked back and forth, the crowd went wild.

They hooted, whistled, clapped, shrieked. When he got up and slid hastily along the wire to the platform, they applauded even louder, as if getting back to safety were something remarkable in itself. The roar of voices outdid the roar of the Falls.

The tightrope walker put the chair down on the platform. Automatically his body stiffened in the position of the artist accepting acclaim. Arms lifted in a graceful arc, feet turned out like a ballet dancer's, back straight, head up, smile. Thank you, thank you, it said, and at the same time, louder, please. He held it while the crowd screamed approval. One, two, three, four, five, six, seven, eight, nine, ten. He dropped the pose and the smile, turned and scuttled down the ladder. Hilke Orvaag was standing at the foot of it. The performer seemed to trip. Hilke's square hands shot out to steady him.

The man was shaking from head to toe. His face was pasty white. Staring at Hilke's ruddy face like a man trying to see something a mile away, he muttered, "I need a glass of beer."

Hilke looked quickly over his shoulder. "Could you need it more than me?" he asked. He put an arm around the man in the pale blue tights. "In the wagon," he whispered. "But my wife don't need to see us." Grinning happily, Hilke hurried the trembling daredevil away from the scene of his triumph.

vii

It was all over. The tourists had climbed back into the train and the little black locomotive had pushed it

down the grade. The people from Kalakwahtie had
gone home by canoe and wagon and the people of
Three Forks and Gold Mountain had headed home
one by one, thinking already of the evening chores.

It was quiet again, and the shadows were lengthening before the afternoon sun. The women sorting out
dishes and bowls and roasting pans at the picnic
tables were too weary to speak. Their aprons were
crumpled and their hair was in their eyes. In a wide
circle around them Indians waited silently for the
scraps. They came forward at a nod, took what the
women handed them, crept back to the watchful ring.

Nils was alone at an empty picnic table. One by
one the wagons were leaving. He should be in his
own, and halfway home. But he waited, because he
could not see Katherine. She should go home with
the Carlsons, but there was Faith. And there was
Jeb, waiting in the wagon. Could she have left with
someone else?

Nils shook his head. He would have seen her
leave, and he had no business thinking about her
anyway. He shouldn't have come today. They didn't
need his help. He had tricked himself into believing
they did. He'd told himself the sight of Katherine
couldn't hurt him; or that if it did now, each meeting
would disturb him less than the last and that was the
only way to get over it. He had studied the crowd of
Seattle people, expecting to see Carl White among
them. That would mean seeing Katherine and Carl
together, and he had thought that would be the kind
of bitter medicine he needed. But Carl hadn't come,
and the sight of Katherine alone shook him so badly
he wondered that when he first loved her he had felt
so little by comparison.

This watching her from a distance—Nils hated
himself for being such a beggar. He had known all

along that he wouldn't even talk to her. When it was over she would climb into the wagon with all the Carlsons. He would watch her until the road turned and they were all out of sight. He had pictured it, prepared himself for it. Perhaps that was why he was waiting so uneasily. She must appear, climb into the wagon, go. Then he could begin his lonely ride home.

The Nelson wagon rolled away, then the Smiths' and the Andersons'. Besides himself there were only the Carlsons now with Jeb stirring impatiently on the wagon seat.

Faith Carlson began calling the children. They appeared from all directions and climbed into the back of the wagon. Nils heard the elder Carlsons talking together. Then Faith questioned one after another of the children. Suddenly Nils was frightened.

He walked quickly toward the Carlsons, his fear doubling as he saw how gratefully they turned toward him. Faith resented him, Jeb would have liked him but didn't dare. It was wrong that they were so eager to see him now.

"Have you seen her?" Faith called even before he'd reached them.

"Not for a while. When did you last. . ."

Faith exclaimed, "Not since the train pulled out!"

Little Johnny sang, "The train, the train! *Choo* choo choo choo *choo* choo choo choo. . ."

Jeb looked at his wife. "Faith, you don't suppose . . ." It was clearly a question he did not expect Nils to understand.

Faith shook her head firmly. "Her leave the *school*?"

Nils winced. They knew her best and they knew it was the school that kept her here. He owned the biggest hop ranch in the world. In a few years the ranch would pay off his debts and he'd be one of the richest men on the Coast. He had everything in the world, but nothing Katherine would see as reason for staying in the Valley.

"Have you looked for her?" Nils gestured up the slope toward the woods.

"I remember she did say something about she'd like to rest quiet for a few minutes." Faith turned to the children. "Not a one of you seen her, for sure?"

They shook their heads. Johnny jumped up and made a locomotive with his hands. "*Choo* choo!"

"I'll find her."

Jeb was at his side as he walked along the river bank, then turned up the hill and circled back through the maples. Neither of them spoke. They found Katherine in the long grass at the far edge of the clearing. Her shoes were off. They stood side by side at her elbow, unbuttoned and toed in as if a pigeon-toed girl had just leaped out of them. Her hair was loose and her apron was crumpled up under her head. She lay on her side with her hand on one arm and her knees drawn up, and she was sound asleep.

Nils and Jeb sighed almost simultaneously, then they looked at each other and smiled.

"Well!" Jeb whispered. "It don't surprise me she fell asleep. After all she's done the last few days."

"I'll take her home."

Nils spoke softly. But there was such urgency in his voice that both he and Jeb were startled. Jeb's smile faded. For the first time in his life Nils felt as if he might be blushing.

"Yes, I will, Jeb. I'll take her home," he repeated. Instinctively he tried to keep Jeb from replying. A commanding forefinger pointed in the direction of the wagons. "No need to wake her up yet. You go home with your family."

Jeb said uncertainly, "*We* could wait. . ."

"I'll take her home!"

"It makes a long ride for you."

"Jeb, I want . . . I've got to talk to her."

Jeb looked at him thoughtfully. Nils faced Jeb, daring him, even asking him, to guess the truth. Jeb knew Katherine as well as anyone in the Valley. He knew Carl White. Nils stood in front of him, grim but defenseless, waiting for Jeb's judgment. His feeling for Katherine was plain, if Jeb could see it. And if he could, what would his opinion be of a man who fell in love with another man's girl?

Jeb said at last, "I guess you got a right to talk to her, if you want to."

Jeb wouldn't try to judge another man. Nils thought, I should have known he wasn't the kind that would. "Thanks, Jeb," he said softly. "I guess you know. . ."

But Jeb did not want to know, if knowing put him to the test of judging. He backed away. "It don't seem right to wake her," he murmured. He hurried down the hill toward the wagons.

Nils sat down on the grass next to Katherine. The sun dropped slowly, the shadows lengthened. The rocky cliffs of Old Hi turned pink with the late afternoon glow. The scratchy voices of the crickets grew louder and the meadowlark's song turned melancholy. Nils' eyes were on Katherine. He pulled a stalk of grass, chewed on the soft end, threw it away, pulled another. As one hour slid into another, he sorted out his thoughts and endured the struggle between conscience and desire.

The sun fell behind the ridge. The trail through the heavy timber would already be dark and dampness would raise from the river. Gently Nils picked up the sleeping Katherine and held her in his arms.

She stirred and opened her eyes. They were dull with fatigue. "I fell asleep."

"Don't wake up." Her head fell back against his shoulder. He carried her down the hill, walking more carefully than he ever had in his life. In the wagon he pulled her close and put his arm around her. She was awake, but she did not pull away. They rode the many miles back to the Carlson farm in sleepy silence.

In the barnyard Nils jumped to the ground and held out his hands. Katherine hesitated, looking down at him like a child wakened from a deep sleep. At last she leaned forward and let herself drop into his arms. He held her, his face against hers. Her hand touched his. It was cold. His own hand closing over it felt the cold stone of the engagement ring. He put her down, wheeled her around toward the house and gave her a gentle push. "Go to bed," he said hoarsely, but watched until the door closed safely behind her. Then he got back into the wagon and let the horses take him home.

CHAPTER TEN

i

TOMMY TINE, Agatha's son, sat on a log in the sunshine and decided that the way things were going the day promised to be just about perfect. First off, there wasn't any school, so a fellow could come down to watch for the *Viking* without playing hooky. Not that Tommy was given to playing hooky, especially. Since Miss Duncan had started teaching almost four years before, only a real emergency, like the first snow, or an extra good fishing day had ever dimmed his faithfulness. Even then it wasn't as if he'd planned it. More that he just happened to change his mind somewhere along the road between home and the schoolhouse. He'd never lied about it afterward. "Didn't go to school today, Mother," he'd say walking right into the kitchen with his string of fish. She never punished him. "Well you better clean them things outside," she'd say, "I don't want to find no salmon tail in my sugar bowl." But she looked so hurt he always wished he hadn't done it. His mother wanted him to be as bookish as Grandfather Martin had been, the one who signed the papers when the Washington Territory was made. Tommy knew she was already saving up for a pair of eyeglasses. He hoped he'd learn to read well enough to use them. He didn't like to disappoint her. So he was glad there was no school today, and he could come down to meet the *Viking* and still go home and look his mother in the eye.

Then there was the weather. Being June it was more likely to be rainy than clear. As his mother said, "We got a right to the sun during July and August but in June, it's doing us a favor." Today the sky was pale blue and there wasn't a cloud to cross over the sun even for a minute. The sunshine ate right into you. It warmed the top of your head and thawed out your joints. It made you happy without knowing why and sleepy all the time. The robins chirped, the meadow-larks sang, the hayfields smelled sweet. Last week the log he was sitting on would have been soggy with rain. The wetness would have soaked through his jeans in no time. His fingers picked lazily at the bark. It was dry and warm, and came off in little rust-colored chips. Tommy sighed with pleasure.

There were so many things he might do today. He could go fishing. He could burn out a little more of the cedar canoe old Indian Doc was showing him how to make. Or he might go find Julie Bengston. Julie always had fine ideas, like building a dam across the creek or hunting for periwinkles. He thought about them all. It was fine to think about them while you sat on a log waiting for the riverboat and did nothing. Because if he didn't move until sundown, if he left the fish in the river and the periwinkles in the swamp pools and the canoe untouched in the woodshed, the best of this perfect day was still waiting at the end of it. Tonight there was a dance at Black River.

Hi Barker would come down from the mountain with his fiddle. If Hilke Orvaag's hotel didn't burn down, they'd still be dancing at breakfast time. People would come by wagon from Gold Mountain and Three Forks. They'd paddle upriver in canoes from Kalakwahtie and the farms below.

Tommy stretched out on the log and closed his eyes. The dance tonight—he might even whirl

around a few times himself, if Julie Bengston would
try it with him. Fishing and periwinkles, Miss Duncan standing in front of the class, the sound of a fiddle
playing, the smell of warm cedar needles, Tom
Stump yelling with his arms beating the air. . .

"Toot!"

Tommy rolled off the log with a thud. That one
short wheeze, like his mother trying to call him when
she was out of breath—that was the *Viking*'s whistle
when she came around the bend. The riverboat was
here at last, and he had been asleep.

He rubbed his eyes hard with the back of his hand.
At the foot of the hill a crowd had gathered around
the boat landing. In a minute the *Viking* would be
alongside and they'd be shoving her cargo out and a
fellow would find plenty to look at. Suddenly Tommy
spotted Teacher, waiting for the boat along with all
the ordinary people. "Gee!" he said, and ran down
the hill toward her.

Tommy skidded to a stop right at Teacher's side.
Grinning broadly, he said, "You're here, too."

"Yes, I am." She smiled at him, but to Tommy it
seemed like a shaky smile, as if she were thinking of
something else and was maybe even a little scared.

"Yep, you're here," he repeated. She wasn't acting natural. It made him uneasy.

"I done that extra lesson at home," he volunteered.

"*Did*, Tommy." She was looking at the *Viking*.
She didn't even look at him when she talked.

"Did," he mumbled, kicking the dirt with a boot
heel. He liked Miss Duncan fine. The only teacher
he'd had before her had given him a first reader and
every time he finished it had made him start over
again at the beginning. He had hated the book so
much he hadn't even learned to read it, and his

mother had twice washed his mouth out with yellow soap because he had called the teacher a pukey. But Miss Duncan was different. After two years in her school he was in the fifth grade, and he'd had a new book every year, not a single one of them a "reader." He liked Teacher too because she wasn't. . .Tommy's mind stumbled when he tried to find the word for what she wasn't. She *was* like Julie Bengston. She rode a horse like a man and played baseball with the kids and she didn't giggle or cry. She didn't talk grown-up, closing you out as if being young meant you weren't quite smart. Tommy's heel stirred the dirt angrily. Miss Duncan had never acted. . .secret. But she was now. He took a few experimental steps to one side, watching her closely to see if she would miss him. She didn't. She was staring at the deck of the *Viking,* so still it was like she was holding her breath. Her face looked funny and stiff. In disgust, Tommy turned and as noisily as he could, walked away.

But he couldn't abandon the riverboat, even for a thoughtless woman. He slid through the crowd to a vantage point on the river bank next to the landing, a perfect spot for looking.

There was old Captain White. He and the man stevedoring for him were already pushing boxes down the plank. There was the captain's son, but he wasn't working this time. In fact, Tommy couldn't remember when he had last seen him on the *Viking.* He was dressed up good enough for a funeral, Tommy decided. Tommy's eyes followed him admiringly. Young Mr. White walked down the gangplank. He seemed to know just where he was going. He didn't look right or left. He went up the hill through the crowd with no more than a nod to anyone. Then he stopped, right in front of Tommy's teacher.

Tommy's stomach contracted unpleasantly. Sure he'd heard the women talking about him and her. "Funny kind of 'engagement' when he ain't been to see her for eighteen, nineteen months," they said. "But she's still wearing his ring." Tommy had taken it all for female talk. It just wasn't possible that Teacher would think of doing something so—so common, as getting married. He watched Carl White extend his arm, saw his teacher smile as she took hold of it. She didn't look like herself. Her smile, her gesture as she put her hand on his arm—suddenly Tommy saw her as just another woman. Teacher, who was to be admired, had crumbled and fallen away. Mr. White and Miss Duncan were walking up the hill now. Very slowly, like they were talking over secrets. Tommy clenched his fists and felt all riled, as if something bad had happened. "Gee whizz darn!" he blurted out.

He bit his tongue guiltily and looked around. He hadn't meant to say anything out loud. No one seemed to have heard him, except one man he hadn't seen before and he was grinning. It was only Julie's father. Tommy gulped with relief. "Oh, it's you, Mr. Bengston. I didn't know you was here too."

Mr. Bengston was all right. He always said the words Tommy was forbidden to use and he wasn't likely to report a simple little Gee Whizz Darn. His mother complained that he had a big heart and a hard head but the way she said it, it sounded like a compliment and that's the way Tommy had always taken it.

Mr. Bengston said, "I like to watch the boat come in, same as you, Tommy."

But he was looking up the hill, where there was nothing to see right now but Mr. White and Teacher, walking together toward town. He had been grinning

when Tommy first saw him, but Tommy thought uneasily that for Mr. Bengston, who laughed at everything, the grin hadn't lasted long at all.

"You going to the dance tonight?" Tommy asked.
He wanted desperately to draw Mr. Bengston's attention back to the landing.

But the question failed. Still watching Carl White
and the teacher, Julie's father said slowly, "I don't
know, Tommy. I don't know if I dare."

Tommy looked at him dumbly. Mr. Bengston was
so big. He was strong, the strongest man in the Valley. What he'd said didn't make sense. It was one of
those grown-up remarks. Behind it lurked the whole
unpleasant, secret grown-up world. Tommy turned
his back on Mr. Bengston, gluing his eyes on the
Viking. He wouldn't look up the hill. He wouldn't
look at Mr. Bengston. It seemed all of a sudden as if
the sun had gone down.

ii

Carl was thinking of the people around them.
Katherine saw it in every motion he made. In the way
his steps were measured as he walked up the hill from
the *Viking*. In the way he allowed no recognition to
break across his face, though she knew he had seen
her even before he got off the boat. In the way he
held out his arm, saying, "You're looking well,
Katherine."

Couldn't he smile? Katherine surprised herself by
feeling irritated. Not guilty or worried or excited or
any of the other emotions she had been suffering ever
since his letter had come the week before. They had
not seen each other for two and a half years. The
whole world had changed in that time but—"You're

looking well, Katherine." "I'm feeling fine," she said curtly.

"You brought the wagon." He didn't pretend it was a question. He was stating a fact, so flatly as to deny the possibility that it might not be true. He had never approved of her riding astride, especially when she had become so hard and skillful a rider. His intonation brought back every quarrel they'd had, and her irritation doubled. I wanted to be nice to him, she thought. Why won't he let me?

"Shall we go?"

They walked up the hill. For the first time Katherine wished she had told Carl everything she had to say in a letter, and sent it to Seattle months, or even years, before. If he could stay away from her for two and a half years, why had she imagined she owed him something? His letters had come at regular intervals, almost as if he had marked the dates on the calendar well in advance. His reason for staying in Seattle had been good—he had to finish his studies. But would a man in love consider that any reason at all?

She had begun so many letters to him and destroyed them all with a feeling of shame. Writing a letter and sending back his ring could be made to sound very honest and proper, but she had felt it would be cowardly. What was "honest" about running away from the moment when she would have to explain her feelings to his face? And so at last she had written, "If you can make this trip without interfering with your studies, I would like to talk with you."

Weeks later his answer came. "My studies are finished now, and I am employed full time by the firm of Bryce and Bennet. I agree that there is much to talk over. Can you meet me in Black River when the *Viking* arrives there a week from Saturday?"

This, then, was the moment she had felt only a coward would avoid. They had met, smiled politely, and were walking arm in arm. Was this the time to say, Carl, I do not love you. I cannot love you. Thank you for everything, but . . . Kindness urged her to reach back two and a half years to the last time they had been together. By acting natural she would assure him that nothing had happened since. But so much had happened, so much which in his deep self-interest he didn't even suspect. "You are working for a law firm?" she said stiffly.

He nodded solemnly. "As I wrote you, the name of the firm is Bryce & Bennet. For a time I will serve as an apprentice."

Katherine thought, why is it hard even now to tell him I don't love him? Because "I don't love you" is an admission that somehow I *haven't* measured up? I was asked to love, I tried to love and failed. Or is it that I know how proud he is. If Carl doesn't love me, it will still hurt him to be rejected. It would be easier for both of us, she thought, if he had come to tell me that he no longer loves me. He would do it so kindly.

Carl was saying ". . . fifteen dollars a week. Many apprentices aren't paid at all."

She nodded. "That's fine. You should be proud." Now, when he was in the midst of describing his success? Was now the time?

"It will give us a modest living."

Her hand tightened convulsively. "I can't go to Seattle!" Once she had been ready with every kind of explanation. She hadn't expected to need them now. Confused, she repeated the stupidity. "I'm sorry, Carl," she murmured, "but I can't go to Seattle."

Of course he would misunderstand. Why wouldn't he, when she had blundered around the truth? "Katherine," he said stiffly, "I believe you heard what I told Mrs. Nelson after the Christmas church service two years ago. I said that was the last time I'd leave the Valley without you, and I meant it sincerely. For three years you have postponed our wedding date because of this. . .little school of yours. Your school has separated us long enough. The school year is finished now. There is no reason why you can't come with me.''

She grasped at the unimportant error. "Oh, no, the term isn't finished *here*! There will be classes all through June and July, to make up for the time the school had to be closed over the winter.''

"Let Nils find another teacher!''

Color rushed to Katherine's face. He blamed everything on the school. Their long separation, the unhappiness that had developed between them before that. She wanted to cry out at the injustice of it, but the strength to do it deserted her. He was wrong, all wrong. Now could she begin to tell him? Later, later, her mind cried silently, I'll talk to him later. "The wagon is right over there,'' she said unsteadily. "In front of the hotel. I wonder who those men are beside it?''

Carl frowned. "They were on the boat. Loggers. Undoubtedly looking for a ride to Gold Mountain.'' He turned to Katherine. "I'll refuse. If we are alone, we can talk.''

Katherine stammered, "We shouldn't refuse!''

Carl shrugged. "Very well, later then.''

Later, yes, later, Katherine's mind cried in silent reply.

iii

The dance began at nine o'clock, more or less, and

would end at dawn, unless the fiddler caught still another wind and played on. The dancers left home after evening chores and were often late for the morning ones.

Being hungry or sleepy was no excuse for leaving early. Everyone brought food. The kitchen table in Hilke Orvaag's hotel was loaded with roasts of ham and venison, crocks of sauerkraut and pickles and bright yellow butter, and loaves of bread. You could eat whenever the idea took you. Chairs and benches lined the dance floor. By midnight many an old man would have dozed off sitting up, hands on his cane and chin on his chest. A dozen children would be stretched out on the benches, one leg drawn up close, the other falling off the bench, their heads resting comfortably in their grandmothers' laps. The only disturbance was the silence when the fiddler stopped to rest a while and the dancers went outside for a breath of air.

Hi Barker had never played better. Everyone was saying it. "Hurray for Hi, hurray for old Hi!" Levi, who never danced, sat on a stool behind his father. Every smile they gave Hi as they danced past, every affectionate nod made the boy's eyes shine with pride. Even little Johnny Carlson paid his tribute. The younger Carlsons were lined up on a bench, their mother and father at one end and Katherine and Carl at the other. Hi had just wound up a fast reel.

At last he handed his violin to Levi and began to stretch his arms and fingers. That meant he would rest a while. Katherine turned to Carl. In the afternoon she had dreaded talking to him, but since then it had been even more unbearable not to be able to. Then there had been the crowd of the children, the chores, the evening meal, the many preparations for the dance.

"Carl, we've been wanting to talk," she said. "Hi has stopped playing. Shall we go outside?"

She took his arm. Quite suddenly the music began again. Carl stopped. "It looks like old Hi doesn't need a rest yet." He pulled Katherine around to face him. "And it's a waltz."

Katherine exclaimed, "But I'd like to talk. . ."

"We can talk while we're dancing." Carl led her onto the floor with a slow, even glide. "*I* can do more than one thing at a time. I'll do the talking. The *Viking* leaves first thing in the morning. We'll have breakfast with the crowd and get on the boat right afterward."

"Carl, I can't!"

He glanced at her dress. It was of brown and white gingham, with full sleeves and two rows of ruffles around the bottom. "You'll look fine, even in Seattle," he said confidently. "You don't own anything worth riding all the way back to Carlsons' for. We can say good-bye to everyone in the morning." His quick gesture was tinged with distaste. "They're certainly all here."

Katherine stiffened. Now, while he had irritated her. "Please, Carl," she said, "may we leave the dance and go outside?"

He looked startled. His smile was gone so quicky she might have knocked it off his face. "If you wish."

Katherine walked across the dance floor and out the front door, Carl behind her. At least, she thought, Nils isn't here to see. Others would notice, nudge each other, smile, but she need not go out into the dark with Carl with Nils' eyes following her.

Outside the air was warm, and sweet with the scent of some invisible Balm of Gilead tree. Spears of lantern light from the hotel windows cut across the darkness.

"Yes, Katherine?" Carl's voice was anxious. It sounded like the Carl she had once talked with during the trip inland from Snohomish City, the boy who knew insecurity and self-doubt and hopelessness. Katherine thought, will I end up by pitying him? She walked out of the irregular circle of light and turned to face him.

They seemed to have fallen into a pocket of blackness. Carl's face was indistinct, but she knew he was looking down at her, waiting. He was afraid. She could feel it as surely as if an uncontrolled spasm had made him clutch her hand. All the tactful phrases, the reasons that were not reasons at all, flashed across her mind. She had such a simple thing to say, and had thought of so many complicated ways to avoid saying it. Carl was waiting.

Would he be angry? Would he destroy her with his retort, in the fury of his injury trying to hurt her as much as she had hurt him? Katherine drew a deep breath and spoke quickly. "I can't marry you," she gasped. "Because I don't love you."

He did not move. In the quivering silence she pulled the diamond ring from her finger and extended it blindly. "I kept wearing it, because it didn't seem right to take it off without your knowing." His hand was there, and she dropped the ring into it. "Carl, I'm very sorry."

"You might have written."

"Carl, I'm sorry. I tried, but a letter seemed a cowardly way to tell you. If you had only come out."

"I was exceedingly busy." His voice was steady. He was a stranger whom she had not hurt but only inconvenienced. "The work that kept me away from you was *important*."

Another slap at her notion that "her little school" was important, too. He was telling her that it was the school, only the school, which had made them strangers to each other. And he believed it. A sigh shuddered through her, escaping in the barest exhalation of breath. After all, it had been so terribly easy.

"I want to thank you, Carl. You have helped me in so many ways."

"Nothing at all." His voice was muffled, as if the darkness choked it off.

She said anxiously, "No, truly, I am grateful to you. For your kindness, when I first came to the Valley. For all your advice."

For loving me. The words came to her, but she held them back. If she didn't love him, what right had she to remind him that he had once loved her? "For everything. . ." Surely there must be something more to say.

"Good-bye, Katherine." His arm moved. Mechanically she responded, and they shook hands. "Good-bye, Carl." He was about to go.

"Oh, Carl," she cried out, "if only. . ."

He turned back. "If only?" There was no eagerness in his voice. There was nothing at all.

The last bit of her old feeling for him died like an echo. She shook her head. "I guess—oh, I don't know."

"Good-bye, then." Even in the darkness she could see the polite inclination of his head.

"Good-bye." She stood still, listening to his footsteps as he walked down the wooden sidewalk in the direction of the *Viking*. The sound ended abruptly. He had stepped off the sidewalk into the dirt street. Still she waited. Hi Barker's fiddle twangled faintly in the distance. It was all over. He was gone. For the first time there was a painful lump in her throat. She walked unsteadily toward the hotel.

The light through the hotel windows made a pale

circle on the sidewalk outside. Just at the edge of it Nils Bengston was standing.

Katherine gasped. He hadn't been at the dance. She had been so thankful for that. Now Carl was gone, it was all over. Her teeth were chattering as if she were cold.

A powerful hand took possession of her elbow and half guided, half propelled her away from the lighted windows, around the hotel into the shadows. There Nils stopped and released her arm.

She felt rather than saw him move toward her, loom over her, so big he seemed to be falling down on her.

"Nils." It was an anguished whisper. She put her hands up to steady herself, to push him away.

"You didn't kiss him good-bye."

Her hands touched his chest, clutched the rough shirt. She looked at him helplessly. "It isn't fair..."

In a mighty sweep his arms pulled her against him. For an instant her body tensed and her hands pushed desperately against his chest. But the secret desire stirred. It spread through her relentlessly. Through her body, down her arms to the fingertips...

Nils kissed her mouth. The shock of feeling was so strong that she could not turn her head away. Her hands crept up to his shoulders, while he kissed her cheeks, her forehead, the soft hollow of her throat.

Inside the hotel Hi Barker's fiddle played a final flourish. "Form your squares!" the old man's voice sang out, and in a second the violin began the fast bright tune of a square dance. "*Honor* your *partner...*"

Katherine pulled away. Nils held her, with her hands pressing uselessly against his chest. "My darling girl," he said huskily, "don't ever run away from me again."

She couldn't speak. "*Now* every*body* circle *round*!" came from the dance floor. She looked up at Nils—the wide eyes, the blunt nose, the hair that had grown so long it curled back behind his ear, the strong mouth. He was a strong man, and yet she had never been so helpless against him as she was in loving him.

"*Ladies* keep a-going and the *men* turn back. . ."

She tried to pull free. In one kiss she had told him her feelings as clearly as if she had whispered them in his ear, but she fought against him with an instinct to save herself. In the distance Hi Barker's scratchy voice sang, "*Pa's* in the pantry, *cows're* in the hay, *take that pretty one* and *bring her this way*. . ."

"Nils. . ."

His hands were gentle, but she might as well have tried her strength against an iron bar. In her fight for independence she had told herself that loving Nils she would be lost forever. Now, weakened by his touch, just his physical size and strength were frightening. If she let herself love him, wouldn't she be surrendering to a man who might want her now, but would never really need her? She had seen her mother destroyed by love. Was her own nature so very different? Nils was so strong, so rich, so . . . invulnerable. What could love add or take away from such a man? I am afraid, she thought desperately. I will be lost. . . .

The moment of indecision lengthened. Her body ached with desire but mind and voice were paralyzed by old fears. "I don't know," she whispered. "I'm afraid. . . ."

Nils' arms dropped to his sides.. "Afraid of loving," he said quietly, as if he had heard what she hadn't been able to say and was simply saying it for her. "Yes, Katherine, I know what it is to be afraid. I have fought against loving you from the day you came to Gold Mountain. *I* am afraid of loving. In spite of that, I *know* that I love you."

Nils turned away. With long rapid strides he was leaving her. Silent, motionless, Katherine watched him go. *Now!* an inner voice urged her. *Now!* Everything hung in balance. To love him forever, or let him walk away.

"Nils!"

His figure had already disappeared around the corner of the hotel. Now he must be on the road. In seconds he would reach his horse and ride away. Like a person bewitched and suddenly free of the spell, Katherine lifted her long full skirts and petticoats and began to run.

When she found him, she was too short of breath to speak. She stood in front of him, skirts clutched in both hands, mouth open as she gulped the cool night air.

Through the hotel windows music and lamplight spilled out into the rutted street. "Chickens in the bread pan kneading up dough, heel and toe and away we go. . . ."

Nils looked down at Katherine with a gaze of intense and silent scrutiny. Still without speaking, he scooped her up with both arms and carried her away. Away from the windows and the dusty road, away from the wagons and the horses waiting patiently at the hitching posts. The fiddler's rollicking notes pursued them, bright and loud at first, fainter as Nils walked around the hotel, across the backyard, past the hotel barn, and on into the orchard.

There under the trees the ground was covered with wild clover. A fresh green sweetness drifted up to mingle with the scent of apple blossoms. Though it was night and cool along the river, here it was warm, as if the earth had absorbed the heat of the sun and now in the dark was releasing it, to rise and blend with the fragrant air.

Nils kneeled, lowered Katherine onto the cushion of clover and new grass and lay down beside her. "Now you know."

"Now I know," she repeated, as if these three simple words, and only these words, were a true and solemn pledge. How could she ever have been afraid? "I *know* I love you. But you must show me. I don't know what to do."

He kissed her gently, holding back the yearning already knotting in his groin and pounding in the blood vessels of his neck. She responded with the chaste kiss of a child. Though he longed to continue the kiss, to demand a deeper response, Nils lifted his head. "You will," he said softly. "You will, when the moment comes."

Resting on his elbow, he drew her closer. Very gently, his fingertips began to caress her. They moved along her cheek, probed the curving recesses of her ears, traced the outline of her chin. They found her mouth, and one forefinger, moistened by the tip of her tongue, ran along her lower lip, back and forth softly, until her lips parted.

Instantly Nils' mouth met hers, and now the kiss was a real union. Lightly at first, his tongue searched the warm cavity. Katherine murmured wordlessly, and suddenly her tongue was responding, flicking in and out of his mouth. Her hands had been resting passively on his shoulders. Now they tightened into fists as they clutched the rough cotton of his shirt.

Though his body throbbed, begging for release, Nils led Katherine slowly towards the moment of complete arousal when she would want him as much as he wanted her. He longed to undress her, to see again the small virginal body he had pulled out of the river, carried to Julian's cabin, stripped and wrapped in blankets. The memory of that night had haunted him. Now it glowed in his mind like an ember suddenly bursting into flame. But he choked back his longing and did nothing more than unbutton and open her blouse.

Through the thin covering of her camisole, his hand felt the softness and warmth of her breasts. He stroked them and felt the nipples harden against his palm. Again Katherine murmured, a low trembling sound without words. Her hands slipped from his shoulders and pressed against the small of his back. Nils' tormented body responded with a fresh surge of almost uncontrollable yearning. God, oh God, he thought. Have I ever wanted to take a woman as much as I do right now. Wait, his mind told him. Wait a little longer. It is beginning for her, but it will be much, much more, if you can wait.

Nils slid one arm under Katherine's shoulders, lifted her off the ground and removed her blouse and camisole. The small perfect mounds of her breasts were faintly visible even in the dark. With a groan he could not supress, Nils kissed them, letting his tongue follow the warm valley between them and linger on the nipples.

In the little wordless exclamation that came up from her throat like a sigh, in the more and more urgent pressure of her hands, Nils sensed her rising excitement. "Yes, Katherine. Yes, yes. . ." Whispering reassurance, he removed the rest of her clothing and quickly took off his own.

Thus far she had followed him eagerly through the gradual revelations of her first lovemaking. But Nils sensed that now they had reached the moment when Katherine, lonely and love-hungry as she was, might panic and retreat. This could be the moment of doubt, a moment when the reality of his naked body would awaken old fears. He knew what kind of agony he would suffer if she rejected him now, but he could stop now, if he had to. Once beyond this moment, there would be no turning back. And he did not want her merely to submit. He did not want her to allow the act of love. He wanted her to match him, in passion as she had in her feisty way of standing up to him at the pie social and the public meeting and a dozen other occasions since their first clash four years before. His body was filled to the breaking point. He wanted the same fierceness from her, thrust for thrust, yearning for yearning, need for need.

Katherine lay very still though her pulse was racing. Nils' powerful arms were propped at her sides, bearing the weight of his body as it hovered over her, barely touching. She felt the earth warm at her back, and smelled the night air laced with the scent of clover. Every part of her body throbbed with self-awareness. Thighs, breasts, belly ached with longing. ''Nils!'' she whispered urgently. ''Nils!'' and her arms wrapped around him, pulling him down.

As their bodies joined, a tide of exaltation swept through her. She met him eagerly, legs opening to receive him, back arching as her breasts begged for his mouth. There was a moment of pain, but it was soon submerged by a flood of emotion nothing could hold back. It was a joyful, exultant feeling, rising from the warm inner region where their bodies were joined and surging through her, wave after wave, as the fierce rhythm of the love act took possession. Faster and faster, jubilant, triumphant. . . . The most powerful wave of all crested in a shattering crescendo. When it broke, they were kissing. They both cried out, mouth to mouth.

In the distance, Hi Barker's fiddle played merrily. In the orchard, everything was still.

iv

As Nils rode home from Black River, his head buzzed with plans for the future. He and Katherine would have the finest wedding the Territory had ever seen. He would build Katherine the biggest house in the Territory. For Katherine he would buy store clothes in Seattle. And if Katherine was going to be mulish about keeping up the school—and he had a strong hunch that she would be—he'd build her a new one. A big school, a much bigger school. . .

The moon had risen. In the barnyard he unsaddled his horse by moonlight, whistling softly to himself. He led the horse to the boxstall. As he opened the door he heard the low whimpering sound of a child crying.

"Julie!"

The crying grew louder at the sound of her name. "Father. . ." she sobbed, lost somewhere in the dark corner of the stall. "Father. . ."

Nils fumbled for a lantern, lit it and turned the flame up to see her face. Julie was crouched in the corner, her back against the wall. Indianlike, her face had gone blank with fear.

Nils went to her quickly, laying his big hand on her shoulder. "What's the matter? What're you doing out here?"

Her body was cold and tensed so hard she was shivering. He pulled her to her feet. "Julie, tell me.

Why are you here? Where's Uncle Julian?''

She whispered, "I don't want to go inside.''

Years ago he had seen Julie's mother as mute with fear as Julie was now. He shook her. "Why not?''

She crumpled suddenly. "Mama came back!'' she sobbed. "And she's terrible sick.''

Nils stared at her. "Mama came back. . .''

"Don't make me go inside!'' Julie was pulling on him with both hands. "I don't want to catch it. Please, father, please. . .''

Mechanically Nils pulled a red handkerchief from his pocket and dried Julie's face. "No,'' he said, "you don't have to go back to the house. I'll bring you a blanket and you can sleep in the loft.''

"She's got the pox fever!'' Julie wailed. "Father, I'm scared!''

Suddenly Nils felt exhausted. If I could just lie down and sleep. "It's all right, baby,'' he said over and over again. "Everything's going to be all right.'' And he patted her head, repeating the empty promise, while within himself he felt nothing could ever be all right again.

CHAPTER ELEVEN

i

THE EPIDEMIC OF small pox swept through the Indian shacks along the river. The people of Gold Mountain rode past quickly and were pursued by the sounds. The wailing of a widowed squaw who paced along the beach, crying her sorrow to the skies for day after day and week after week. The guttural chant of the doctor as he treated his patient, the sudden screech, the long moan, when another one died. The white settlers shivered and prayed.

As coastal Indians always had, the Valley Indians looked for a cure in their sweat houses. They dug them into the mud of the riverbank, like industrious farmers building potato cellars. Around the shallow hole they piled fieldstones some two or three feet high, laying rough boards across the top as a roof. A bonfire blazed nearby. They heated large stones in it, and with heavy green poles rolled them into the sweat house. Water was poured onto the red hot stones, and cedar branches spread over them. Naked, the feverish Indian crawled through the low door and pulled it tight behind him. When the heat and steam had become insufferable, he burst through the door and leaped into the river.

Whatever disease the white man had visited upon them—measles, smallpox, influenza—the Indian treated it in the same way. Gold Mountain's white children grew used to the sight of a naked brown body plunging into the icy river, a cloud of steam pouring from the open mouth of the hovel from which he'd come. They leaped into the water in two's and three's, crazy with fear. They splashed around helplessly, out of their heads with fever. Most of them crawled out to die before old Indian Doc could begin his chant.

The Snoqualmies buried some of their dead as the Catholic father had taught them, in graves made sacred by the cross he had made of saplings and planted in the center of the burial ground. Others carried the bodies to the hill above the river, stretching them out on the upper limbs of the tallest trees or burying them on the highest ground. It was a spot the white boys had often visited in search of blue and white burial beads, but they stayed far away from it now. The whites who saw the mourning processions hurried away, as if the very sight of them might pass along the fever. There had been hundreds of Indians on the prairie above the Falls. No one knew how fast they were dying. No one cared, except to pray that the plague would not touch him.

At the hop ranch the hired help had recognized Indian Mary's disease the moment she walked into the barnyard. They had fled like field mice before a hungry owl. Bedrolls lay cold in the bunkhouse, spiders spun webs over the clothing on the nails along the wall. The Valley knew that only Uncle Julian had stayed, though the last of the foremen to saddle up had tried to drag the old man along with him. "You've seen smallpox," the foreman said. "It ain't a pretty way to die." But death in that form hadn't seemed half as close to Julian as the death that shadowed him every day; death for an old and ailing man lay in the next step, the next bite, even the next breath. So he stayed. There was the biggest hop ranch in the world, only three months from harvest time, and Nils Bengston was trying to run it alone, with the help of a senile old man, a little girl and a dying wife.

For the first time there were people who felt sorry for him. What right had that Indian woman to come back, they asked each other? Mary had left him so often and finally deserted him altogether. It had been four years since she had been Nils' wife; everyone knew there were "papers" dissolving the marriage at the district court in Seattle, though it had been a couple of years before Nils would agree to ask for them. Now, eaten with pox fever, she had turned to him. "Nils ought to send her packing," the whites agreed. "She ran off to her own people. Why don't he make her go back to 'em now?" But they knew he hadn't. "He's crazy," they said to comfort themselves, because they felt sorry for him and it was an unusual feeling to have toward Nils.

No one dared visit the hop ranch. Some slowed down at the spot where the road passed the entrance, peering toward the buildings to see what movement there might be. But they never saw anything; the long storehouses, the kilns and sheds, the barns, woodhouses, the farmhouse, the rows of bunkhouses, looked deserted. Death seemed close even by daylight and the rider always leaned forward in the saddle and spurred his horse to a gallop. No one but Nate Tarpee had ever talked with anyone at the ranch.

Riding past the entrance he saw Julie, peering at him from behind a stump. At his approach she darted back into the lane.

Conscience, and curiosity, stirred him to call out, "You sick?"

Julie shook her head.

"Your Pa sick?"

Julie shook her head a second time. "I'm not supposed to be here."

"You lack for something?" His horse took a step toward Julie. The movement put her to flight. "Want me to leave off something for you here at the road?" he called after her, but she was running toward the house.

Nate hesitated, his hand uncertain on the reins. But he had seen smallpox. "Leave the big Swede be," he muttered, with an uncomfortable tight feeling in his throat. "Let him run his two square miles of land by himself. He can do it." And he turned his horse and rode away as fast as he could.

ii

On the tenth day Mary died. Miraculously, Julie and old Uncle Julian were well. Nils had ordered them to eat and sleep in one of the bunkhouses, and to stay as far from him as they did from Mary. He alone cared for her, until day and night, even time and place, ran together in the confusion of weariness. He did not know exactly when she died. He had fallen asleep in a chair. He awoke suddenly, thinking she had cried out. "Mary?" he whispered. His body felt heavy; it seemed to take all his strength to stand and walk to the bed. There was a sharp ringing in his ears. He shook his head angrily to get rid of it. "Mary?" he said again, and then he saw that she was dead.

He looked down at her, and a violent shudder went through him. He had hardly known this woman he had cared for. "We'll go home," he had told her once. "There the sickness will never touch you. I will keep you safe forever." For ten days of hell he had kept some kind of faith with that promise, uttered so many years before to a young Indian girl he could only half remember. Loyalty—he had felt he owed her that much for not loving her. This was the end of it. Her face was swollen hideously. Disease had bloated the nostrils, the mouth, the cheeks . . .The taste of bile rose in Nils' throat. He swallowed, fighting against shudders that seemed to be attacking him in a series. He must bury her, he told himself, and it should be done right away. It was no time for mourning. He dared not even go close enough to Julie to tell her that her mother was gone. He pulled the gray and red blanket over Mary's face, turned and walked heavily to the barn.

He found shovel, boards, saw, nails, a hammer. With great pains he fashioned a coffin. The work went slowly. The feeling of heaviness grew worse with every moment; moving at all was an almost insurmountable problem. He concentrated on it, watching his hands fixedly. He sawed the boards, nailed them together, tested the joints for strength. When he was through he loaded the box onto the back of the wagon and went back into the house. Dread of the task slowed him down; fear of not finishing it speeded him. As gently as he knew how he wrapped Mary in all the blankets on the bed, and carried her out to the wagon.

The effort made him weak and he began to tremble. He lowered her into the box, nailed the top boards into place. He despised the weakness that had hit him, and began to race against it. The burial spot must be as far from the ranch buildings as possible. That was the only clear thought his mind would give him. He hitched the team to the wagon, drove them straight across a field of sprouting oats to a rocky spot high above the river. The water had never risen this high, and the nearest dwelling was miles away. She would not be disturbed here. In the distance were the apple orchards which he had planted when Mary was a young girl, a laughing, slender, chief's daughter, who once had teased her stepmother by rocking the canoe.

Nils paced off the grave, and began digging. The surface dirt was thin. Underneath were the round boulders of an ancient river bed. He bent his back against the weight of them. Sweat burst out of him, and his strength seemed to leave him with it. He worked frantically.

At last the hole was big enough. He lifted the coffin onto his shoulder, lowered it into place. He was trembling. Hurriedly he groped for the shovel, scooped the dirt onto the box with frantic, unsteady sweeps of his arms. The hole was filled, and the last shovelsful made an uneven mound above the grave. Nils' teeth were chattering; he clenched his jaw and still could not stop the sound. It was done. He threw the shovel into the back of the wagon, and clutched suddenly at the bang board, leaning forward against it. Shudder after shudder ripped through him. He held on tight, wishing angrily for the strength to curse out loud. The worst of it passed, and he pulled himself onto the wagon seat and turned the horses home. It was done. He rode with his elbows on his knees, head down, eyes closed.

In the barnyard the horses stopped by themselves. Nils straightened and stared witlessly at the house and barns. He hadn't been asleep, he was sure of it, but he couldn't remember the ride home. His head throbbed painfully. The thought kept hammering at him that he would have to burn his clothes and bathe before he got near Julie. If he scubbed himself hard, if he destroyed everything he'd worn, even his boots, perhaps he would not carry the sickness to her. . .

He stood up, rocking unsteadily. Right away, he thought, right fast before Julie comes near. Let the horses stand in harness for a while. He saw the door of the bunkhouse open and Julie step out.

"No!" he shouted. It seemed as if his voice weren't carrying at all. "No, stay there!" He lifted both hands to wave her back. She hesitated. He would have to get down from the wagon, call her again . . . "Baby . . ." Nils took a step, but his legs didn't hold him. He grabbed for the dashboard. His fingers touched it and slid away as his great body crumbled and fell unconscious to the wagon floor.

iii

Katherine and Faith Carlson were in the kitchen when Julie rode in.

Faith exclaimed, "My goodness, it's Julie Bengston. Why . . ."

Katherine ran to the door. "Where are the children?"

"In the woods," Faith said distractedly. "Or the shed, maybe. Oh my goodness, I don't know."

"You watch for them. Keep them away. I'll talk to Julie."

It didn't take Julie long to tell Katherine what was wrong. She didn't explain why she had come to her teacher rather than to others. "*You* help us." She made the request as confidently as if she were asking for the right answer to an arithmetic problem.

Katherine nodded with all the authority of a teacher before her class. "You go back home," she said firmly, "and stay with your father. Cover him with a blanket. Be sure he doesn't get cold. I'll get the doctor."

Without a word Julie wheeled her pony around and raced back along the trail. Katherine ran into the house for a shawl, then across the clearing to where her pony grazed. Jeb had the wagon in Gold Mountain. No time now to worry about how she would get Dr. Meade up the hill to the hop ranch. She grabbed the halter rope and leaped onto the pony's smooth back. Only this time Nils could not help her.

In Black River she found Dr. Meade in back of the hotel, bandaging a gash on the leg of Hilke Orvaag's big bay horse. The doctor was on his knees. He squinted up at her through bushy black eyebrows. "Well, it's the teacher and she caught me doctoring a horse. I'm not ashamed of it. They pay up faster than some humans. Who's having a baby, Miss Duncan? I hope you forgot your ladylike sensibilities enough to ask the right question this time."

"Nils Bengston is sick."

The doctor tied the bandage with a quick little jerk, and got slowly to his feet. "*Nils* is sick." He knew what it meant. Hilke, standing beside him with his mouth open, knew, too. "Aahh. . ." The doctor sighed. His satchel stood open on a stool. He went to it and scowled at its interior. "Mmm."

Katherine burst out, "Doctor, will you come, please?"

The doctor looked at her sideways. "I have a lot of patients, Miss Duncan. They're not all horses. Most of them I can do something for and every now and then I save a life. There's almost nothing I could do for Nils."

Katherine cried, "But you're the only doctor!"

The man nodded. "That's just it. Who will take

care of all the other people?''

''Then you don't go to see Nils?'' Hilke Orvaag asked incredulously.

''Of course I'm going!'' the doctor bellowed suddenly. ''You knew I never turned anyone down in my life. I just don't want this young lady to think she can ride down here and drag me up to Gold Mountain every two years.'' He scowled at Hilke. ''Saddle that big black of yours. I been riding some and it don't seem to hurt my leg any worse than falling in and out of ruts in some old farm wagon.''

A loud sigh escaped from Katherine. ''Thank you, Dr. Meade.''

The doctor wheeled toward her. ''Why are you so anxious about the big bully of a Swede?''

Katherine flushed. Hilke was staring at her. Suddenly his face broke into a knowing grin and he hurried toward the barn. The doctor's eyebrows seemed to be point at her accusingly. ''I. . .''

''Never mind,'' he said curtly. ''I'm not interested in your personal follies.'' He closed his satchel with a loud snap. ''You haven't been to the hop ranch?''

Katherine shook her head.

''Not near Nils?''

''No.''

The doctor nodded. ''Good. Now get on your pony and ride back to Carlsons' and don't you go near that ranch, even if you love that man enough to die for him. He might not live to appreciate it.'' He thumped his pockets energetically. ''Fever pills, yes. Eyeglasses, yes. . .'' He glared at Katherine. ''Well, go on. I can find my way up the Valley. Good-bye.''

''Good-bye.'' Katherine walked away reluctantly. She turned back. ''If there's something I can do,'' she said in a small voice. ''If there's any way at all I can help. . .''

"He's not going to have a baby," the doctor snapped. He looked at Katherine's face and his voice softened. "My dear girl," he said gently. "there's nothing you can do. Nothing at all. But you could do a lot of harm to all those little Carlson youngsters if you didn't stay away."

The doctor's sudden kindness was unbearable. Katherine burst into tears. "I love him!"

The doctor's hand touched her shoulder. "I'll tell him," he said simply. "Now go home."

iv

Dr. Meade arranged the strips of side meat in the big iron spider and reflected that the practice of medicine involved so little of what he had learned at medical school. He'd graduated after eleven months. The wonderful thing about higher education, he mused, is that so much of it sticks with you even after you're smart enough to forget it. If he was a good doctor now it was because he had learned so much since college. And because he could cook, shoot straight, speak Chinook and had no use for liquor. He grinned. How would that have looked on his diploma?

He set the spider over the coals, pushing it back and forth on its long legs until it rested evenly on the hearth. Come to think of it, who cared what was on his diploma, or even whether he had one? The Territorial Legislature—he laughed. He had paid two dollars at the county auditor's, shown his diploma and signed his name. So much for the law. He wasn't nursing the legislature, he was nursing people, as he always had. He'd been a post doctor in Idaho, a doctor in the range country of Montana. The Valley was a civilized place by comparison.

Wherever he'd been , his patients had trusted him. You do, the doctor thought wryly, if there's only one doctor and you've ridden from ten to eighty miles to get him. They didn't ask where you'd studied, and the two dollars you paid the county meant nothing to them. Old Mark Bliss was called "doctor" simply because he had strong hands. The "rubbing doctor," they had named him back in Idaho, and paid a silver dollar for a healing rub. Years before little Mrs. John Tobias had put two medical kits in the wagon when she and her husband left Iowa for Oregon. Those kits made her the "doctor" for the whole train and she'd been mending and healing and delivering infants ever since. Lucy Grant hadn't gone to medical school to learn about bread and milk and poultices, which she prescribed for every ailment known to man, but she'd never lost a childbirth and she was as deeply trusted as he, even if she was a woman. Patching a man's head after the Indians had lifted his scalp, cutting off frostbitten toes without anaesthetic—no, they hadn't said much about that back east in medical school.

The doctor picked up a long hunting knife. Potatoes were roasting under a thin covering of hot ashes. One by one he speared them with the point of the knife and dragged them to the edge of the hearth. If I'd married, he reflected, I wouldn't be such a good cook, and that would mean that in cases like this I wouldn't be such a good doctor. Nils was far too sick to eat. He was in the bedroom with damp towels over his forehead, if he hadn't already thrown them off in the delirium of his fever. But that little Julie had been hungry when he came and too grieved by her mother's death to feed herself properly. Old Uncle Julian had become too witless to think of food when he wasn't hungry himself. Julie was sure to eat, once he got her started. At the moment feeding the child was a doctor's job as much as worrying about what to do for her father.

He didn't know, and that irritated him. He knew many a doctor who would have soothed himself during the past few days with a little whiskey. But that was one of the four ways in which Doc Meade had lived up to his oath and his diploma and himself. He scarcely knew the taste of liquor.

Not that he hadn't administered it, if there was a reason. The day, for example, when Luther Anderson fell from his hayloft and broke his legs in so many places a country doctor would hardly know where to put the splints. Doc Meade saw that if the man was to walk again, he would have to be treated in a hospital in Seattle.

The eldest Anderson boy drove the wagon. Dr. Meade and the groaning Luther were in the back. It was a long ride over a trail so rough that most wagons broke down at least once before they got to Seattle. Doc had carried a quart of whiskey in his satchel that day, and praised heaven for having it. The man had been in severe pain. Whenever he regained consciousness the good doctor forced open his mouth and poured half a tumbler of whiskey down his throat.

"My legs!" the man would moan as he awakened.

"Liquor is the servant of man," Dr. Meade replied, and tipped the bottle into his mouth. He had often said later that by the time they reached the hospital the doctors could have transplanted Luther's arms and legs without anaesthetic and Luther would have smiled.

The meat was beginning to sizzle. The doctor shook the pan a little, to see it didn't stick. Then he went to the bedroom door.

Julie was squatted beside her father's bed. Her eyes were round and blank. In pain and in fear, the doctor thought, the Indian comes out strongest. He should scold her for sitting by her father. But what was the use, when she had undoubtedly been near him the week before? If it was smallpox. . .The doctor frowned. There wasn't anything on his diploma that said he couldn't catch disease. In thirty years of practice it seemed as if he'd had everything his patients had ever had, except a baby. If it was smallpox, he and Nils and Julie and the old man Julian might easily die together.

But was it? Nils had been ill for two days now. His fever had been high, his pulse quick. In his rational movements he had complained of headache and pains in his back. But there was no rash. Perhaps it was too early, but if the dusky red spots had not appeared by morning. . .The doctor sighed. Then it wouldn't be smallpox. Nils was wasting with the fever; he was out of his mind most of the time. Whatever the illness, such a fever might easily kill him whether or not the doctor knew what to call it.

"Get up, girl, and wash," he said gruffly. "I'm hungry but I won't eat unless you do."

Julie went outside. Obedience, a natural sense of courtesy—they were strong in her, the doctor noted, and besides she's a hungry little girl. He picked up a potato with the tip of his hunting knife; with a second knife cut off the crusty black covering. When he opened it on her plate a delicious steam rose. He used his hunting knife to scoop butter from the crock and cut it into the potato. With the same knife he speared several strips of side meat and carried them from the hearth to her plate. He pushed the knife's point through a cold biscuit and held it out to her. She pulled it off and began chewing on it. In the same way the doctor filled his own plate. They ate in silence. Julie's plate was empty before his.

"Now go to bed," the doctor said. He didn't believe in deceiving people, but the little girl's wide, unhappy eyes made him tell a downright lie. "Your father's going to start getting better tomorrow. I want you to be wide awake so you can help take care of him." When Julie was asleep, the doctor pulled a chair up next to Nils' bed and settled himself for the night.

By noon the next day he was sure Nils did not have smallpox. But he was plainly failing. The doctor watched him anxiously, cooling him with damp towels and trying to force a little lukewarm tea into his mouth with a spoon. Convulsions, a coma—it would be one or the other, the doctor thought, unless the fever broke. Nils talked deliriously, then lapsed into half-consciousness, his mouth moving and his eyes fixed blindly on the ceiling. That poor little schoolteacher, the doctor thought. What a confession it was for her to say she loved him, and now he's going to die before I've had a chance to tell him. The doctor was feeling for Nils' pulse when Brother Bill walked into the room.

He put Nils' hand down gently and turned to the big evangelist. "What are you doing here?" he whispered.

"I got to Black River this morning. They told me Nils was dying of the smallpox. I walked up right away."

The doctor shook his head. "Not smallpox."

Brother Bill looked down at Nils. "What is it?"

Doc Meade shrugged. "I don't know. I suppose *you'd* say God alone knows."

Brother Bill said simply, "Yes, I would." He moved toward the bed.

The doctor stepped in front of him. "Stay back, Bill. No use in your. . ."

Brother Bill got past him without actually shoving him aside. "I come to pray with him. He pushed his hair back from his eyes and got down on his knees beside the bed.

"Get out of here, Bill. I don't know what this fever is, but it might be something you could catch."

"You're here, Doc."

"Because I'm a doctor."

"Haven't you ever caught anything?"

"I've had everything," the doctor snapped. "But it's my business to be here."

Brother Bill said, "The man's dying. That means I got more business here than you have." He nodded solemnly toward the bedroom door. "So *you* get out. If you stay you got to get down on your knees. I'm going to pray."

The doctor looked from the evangelist's big, homely face to the unconscious body of his patient. At times doctoring isn't even a matter of medicine, he thought bitterly, and they didn't teach me that in medical school, either. He bent one knee and wearily let himself down to the floor. Bill's prayer began. "Our Lord in heaven. . ." The doctor rested an elbow on his knee, and covered his face with his hand.

v

Nils came out of the semicoma briefly that afternoon. He turned his head and looked at Brother Bill, though his eyes did not seem to focus clearly.

"Can you hear me, Nils?"

Nils' voice answered him weakly. "Quit your shouting. My head aches."

"I'm glad you're awake. Will you pray with me now, Brother Nils?"

Nils' breathing was so labored that his voice came out unevenly. "Am I that bad? Doc think I'm dying?"

"You should be prepared."

"Where's Doc?" Nils' voice had fallen to a whisper.

"Sleeping in the next room. He ain't more than catnapped the past two, three days." He cleared his throat. "Pray with me, Nils."

Nils closed his eyes. "So I'm dying."

"You've been a sinful man, Nils Bengston. But God receives all those who repent."

Nils' lips barely moved. "You trying to get me into heaven, Bill?"

The evangelist nodded. "Heaven is the life after death, where all is beautiful and good."

With a sudden movement Nils pulled himself up on one elbow. "If everybody gets changed I wouldn't know my friends." He fell back, exhausted by the effort.

Brother Bill looked at him uncertainly. "Well, it don't say exactly that everybody's *changed*."

"If they ain't, then heaven's full of stupid people." Nils' eyes were bright. The pupils had dilated so wide the eyes looked black. He was breathing hard. With a great effort he put both hands behind him and pushed himself to a sitting position. A shadow of his old grin flickered across his face. "It don't sound good to me, Bill," he gasped. "I changed my mind. I'm not going to die."

Brother Bill felt the demon of his temper stirring. "God will decide whether you live or die," he said loudly, "not you. I came here to pray with you. Now bow your head like a Christian."

"I'm not going to die!" Nils repeated weakly. "I'd rather own the biggest hop ranch in the world."

"Bow your head!"

Nils stared glassily at Brother Bill. "Nobody's going to pray over me," he whispered, "least of all a twenty-five-cent walking preacher."

That was too much. Brother Bill had often heard Nils' estimate of him: twenty-five cents a mile but not a penny for preaching. For the first time in years the temper got away from him completely. "Bow your head and pray!" he bellowed, threatening Nils with both fists, "Or with the help of God I'm going to beat your ears off!"

The shout brought Doc Meade running to the room. He saw Brother Bill leaning over the bed, his face white with anger, and Nils sitting straight up with a wide grin on his face. "Dear Lord," he muttered, as if he had come in specifically to lead off the prayer. He went to the bed and felt Nils' wrist, his forehead, his heart, but even as he did it he knew the fever had broken and Nils would live.

CHAPTER TWELVE

i

THE LAST DAY of school was to be a July fourth program. Every pupil would be in it. The big Smith boy who had given up chewing tobacco in order to sit through class. The little three- and four-year-olds, who attended the first grade because their mothers didn't want to fuss with them at home and kept right on attending it until they knew by heart all the pictures in all the books. The "good students," like Julie Bengston and Levi Barker and Tommy Tine.

The program was to be held in the new school, and for that reason was like none Gold Mountain had ever anticipated before. It called for a new dress, if possible. Mothers dyed buttercloth or ripped up dresses of their own if they couldn't afford to buy a length of goods at Nate Tarpee's store. For the new schoolhouse was as different as silk is from homespun. It had a store-boughten look.

Instead of a dirt floor, one walked on smooth planks. The old wood shutters had been replaced by real glass windows. There was a big, potbellied stove with a tin chimney instead of a crude hearth of fieldstone and clay. In the old school a thirsty child had had a choice between the river or a bottle of water from home. A row of jars had stood on a bench at the back of the room, with initials scratched into each metal top. Now there was a well, and a shiny bucket of water with an equally shiny dipper hanging from a nail above. There were even two outhouses, one for girls, one for boys. No question but that the new schoolhouse was one of the best in the county. How many had blackboards the size of a wall and real sheepskin erasers?

Julie and Tommy Tine were to say one of the longest poems, or so Teacher had said before Julie left school because of the smallpox. Nils heard of it from Tommy's mother, Agatha, who arrived at the hop ranch with a wagonload of food the same day Doc Meade left it. "I passed Doc on his way home this morning," Agatha said. "He said you wasn't bad sick any more but more'n likely you'd soon be bad hungry. It's a good thing I come. You look skinny as a garter snake and just about as strong."

Before she left she had filled the cooler with smoked ham and venison, butter, two or three round hard loaves of bread, a couple of pies and preserves to last a winter. She had declared that the ranch was well rid of the lily-livered cook who ran off with the foremen; he put so little by he must have been planning to starve them anyway. She had also passed along the information that Doc Meade had a message for Nils and forgot it. "Nothing important," the doctor had promised her, with a sharp look in his eye. Also, she concluded, there was a school program in a couple of days, and Tommy couldn't be in it unless Julie was, because they were to say a poem together.

"I'll send Julie back to school tomorrow," Nils said.

"I'll come over, if you need someone to fix for you."

"When I want a woman around here," Nils retorted, "I'll pick her out myself."

Agatha snorted. "Too bad you had to go and get

sick, with the big school program only two days away. You'll miss it."

"I never missed school, or any part of it."

"Ha!" Agatha eyed him narrowly. "It just calls attention to your ignorance, to act like you're proud of it."

"I'm ignorant," Nils snapped, "but I'm rich. I got the biggest hop ranch in the world. I can afford to hate school."

"And schoolteachers." Agatha's little round mouth closed tightly as she scanned his face.

"You're a fat old busybody." Nils lay back and closed his eyes. "If my legs would hold me, I'd go to the program, just for Julie's sake. That'd be the only reason. Miss Duncan is a bright one, and a good one, for being a schoolmarm, but me and her don't look at anything the same way and we never will. I'm tired, Ag. Now that you brought me all that good grub, why don't you go on home?"

"I'll tell you about the program afterward."

Nils shook his head warily. "No hurry, Ag, no hurry."

ii

Katherine stood at the window, watching the road on which the wagons would soon appear. The school desks had been crowded together in the middle of the floor and benches from the old school placed along the walls for the parents. Everything was in place. The globe, the American flag, the Bible for opening reading and the harmonica with which to start the songs. American flags, cut, pasted and colored were pinned to the back wall; the front wall, which was taken up entirely by a blackboard, was appropriately decorated with crude chalk drawings of minutemen and their muskets. All in readiness, Katherine thought, even to Teacher's new dress.

She touched the soft folds of the skirt affectionately. It was made of green delaine, a light wool muslin with a little leaf pattern woven right into the fabric. It was the first good dress she had made since she came to the Valley. Her mother had often spoke of the delaine dresses she had worn before her marriage, fashionable dresses that had one by one been lost or worn out and never replaced. Katherine had planned this new dress for months. In the very beginning she had decided that it must be of delaine.

The sin of pride—Brother Bill would call it that, Katherine thought. But it seemed as if she had always had an uncommon need for her pride. She had chosen a course four years before and kept to it, but pride had protected her, spurred her, goaded and strengthened her, every step of the way. The first was taken the day she defied her father and all her aunts and uncles with the announcement that she was going to become a teacher. A skinny little seventeen-year-old with scarcely five whole terms of schooling behind her—it had been a crazy, a proud, thing to do. Yet the best of everything she had done since had been accomplished in the same way, as if she had found a pattern that day she stared down her elders, a pattern that was her own. Decide on the impossible, and be too proud to give it up.

Pride had built this new school, but it was a good kind of pride, the kind even Brother Bill approved of. The shared feeling of a hundred neighbors, which built good things and brought good people together. "Teacher deserves it," the Valley people said, like parents tolerating their child's whim because she's been such a good girl. No one had dreamed there could be such a school here, but teacher had worked hard and done it in four years. It would be closer to the truth, Katherine thought wistfully, to say that I've done it in twenty-one.

For the new school and even her delaine dress was an answer not only to Nils Bengston who had once said he'd send her back to Seattle, or to Carl White who had begged her to give it up, or to ignorance or poverty or anything else in the Valley that had stood in her way. To Katherine this day was part of the lifetime of Katherine Fairfield Duncan, born twenty-one years ago in a sod house in Kansas.

"School" had been such a changeable word. Once it had meant the neighbor's kitchen, where a mother born in Boston ransacked her memory for the bits of learning she passed on to a class of Katherine, Teddy and five children of her own. For a few weeks it had been part of an old fort. The outside walls of the school had been pock-marked by the impact of hundreds of bullets, and the pupils had played in the charred remnants of the other buildings. School in a barn, in a kitchen, in a sod house or an abandoned log cabin. Teachers who ended the term to butcher the hog or work along a trap line or boil a year's crop of maple sugar or give birth to a new baby. Schools without books, without pencils, without heat, where the winter cut through the unchinked walls so that your mind felt as stiff as your fingers and toes. From now on the children of Gold Mountain would have a school that was a school and something more, a teacher who was a teacher above all else. That had been the goal, glimpsed when she was too young and untrained even to receive a proper teaching certificate, and kept before her ever since because she was too stubborn to settle for anything less. That's where pride had taken her, straight up the road toward the impossible. The people of Gold Mountain had gone with her, determined as she was to give their children something they had missed themselves. We have come a long way, Katherine reflected, glancing around the sunlit school room. So far that in a few years no one will remember what it was we struggled so hard to leave behind.

A wagon appeared around the bend of the road. Katherine felt a sudden tight sensation in her stomach. Squinting, she tried to make out the driver. Mr. Nelson. . .She sighed. She did not expect Nils to come. But thinking of Nils was as unavoidable as thinking at all; she thought about him hardest when she was reminding herself to put him out of her mind. He was still in bed, but he was well enough to send for her and she had made up her mind to go to him if he did. But he hadn't, and that seemed to prove that even when he was physically weak and ailing he felt no need of anyone outside himself. She wanted to see him, yet . . . yet, she was afraid to face him. Katherine straightened her bodice with a nervous gesture, and went to the door to welcome the Nelsons.

One after another the families of Gold Mountain arrived. The children's faces were shiny. The girls' hair had been brushed from their faces hard enough to pull their mouths into a smile. The boys smelled of soap and shoe grease. Many of them had new haircuts, with a white strip showing between their summer's sunburn and their new hairline. The children raced for their own school desks while their parents found places along the wall. Katherine was about to open the program when still another wagon came into the yard. In it were Nils Bengston and Julie.

Katherine whirled around and flew to her desk. "We'll begin," she said in a choked voice. No one heard her, but at least she was away from the door so she would not have to meet him. She picked up a ruler and rapped it sharply on the desk. "We'll begin," she repeated more loudly. The children closed their mouths and faced her, every one a perfect student now that their parents were here.

The door opened. All heads turned toward Nils and Julie. Katherine's gaze followed reluctantly. Julie's face was bright with a smile. Nils stood behind her. His face was pale and there was a boniness to it which illness had uncovered. But he still looked like a puzzled giant, his shoulders hunched forward as if the room were not quite big enough. Katherine felt a wave of heat flow into her face. She nodded silently.

Julie took her father's hand. "Over here," she whispered. Nils let Julie lead him to a place at the back of the room. With her eyes on Katherine's face Julie put a solemn good-scholar look in place of her smile and took a seat in the middle of the room.

He came after all. . .Katherine picked up the Bible. Her finger felt for the place mark. Will he speak to me afterward? she thought. What will he say, what will I say to him? She looked blindly into the open book. No moment in her four years in the Valley had been quite as hard as this one, when she must hold the book though her hands trembled, read aloud though her voice shook, and face the crowd in front of her, though Nils was among them and she could think of nothing but how much she loved him.

iii

The duet sung by Julie Bengston and Tommy Tine was the last number on the program. Julie jumped up at Katherine's signal. Nils looked at her, suddenly anxious about how she would appear. He analyzed her dress and the dresses of the other girls, and concluded that it was all right even if it was red. Her stockings—he stared at them, wondering why he hadn't noticed them before. Wide, bright stripes ran all the way around them. In a flurry he peered at the legs of the other little girls. Two of them had striped stockings just like Julie's. He had to repress a sigh. For years he had trusted Agatha to buy Julie's clothes. She had done all right.

Tommy Tine's face was pink and his ears looked enormous and very red. He had slid down in his seat so far that he seemed to be resting on his shoulder blades. Katherine repeated the signal to stand up and come forward. He stared at her blankly and didn't move. Agatha's face was as red as his. She was pulling in her breath to yell across the room when Julie reached down and took Tommy by the arm. She whispered hoarsely, "You get up, Tommy Tine, or I'll never speak to you again." With a long groan Tommy stood up and followed Julie to the front of the room.

Katherine picked up the mouth organ and sounded a note. Julie's sweet, clear voice repeated the sound obediently, but Tommy was staring over the heads of the audience as if suddenly fascinated by something at the back of the room. Julie's elbow nudged him lightly. He jumped and began to sing.

"Fair lady, I will buy you a penny's worth of pins,
To pin up your laces and many other things,
If you'll walk, walk with me, anywhere, any-
    where,
If you'll walk, walk with me, anywhere."

Tommy stopped abruptly. Instantly Julie lifted her chin and sang:

> "Kind sir, I won't accept of your penny's worth
>   of pins,
> To pin up my laces and many other things,
> Nor I won't walk with you, anywhere, anywhere,
> Nor I won't walk with you, anywhere."

This time Nils could not hold back his sigh. "Aahh. . ." he said out loud, sliding down on his spine and shoving his hands into his pockets. She knew *her* part of it, all right. If she had made any mistakes, you couldn't tell it.

> "Fair lady, I will buy you a pretty golden chain,
> To hang around your neck when you trip across
>   the plain,
> If you'll walk, walk with me anywhere, any-
>   where,
> If you'll walk, walk with me, anywhere."

Tommy's voice trailed off and his glance wandered over the room. Julie sang out brightly:

> "Kind sir, I won't accept of your pretty golden
>   chain,
> To hang about my neck when I trip across the
>   plain,
> Nor I won't walk with you, anywhere, anywhere,
> Nor I won't walk with you, anywhere."

Tommy was looking out the window.
"Tommy!" Julie hissed.
"Fair lady, I will buy you a silk gown five yards long!" Tommy exclaimed. He stumbled, forgetting.

He wheeled around to look at Katherine.

"To trail the ground. . ." she whispered.

"To trail the ground!" Tommy shouted.

Quickly Julie sang, "Kind sir, I won't accept of your rich silken gown, with five long yards to trail along the ground. . ."

Nils grinned. Julie knew it better than Tommy, anyone could see that. Better not to say anything about it to Agatha. His gaze moved to Agatha Tine. It's a shame, he thought, but he was grinning.

"Fair lady, I will give you the key to my chest,
Gold or silver, whichever you love the best. . ."

And Julie answered saucily, "Kind sir, I won't accept of the key to your chest. . ."

As Julie finished Tommy seemed to come to life. He stood up straight and frowned mightily. "Fair lady, I will give you the keys to my heart," he sang out, directing the offer in the opposite direction from Julie.

He must be coming to the end, Nils thought. He's like a horse riding for the barn.

"To keep with you forever until death do us part. . ."

"Kind sir, I *will* accept of the keys to your heart,
To keep with me forever till death do us part,
And I'll walk, walk with you, anywhere, anywhere,
And I'll walk, walk with you, anywhere."

Tommy and Julie stood before the crowd with bright expectant looks on their faces. They were out of breath. Nils brought his hands together in a resounding clap, and everyone else followed. Nils looked around proudly, noting how many people were smiling at Julie.

The program was over. As Katherine stood up and thanked them for coming, Nils' preoccupation with Julie ended abruptly. The children fell over each other in their effort to get their wraps on first and to be first out the door. Their parents got up slowly, smiling to themselves. Katherine stood at the door like Preacher Bill, and no couple left without stopping to congratulate her.

At the back of the room Nils let one person after another push past him. He hadn't an idea in his head of what to say to her. He felt bare. Anger and deliberate laughter had always been handy when he needed protection, but he couldn't even begin to arouse them with his whole being shouting that she was beautiful. What could he say to her? "I love you. I've been trying not to for well on to four years and it doesn't work." That night at the dance in Black River, he had made love to her with feeling he had never known before, and she had shown feeling as strong as his own. He couldn't have been mistaken, but that was weeks ago. She hadn't come to him, she hadn't said it was the same, now. Julie touched his arm. He looked at her confusedly.

"Father, everybody's going!"

"Oh, sure." Katherine was waiting at the door. She had spoken to everyone else. "Sure," Nils repeated mechanically.

Julie's hand pulled him down. "Everyone else said something nice to Teacher," she whispered urgently.

Nils walked to the front, Julie jerking his hand to make him move faster. But he went in slow motion, his feet dragging, his eyes on Katherine's face. Katherine didn't move. How green her eyes are, he thought, like river water when the sun goes through it. "I. . ."

She was so very still. Her wide eyes looked at him solemnly. "I want to thank you," he began. Her mouth—he found he couldn't stop looking at it. The lower lip was rounded, moist along the rim. He had kissed her.

Katherine moved, picking up a pile of papers and hurriedly pulling one out. Nils saw that her hands trembled. "This is Julie's last English composition," she said, in a tight little voice. "I thought you'd like to read it."

Bitterness flooded through him. He wanted to hurt her, to destroy her with one devasting word or one murderous blow. His throat tightened so he could hardly speak; for the first time since he had got out of bed and dressed for the program, weakness returned. He gritted his teeth, forcing himself to stand without support. Anger would have been comforting; this feeling of nakedness was unbearable. "Miss Duncan," he said at last, "I can't read or write."

Julie whispered, "Father, you're supposed. . ."

Nils answered her by bolting through the door and across the schoolyard to the wagon. With Julie stoically silent beside him, he turned the horses onto the road and whipped them into a trot.

The wagon creaked alarmingly, jolting in and out of the sun-baked ruts. Under his breath, Nils began to curse. With each word his pulse quieted and his strength returned. The hop ranch buildings were only a few rods distant when Nils jerked the horses to a halt. Julie's startled voice said, "Father, what are you doing now?" Nils growled wordlessly and turned the horses back the way they'd come. "Forgot something," he gasped as the wagon slammed in and out of a hole, and he lay the reins hard across the horses' backs. The return trip was as fast, as tense and as silent as the departure had been. In the schoolyard Katherine's pony was still tethered to an alder. Nils threw the reins into Julie's hands, and leaped to the ground as if he'd never known a sick day in his life.

He ran across the yard and pushed the schoolhouse door open so hard it hit the wall with a crash. Katherine was at the desk. And then she was in his arms.

He kissed her in a frenzy. "Sweetheart," he whispered, "sweetheart. . ."

The summer sun shot bright shafts of light into the room. Outside the horses whinnied. Her mouth was soft. He kissed her cheek, and felt her breath warm against his ear.

He stopped kissing her but he could not let her go. He held her gently, and talked to her over her head. "You got a pretty dress," he said. "The color of your eyes. Did you know it was?"

She nodded, her chin rubbing against his chest.

He grinned. "Too bad you're such a dried-up little old schoolmarm. Heart like a stone and head full of letters and numbers. Poor little thing. Don't even know she's got beautiful big eyes."

Katherine giggled, somewhere below his lapel.

Nils kissed the top of her head. "I love you, Kate."

"Not Kate!"

Laughing, Nils tilted her head back and kissed her on the mouth. Her hands tightened on his shoulders. He kissed her again. Her lips parted and she seemed to melt into him. He kissed her throat, and caught the sweet odor of her body. Suddenly he held her at arm's length. "Did that Carl ever kiss you?"

Katherine's eyes widened. "What do you mean? We were engaged. But he never called me Kate."

Katherine burst into laughter.

Muttering angrily, Nils drew her back into his arms. "Then I will."

She drew back. "Julie. . .Isn't Julie outside?"

"She'll wait." But the mention of Julie reminded him of the composition paper. "I can't read or write," he said flatly.

Katherine nodded. "That's what you said."

Nils said brusquely, "Maybe you guessed it before."

"No."

"I could learn."

Katherine's eyes filled with tears. "Would you?" she asked softly. "Why?"

"I want to marry you."

They looked at each other. After a moment Katherine tried to speak, and then only shook her head and smiled. Nils sat down on the nearest bench and pulled her into his lap. "I'm going to learn how to read and write," he said. "And I'm going to build you a house. Then we'll get married. We'll have the biggest wedding in the Territory."

Katherine laughed. "You have a house."

"It's not big enough," Nils said curtly. He frowned at her. "Did you ever live in a nice house?"

"Once," Katherine said wistfully, "in Seattle, before I came here. It burned down."

Little by little, she told him about the big white house on the hill. The house with glass windows in every room, with the carved newel post and the crystal lamps and the naked godesses over the mantelpiece.

Nils listened attentively. "I'll build one just like that," he said when she was finished. "Only bigger."

Katherine shook her head. "No. That kind of house was my mother's dream. For many years I thought it was mine, too. But it isn't. Just an ordinary house. . ."

Nils held her tightly by the shoulders. "Listen here, Kate. I own the biggest hop ranch in the world. An ordinary house isn't enough. I'll build you a house they'll talk about in Seattle. When it's done, we'll get married." He grinned. "Engaged in the morning, married that afternoon."

Katherine's mouth opened to object. He kissed her. "The biggest house in the Territory."

She shook her head but Nils saw that her eyes were sparkling. "How about learning to read and write? Are you going to do that better than anyone in the Territory, too?"

Nils frowned. "How long does it take?"

"That depends on how hard you work at it," Katherine said soberly, a smile twitching at the corners of her mouth. "And how bright you are."

"It will take a year to build the house. Maybe more, to furnish it right. Do you think I'll be writing and reading in that time?"

Katherine shrugged. "I don't know. Who's going to teach you?"

Nils shook her. "You are, by golly."

"During school hours?"

"No!" Nils howled. "After school. At night. Any other time."

"Well, I don't know," she said, grinning wickedly. "I might not have the time."

"We can start right now."

Katherine's head tilted sideways as she looked up at him. He leaned forward but she slipped out of his hands and went behind the teacher's desk.

"Sit right there," she commanded, pointing to the school desk in front of her. Nils sat down, forcing his tremendous body into the little desk.

Katherine picked up a piece of chalk and wrote a series of letters on the blackboard. "Now," she said briskly, turning to look down at her giant pupil, "pay close attention. This is the letter A. . ."

In time Julie got cold and came into the schoolhouse to see what had happened. She saw her father doubled up in a sixth-grader's desk, slowly reciting the ABC's.

CHAPTER THIRTEEN

i

THE HOUSE NILS BENGSTON built for Teacher was fabulous from the moment the first shovel of dirt was moved for the foundation. The people of Gold Mountain watched a hanging garden of Babylon, a sphinx at Giza, a gem-studded Taj Mahal, spring from ground that had cost two and a half dollars an acre.

It was just like Nils to build a house like that, they all said. There were dwellings like it in Seattle, and some claimed to have seen its twin in San Francisco. But everything about Nils' house for Katherine was bigger, more ornate, or had been brought from more distant places than anything they could remember.

It was no secret now that Nils was in debt, that the unbelievable house was pushing him into debt still deeper. But that was Nils. They said it with admiration but also with such awe as they might feel if he were poised to dive over the Falls. Another good hop year would set him straight, his enemies grinned uneasily, and his friends dared not talk about it. Nils himself closed his eyes to worry. It was a powerful love, they whispered, which could make him so blind.

The house was built on high ground above the

river, in a clearing just below the spot where the three forks met to form the wide, swift Snoqualmie. It faced the mountain. To the north of the house was heavy timber and the swamp land where Indians had once picked wild cranberries. A man from Vermont had claim to it now, and was shipping the berries out to Seattle. To the south, the long miles of hops. To the west, the Falls. And straight ahead, the mountain, craggy, purple-black, against the unending sky.

The house went up slowly, for at each stage Nils refused the materials at hand if something difficult to obtain could be substituted. When he had first come to the Valley many families lived right on the dirt. The better homes boasted puncheon floors or floors of rough, hand-split cedar. There were three stories in the house for Katherine, and the floors throughout were made of white oak from Minnesota.

The hearth of the typical homestead cabin was of mud and fieldstone, or more often simply of sticks laid one above the other and plastered on the inside with clay. In Nils' house there was a fireplace in every room, each with a heavy facing and mantel-piece of white Vermont marble. The huge fireplace in the drawing room was a degree more elegant. It was finished with Italian marble, the fine-grained, faintly gray-streaked stone of Carrara. Sloe-eyed goddesses with large breasts and little drapery swam over the mantelpiece; a huge gilt-framed mirror hung between them, briefly recording the expressions of those who stared.

Fish oil lamps, tallow dips or a saucer of oil had lighted the cabins when the Tarpee brothers settled in Gold Mountain, and even now there was many a family which had never owned a kerosene lamp. In Nils' house light came from hundreds of candles, glittering in crystal chandeliers as big around as the wheels of an ox cart. In the bedrooms were kerosene lamps with ornate, hand-painted globes.

Nils himself had built or helped to build a dozen homes with no plan to follow but the one in the owner's head. What settler couldn't pace off the walls, cut timber, roof it over, and move into it while the moss and mud were still wet in the chinks? But before a board could be cut for Nils' house for Teacher, an architect must be brought in from San Francisco. His was an awe-inspiring plan, to Gold Mountain old-timers breathtakingly foolish. Everyone knew a ceiling should be low to keep the heat in but in Nils' house they were twelve feet from the floor. Windows should be high so that the stock would not break them, small because glass was a luxury and the oiled paper or thin white cloth used in its place let in both wind and rain. The windows of the house for Teacher were as big as doors. On the first floor they began just above the floor. Who else would build a castle like that on borrowed money, with hop prices going down and the dreaded hop louse spreading from field to field?

Nils laughed at anyone who questioned him. "My wife is going to have the biggest house in the Territory."

"Have you got money enough?" they asked, if they dared question him at all.

That made Nils roar with laughter. "Of course not!" he'd answer. "I've never had enough money for anything. But half of Gold Mountain belongs to me and there's a long list of properties in Three Forks and Black River with my name on them. I've got a sawmill and a shingle mill. I'm in the logging business, and I sold five thousand bushels of apples last year. When I come to the Valley I had two pair of britches and a winter's wages from rafting timber. Have I got money enough? Ha! Are you trying to tell me I don't know what I'm doing?''

He laughed at Agatha, ignored the Nelsons and Andersons, outshouted Nate Tarpee, and would not listen to Katherine at all.

Katherine's uneasiness was sharper than anyone else's. This extravagant house was for her and she was afraid from the moment the studdings were erected. There were great square pillars, heavy enough to support a medieval castle.

Nils would not show her the plan. ''Bad luck to let a lady see her wedding present ahead of time.''

Katherine retorted that he didn't believe in bad luck, or good luck, for that matter. Hadn't he often said ''luck'' was something a weak man talks about to explain why he'd failed?

Nils' answer was to pick her up and swing her around so that she had to clutch at him like a child riding pickaback, or fall to the ground. ''I'll show you where the rooms will be,'' he said, bracing her legs around his waist, his big hands holding her by the ankles.

''Nils!'' she gasped, looking down to see if her petticoats were showing.

''Now this is the front door,'' he said, ignoring the protest, ''and this is the—the foyer, or something.''

Nils' education kept apace with the building. He appeared at the schoolhouse two or three afternoons a week, his primer and speller strapped together and tied to the back of his saddle. The first time several of the bigger boys lingered in the schoolroom, pretending to be busy with extra lessons, Nils picked them up two at a time and threw them out the door.

As a scholar Nils proved to be slow or quick, depending on his private opinion of the subject. While he was studying from a first-grade primer reading was difficult. He said the story was silly. When Katherine gave him copies of the *Times* or the *Press* or the *Post-Intelligencer,* he turned to the financial columns and learned rapidly. Arithmetic was easy from the first. He had always kept hop ranch accounts in his head and had often corrected the errors old Uncle Julian made on paper. He could read market reports and shipping news in the newspapers while he was still stumbling over the Sermon on the Mount and the Twenty-third Psalm.

"You learn only what you want, and no more," Katherine scolded.

"Does that make me a fool?" Nils asked, grinning. "I'm only doing this because I want you."

"If you studied what you don't like the way you study what you do like, you could teach school."

Nils choked. "Woman, if you knew what I used to say about schoolteachers."

Month moved into month, and the wonder of Nils Bengston's house for Teacher grew. Round turrets were built into the four corners of the house, each topped with an elaborately carved cupola, each of a different design. The building bristled with wrought ironwork and wood carving. By spring it had been painted white, and work on the inside began.

Oak, marble, crystal. Blood red wallpaper with golden plumes. Overstuffed furniture with heavy oak carving and upholstery of fine black horsehair or deep red velvet. As each new addition was made, Katherine's apprehension grew. She told herself she should not listen to the others, for Nils himself was confident. Why should she feel that he was wrong and those without confidence were right? Besides, no one could stop him. He *would* build this house. It was a natural expression of his desire for the biggest of everything, as if his physical size required a world bigger, more daring than anyone else's.

"School year 1889-90" in Katherine's notebook had just begun when the first load of furniture arrived at Black River. It had been shipped on the *Viking*, each piece of it so heavily crated that the box weighed as much as the contents. That afternoon Nils stopped at the schoolhouse.

He came through the door like a man who has never known the barrier he couldn't push aside. The children waited gleefully for him to kiss Teacher. They'd seen him do it and Teacher's face was already bright pink as if she were afraid he might.

"Class dismissed," Teacher said in a particularly firm voice.

"Sure, kids, go on home," Nils commanded, waving "shoo" at them with both hands.

They scuttled through the door, then looked back to see if he were really going to. Grinning, Nils kicked the door shut with the toe of his boot.

"Nils, really."

He pulled her into his arms and kissed her. *"Really,"* he whispered mockingly and kissed her again. "Yes, *really.*"

"Where is your primer?"

He grinned at her crookedly. "I didn't come for no reading lesson."

"*Any* reading lesson."

"Don't be so prissy. I got something for you."

Katherine looked at his empty hands.

"Not here. Lock this place up and come with me."

They rode through the hop fields toward the river. The house was visible from a distance. Its fancy cupolas pointed skyward like church spires, high above the roofs of the stables and barns and sheds nearby. Its white paint glistened in the afternoon sun.

"In the house? Katherine called.

Nils nodded. "A surprise."

They tethered their horses to a fine brass hitching post, walked through the iron gate to the house. Gardeners had been working. Grass had been sown the moment the outside construction was done in the spring, and now they had clipped it to unnatural smoothness. Shrubs had been planted to form alleys and circles and other patterns, and had been trimmed in various geometric shapes. Katherine knew Nils was proud of them because he had brought the Italian gardener all the way from Portland. Nils opened the door for her.

The hallway was full of heavy crates. Only one of them had been opened. "Here it is," Nils said, pulling her past the boxes into the parlor.

It was an organ. Katherine looked at it unbelievingly. Scrolls and fancy lattice work adorned the sides and every inch of the massive back and top was carved. Brass candlesticks were attached to fancy brass arms fitted into holes in the woodwork, and swung over the keyboard in a half-circle. Gently Katherine took hold of the carved knob and slid back the panel which hid the keys. The ivory had the sheen of old satin.

"Oh. . ." she breathed. "Oh, my. . ."

Nils looked at it as admiringly as she. "Just think," he said, "it come all the way around Cape Horn."

Katherine's eyes were misty as she smiled at him. Nils had often said that a donkey had more music in him than he did. The organ was wonderful to her because it was music; to him because it had come twelve thousand miles. It was the finest gift he could buy her because it had been the hardest to get.

"Miller Organ Company," she read softly, her finger tracing the ornate gold lettering. "Lebanon, Pennsylvania."

"Cost three times as much to send it," Nils said jubilantly, "as it cost for the danged thing itself."

A feeling of apprehension shook her. "Nils, the cost. I'm worried."

Nils frowned. "Why?"

"I keep hearing. . ."

"Who have you been listening to?" he burst out angrily. "You sound like one of my foremen."

Katherine stared at him. Why did he protest so bitterly? "Perhaps they don't know what they're saying. . ."

Nils shrugged. "Maybe they do and maybe they don't. I've never had a foreman," he said, one hand tightening into a fist, "who didn't take a nickel's worth of truth and cover it over with a dollar's worth of lies."

"They said there were lice on the hops."

She waited for the burst of laughter or the fit of anger. But he only shrugged again, not quite facing her. "There are."

"No!" She had heard people talk of the diseasing aphids ever since she came to the Valley. The danger had grown in her mind until now it seemed to be the most dreaded thing in the world.

"We're spraying the fields," Nils said. "We'll get rid of them."

"But the crop. . ."

"It's a good crop. Maybe the biggest we've had. We won't miss what we lose to the lice."

Katherine cried out, "Nils, is that true?"

He turned toward her and lifted her chin with his forefinger. "Do you like the organ?"

She nodded, too choked to speak.

He kissed her gently. "Do you like the house?"

"Oh, darling. . ."

He looked straight into her eyes. "Katherine, if you love me, let's get married."

"Yes," she whispered. The ache in her throat was unbearable. Nils might fail; the realization hit her hard and grew instantly into certainty that he would. But he was grinning again, as Nils Bengston, who had never failed at anything, always grinned. He wanted her to marry him. Nothing, nothing, not a single gloomy whisper or the faintest shadow of fear would be allowed to spoil that.

"Right after the hop harvest," he was saying. "We'll wait till the Yakimas have gone back over the mountain and the rest of the pickers have cleared out and the last bale is on its way to England. Then we'll have our wedding. Right here. The biggest, fanciest wedding in the Territory. Maybe, by then, in the State. Washington becomes a state and Teacher becomes a bride."

Katherine tried to smile. Instead she hid her face against his chest. "Can you read your book straight through?"

"Almost as good as little Johnny Carlson," he said, laughing.

Right after the hop harvest—would Nils be laughing then? Katherine put her arms around his neck and held him tightly. "Please God," she whispered, fighting back the tears, "if only. . ."

"What was that?"

She lifted her face. "Kiss me," she answered in a husky voice. He bent his head. Clinging to him, Katherine closed her eyes.

ii

Nils felt the package he had stuffed into his coat pocket. Still there, he thought, though there was no reason at all why it shouldn't be. He walked up the plank and stepped onto the deck of the riverboat *Viking*. Old Cap White was inside at the wheel. Nils waved absently. He was uneasy. It was such an unusual feeling that he hardly knew how to manage it. It was vague, it was baseless, but it was persistent. He frowned, both irritated and puzzled. He'd heard things in Seattle that weren't good news for the owner of a hop ranch but he'd had problems before. Trouble had always stirred him up, not depressed him.

It was the way Seattle had looked, he told himself. A hundred and twenty acres burned to the ground, every business house in the city leveled except a few on the east side of Second Avenue. They were rebuilding it. Even without a wharf or a warehouse in which to store supplies shipped into the stricken city, the buildings were going up fast. Half the stores were still tents; the gift bulging in his coat pocket had come off a packing box counter in a canvas store. But what of it, Nils thought impatiently. Seattle people were hopeful, not gloomy. Why was he so down at the mouth?

He walked across the deck to the railing. Leaning

forward on both hands he stared at the gray river. He felt nervous because he had made a trip to Seattle in the midst of the hop-picking season. That might be it. But that didn't make sense either. He had ridden to Seattle every week of every hop-picking season the ranch had seen. The Indians must be paid in silver dollars and he didn't trust anyone else to pick up that much money and carry it for twenty-eight miles. He had driven a box wagon containing three or four thousand dollars all the way out from Seattle alone, with nothing but nerve and a one-shot rifle to protect him. He'd never felt a shadow of the feeling that nagged him now. He was . . .worried. Nils guffawed. He hated the word. Worry—that was a disease that attacked the minds of weak men and old women. He cursed softly and went into the cabin to talk to the captain.

Old Captain White was puffing at the *Viking*'s controls. The boat pulled away from the wharf, easing out slowly into the current. The captain's beard had grown white in the past few years and his black eyes seemed to have sunk deeper behind his high cheekbones. The scowlike *Viking* shuddered as she hit the full force of the current. Grunting, the captain pulled the wheel around and steadied it against his belly. "Upstream," he muttered. "Never did like this trip upstream. Don't get the chance to keep my pipe lit like I should."

Nils grinned. The old captain was getting crotchety. Nils' own uneasiness disappeared instantly. "I'll take the wheel for you, Cap."

"Keep your hands off." The old man braced the wheel with one elbow, twisted sideways to reach for his pipe. "How come you didn't take the train?"

"I did, going in."

"Sure, sure," the captain said accusingly, waggling his head.

"The railroad's hurting you, eh? Business poor?"

"Business is dead." The old man shrugged. "Why would a sensible person ride with me, when the train makes a straight thirty-mile trip in only three, four hours?" He gestured toward the deck. "How many passengers you see out there? Five, six? How much freight? The kids don't even come down to meet the boat anymore."

"You must of seen it coming?"

The old man snorted loudly. "Sure I seen it coming. It had to happen. I know I got to die some day, too, but that don't mean I'd like someone to put a bullet through me."

"It's too bad, Cap." Nils looked affectionately at the old man. It *was* too bad, but wasn't he working against the captain as much as anyone else? Last year the hops had been shipped by riverboat. This year they would be loaded right onto the spur line and sent to Seattle on the railroad. Times had changed. If change had made a failure out of Captain White, it was his tough luck, but maybe it was his fault, too. Nils despised failures, but he liked the old man. "Look here, Cap," he said gently, "what are you going to do? How are you fixed?"

Cap shrugged. "I can't even sell her for what she's worth. Too old, too flat, that's what I keep hearing. Even the river's working against me, it looks like. She's filling up so bad there's hardly a clear channel. That's what happens when you cut the timber." Frowning, he tried to relight his pipe. "I'm going to tie this good old tub up along the bank somewheres," he said simply, "maybe down by Kalakwahtie where you can see Mount Rainier now they got the big trees down. I'll live on her. I got enough put away for beans and coffee. I can grow my own tobacco.''

Nils frowned. Cap was giving up, and for some reason his own uneasiness returned. "Carl can help you.''

The captain squinted up at him. "Uh," he grunted. "Maybe you didn't know he went down to Frisco, first steamer that left after the fire. He said that was the end of Seattle. He's married, too. Anyways, Carl and me don't look at things eye to eye. I wouldn't want to shame him.'' Suddenly the captain's eyes sparkled. "Say, you took his girl away from him, didn't you? Getting married in a couple of weeks, ain't you?''

Nils nodded. When the old man spoke of Katherine and Carl together, he felt shooting pains of jealousy. If the captain had been younger or had anything like a smile on his face, he would have cracked his jaw. "I hope things work out for you, Cap," he said brusquely. "It won't seem right when the *Viking* don't pull into Black River any more.''

"Don't cry over me," the old man snapped. "You're worse off'n I am.''

Nils was startled. If he had been sitting peacefully in the hop ranch yard and an Indian arrow had come out of nowhere, striking him, its feather tip quivering with the impact as the first waves of pain went out through his body. . ."What are you talking about?''

"What have I got to lose?" the captain asked sourly. "An old sidewinder of a boat. I'm too old to want much, anyways.'' He squinted at Nils. "But you're an ambitious man.''

"You sound like one of my foremen.'' Instantly Nils realized that he had once said the same thing to Katherine. If the whole world was beginning to sniff

failure. . ."From the day the first plant showed
through the dirt they've been promising me there
would be lice in the hops," Nils said. "Now we got a
little of it. That don't mean the ranch will fail. We can
take care of it. "We *are* taking care of it." He looked
closely at the captain. "Now just why," he went on,
angry now, "would that make me so bad off that you
have to worry about me?"

The old man shrugged. "If the *Viking* was to sink
right here and now it wouldn't hurt the Valley a bit,
because there's already something come in to take its
place. But if the hop ranch was to go under, it would
be a terrible loss to everyone."

"Go under?" Nils shouted, letting his anger take
over completely. "Because of a few lice, when we
got a crop so big. . ."

The captain waved his hand. "Don't keep shouting
hop lice at me," he said calmly. He took his pipe out
of his mouth and frowned at the cold bowl, his little
eyes crossing slightly as they looked down his nose.
"There's more than one way to kill a cat."

Nils watched the captain working over his pipe as
if there were nothing to equal the job in importance.
A sign of age—Nils felt sorry for him. His clothes
were shabby, his back humped, his once powerful
shoulders were losing their strength. His boat was
aging and so was he, and together they would rot on
the bank at Kalakwahtie. No wonder, Nils thought,
that he's looking for someone else to feel sorry for.
His anger at the old man vanished before a pleasant
feeling of superiority. Old Captain White was like a
memory of his youth. A symbol, a picture, a beloved
character out of earlier, different times. Nils thought
of Katherine. But not of better times, for he had
never had so much before. His ranch, his millions,

his house, and now, his wife. . .

His hand went instinctively to his pocket, feeling for the outline of his wedding gift for Katherine. It was a pair of little gold slippers, sparkling with stones of many different colors. He had wanted them for her so badly that he hadn't been able to hide his eagerness and their price had been fantastic. Every saleable item in Seattle was costly now, either because all others of it kind had been burned up or because it was one of the few things that hadn't been. The slippers would be Katherine's wedding shoes. They were extravagant and therefore just right for the wife of one of the wealthiest men in the Territory, the mistress of a thirty-room house. Nils' fingers pressed against the package, feeling the jeweled studdings through the wrapping paper. The existence of the shoes, the feel of them, was reassuring. The shoes were real. The captain's fear, his own uneasiness, were as unsound as a bad dream. He nodded at the old man and went back on deck, his hand clamped tightly around the slippers.

iii

Nils Bengston's house for Teacher had been built with oak from Minnesota and marble from Vermont and crystal from Boston, but Gold Mountain regarded Teacher's wedding day as a thoroughly Gold Mountain affair.

November first was the date. Preparations began weeks beforehand. Since Katherine had no relatives in the Valley, the dozens of families whose children she had taught took possession of her wedding day.

Ceremony, dress, food—Gold Mountain jealously took all those matters unto itself.

In years past many a young couple had postponed their wedding for months until the preacher came through. Others had ridden thirty miles to Seattle so that some strange minister might bless their union. But this, the Valley knew, was no usual affair, and so Jeb Carlson made a fifty-mile horseback ride to catch up with Brother Bill and see that he would appear in Gold Mountain for the ceremony.

Agatha Tine took charge of the food. Some of the other women worried about what should be served in a mansion such as Nils had built, but to Agatha a wedding supper lighted by crystal chandeliers was a feed, just like any other. Cakes, cookies, roasts of meat, turkeys and chickens, crocks of potato salad and pickles—and plenty of all of them.

Only a few things were brought in from Seattle. The champagne, because having read a newspaper story about a party in San Francisco, Nils insisted on having it. The satin and lace for Katherine's wedding gown, the candied fruits for the wedding cake, a string of pearls for the bride. . ."What shall I send for?" Nils asked Katherine again and again. "Don't you want something more?"

"I have everything."

He looked down at her, gently put his hands on her shoulders. "You can have anything you want," he said. "You got to tell me because I'm nothing but a backwoods logger and I just don't know."

She shook her head. "Nils, truly. . ."

"Jewelry?" he asked anxiously, just barely shaking her. "If they haven't got it in Seattle, they'll have it in Frisco. I'll send for it. Some kind of dress goods? You think the house needs more furniture?"

She smiled. "No, no, no. . ."

He looked into her face, frowning in his intensity.
"What do *you* want, Nils?"

He looked surprised. He glanced around the richly
furnished drawing room, through the long windows
to the hop fields stretching forever and ever outside.
"What could I want for?" he mused, still looking
through the window. He turned back to her and
pulled her into his arms. "I've got everything," he
said, holding her tightly. "The biggest hop ranch and
the littlest wife."

There were no wedding invitations. No one tried to
make a list of guests. Everyone in the Valley understood that he was invited whether he lived in Gold
Mountain, Three Forks, Black River, or Kalakwahtie, whether he owned a Sunday suit or would
have to come in denim and logging boots, whether he
could look Nils Bengston in the eye or still owed him
money.

For the first time in a year Katherine tried to reach
her father. Again she failed. If her letters to him were
delivered, he did not answer them. He had always
talked easily, written with difficulty. She wrote to her
aunts and uncles in Oregon, and they replied as they
had before. They had seen him only once in five
years, when he had been talking of silver mining in
Colorado. God's will be done, they wrote, and all the
children were doing fine.

They could not come to the wedding, of course, for
the trip was too long and too dangerous. But
Katherine's intended had been generous indeed in
sending the fare and they'd use the money for
clothes, a more sensible way to spend it anyway,
didn't she agree? Teddy's letter had a different ring to
it. The steamship company had transferred him to

San Francisco, where he was a clerk in their business office. He'd been married for three months now and his wife was carrying a child but they'd both be in Gold Mountain for the wedding if they had to build their own raft.

"He's all right," Nils said when Katherine read the letter. "I'll send him money for the trip."

"Nils, he wouldn't take it."

Nils frowned. "No?"

Katherine shook her head firmly, "No."

Nils grinned. "The Duncans sure made their kids ornery."

"Proud."

Nils shrugged, "What's the difference?"

Katherine's eyes snapped. "Don't you know? Is there anyone more proud than you?"

Nils burst out laughing. When she tried to slap him he kissed her. "I'm not proud," he said against her ear, "I'm just rich."

iv

Katherine dressed slowly for the wedding. She was alone in the big master bedroom. Faith Carlson, Agatha, Hannah, Julie Bengston, Mrs. Nelson, and a half dozen other women had left her so that she would rest for an hour or so. They were in the kitchen now, undoubtedly arguing about whether it was time to come upstairs and waken her.

She smiled wistfully. She had tried to sleep. She had lain back in the huge four-posted spool bed, pulled the coverlet up to her chin and dutifully closed her eyes. But then the fears that had been plaguing her were worse than ever. Faces she didn't want to

see danced in the darkness. Words she wanted to
forget sang monotonously in her ears. Agatha, Faith
and Jeb Carlson, the hop ranch foreman, Nate Tarpee, everyone, everyone had heard it. Everyone was
whispering it.

Something terrible had happened to Washington
hopgrowers. Nils Bengston's crop, the one which
could set him straight or make a pauper of him, had
been dried and baled and shipped to Seattle, but it
was still there. Why, if Nils had found a buyer?

Nils refused to discuss it. Hop ranches from the
Skagit to the Duwamish were going under. Growers
were getting less than one hundred dollars an acre for
hops when every acre they grew on had been cleared
for five hundred more. The Chinese were buying up
hop ranches and wealthy men were going into bank-
ruptcy. But Nils laughed and said, "November first
is my wedding day. Only thing I'm worried about is
whether me and Brother Bill get in a fist fight before
he gets us properly married."

Katherine tried to think of the way Nils grinned,
the way he laughed, the way he picked her up and
kissed her and told her not to sound like a foreman.
He owned the biggest hop ranch in the world, he
would soon be the wealthiest man in the state of
Washington, and she would be mistress of the most
elegant house west of the Mississippi, so smile, he
said, and kiss me.

But he had made extra trips to Seattle this week.
He answered all her questions by pointing out how
harmless the hop lice had been and what a large crop
they'd had, but his voice was rough when he cut off
her queries about where and how he would sell it.
Meanwhile there were whispers, broad hints, sympathetic or curious glances. No one knew anything

for sure, but no one could keep silent. People spread
the disaster news swiftly and anxiously, like thieves
passing along stolen goods. It was no use trying to
sleep with her mind so full of it.

Under the soft coverlet Katherine's body lay stiff
as a cedar post and every time she closed her eyes
they snapped open again and she found herself staring sightlessly at the gold drapery overhead. Nils said
he had nothing on his mind but his wedding day. He
made her anxiety seem ridiculous. Offering sympathy would be calling him a liar. Unless he came to
her . . . Katherine threw back the coverlet and got out
of bed. Perhaps her fears were truly groundless. No
one but Nils knew whether the whispered reports
were true, and Nils laughed. She went to the huge gilt
dressing table by the window and sat down.

The mirrors showed how pale she was. With
thumb and forefinger Katherine impatiently pinched
her cheeks. In two hours she thought, we will be
married. She picked up her hairbrush. It might help
to go through the soothing ritual of brushing her hair.
In two hours. . . .

She dropped the hairbrush and crossed the room.
Her wedding gown was spread over two chairs, the
veil and train of lace across two more. On the dressing table was a Juliet cap of pearls to which the train
would be attached. Katherine picked up the cap. She
turned it around thoughtfully. A cap of pearls. Had it
been some childhood dream of her own which made
her choose such an ornament, or an old wish of her
mother's, absorbed so long ago that it had become a
wish of her own? Suddenly Katherine saw her
mother's face. The picture was sharper than that of
the faces of Agatha and Faith whom she had seen less
than an hour before. The deep worry lines across her

forehead, the weary set of her chin, the look of hope and then hopelessness, about the eyes. "If I could just know for sure," her mother might be saying, "that I could do the washing of a Monday morning."

Katherine looked around the room, from the marble fireplace to the beautiful mahogany bed, to the gold-framed mirror and dark red carpet. "A house with glass windows," she could hear Angus pleading in a shrill little boy's voice. "Papa, did you say we'd have a house with glass windows?" The shadow in the corner was herself, a little girl with a pale face and angry eyes, carrying an armload of dried cow dung to start a fire for her mother's tea. "Some day," that little girl was sobbing, "some day I'll have a real house all my own."

Katherine got up and went to the window. The men were outside, Teddy and Nils and Brother Bill and Jeb Carlson and others who had been helping with the preparations. Their women were in the kitchen. Katherine frowned. With Nils was a stranger, or at least a man she did not know, whose face had a puzzling familiarity to it. There would be so many here today whom she might know only by sight. Why should the presence of a stranger be so disturbing? And yet an uncomfortable tightness settled in her chest. They were talking earnestly. She studied them, her pulse pounding out a warning. A friend of Nils', a traveler, perhaps a cattleman from Kittitas. Teddy appeared, joining Nils and the stranger. Then Jeb, then Ole Nelson. They formed a silent circle, hands in pockets, faces solemn. The stranger talked, talked, talked.

Nils was listening. The picture was wrong. All at once, Katherine knew why. She had never seen Nils so motionless, so silent. She had never seen him listen for so long without once laughing.

Katherine whirled away from the window and ran to the bedroom door. Leaning over the bannister she called, "Faith!" Below a door opened, closed, there were running steps along the hall. Faith stood at the foot of the stairway and looked up at her.

"Faith."

Faith was crying.

Katherine stared at her. She felt cold, almost numb. "Faith," she said in a hollow voice, "will you come up here a minute?"

Faith climbed the stairs slowly. She walked past Katherine and into the bedroom. Katherine closed the door with exaggerated care and leaned against it, holding tightly to the doorknob. "Who is that man?"

Faith shook her head. "I don't know exactly. He rode out from Seattle."

"He's in business with Nils in some way."

"Oh, I don't know just how," Faith sobbed. "Oh, Katherine."

Katherine said doggedly, "He came to tell Nils something about the hops."

"Yes, yes." Faith covered her face with both hands. Tears came through the fingers, spotting the bodice of her dress.

Katherine took hold of Faith's wrists and pulled her hands down. Faith's plain face quivered in her misery. "Faith, listen," Katherine said. "You've got to tell me what they're talking about, whatever you heard. Soon I'll be talking to Nils. I've got to be ready."

Faith fought a new wave of sobs. She looked blankly at Katherine, collecting herself with an effort.

Katherine's hands tightened on her wrists. "Tell me!" she said harshly.

Faith's body shuddered with the last sob. "Something happened to the price of hops,'' she said dully. ''The man come to tell Nils they can't get but six cents a pound for them. I heard Nils say it cost eight cents a pound to grow them.''

Katherine released Faith's hands, and they dropped lifelessly. ''I'm not sure,'' Katherine said huskily, ''that I quite understand what that means.''

''Jeb says Nils got a dollar and a quarter a pound last year.''

''Aahh. . .''

Tears came back to Faith's eyes. ''The wedding,'' she cried, ''the beautiful wedding.''

Katherine turned and walked to the dressing table. She picked up her brush and mechanically began pulling it through her hair. ''I'd better start getting dressed for it.''

''We're not going to have the wedding!''

Katherine wheeled around to face her. ''The wedding, the party, the champagne, the dancing, every bit of it.'' She waved the hairbrush at Faith. ''Now go wash your face and take off your apron and get ready. Don't let Nils see you looking like that!''

''If he's lost everything, everything. . .''

''He hasn't!''

Faith cried, ''Oh Katherine, the man said. . .''

Katherine said sharply, ''I don't care what the man said. This is my wedding day.'' She lifted the hairbrush, brandishing it like a man holding a lion off with a saber.

''I'll help you dress.''

Katherine shook her head. There was such a painful lump in her throat that she couldn't say much more. ''I'd like to be alone for a while.'' She touched Faith's hand. ''Faith, I'll have to talk to Nils. I've got to think what to say.''

Faith turned and ran out.

Katherine sat down at the edge of the bed. A moment before she had to fight to keep from crying, but she was past that now. Crystal and marble and satin surrounded her, and Nils had lost everything. Think, she told herself, think. Everything depends on whether you can help him now.

If he has lost everything, she thought in anguish, can I help him without losing him?

v

For an hour she sat there, measuring herself against the crisis she had to meet. She thought of so many things, so many which had nothing to do with Nils or the failure of the hop ranch or even with herself as she was now. Think, she told herself, think.

Nils had failed. The cornerstone of his little empire had been knocked out and when debts were paid and property sold there would be nothing left for him but rubble. Failure, which he despised so deeply that anyone who had ever failed was to him despicable—on his own wedding day the worst of all possible things had happened to him. To anyone else it would have been a lighter blow.

But it was not so with her. For me, Katherine reflected, nothing could be as terrible as the loss of Nils himself. Nils' world had been destroyed; hers had not been touched. Now, at last, she was the stronger of the two.

He needed her now; he had only wanted her before. But needing another person, even the woman he loved—could Nils be humbled to that degree without hating her? "No one ever cut him down to size," old Uncle Julian had said. "Lot of people would like to, but I'm not one of them. Nils is a big man. He was built to be king. If he was to be cut down I don't think I'd like to see it." This, then, was the true shape of the crisis. Katherine sat on the edge of the big bed, still as a doll, asking herself if she could meet it.

How ill prepared she would have been when she first came to the Valley. She thought back over the dreams she had cherished, the little-girl dreams, the petulant, unhappy, never-fulfilled dreams of her mother. She had had only one ambition then, and that was to live in a world where nothing unexpected could happen. Like an extension of her mother's pathetic plea to know for sure that she could always start the washing of a Monday morning, the younger Katherine's world was to have been a neat and proper place. It was to be hemmed in; by making it smaller and smaller, neater and neater, the fears of her youth were to be closed out forever.

No child would ever spend a week putting wheat kernels through an old coffee grinder. No little girl would roam the prairie looking for cow chips. There would not be this house and then that one, coming so fast one after another that a child could not say where he came from. Such were the materials with which she had built her dream, the negative desires, the things she prayed would not be.

When she came to the Valley five years before, she had looked at everything through the mist of this dream. As she had all her life, she saw only the things that were not good enough; she had understood no experience but the experience of disappointment. She had hated and feared Gold Mountain because even more than the hateful places of her childhood it was crude and poor and terrifying. That Katherine Duncan who had spent her last dollar on a pair of silly pink gloves because they would make her look like a lady, rather than on the umbrella which would have kept her dry—*that* Katherine could not have helped Nils, for she hadn't been even a big enough person to love him.

But now, now at the moment of crisis, she had five years in the Valley behind her. Five years of preparation, begun the day she got wet enough to admit she should have bought an umbrella instead of the pink gloves. Perhaps she had never been truly helpless, but she had been obsessed by an old-maidish conviction that she should be. Gold Mountain had taken that out of her. Everything that had happened to her here, the good and the bad, the tragic and the trivial, stood solidly behind her now. Nils' Katherine was not that scary creature with the pink gloves, Nils' Katherine was the girl whom Gold Mountain had trained to be equal to him.

She was the girl who stood up in a public meeting to bid against a man for her job; who had cooked in a logging camp and attacked an Indian beggar with a stack of hot cakes and a soup ladle; who had taught a second grade full of sixteen-year-olds; had learned to travel alone with a lamp for light, an umbrella for rain and a gun for everything else. *She* could help Nils, and it was time to do it.

She slid off the edge of the bed, quickly pulled on a soft flannel wrapper, and going to the top of the stairs called down to ask for Nils.

vi

Nils, who always slammed doors, closed the bedroom door quietly. Katherine waited for his usual greeting—one great sweep of an arm which pulled her against him, a quick "Hello, Kate," and a grin just before he leaned down to kiss her. But he did not move to touch her. He had always carried himself carelessly, as if to contradict the braggadocio of his size. But his shoulders were almost too square now, his posture too consciously upright. Hands and face were still. He showed nothing at all, except in his eyes.

Katherine felt her throat constrict, fiercely fought down the desire to cry out. She went to Nils and taking both his hands, pulled him forward to a pair of chairs. She sat down, forcing him to sit opposite her.

"You don't know what to do," she said simply.

"They waited a long time. But they always said I'd outreach myself someday."

They—Katherine recognized the "they" he had spoken of so often. The nameless ones whom he imagined were always waiting for his failure. Nils had done a lot to prove how wrong "they" were. "How bad . . . is it?"

Nils said dully, "It couldn't be worse."

"This year's crop can't be sold?"

"I'll end up paying $50,000," he said in a strange, hoarse voice, "for the pleasure of growing it."

"But your other property, such as the sawmill and the timber claims and the store?"

Nils looked directly into her eyes. "Kate," he said, "I don't own them, not half as much as the banks in Seattle."

"Mortgaged. . ."

Nils grinned crookedly, though the misery was in his eyes. "Everything. With the hop ranch doing so well I knew bankers who would loan me money on Old Hi."

Katherine grabbed his hands. "Nils, you didn't mention this house."

Nils frowned. "It wouldn't help. They don't like to loan money on a house. Not productive, doesn't earn anything. And a house like this, way out here?" He gestured toward the gold-framed mirrors, the golden brocade, the mahogany woodwork. "Even if I was to get a mortgage on it, it wouldn't begin to pay off what I owe. They've already figured on what they're going to do with the hop ranch when they take it over."

"Then the house *is* free and clear? They won't take it, too?"

Her excitement puzzled him. Some of the unhappiness went out of Nils' face. "Well, yes, just the house itself, maybe a little strip of land around it."

"You could let them take the hop ranch, take the hotel and the farms and the shingle mill and all the rest. . ."

"Let them?" Nils said dryly. "They don't have to ask permission."

"But you'd still have the house."

Nils grinned. Katherine saw that her voice and manner were shocking him into aliveness. "Why yes," he said, "I'll still have the house. Not a bad place to starve in. Why do you keep talking about the house?"

He was wide awake now, trying to figure her out. How could she ever have thought there could be trouble bigger than he was? She jumped up, sat on his lap and threw her arms around him. "Then my idea will work," she said excitedly. "I wasn't sure because I didn't know about the mortgages and things."

"I never heard you talk like this before," Nils said gruffly. "What do you know about mortgages?"

Katherine giggled. Her feeling of relief was almost

unbearable. "My father brought more of them home than he did meat and potatoes." She kissed him, and with her face hidden against his shoulder said quickly, "We'll change our house into a hotel."

"What!" Nils bellowed. He tried to get up but Katherine grabbed the arms of the chair and holding on tight said, "If you get out of this chair I'll scream, and you know what they'll think downstairs!"

"Kate!" Nils exclaimed, falling back against the chair. "A fine thing for a schoolteacher to say."

"Nils, you know how many people are coming into the Valley now that the railroad runs out all the way. Drummers, especially. Nate Tarpee says he's seen twenty to thirty of them in a day. There are so many hunters and fishermen and tourists now. Ever since the railroad got to Gold Mountain, there have been more of them every month. There are many wealthy families in Seattle, people who take vacations. They would come out here if there were a nice enough hotel. A hotel such as this house would make would be a reason to come in itself. Don't you see? We'd be famous!

"Perhaps you could keep some of the hop ranch horses and a wagon or two. Or somehow we'd get money to buy a rig and hire a driver. He could meet the trains, take drummers and travelers wherever they wanted to go. They're hiring in Kirkland now. Wouldn't they rather go to the end of the line and get a rig there? That's two businesses already, a hotel and a livery stable." Katherine stopped.

Nils was frowning fearfully. "You sure got a lot to say."

"I've been thinking."

"A *hotel*. I bought the best of everything for this house. Marble from Italy, hardwood from Minnesota, an organ that come all around Cape Horn. . ." He looked at her silently for a moment and then he shook his head. "This is your house, Kate. It's the biggest, finest house in the state of Washington. I lost the ranch but I won't give up the house, too."

"We wouldn't be giving it up. We'd be keeping it." Katherine looked at him earnestly. "Nils, whatever happens, I wouldn't want to leave the Valley, would you?"

"You said you'd been thinking," Nils said quietly. "For the past two weeks I've been thinking, too. Not very straight or clear, because I wouldn't admit anything." He looked toward the long windows, through which the dark stretch of the Valley and the great barren rock of Old Hi could be seen. "One thing I did decide for sure, and that was that I would not leave the Valley."

"That's what I decided, too." Katherine put her hand against his cheek and turned his head back so that he had to look at her. "We want to stay. This is our place. But the place itself is changing. Remember what you said about old Captain White? He's a failure, you said, because he couldn't move along with the times. We know it's the railroad that's changing things. Because of the railroad there will be a need for a hotel, a need for a livery stable. So here we are, with the changing times handing us opportunity on a platter. Why don't we take it and move along with them?"

Nils' blue eyes cleared. There was a look of expectancy about his weathered face. "Gabby little thing, ain't you," he muttered. "But what if I can't even raise the money for rigs and horses?"

"We'll mortgage the house."

His look was one of sheer amazement. "*Mortgage* the house I built for you," he murmured, but she could see it was beginning to strike him funny. No, she needn't have been afraid. Nils had never failed, even now. She said brightly, "I have never lived in a house that wasn't."

"Mortgages, hotels, livery stables. What all have you got in that red head of yours?" His arms went around her and he held her tightly. "I love you, Kate."

"The Gold Mountain Hotel. . ."

She saw his jaw tighten, and a mulish desperation darkened his eyes. He looked at her with such intensity that she stiffened, consciously bracing herself against the impact of the glance. Her heart pounded furiously as she waited for him to speak. Suddenly his face softened. He kissed her, whispering to her. "Kate, Kate, a few years ago if I'd lost the hop ranch I would have killed myself. Now all I want to do is to get married."

She clung to him. "I was so afraid you wouldn't want me any more."

"I didn't," he said dryly, "until I found out you know so much about mortgages. Now I can't afford to give you up."

Laughing, she went back to her dressing table and sat down on the ornate little gilt stool. The face in the mirror was not the one she had seen there an hour earlier, with pale cheeks, anxious eyes, and grim determination written all over her mouth and chin. Now her cheeks were flushed and her eyes were bright and curious.

"Everything will be all right," she announced, more to herself and the world than to Nils, who had followed her and was looking over her shoulder. "But I really must brush my hair."

She untied the green ribbons knotted at the ends of her braids and shook her head vigorously from side to side. Free of restraint, the well disciplined braids flew apart and became a silky red-gold cape that covered her shoulders, half hid her face, and fell all the way to her waist. Head tilted, she began the rhythmic ceremony. One hand brushed, the other smoothed. With each long stroke, the hair snapped and lifted, as if it were alive and might float away.

For some time Nils watched in silence. Even when he caught her hand in mid-air and took away the hairbrush, neither of them spoke. Slowly, awkwardly at first, he drew the brush through her long hair. Soon his motions were as graceful as her own.

"I've been wanting to do this," he said, looking over her shoulder at her mirror face. Katherine's green eyes softened as she smiled at Nils' reflection. "You've been spying on me? Watching me in the privacy of my bedroom? Shame on you, Nils Bengston."

Nils put down the hairbrush. "I refuse to apologize. For what I've done, or for what I'm going to do now." He lifted her off the stool and swung her up into his arms as easily as he would toss a ball. Peering solemnly into her face, he said, "Well, I was right. The real Katherine Duncan is just as funny looking as the one in the mirror."

In mock anger, Katherine retorted, "What a fine thing to tell a lady on her wedding day! You'd better not let my husband hear you say that."

"I'm not afraid of *him*." His arms tightened around her as he turned away from the window and the dressing table and walked across the room.

"Why are you always picking me up and carrying me?"

"Because you fly around so fast it's the only way I know for sure where you are." Still holding her, Nils sat down on the edge of the big four-posted bed. With one hand, he turned her face toward his and kissed her, on the mouth, on the throat, on the forehead.

Against his cheek, Katherine murmured, "I should be getting into my wedding dress."

"That's the only reason I'm taking off your nightclothes," Nils replied. "I'm helping."

"But you're taking off your own clothes, too."

"I am?" Nils looked down at his naked body and frowned mightily. "By God, Katherine, you're right. I am."

The playful laughter faded slowly, like the distant sound of a train whistle moving farther and farther away and finally melting into silence. They lay side by side, caressing each other's body with sensitive fingertips exploring the hollows, the soft places, the warm responsive flesh. Little by little their touching was more demanding, their kisses deeper. Together they reached the peak of excitement where nothing mattered, nothing existed, except the driving need to enter and be entered, to continue the climb, on and on, up and up, to the final moment when they were locked together in the last great cleansing explosion, and then lay back, in peace.

For a long time, Nils held Katherine close against him, her head resting in the crook of his arm. She studied his profile, musing about their future, wondering how she could know so little about this big, stubborn, laughing man and at the same time feel she had known him forever.

As she watched, she saw his expression change. The drowsy daydreamer departed abruptly. Nils the master planner, the owner of the biggest hop ranch in the world and the finest house in the Territory, lay beside her, looking straight up with such intense concentration she had the ridiculous feeling that complete blueprints for his next big venture must be painted on the ceiling. She moved against his body. She kissed his cheek. He patted her arm absentmindedly, without turning his head.

"Nils!" She sat up and thumped the bed with both fists. "Nils! What are you thinking about?"

"About the hotel," he said. "You know, we could make it the biggest finest vacation hotel on the whole Pacific Coast. They'd hear of it all the way to San Francisco. What other hotel would have gold curtains and all that fancy crystal? Should we call it the Gold Mountain Hotel, do you think, or does Bengston's Hotel sound all right?"

Katherine slid off the bed, walked to the dressing table and for the third time that day, though the first without any clothes on, she began to brush her hair. She was laughing so hard she was afraid he would notice. She'd have to hold it in for a moment, let him finish his dream plans.

Bengston's Hotel, of course. Did he really think she would believe there was a choice? Nils would be up soon, for it wouldn't take long for the biggest dreamer in the Territory to design the biggest finest vacation hotel on the whole Pacific

Coast, and that done, the Nils who was about to take a wife would rise and put on his wedding suit and they would go downstairs and get married.

CHARLOTTE PAUL is a native of the Pacific Northwest, though she is a graduate of Newton High School (Newton, Massachusetts) and Wellesley College, and for twenty-five years of her very active and creative life she has lived east of the Mississippi, one spot being as far east as Dresden, Germany, where she studied dance with Mary Wigman. She says her writing career began the day she learned to read and that her first (and unpublished) story was written in the attic cubbyhole of the Paul home in Longview, Washington, a niche designated as her "study".

After graduation from Wellesley with a B.A. degree and honors in English Composition, she became assistant foreign news editor for the Chicago Daily *Times* and later that paper's roving correspondent in the Caribbean. For three years she served in an editorial and re-write capacity for *Esquire-Coronet* in Chicago.

Twenty-five years as a freelance writer produced countless articles and short stories for national magazines, as well as five books—three novels and two works of non-fiction. Most of her work has been translated into several foreign languages, and several of them have been book club selections.

In 1962, Charlotte Paul took up a new career when the governor of the state of Washington appointed her to the Washington State Board of Prison Terms & Paroles, the only woman on a five-man board. Two years later, after appointment by President Johnson, she moved to Washington, D.C., and began a six-year term as the "eighth man" on the U.S. Board of Parole. She has calculated that in six years of conducting interviews with federal prisoners, she has spent 24 months in men's penitentiaries.

Retiring from government service in the fall of 1970, she and her husband, Robert W. Reese, a long-time writer and public affairs officer for the Treasury Department, settled in the San Juan Islands, off the northern coast of the state of Washington, and Mrs. Reese went back to her first professional love—writing, particularly writing of fiction. The highly successful result of her first two years back at the typewriter was *Phoenix Island,* which has sold close to a million copies.

Charlotte Paul claims that her only hobby is work, but she admits to spending her leisure time hunting wild mushrooms, collecting edible weeds, and hauling driftwood for the two big fireplaces in the Reeses' sprawling cedar house where the front windows look out towards the Pacific and the snow-covered range of the Olympic Mountains. She also plays a mean piano, 1940s style, and occasionally gets together with a local bull fiddler and local guitarist to lift the roof off the local pub. She has three sons—Hiram Paul Groshell, public defender, John Paine Groshell, pro and part owner of a golf course outside Seattle, and Robert J. Reese, investigator for an insurance company. And three grandchildren.

AND two bassets and one cairn terrier.

There are a lot more
where this one came from!

The Gothic Magic of Anne Maybury

Just $1.25 each

The Brides of Bellenmore

Falcon's Shadow

Green Fire

House of Fand

I Am Gabriella

The Night My Enemy

The Pavilion at Monkshood

Shadow of a Stranger

Someone Waiting

Stay Until Tomorrow

Whisper in the Dark

The Winds of Night

Available wherever paperbacks are sold or use this coupon.

AN Agatha Christie CHRONOLOGY

NANCY BLUE WYNNE

The only one volume listing of every Christie novel, short story and collection, including plot outlines of MURDER ON THE ORIENT EXPRESS and major and lesser known works.